MODERN
REAL ESTATE
PRACTICE IN TEXAS

SIXTEENTH EDITION

Cheryl Peat Nance, EdD, DREI, CREI | with Loretta DeHay, Contributing Editor

Dearborn
Real Estate Education

This publication is designed to provide accurate and authoritative information in regard to the subject matter covered. It is sold with the understanding that the publisher is not engaged in rendering legal, accounting, or other professional advice. If legal advice or other expert assistance is required, the services of a competent professional should be sought.

President: Dr. Andrew Temte
Chief Learning Officer: Dr. Tim Smaby
Executive Director, Real Estate Education: Melissa Kleeman-Moy
Development Editor: Adam Bissen

MODERN REAL ESTATE PRACTICE IN TEXAS, SIXTEENTH EDITION
©2014 Kaplan, Inc.
Published by DF Institute, Inc., d/b/a Dearborn Real Estate Education
332 Front St. S., Suite 501
La Crosse, WI 54601

Printed in the United States of America

ISBN: 978-1-4754-2183-5 / 1-4754-2183-4
PPN: 1510-0616

Contents

Preface

Although the real estate industry is making rapid technological changes, a basic knowledge of real estate laws, practices, and terminology is still essential for anyone desiring to enter the field. *Modern Real Estate Practice in Texas*, now in its 16th edition, is the recognized authority for accurate, comprehensive information in a student-friendly format. Whether you are preparing for a state licensing examination, fulfilling a college or university requirement, looking for specific guidance about buying a home or an investment property, or simply expanding your understanding of this fascinating field, you can rely on *Modern Real Estate Practice in Texas*. If your goal is a license, this text covers all the topics required by the Texas Real Estate License Act to be included in a principles core course, with both national and state-specific content. In addition to helping you prepare to enter the real estate industry, this book can become an integral part of your professional reference library when you start to work.

This is a great time to get into the industry; you have an opportunity to train and get experience for the really busy times ahead. In addition, Texas may be just the market in which to begin. Texas became the United States' second-largest economy during the past decade (displacing New York state) with our share of the U.S. economy reaching 8.3% in 2010 (Dennis Cauchon, *USA Today*, June 21, 2011). Texas consistently ranks first or second in CNBC's "America's Top State for Business," an annual study that scores each state on 55 different measures of competitiveness (2013).

Today's real estate market is challenging and complex, and real estate students are increasingly sophisticated, demanding a high level of expertise and efficiency. The 16th edition of *Modern Real Estate Practice in Texas* meets those expectations. In response to the growing body of laws that govern the practice of real estate, this edition contains revisions and features designed to make it an even more effective tool, no matter what your goal.

FEATURES

This edition contains revisions brought about by the 83rd Legislative Session in 2013, as well as changes in state and federal government regulations and industry practice and procedure. In addition, the book has been enhanced by

- *"hot issues"* such as fair housing, discrimination, ethics, Dodd-Frank Act, and the new loan estimate and closing disclosure forms;
- *examples* to illustrate key concepts and provide real-life explanations for further clarification of real estate principles;
- *math concepts* at relevant points in the chapters—where they would normally occur in a transaction—to help illuminate the real-life application of the mathematics of real estate;
- a basic *real estate math primer*, Chapter 19;

■ *margin notes* to help direct attention to important vocabulary terms, concepts, study tips, and related news;

■ *detailed rationales* for the answers to end-of-chapter review questions; rationales are available exclusively online at www.dearborn.com through the **Instructor Resource Guides** link.

For information on obtaining a real estate license—including a guide to the license application process, tips for selecting a broker, and passing the state exam—visit a special student section on the Dearborn instructor resources page. Students may also download a practice state exam, modeled on the latest testing format. Obtain these resources at http://resources.dearborn.com/instructor-resources. The access PIN is 147832.

A FINAL NOTE

The fundamental goal of *Modern Real Estate Practice in Texas* is to help students understand the dynamics of the real estate industry and to assist them in preparing for the licensing exam. This text provides the tools necessary to develop a foundation for advanced study in the general practice of real estate or in any one of the real estate specialties. To derive the maximum benefit from this textbook, become familiar with the key terms listed at the beginning of each chapter and the definitions included in the glossary. The questions at the end of each chapter provide an opportunity to apply the principles presented in the text.

We like to hear from our readers. Like the dozens of Texas real estate instructors who have helped to develop this and previous editions, like the real estate professionals who have shared their expertise, you are a partner in the *Modern Real Estate Practice in Texas* series. The only way we can be sure we've succeeded—and know what we need to improve—is if you tell us.

Your comments are invaluable. Has your understanding of the real estate industry increased? How did you do in your course or on your real estate license exam? Which features of the text were most helpful to you? What additional or different information would improve the book?

Thank you for your help and for joining the ranks of successful *Modern Real Estate Practice in Texas* users!

Modern Real Estate Practice in Texas was originally adapted from the classic text, *Modern Real Estate Practice* by Galaty, Allaway, and Kyle (1959), which has provided more than 3 million readers with a critical edge as they enter the world of real estate. Permission to use the material in *Modern Real Estate Practice* has been granted to the author of this 16th Edition of *Modern Real Estate Practice in Texas*.

The 25 chapters herein cover the broad subject of real estate, together with real estate law and operating procedures that apply to the State of Texas. Real estate practice in each state is controlled by federal laws and regulations, as well as the respective state laws, regulations, and court decisions. Additionally, the practice of real estate in any specific location in Texas may be influenced by local agencies, bureaus, and organizations such as county and city governments or local real estate associations.

Statements of law in this book are general summaries that are not intended to substitute for an experienced legal counsel. Unique situations require specific application of the law. Therefore, this text should be used only as a general guideline and not as a final statement of the law on any given matter. The author and the editors assume no responsibility for any errors, omissions, or inadvertent misinterpretations of the law.

Acknowledgments

We would like to thank the following individuals who have reviewed and contributed to this edition of *Modern Real Estate Practice in Texas*:

- Linda Brothers, Escrow Officer, First American Title Company
- C. Wallace Cater, Certified General Real Estate Appraiser, San Jacinto College
- Bill Chudej, CCIM, CPM, President, FIMC Commercial Realty
- Ken Combs, Professor, MBA, CREI, GRI, Del Mar College
- Greg Glenn, Broker, Prudential Ada REALTORS®
- Norman E. Gutzmer, Attorney, Miller and Gutzmer Attorneys
- Travis Loe, SRA, Appraiser, The Steve Rogers Co.
- John F. Waldron, J.D., Program Coordinator, Real Estate Program, San Antonio College, Department of Business
- Sue Williams, Executive Director, Real Estate Institute of Corpus Christi, Inc.
- Theda Redwine, MBA, North Lake College Real Estate Program Coordinator

Special thanks is extended to the various state agencies that reviewed sections of this book and to the following groups for permission to use materials or forms: Texas Association of REALTORS® and Texas Real Estate Commission.

Sincere gratitude goes to the late G. E. Irby, Texas series advisor to Real Estate Education Company® and author of the fifth and sixth editions of this book.

About the Author

Cheryl Peat Nance is the author of *Modern Real Estate Practice in Texas*. She holds a BBA degree from Texas Tech University, an MBA degree from West Texas State University, and an EdD in business education from Texas Tech University. Nance has been a real estate practitioner in Amarillo, Texas, since 1978 and began teaching real estate license-preparation classes at Amarillo College in 1985. She holds the Distinguished Real Estate Instructor (DREI) designation from the Real Estate Educators Association (REEA) and the Certified Real Estate Instructor (CREI) designation from the Texas Real Estate Teachers Association (TRETA). She served as the instructional coordinator for the CREI program in Texas from its inception in 1994 through 1999, is a past president of TRETA (1992 conference year), and was approved as a senior instructor for the Real Estate Educators Association. Nance is the owner-broker of the Amarillo-based Real Estate Investment Group and CJ Investments, a property management company. She is the 1995 recipient of the John Mead Faculty Excellence Award from Amarillo College and has received both the Don Roose Award of Excellence (1999) and the Lifetime Achievement Award (2009) from TRETA.

Dearborn Real Estate Education would like to thank Cheryl Nance for her high quality and diligent work on Modern Real Estate Practice in Texas *for the past nine editions. Her meticulousness, craft, and commitment to education are remarkable.*

ABOUT THE CONTRIBUTING EDITOR

Loretta DeHay is an attorney in private practice in central Texas with an extensive background in real estate regulation and government administration. She retired in August 2013 from the Texas Real Estate Commission (TREC), where she started as the director of enforcement and later served as general counsel and assistant administrator. Before working for TREC, DeHay worked for the Texas Attorney General's office. DeHay has served on the board of directors for the Association of Real Estate License Law Officials and the regional chapter of the General Counsel Forum.

CHAPTER

1

Introduction to Modern Real Estate Practice

■ **LEARNING OBJECTIVES** *When you have completed this chapter, you will be able to*

- **identify** the various careers available in real estate and the professional organizations that support them;
- **describe** the five uses of real property;
- **list** the seven sources of real estate law and give an example of each; and
- **define** the following *key terms*:

agricultural real estate	National Association of REALTORS® (NAR)	seven sources of law
broker		special-purpose real estate
commercial real estate	precedent	
common law	Realtist	Texas Real Estate Commission (TREC)
industrial real estate	REALTOR®	Texas Real Estate License Act
mixed use real estate	residential real estate	
	salesperson	

OVERVIEW

Real estate transactions take place all around us, all the time. A commercial leasing company rents space in a mall to an electronics store. The owner of a building rents an apartment to a retired couple. An appraiser gives an expert opinion of the value of 100 acres of farmland, which is now surrounded by residential subdivisions. A bank lends money to a professional corporation so that it can purchase a medical office building. And, of course, the typical American family sells its old house and buys a bigger one.

Real estate is big business, involving billions of dollars every year in the United States alone. Because real estate is a heavily regulated market, the real estate practitioner must be familiar with the many sources of law on the federal, state, and local levels.

This chapter introduces students to the industry in general, as well as to many legal considerations that affect today's real estate professional.

REAL ESTATE—A BUSINESS OF MANY SPECIALIZATIONS

Brokerage

The business of bringing together people who are interested in making a real estate transaction is *brokerage*. Typically, the **broker** acts as an *agent* of the buyer or the seller (or both) in negotiating the sale, purchase, or rental of property. A **salesperson** is a licensee employed by or associated with a broker who conducts brokerage activities on behalf of the broker for a fee or commission. Residential brokerage involves the sale and purchase of a residential property. Other types of real estate brokerage, such as property management, apartment locating, commercial brokerage, and the sale of farm and ranch property, require specialization and sometimes additional education and experience to maintain competency in that area.

Brokerage is discussed further in Chapter 5, and Chapter 23 provides a more detailed analysis of commercial, farm and ranch, and other real estate specializations and related disciplines. Property management will be extensively discussed in Chapter 22.

Despite the size and complexity of the real estate business, many people think it only consists of brokers and salespersons. In reality, the real estate industry is much bigger than that and encompasses a wide variety of related disciplines interacting together. Basic knowledge of the real estate–related disciplines helps to maintain a better understanding of the real estate business in general.

Real Estate–Related Disciplines

Some real estate–related disciplines include appraising, lending and financing, property inspection, property development, real estate counseling, real estate education, title insurance and abstracting, urban planning, petroleum landsmen and women, and easement and right-of-way registrants. Real estate financing and licensing of mortgage professionals are examined in Chapters 15 and 16. The other specializations and related disciplines or industries will be further discussed in Chapter 23.

Uses of Real Property

Just as there are many areas of specialization within the real estate industry, there are many different types of property in which to specialize (see Figure 1.1). Real estate generally can be classified as

- ■ **residential**—all property used for housing, from small city lots to acreage, both single-family and multifamily, in urban, suburban, and rural areas;
- ■ **commercial**—business property, including offices, shopping centers, stores, theaters, hotels, and parking facilities;
- ■ **industrial**—warehouses, factories, and land in industrial districts;
- ■ **agricultural**—farms, timberland, pastureland, ranches, and orchards;
- ■ **special-purpose**—places of worship, schools, cemeteries, and government-held lands; or
- ■ **mixed-use**—any lawful combination of the other five basic categories of real property permitted by local zoning.

FIGURE 1.1: Uses of Real Property

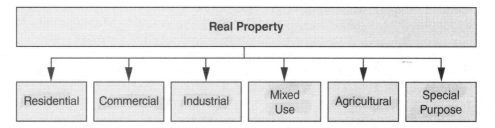

The market for each of these types of properties can be further subdivided into (1) the sales market, which involves the transfer of title, and (2) the rental market, which involves the use of space on a lease basis.

I N   P R A C T I C E   Although in theory a real estate person or firm can perform all these services and handle all six classes of property, this is rarely done, except in small towns. Most real estate firms tend to specialize in one class to some degree, especially in urban areas. Specializations in the real estate industry and related disciplines will be more thoroughly addressed in Chapter 23.

Education Standard Advisory Committee

The Texas Legislature created the Education Standard Advisory Committee (ESAC) by amending TRELA in 2011 under Senate Bill 747. The mission of the ESAC is to regularly review and revise curriculum standards, course content requirements, and instructor certification requirements for core and continuing education courses. The committee consists of seven members who have been actively engaged in the practice of real estate for at least five years before appointment; four members who are either owners of real estate schools that are accredited by TREC and provide core or continuing education, or approved instructors; and one public member. The chair of the Commission may also appoint a nonvoting Commission-member liaison.

At its first meeting, the ESAC developed a process for reviewing existing core courses and textbooks, comparing course materials to the topics required by TRELA for each course, and creating a detailed list of subtopics with time periods ascribed to each subtopic. The committee began its review of each core course by first focusing on the principles of real estate. They extensively surveyed a selection of textbooks on the principles of real estate, including this book, comparing the texts to the topic areas required by TRELA for principles, and finally recommended a revised curriculum for the Principles of Real Estate I and II, consisting of two 30-hour courses with very specific subject matter requirements. The Real Estate Commission adopted the new curriculum requirements for Principles I and II in the Rules.

This edition of *Modern Real Estate Practice in Texas* incorporates all the required curriculum changes. Chapter 6, which concerns fair housing laws, was substantially rewritten to comply with the new requirements. In addition, Chapter 23 was added to provide an in-depth discussion of real estate specializations.

The ESAC has also recommended, and the Commission has adopted by rule, new curriculum requirements for 30-hour courses in Law of Agency, Promulgated Contracts, and Law of Contracts. As of this writing, the ESAC was in the process of recommending curriculum requirements for adoption by the Commission for a 30-hour finance course.

The ESAC is also working on ways to improve classroom, correspondence, and alternative-delivery courses. The ESAC intends to review all core course curriculum content, course fees and approval processes, methodologies of course delivery (including classroom, correspondence, alternative delivery, webinars, and combinations thereof), instructor and provider qualifications, and alternative ways of measuring student mastery of a subject, besides examination.

After the ESAC addresses all the required core courses, it will begin a review of the required continuing education courses in a similar manner. At the same time, it continues to examine the other items described here and will make recommendations for rule changes to the Commission as necessary to improve the quality of real estate education in Texas.

REAL ESTATE LAW

The purchase of real estate is an entirely different type of transaction from the purchase of personal property such as groceries, clothing, fuel, automobiles, or television sets. Although every type of sales transaction creates a change of ownership involving certain relatively simple legal problems, even the simplest of real estate transactions brings into play a body of complex laws.

Real estate brokers and salespersons must have a broad understanding of law and how various laws affect real estate activities. However, if legal questions or problems arise, the real estate practitioner must advise the parties to consult an attorney, preferably one who specializes in real estate law.

Sources of Real Estate Law

Generally, in the United States, **seven sources of law** affect the ownership and transfer of real estate (see Figure 1.2). These sources are the Constitution of the United States; laws passed by Congress; federal regulations adopted by the various agencies and commissions created by Congress; state constitutions; laws passed by state legislatures; ordinances passed by cities, towns, and other local governments;

and court decisions. Because the Spanish, Mexican, and French flags are among the "six flags over Texas," the laws of those countries have influenced the development of Texas legal principles. Texas has adopted the English common law for certain rules, such as riparian water rights, and has drawn heavily on Spanish law for doctrines such as community and separate property.

FIGURE 1.2:   Sources of Real Estate Law

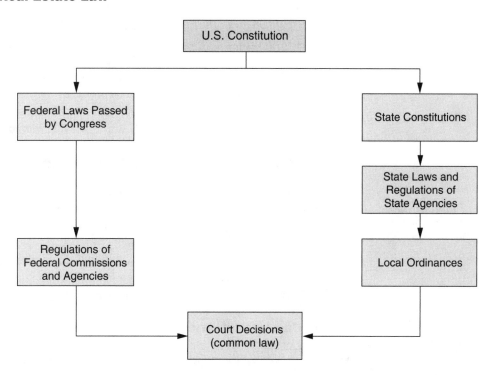

The primary purpose of the *U.S. Constitution* and the individual *state constitutions* is to establish the rights of citizens and delineate the limits of governmental authority. For example, the Fourteenth Amendment to the U.S. Constitution provides civil rights protections that serve as the basis for federal fair housing legislation; homestead and community property laws derive from the Texas constitution.

Laws passed by Congress and by *state and local legislative bodies* may establish specific provisions, or they simply may set broad standards of conduct and establish administrative enforcement agencies. Federal fair housing laws prohibiting discrimination are examples of laws passed by the U.S. Congress; the Texas Real Estate License Act, which regulates real estate professionals, is a state statute passed by the Texas Legislature. Some laws may apply only to a specific type of property. For example, some landlord-tenant laws differ between residential and commercial properties.

Governmental agencies that enact rules and regulations range from the Federal Housing Administration to the Texas Real Estate Commission to local zoning boards. The regulations passed by these agencies are a means of implementing and enforcing legislative acts; they provide detailed information regarding legal and illegal actions and practices; they designate penalties and violations; and they expand on the law and have the effect of law.

Decisions handed down by federal, state, and municipal courts serve to clarify and interpret laws, regulations, and constitutional provisions. By applying and interpreting the laws in relation to a specific event, a court decision expands the meaning of the law, establishing a **precedent** that may be used as a standard in subsequent similar cases. However, the courts are not always bound by established precedent. Courts in one jurisdiction (area of authority) may not be bound by the decisions of courts in other jurisdictions. Furthermore, a court with superior authority in its jurisdiction may, at its discretion, reverse the ruling of a lower court.

Real estate ownership and transfer are affected by **common law**, which is the body of rules and principles founded on tradition and court decisions. It is derived mainly from practices developed in England and, as it applies to the United States, dates back to practices in effect during the American Revolution.

Some remedies provided under common law were considered too harsh, and as a result, *courts of equity* evolved to provide relief on the basis of equitable principles. Although Texas does not have separate courts of law and equity, Texas judges are permitted to grant both legal and equitable remedies to ensure justice.

Laws Affecting Real Estate Practice

Federal Laws
- Capital gains tax law
- Fair housing law
- Equal credit law
- Real estate settlement law

The general sources of law encompass a number of specific areas that are important to the real estate practitioner. These include the *law of contracts*, *general property law*, *landlord-tenant law*, the *law of agency* (which covers the obligations of a broker to the person who engages his services), the *real estate license law*, and *consumer protection laws*. All these areas will be discussed in this text.

The Purpose of Real Estate License Laws

State Laws
- Contract law
- General property law
- Landlord-tenant law
- Agency law
- Real estate license law
- Consumer protection law

Because real estate brokers and salespersons engage in the business of handling other people's real estate and money, the need to regulate their activities has long been recognized. In an effort to protect the public from fraud, dishonesty, or incompetence in the buying and selling of real estate, all states, the District of Columbia, and all Canadian provinces have passed laws that require real estate brokers and salespersons to be licensed. The first real estate license law was passed in California in 1919.

Real Estate License Requirements in Texas

The first law to regulate real estate brokerage in Texas, the *Texas Real Estate Dealers Act*, was passed in 1939. The law that currently regulates real estate in Texas is the **Texas Real Estate License Act**, passed by the Texas Legislature in 1949. The act has been revised many times, most recently in 2011, and is administered by the **Texas Real Estate Commission (TREC)**.

The Texas Real Estate Commission (Commission) is a self-directed, semi-independent state agency. The nine-member Commission is composed of six broker members and three public members appointed by the governor for six-year staggered terms. One of the broker members serves as the chair and is appointed by the governor. The Commission oversees the licensing and certification of real estate salespersons and brokers, home inspectors, and right-of-way registrants; the registration of time-share developments and home warranty companies; the accreditation of prelicense and continuing education providers; and the approval of real estate courses and instructors.

The Texas Appraiser Licensing and Certification Board (TALCB) is an independent nine-member board housed within the Texas Real Estate Commission that licenses real estate appraisers in Texas under state and federal laws.

The combined mission of the state agency, as articulated on its websites, is as follows:

> The agency exists to safeguard the public interest and protect consumers of real estate services. In accord with state and federal laws, the agency oversees real estate brokerage, appraisal, inspection, home warranty and timeshare interest providers. Through education, licensing and regulation, the agency ensures the availability of qualified and ethical service providers, thereby facilitating economic growth and opportunity in Texas.

Persons who deal only with their own property are not required to hold a real estate license. However, any person who, for compensation or the promise of compensation, lists or offers to list; sells or offers to sell; buys or offers to buy; negotiates or offers to negotiate—either directly or indirectly—for the purpose of bringing about the listing, sale, exchange, purchase, option to purchase, auction, rental, or leasing of real estate is required to hold a valid real estate broker's license.

Exceptions to the licensing requirements include an attorney licensed in Texas; a person acting under a duly authorized power of attorney to conduct a single real estate transaction; a public official acting in his official capacity; a licensed auctioneer conducting a real estate auction, so long as the auctioneer does not engage in other brokerage activity; a person acting under a court order or under a will or trust; an employee of a builder or owner; an onsite manager of an apartment complex; transactions involving the sale, lease, or transfer of mineral interests or cemetery lots; transactions involving the lease or management of a hotel or motel; and foreclosure transactions.

A real estate license applicant must possess certain stated personal and educational qualifications and must pass an examination to prove adequate knowledge of the business. In addition, to qualify for license renewal and continue in business, the licensee must pay renewal fees, follow certain prescribed standards of business conduct and meet continuing education requirements.

Chapter 5 thoroughly addresses the duties and responsibilities of real estate brokers and salespersons to clients and consumers by introducing the concepts of real estate brokerage and the law of agency. Chapter 8 provides an in-depth discussion of the Texas Real Estate License Act and Rules of the Commission. These laws and regulations provide the framework for obtaining and maintaining a real estate license, including a laundry list of prohibited practices such as negligence, misrepresentation, failing to disclose, and publishing misleading advertising. The act and the Rules also include the procedures that must be followed for consumers to file disciplinary complaints against licensees for violations of the act and the Rules and to file for reimbursement from the Real Estate Recovery Trust Account for unpaid judgments against a licensee.

The Texas Real Estate License Act requires that the license examination "be of scope sufficient in the judgment of the commission to determine that a person is competent to act as a real estate broker or salesperson in a manner to protect the interest of the public." Chapter 7 more fully describes the License Act and the required education and sponsorship standards.

PROFESSIONAL ASSOCIATIONS

Professional associations for various real estate specializations are listed in Figure 1.3. The organizations include, among others, the Appraisal Institute, the National Association of Real Estate Brokers, the National Association of REALTORS®, the Texas Association of Real Estate Inspectors, the Texas Land Title Association, and the Texas Real Estate Teachers Association. The members of the National Association of Real Estate Brokers (NAREB) are known as **Realtists**.

FIGURE 1.3: Professional Associations

Organization	Web Site
American Institute of Architects	www.aia.org
American Planning Association	www.planning.org
Appraisal Institute	www.appraisalinstitute.org
Asian Real Estate Association of America	http://www.areaa.org/
Building Owners and Managers Association International	www.boma.org
International Council of Shopping Centers	www.icsc.org
National Association of Exclusive Buyer Agents	www.naeba.org
National Association of Hispanic Real Estate Professionals	http://nahrep.org/
National Association of Home Builders	www.nahb.org
National Association of Real Estate Brokers	www.nareb.com
National Association of REALTORS®	www.realtor.org
Texas Apartment Association	www.taa.org
Texas Association of Mortgage Professionals	www.ttamp.org
Texas Association of Real Estate Inspectors	www.tarei.com
Texas Association of REALTORS®	www.texasrealestate.com
Texas Land Title Association	www.tlta.com
Texas Mortgage Bankers Association	www.texasmba.org
Texas Real Estate Teachers Association	www.treta.org
Women in Mortgage Banking	http://www.americanbanker.com/women-in-banking/

The largest real estate trade organization is the **National Association of REALTORS® (NAR)**, founded in 1908. It serves members' interests by keeping them apprised of developments in their field, publicizing the services of members, improving standards and practices, and recommending or taking positions on public legislation and regulations affecting the operations of members and member firms. NAR also sponsors various affiliated institutes and societies that offer professional designations to brokers, salespersons, and others who complete required courses in areas of special interest. Some of the NAR institutes and societies and their designations are listed in Figure 1.4. In addition to the professional designations, NAR offers several certifications, among them an "At Home with Diversity" certification, "e-PRO" certification for internet professionals, Real Estate Professional Assistant certification, Resort and Second-Home Property Specialist certification, and Short Sales and Foreclosures Resource certification.

FIGURE 1.4: National Association of REALTORS® Institutes, Societies, and Professional Designations

Institute	Designation
CCIM Institute	CCIM—Certified Commercial Investment Member
Council of Real Estate Brokerage Managers	CRB—Certified Real Estate Brokerage Manager
Council of Residential Specialists	CRS—Certified Residential Specialist
Counselors of Real Estate	CRE—Counselor of Real Estate
Green REsource Council	Green Designation
Institute of Real Estate Management (IREM)	CPM—Certified Property Manager
	AMO—Accredited Management Organization
	ARM—Accredited Residential Manager
	ACoM—Accredited Commercial Manager
National Association of REALTORS® (NAR)	GRI—Graduate, Realtor® Institute
	CIPS—Certified International Property Specialist
	RAA—Residential Accredited Appraiser
	GAA—General Accredited Appraiser
	RCE— Realtor® Association Certified Executive
Real Estate Buyer's Agent Council (REBAC)	ABR—Accredited Buyer's Representative
REALTORS® Land Institute (RLI)	ALC—Accredited Land Consultant
Society of Industrial and Office REALTORS®	SIOR—Society of Industrial and Office REALTORS®
SRES Council	SRES—Seniors Real Estate Specialist
Women's Council of REALTORS® (WCR)	PMN—Performance Management Network

Only members of NAR may be called REALTORS®; other agents are simply *real estate licensees* or *agents*.

NAR is composed of state, regional, and local associations. Members must hold a real estate license, subscribe to a strict Code of Ethics, and are known as **REALTORS®** (a registered trademark). The Texas Association of REALTORS® (TAR) is affiliated with NAR and works closely with local associations of REALTORS® in developing the interests of individual REALTORS® and the buying and selling public. Membership in NAR and TAR is voluntary. Only members of NAR may be called REALTORS®; other agents are simply *real estate licensees* or *agents*. NAR has two internet sites: www.realtor.com contains tools and resources primarily for consumers, and www.realtor.org has information for real estate professionals.

WEBLINK @ www.realtor.com and www.realtor.org

IN PRACTICE   With more than 80,000 members, the Texas Association of REALTORS® (TAR) represents all aspects of real estate in Texas. For more information about Texas REALTORS®, consult one of the following websites or locate an association in your area at the TAR site:

- Austin Board of REALTORS®, www.abor.com
- Houston Association of REALTORS®, www.har.com
- MetroTex Association of REALTORS®, www.dfwrealestate.com
- San Antonio Board of REALTORS®, www.sabor.com

WEBLINK @ www.texasrealestate.com

SUMMARY

Although selling and leasing are the most widely recognized activities of the real estate business, the industry also involves many other services, such as appraisal, apartment locating, property inspection, property development, counseling, property financing, education, title work, and urban planning. The highly complex and competitive nature of the real estate industry requires that a practitioner be competent in a number of fields.

Real property can be classified according to its general use as residential, commercial, industrial, agricultural, mixed-use, or special-purpose. Although many brokers deal with more than one type of real property, they usually specialize to some degree.

Even the simplest real estate transactions involve a complex body of laws. In the United States, the seven sources of law are the U.S. Constitution, laws passed by Congress, federal regulations, state constitutions, laws passed by state legislatures, local ordinances, and court decisions.

Much of real property law is based on common law practices developed in England. Common law includes rules and principles founded on custom and prior court decisions. Spanish law also has influenced Texas real estate law.

The real estate business is a dynamic industry that employs hundreds of thousands of professionals. Every state, the District of Columbia, and every Canadian province have some type of licensing requirement for real estate brokers and salespersons. The Texas Real Estate License Act regulates real estate in Texas.

Various professional organizations afford the licensee an opportunity to stay current on issues related to real estate. Some of these organizations are the National Association of REALTORS®, the Texas Association of REALTORS®, local associations of REALTORS®, and the National Association of Real Estate Brokers.

CHAPTER 1 QUESTIONS

1. Professional associations of specialists in various fields of real estate activity were organized to serve the interests of their members. Which is *NOT* generally a service expected of such organizations?
    a. Keeping members informed of developments in their field
    b. Improving standards and practices
    c. Providing a clearinghouse of information
    d. Passing laws to regulate brokers and salespersons

2. There are seven sources of law in the United States. Which is *NOT* an example of one of them?
    a. Local zoning laws
    b. FHA/VA regulations
    c. Court decisions
    d. Precedent set by decisions of the city council

3. Laws passed by Congress and various state legislatures may
    a. not designate penalties and violations.
    b. set precedents for future court decisions.
    c. authorize agencies to pass rules and regulations to enforce the provisions of the law.
    d. clarify and interpret court decisions.

4. The legal concept of precedent
    a. applies only to state court decisions.
    b. must always be followed by judges when formulating court decisions.
    c. grew out of common law.
    d. binds courts in all jurisdictions, regardless of superior authority.

5. Constitutional provisions
    a. establish the rights of citizens and delineate government authority.
    b. set down specific provisions on every issue.
    c. can be waived by signing a release.
    d. designate penalties and violations.

6. Real estate license laws
    a. are consistent from state to state.
    b. apply only to licensed brokers.
    c. were passed to protect the public from the possible fraud, dishonesty, and incompetence of unscrupulous brokers and salespersons.
    d. apply to persons who sell their own property.

7. Common law
    a. is derived from practices developed in the Spanish Empire.
    b. has no effect on today's real estate practices.
    c. includes both custom and court decisions in its application today.
    d. establishes the limitations of municipal court decisions.

8. A REALTOR® is
    a. a specially licensed real estate professional who acts as a point of contact between two or more people in negotiating the sale, purchase, or rental of property.
    b. any real estate broker or salesperson who assists buyers, sellers, landlords, or tenants in any real estate transaction.
    c. a real estate licensee who is a member of the National Association of REALTORS®.
    d. a member of the National Association of Real Estate Brokers who specializes in residential properties.

9. Which is an example of commercial real estate?
    a. An office building converted to low-income housing
    b. An apartment for rent
    c. Retail space for lease
    d. A factory

10. Peyton is a real estate broker in a large metropolitan area. Chances are his real estate firm
    a. deals in most or all the various real estate specializations.
    b. deals only in farm property.
    c. deals only in insurance.
    d. specializes in only one or two types of property.

11. Which is an example of special-purpose real estate?
    a. A public library
    b. A shopping center
    c. An industrial park
    d. An apartment complex

12. Brenda holds a real estate license and has several years of experience in the industry. However, she has "retired" from actively marketing properties and now helps clients choose among the various alternatives involved in purchasing, using, or investing in property. What is her profession?
    a. Real estate counselor
    b. Real estate appraiser
    c. Real estate educator
    d. REALTOR®

Detailed rationales for the end-of-chapter review questions are available online at www.dearborn.com through the *Instructor Resource Guides* link.

CHAPTER 2

Real Property

OVERVIEW

Will Rogers often is quoted as saying, "Buy land—they ain't making any more of the stuff!" The preamble to the National Association of REALTORS® Code of Ethics begins with the words "Under all is the land. . . ." We see it, touch it, and refer to it every day, but what exactly is land? When we own it, do we own just the ground beneath our feet and, if so, how deep does this ownership go? What about the trees we sit under and the air we breathe—are these a part of the land also?

This chapter discusses the nature and characteristics of real estate, as well as the similarities and distinctions among land, real estate, and real property. In addition, the chapter illustrates the distinctions between real estate and personal property and shows how an item of personal property can be converted into real property, and vice versa.

LAND, REAL ESTATE, AND REAL PROPERTY

The words *land*, *real estate*, and *real property* commonly are used to describe the same commodity. In the broader sense, they appear to be interchangeable; however, their technical meanings have subtle but important differences.

Land

The term *land* refers to more than just the surface of the earth; it includes the underlying soil and things that are attached permanently to the land by nature, such as trees and water. From a legal standpoint, land ownership also includes possession and control of the minerals and substances below the earth's surface, together with the airspace above the land.

Thus, **land** is defined as *the earth's surface extending downward to the center of the earth and upward to infinity, including things permanently attached by nature, such as trees and water* (see Figure 2.1).

FIGURE 2.1:   Land, Real Estate, and Real Property

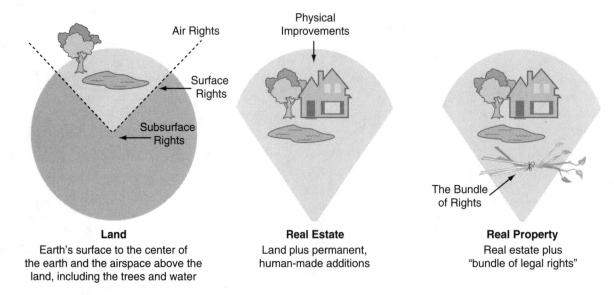

Land
Earth's surface to the center of the earth and the airspace above the land, including the trees and water

Real Estate
Land plus permanent, human-made additions

Real Property
Real estate plus "bundle of legal rights"

Real Estate

The term *real estate*, or *realty*, is somewhat broader than *land* and includes not only the physical components of the land as provided by nature but also all man-made permanent improvements on and to the land. In actual practice, the word **improvement** applies to the buildings erected on the land as well as to streets, utilities, and sewers (referred to as *infrastructure*) and other man-made additions to the property.

Real estate, therefore, is defined as *the earth's surface extending downward to the center of the earth and upward into space, including all things permanently attached to it by nature or by people* (see Figure 2.1).

Real Property

The term *real property* is broader still; it refers to the physical surface of the land, what lies below it, what lies above it, and what is permanently attached to it, as well as to the *legal rights of real estate ownership*, often described as the **bundle of legal rights**. The bundle of legal rights (see Figure 2.2) includes the right to *control* the property within the framework of the law, the right of *exclusion* (to keep others from entering or occupying the property), the right of *possession*, the right of *disposition* (to be able to sell or otherwise convey the property), and the right of *enjoyment* (to use the property in any legal manner). Within these ownership rights are included further rights: to mortgage or encumber; lease or license; cultivate or mine; will, dedicate, or give away; and share, trade, or exchange.

FIGURE 2.2: The Bundle of Legal Rights

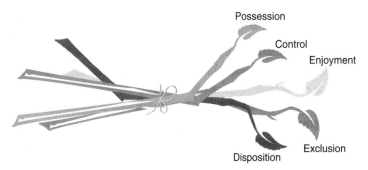

Possession
Control
Enjoyment
Exclusion
Disposition

Thus, **real property** is defined *as the earth's surface extending downward to the center of the earth and upward into space, including all things permanently attached to it by nature or by people, as well as the interests, benefits, and rights inherent in the ownership of real estate* (see Figure 2.1).

IN PRACTICE   Although real estate and real property have different meanings as described, they are used interchangeably in everyday use. People use the term *real estate* when referring to buying or selling homes, office buildings, or land. Thus, in casual usage, real estate generally includes the legal rights of ownership specified in the definition of real property. For simplicity, the term *real estate* will be used in this textbook.

Subsurface and Air Rights   Ownership of land can be *laterally severed* into subsurface rights, surface rights, and air rights. The owner of **surface rights** (the rights to use the surface of the earth) does not always control the subsurface or air rights to the property.

Lateral severance—separates subsurface, surface, and air rights

Subsurface rights are the rights to the natural resources below the earth's surface. Texas recognizes as separate estates oil and gas (as one right) and other mineral rights. Underground water is considered part of the surface estate.

For example, a landowner may sell to an oil company the rights to any oil and gas found in the land. Later, the same landowner can sell the remaining interest to a purchaser but, in the sale, reserve the rights to all coal that may be found in the land. After these sales, three parties have ownership interests in this real estate: (1) the oil company owns all oil and gas, (2) the seller owns all coal, and (3) the purchaser owns the rights to the rest of the real estate.

In Texas, when subsurface rights are sold separately from surface rights, the mineral interest is considered dominant over the surface interest. Owners of mineral rights are legally entitled, unless otherwise specified, to reasonable entry onto the property of the surface owner to extract the minerals for which they hold subsurface rights. Typically, a general grant of mineral rights does not include any substance such as iron ore, strip-mined coal, limestone, or gravel, the removal of which would substantially spoil or deplete the surface lands. These substances would belong to the holder of the surface rights.

Air rights, the rights to use the air above the land, may also be sold or leased independently of the land. They can be an important part of real estate, particularly in large cities where air rights over railroads have been purchased or leased to construct office buildings such as the Met Life Building in New York City and the Merchandise Mart in Chicago. For the construction of such buildings, developers must acquire not only the air rights above the land but also numerous small portions of the land's surface for the building's foundation supports.

Because land for development is relatively plentiful in Texas cities, it is more common for air rights to be granted by a public entity through a license agreement for a nominal fee rather than through sale or lease. For example, the Galleria in Houston built shops and a walkway over a city street in "air rights" granted from the City of Houston through a license agreement. Institutions within the Texas Medical Center in Houston have a similar license agreement for pedestrian walkways over streets to connect buildings within its complex. In addition, the downtown businesses have a license agreement with the City of Houston, which gives them "subsurface rights" to build and maintain a public pedestrian tunnel system.

IN PRACTICE   Although a property owner has the rights to the air upward to infinity, the courts permit reasonable interference with these rights for aircraft, so long as the owner's right to use and occupy the land is not unduly lessened. Texas law has provided air easements over land near commercial airports for the benefit of the airports, including height restrictions for buildings to prevent interference with airborne operations. To enhance citizens' rights, city zoning ordinances restrict residential development in noise-impacted areas. However, if an airport is built near an existing residential area, the airport owner (a city, county, or other entity) would be required to soundproof existing homes, to make a financial settlement with homeowners in the noise-impacted area, or to buy the homes and raze them to make room for possible commercial development.

REAL PROPERTY VERSUS PERSONAL PROPERTY

Personal property = personalty = chattel

Property may be classified as either real or personal. As noted, real estate is defined as a part of the earth, including the permanent additions or growing things attached to it, the airspace above it, and the minerals below it. **Personal property**, sometimes called **personalty**, is all property that does not fit the definition of real estate. Thus, personal property has the unique characteristic of being *movable*. Items of personal property, also called **chattels**, include such tangibles as chairs, tables, clothing, money, bonds, and bank accounts (see Figure 2.3).

FIGURE 2.3:   Real Versus Personal Property

Real Estate or Real Property

Land and anything permanently attached to it

Personal Property

Movable items not attached to real estate; items severed from real estate

Fixture

Item of personal property converted to real estate by attaching it to the real estate with the intention that it become permanently a part thereof

Trade Fixture

Item of tenant-owned personal property attached to real estate and used in a business; legally removable by tenant

Title to real estate passes by a recordable document such as a deed or will, whereas title to personal property usually passes by a bill of sale.

It is possible to change an item of real estate to personal property by **severance**. For example, a growing tree is real estate, but if the owner cuts down the tree for firewood, thereby severing it from the earth, the tree becomes personal property.

The reverse situation, changing personal property into real estate, also is possible. If an owner buys cement, stones, and sand and constructs a concrete walk on his parcel of real estate, the component parts of the concrete, which were originally personal property, are converted into real estate by **attachment** because they have become a permanent improvement on the land.

Manufactured Housing

The distinction between real and personal property is not always obvious. A manufactured home (mobile home), for example, is generally considered to be personal property because it is movable. In Texas, a manufactured home may be considered real estate *but only if* (a) the owner of the home has elected to treat the home as real property, (b) a certified copy of the "statement of ownership and location" for the home has been filed by the owner in the real property records of the county in which the home is located, and (c) both the Texas Department of

Housing and Community Affairs (TDHCA) and the county's chief tax appraiser have been notified of the filing (House Bill 1510, 2011).

In addition, for an owner to treat a manufactured home as real property, the home must be attached (a) to land owned by the owner of the manufactured home (through a deed or a contract for deed) *or* (b) to land leased to the owner of the home under a long-term lease. It must be attached by means of a stabilization system, which may or may not be a permanent foundation (Manufactured Housing Rules, Subchapter B, Section 80.21).

Owners of manufactured homes are entitled to obtain a homestead tax exemption regardless of whether they have elected to treat the home as real property or personal property and regardless of whether the home is listed on the tax rolls with the real property to which it is attached or separately.

Real estate brokers or salespersons do not have to obtain a special license to sell manufactured homes (even when such homes are not classified as real property), as long as they conduct negotiations for a consumer while acting as the consumer's broker or salesperson. For more information, contact the Manufactured Housing Division of the Texas Department of Housing and Community Affairs at 800-500-7074 or search the website. Additional consumer resources are available on the U.S. Department of Housing and Urban Development (HUD) website through the "Buy a Home" link.

WEBLINK @ www.tdhca.state.tx.us/ and www.hud.gov

IN PRACTICE   For a complete copy of House Bill (H.B.) 1510 and others passed in legislative sessions since 1989, visit the Texas Legislature's website: www.capitol.state .tx.us.

Plants and Minerals

> The term used for plants that do not require annual cultivation (real estate such as trees and shrubbery) is *fructus naturales* (fruits of nature). Emblements (personal property such as a wheat crop) are known as *fructus industriales* (fruits of industry).

Trees and crops generally fall into one of two classes. Trees, perennial shrubbery, and grasses that do not require annual cultivation are considered real estate and are sometimes called **fructus naturales** (fruits of nature). Annual plantings or crops of wheat, corn, vegetables, and fruit are known as **emblements** or **fructus industriales** (fruits of industry) and are generally considered personal property. As long as an annual crop is growing, it will be transferred as part of the real property unless other provisions are made in the sales contract.

As previously noted, ownership of real estate usually includes rights not only to the surface of the ground but also to the minerals and substances below the surface. When an owner drills into land, discovers oil, and stores the oil in tanks ready for transport, the oil is converted from real estate to personal property. In the case of minerals, it is customary to specify in a sales contract what is *not* included in the sale by providing for

- a **reservation** indicating an interest being retained by the seller, such as a mineral right or an access easement, *or*
- an **exception** indicating a deficiency in the grantor's title, such as a mineral interest held by a previous owner.

Fixtures

Legal Tests of a Fixture
1. Intent
2. Adaptation to real estate
3. Method of annexation

An article that was once personal property but has been so affixed to land or to a building that the law construes it to be part of the real estate is a **fixture**. Examples of fixtures are heating units, elevator equipment in highrise buildings, kitchen cabinets, lighting fixtures, plumbing fixtures, and garage door openers. Almost any item that has been added as a *permanent part* of a building is considered a fixture and is automatically included with the real property when a sale occurs, unless other provisions are made in the sales contract. Paragraph 2 of the real estate sales contract shown in Chapter 12 (Figure 12.3) lists additional property considered fixtures in Texas.

Legal Tests of a Fixture   A *written agreement* between parties to a contract is the one certain way to avoid a dispute between a buyer and a seller, or a landlord and a tenant, about whether a particular item should remain with the property as a part of the real estate. Although the Texas standard sales contract forms specify what normally constitutes a fixture, the real estate broker or salesperson should ensure that a sales contract includes a list of all articles included in the sale, particularly if any doubt exists as to whether they are permanently attached fixtures. Some of the articles that might cause confusion between buyers and sellers include satellite dish systems and equipment, carpeting that is not tacked down, ceiling fans, kitchen appliances, artificial fireplace logs, and cabinetry, such as a bookcase, that seems to be affixed to the wall but is actually freestanding.

Absence of a written agreement will necessitate the court's intervention to determine whether an article is personal property or a fixture, and therefore part of the real estate. The three legal tests of a fixture are based on

- the intention of the parties,
- the adaptation of the article to the real estate, and
- the mode and permanence of annexation.

The *intent of the parties* at the time an article was attached is generally considered the most important factor in a court's deciding whether an article is a fixture. Did the person who installed the item intend it to remain permanently on the property or to be removable in the future? For example, a property owner who sets the post of a gas grill in concrete *appears to intend* for the grill to be permanent. However, if a short pipe with a larger diameter were to be set in concrete and the pipe for the gas grill simply set into the larger pipe, would the intent be permanence?

The *adaptation of an article* to use in a particular building is another test of a fixture: has it been customized for this home or is it a standard purchase item? Is the item being used as real property or personal property? For example, a fireplace screen custom built for an oval fireplace opening is considered a fixture, a portion of the real estate that should be included in the purchase of a home. A fireplace screen of a standard size that was purchased ready-made and simply placed on the hearth is not automatically considered a fixture. A refrigerator is usually considered personal property; but if its front has been adapted to match the kitchen cabinetry, it becomes a fixture.

The *mode and permanence of annexation*, or attachment, provides another basis for court decisions. How permanent is the method of attachment? Can the item be removed without causing damage to the surrounding property? An item attached by permanent means, such as cement, nails, or bolts, becomes a fixture. For instance, a furnace, although removable, is usually attached in such a way that it cannot be taken out without causing extensive damage to the property; it is, therefore, a fixture.

Trade Fixtures An article owned by a tenant and attached to a rented space or building for use in conducting a business is a **trade fixture**. Examples of trade fixtures are bowling alleys, store shelves, bars, and restaurant equipment. Agricultural fixtures such as chicken coops and toolsheds are also included in this definition (see Figure 2.3). Trade fixtures are considered personal property of the tenant and, as such, must be removed on or before the expiration of the lease, without seriously damaging the building. Trade fixtures not removed become the real property of the landlord. Acquiring property in this way is known as *accession*.

> *Trade fixtures* are personal property if removed on or before the expiration of a lease.

FOR EXAMPLE Paul's Pizza leases space in a small shopping center. Paul bolted a large iron oven to the floor of the unit. If Paul's Pizza relocates, Paul will be able to take his pizza oven with him if he can repair the bolt holes in the floor. On the other hand, if the pizza oven were set in concrete and welded to metal bracing on the wall, Paul might not be able to remove it without causing structural damage. In that case, the oven would be considered a fixture.

Trade fixtures differ from other fixtures in the following three ways:

- Fixtures belong to the owner of the real estate, but trade fixtures usually belong to, and are installed by, tenants for their use.
- Fixtures are considered a permanent part of a building, but trade fixtures are removable. Trade fixtures may be affixed to a building so as to appear to be fixtures (real estate); however, due to the relationship of the parties (landlord and tenant), the law gives a tenant the right to remove trade fixtures if the removal is completed before the lease expires and if the rented space is restored to approximately its original condition. Leases usually require that upon expiration of a lease the tenant return the premises to the landlord in as good condition as at the beginning of the lease, except for reasonable wear and tear and damage by the elements.
- Fixtures legally are construed to be real estate, but trade fixtures legally are construed to be personal property. Trade fixtures are not included in the sale or mortgage of real estate, except by special agreement.

SUMMARY

Although most people think of land as the surface of the earth, this word really applies not only to the earth's surface but also to the mineral deposits under the earth and the air above it, including things permanently attached by nature. The term *real estate* expands this definition to include human-made improvements attached to the land. *Real property* is the term used to describe real estate plus the "bundle of legal rights" associated with its ownership.

The same parcel of real estate may be laterally severed and thereby owned and controlled by different parties—one owning the surface rights, one owning the air rights, and another owning the subsurface rights.

All property that does not fit the definition of real estate is classified as personal property, or chattel. When articles of personal property are permanently affixed to land, they may become fixtures and as such are considered a part of the real estate.

However, personal property attached to real estate by a tenant for the tenant's business is classified as a trade fixture and remains personal property if removed before the lease expires and without damaging the property.

CHAPTER 2 QUESTIONS

1. A construction firm builds an office center over a railroad right-of-way. This means that
   a. the developer must purchase from the railroad all land under the office center.
   b. trains can no longer operate on the tracks under the building during business hours if the noise disturbs the occupants of the office center.
   c. the construction firm has built the office center using the subsurface rights to the property.
   d. the developer must purchase or lease some land and air rights from the railroad.

2. The term *fructus naturales* refers to which of the following?
   a. Annual crops
   b. Real estate
   c. Fruits of industry
   d. Emblements

3. John purchases a parcel of land and sells the rights to any oil, gas, and minerals located in the ground to an exploration company. This means that he owns all rights to this property *EXCEPT*
   a. air rights.
   b. surface rights.
   c. subsurface rights.
   d. water rights.

4. Manufactured housing
   a. is generally considered real property.
   b. may be considered real property if it is sold in conjunction with a parcel of land.
   c. may be considered real property even if it is not permanently attached to land.
   d. may not be considered real property if it is attached to leased land.

5. A store tenant firmly attaches appropriate appliances for his restaurant business on leased premises. Which statement is *TRUE*?
   a. The appliances are trade fixtures and will be sold as part of the building if the building is sold during the lease term.
   b. The appliances are trade fixtures and must be removed before the lease expires.
   c. The appliances may not be removed without the landlord's permission.
   d. The appliances become the landlord's property on installation.

6. Real estate, by definition, includes many elements and parts. Which items would be a part of real estate?
   a. Chattel
   b. Patio furniture
   c. Farm equipment
   d. Growing trees

7. Which *BEST* defines real property?
   a. Land and the air above it and the subsurface below it
   b. Land and all that there is above or below the surface, including all things permanently attached to it and legal rights associated with it
   c. Land and the buildings permanently affixed to it
   d. Land and all the legal rights associated with it

8. A fixture is
   a. any item that is not a permanent part of the building.
   b. real estate that at one time was personal property.
   c. an item installed by a tenant for temporary use.
   d. not included in the sale or mortgage of real estate.

9. The definition of land includes all *EXCEPT*
   a. minerals in the earth.
   b. the air above the ground up to infinity.
   c. buildings.
   d. trees.

10. Miguel and Celia are adding an enclosed front porch to their home. The lumber dealer with whom they are contracting has just unloaded a truckload of lumber in front of their house that will be used to build the porch. At this point, the lumber is considered

a. a fixture.
b. real property.
c. personal property.
d. real estate.

11. When the new front porch, as described in question 10, is completed, the lumber that the dealer originally delivered will be considered

a. personal property.
b. real estate.
c. chattel.
d. emblements.

12. Suppose that halfway through the construction of the new front porch, as described in question 10, work is delayed indefinitely because of unforeseen difficulties. At this point, the lumber the dealer originally delivered would be considered

a. personal property if it has been used in the construction of the porch.
b. real estate if it has been used in the construction of the porch.
c. real property of the contractor.
d. real property of the dealer.

13. Man-made, permanent additions to land are called

a. chattels.
b. emblements.
c. improvements.
d. fructus naturales.

14. Real estate may be converted into personal property by

a. severance.
b. accession.
c. a bill of sale.
d. inference.

15. Steven rents a detached, single-family home under a one-year lease. Two months into the rental period, Steven installs permanent awnings over the building's front windows to keep the sun away from some delicate hanging plants. Which statement is *TRUE*?

a. Because of their permanent nature, the awnings are considered personal property.
b. The awnings are considered fixtures and may not be removed by the tenant.
c. The awnings are now the personal property of the owner.
d. The awnings are considered trade fixtures and may be removed by the tenant.

16. Real estate is often referred to as a *bundle of legal rights*. Which is *NOT* among these rights?

a. Right of exclusion
b. Right to use the property for illegal purposes
c. Right of enjoyment
d. Right to sell or otherwise convey the property

17. When a person purchases real estate from a seller,

a. she is actually buying the legal rights to the property that were previously held by the seller.
b. the seller cannot legally retain any rights of ownership.
c. the mineral rights remain with the original owner of the property.
d. he must buy subsurface, air, and surface rights.

Detailed rationales for the end-of-chapter review questions are available online at www.dearborn.com through the *Instructor Resource Guides* link.

The Real Estate Market

■ **LEARNING OBJECTIVES** *When you have completed this chapter, you will be able to*

- **list** and describe the physical and economic characteristics of real estate;
- **explain** the operation of supply and demand in the real estate market;
- **identify** the economic, political, and social factors that influence supply and demand and the real estate cycle; and
- **define** the following *key terms*:

abatement	demographics	price
business cycle	market	subjective value
cost	objective value	supply
demand		

OVERVIEW

The real estate business is more than the neighborhood storefront with the Realty sign hanging in the window. Real estate is a national industry that has worldwide economic influence.

This chapter discusses the physical and economic characteristics of real estate and explains the concept of value, particularly how value is tested by the influences of supply and demand in the real estate market.

CHARACTERISTICS OF REAL ESTATE

Real estate possesses seven basic characteristics that determine its value and affect its use: relative scarcity, improvements, permanence of investment, area preference, immobility, indestructibility, and nonhomogeneity. These characteristics fall into two broad categories: economic and physical.

Economic Characteristics

> **Economic Characteristics of Real Estate**
> - Relative scarcity
> - Improvements
> - Permanence of investment
> - Area preference

The economic characteristics of land affect its investment value. They are
- relative scarcity,
- improvements,
- permanence of investment, and
- area preference.

Relative Scarcity   Although land as such is neither scarce nor rare, scarcity in an economic sense means that the total supply of land is fixed. Even though a considerable amount of land remains unused, land in a given location or of a particular quality is in short supply in some areas, such as downtown Houston.

Improvements   Construction of an improvement on one parcel of land can affect the value and use of a particular parcel of land, as well as that of neighboring tracts and whole communities. For example, the construction of a steel plant or the building of an atomic reactor can directly influence a large area. An improvement can be new construction or a modification, and it can influence other parcels favorably or unfavorably.

Permanence of Investment   The capital and labor used to build an improvement represent a large, fixed investment. Although older buildings can be razed to make way for newer buildings, improvements such as drainage, electricity, water, and sewerage remain. The return on such investments is long-term and relatively stable and usually extends over what is called the *economic life* of the improvement. Consequently, real estate investment and land-use decisions must consider the usefulness of improvements 20 to 30 years into the future.

Area Preference   This economic characteristic, sometimes called *situs*, does not refer to a particular geographic location but rather to people's choices and preferences for a given area. The unique quality of personal preference results in different values for similar units. Area preference is the reason that some residential purchasers pay more for a corner house lot than for a lot of the same size located in the middle of the block—and other purchasers might pay less. *Area preference is the most important economic characteristic of land.*

F O R   E X A M P L E   A river runs through Bedford Falls, dividing the town more or less in half. On the north side of the river, known as North Town, houses sell for an average of $150,000. On the south side of the river, known as Southbank, identical houses sell for more than $200,000. The only difference is that homebuyers think that Southbank is a better neighborhood, even though no obvious difference exists between the two equally pleasant sides of town.

Physical Characteristics

The three basic physical characteristics of land are
■ immobility,
■ indestructibility, and
■ nonhomogeneity.

Immobility   Land, which is the earth's surface, is immobile. Some of the substances of land are removable, and its topography can be changed, but *the geographic location of any given parcel of land can never be changed. The location is fixed.*

Because land is immobile, real estate markets tend to be local in character. In addition, local governments are supported largely by property taxes on real estate. The fixed amount of land in a given area enables the local government to rely on a certain amount of annual revenue from property taxes, which in turn allows the government to make long-range plans based on the projected income.

Indestructibility   Land is also *indestructible*. This permanence of land, coupled with the long-term nature of improvements, tends to stabilize investments in real estate. Of course, the fact that land is indestructible does not change the fact that the improvements on land depreciate and can become obsolete, which may dramatically reduce the land's value. Because land is indestructible, it cannot be depreciated and is not insurable.

Nonhomogeneity   No two parcels of land are ever exactly the same. Although they may be substantially similar, *all parcels differ geographically* because each parcel has its own location and, therefore, its singular legal address (enabling, among other things, a seller's transfer of property or a lender's placing a lien to ensure loan repayment). This characteristic may also be called *heterogeneity*.

Characteristics Define Land Use

The various characteristics of a parcel of real estate affect its desirability for a specific use. Some specific physical and economic factors that affect land use include
1 contour and elevation of the parcel, known as *topography*;
2 prevailing winds;
3 transportation;
4 public improvements; and
5 availability of natural resources (such as water).

For example, hilly or heavily wooded land would need considerable work before it could be used for industrial purposes but it would be ideally suited for residential use. Likewise, flat land located along a major highway would be undesirable for residential use but would be well-located for industrial, office, or commercial use.

REAL ESTATE—THE BUSINESS OF VALUE

Subjective value: A desk with an estimated cost of $30,000 reportedly sold for $1.3 million at the estate sale of Jacqueline Kennedy Onassis.

The economic and physical characteristics of real estate form the underlying basis for the determination of value. *Value* can be defined as *the amount of goods or services considered to be a fair and suitable equivalent for something else.* It also has been described as the present worth of future benefits arising from the ownership of real property.

Value is based on objective and subjective factors. For example, a house fitted with a marble entrance hall and hardwood floors would have a greater **objective value** than a house with only rough concrete floors. **Subjective value**, on the other hand, is affected by the relative worth an individual places on a specific item. Thus, a house may be beautifully designed and constructed with expensive materials and still be of no value to someone who does not want such a home.

A given parcel of real estate may have many different kinds of value at the same time—for example, market value (used to estimate selling price), appraised and taxable values (used for property taxes), insured value, mortgage value, and depreciated value.

Often, value is not the same as price, nor is it the same as cost. **Price** is the amount of money ultimately paid for a property; **cost** is the capital outlay for land, labor, materials, and profits necessary to bring a property into existence.

Supply and Demand

Supply and price move in opposite directions.

Demand and price move in the same direction.

A **market** is a place where goods can be bought and sold. A market may be a specific place, or it may be a worldwide economic system for moving goods and services around the globe. In either case, the function of a market is to provide a setting in which supply and demand can establish market value, making it advantageous for buyers and sellers to trade.

The economic forces of supply and demand continually interact in the market to establish and maintain price levels. Essentially, *when supply goes up, prices drop* as more sellers compete for buyers; *when demand increases, prices rise* as more buyers compete for the product (see Figure 3.1). When both supply and demand increase, real estate prices tend to remain stable. Although no one can accurately predict changes in real estate values, understanding what causes prices to go up and down can be helpful to the real estate practitioner.

FIGURE 3.1: Supply and Demand

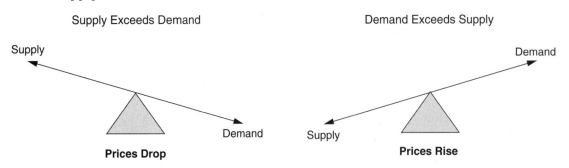

Supply can be defined as *the amount of goods offered for sale within the market at a given price during a given time period.* To be a part of the available supply, land must be readily adaptable to the desired purpose at a price the market will bear. For example, very rocky land located near a city could be considered part of the supply of land available for residential housing only if the market prices of homes in the area were high enough to absorb the cost of removing the rocks before construction.

Demand can be defined as *the amount of goods consumers are willing and able to buy at a given price during a given time period.* In real estate, demand is based on the benefits that can be derived from using land for a specific purpose. For example, an investor who buys a corner lot in a business district to construct an office building buys the land for the rental income it will generate.

Supply Factors
■ Labor force
■ Construction costs
■ Government controls
■ Government financial policies

Factors Affecting Supply

A number of factors affect supply in the real estate market. Some of the major factors include the labor force, construction costs, and government controls and financial policies (see Figure 3.2).

FIGURE 3.2: Factors Affecting Supply and Demand

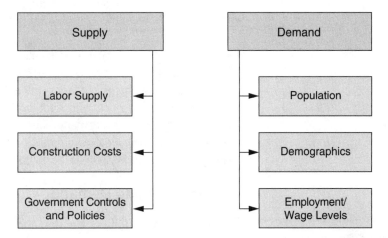

Labor Force and Construction Costs   A shortage of skilled labor or building materials or a significant increase in the cost of labor or materials can decrease the amount of new construction. The impact of labor supply and price levels depends on the extent to which higher costs can be passed on to the buyer in the form of higher purchase prices.

Technological advances that result in less expensive materials and more efficient means of construction may counteract some price increases.

Government Controls and Financial Policies   Government monetary policy can have a substantial impact on the real estate market. The Federal Reserve Board establishes a *discount rate* of interest for the money it lends to commercial banks. That rate has a direct impact on the *interest rates* the banks charge to borrowers. Obviously, interest rates charged to builders, homebuyers, and commercial property developers play a significant part in determining the supply of real estate available. Government agencies such as the Federal Housing Administration (FHA) and Ginnie Mae (the Government National Mortgage Association) determine the terms and conditions under which money is available to lenders for mortgage loans (see Chapter 16). The Consumer Financial Protection Bureau (CFPB) was created by the Dodd-Frank Wall Street Reform and Consumer Protection Act of 2010 (the Dodd-Frank Act), signed into law on July 10, 2010. The Dodd-Frank Act transferred oversight of several federal consumer protection laws to the CFPB—such as the Real Estate Settlement Procedures Act (RESPA), Home Ownership and Equity Protection Act (HOEPA), and Truth in Lending Act (TILA)—and the agency was given broad authority to write rules to protect consumers from unfair or deceptive financial products and practices (see Chapter 16).

Virtually any government action can have some effect on the real estate market. For instance, federal environmental regulations may increase or decrease the supply and value of land in a local market.

Local governments also influence supply. Land-use controls, building codes, zoning ordinances, and taxation policies help shape the character of a community and control the use of land. And they can have either positive or negative effects. High taxes may deter investors. On the other hand, tax incentives or tax **abatements** can attract new businesses and industries by reducing or eliminating their property taxes. Increased employment and expanded residential real estate markets should result from these new enterprises—encouraging developers to increase the supply of houses and commercial properties.

IN PRACTICE Tax abatements were credited with creating or retaining more than 100,000 jobs in Texas between 1997 and 2007. Although taxing entities authorize and consent to tax abatements, the task of attracting new business to a community is often the result of hard work by publicly funded, local economic development foundations or organizations. Under the terms of many incentive or tax abatement agreements, a private firm may have to reimburse local governments or taxing entities if it does not meet agreed-upon performance standards, such as the number of jobs to be created.

Factors Affecting Demand

Factors that tend to affect the demand for real estate include population, demographics, and employment and wage levels (see Figure 3.2).

Demand Factors
■ Population
■ Demographics
■ Employment levels
■ Wage levels

Population Shelter is a basic human need. The demand for housing grows with the population; and as housing needs grow, the demand for industrial and commercial areas also should increase. Although the total population of the country continues to rise, the demand for real estate increases faster in some areas than in others. In some locations, however, growth has ceased altogether or the population has declined. This may be due to economic changes (such as plant closings), social concerns (such as the quality of schools or a desire for more open space), or population changes (such as shifts from colder climates to warmer climates). The result can be a drop in demand for real estate in one area and an increased demand elsewhere.

Demographics The study and description of a population is **demographics**. The characteristics of the population in a community are major factors in the quantity and type of housing in demand. Family size, the ratio of adults to children, the number of retirees, family income, lifestyle, and the growing number of single-parent and "empty nester" households are all demographic factors that contribute to the amount and type of housing needed.

IN PRACTICE   The coming of age of Generation Y/millennials/echo boomers (the children of baby boomers) is expected to be one of the most important demographic trends to influence the real estate market over the next decade. Roughly 80 million children were born between 1982 and 1995 and either are or soon will be renting their own apartments and buying their own homes.

Employment and Wage Levels   Decisions about whether to buy or rent and how much to spend on housing are closely related to income. When job opportunities are plentiful, wages are competitive, and an employee feels secure in a job, demand for housing is likely to increase. When job opportunities are scarce or wage levels low, demand for real estate usually drops. The market might, in fact, be affected drastically by a single major employer's moving in or shutting down. Therefore, licensees must be aware of the business plans of local employers.

CYCLES

Business cycles:
- Expansion—growth
- Recession—slow down
- Depression—the bottom
- Revival—recovery

Over the years, business activity as measured by the gross domestic product (GDP) has had its ups and downs. These irregular fluctuations in activity are called **business cycles**. They are caused by both internal forces (such as employment levels and consumer and investment spending) and external forces (such as wars, oil embargoes, and global economic forces). The business cycle generally can be characterized by four stages: *expansion* (growth or economic boom), *recession* (contraction; general slowdown in economic activity), *depression* (the bottom or trough of the cycle), and *revival* (recovery; bringing the economy back to life after a depression and leading into a period of expansion). Movements within the cycle generally are gradual but can be very sudden (see Figure 3.3).

FIGURE 3.3: The Business Cycle

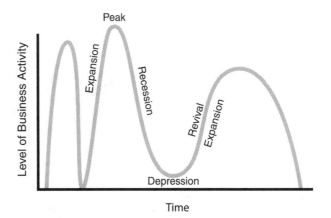

To analyze the patterns of business cycles, a number of trends can be considered simultaneously. The long-term trend (referred to as the *secular trend*) tends to be smooth and continuous. It is most affected by basic influences such as population growth, technological advances, capital accumulation, et cetera. Within this overall pattern are business cycles of varying lengths. Various segments or industries within the economy may have shorter cycles with different timing and different characteristics. Generally, residential real estate sales data reflect seasonal cycles with increases during spring and summer months—influenced by climatic conditions, vacation patterns, school schedules, and similar factors.

The Real Estate Cycle

> The real estate market is local in nature and generally slow to adjust to changes in supply and demand.

Because of the characteristics of nonhomogeneity and immobility, the real estate market generally is slow to adjust to sudden variations in supply and demand. The product cannot be transferred to another market, so an oversupply usually causes prices to drop. Because there is considerable lag time between the conception of real estate development and completion of construction, increases in demand may not be met immediately. Additionally, the number of "housing starts" can lead the economy either into a recession or out of a depression because the housing industry is very sensitive to changes in interest rates. A "tight" monetary policy during a period of expansion or inflation may drive the housing industry into a recession before affecting the rest of the economy. In contrast, an "easy" monetary policy, which results in lower interest rates, generally spurs consumer buying of residential real estate and may enable the home construction sector to lead the economy out of a recession.

SUMMARY

The unique nature of land is apparent in both its economic and physical characteristics. The economic characteristics consist of scarcity, improvements, permanence of investment, and area preference. The physical characteristics are immobility, nonhomogeneity, and indestructibility.

The foundation of the real estate business is value, to which every real estate specialization relates directly or indirectly. A property's value is the present worth of its future benefits. Value is not the same as price, which is determined in the marketplace.

A market is a place where goods and services can be bought and sold and relatively stable price levels established. The ideal market allows for a continual balancing of the forces of supply and demand. Because of its unique characteristics, real estate is relatively slow to adjust to the forces of supply and demand.

Supply can be defined as the amount of goods available in the market for a given price. Demand is defined as the amount of goods that consumers are willing to buy at a given price. The supply of and demand for real estate is affected by many factors, including population changes, demographics, wage and employment levels, construction costs and availability of labor, and government monetary policy and controls.

In the United States, fluctuations in business activity are observed in cycles. Business cycles generally have four stages: expansion, recession, depression, and revival. Stages of the real estate cycle are similar to. Stages of the real estate cycle are similar to—but do not necessarily coincide with—those in the overall business cycle.

CHAPTER 3 QUESTIONS

1. *Value* is best defined as
   a. the highest price that a property will bring.
   b. capital outlay for land, labor, materials, and profits.
   c. a measure of the present worth of future benefits as perceived by each person.
   d. the amount a buyer agrees to pay and a seller agrees to accept.

2. The factors that influence the demand for real estate include
   a. wage levels and employment opportunities.
   b. local government ordinances.
   c. scarcity of building materials.
   d. labor supply.

3. Business cycles
   a. recur at regular intervals.
   b. cannot be regulated by government fiscal and monetary policy.
   c. involve periods of expansion, recession, depression, and revival.
   d. occur simultaneously throughout the state.

4. A factor that affects supply in the real estate market is
   a. construction costs.
   b. population.
   c. wage levels.
   d. demographics.

5. The real estate market is considered local in character because
   a. parcels of land are likely to be similar and confusion could occur concerning similar parcels in two different locations.
   b. each state has its own licensing requirements for real estate salespersons.
   c. land is fixed, or immobile.
   d. local taxation policies affect real estate values.

6. In general, when the supply of a certain commodity increases
   a. prices tend to rise.
   b. prices tend to remain level.
   c. prices tend to drop.
   d. demand tends to drop.

7. *Price* is best defined as the
   a. highest dollar amount a property will bring.
   b. most likely amount a property will bring.
   c. capital outlay for land, labor, materials, and profits.
   d. amount a buyer agrees to pay and a seller agrees to accept.

8. Compared with typical markets, the real estate market
   a. is relatively quick to adapt to the forces of supply and demand.
   b. is national in scope.
   c. is relatively slow to adjust because of its nonhomogeneity and its immobile characteristics.
   d. does not have the problem of oversupply.

9. In general terms, the term *market* refers to which of the following?
   a. A place where buyers and sellers come together to establish prices
   b. The amount of goods available at a given price
   c. An estimate of the selling price
   d. The amount of goods bought at a given price

10. Which is an example of an economic characteristic of land?
    a. Immobility
    b. Nonhomogeneity
    c. Improvements
    d. Indestructibility

11. The term *area preference* refers to
    a. a physical characteristic of land.
    b. nonhomogeneity.
    c. relative scarcity.
    d. an economic characteristic of land.

12. Which physical and economic factors would *NOT* be a consideration for a land developer in determining the optimum use for a parcel of land for industrial purposes?
    a. Transportation
    b. Natural resources available
    c. Public improvements
    d. Indestructibility

13. The term *nonhomogeneity* refers to
    a. land's durability and indestructibility.
    b. capital expenditures represented by a fixed investment.
    c. the fact that no two parcels of land are exactly alike.
    d. the fact that the geographic location of land cannot be changed.

14. Relative scarcity implies that
    a. land available for development is scarce throughout Texas.
    b. land available for development may be in short supply in some areas.
    c. families may place different values on similar properties.
    d. families may prefer one area of a city over another.

Detailed rationales for the end-of-chapter review questions are available online at www.dearborn.com through the *Instructor Resource Guides* link.

Concepts of Home Ownership

When you have completed this chapter, you will be able to

- **identify** the various types of housing choices available to homebuyers;
- **describe** the issues involved in making a home ownership decision;
- **discuss** the primary considerations for determining housing affordability;
- **explain** the tax benefits of home ownership;
- **distinguish** the various types of homeowners insurance policies and relate them to property-damage claims;
- **describe** the requirement for and the coverage provided by a flood insurance policy; and
- **define** the following *key terms:*

capital gains	equity	homeowners insurance
coinsurance clause	Federal Emergency	policy
deductible clause	Management Agency	investment
endorsement	(FEMA)	

OVERVIEW

To rephrase an old quotation, a home is not a house—not necessarily, anyway. Although the term *home ownership* once referred mainly to detached single-family dwellings, today's homebuyer can choose among many different types of housing designed to satisfy individual needs, tastes, and financial capabilities.

This chapter discusses the various types of housing available, as well as the factors a potential homeowner must consider in deciding what, where, and how much to buy. The chapter also covers the many tax benefits available to homeowners and the forms of property insurance designed to protect one of the biggest investments of a lifetime. Note that this chapter is devoted to the ownership of a *residence*; the ownership of income-producing property is discussed in Chapters 22 and 25.

HOME OWNERSHIP

A home is the single-largest purchase most Americans make. Historically speaking, it is an investment that can both appreciate in value and provide federal income tax deductions. Even in declining markets, home ownership offers intangible benefits that may be no less valuable: pride, security, a sense of belonging to the community, and a symbol of financial success.

In the past, most homes were single-family dwellings bought by married couples with small children. Today, however, social, demographic, and economic changes have altered the residential real estate market considerably. Many of today's real estate buyers are *single* men and women; many are *empty-nesters*, married couples whose children have moved away from home. Others are unmarried couples and married couples who choose not to have children. Still others are friends or relatives who plan to co-own a home rather than share an apartment lease.

Type of Housing

Patio homes or **cluster homes** are attached dwellings that may be condos or town houses, based on the ownership of the land underneath the units.

As our society evolves, the needs of its homebuyers become more specialized. In addition to the traditional single-family dwelling, the homebuyer can select from the housing types listed in the following paragraphs.

A *condominium* is a popular form of residential ownership, particularly for people who want the security of owning property but do not want the responsibilities of caring for and maintaining a house. Ownership of a condominium—which shares party walls with other units—involves individual ownership of the airspace within the unit itself, plus shared ownership of common facilities such as halls, elevators, and the land as undivided interests.

A *cooperative* is similar to a condominium in that it involves units within a larger building with common walls and facilities. However, an owner of a cooperative unit owns not the unit itself but shares of stock in the cooperative (a type of corporation) that holds title to the building. In return for stock in the cooperative, owners receive a proprietary lease, which entitles them to occupancy of a particular unit in the building.

Town houses, similar to single-family houses, are constructed on lots owned by the individual homeowners—but the homes are joined to each other. They may be connected by a common wall (usually a firewall), or they may be freestanding homes separated by airspace and attached to each other by exterior shingles and brick or siding. The names of some condominium projects indicate that they are town houses when in reality, if the land is not owned by the individual homeowners, they are condominiums. An examination of the legal description will reveal whether the property is a town house or a condominium (see Chapter 10).

A *planned unit development* (PUD) is a project or subdivision that consists of common property and improvements that are owned and maintained by an owners association for the benefit and use of the individual housing units within the project. For a project to qualify as a PUD, the owners association must require automatic, nonseverable membership for each unit owner and provide for mandatory assessments to maintain the common areas.

Converted-use properties are existing structures, such as factories, office buildings, hotels, schools, and churches, that have been converted to residential use as either rental or condominium units. Rather than demolish old structures to make way for new ones, developers often find it aesthetically and economically appealing to renovate the existing buildings into affordable housing. In this manner, an abandoned factory may be transformed into luxury loft condominium units and old warehouses converted to restaurants and shopping areas.

Retirement communities are widely accepted in Texas. They lend themselves particularly well to areas with mild weather conditions. In addition to residential units, retirement communities often provide shopping, exercise, recreational opportunities, restaurants, and, in some cases, health care facilities.

Mixed-use developments that combine condominium or apartment living with shopping and recreation facilities either in one building or in a group of buildings are popular, especially in metropolitan areas close to a central city. These complexes usually are self-contained and include—along with housing—office space, retail stores, restaurants, theaters and other entertainment facilities, gyms, swimming pools, parks, concierge services, and other attractive and convenient features.

Manufactured homes (formerly known as *mobile homes*) are built in manufacturing plants and transported on permanent chassis to manufactured home dealerships and then to purchasers' homesites, where they are connected to gas, water, and electricity. The homes are generally permanently attached to a foundation on land owned or leased by the manufactured home purchaser or semipermanently attached to a foundation in a "housing park." Housing parks often offer complete residential environments with permanent community facilities. Newer models of manufactured homes couple relatively low cost with increased living space, making them an attractive alternative to the conventionally constructed residence.

Modular and *prefab* or *kit homes* are constructed with large wall and roof components that are built in factories. The pieces are trucked from a factory to a building site and lifted into place with a crane. Then workers finish the structure and install plumbing, wiring, and amenities. Modular homes can generally be built at a fraction of the time and cost for conventional construction and often enable buyers to take part in designing their homes without having to start from scratch with an architect.

Through *time-shares*, multiple purchasers share ownership of a single property, usually a vacation home. Each owner is entitled to use the property for a certain period each year, but many time-share trade agreements exist among developers of this type of property, allowing owners to vacation at various sites. In addition to the purchase price, each owner pays an annual maintenance fee.

Location

Once a buyer has determined the type of housing desired, the physical appearance of a house and its location are probably the most important factors in selecting a home. The elements that contribute to the desirability of a community go beyond geographic area. Five major factors influence the choice of location:

1. *Employment opportunities*—Industrial and commercial development offering vocational opportunities is essential if a community is to grow.
2. *Cultural advantages*—Schools, colleges, places of worship, libraries, theaters, museums, zoos, sports attractions, and parks all constitute a powerful sociological attraction to a given community.
3. *Governmental structure*—Police and fire protection, sanitation, and utilities (water, gas, and electricity) add to an area's desirability, as do various quasimunicipal authorities such as ports, public transportation, antipollution practices, and forest preserves. Real estate tax rates and a city's plan for and attitude toward growth may affect an area either positively or negatively.
4. *Social services*—The availability and quality of hospitals, clinics, community centers, and similar facilities also attract buyers to a community.
5. *Transportation*—A community's accessibility to people and goods depends on available air, rail, and highway systems. In recent decades, the automobile and truck dominated the transportation industry and made it possible to open new areas for commercial and residential development. Higher energy costs and increased pollution, however, have made the development of better mass transit facilities a greater priority, especially in urban areas. When gasoline prices rise sharply, the railroad attracts renewed interest as an economical means of moving people and freight.

FOR EXAMPLE   A buyer in Dallas, because of the commute time, might choose a location close to employment. Another buyer might choose a location based on a school district; and a retired buyer might choose a location near medical facilities.

The Real Estate Center at Texas A&M University maintains a website that contains housing and economic information for each area of Texas.

WEBLINK @ www.recenter.tamu.edu

HOUSING AFFORDABILITY

> The highest homeownership rate nationwide is for those 65 or older—81.2%

In the 1950s, only 55% of Americans owned their homes. Over the ensuing 50 years, homeownership rates grew to 69.2% during the housing boom of 2004. Even through the recent job loss and foreclosure problems, the U.S. homeownership rate in 2013 was 65.3%—with 63.5% of Texas households owning their homes. Certainly not everyone wants to or should own a home. Home ownership involves substantial commitment and responsibility, and the flexibility of renting suits some individuals' needs. People whose work requires frequent moves or whose financial position is uncertain benefit particularly from renting. Renting also provides more leisure time by freeing tenants from management and maintenance responsibilities.

Those who choose to take on the responsibilities of home ownership must evaluate many factors before they decide to purchase a particular property: mortgage terms, ownership expenses, ability to pay, and other investment considerations. It is often the responsibility of the real estate broker or salesperson to guide prospective homeowners in this process and to help them arrive at acceptable choices.

Mortgage Terms

A variety of factors contributed to the housing crisis of the late 2000s. Among them were the following: (1) the liberal mortgage terms of the 1990s to the mid-2000s, (2) the large number of subprime loans (those offered to less-creditworthy borrowers), (3) no- or low-documentation loans, and (4) resets on adjustable-rate loan payments coupled with rising interest rates.

As a result of the increased number of foreclosures, most lenders have returned to more traditional lending practices with more conservative borrower and property qualifying practices (see Chapter 16). However, achieving the dream of home-ownership can still be a reality for qualified borrowers. The National Association of REALTORS® Housing Affordability Index was 165.4 in October 2013. The index means that a family earning the median income has 165.4% of the income necessary to qualify for an 80% conventional loan on a median-priced existing single-family home.

Ownership Expenses and Ability to Pay

Memory Tip

The basic costs of owning a home are mortgage **P**rinciple and **I**nterest, **T**axes, and **I**nsurance, easily remembered by the acronym **PITI**.

Home ownership involves many expenses, including utilities (such as electricity, natural gas, and water), trash removal, sewer charges, and maintenance and repairs. Owners also must pay real estate taxes, buy property insurance, and repay the mortgage loan with interest. Income lost because money invested in a home is not available for income-producing investments is also a cost of home ownership.

To determine whether a prospective buyer can afford a certain purchase, lenders may use a conservative rule-of-thumb formula to calculate the borrower's debt-to-income ratio (DTI ratio): the monthly cost of purchasing a home (the housing expense or front-end ratio—mortgage principal plus interest on the remaining balance plus $\frac{1}{12}$ of annual taxes and insurance) should not exceed 25 to 28% of a borrower's gross (pretax) monthly income. The payments on all debts (the total debt or back-end ratio) should not exceed 33 to 36% of gross monthly income. Which qualifying ratios a specific lender uses and how strictly the formulas are applied, however, depend on such factors as the type of loan, amount of down payment, potential future earnings, number of dependents, credit history, and general economic conditions.

FOR EXAMPLE   Prospective homebuyers want to know what amount they can afford to spend to purchase a house. The buyers have a gross monthly income of $3,000. If the lender uses a housing expense ratio of 28% and a total debt ratio of 36%, the buyers' maximum PITI payment would be calculated as follows:

$3,000 gross monthly income × 28% = $840 maximum PITI payment

$3,000 gross monthly income × 36% = $1,080 total debt allowed (including PITI payment and other debt expense)

Investment Considerations

Investing in a home offers several financial advantages. First, the mortgaged property represents an **investment**. If the property's value increases, a sale could bring in more money than the owner paid—resulting in a long-term gain. Of course, if the property's value decreases, the owner could owe more money than was borrowed initially. The second financial advantage of home ownership is the tax deductions available to homeowners. Third, as the total mortgage debt is reduced through monthly principal payments, the owner's actual ownership interest in the property increases (as long as property values remain the same or increase). This increasing ownership interest is called **equity** and represents the current market value of the property minus any loans. However, equity buildup from loan repayment is gradual in the early years of the mortgage because most of the monthly payment is applied to the interest on the loan rather than to the principal. Equity builds faster if the property value rises.

FOR EXAMPLE   A homeowner purchased his home five years ago for $150,000, making a $15,000 down payment and financing it with a $135,000 loan at 6%. After making 60 monthly payments, the loan balance is $125,623.61. Assuming the property value has neither gone up nor down, the homeowner's equity may be calculated as follows:

$150,000 current market value – $125,623.61 loan balance = $24,376.39 equity

IN PRACTICE   As with other types of investments, real estate can be subject to negative market forces. The market value of an investment can decrease as well as increase, even to the point that the loan balance exceeds the market value. This is a serious concern to lenders, mortgage loan insurers, and investors and should be considered by prospective owners.

Research Sources

Buyers, sellers, and real estate agents can access a wealth of information through the internet. Consumer-oriented sites may contain "homes for sale," "finding a real estate agent," "financing options," "offer and closing," "moving," "owning," and "avoiding foreclosure." Most sites include calculators and worksheets to assist in the "buy versus rent" decision or to determine how much money a buyer can borrow. HUD's YouTube channel has three homebuyer videos: "Shopping for Your Home," "Shopping for Your Loan," and "Closing the Deal." NAR's HouseLogic site is designed to help homeowners maintain and enhance home values.

WEBLINK @
www.realtor.com
www.fanniemae.com
www.freddiemac.com
www.houselogic.com
www.realestate.msn.com
www.move.com
http://realestate.yahoo.com
www.realestateabc.com
www.youtube.com/HUDchannel
zillow.com
trulia.com
redfin.com

TAX BENEFITS FOR HOMEOWNERS

To encourage and enhance the viability of home ownership, the federal government allows homeowners certain income tax advantages. Besides mortgage interest, a homeowner may deduct real estate taxes and certain other expenses from gross income. Homeowners' tax benefits are summarized in Figure 4.1.

Income Tax Deductions

For income tax purposes, homeowners are entitled to five deductions from their gross income:

- Mortgage *interest* payments on first and second homes, subject to limitation
- Real estate taxes
- Certain loan origination fees
- Loan discount points. The criteria for deducting discount points include, among others: the mortgage must be secured by the taxpayer's *principal* residence, the points must be paid in cash at closing, and there must be a charge for the use of money (interest, *not* fees), which is computed as a percentage of the loan principal. Otherwise, discount points are prorated over the term of the loan.
- Mortgage insurance provided by the U.S. Department of Veterans Affairs, the Federal Housing Administration, or the Rural Housing Service, and private mortgage insurance (PMI) for homebuyers with adjusted gross incomes up to $100,000 ($50,000 if single or married filing separately), subject to limitation

FIGURE 4.1: Homeownership Tax Benefits

Capital Gains
- Up to $500,000 exclusion of profit on the sale of a home owned and occupied as a principal residence for at least two of the five years before the sale ($250,000 for a single taxpayer)
- Exclusion of profit allowed on each sale of a principal residence but not more often than every two years
- Long-term capital gains tax rates are 20% (in the upper brackets, above 39.5%), 15% (in the 25%, 28%, 33%, or 35% brackets) or 0% (in the 10% and 15% brackets) through 2013

Income Tax Deductions
- Loan interest on first and second homes, subject to limitation
- Real estate taxes
- Loan origination fees
- Some loan discount points
- Some mortgage insurance premiums

First-Time Homebuyers
- Penalty-free withdrawals up to $10,000 from an IRA for first-time homebuyers

Estate Tax Exemption
- Up to $5.25 million per person through 2013.

IN PRACTICE   The American Taxpayer Relief Act of 2012 extended the deductibility of mortgage insurance premiums for the 2013 tax year, subject to limitation. Check for changes relating to all homeowners' income tax deductions at www.irs.gov/taxtopics and scroll down to the itemized deductions entries.

Capital Gains

Capital gains are the *profits* realized from the sale or exchange of an asset, including real property. To stimulate investment in the economy, Congress at various times has allowed part of a taxpayer's capital gains to be free from income tax.

With the passage of the Taxpayer Relief Act of 1997 and its implementation for sales made on or after May 7, 1997, married homeowners who file jointly are able to exclude up to $500,000 of capital gains realized on the sale or exchange of a principal residence. For single homeowners, the maximum exclusion is $250,000. The exclusion is allowed each time a homeowner sells or exchanges a principal residence but generally no more frequently than once every two years.

> Married homeowners filing jointly may exclude up to $500,000 of capital gains if the property was a principal residence that was owned and used at least two years of the five preceding the sale—not necessarily continuously.

To be eligible for the exclusion, a homeowner must have owned the residence and occupied it as a principal residence for two years or more during a five-year period ending on the date of the sale. A homeowner who fails to meet these requirements because of an employment change, health, death, natural or man-made disasters, acts of war (including terrorist attacks), divorce or legal separation, or other unforeseen circumstances is able to exclude the fraction of the $500,000 ($250,000 for a single taxpayer) that is equal to the fraction of two years that these residency requirements are met. In the case of persons filing jointly but not sharing a principal residence, an exclusion of $250,000 is available on a qualifying sale or exchange of the principal residence of one of the spouses. Similarly, if a single person who is otherwise eligible for an exclusion marries someone who has used the exclusion within the two years prior to the marriage, the newly married, eligible homeowner will be allowed a maximum exclusion of $250,000. Once both spouses satisfy the eligibility rules and two years have passed since the last exclusion was allowed to either of them, the taxpayers may exclude $500,000 of gain on their joint return. Upon the death of one spouse, the surviving spouse has up to two years after the spouse's death to sell the main home and receive $500,000 in tax-free capital gains—as long as the ownership and use tests were met by both spouses prior to the death. When a former second home is sold, some portion of the gain may be taxable, even when the owner has lived in the home for the required two of the previous five years. Effective January 1, 2009, individuals who convert a second home to a principal residence and then later sell that property will have to compute, based on the use of the property, the portion of the gain that is subject to capital gains taxes and the portion of the gain that can be excluded from capital gains taxes. Any gain attributable to use as a second home or rental property will be taxed at capital gains tax rates. Any gain attributable to use as a principal residence will remain excludable, up to the $250,000/$500,000 limits.

For most homeowners, the net result of the Taxpayer Relief Act of 1997 is that *they will never pay capital gains tax on the sale of their homes*. Concerns about the capital gains consequences of a sale are effectively eliminated for most homeowners. Sellers of higher-bracket homes who have accumulated profits that exceed $500,000 ($250,000, single taxpayer) will continue to face federal capital gains taxation for the gains over that exclusion.

Starting in 2013, the top tax rate is 20% on long-term capital gains (assets held for more than one year) for taxpayers in the new 39.6% tax bracket, 0% for taxpayers in the 10% and 15% tax brackets, and 15% in the 25%, 28%, 33%, or 35% tax brackets.

First-Time Homebuyers

To meet down payment and closing cost requirements, a first-time homebuyer (someone who has not owned a home for two years) may make a penalty-free withdrawal from a tax-deferred individual retirement account (IRA). The limit on such withdrawals for a first-time homebuyer is $10,000.

Income tax credits were available for first-time homebuyers in 2008, 2009, and 2010. For purchases from April 8, 2008, through December 31, 2008, tax credits received (up to $7,500) must be repaid, without interest, over a 15-year period. Tax credits of up to $8,000 on purchases after December 31, 2008, and before May 1, 2010 (with contract closing dates up to July 1, 2010), do not have to be repaid, provided the home remains the buyer's main home for 36 months after the purchase date.

Estate Tax Exemption

An estate tax exemption is the amount an individual can leave to heirs tax free. The American Taxpayer Relief Act of 2012, signed into law on January 2, 2013, permanently extended a $5 million per person estate tax exemption indexed to inflation ($5.25 million in 2013). For estates that exceed $5 million per person, assets over that amount will be taxed at a 40% rate.

IN PRACTICE   The homeowner tax benefits in this section are those included in the Tax Relief Act of 2012. However, IRS regulations are subject to revision and official interpretation. Consult the Internal Revenue Service, a certified public accountant, or a tax lawyer for further information on, and precise applications of, these and other income tax issues. *It is illegal for a real estate licensee to give tax or legal advice to clients or customers, unless the licensee is also a tax specialist or licensed attorney.*

WEBLINK @ www.irs.gov

HOMEOWNERS INSURANCE

Home ownership represents a significant financial investment, and homebuyers usually *want* to insure their property to protect this investment. If the property is used to secure a loan, lenders usually *require* that a homeowner obtain insurance. A lender cannot require a borrower to purchase homeowners or other residential property insurance coverage in an amount that exceeds the replacement value of the dwelling and its contents (excluding the fair market value of the land), regardless of the amount of the mortgage. However, insurance companies may require that properties purchased below replacement cost (as might be the case in foreclosure or other distress sale situations) be insured at market value rather than at purchase price.

Characteristics of Homeowners Packages

Although it is possible for a homeowner to obtain individual policies for fire or windstorm, injury to others, and theft of personal property, most buy a package

homeowners insurance policy to cover all these risks on owner-occupied property. A Texas homeowners policy combines five different types of coverage:

1. *Dwelling*—pays for damage to the house and any outbuildings, such as detached garages and storage sheds.
2. *Personal property*—pays when household items, including furniture, clothing, and appliances, are damaged, stolen, or destroyed.
3. *Liability*—provides $25,000 in coverage if homeowner is sued and found legally responsible for someone else's injury or property damage; if a property owner wants more liability coverage than a homeowners policy provides, a separate umbrella liability policy can be purchased.
4. *Medical payments*—pays medical bills for people hurt on the homeowner's property; a basic homeowners policy pays $500 in medical bills.
5. *Loss of use*—pays living expenses if a home is too damaged to live in during repairs (if the damage was due to a covered loss).

Types of Homeowners Insurance Policies

Insurance companies may sell several types of policies in Texas, each with a different level of coverage. Three of the policy forms are standardized: the HO-A, HO-B, and HO-C. Policy language and coverage provided by these basic policies are the same for all insurance companies; however, rates charged for the policies vary from company to company. Figure 4.2 lists the losses covered by most homeowners policies; such policies do not cover flood, earthquake, war, or nuclear attack. The basic types of policies sold in Texas include the following:

- *HO-A policies* provide limited *actual cash value coverage* of the home and its contents. Only the types of damage specifically listed in the policy are covered.
- *HO-A amended policies* provide more extensive coverage than the base HO-A policy but less coverage than an HO-B. HO-A amended policies are not standardized; coverage provided varies from one company to another.
- *HO-B policies*, the most common homeowners policies, provide *replacement cost coverage* for most types of damage *to the real property*, except claims specifically excluded in the policy. They provide *actual cash value coverage for personal property* unless endorsed to provide replacement cost coverage.
- *HO-C policies* provide the most extensive coverage but are more expensive than other types of policies.
- *Approved alternative policies* offer varying levels of coverage, are different from one company to another, and are sold only with the approval of the Commissioner of Insurance.

FIGURE 4.2: What Homeowners Policies Do and Do Not Cover

Most Policies Cover Losses Caused by	Most Policies Do Not Cover Losses Caused by
Fire and lightning	Flooding
Aircraft and vehicles	Earthquakes
Vandalism and malicious mischief	Termites
Theft	Insects, rats, or mice
Explosion	Freezing pipes while the house is unoccupied (unless the water was turned off or the building was heated)
Riot and civil commotion	
Smoke	Wind or hail damage to trees and shrubs
Windstorm, hurricane, and hail (except property on the Gulf Coast)	Losses if the house is vacant for 60 days or more
	Wear and tear or maintenance
Sudden and accidental water damage	

An insurance company may modify a homeowners policy through **endorsements**, most often including glass breakage; replacement cost on personal property; and increased limits on jewelry, fine arts, camera and computer equipment, and radio and television satellite dishes and antennas.

Insurance companies may also exclude coverage for certain losses. Policies for properties located on the Gulf Coast would usually include an endorsement excluding coverage for wind and hail damage. The Texas Windstorm Insurance Association (TWIA) provides coverage for properties located in the 14 Texas coastal counties and parts of Harris County on Galveston Bay when insurance companies exclude it from homeowners and other property policies. However, some Gulf Coast residents may be required to purchase flood insurance on their property before they are eligible for a TWIA policy. For more information, contact TWIA at 1-512-899-4900 or visit its website.

IN PRACTICE   The HO-A policy offers no coverage for damage caused by water leaks—whether from sudden and accidental leakage from plumbing, heating or air-conditioning, or from continuous and repeated seepage. Some, but not all, of the other approved policy forms cover damage from sudden and accidental water leaks and from continuous or repeated leakage; and they offer some basic but limited mold coverage. For a comparison of the coverage provided by policy forms approved for sale in Texas, visit the website of the Office of Public Insurance Counsel.

WEBLINK @
www.opic.texas.gov
www.tdi.texas.gov
www.twia.org

Claims

HO-A policies only provide actual cash value coverage unless the homeowner has bought an endorsement to provide for replacement cost coverage. Actual cash value is the replacement cost of the property minus depreciation. With actual cash value coverage, a homeowner might not be able to completely repair or rebuild a home.

HO-B and HO-C policies (and some amended HO-A policies) provide replacement cost coverage for the house up to the policy's dollar limits. Replacement cost is the amount needed to rebuild or repair a home, based on current construction costs. It does not include the value of the land. To receive full payment (minus the deductible) for a partial loss, such as a hail-damaged roof, a **coinsurance clause** in the policy requires that the property be insured for *at least 80% of its replacement cost*.

For example, a homeowner's dwelling that has been damaged by fire has a replacement cost of $100,000 (excluding the lot) and a repair estimate for $71,000 damage. If the homeowner carries at least $80,000 insurance on the dwelling ($100,000 × 0.80), the claim against the insurance company can be for the full $71,000.

If the homeowner carries coverage of less than 80% of the full replacement cost of the dwelling, the loss will be settled either for the actual cash value (cost of repairs less depreciation) or for a prorated amount calculated by dividing the percentage of replacement cost actually covered under the policy by the minimum coverage requirement (usually 80%), whichever is greater. For example, if the building is insured for only 60% of its value and there is a $71,000 loss, the insurance company will pay only $53,250 (60% ÷ 80%, or 75% of $71,000 = $53,250).

In any event, *the total settlement cannot exceed the face value of the policy*—unless an endorsement to the policy specifies otherwise. Because of coinsurance clauses, homeowners periodically should review all policies to be certain that the coverage is equal to at least 80% of the current replacement cost of their homes unless the policy contains an "inflation clause," which automatically adjusts the amount of coverage. A check from an insurance company for damages to mortgaged property will be payable to both the owner and the lender.

To discourage the filing of a large number of small claims, which would take a significant amount of paperwork and expense to handle, **deductible clauses** are included in insurance policies. In general, the larger the deductible, the lower the premium.

IN PRACTICE Companies may use a number of criteria to establish a policy premium. These include the following:

- *The age and condition of the home.* Older homes and homes in poor condition generally are more expensive to insure. Companies may refuse to insure homes in poor condition, but they cannot deny coverage solely because of a home's age or value.

- *The home's replacement cost.* Because the policy will pay to rebuild the home if it is destroyed by a covered loss, premiums are more expensive for homes with a high replacement cost.

- *The construction materials used in the home.* Homes built primarily of brick are less expensive to insure than frame homes.

- *The location of the home.* Premiums will likely be higher for homes in areas with a high frequency of storms (such as tornados or hailstorms) or with a high incidence of theft.

- *Availability of local fire protection.* Homes with access to good fire protection services get better rates.

- *The homeowner's claims history.* Companies will charge more if claims have been filed in the past—unless the claim resulted from a loss by natural causes or was appliance-related water damage that was properly remediated, inspected, and certified by a person experienced in remediation of water damage. Many companies use the Comprehensive Loss Underwriting Exchange (CLUE) to review an applicant's claims history. CLUE lists the property insurance claims by houses and by individuals for the preceding three years. After incurring property damage, a homeowner should initially contact the insurance company to make an *inquiry*, discussing the terms of coverage on a specific loss. Then the homeowner should ask the insurance agent how filing a claim would affect the CLUE report, the policy premium at renewal time, and the future insurability of the property. An inquiry does not affect a CLUE report; a *claim* does. For less expensive losses, it may be cheaper in the long run for the homeowner to pay for the repairs rather than file a claim, especially if the cost of repairs is not much more than the deductible amount. A property insurance company may offer a premium discount if the homeowner has filed no property damage claims for three consecutive years.

■　*The homeowner's credit score.* Companies may consider a homeowner's credit score when deciding whether to issue a policy and what to charge for it. However, a company cannot refuse to sell a policy or cancel or refuse to renew a policy solely on the basis of credit.

National Flood Insurance Program

> Texas Water Development Board is responsible for state administration and management of local participation in the National Flood Insurance Program.

In the face of mounting flood losses and escalating costs of disaster relief, Congress established the National Flood Insurance Program (NFIP) in 1968. One of the primary goals of the program is to reduce future flood damage through effective floodplain management. In exchange for a community's adopting and enforcing NFIP floodplain management regulations, the NFIP makes federally backed flood insurance available for purchase by homeowners, renters, and business owners in the community.

As a program within the **Federal Emergency Management Agency (FEMA)**, the NFIP is administered by the Federal Insurance Administration (FIA). FEMA sets rates and coverage limits, establishes eligibility requirements for flood insurance, and issues detailed Flood Insurance Rate Maps (FIRMs), establishing flood zones and rates for each participating community. Federal law requires that owners of properties on which a "structure" is located in a floodplain area obtain flood insurance if properties are financed by loans provided, regulated, or insured by the federal government or purchased by Fannie Mae or Freddie Mac secondary mortgage market agencies. As a condition for making a loan, an individual lender may require flood insurance if any part of the property is in a flood zone. All types of buildings—residential, commercial, industrial, and agricultural—are required to maintain this coverage for either the value of the improvement or the amount of the mortgage loan, subject to the maximum limits available.

Annual flood insurance policies can be written directly with the NFIP or any licensed property insurance carrier. In participating communities, the NFIP also offers the Preferred Risk Policy for any one-unit to four-unit dwelling not existing in a floodplain area and not having more than one previous flood loss in excess of $1,000.

The NFIP defines flooding as a general and temporary condition during which the surface of normally dry land is partially or completely inundated by water. Covered losses include

■　an overflow of inland or tidal waters,

■　an unusual and rapid accumulation or runoff of surface waters,

■ mudslides or mudflows on the surface of normally dry land areas, and
■ the collapse of land along the shore of a body of water (under certain circumstances).

Flood policies exclude coverage for many of the same types of property as those that are not covered by fire insurance. The list includes such items as money, lawns, livestock, motorized vehicles, fences, swimming pools, and underground structures and equipment. More information about the National Flood Insurance Program can be obtained from the FEMA website or by calling 1-888-379-9531.

Biggert-Waters Flood Insurance Reform Act of 2012   The Biggert-Waters Flood Insurance Reform Act of 2012 changed the way that FEMA and other related agencies manage the National Flood Insurance Program, which may mean premium rate increases for some policyholders. Key provisions of the legislation include
■ raising NFIP rates to reflect true flood risk,
■ making the program more financially stable, and
■ changing how the Flood Insurance Rate Map (FIRM) updates impact policyholders.

WEBLINK @
www.floodsmart.gov
www.fema.gov/flood-insurance-reform

IN PRACTICE   In September 2008, Hurricane Ike, the most destructive storm ever to hit Texas, slammed into the Texas coast with storm surges up to 17 feet. Remnants of Ike produced heavy rainfall and flooding all the way to the Great Lakes. It was the fourth-costliest hurricane to strike the United States, causing $20.3 billion in damages while taking 48 lives. The costliest, and one of the deadliest, hurricanes to ever strike the U.S. was Hurricane Katrina in 2005, which caused at least $81 billion in damages and took more than 1,500 lives.

SUMMARY

Current trends in home ownership include traditional single-family homes, condominiums, cooperatives, town houses, planned unit developments, converted-use properties, retirement communities, mixed-use developments, manufactured homes, modular homes, and time-shared occupancy of vacation homes. A prospective homebuyer should note a house's specific characteristics and evaluate the desirability of the community based on its cultural activities, employment opportunities, recreational and social facilities, and transportation (among others).

Prospective buyers should be aware of both the advantages and disadvantages of home ownership. Although a homeowner gains financial security and pride of ownership, the costs of ownership—both the initial price and the continuing expenses—must be considered.

An income tax benefit available to homeowners is the deduction of mortgage interest payments and property taxes from their federal income taxes. Married homeowners who file jointly are able to exclude up to $500,000 of capital gains on the sale or exchange of a principal residence. A homeowner must have owned the residence and occupied it as a principal residence for at least two of the five years prior to the sale or exchange. For gains exceeding $500,000, the tax rate has been capped at 15% for most taxpayers; however, the rate is subject to change.

To protect their real estate investment, most homeowners purchase a standard homeowners insurance policy that includes the dwelling, personal property, liability, medical payments, and loss-of-use coverage and can be extended to cover other risks. Most homeowners policies contain a coinsurance clause that requires that the property be insured for at least 80% of its replacement cost. If this percentage is not met, the policyholder may not be reimbursed for full repair costs if a loss occurs. In addition to homeowners insurance, the federal government makes flood insurance mandatory for people who wish to obtain federally regulated or federally insured mortgage loans on properties in flood-prone areas.

CHAPTER 4 QUESTIONS

1. The real cost of owning a home includes expenses that many people tend to overlook. Which is *NOT* a cost or an expense of owning a home?
   a. Interest paid on borrowed capital
   b. Homeowners insurance
   c. Maintenance and repairs
   d. Taxes on personal property

2. If a single person who is eligible for a tax exclusion marries someone who has used the exclusion within the two years before the marriage, what is the maximum exclusion she may claim?
   a. $500,000
   b. $125,000
   c. $175,000
   d. $250,000

3. The difference between the mortgage owed on a property and the property's current market value represents the homeowner's
   a. tax basis.
   b. equity.
   c. replacement cost.
   d. capital gain.

4. When choosing a location in which to live, a homebuyer is *LEAST* likely to be influenced by the area's
   a. transportation facilities.
   b. employment opportunities.
   c. availability of medical facilities.
   d. street signage.

5. A homeowners insurance policy excludes
   a. the cost of medical expenses for a person injured in the policyholder's home.
   b. riot and civil commotion.
   c. theft.
   d. flood damage.

6. A building that is remodeled into residential units and no longer used for its original purpose is a
   a. converted-use property.
   b. cooperative.
   c. planned unit development.
   d. modular home.

7. In a homeowners insurance policy, the term *coinsurance* refers to
   a. the specific form of policy purchased by the owner.
   b. the stipulation that the homeowner must purchase insurance coverage equal to at least 80% of the replacement cost of the structure to be able to collect the full insured amount in the event of a loss.
   c. the stipulation that the homeowner must purchase insurance coverage equal to at least 90% of the replacement cost of the structure to be able to collect the full insured amount in the event of a loss.
   d. additional insurance held by the homeowner other than the homeowners policy.

8. Federal flood insurance is
   a. required in certain areas to insure against flood damage for 100-year floodplain properties financed by federally related mortgage loans.
   b. a common part of a homeowners insurance policy.
   c. an option available to the homeowner on properties financed by FHA or VA mortgage loans.
   d. optional for most homes in flood-prone areas.

9. Under the provisions for liability coverage in a homeowners insurance policy, the insurance company may settle a claim for
   a. physical damage to the insured's property.
   b. funeral expenses for the insured's child.
   c. personal injury to a delivery person who is injured on the insured's property.
   d. flood damage.

10. A town house is most closely associated with which of the following types of housing?
    a. Highrise development
    b. Cooperative
    c. Converted-use property
    d. Single-family residence

11. As a conservative rule of thumb, many mortgage lenders will not make a loan in which the DTI housing expense ratio exceeds what percentage of a borrower's monthly income?
    a. 25 to 28%
    b. 33 to 36%
    c. 20%
    d. 30%

12. Under the Taxpayer Relief Act of 1997, the profit homeowners receive from the sale of their residence
    a. is never taxable.
    b. is always considered "taxable gain" for tax purposes.
    c. can be excluded from taxation (up to specified limits) if a couple has occupied the residence for at least two years before the sale.
    d. cannot be excluded from taxation for a couple if one spouse has previously taken the exclusion.

13. A homeowner sold his house for $127,500. The house had been purchased new three years earlier for $75,000. Assuming there are no adjustments to the purchase price and no expenses of sale, what is the homeowner's gain on this transaction?
    a. $53,250
    b. $52,500
    c. $51,750
    d. $75,000

14. In question 13, how much of the gain will be subject to income tax?
    a. All of it
    b. $20,700
    c. $21,300
    d. None of it

15. Brendon and Sara, a married couple, ages 36 and 38, sell their home and realize a gain from the sale. If certain conditions are met, the tax levied on the profit from the sale may be
    a. excluded up to $250,000 if one spouse has used the exclusion in the last two years.
    b. excluded up to $500,000 if the couple occupied it as a residence for one year prior to the sale.
    c. excluded up to $500,000 if both spouses have used the exclusion within two years prior to their marriage.
    d. excluded up to $500,000 if one year has passed since the last exclusion.

16. A development that includes office space, stores, theaters, and apartment units is an example of a
    a. planned unit development.
    b. mixed-use development.
    c. converted-use property.
    d. cooperative.

Detailed rationales for the end-of-chapter review questions are available online at www.dearborn.com through the *Instructor Resource Guides* link.

CHAPTER

5

Real Estate Brokerage and the Law of Agency

■ **LEARNING OBJECTIVES**   *When you have completed this chapter, you will be able to*

■ **explain** the types of agencies and the processes by which agency can be created and terminated;

■ **describe** an agent's duties to a principal, a principal's duties to an agent, and an agent's duties to customers, as well as a broker's duties related to minimum service standards;

■ **identify** the broker's role in the disclosure of agency relationships and the types of agencies and the types of agency relationships and agency responsibilities created by Texas statute;

■ **distinguish** employees from independent contractors and explain why the distinction is important;

■ **list** the requirements for broker compensation and some common situations in which a broker would or would not be entitled to a commission;

■ **describe** the various types of antitrust violations common in the real estate industry;

■ **explain** the provisions of the Texas Deceptive Trade Practices Act—Consumer Protection Act (DTPA) and its applicability to actions of real estate agents; and

■ **define** the following *key terms*:

agency	commission	listing agreement
agency by ratification	consumer	misrepresentation
agent	customer	principal
antitrust laws	employee	procuring cause
appointed licensee	express agency	puffing
broker	fiduciary relationship	ready, willing, and able buyer
brokerage	fraud	special agent
buyer representation agreement	general agent	subagent
caveat emptor	implied agency	Texas Deceptive Trade Practices—Consumer Protection Act
client	independent contractor	
commingle	intermediary broker	
	law of agency	

OVERVIEW

The business of bringing buyers and sellers together in the marketplace is **brokerage**. In the real estate business, a **broker** is defined broadly as a person who is licensed to buy, sell, exchange, or lease real property *for others* and to *charge a fee* for services.

This chapter discusses the complex legal relationships among buyers, sellers, and brokers in real estate. The chapter also examines the nature of the real estate brokerage business.

THE LAW OF AGENCY

> An agent is a person authorized to act on behalf of another.

The **law of agency** defines the rights and duties of the parties in a real estate transaction—the principal, the agent, and the customer. The **principal**, or **client**—the person who employs the broker—may be a seller, a prospective buyer, an owner who wishes to lease the property, or a person seeking property to rent. The real estate broker acts as the **agent** of the principal, and may use other licensed brokers to assist as **subagents**. Agents and subagents have a fiduciary relationship with a principal—one in which a licensee has a legal requirement to act in the client's best interest and with the utmost good faith. The principal usually compensates the broker with a **commission** or fee. This compensation is contingent on the broker's performing successfully the service for which he was employed, which generally is negotiating a transaction with a third party or **customer**—a prospective purchaser, seller, lessor, or lessee—who is ready, willing, and able to complete the contract.

> An agent works *for* the *client* and *with* the *customer*.

In traditional real estate sales transactions, the broker is hired by sellers to market their real estate. In this situation, the broker is an *agent* of the sellers; the sellers are the broker's *clients*. Unless otherwise agreed on, buyers who contact a broker to review properties listed with the broker's firm are merely the broker's *customers*. Though obligated to deal honestly and fairly with all parties to a transaction [TREC Rule 535.156(b)], the broker is strictly accountable *only to the principals*—in this case, the sellers. The broker must never mislead buyers into thinking that they are being represented by the broker. To clarify the role of the broker or salesperson, the Texas Legislature requires licensees to make clear to all parties which party they are acting for (TRELA 1101.652(b)(7); 1101.558(b)). It is becoming increasingly common for brokers to represent buyers for a fee, and in this situation, the statute requires that the broker disclose the buyer agency to the sellers and the sellers' agent, if the seller has one.

Section 1101.557 of the Real Estate License Act provides that a *broker* who represents a party in a real estate transaction or who lists real estate for sale under an *exclusive agreement* for a party *is that party's agent.* An agent

- must inform the client if *material information* related to a transaction to list, buy, sell, or lease is received by the agent, including the receipt of an offer;
- shall, at a minimum, answer the client, sell, or lease *present* any offer to or from the client;
- may not instruct another broker to *negotiate* directly with the client (seller, landlord, buyer, or tenant); however, another broker may *deliver* an offer to the agent's client if
  — the agent consents to the delivery,
  — a copy of the offer is sent to the agent, and
  — the other broker does not *negotiate* or attempt to negotiate the contract; and
- shall be a *party* to a lease or sale if she is operating under a power of attorney or property management agreement.

IN PRACTICE   These minimum service duties to the principal are required under Texas law, regardless of the fee charged by the broker. A broker may negotiate a fee but may not contract to provide a lesser level of service to clients.

Types of Agencies

> **Memory Tip**
>
> *General agent*—represents a principal in *general* (broad range) matters
>
> *Special agent*—represents a principal only for *special* matters, such as the sale of a house

The authorized activity of an agent is as simple or as complex as the principal dictates and the agent consents to. An agent may be classified as a general agent or a special agent, based on the authority delegated.

A **general agent** is empowered to represent the principal in a *broad range of matters* and may bind the principal to any contracts within the scope of the agent's authority. The real estate broker typically does *not* have this scope of authority as an agent in a real estate transaction. However, the relationship between a broker (as a principal) and the broker's salesperson (as an agent) is usually a general agency relationship. The relationship of a property manager to a property owner is also an example of general agency.

A **special agent** is authorized to represent the principal in *one specific act or business transaction, under detailed instructions.* A real estate broker is usually a special agent. If hired by a seller, the broker is limited to finding a "ready, willing, and able" buyer for the property. A special agent for a buyer has the limited responsibility of finding a property that meets the buyer's criteria. As a special agent, the broker may not bind or obligate the principal (client).

CREATION OF AGENCY

Agency is created at the broker level, not the salesperson level. The real estate broker-seller relationship generally is created by an employment contract, commonly referred to as a **listing agreement** (see Chapter 13). A broker-buyer agency relationship is created by a **buyer representation agreement**.

Written listing agreements and buyer representation agreements are examples of **express agency**, in which the parties state the contract's terms and express their intentions. On the other hand, a broker's *actions* may create an **implied agency** relationship. Buyers can easily assume that when they contact a salesperson to show them property, the salesperson becomes "their agent." An implied agency with the buyer can result if the words and conduct of the salesperson do not dispel this assumption.

Agency by ratification is an agency "after the fact." For instance, an agent who obtains a purchase contract for a property that has not been listed might be considered an agent by ratification if the seller subsequently ratified, or agreed to, the contract.

Although a written express agency listing agreement usually is preferred, having a written contract is not a requirement for creating an agency relationship. The primary ingredients in creation of agency are

1. delegation of authority by the principal,
2. acceptance of such by the agent,
3. reliance on the agent by the principal, and
4. control of the agent by the principal.

Notice that compensation of the agent is not required; at best, it merely *indicates* an agency relationship. This means that the agent can work for nothing or be paid by anyone. In fact, the agent can be paid by either party, so long as the legally required disclosures are made.

A prudent real estate broker will not rely on an oral agreement from the principal but will require that all agreements be in writing and signed by the principal because oral agreements are unenforceable in court.

Termination of Agency

Generally, an agency relationship may be terminated at any time. An agency may be terminated by the acts of the parties or by operation of law for any of the following reasons:

- Death or incapacity of either party (notice of death is not necessary)
- Destruction or condemnation of the property
- Expiration of the term of the agency
- Mutual agreement to terminate the agency (must be written)
- Renunciation by the broker or revocation by the owner
- Bankruptcy of the owner if title transferred to receiver
- Completion or fulfillment of the purpose for which the agency was created

Agency cannot be assigned without the consent of the principal because agency creates a personal obligation. Agency cannot be terminated wrongfully to avoid paying a fee.

Agent's Responsibilities to Principal

As mentioned previously, the role of a broker as the agent of the principal is a **fiduciary relationship**—one in which the agent is placed in a position of trust and confidence and normally is responsible for the money and/or property of another. In addition to the fiduciary duties owed as a result of the listing agreement, a buyer representation agreement, the Real Estate License Act, and/or TREC Rules, the broker owes the principal certain common law duties. They are not simply moral or ethical; they are the law—the *law of agency*. The agent owes the principal the duties of *care, obedience, accounting, loyalty,* and *disclosure.*

ligal duty to a principle or client.

Care   As an agent, the broker must exercise a reasonable degree of care while transacting business entrusted to the broker by the principal, and the broker is liable to the principal for any loss resulting from the broker's negligence or carelessness. If the agent represents the seller, care includes helping the seller arrive at an appropriate and realistic listing price, making reasonable efforts to market the property (such as advertising and holding open houses), and helping the seller evaluate the terms and conditions of offers to purchase. If the agent represents the buyer, care includes helping the buyer locate a suitable property; evaluate property values, neighborhood, and property conditions; and weigh financing alternatives, offers, and counteroffers—with the buyer's interests in mind.

Obedience   The broker is obligated to act in good faith at all times, obeying the principal's instructions. The broker, however, is not required to obey unlawful or unethical instructions because illegal acts do not serve the principal's best interest.

FOR EXAMPLE   A seller tells a broker that she will not sell to a member of a particular minority group. Because refusing to show a property to someone on the basis of race is illegal, the agent cannot follow the seller's instructions.

Accounting   The broker must be able to report the status of all funds received from or on behalf of the principal. The Texas license law requires that brokers give accurate copies of all documents to all parties affected. In addition, the license law and related rules require that brokers deposit all funds entrusted to them in a special trust, or escrow, account "by the close of business of the second working day after execution of the contract by the principals." The law also makes it illegal for brokers to **commingle**, or mix, such monies with personal funds.

Loyalty   The broker owes the principal the utmost loyalty. An agent must always place a principal's interests above those of the agent and above those of others with whom the agent deals. Thus, an agent cannot disclose information such as the principal's financial condition, the fact that the principal (if the seller) will accept a price lower than the listing price for the real estate, or any similar *confidential* facts that might harm the principal's bargaining position. On the other hand, loyalty dictates that the broker (if representing the seller as agent or subagent) must disclose to the seller any statements made by a buyer that reflect willingness to raise the offer if an initial offer is not accepted.

Texas law forbids brokers or salespersons to buy property listed with them for their own accounts; for accounts in which they have a personal interest; for a parent, child, or spouse; for a business entity in which the license holder is more than a 10% owner; or a trust for which the license holder is a trustee or of which the licensee's spouse parent or child is a beneficiary without first notifying the principal of such interest and receiving consent [TREC Rule 535.144]. Likewise, by law neither brokers nor salespersons may sell property in which they have a personal interest, as described, without so informing the purchaser.

A broker owes the client a full, fair, and timely disclosure of *all known facts relevant to the transaction.*

Disclosure   It is the broker's duty to keep the principal fully informed at all times of *all* facts or information the broker obtains that could affect the principal's decisions. The broker may be held liable for damages for failure to disclose such information. For example, an *agent for the seller* has a duty to disclose

■   the agent's opinion of the market price of the property;

■   all offers received (unless the seller has specifically instructed the listing broker, in writing, to do otherwise);

■   the identity of prospective purchasers, including any relationship the agent has with them;

■   the ability of a purchaser to complete the sale or offer a higher price;

■   any interest the broker has in the buyer (such as the buyer's asking the broker to manage the property after it is purchased); or

■   the buyer's intention to resell the property for a profit.

An *agent for a buyer* must inform the buyer of deficiencies of a property, as well as sales contract provisions and financing that do not suit the buyer's needs. The broker would suggest the lowest price that the buyer should pay based on comparable prices, regardless of the listing price. The agent would disclose information about how long a property has been listed or why the seller is selling if it would affect the buyer's ability to negotiate the lowest purchase price. Note that this information, if the agent were representing the seller, would violate the agent's fiduciary duty to the seller.

IN PRACTICE   Because fiduciary obligations cannot be taken lightly, it is crucial that brokers exercise the right to reject any proposed agency relationship that in their judgment violates legal or ethical standards.

Principal's Responsibilities to Agent

The principal also owes certain duties to the agent or broker. Among these are compensation, information, indemnification, and availability.

Compensation   The principal is liable for compensating the broker by paying the specified fee on completion of the broker's duties. This means that the principal must pay a commission or fee when the broker has performed the broker's portion of the listing agreement and produced a buyer who is ready, willing, and able to purchase.

Information   The principal must furnish accurate information requested by the broker. The broker is entitled to rely on such information, unless he has reason to know of its falsity.

Memory Tip

The four common law duties of a principal (client) to an agent may be remembered by the acronym **CIIA**: **C**ompensation, **I**nformation, **I**ndemnification, and **A**vailability.

Indemnification   The principal agrees to indemnify or reimburse the broker if the broker suffers financial injury while performing duties as broker. This means the broker is "held harmless" during the agency relationship.

Availability   The principal must be available at reasonable times to consider offers, accept notices, or permit the showing of the property. If the principal will not be available, arrangements must be made to ensure accessibility for the broker.

Agent's Responsibilities to Customers

Even though an agent's primary responsibility is to the principal, the agent also has duties to third parties, or customers—duties of reasonable care and skill, honest and fair dealing, and disclosure of known material facts about the property. Brokers must carefully monitor statements they or their staff members make about a parcel of real estate. Statements of opinion are permissible so long as they are offered as opinions and without any intention to deceive. Making exaggerated or unsubstantiated statements of value when selling real estate is called **puffing**. Although permissible under agency law, statements of opinion and puffing should be avoided because of possible claims under the *Deceptive Trade Practices Act* that they mislead the consumer.

Brokers and salespersons must secure accurate information to avoid **misrepresentation**, the *unintentional* misstatement of a fact. Additionally, they must ensure that none of their statements can be interpreted in any way as involving fraud. **Fraud** is the *intentional* misstatement of a material fact made for the purpose of harming or taking advantage of another person, inducing that person to enter into a contract relying on the false representation. In addition to false statements about a property, the concept of fraud covers intentional concealment or nondisclosure of important facts. If a contract to purchase real estate is obtained as a result of fraudulent misstatements made by a broker or his salespersons, the contract may be disaffirmed or rescinded by the purchaser. In such a case, the broker will lose a commission. If either party suffers loss because of a broker's misrepresentations, the broker also can be held liable for damages. If the broker's misstatements are based on the owner's inaccurate statements to the broker, however, the broker may be entitled to a commission even if the buyer rescinds the sales contract.

Parties to and licensees in a transaction are protected from liability for the misrepresentation or concealment of material facts by each other or by a subagent unless the party or licensee knew of the falsity of the misrepresentation or concealment and failed to disclose that knowledge. However, brokers are always responsible for the acts or omissions of their salespersons.

Brokers and salespersons should know that the courts have ruled that a seller is responsible for revealing to a buyer any *hidden*, or *latent*, defects in a building. A 2006 Texas court of appeals case defined a *"defect of the property"* as an irregularity in a surface or a structure that mars its appearance or causes some tangible aspect of the property, whether it's physical appearance or structure, to weaken or fail (*Coldwell Banker Whiteside v. Ryan Equity, 181 S.W. 3d 879*). *A latent defect is one that is known to the seller but not to the buyer and that is not discoverable by ordinary inspection.* As an agent of the seller, a broker is likewise responsible for disclosing known latent defects. Buyers have been able to either rescind the sales contract or receive damages in such instances. Examples of such circumstances are cases in which a buried drain tile caused water to accumulate, a driveway was built partly on adjoining property, or a house was built over a ditch that was covered with decaying timber. Section 1101.556 of the *Texas Real Estate License Act* releases a seller or a seller's agent from the duty to disclose information related to whether a death by natural causes, suicide, or accident unrelated to the condition of the property occurred on the property. Presumably other conditions related to any stigma attached to the property (e.g., murder or molestation on the property or a reputation for being haunted) would have to be disclosed.

Puffing = opinion

Misrepresentation = unintentional untruth

Fraud = intentional untruth or nondisclosure

An agent must disclose to a buyer-customer *all material facts about the condition of the property*, such as known structural defects, building code violations, and hidden dangerous conditions.

FOR EXAMPLE   Case 1: While showing a potential buyer an average-looking house, a broker described even its plainest features as "charming" and "beautiful." Because the statements were obviously the broker's personal opinions, designed to encourage a positive feeling about the property (or puff it up), their truth or falsity probably would not be an issue.

Case 2: A broker was asked by a potential buyer whether a particular neighborhood was safe. Although the broker knew that the area was experiencing a high rate of violent crime, he assured the buyer that no problem existed. He also neglected to inform the buyer that the lot next to the house the buyer was considering had been sold to a waste disposal company for use as a toxic dump. Both the statement and the omission are examples of fraud.

IN PRACTICE   Because of the enormous exposure to liability that real estate licensees have under the law, some brokers purchase errors and omissions insurance policies for their firms. In fact, Section 1101.453 of Real Estate License Act now requires errors and omissions insurance in certain instances. If the designated broker for a brokerage firm does not own at least 10% of the firm, the firm must have errors and omissions insurance of at least $1 million. Similar to medical malpractice insurance, such policies generally cover liabilities for errors, mistakes, and negligence in the usual listing and selling activities of a real estate office. They do not cover intentional acts or trebling or multiplication of damages under the Texas Deceptive Trade Practices Act.

AGENCY POSITIONS AND DISCLOSURE

The Real Estate License Act defines four positions a broker might take when doing business with a seller, a buyer, a landlord, or a tenant. The law requires that "a licensee shall provide to a party to a real estate transaction at the time of the first substantive dialogue with the party" a "written statement" that sets forth generalized information relative to seller representation, subagency, buyer representation, and the intermediary position (see Figure 5.1, Information About Brokerage Services). The statutorily prescribed written statement does not require signatures, dates, or licensee names and may be printed in any format that uses at least 10-point type. It is not required if

- the proposed transaction is for a *residential* lease for not more than one year and no sale is being considered (this exemption does not apply to commercial leases), or
- the licensee meets with a party who is represented by another licensee.

Four Statutory Agency Positions
- Seller's agent
- Subagent
- Buyer's agent
- Intermediary

Substantive dialogue means a meeting or written communication that involves a substantive discussion relating to specific real property. A face-to-face meeting with a prospective client in which properties are discussed is a substantive dialogue. In addition, any written correspondence, including email or other electronic means, about specific properties constitutes a substantive dialogue. A telephone conversation by itself may not (but could) constitute a meeting that would require providing the form. In any event, any written follow-up or face-to-face meeting would require that the client receive the form. A substantive dialogue requiring an agent to give a party the Information About Brokerage Services form does not include a meeting at an open house or a meeting that occurs after the parties have signed a contract. However, the Real Estate License Act does require that agents *disclose* to persons visiting an open house (either orally or in writing) that they represent the seller [Section 1101.558].

FIGURE 5.1:   Information About Brokerage Services

for Substahtial Convertation   10-10-11

Approved by the Texas Real Estate Commission for Voluntary Use
Texas law requires all real estate licensees to give the following information about brokerage services to prospective buyers, tenants, sellers and landlords.

Information About Brokerage Services

Before working with a real estate broker, you should know that the duties of a broker depend on whom the broker represents. If you are a prospective seller or landlord (owner) or a prospective buyer or tenant (buyer), you should know that the broker who lists the property for sale or lease is the owner's agent. A broker who acts as a subagent represents the owner in cooperation with the listing broker. A broker who acts as a buyer's agent represents the buyer. A broker may act as an intermediary between the parties if the parties consent in writing. A broker can assist you in locating a property, preparing a contract or lease, or obtaining financing without representing you.   A broker is obligated by law to treat you honestly.

IF THE BROKER REPRESENTS THE OWNER:
The broker becomes the owner's agent by entering into an agreement with the owner, usually through a written - listing agreement, or by agreeing to act as a subagent by accepting an offer of subagency from the listing broker. A subagent may work in a different real estate office. A listing broker or subagent can assist the buyer but does not   represent the buyer and must place the interests of the owner first. The buyer should not tell the owner's agent anything the buyer would not want the owner to know because an owner's agent must disclose to the owner any material information known to the agent.

IF THE BROKER REPRESENTS THE BUYER:
The broker becomes the buyer's agent by entering into an agreement to represent the buyer, usually through a written buyer representation agreement. A buyer's agent can assist the owner but does not represent the owner and must place the interests of the buyer first. The owner should not tell a buyer's agent anything the owner would not want the buyer to know because a buyer's agent must disclose to the buyer any material information known to the agent.

IF THE BROKER ACTS AS AN INTERMEDIARY:
A broker may act as an intermediary between the parties if the broker complies with The Texas Real Estate License Act. The broker must obtain the written consent of each party to the transaction to act as an intermediary. The written consent must state who will pay the broker and, in conspicuous bold or underlined print, set forth the broker's obligations as an intermediary. The broker is required to treat each party honestly and fairly and to comply with The Texas Real Estate License Act.   A broker who acts as an intermediary in a transaction:

(1) shall treat all parties honestly;

(2) may not disclose that the owner will accept a price less that the asking price unless authorized in writing to do so by the owner;

(3) may not disclose that the buyer will pay a price greater than the price submitted in a written offer unless authorized in writing to do so by the buyer; and

(4) may not disclose any confidential information or any information that a party specifically instructs the broker in writing not to disclose unless authorized in writing to disclose the information or required to do so by The Texas Real Estate License Act or a court order or if the information materially relates to the condition of the property.

With the parties' consent, a broker acting as an intermediary between the parties may appoint a person who is licensed under The Texas Real Estate License Act and associated with the broker to communicate with and carry out instructions of one party and another person who is licensed under that Act and associated with the broker to communicate with and carry out instructions of the other party.

If you choose to have a broker represent you, you should enter into a written agreement with the broker that clearly establishes the broker's obligations and your obligations. The agreement should state how and by whom the broker will be paid. You have the right to choose the type of representation, if any, you wish to receive. Your payment of a fee to a broker does not necessarily establish that the broker represents you. If you have any questions regarding the duties and responsibilities of the broker, you should resolve those questions before proceeding.

Real estate licensee asks that you acknowledge receipt of this information about brokerage services for the licensee's records.

_____

Buyer, Seller, Landlord or Tenant   Date

Texas Real Estate Brokers and Salespersons are licensed and regulated by the Texas Real Estate Commission (TREC). If you have a question or complaint regarding a real estate licensee, you should contact TREC at P.O. Box 12188, Austin, Texas 78711-2188 , 512-936-3000 (http://www.trec.texas.gov)

TREC No. OP-K

The following is a summary of broker agency positions:

- A broker who lists the property for sale or lease represents the owner as a *seller's agent*, usually through a written listing agreement (see Chapter 13).
- A broker who acts as a *subagent* represents the owner in cooperation with the listing broker; a subagent is not sponsored by or associated with the listing broker.
- A broker who acts as a *buyer's agent* represents the buyer, usually through a written buyer representation agreement (see Figure 5.2).
- A broker must agree to act as an *intermediary* if agreeing to *represent* both a buyer and a seller in a transaction. Each party to the transaction must give written consent to the broker's acting as an intermediary. An **intermediary broker** may appoint a licensed associate (**appointed licensee**), with the written consent of the parties, to communicate with and carry out instructions of each party. The written consent must state who will pay the broker and set forth the broker's obligations. The intermediary broker (or appointed licensee)
  - must treat all parties honestly,
  - may not disclose that the owner will accept a price less than the asking price,
  - may not disclose that a buyer will pay a price greater than submitted in a written offer,
  - may not disclose any confidential information or any information a party specifically instructs the broker in writing not to disclose unless otherwise instructed or required to do so, and
  - must comply with the Texas Real Estate License Act.

Only a broker can act as an intermediary. The intermediary broker must act fairly and impartially and is *not* allowed to give advice or opinion. However, if a broker appoints associated licensees to work with the parties, each appointed licensee may provide advice or opinions to the party to which the licensee has been appointed but may not disclose confidential information prohibited in the previous section.

FOR EXAMPLE   A broker obtains a listing agreement with a seller and becomes the seller's agent. A salesperson in the broker's office has a client (with a signed buyer representation agreement with the broker's firm) who expresses an interest in the property. A potential conflict of interest exists because the broker has an agency relationship with both parties. Unless the broker refers either the buyer or the seller to another real estate firm, the broker will have three possible courses of action, according to the Texas Real Estate Commission:

- The firm, acting through the salesperson or the broker, could represent one of the parties and work with the other party (probably the buyer) as a customer rather than as a client, terminating the buyer representation agreement or listing agreement.

- If the firm has obtained permission in writing from both parties to be an intermediary and to appoint licensees to work with the parties, the broker could appoint licensees to work with each party. The buyer's agent could not be appointed to work with the seller nor could the broker as intermediary represent the seller. Another licensee would have to be appointed to work with the seller. The broker would immediately obtain the written consent of both parties, explain how the intermediary relationship will alter the original relationship with the clients, and provide written notice of the appointment to all parties involved in the transaction.

■ If the firm has obtained permission in writing from both parties to be an intermediary but does not appoint different associates to work with the parties, the salesperson or the broker could function as a representative of the firm, working with both parties in a neutral manner but being careful not to favor one over the other or to provide advice or opinion to either of them.

A licensee who has an established agency relationship with one party in a proposed transaction must disclose that representation either orally or in writing at the time of the licensee's first contact with

■ another party to the transaction, or

■ another licensee who represents another party to the transaction.

IN PRACTICE   While licensees often attempt to meet the statutory disclosure requirement by providing a boilerplate link to the disclosure in an email or text to a client or prospective client, it can be difficult to prove that the disclosure was timely received. Although the statute does not require that a licensee obtain a client's signature to acknowledge that the disclosure was received, it may be prudent in such cases for the licensee to ask the client to respond by return email or text that the disclosure was received.

IN PRACTICE   The Information About Brokerage Services statement is intended to inform sellers, buyers, landlords, and tenants about the statutorily created alternative methods for doing business with a real estate broker. It must state, "You have the right to choose the type of representation, if any, you wish to receive." This means that the consumer who feels competent to function without representation may elect to have no representation. The Texas Real Estate License Act provides for the suspension or revocation of a licensee "for failing to make clear, to all parties to a transaction, which party he is acting for …" Although agency law permits disclosure to "another party" or "another licensee" to be made orally or in writing, a broker may want licensed associates to make the agency disclosure in writing as an affirmative defense against a charge of fraud or deceptive trade practice.

Single agency exists when the agent represents only one party to the transaction—a buyer or a seller. A broker must agree to act as an *intermediary* if the broker agrees to represent both a buyer and a seller in a transaction (§ 1101.561 of the License Act). However, if an agent has an express agreement with a seller and an implied agreement with a buyer, an *undisclosed dual agency* relationship would exist under common law. An undisclosed dual agency relationship is always illegal because it violates the common law duties of loyalty and disclosure and the requirement for informed consent of all parties. For more information about agency disclosure, go to the Texas Real Estate Commission website: www.trec.texas.gov; then choose FAQs, Enforcement FAQs, and Disclosure of Agency.

FIGURE 5.2: Residential Buyer/Tenant Representation Agreement

TEXAS ASSOCIATION OF REALTORS®
**RESIDENTIAL BUYER/TENANT REPRESENTATION
AGREEMENT**
USE OF THIS FORM BY PERSONS WHO ARE NOT MEMBERS OF THE TEXAS ASSOCIATION OF REALTORS® IS NOT
AUTHORIZED.
©Texas Association of REALTORS®, Inc.
2014

1. **PARTIES:** The parties to this agreement are:

    Client:_____

        _____
        Address:_____
        City, State, Zip:_____
        Phone:_____Fax:_____
        E-Mail:_____

    Broker:_____

        _____
        Address: _____
        City, State, Zip: _____
        Phone:_____Fax: _____
        E-Mail: _____

2. **APPOINTMENT:** Client grants to Broker the exclusive right to act as Client's real estate agent for the purpose of acquiring property in the market area.

3. **DEFINITIONS:**
    A. *"Acquire"* means to purchase or lease.
    B. *"Closing"* in a sale transaction means the date legal title to a property is conveyed to a purchaser of property under a contract to buy. "Closing" in a lease transaction means the date a landlord and tenant enter into a binding lease of a property.
    C. *"Market area"* means that area in the State of Texas within the perimeter boundaries of the following areas: _____
       _____
       _____
       _____.
    D. *"Property"* means any interest in real estate including but not limited to properties listed in a multiple listing service or other listing services, properties for sale by owners, and properties for sale by builders.

4. **TERM:** This agreement commences on _____ and ends at 11:59 p.m. on _____.

5. **BROKER'S OBLIGATIONS:** Broker will: (a) use Broker's best efforts to assist Client in acquiring property in the market area; (b) assist Client in negotiating the acquisition of property in the market area; and (c) comply with other provisions of this agreement.

6. **CLIENT'S OBLIGATIONS:** Client will: (a) work exclusively through Broker in acquiring property in the market area and negotiate the acquisition of property in the market area only through Broker; (b) inform other brokers, salespersons, sellers, and landlords with whom Client may have contact that Broker exclusively represents Client for the purpose of acquiring property in the market area and refer all such persons to Broker; and (c) comply with other provisions of this agreement.

FIGURE 5.2:   Residential Buyer/Tenant Representation Agreement (continued)

Buyer/Tenant Representation Agreement between _____

7.   REPRESENTATIONS:

A. Each person signing this agreement represents that the person has the legal capacity and authority to bind the respective party to this agreement.

B. Client represents that Client is not now a party to another buyer or tenant representation agreement with another broker for the acquisition of property in the market area

C. Client represents that all information relating to Client's ability to acquire property in the market area Client gives to Broker is true and correct.

D. Name any employer, relocation company, or other entity that will provide benefits to Client when acquiring property in the market area: _____.

8.   INTERMEDIARY: *(Check A or B only.)*

❑   A. <u>Intermediary Status</u>: Client desires to see Broker's listings. If Client wishes to acquire one of Broker's listings, Client authorizes Broker to act as an intermediary and Broker will notify Client that Broker will service the parties in accordance with one of the following alternatives.

1) If the owner of the property is serviced by an associate other than the associate servicing Client under this agreement, Broker may notify Client that Broker will: (a) appoint the associate then servicing the owner to communicate with, carry out instructions of, and provide opinions and advice during negotiations to the owner; and (b) appoint the associate then servicing Client to the Client for the same purpose.

2) If the owner of the property is serviced by the same associate who is servicing Client, Broker may notify Client that Broker will: (a) appoint another associate to communicate with, carry out instructions of, and provide opinions and advice during negotiations to Client; and (b) appoint the associate servicing the owner under the listing to the owner for the same purpose.

3) Broker may notify Client that Broker will make no appointments as described under this Paragraph 8A and, in such an event, the associate servicing the parties will act solely as Broker's intermediary representative, who may facilitate the transaction but will not render opinions or advice during negotiations to either party.

❑   B. <u>No Intermediary Status</u>: Client does not wish to be shown or acquire any of Broker's listings.

Notice: If Broker acts as an intermediary under Paragraph 8A, Broker and Broker's associates:

♦ **may not disclose to Client that the seller or landlord will accept a price less than the asking price unless otherwise instructed in a separate writing by the seller or landlord;**

♦ **may not disclose to the seller or landlord that Client will pay a price greater than the price submitted in a written offer to the seller or landlord unless otherwise instructed in a separate writing by Client;**

♦ **may not disclose any confidential information or any information a seller or landlord or Client specifically instructs Broker in writing not to disclose unless otherwise instructed in a separate writing by the respective party or required to disclose the information by the Real Estate License Act or a court order or if the information materially relates to the condition of the property;**

♦ **shall treat all parties to the transaction honestly; and**

♦ **shall comply with the Real Estate License Act.**

9.   COMPETING CLIENTS: Client acknowledges that Broker may represent other prospective buyers or tenants who may seek to acquire properties that may be of interest to Client. Client agrees that Broker may, during the term of this agreement and after it ends, represent such other prospects, show the other prospects the same properties that Broker shows to Client, and act as a real estate broker for such other prospects in negotiating the acquisition of properties that Client may seek to acquire.

10. CONFIDENTIAL INFORMATION:

A. During the term of this agreement or after its termination, Broker may not knowingly disclose information obtained in confidence from Client except as authorized by Client or required by law. Broker may not disclose to Client any information obtained in confidence regarding any other

FIGURE 5.2: Residential Buyer/Tenant Representation Agreement (continued)

Buyer/Tenant Representation Agreement between _____

person Broker represents or may have represented except as required by law.

    B. Unless otherwise agreed or required by law, a seller or the seller's agent is not obliged to keep the existence of an offer or its terms confidential. If a listing agent receives multiple offers, the listing agent is obliged to treat the competing buyers fairly.

11. BROKER'S FEES:

    A. <u>Commission</u>: The parties agree that Broker will receive a commission calculated as follows: (1) ____% of the gross sales price if Client agrees to purchase property in the market area; and (2) if Client agrees to lease property in the market area a fee equal to *(check only one box)*: ❑ _____% of one month's rent or ❑ _____% of all rents to be paid over the term of the lease.

    B. <u>Source of Commission Payment</u>: Broker will seek to obtain payment of the commission specified in Paragraph 11A first from the seller, landlord, or their agents. **If such persons refuse or fail to pay Broker the amount specified, Client will pay Broker the amount specified less any amounts Broker receives from such persons.**

    C. <u>Earned and Payable</u>: A person is not obligated to pay Broker a commission until such time as Broker's commission is *earned and payable*. Broker's commission is *earned* when: (1) Client enters into a contract to buy or lease property in the market area; or (2) Client breaches this agreement. Broker's commission is *payable*, either during the term of this agreement or after it ends, upon the earlier of: (1) the closing of the transaction to acquire the property; (2) Client's breach of a contract to buy or lease a property in the market area; or (3) Client's breach of this agreement. If Client acquires more than one property under this agreement, Broker's commissions for each property acquired are earned as each property is acquired and are payable at the closing of each acquisition.

    D. <u>Additional Compensation</u>: If a seller, landlord, or their agents offer compensation in excess of the amount stated in Paragraph 11A (including but not limited to marketing incentives or bonuses to cooperating brokers) Broker may retain the additional compensation in addition to the specified commission. Client is not obligated to pay any such additional compensation to Broker.

    E. <u>Acquisition of Broker's Listing</u>: Notwithstanding any provision to the contrary, if Client acquires a property listed by Broker, Broker will be paid in accordance with the terms of Broker's listing agreement with the owner and Client will have no obligation to pay Broker.

    F. In addition to the commission specified under Paragraph 11A, Broker is entitled to the following fees.
        1) <u>Construction</u>: If Client uses Broker's services to procure or negotiate the construction of improvements to property that Client owns or may acquire, Client ensures that Broker will receive from Client or the contractor(s) at the time the construction is substantially complete a fee equal to:_____.
        2) <u>Service Providers</u>: If Broker refers Client or any party to a transaction contemplated by this agreement to a service provider (for example, mover, cable company, telecommunications provider, utility, or contractor) Broker may receive a fee from the service provider for the referral.
        3) <u>Other</u>:_____
_____
_____.

    G. <u>Protection Period</u>: "Protection period" means that time starting the day after this agreement ends and continuing for _____ days. Not later than 10 days after this agreement ends, Broker may send Client written notice identifying the properties called to Client's attention during this agreement. If Client or a relative of Client agrees to acquire a property identified in the notice during the protection period, Client will pay Broker, upon closing, the amount Broker would have been entitled to receive if

FIGURE 5.2:   Residential Buyer/Tenant Representation Agreement (continued)

Buyer/Tenant Representation Agreement between _____

this agreement were still in effect. This Paragraph 11G survives termination of this agreement. This Paragraph 11G will not apply if Client is, during the protection period, bound under a representation agreement with another broker who is a member of the Texas Association of REALTORS® at the time the acquisition is negotiated and the other broker is paid a fee for negotiating the transaction.

   H. Escrow Authorization: Client authorizes, and Broker may so instruct, any escrow or closing agent authorized to close a transaction for the acquisition of property contemplated by this agreement to collect and disburse to Broker all amounts payable to Broker.

   I. County: Amounts payable to Broker are to be paid in cash in _____ County, Texas.

12. MEDIATION: The parties agree to negotiate in good faith in an effort to resolve any dispute that may arise related to this agreement or any transaction related to or contemplated by this agreement. If the dispute cannot be resolved by negotiation, the parties will submit the dispute to mediation before resorting to arbitration or litigation and will equally share the costs of a mutually acceptable mediator.

13. DEFAULT: If either party fails to comply with this agreement or makes a false representation in this agreement, the non-complying party is in default. If Client is in default, Client will be liable for the amount of compensation that Broker would have received under this agreement if Client was not in default. If Broker is in default, Client may exercise any remedy at law.

14. ATTORNEY'S FEES: If Client or Broker is a prevailing party in any legal proceeding brought as a result of a dispute under this agreement or any transaction related to this agreement, such party will be entitled to recover from the non-prevailing party all costs of such proceeding and reasonable attorney's fees.

15. LIMITATION OF LIABILITY: Neither Broker nor any other broker, or their associates, is responsible or liable for any person's personal injuries or for any loss or damage to any person's property that is not caused by Broker. Client will hold broker, any other broker, and their associates, harmless from any such injuries or losses. Client will indemnify Broker against any claims for injury or damage that Client may cause to others or their property.

16. ADDENDA: Addenda and other related documents which are part of this agreement are:
   ☑ Information About Brokerage Services   ❑ Protect Your Family from Lead in Your Home
   ❑ Protecting Your Home from Mold   ❑ Information about Special Flood Hazard Areas
   ❑ Information Concerning Property Insurance   ❑ For Your Protection: Get a Home Inspection
   ❑ General Information and Notice to a Buyer   ❑ _____

17. SPECIAL PROVISIONS:

18. ADDITIONAL NOTICES:

   A. **Broker's fees and the sharing of fees between brokers are not fixed, controlled, recommended, suggested, or maintained by the Association of REALTORS® or any listing service.**

   B. **In accordance with fair housing laws and the National Association of REALTORS® Code of Ethics, Broker's services must be provided without regard to race, color, religion, national origin, sex, disability, familial status, sexual orientation, or gender identity. Local ordinances may provide for additional protected classes (for example, creed, status as a student, marital status, or age).**

FIGURE 5.2: Residential Buyer/Tenant Representation Agreement (continued)

Buyer/Tenant Representation Agreement between _____

C. Broker is not a property inspector, surveyor, engineer, environmental assessor, or compliance inspector. Client should seek experts to render such services in any acquisition.

D. If Client purchases property, Client should have an abstract covering the property examined by an attorney of Client's selection, or Client should be furnished with or obtain a title policy.

E. Buyer may purchase a residential service contract. Buyer should review such service contract or the scope of coverage, exclusions, and limitations. The purchase of a residential service contract is optional. There are several residential service companies operating in Texas.

CONSULT AN ATTORNEY: Broker cannot give legal advice. This is a legally binding agreement. READ IT CAREFULLY. If you do not understand the effect of this agreement, consult your attorney BEFORE signing.

_____
Broker's Printed Name   License No.

_____
❏ Broker's Signature   Date
❏ Broker's Associate's Signature, as an authorized agent of Broker

_____
Broker's Associate's Printed Name, if applicable

_____
Client's Printed Name

_____
Client's Signature   Date

_____
Client's Printed Name

_____
Client's Signature   Date

NATURE OF THE BROKERAGE BUSINESS

Texas real estate license law regulates many of the day-to-day business operations of a real estate brokerage. Such matters include location of a definite, regular place of business for the firm; use of business signs; requirements for establishing and maintaining branch brokerage offices; proper accounting procedures; correct handling of client trust fund accounts; and the specific manner of execution and retention of documents involved in the real estate transaction. However, it is up to the broker to set effective written policies for every aspect of the brokerage operation: hiring of employees and salespersons, determination of compensation, and direction of staff and sales activities, as well as procedures to follow in carrying out agency duties. In addition, Section 535.2 of the TREC Rules requires that a brokerage firm have specific written policies and procedures addressing such things as the scope of the sponsored salespersons' activities; license status; compensation; changes to the License Act, Rules, and promulgated contract forms; continuing education; competency; advertising; and maintenance of trust accounts and client records.

Broker-Salesperson Relationship

Although brokerage firms vary widely in size, few brokers perform their duties without the assistance of salespersons. Consequently, much of a business's success hinges on the broker-salesperson relationship.

If an agent is to receive a fee from a vendor (such as a cable provider) who is being paid by a party the agent does not represent, the agent must get permission from that party and the agent's client to receive the fee.

A real estate salesperson is any person licensed to perform real estate activities on behalf of a licensed real estate broker. The salesperson can carry out only those responsibilities assigned by the broker with whom the salesperson is licensed—and all activities must be performed in the name of the supervising broker. Unless the scope is limited or revoked in writing, a broker is responsible for the authorized acts of persons licensed under the broker, even when the salesperson does not work out of the broker's main office. If a broker permits a sponsored salesperson to conduct activities beyond the scope explicitly authorized by the broker, the broker is responsible for those acts.

A broker is licensed to act as the principal's agent and thus can collect compensation for performing assigned duties. A salesperson, on the other hand, has no authority to make contracts or receive compensation directly from a principal. All compensation to the salesperson must be paid with the knowledge and written consent of or through the sponsoring broker or through the broker under whom the salesperson was licensed at the time the right to compensation was earned. *Remember that agency with the principal is at the broker level.*

Employee Versus Independent Contractor   Brokers engage salespersons as either employees or independent contractors. Whether a salesperson operates under the broker as an employee or as an independent contractor affects the structure of the salesperson's responsibilities and the broker's liability to pay and withhold taxes from the salesperson's earnings (see Figure 5.3).

FIGURE 5.3: Employee Versus Independent Contractor

Employee	Independent Contractor
Must have income tax and Social Security withheld from wages by broker	Assumes responsibility for paying own income tax and Social Security
May receive "employee benefits" from broker	Cannot receive any "employee benefits" from broker
	Must have a written contract
	Must be compensated on production

The nature of the employer-employee relationship allows a broker to exercise certain *controls* over salespersons who are employees. Persons who are required to comply with instructions about when, where, and how they are to work is ordinarily an **employee**. The broker may require that an employee adhere to regulations concerning such matters as working hours, office routine, and dress or language standards. As an employer, a broker is required by the federal government to withhold Social Security tax and income tax from wages paid to employees. Employing brokers are also required to pay unemployment compensation tax on wages paid to one or more employees, as defined by state and federal laws. In addition, such brokers may be required to provide employees with such benefits as health insurance and profit-sharing plans.

A broker's relationship with an independent contractor is different. The **independent contractor** salesperson operates more freely than an employee. Through a written policies and procedures manual that a salesperson is required to follow, the broker may control *what* the independent contractor does, but not *how* it is done. The independent contractor assumes responsibility for paying any required income and Social Security taxes, health insurance (if coverage is desired), travel expenses, and supplies needed for work and receives nothing from the broker that could be construed as an employee benefit, such as paid vacation time.

The IRS is authorized to investigate the independent contractor/employee relationship in brokers' offices. To determine whether a person is an independent contractor or employee, all evidence of control and independence must be considered. The "IRS Independent Contractor Test" evaluates the evidence of the degree of control and independence in three categories: behavioral control, financial control, and the type of relationship between the parties. IRS Publication 15-A (December 2013) further defines licensed real estate agents as *statutory nonemployees* who are treated as self-employed for all federal tax purposes, including income and employment taxes, *if*

- substantially all payments for their services as real estate agents are directly related to sales or other output, rather than to the number of hours worked, and
- their services are performed under a written contract providing that they will not be treated as employees for federal tax purposes.

IN PRACTICE   A broker should have an independent contractor agreement drafted and reviewed by an attorney to ensure its compliance with federal law and should negotiate such an agreement with each independent contractor salesperson. The broker must be aware, however, that written agreements carry little weight with an IRS auditor if the actions of the parties contradict the provisions of the contract. Specific legal and tax questions regarding independent contractors should be referred to a competent attorney or accountant.

Compensation

Broker's Compensation   The broker's compensation is specified in the listing agreement, the buyer representation agreement, the management agreement, or other contract with the principal. Compensation usually is in the form of a commission, professional service fee, or brokerage fee computed as a *percentage of the total amount of money involved*—and the amount or rate of compensation is always negotiable between the principal and the broker. A commission typically is considered *earned* when the broker *performs* under the terms of the listing contract or buyer representation agreement—when a completed sales contract has been signed by a ready, willing, and able buyer and accepted by a seller. If the listing contract or buyer representation agreement expires before the closing date of the earnest money contract, the broker's commission still is vested; that is, it is not necessary for the listing contract or buyer representation agreement to be extended to include the closing date. Most sales commissions are *payable* when the sale is consummated by delivery of the seller's deed or immediately on default by the seller.

> To be a *procuring cause*, the broker must have started a chain of events that resulted in a sale.

According to common law, to be entitled to a sales commission, selling brokers must be able to show that they were the **procuring cause** of a sale—that the broker had taken action to start or cause a chain of events that resulted in the sale. Section 1101.806 of the Texas Real Estate License Act lists three *requirements* for compensation:

- The person held a valid real estate broker's license.
- The agreement to pay was in writing and signed by the party to be charged.
- The broker or salesperson advised the buyer in writing before closing that the buyer should obtain or be furnished with a title insurance policy or have the abstract covering the subject property examined by an attorney of the buyer's choice.

> A broker may be due a commission if a transaction is not closed because of the principal's (client's) default.

On accepting an offer from a ready, willing, and able buyer, the seller is technically liable for the broker's commission regardless of whether the seller completes the sale, unless the broker knew or should have known the buyer was not financially able to complete the purchase. A **ready, willing, and able buyer** is one who is prepared to buy on the seller's terms and ready to take positive steps toward consummation of the transaction. A broker who has produced such a buyer is usually still entitled to a commission if the transaction is not consummated for any of the following reasons:

- The owner has a change of mind and refuses to sell.
- The owner's spouse refuses to sign the deed.
- The owner's title is defective.
- The owner commits fraud with respect to the transaction.
- The owner is unable to deliver possession within a reasonable time.
- The owner insists on terms not in the listing (for example, the right to restrict the use of the property).
- The owner and the buyer agree to cancel the transaction.

There are, however, some situations in which a broker would not be entitled to a commission, including the following:

■ Failure to give the required title notice to the buyer. The required title notice is a part of the Texas promulgated sales contracts; however, if a licensee uses any contract form other than one promulgated by TREC, the title notice must be given by the licensee either separately or in the contract to purchase. In addition to losing a commission, the agent's real estate license may be revoked or suspended.

■ Failure to state an amount or percentage rate of commission in a listing contract. The rate of a broker's commission is *negotiable in every case*. If the commission rate was not negotiated, the broker may be unable to collect any fee at all.

■ Failure (without fault) on the part of the seller to deliver title assurance (an abstract or title insurance policy) to the buyer.

If a person makes a referral with the expectation of receiving cash, discounts, or gifts valued over $50, that person must be licensed.

The Texas Real Estate License Act prohibits a real estate licensee from paying a commission, fee, or other valuable consideration to a person who is not licensed as a salesperson or broker for services as a real estate agent. This includes a prohibition against sharing a sales commission with an unlicensed business entity or with an attorney who is not licensed by TREC. An attorney who is not licensed by TREC but performs brokerage services in a transaction must negotiate for a commission or fee from one of the principals to the transaction. Prohibited *valuable consideration* includes items of personal property (such as a television) and other premiums (vacations, rent, bonuses, and discounts) as well as finders' fees. A *gift* is permissible as long as the retail value does not exceed $50; however, a cash payment in any amount is a violation of TREC Rules. A gift certificate worth no more than $50 is permitted as long as it cannot be exchanged for cash. Under certain circumstances, it is legal for a broker to *rebate* a portion of the commission to the principal if the payment is strictly a rebate and is not made for a real estate service, such as a referral. The rebate may be in any form such as cash, gift certificates, appliances, frequent flyer certificates, et cetera.

"Loser pays" legislation passed in 2011 permits a judge to dismiss a meritless lawsuit and requires the plaintiffs to pay the defendant's attorneys' fees and court costs (H.B. 274).

Under statutorily defined circumstances, a real estate broker or licensed or certified real estate appraiser can file a lien on commercial real estate for commissions earned but not yet paid. The commission must exceed $2,500, and the broker or appraiser must have disclosed the right to the lien in the fee agreement.

Salesperson's Compensation   A salesperson's compensation is set by mutual agreement between broker and salesperson, and that agreement must be in writing. A broker may agree to pay a salary (generally to an employee) or a share of the commissions from transactions originated by a salesperson (generally to an independent contractor). If a salesperson has a drawing account against earned commissions, the salesperson should sign a note for each draw to preserve the independent contractor status.

Usually, the higher the commission split to the agent, the more expenses the broker will require the agent to pay. In a *100% commission firm*, all salespersons who achieve a predetermined sales quota receive 100% of the commissions from the sales they negotiate and pay a monthly service charge to their broker (to cover the costs of office space, telephones, and other overhead expenses).

IN PRACTICE Top real estate producers often employ personal assistants to enable them to be more productive. Unlicensed assistants may perform myriad tasks, among them: answering phone calls, maintaining records, handling correspondence, scheduling appointments, and serving as hosts or hostesses at open houses. They may not, however, engage in any activity for which a license is required (such as interviewing prospects, showing property, soliciting prospects or listings, or controlling the acceptance or deposit of rent from a resident of a single-family residential property unit); and they may not at any time respond to inquiries about a property when the response requires communication of information that has not been specifically advertised. Personal assistants may be licensed or unlicensed but generally work under the direction and control of the real estate agent. As such, they are usually considered employees and are paid hourly. For more information about using unlicensed assistants in real estate transactions, check the TREC website at www.trec.texas.gov and choose News and Public Data; then Topics of Special Interest.

Antitrust Laws

Antitrust violations include these:
- Price-fixing
- Boycotting a competitor
- Allocation of customers or markets

The real estate industry is subject to federal and state **antitrust laws**. These laws prohibit monopolies and contracts, combinations, and conspiracies that unreasonably restrain trade. The most common antitrust violations that can occur in the real estate business are price-fixing, boycotting competitors, and allocating customers or markets.

Price-fixing is the practice of setting prices for products or services rather than letting competition in the open market establish those prices. In real estate it occurs when brokers agree to set sales commissions, fees, or management rates, and it is illegal. Brokers must independently determine commission rates or fees only for their own firms. These decisions must be based on the broker's business judgment and revenue requirements without input from other brokers.

The broker's challenge is to avoid any impression of attempts at price-fixing, as well as the actual practice. Hinting in any way to prospective clients that there is a "going rate" of commission or fee implies that rates are in fact standardized. A broker must clarify to clients that the rate stated is only what that firm charges. Likewise, discussions of rates among licensees from different firms could be construed as a price-fixing activity and should be avoided.

Multiple listing organizations, boards of REALTORS®, and other professional organizations may not set fees or commission splits, nor are they allowed to deny membership to brokers based on the fees the brokers charge. Either practice could lead the public to believe that the industry sanctions the illegal practice of restricting open-market competition.

Boycotting competitors results when brokers are unfairly excluded from real estate professional associations or when two or more businesses conspire against other businesses or agree to withhold their patronage to reduce competition. For example, an agreement among brokers not to work with measured-service brokers (MSBs), also known as "discount" brokers, or with buyer brokers would be illegal.

Allocation of customers or markets involves an agreement between brokers to divide their markets and refrain from competing against each other. Illegal allocations may take place on a geographic basis, with brokers agreeing to specific territories within which they will operate exclusively, or the division may take place along other lines. For example, if two brokers agree that one will handle residential properties under $100,000 in value and another will handle residential properties over $100,000 in value, the resulting allocation of markets would be illegal.

The penalties for such acts are severe. Individuals found guilty of violating antitrust laws may be charged with either a misdemeanor or a felony, depending on the severity of the violation, punishable by a maximum $1 million fine and 10 years' imprisonment. For corporations, the penalty may be as high as $100 million. In a civil suit, a person who suffered a loss because of the antitrust activities of a guilty party may recover triple the value of actual damages plus attorneys' fees and costs.

TEXAS DECEPTIVE TRADE PRACTICES—CONSUMER PROTECTION ACT

At one time, real estate transactions were governed solely by the maxim **caveat emptor**, Latin for "let the buyer beware." Through this principle, the courts charged the buyer with the responsibilities of inspecting the property and searching the public records to ascertain interests of other persons, including the rights of parties in possession.

Because of growing concern about consumer protection in the United States, the courts have modified the caveat emptor principle by placing more responsibility on the seller. Sellers of residential property in Texas are required to deliver a Seller's Disclosure Notice to a buyer on or before the effective date of a contract to disclose, among other things, the seller's knowledge of the property condition, along with a list of appliances and whether they are working (see Chapter 13). Consumer protection applies to the real estate agent, too. Texas licensees have an affirmative duty imposed by the Real Estate License Act to disclose known latent or hidden defects, and they can be held liable for false or misleading statements made about the property.

The DTPA protects consumers against false, misleading, or deceptive acts or practices of sellers or real estate agents.

In Texas, consumer rights are also protected by the **Texas Deceptive Trade Practices—Consumer Protection Act (DTPA)**, Chapter 17, Subchapter E, Business and Commerce Code. This act declares, among other things, that "false, misleading or deceptive acts or practices" in the advertising, offering for sale, selling, or leasing of any real or personal property are unlawful. As set forth in the act, false, misleading, or deceptive acts or practices are included in a "laundry list" of 27 items; some of them are as follows:

- Representing that something is new or original when it is not or that it is of a particular quality when it is not
- Advertising property with no intention of selling the property as advertised
- Making false statements of fact concerning the reasons for a price reduction
- Misrepresenting the authority of an agent to negotiate the final terms of a sales contract
- Representing that a warranty guarantees or confers rights or remedies not included
- Representing that work has been done on real or personal property when the work has not been done

The Texas Legislature in 2011 sought to reduce frivolous lawsuits against real estate brokers and salespersons by providing that the DTPA does not apply to claims arising from an act or omission by a broker or salesperson, with certain exceptions (S.B. 1353, 2011). The three circumstances under which the DTPA *does apply* to the actions of real estate agents are

- "an express misrepresentation of a material fact that cannot be characterized as advice, judgment, or opinion";
- a failure to disclose information concerning goods or services that was known at the time of the transaction if the failure to disclose such information was intended to induce the consumer into a transaction into which the consumer would not have entered had the information been disclosed; or
- "an unconscionable action or course of action that cannot be characterized as advice, judgment, or opinion."

In a DTPA suit, the consumer must prove that the deceptive act was the producing cause of damages. The suit must be commenced within two years after a false, misleading, or deceptive act or practice occurred—or within two years after the consumer discovered, or should have discovered, the deceptive act or practice. With the exception of residential property, the DTPA does not apply to transactions that exceed $100,000 where there is a written contract and the consumer is represented by legal counsel.

By statute, consumers may waive their rights to bring a suit under the DTPA. However, court opinions consistently uphold that "any waiver by a consumer of the provisions of the subchapter is contrary to public policy and is unenforceable and void." Therefore, all of the following strict requirements must be met for the waiver to be valid and enforceable:

- The waiver must be in writing and signed by the consumer.
- The consumer must not be in a significantly disparate bargaining position.
- The consumer must be represented by legal counsel (not referred by the defendant or an agent of the defendant) in seeking or acquiring the goods or services.
- The waiver must be conspicuous and in boldface type at least 10 points in size.
- The waiver must be in substantially the promulgated form under the heading "Waiver of Consumer Rights."

Either party to a lawsuit filed under the DTPA may file a motion to compel mediation of the dispute. Defenses to the DTPA include (1) a reasonable offer of settlement within specified time limits, (2) written notice to the consumer prior to consummation of the sale that the broker is relying on written information prepared by others, and (3) the impossibility of the broker's knowing that the information was false or inaccurate. The act also permits recovery of court costs and attorneys' fees if the lawsuit was ruled frivolous or harassing.

Recovery under the DTPA is limited to economic damages—costs of repair and replacement. However, if the defendant is found to have committed the act *knowingly*, then damages for mental anguish may also be awarded (and in some cases, up to three times the amount of economic damages). If the defendant is found to have committed the act *intentionally*, then the economic and mental anguish damages may be trebled. In addition to consumer compensation, the DTPA allows for civil penalties of up to $20,000 per violation, with an additional penalty of up to $250,000 for deceptive acts or practices that target the elderly. Note that an errors and omissions insurance policy purchased by a broker will not cover fraud or intentional violations of the DTPA. (*St. Paul Insurance Company v. Bonded Realty, Inc.* 583 S.W.2d 619 [Tex. 1979] p. 141.)

A **consumer** is defined by the DTPA as an individual, partnership, corporation, or Texas government agency "who seeks or acquires, by pur-chase or lease, any goods or services." Businesses with assets of $25 million or more are not *consumers* under the DTPA.

Under Section 1101.805 of the License Act, parties to a contract and licensees are protected from liability for misrepresentation or concealment of material facts by each other or by a subagent unless the party or licensee knew of the falsity or concealment. A defendant who is only marginally at fault in a claim will be liable to the consumer for that defendant's percentage of responsibility. In addition to proportionate responsibility, a defendant may be held jointly and separately responsible for *all* damages recoverable by the claimant if (a) the defendant's percentage of responsibility is greater than 50% or (b) the defendant, with specific intent to do harm to others, acted with another person to engage in a felony of the third degree or higher—including forgery, misapplication of fiduciary property, or securing execution of a document by deception. However, proportional responsibility laws do not diminish the broker's liability for the acts of the broker's salespersons, for whom the broker is still fully responsible.

FRAUD IN REAL ESTATE AND STOCK TRANSACTIONS STATUTE

In addition to an agent's responsibilities under the Texas Real Estate License Act and the DTPA, the Fraud in Real Estate and Stock Transactions Statute, Article 27.01, Business and Commerce Code, states that any person who stands to gain financially from a transaction is assumed to have knowledge of all aspects of the transaction. Clearly this includes sellers, brokers, and salespersons. Whereas common-law fraud is limited to the intent to deceive, among other elements, statutory fraud covers innocent misrepresentations as well as unfulfilled promises. The act provides for actual and punitive damages against not only the person making the misrepresentation or promise but also against any person who benefits from the transaction, has actual knowledge of the falsity, and fails to reveal it. This means that a broker or a seller who is aware of the wrongful acts of another broker or seller can be liable for those acts if a benefit is received.

Extreme care should be taken in handling all phases of a real estate transaction. Carelessness in the performance of a real estate agent's duties can result in expensive litigation. Costly court actions may be avoided if all parties exercise great care and employ competent legal counsel when it is needed.

SUMMARY

Real estate brokerage is the business of bringing together people who wish to buy, sell, exchange, or lease real estate. An important part of real estate brokerage is the law of agency. A real estate broker is the agent, hired by the seller or by the buyer, to sell or find a particular parcel of real estate. The person who hires the broker is the principal. The principal and the agent have a fiduciary relationship under which the agent owes the principal the duties of care, obedience, accounting, loyalty, and disclosure. In the absence of a buyer representation agreement or a signed agreement for the broker to act as an intermediary, the broker's sales staff and cooperating brokers and their staffs are presumed to represent the seller.

The broker's compensation in a real estate sale generally takes the form of a commission, which is a percentage of the real estate's selling price. The broker is considered to have *earned* a commission when she procures a ready, willing, and able buyer for a seller. The commission is *payable* on closing or, under certain circumstances, on the seller's breach of contract.

A broker may hire salespersons to assist in this work. Salespersons work on the broker's behalf as either employees or independent contractors.

Real estate license laws regulate many of the general operations of a real estate brokerage. In addition, state and federal antitrust laws prohibit brokers from conspiring to fix prices, boycott competitors, or allocate customers or markets.

In Texas, buyers of real estate are protected by the Texas Deceptive Trade Practices—Consumer Protection Act. This act prohibits real estate brokers and other providers of goods and services from deceiving or misleading consumers.

CHAPTER 5 QUESTIONS

1. A real estate broker acting as the special agent of the seller
   a. is obligated to render faithful service to the seller.
   b. can disclose personal information to a buyer if it increases the likelihood of a sale.
   c. can agree to a change in price without the seller's approval.
   d. can accept a commission from the buyer without the seller's approval.

2. An agency relationship may be terminated by all of the following means *EXCEPT*
   a. the owner decides not to sell the house.
   b. the broker discovers that the market value of the property is such that he will not make an adequate commission.
   c. the owner dies.
   d. the broker secures a ready, willing, and able buyer for the seller's property.

3. A real estate broker loses the right to a commission if she
   a. fails to advertise the property.
   b. is not licensed when a sale occurs.
   c. produces a ready, willing, and able buyer.
   d. does not personally market and sell the listing.

4. A real estate broker who engages salespersons as independent contractors must
   a. withhold income tax and Social Security from all commissions earned by them.
   b. require them to attend sales meetings and to participate in office insurance plans if the broker requires other salespersons hired as employees to do so.
   c. refrain from controlling how the salesperson conducts business activities.
   d. provide employee benefits.

5. The statement "a broker must be employed to recover a commission for services" means that the
   a. broker must work in a real estate office.
   b. seller must have signed an agreement to pay a commission to the broker for selling the property.
   c. broker must have a salesperson employed in the office.
   d. broker must have signed the listing agreement.

6. A real estate broker hired to sell a parcel of real estate must
   a. comply with the owner's instructions even if the broker believes they are unethical.
   b. be available at any time to show the property.
   c. disclose a customer-buyer's comment that he will pay up to $70,000 if the seller makes a counteroffer.
   d. keep confidential a customer-buyer's comment that he will pay up to $70,000 if the seller makes a counteroffer.

7. As an independent contractor for a real estate broker, a real estate salesperson has the authority to
   a. act as an agent for another person.
   b. assume only responsibilities assigned by the broker.
   c. act independently when disagreeing with the broker.
   d. make contracts and receive compensation directly from the principal.

8. Reckless disregard for truth with the intent to obtain a financial advantage over another is a definition of
   a. the Deceptive Trade Practices Act.
   b. fraud.
   c. procuring cause.
   d. puffing.

9. Alice is a real estate broker. Rich lists a home with Alice for $89,500. Later that same day, Robert comes into Alice's office and asks for general information about homes for sale in the $80,000 to $100,000 price range. Based on these facts, which statement is *TRUE*?

   a. Both Rich and Robert are Alice's customers.

   b. Rich is Alice's client; Robert is a customer.

   c. Alice owes fiduciary duties to both Rich and Robert.

   d. If Robert asks Alice to be a buyer's representative, Alice must decline because of the pre-existing agreement with Rich.

10. Tomas, a licensed broker, learns that his neighbor, Paul, wishes to sell his house. Tomas knows the property well, and while Paul is out of town for a week, Tomas convinces Barney to buy the property. Tomas obtains Barney's signature on a purchase offer, together with a check for an earnest money deposit. When Paul returns, Tomas presents Barney's offer. In this situation,

    a. Paul is not obligated to pay Tomas a commission.

    b. Barney is obligated to pay Tomas a commission for locating the property.

    c. Paul must pay Tomas a commission.

    d. Tomas has become a subagent of Paul.

11. Which statement *BEST* describes the role of an intermediary broker?

    a. The broker represents both the buyer and the seller and may disclose confidential information from either unless instructed not to do so.

    b. The broker is paid by the seller and must not disclose any confidential information to the buyer.

    c. The broker is acting on behalf of both the buyer and the seller and must not disclose any confidential information to either party without written permission.

    d. The broker is bound by the Texas Real Estate License Act to represent the buyer and must communicate with and carry out the buyer's instructions.

12. Which would *NOT* be considered a violation of antitrust laws?

    a. Brokers representing the Temple, ABC, and All-American Property Management companies decide to de-escalate their current price war by charging more uniform rates.

    b. Salespersons Joe and Emma Marie, working on behalf of two local firms, agree that Joe should seek listings only from the east side of town and Emma Marie should seek listings only from the west side of town.

    c. Brokers throughout the city set their commission rates unilaterally without consulting competitors.

    d. A local association of apartment managers decides to charge a set rate for management services.

13. The legal relationship between broker and seller is generally a(n)

    a. special agency.

    b. general agency.

    c. implied agency.

    d. agency by ratification.

14. Broker Duncan lists Sam and Adele's house for $87,000. Adele has been transferred to another state, and the couple must sell their house within three months. To expedite the sale, Duncan tells a prospective buyer who is calling on the ad that the couple will accept at least $5,000 less for the house. In this situation, Duncan

    a. has not violated his agency responsibilities to Sam and Adele.

    b. should not have disclosed this information to the prospective buyer, because it is not in the sellers' best financial interests.

    c. has acted prudently because he is the buyer's agent.

    d. Duncan is only obligated to produce a ready, willing, and able buyer.

Detailed rationales for the end-of-chapter review questions are available online at www.dearborn.com through the *Instructor Resource Guides* link.

CHAPTER

6

Fair Housing Laws and Ethical Practices

■ **LEARNING OBJECTIVES**   *When you have completed this chapter you will be able to*

- **describe** the historical development of fair housing laws;
- **identify** the classes of people who are protected against discrimination in housing by various federal laws;
- **explain** how fair housing laws address a variety of discriminatory practices;
- **identify** the exemptions allowed in the Fair Housing Act;
- **list** at least three examples of housing discrimination that HUD has addressed in regulations;
- **explain** how complaints against discriminatory practices are enforced in Texas;
- **distinguish** the protections offered by the Fair Housing Act and subsequent amendments, the Equal Credit Opportunity Act, the Home Mortgage Disclosure Act, and the Community Reinvestment Act;
- **discuss** the Fair Housing Act's prohibition of discriminatory advertising;
- **recognize** words and phrases that violate the Fair Housing Act; and
- **describe** the requirements of the Canons of Professional Ethics of the Texas Real Estate Commission; and
- **define** the following *key terms:*

Americans with
  Disabilities Act (ADA)
blockbusting
Civil Rights Act of 1866
Code of Ethics
Community Reinvestment
  Act (CRA)
discriminatory housing
  practices
Equal Credit Opportunity
  Act

Fair Housing Act of 1968
familial status
handicap
Home Mortgage
  Disclosure Act
protected classes
redlining
residential real estate–
  related transaction
steering

Texas Fair Housing Act
Texas Real Estate
  Commission Canons of
  Professional Ethics
Texas Workforce
  Commission Civil Rights
  Division (TWCCRD)
U.S. Department of
  Housing and Urban
  Development (HUD)

OVERVIEW

Federal and state fair housing laws ensure equal opportunity in housing for buyers and renters by making it unlawful to refuse to sell to, rent to, or negotiate with any person based on certain physical characteristics, religion, or family status. In addition to requiring compliance with fair housing laws, the Texas Real Estate License Act also requires that licensees adhere to certain ethical practices. A real estate licensee must demonstrate more than industry knowledge—the licensee's ethics, or business principles, must be above reproach. This chapter deals with fair housing laws and codes of ethical practices as they apply to the real estate business.

The Texas Real Estate License Act, as contained in Section 1101.354 of the Texas Occupations Code, requires that all license applicants show evidence of satisfactory completion of three classroom hours of instruction on laws governing fair housing, community reinvestment, and equal credit opportunity. All three of these topics are discussed in this chapter, as well as such additional matters as equal opportunity in housing, housing discrimination, and housing credit discrimination.

EQUAL OPPORTUNITY IN HOUSING

Brokers and salespersons who offer residential property for sale must be aware of federal, state, and local laws pertaining to human rights and nondiscrimination. *Laws governing fair housing,* also known as *equal opportunity housing* and *open housing,* generally prohibit undesirable and discriminatory activities. Fair housing laws affect every phase of the real estate sales process from listing to closing, *and all brokers and salespersons must comply with them.* The goal of legislators who have enacted fair housing laws and regulations is to create an unbiased housing market—one in which every homeseeker has the same opportunity to buy any home in the area of his choice, provided the home is within the homeseeker's financial means. Potential licensees must be aware of unethical and illegal housing practices so they can avoid them. Failure to comply with fair housing practices is not only a criminal act but also grounds for license revocation or suspension.

THE EVOLUTION OF FEDERAL FAIR HOUSING LAWS[1]

The Declaration of Independence proclaimed that all people have certain human rights. The "pursuit of happiness," for most of us, means the opportunity to own our home or live where we choose. However, the blessings of liberty have eluded millions of Americans who have struggled through the years to attain the American Dream.

Although the signers of the Declaration stated that "all men" should be considered equal, it became apparent that persons of African descent would not be accorded any rights or freedoms. Article 1 of the U.S. Constitution, adopted in 1787, quantified slaves as "three-fifths" of a person in determining a state's population for congressional representation.

The rights of African Americans were further eroded by the 1857 Supreme Court case of *Dred Scott v. Sanford*. The decision declared that no black, free or slave, could claim U.S. citizenship and that blacks had no rights that whites were bound to respect. In addition, the ruling stated that Congress could not prohibit slavery in any U.S. territory. The ruling was influential because it built angry resentment in the North and moved the nation closer to civil war. It also paved the way for the passage of the Fourteenth Amendment to the U.S. Constitution in 1868, which extended full citizenship and civil rights to African Americans. The amendment also guaranteed all persons due process and equal protection under the law.

Following the Civil War (1861–1865), the Thirteenth Amendment, enacted in 1865, formally abolished slavery.

The following year, the Reconstruction Congress passed the **Civil Rights Act of 1866,** which guaranteed equal rights under the law. The act specifically provided the following:

> All citizens of the United States shall have the same right, in every State and Territory, as is enjoyed by white citizens thereof to inherit, purchase, lease, sell, hold, and convey real and personal property.

For more than a century, the Civil Rights Act of 1866 would be of little importance in combating housing discrimination, primarily because courts interpreted the law to prohibit public, or governmental, discrimination only. (See Figure 6.1.) Not until 1968 would the Supreme Court rule, in *Jones v. Mayer*, that the act

> bars all racial discrimination, private as well as public, in the sale or rental of property, and that the statute, thus construed, is a valid exercise of the power of Congress to enforce the Thirteenth Amendment.

Today, the act is still good law and is often used in fair housing discrimination lawsuits, especially in situations not subject to the Fair Housing Act.

In a major setback in the struggle for racial equality, the Supreme Court's 1896 decision in *Plessy v. Ferguson* opened the door for institutionalized segregation. The famous "separate but equal" doctrine legalized the separation of the races in everything from schools to public accommodations. facilities were indeed separate, but rarely equal. The Supreme Court finally overturned the doctrine in the

---

[1]   Substantial portions of this chapter are quoted or adapted from Marcia L. Russell, *Fair Housing Fourth Edition*, (La Crosse: Dearborn Real Estate Education, 2012).

1954 landmark decision in *Brown v. the Topeka Board of Education*. This ruling outlawed the separation of the races in public schools, and it was soon followed by other rulings outlawing the separation of the races. The Court made clear that all forms of government-endorsed segregation violated the Fourteenth Amendment.

In 1948, the U.S. Supreme Court held in *Shelly v. Kraemer* that enforcement of racially restrictive covenants by state courts violated the equal protection clause of the Fourteenth Amendment. Thus, persons were precluded from using the judicial system to enforce racial discrimination.

FIGURE 6.1:   History of Residential Segregation

1920s	Whites who controlled the housing industry implemented a series of techniques designed to segregate the black population. These techniques included (1) racial zoning; (2) restrictive covenants; and (3) discriminatory sales, rental, and financing practices.
1930s	Segregation was perpetuated by federal policies that encouraged racial discrimination in federally assisted housing.
1940-'50s-'60s	The age of industrialization and urbanization brought millions of black families to cities in both the South and the North. The primary method of providing housing opportunities was through "blockbusting" neighborhoods next to ghettos.
1960s	Geographic regions throughout the United States experienced an increase in residential segregation by race.
1980s	A HUD study estimated that approximately 2 million incidents of housing discrimination were occurring every year.

Source: Russell, Marcia L. *Fair Housing Fourth Edition* (La Crosse: Dearborn Real Estate Education, 2012), 3.

It is naive to think that 50 years of segregated housing patterns and institutionalized discrimination would be reversed with the passage of fair housing laws. Housing segregation has multiple causes, such as economic factors and personal preference to live with persons of the same race. However, the primary cause of the patterns of racial segregation identified in metropolitan areas must be attributed to discrimination.

The history of residential segregation in America also established the necessity to pass laws that prohibited discrimination in order to ensure a housing market that provides equal opportunity in housing to all.

On November 20, 1962, President John F. Kennedy issued Executive Order 11063, "Equal Opportunity in Housing." The order prohibited discrimination in the sale, rental, or use of all residential property that was owned, operated, or financed by the federal government. The order had little impact because it did not provide for judicial enforcement.

The Civil Rights Act of 1964 prohibited discrimination in public accommodations; in all federally assisted programs; and in employment on the basis of race, color, religion, sex, or national origin.

The year 1968 marked the beginning of the modern era of fair housing law in this country. On March 1, 1968, the National Advisory Commission on Civil Disorders published *The Kerner Report*, which showed that America was moving toward two societies, one black and one white—separate and unequal.

President Lyndon B. Johnson first introduced fair housing legislation in 1966. The three-year debate culminated in the passage of the federal Fair Housing Act. The new law was not the result of careful congressional consideration; rather, it was the product of an intense debate occurring over a relatively short period, against a background of dramatic national events. On April 4, 1968, Dr. Martin Luther King Jr. was assassinated in Memphis, Tennessee. Johnson, in urging unity and peace, said, "America is shocked and saddened by the brutal slaying." King was the symbol of the nonviolent civil rights protest movement.

Although the Senate had passed an amended version of the Fair Housing Bill on March 11, 1968, there was little hope that the bill would pass the House of Representatives. After King's assassination, however, the House hastily passed the Fair Housing Act. Johnson signed the Civil Rights Act of 1968 (also known as the **Fair Housing Act of 1968**) into law on April 11, 1968.

The 1968 law prohibited discrimination on the basis of race, color, religion, and national origin. The act was, for the most part, ineffective in combating housing discrimination. The enforcement mechanisms were simply too weak to have any perceptible impact on housing discrimination.

In 1974, Congress passed the Housing and Community Development Act, which added sex as another basis on which discrimination was prohibited. This prohibited basis includes sexual harassment but not sexual orientation. This act also created a new set of housing assistance programs for lower-income families, the Section 8 programs.

The 1988 Fair Housing Amendments Act, which represented the most important development in fair housing law in the 20 years since the Civil Rights Act of 1968, extended federal civil rights protection to families with children and to persons with physical and mental disabilities. (See Figure 6.2.) The act also greatly strengthened the enforcement mechanisms and gave the Department of Housing and Urban Development (HUD) greater enforcement power. Monetary awards became available for actual damages, as well as for noneconomic injuries such as embarrassment, humiliation, inconvenience, and mental anguish. In addition, the cap of $1,000 on punitive damages was removed in federal district court actions.

FIGURE 6.2: Evolution of the Protected Classes

Race, color, religion, national origin	The Fair Housing Act of 1968
Sex	The 1974 Housing and Community Development Act
Persons with physical or mental handicaps; families with children	The 1988 Fair Housing Amendments Act

Source: Russell, Marcia L. *Fair Housing Fourth Edition* (La Crosse: Dearborn Real Estate Education, 2012), 4.

The 1988 Fair Housing Amendments Act passed by overwhelming margins in both the House and the Senate, and was signed into law by President Ronald Reagan on September 13, 1988. The effective date of the act was March 12, 1989.

With the passage of the 1988 Amendments Act, the fair housing laws were applied to the banking and insurance industries for the first time.

The 1995 Amendment to the Fair Housing Act, entitled the Housing for Older Persons Act of 1995 (HOPA), repealed the significant facilities and services requirements designed to meet the physical and social needs of older persons and made several changes to the 55-and-older familial status exemption. Since the 1988 amendments, the Fair Housing Act has exempted from its familial status provisions properties that satisfy the act's 55-and-older housing condition.

HOPA called on HUD to implement rules for verifying the age of occupants. The amendment also prohibits the awarding of monetary damages against persons who reasonably believed, in good faith, that the property, as housing for older persons, was exempt from the familial status provisions of the Fair Housing Act.

HOUSING DISCRIMINATION

The Fair Housing Act prohibits the following **discriminatory housing practices**[2]:

- To refuse to sell or rent after the making of a bona fide offer, or to refuse to negotiate for the sale or rental of, or otherwise make unavailable or deny, a dwelling to any person because of race, color, religion, sex, familial status, or national origin
- To discriminate against any person in the terms, conditions, or privileges of sale or rental of a dwelling, or in the provision of services or facilities in connection therewith, because of race, color, religion, sex, familial status, or national origin

Note:

The first two provisions do not include handicap as a protected class. The 1988 Fair Housing Amendments Act added several new provisions that deal exclusively with protections for this class. The reason for treating handicap discrimination in this way was apparently to clarify that the law does not condemn housing that is available only to persons with physical or mental disabilities.

> **The *Fair Housing Act* prohibits discrimination based on**
> - race,
> - color,
> - religion,
> - sex,
> - handicap (disability),
> - familial status, and
> - national origin.

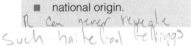

- To make, print, or publish, or cause to be made, printed, or published any notice, statement, or advertisement, with respect to the sale or rental of a dwelling, that indicates any preference, limitation, or discrimination based on race, color, religion, sex, handicap, familial status, or national origin, or an intention to make any such preference, limitation, or discrimination
- To represent to any person because of race, color, religion, sex, handicap, familial status, or national origin that any dwelling is not available for inspection, sale, or rental when such dwelling is in fact so available
- For profit, to induce or attempt to induce any person to sell or rent any dwelling by representation regarding the entry or prospective entry into the neighborhood of a person or persons of a particular race, color, religion, sex, handicap, familial status, or national origin
- To discriminate in the sale or rental, or to otherwise make unavailable or deny, a dwelling to any buyer or renter because of a handicap of
  — that buyer or renter;
  — a person residing in or intending to reside in that dwelling after it is so sold, rented, or made available; or
  — any person associated with that buyer or renter

---

[2]   The listed discriminatory housing practices are quoted from 42 U.S.C. §§ 3601–3619.

- To discriminate against any person in the terms, conditions, or privileges of sale or rental of a dwelling, or in the provision of services or facilities in connection with such dwelling, because of a handicap of
  - that buyer or renter;
  - a person residing in or intending to reside in that dwelling after it is so sold, rented, or made available; or
  - any person associated with that buyer or renter
- To refuse to permit, at the expense of the handicapped person, reasonable modifications of existing premises occupied or to be occupied by such person if such modifications may be necessary to afford such person full enjoyment of the premises, except that in the case of a rental, the landlord may, where it is reasonable to do so, condition permission for a modification on the renter agreeing to restore the interior of the premises to the condition that existed before the modification, reasonable wear and tear excepted
- To refuse to make reasonable accommodations in rules, policies, practices, or services, when such accommodations may be necessary to afford a handicapped person equal opportunity to use or enjoy the dwelling
- To fail to design and construct covered multifamily dwellings for first occupancy after March 12, 1991, that are accessible to and usable by handicapped persons
- To deny any person access to or membership or participation in any multiple-listing service, real estate brokers organization, or other service, organization, or facility relating to the business of selling or renting dwellings, or to discriminate in the terms or conditions of such access, membership, or participation, on account of race, color, religion, sex, handicap, familial status, or national origin
- For persons whose business includes engaging in residential real estate–related transactions, to discriminate against any person in making available such a transaction, or in the terms or conditions of such a transaction, because of race, color, religion, sex, handicap, familial status, or national origin

EXEMPTIONS

The Fair Housing Act contains seven exemptions with respect to property transactions not subject to the act's general mandate of nondiscriminatory treatment. It is important to note, however, that a housing provider exempt from coverage under the Fair Housing Act may still be liable for racial discrimination under the Civil Rights Act of 1866. The Civil Rights Act of 1866 is still good law and contains no exemptions to coverage. In addition, *no exemptions apply when a real estate licensee is involved in a transaction.*

- *Religious organizations*—A religious organization may discriminate with respect to its noncommercial property, provided that the religion itself doesn't discriminate on the basis of race, color, or national origin. The exemption also applies to a nonprofit institution operated in conjunction with a religious organization. This exemption is quite limited and has generated very little litigation.
- *Private clubs*—The act does not prohibit a private club, not in fact open to the public, from limiting the rental or occupancy of noncommercial lodgings to members. Courts have held that Congress deliberately used the word

lodging and not dwelling to limit the exemption to temporary accommodations. This exemption, then, appears to be narrowly construed to cover temporary rooming facilities of social organizations, such as university clubs.

- *Occupancy standards*—The act does not limit "the applicability of any reasonable local, state, or federal restrictions regarding the maximum number of persons permitted to occupy a dwelling." The occupancy standard provision was added in 1988 at the same time families with children became a protected group and appears to be included primarily to alleviate concerns that housing providers would have to accommodate families to the extent of violating other occupancy laws.
- *Drug conviction*—The act does not prohibit conduct against a person because that person has been convicted in a court of law for the illegal manufacture or distribution of a controlled substance. The exemption was intended to allow landlords to protect tenants by refusing to provide housing to persons convicted of distributing or manufacturing illegal drugs.
- *Familial status*—Discrimination based on familial status will not apply to housing qualifying for exempt status as housing for older persons. This type of housing may allow children, but would not violate fair housing laws by excluding them. Racial and other prohibited forms of discrimination are not allowed in the housing for older persons. The exemptions for housing for older persons include the following:
  — Housing provided under any state or federal program that the secretary of HUD has determined is specifically designed and operated to assist elderly persons
  — Housing intended for and solely occupied by persons 62 years of age or older
  — Housing intended and operated for occupancy by at least one person 55 years of age or older per unit in at least 80% of the units
- *Single-family housing*—The sale or rental of a single-family house by the owner will be exempt from coverage, provided that the following conditions are met:
  — The owner does not own or have any interest in more than three single-family houses at any one time.
  — The house is sold or rented without the services of a real estate agent or the facilities of any person in the business of selling or renting dwellings. The exemption will apply to one sale or rental within a two-year period, unless the owner was the most recent occupant.
  This exemption does not apply if a person in the real estate business is involved or if discriminatory advertising is used.
- *Mrs. Murphy's exemption*—The act does not cover owner-occupied dwellings designed for occupancy by no more than four families living independently of each other.

A single-family homeowner, or a "Mrs. Murphy," is still liable for racial discrimination under the Civil Rights Act of 1866.

HUD REGULATIONS

The 1988 Fair Housing Amendments Act contains provisions giving HUD the authority to issue rules to implement the Fair Housing Act. HUD's regulations are based, in part, on 20 years of housing discrimination cases originating under the 1968 act. In 1972, the Supreme Court ruled in *Trafficante v. Metropolitan Life Insurance Co.*, the very first decision involving the Civil Rights Act of 1968, that interpretations of the act by HUD are entitled to a good deal of weight in construing the statute. This is because HUD is the primary agency responsible for implementing and administering the act. The regulations went into effect on March 12, 1989, and provide a tremendous amount of authoritative material concerning the meaning of the Fair Housing Act[3].

Unlawful to Sell or Rent or to Negotiate for the Sale or Rental

Prohibited actions under this section include the following:
- Failing to accept or consider a bona fide offer because of race, color, religion, sex, handicap, familial status, or national origin
- Refusing to sell or rent a dwelling to, or negotiate for the sale or rental of a dwelling with, any person because of protected class status
- Imposing different sales prices or rental charges for the sale or rental of a dwelling upon any person because of membership in a protected class
- Using different qualification criteria or applications, or sale or rental standards or procedures, such as income standards, application requirements, application fees, credit analysis, or sale or rental approval procedures, based on protected class status
- Evicting tenants because of their race, color, religion, sex, handicap, familial status, or national origin, or because their guests are members of a protected class

Discrimination in Terms, Conditions, and Privileges, and in Services and Facilities

Prohibited actions under this section include the following:
- Using different provisions in leases or contracts of sale, such as those relating to rental charges, security deposits, and the terms of a lease, and those relating to down payment and closing requirements, because of race, color, religion, sex, handicap, familial status, or national origin
- Failing or delaying maintenance or repairs of sale or rental dwellings because of membership in a protected group
- Failing to process an offer for the sale or rental of a dwelling or to communicate an offer accurately because of protected class status
- Limiting the use of privileges, services, or facilities associated with a dwelling because of race, color, religion, sex, handicap, familial status, or national origin
- Denying or limiting services or facilities in connection with sale or rental of a dwelling because a person failed or refused to provide sexual favors

---

[3]   Provisions of the Fair Housing Amendments Act noted in this section are adapted or quoted from 42 U.S.C. §§ 3601 et seq.

Other Prohibited Sale and Rental Conduct

Prohibited actions under this section include the following:

- Restricting or attempting to restrict the choices of a person by word or conduct in connection with seeking, negotiating for, buying, or renting a dwelling so as to perpetuate, or tend to perpetuate, segregated housing patterns based on membership in a protected class
- Engaging in any conduct related to the provision of housing or of services or facilities that otherwise makes unavailable or denies dwellings to protected persons
- Discouraging any person from inspecting, purchasing, or renting a dwelling on account of race, color, religion, sex, handicap, familial status, or national origin by exaggerating drawbacks and failing to inform any person of desirable features of a dwelling or neighborhood
- Communicating to any persons that they would not be compatible with existing residents of a community because of their protected class status
- Assigning any person to a particular section of a community, neighborhood, or dwelling, or to a particular floor of a building because of race, color, religion, sex, handicap, familial status, or national origin, a practice also known as steering
- Employing codes or other devices to segregate or reject applicants, purchasers, or renters or refusing to take or show listings of dwellings in certain areas because of race, color, religion, sex, handicap, familial status, or national origin
- Refusing to provide municipal services or property or hazard insurance for dwellings or providing such services or insurance differently because of race, color, religion, sex, handicap, familial status, or national origin

Discriminatory Representations on the Availability of Dwellings

Prohibited actions under this section include the following:

- Indicating through words or conduct that a dwelling that is available for inspection, sale, or rental has been sold or rented
- Representing that covenants, or other deed, trust, or lease provisions that purport to restrict the sale or rental of dwellings because of protected class status, preclude the sale or rental of a dwelling to any person from a protected class
- Enforcing covenants or other deed, trust, or lease provisions that preclude the sale or rental of a dwelling to any person because of membership in a protected class
- Limiting information, by word or conduct, regarding suitably priced dwellings available for inspection, sale, or rental to members of a protected group
- Providing false or inaccurate information regarding the availability of a dwelling for sale or rental to any person, including testers, regardless of whether such person is actually seeking housing, based on protected class status

Blockbusting

Prohibited actions under this section include the following:

- For profit, to induce or attempt to induce a person to sell or rent a dwelling by representations regarding the entry or prospective entry into the neighborhood of members of a particular protected group
- In establishing a discriminatory housing practice under this section, it is not necessary that there was in fact profit, as long as profit was a factor for engaging in the blockbusting activity
- Engaging in conduct, including uninvited solicitations, that conveys to a person that a neighborhood is undergoing or is about to undergo a change in the race, color religion, sex, handicap, familial status, or national origin to encourage the person to offer a dwelling for sale or rental
- Encouraging any person to sell or rent a dwelling by asserting that the entry or prospective entry of persons of a particular protected class will result in undesirable consequences for the project, neighborhood, or community, such as an increase in criminal or antisocial behavior or a decline in the quality of schools or other services or facilities

Steering

Steering is the *channeling* of homeseekers to particular areas on the basis of race, religion, country of origin, or other protected class, either to maintain the homogeneity of an area or to change the character of an area in order to create a speculative situation. Steering often is difficult to detect, however, because the steering tactics can be so subtle that homeseekers are unaware that their choice has been limited. Steering also may be done unintentionally by agents who are not aware of their own biased assumptions. Nevertheless, an unintentional offense is still a violation of fair housing laws. A complainant does not have to prove guilty knowledge or specific intent—only the fact that discrimination occurred.

HUD regulations strongly endorse the view that the Fair Housing Act condemns steering. According to HUD's general definition of steering, it is unlawful on the basis of race or any other prohibited ground

> to restrict the choices of a person by word or conduct in connection with seeking, negotiating for, buying, or renting a dwelling so as to perpetuate, or tend to perpetuate, segregated housing patterns, or to discourage or obstruct choices in a community, neighborhood, or development.

The four specific examples of prohibited actions under this general definition of illegal steering are as follows:

- Engaging in any conduct related to the provision of housing or of services or facilities that otherwise makes unavailable or denies dwellings to protected persons
- Discouraging any person from inspecting, purchasing, or renting a dwelling on account of race, color, religion, sex, handicap, familial status, or national origin by exaggerating drawbacks, and failing to inform any person of desirable features of a dwelling or neighborhood

■ Communicating to any persons that they would not be compatible with existing residents of a community because of their protected class status

■ Assigning any person to a particular section of a community, neighborhood, or dwelling, or to a particular floor of a building, because or race, color, religion, sex, handicap, familial status, or national origin, a practice also known as steering

Discrimination in Residential Real Estate–Related Transactions

It is illegal for any person or other entity whose business includes engaging in residential real estate–related transactions to discriminate against any person in making available such a transaction or to make changes in the terms or conditions of the transaction because of a person's status in a protected class. The term *residential real estate–related transaction* means

■ the making or purchasing of loans or providing other financial assistance for purchasing, constructing, improving, or maintaining a dwelling (included in this section are loans secured by residential real estate); and

■ the selling, brokering, or appraising of residential real property.

Prohibited actions under this section include the following:

■ Refusing to provide information to any person concerning the availability of loans or other financial assistance or providing information that is inaccurate or different because of membership in a protected class

■ Refusing to purchase loans, debts, or securities or imposing different terms and conditions for such purchase to persons of a protected group

■ Using different policies, practices, or procedures in evaluating or determining creditworthiness of any person in connection with the provision of any loan or other financial assistance for a dwelling because that person is a member of a protected class

■ Determining the type of loan or other financial assistance to be provided with respect to a dwelling or fixing the amount, interest rate, duration, or other terms for the loan or other financial assistance because of membership in a protected group

IN PRACTICE   The term **redlining** refers to the practice of refusing to make loans or otherwise denying financial assistance for housing in particular areas. The courts have defined *redlining* as mortgage credit discrimination based on the characteristics of the neighborhood surrounding the would-be borrower's dwelling. The term was derived from the practice of loan officers who would evaluate home mortgage applications by relying on a residential map where integrated and minority areas were marked off in red as poor risk areas.

The Fair Housing Act also prohibits insurance redlining, discriminating in the provision of homeowners insurance based on the characteristics of the neighborhood where the home is situated.

Unlawful practices in the selling, brokering, or appraising of residential real property include

■ an appraisal that improperly takes into consideration race, color, religion, sex, handicap, familial status, or national origin in estimating value; and

■ using an appraisal that improperly takes into consideration the protected classes in estimating value in connection with the sale, rental, or financing of a dwelling where the person knows or reasonably should know that the appraisal was based on discriminatory factors.

Nothing in this section prohibits a person engaged in the business of making or furnishing appraisals of residential real property from taking into consideration factors other than race, color, religion, sex, handicap, familial status, or national origin.

IN PRACTICE   Section 818 of the Fair Housing Act makes it unlawful to "coerce, intimidate, threaten, or interfere with any person in the exercise or enjoyment of, or on account of his having exercised or enjoyed, or on account of his having aided or encouraged any other person in the exercise or enjoyment of any right granted or protected by" the statute.

Familial Status Discrimination

The Fair Housing Act makes no distinction between the level of protection afforded to victims of familial status discrimination and that afforded victims of racial discrimination. HUD regulations state that "families with children must be provided the same protections as other classes of persons" protected by the Fair Housing Act. Housing providers remain free, however, to refuse to deal with families based on legitimate criteria, such as evicting a family because of excessive noise or property damage that can be attributed to their children.

The law broadly defines **familial status** to include anyone younger than 18 being domiciled with
- a parent or another person having legal custody of such individual, or
- the designee of such parent or other person having such custody with the written permission of such parent or other person.

The protections against discrimination on the basis of familial status also apply to any person who is pregnant or in the process of securing legal custody of any individual younger than 18.

The Fair Housing Act's ban on family status discrimination also prohibits advertising that indicates any preference, limitation, or discrimination based on protected class status. Thus, photographs or words indicating that children are not welcome would be actionable under the law. Conversely, phrases such as "kids ok" would show an illegal preference for families with children.

Disparate Treatment and Disparate Impact Theories of Discrimination

The disparate treatment theory of housing discrimination is easily understood because these cases typically involve intentional acts of discrimination directed at those protected by the law. Evidence of the discriminatory motive may be direct, as in a case with open hostility directed toward the minority or other protected group, or circumstantial, which is more often the case. Circumstantial evidence is evaluated based on the housing provider's business practices, with particular emphasis on statistical information regarding the past record of dealing with the protected class.

Aggrieved persons must establish that

- they are a member of a protected class,
- they were financially qualified to obtain the property,
- they were rejected by the defendant, and
- the housing opportunity remained open after the rejection.

The defendant must come forward with evidence of some legitimate nondiscriminatory reason for refusing to deal with the plaintiff.

The disparate impact theory of housing discrimination requires no evidence of discriminatory intent. Disparate impact cases generally involve policies or laws that cause disproportionate harm to members of a protected class. This form of discrimination can be subtle and even unconscious, but when the conduct at issue has a significant statistical effect of disfavoring those protected by law, the result is illegal discrimination. The defendant must present evidence of a business necessity to justify the challenged conduct. It is important to note that applying the criteria to everybody is not sufficient to demonstrate compliance with the Fair Housing Act. The disparate impact theory provides the means of holding housing providers liable for the results of their conduct.

HUD's Disparate Impact Rule

In February 2013, HUD issued its "disparate impact rule," implementing what it called longstanding interpretations of the Fair Housing Act "to prohibit practices with an unjustified discriminatory effect, regardless of whether there was an intent to discriminate." The rule establishes a three-part test to prove a disparate impact violation of the Fair Housing Act even where the practice is facially neutral.

Under the rule, a practice is considered to have a discriminatory effect "where it actually or predictably results in a disparate impact on a group of persons or creates, increases, reinforces, or perpetuates segregated housing patterns because of race, color, religion, sex, handicap, familial status, or national origin." Using the three-part test, the plaintiff must first prove that the practice has a discriminatory effect on a protected class or characteristic. Once the plaintiff establishes the discriminatory effect, the second part of the rule requires that the defendant show that the practice is necessary to serve "substantial, legitimate, nondiscriminatory interests" and that the interests cannot be served with a less discriminatory alternative practice. If the defendant proves that the practice protects a legitimate interest, the plaintiff may still prevail under the third part of the test, which requires the plaintiff to prove that such interest could be protected by a less discriminatory practice.

In June 2013, two insurance trade associations sued HUD on the rule, alleging, in part, that the Fair Housing Act only prohibits intentional discrimination, based on the plain language of the law. The case had been on hold pending the outcome of related U.S. Supreme Court litigation regarding disparate impact claims under the Equal Credit Opportunity Act, which was recently settled. The HUD lawsuit is pending in Federal District Court in Washington, D.C.

Note:

The key to proving a disparate impact claim is statistical evidence showing that the defendant's practice has a greater impact on protected class members than on others. In *Betsey v. Turtle Creek Associates* (4th Cir. 1984), the court held that a landlord's policy of evicting families with children from one of its buildings had a "substantially greater adverse impact on minority tenants." Real estate professionals must be aware that seemingly innocent actions might constitute unlawful discrimination under the disparate impact theory.

DISABILITY DISCRIMINATION

The Congress that passed the 1988 Fair Housing Amendments Act recognized the need to define and protect the rights of the disabled throughout American society. Persons with physical and mental disabilities had been denied housing because of misperceptions, ignorance, and outright prejudice. The decision to add disability discrimination to the Fair Housing Amendments Act was seen as a strong statement concerning the exclusion of persons with disabilities from the American mainstream. A House Judiciary Committee report stated that the new law "repudiates the use of stereotypes and ignorance, and mandates that persons with handicaps be considered as individuals."

The 1988 Fair Housing Amendments Act defined the term *handicap* very broadly, and added prohibitions against discrimination based on handicap to nearly every existing provision of the act. In addition, several new provisions were added that deal exclusively with disability discrimination. Much of the language and definitions contained in the 1988 Fair Housing Amendments Act can be traced to the Rehabilitation Act of 1973. The act prohibits discrimination against the disabled in programs or activities that receive federal financial assistance, including housing programs receiving federal funds.

Definition of Handicap

The Fair Housing Act defines **handicap** as

- a physical or mental impairment that substantially limits one or more of a person's major life activities,
- a record of having such an impairment, or
- being regarded as having such an impairment.

The definition excludes transvestites and persons who are engaging in the illegal use of drugs.

A physical impairment is any physiological disorder or condition, cosmetic disfigurement, or anatomical loss affecting one or more of the following body systems: neurological, musculoskeletal, specific sense organs, respiratory (including speech organs), cardiovascular, reproductive, digestive, genitourinary, hematologic and lymphatic, skin, and endocrine.

A mental impairment is any mental or psychological disorder, such as mental retardation, organic brain syndrome, emotional or mental illness, and specific learning disabilities.

HUD regulations define the term *physical or mental impairment* to include, but not be limited to, such diseases and conditions as orthopedic, visual, speech, and hearing impairments; cerebral palsy; autism; epilepsy; muscular dystrophy; multiple sclerosis; cancer; heart disease; diabetes; human immunodeficiency virus infection; mental retardation; emotional illness; drug addiction (other than addiction caused by current illegal use of a controlled substance); and alcoholism.

> Nothing in the Fair Housing Act requires that a dwelling be made available to an individual whose tenancy would constitute a direct threat to the health or safety of other individuals, or whose tenancy would result in substantial physical damage to the property of others.

Major life activities means functions such as caring for oneself, performing manual tasks, walking, seeing, hearing, speaking, breathing, learning, and working.

HUD REGULATIONS REGARDING DISCRIMINATION AGAINST THE HANDICAPPED

HUD regulations and the Fair Housing Act contain the same general prohibitions against discrimination because of handicap. Prohibited actions under this section are as follows:

- To discriminate in the sale or rental of, or to otherwise make unavailable or deny, a dwelling to any buyer or renter because of a handicap of
  - that buyer or renter;
  - a person residing in or intending to reside in that dwelling after it is so sold, rented, or made available; or
  - any person associated with that buyer or renter
- To discriminate against any person in the terms, conditions, or privileges of sale or rental of a dwelling, or in the provision of services or facilities in connection with such dwelling, because of a handicap of
  - that buyer or renter;
  - a person residing in or intending to reside in that dwelling after it is so sold, rented, or made available; or
  - any person associated with that buyer or renter

DESIGN AND CONSTRUCTION REQUIREMENTS FOR NEW HOUSING

The 1988 Fair Housing Amendments Act requires that all covered multifamily dwellings first occupied after March 13, 1991, be designed and constructed with certain accessibility-enhancing features, including a building entrance on an accessible route. Covered multifamily dwellings include buildings consisting of four or more dwelling units, if such buildings have one or more elevators, and ground-floor dwelling units in other buildings consisting of four or more dwelling units. On March 6, 1991, HUD published the "Fair Housing Accessibility Guidelines" in the Federal Register to provide technical assistance to builders, developers, and others in the development chain.

Accessibility Features

The following features are mandated for new multifamily dwellings:
- Public and common use areas must be "readily accessible to and usable by handicapped persons."
- All doors designed to allow passage into and within all premises must be sufficiently wide to accommodate persons who use wheelchairs.
- There must be an accessible route into and through the dwelling unit.
- Light switches, electrical outlets, thermostats, and other environmental controls must be placed in accessible locations.
- Reinforcements must be installed in bathrooms to allow for the later installation of grab bars.
- Kitchens and bathrooms must be designed to allow people in wheelchairs to maneuver about the space.

FAIR HOUSING CONCERNS AND AIDS DISCLOSURES

The 1988 Fair Housing Amendments Act established persons with handicaps, which includes those diagnosed with AIDS, as a new protected class. It is illegal to discriminate against people with handicaps, just as it is illegal to discriminate on the basis of race, color, religion, sex, national origin, or familial status. The legislative history of the Fair Housing Act makes it clear that Congress intended coverage to include persons suffering from communicable diseases such as AIDS.

According to HUD, it is illegal for real estate agents to make unsolicited disclosures that a current or former occupant of the property has AIDS. If a prospective purchaser directly asks an agent if a current or former occupant has AIDS, and the agent knows this is in fact true, HUD advises that the agent should not respond.

Real estate agents who respond to this question by providing information regarding the AIDS status of a current or former occupant run the risk of violating the fair housing laws. The best response is to tell the purchasers to pursue the investigation on their own if they have determined this information to be relevant to their decision to purchase the property.

THE AMERICANS WITH DISABILITIES ACT

The **Americans with Disabilities Act** (ADA) was signed into law on July 26, 1990, by President George H. W. Bush and has been called the most comprehensive civil rights legislation to be enacted in the last quarter century. The purpose of the ADA is to eliminate discrimination directed toward the approximately 43 million individuals with disabilities and allow them to enter the social and economic mainstream of society. This will be accomplished by providing equal opportunities in employment, transportation, access to goods and services offered by both the public and private sector, and communications.

The ADA was not intended to cover housing, and it specifically exempts "facilities that are covered or expressly exempted from coverage under the Fair Housing Act of 1968." However, the ADA could be applied to facilities that operate a "place of public accommodation," which would be covered by Title III, such as the rental office in an apartment complex. Title III mandates that public facilities, goods, and services must be accessible to persons with disabilities. Public accommodations must remove architectural barriers whenever readily achievable; make reasonable changes in policies, practices, and procedures; and provide auxiliary aids or services unless to do so would result in an undue burden, or would pose a direct threat to the health or safety of others.

HUD ISSUES GUIDANCE ON LESBIAN, GAY, BISEXUAL, AND TRANSGENDER (LGBT) HOUSING DISCRIMINATION COMPLAINTS

On July 1, 2010, HUD announced a "new policy that provides LGBT individuals and families with further assistance when facing housing discrimination. The new guidance treats gender identity discrimination as gender discrimination under the Fair Housing Act, and instructs HUD staff to inform individuals filing complaints about state and local agencies that have LGBT-inclusive discrimination laws," according to HUD press release no. 10-139. Approximately 20 states and the

District of Columbia, as well as more than 200 cities, towns, and counties, have additional protections that prohibit discrimination against LGBT individuals.

The HUD press release provides examples of situations that may be jurisdictional under the Fair Housing Act. These examples are as follows:

■ "If a man alleges that he is being evicted because he is gay and his landlord believes he will infect other tenants with HIV, then the allegation of discrimination may be jurisdictional under the Fair Housing Act based on disability, because the man is regarded as having a disability, HIV/AIDS."

■ "Similarly, if a female prospective tenant is alleging discrimination by a landlord because she wears masculine clothes and engages in other physical expressions that are stereotypical made, then the allegations may be jurisdictional under the act as discrimination based on gender."

EQUAL ACCESS TO HOUSING IN HUD PROGRAMS REGARDLESS OF SEXUAL ORIENTATION OR GENDER IDENTITY

According to HUD, a final rule, effective March 5, 2012, "implements policy to ensure that its core programs are open to all eligible individuals and families regardless of sexual orientation, gender identity, or marital status." Owners and operators of HUD-funded housing, or housing insured by HUD, are prohibited from inquiring about an applicant's sexual orientation or gender identity, or denying housing on that basis.

The term *family* is slightly reorganized in the opening clause to read as follows: "Family includes but is not limited to the following, regardless of actual or perceived sexual orientation, gender identity, or marital status."

The rule adds sexual orientation and gender identity to the characteristics that an FHA lender may not take into consideration in determining the adequacy of a mortgagor's income.

The language of the final rule says that "it is important not only that HUD ensure that its own programs do not involve discrimination against any individual or family otherwise eligible for HUD-assisted or -insured housing, but that its policies and programs serve as models for equal housing opportunity." The rule as published in the Federal Register can be accessed at the website of the Government Printing Office.

The HUD website on Fair Housing and Equal Opportunity can be accessed at www.hud.gov/fairhousing. This site provides additional contact information, and the brochure *Fair Housing—Equal Opportunity for All* may be downloaded at www.hud.gov/offices/adm/hudclips/forms/files/1686.pdf.

TEXAS FAIR HOUSING LAWS AND ENFORCEMENT OF FAIR HOUSING LAWS

The **Texas Fair Housing Act** is located in Chapter 301 of the Texas Property Code. The fair housing laws allow any aggrieved party to file a complaint against discriminatory practices and to pursue enforcement through administrative proceedings, attorney general litigation, or private litigation. Lawsuits brought under the Civil Rights Act of 1866 must be taken directly to a federal court. Other fair housing complaints are enforced as outlined in the following sections.

Administrative Proceedings

A complaint can be filed with the **Texas Workforce Commission Civil Rights Division (TWCCRD)** or with the **U.S. Department of Housing and Urban Development (HUD)**. An aggrieved person who believes illegal discrimination has occurred may file a complaint within one year after the alleged act. If the complaint is filed with HUD, it will be referred to the Texas Workforce Commission Civil Rights Division because Texas has a HUD-approved "substantially equivalent" fair housing program that allows complaints to be heard at the state level rather than at the federal level. Under the Texas Fair Housing Act of 1989, the TWCCRD has 100 days to investigate the complaint, to begin a process of conciliation (attempting to obtain an agreement ending the dispute), and to file a report of its findings. If no conciliation agreement is reached during the 100-day period, the TWCCRD must dismiss the complaint or file charges. If charges are filed, the aggrieved party has 20 days to exercise an election to take the matter to a state district court for a jury trial. If the aggrieved party does not choose to go to court, the case is assigned to an administrative law judge (ALJ). An ALJ makes recommendations to the Texas Workforce Commission Civil Rights Division for resolution of the dispute. An ALJ has the authority to award actual damages to the aggrieved person and to impose monetary penalties. The penalties range from up to $10,000 for the first offense to $25,000 for the second violation within five years and $50,000 for further violations within seven years. An ALJ also has the authority to issue an injunction to order the offender to either take action (such as renting an apartment to the complaining party) or to refrain from taking action (such as to stop conducting business in a discriminatory manner).

Civil Litigation

> Fair housing complaints are filed with the Texas Workforce Commission Civil Rights Division (TWCCRD).

Civil action may be initiated through

- *the attorney general*: If the aggrieved party elects to have a jury trial, the TWCCRD will notify the Texas attorney general, who has 30 days to file a civil action in state district court on behalf of the complainant.
- *private litigation*: An aggrieved party may bring a private enforcement action in state or federal district court within two years of the discriminatory action. The private lawsuit can be filed even though an administrative complaint is filed with the TWCCRD. If a conciliation agreement is entered on the complaint or if a hearing commences before an ALJ, the private lawsuit must be terminated. The court can grant injunctions, actual and punitive damages, and other appropriate equitable remedies.
- *the Department of Justice*: When there is reason to believe that a person or entity is engaged in a "pattern or practice" of discrimination or when a denial of rights to a group of persons raises an issue of general public

importance, the U.S. attorney general may commence a civil action in a U.S. district court. If force or threat of force is used to deny or interfere with fair housing rights, the Department of Justice may also institute criminal proceedings. Most pattern or practice cases involve claims of race discrimination.

At least six Texas cities have fair housing ordinances that have been ruled substantially equivalent to the federal law—Dallas, Ft. Worth, Garland, Corpus Christi, Austin, and San Antonio. Although violation of a local ordinance may only be punishable by a fine, the effects of even the smallest violation for a real estate licensee are obviously significant.

Two other Texas statutes deal with fair housing or discrimination. One stipulates that, regardless of the provisions contained in a deed restriction, no state court can enforce a discriminatory provision. The second statute is part of the Real Estate License Act (Section 1101.652(b)(32)) and prohibits housing discrimination by a licensee. Violation of this statute subjects the licensee to potential civil action as well as license suspension or revocation.

Implications for Brokers and Salespersons

The real estate industry is largely responsible for creating and maintaining an open housing market. Brokers and salespersons are a community's real estate experts. Along with the privileges of profiting from real estate transactions come the social and legal responsibilities to ensure that everyone real estate are protected. Licensees and the industry must be publicly conspicuous in their commitment to the principles of fair housing.

Fair housing is the law. The consequences for anyone who violates the law are serious. In addition to the financial penalties, the livelihood of real estate brokers or salespersons will be in danger their license is suspended or revoked. Remember: that a fair housing offense was unintentional is no defense; only the fact that discrimination did occur has to be proven. Beyond being the law, fair housing is *good business*. It ensures the greatest number of properties available for sale and rent and the largest possible pool of potential purchasers and tenants.

All parties deserve the same standard of service. Everyone has the right to expect equal treatment. A good test is to answer the question, "Are we doing this for everyone?" If an act is not performed consistently, or if an act affects some individuals differently from others, it could be construed as discriminatory.

Standardized practices include careful recordkeeping for each customer: needs analysis, financial analysis, properties suggested, houses shown, documentation of all conversations. Besides helping to avoid fair housing violations, these practices are simply good business and may well translate into a larger client base.

Under the Fair Housing Initiatives Program (FHIP), real estate offices may be visited by testers or checkers, undercover volunteers who investigate whether customers and clients are treated equally and are offered the same free choice within a given price range. The courts have held that such practice is permissible, as it is the only way to test compliance with the fair housing laws.

FEDERAL FAIR LENDING LAWS

Equal Credit Opportunity Act

As enacted in 1974 and amended in 1976, the **Equal Credit Opportunity Act** (ECOA) was the first in a series of fair housing lending laws designed to make credit available to every financially qualified applicant. It applies to a person or an institution that makes loans on a regular basis as a part of its usual business; it does not apply to a seller who agrees to carry back a note.

Most mortgage lending cases brought by the Department of Justice under the ECOA involve claims of discrimination based on race or color.

The ECOA prohibits lenders and others who grant or arrange credit to consumers from discriminating against credit applicants on the basis of race, color, religion, national origin, sex, marital status, age (provided the applicant is of legal age), or dependence on public assistance. (See Figure 6.3.) Credit applicants must be judged only by criteria based on income, net worth, job stability, and credit rating. All rejected applicants must be notified, in writing and within 30 days, of the *basic* reasons for denial or termination of credit stability, and credit rating. All rejected applicants must be notified, in writing and within 30 days, of the basic reasons for denial or termination of credit—unless the denial was based on a consumer's credit score. In that event, the rejection notice must also include the numerical credit score obtained and related credit scoring information (Dodd-Frank Act, 2010). If rejected applicants want specific reasons for denial (other than credit scores), they must request that information from the creditor in writing within 60 days. The ECOA and implementing rules provide that a lender must disclose to a borrower that the borrow is entitled to receive a copy of an appraisal report. The rules also require that a lender promptly provide to a borrower a copy of a home appraisal after it is completed, regardless of whether credit is extended or denied.

FIGURE 6.3: Federal Fair Housing Laws

Legislation	Race	Color	Religion	National Origin	Sex	Age	Disability	Familial Status	Marital Status	Public Assistance Income
Civil Rights Act of 1866	•	•								
Fair Housing Act of 1968 (Title VIII)	•	•	•	•						
Housing and Community Development Act of 1974	•	•	•	•	•					
Fair Housing Amendments Act of 1988							•	•		
Equal Credit Opportunity Act of 1974 (lending)	•	•	•	•	•	•			•	•

IN PRACTICE The Federal Trade Commission offers this "special note to women": "A good credit history—a record of how you paid past bills—often is necessary to get credit. Unfortunately, this hurts many married, separated, divorced, and widowed women. There are two common reasons women don't have credit histories in their own names: they lost their credit histories when they married and changed their names; or creditors reported accounts shared by married couples in the husband's name only. If you are married, divorced, separated, or widowed, contact your local credit bureau(s) to make sure all relevant information is in a file under your own name."

Home Mortgage Disclosure Act

The purpose of the **Home Mortgage Disclosure Act** (HMDA), effective December 31, 1975, is to provide the public and government officials with data to show whether lenders are serving the housing needs of the neighborhoods and communities in which they are located. Each institution must make its mortgage loan disclosure statement available to the general public. Before the disclosure law, some lenders limited the geographic scope of their home loans based on economic or ethnic characteristics of the neighborhoods, a practice known as redlining—certain areas were excluded from eligibility for home loans as though "red lines" were drawn around them.

> Lenders must ask telephone applicants for monitoring information regarding race or national origin, gender, and ethnicity. A borrower is not required to give it.

The HMDA requires mortgage lenders to collect and report data to assist in identifying possible discriminatory lending practices: the race or ethnicity, sex, and income of mortgage applicants, as well as the type of loan they want, where the property is located by census tract, and whether the application was approved, denied, or withdrawn. On certain "high-priced loans" (higher-risk loans), lenders are also required to report the "spread" between the interest rate given and the interest rate that would have been available for a lowest-risk loan. Included with the interest rate data, the lender must report lien status (whether a first or secondary lien) as partial documentation for pricing disparities.

IN PRACTICE The requirement to disclose loan-pricing information was motivated by public and bank regulatory concerns about predatory lending practices. HMDA data enables regulators to look beyond *general* fairness in lending issues and may be used to document charges of discriminatory practices within geographic areas and across racial and ethnic groups.

Community Reinvestment Act

In 1977, Congress passed yet another law dealing with lending practices—the **Community Reinvestment Act** (CRA). Prior to CRA enactment, lenders commonly made loans wherever they felt the risks were lowest and the returns were highest. However, the CRA requires that lenders serve their local communities first—to meet the deposit and credit needs of their low-income and moderate-income housing communities, participate and invest in local community development and rehabilitation projects, and participate in loan programs for housing, small businesses, and small farms.

Each affected lending institution is required to post in a public place in its facilities a Community Reinvestment Act Notice that discloses to potential customers the lending policies of the institution as well as informs customers of their rights under CRA. Additionally, the Community Reinvestment Act requires any federally supervised financial institution to prepare an annual statement containing

- a definition of the geographical boundaries of its community,
- an identification of the types of community reinvestment credit offered (such as residential housing loans, housing rehabilitation loans, small-business loans, commercial loans, and consumer loans), and
- comments from the public about the institution's performance in meeting it community's needs.

IN PRACTICE Regulatory responsibility for the ECOA, HMDA, and CRA has been transferred to the new Consumer Financial Protection Bureau (CFPB). Laws regulating real estate financing are introduced in Congress each year, and recent changes can be found online. Additional financing legal issues will be discussed in Chapter 16—from mortgage disclosures to mortgage fraud and beyond.

FAIR HOUSING ADVERTISING

Section 804(C) of the Fair Housing Act makes it unlawful "to make, print, or publish, or cause to be made, printed, or published, any notice, statement, or advertisement, with respect to the sale or rental of a dwelling, that indicates any preference, limitation, or discrimination because of race, color, religion, sex, handicap, familial status, or national origin, or an intention to make such preference, limitation, or discrimination."

This prohibition applies to all advertising media, including newspapers, magazines, television, radio, and the internet. HUD has found newspapers in violation of the Fair Housing Act for publishing discriminatory advertisements and therefore has concluded that it is illegal for websites to publish discriminatory advertisements as well. In order to ensure that websites do not provide an open market for unlawful discriminatory conduct, HUD continues to investigate allegations that websites have published discriminatory advertisements on the internet.

THE *HUNTER* CASE

It is important to note that a homeowner or a landlord whose dwelling is exempt from coverage under the Fair Housing Act is not free to employ discriminatory advertising. In 1972, the court of appeals noted in *United States v. Hunter* that though free to indulge their discriminatory preferences in selling or renting that dwelling, housing providers do not have the right to publicize that intent to discriminate. The *Hunter* decision was significant because it established judicial guidelines with respect to understanding the meaning of the Fair Housing Act's prohibited practices concerning discriminatory advertising. The *Hunter* opinion also established three important points about Section 804(C):

- That it applies to newspapers and other media
- That the provision does not violate the First Amendment's guarantee of freedom of the press
- That whether or not an advertisement violates the act will be determined by how an ordinary reader would interpret the ad

The antidiscrimination mandate of this provision has a significant impact on the housing industry because it outlaws virtually every discriminatory notice, statement, and advertisement that relates to a housing transaction. Thus, statements made by housing providers that attempt to either encourage or discourage homeseekers from buying or renting in a particular building or neighborhood because of membership in a protected class would violate the law. For example, statements indicating that blacks are not welcome or would not be compatible with existing tenants would be prohibited. The practice of steering homeseekers to certain areas, as well as any discriminatory language contained in restrictive covenants in deeds, would violate the Fair Housing Act.

HUD ADVERTISING GUIDELINES

In 1989, HUD published advertising guidelines (Appendix I to Part 109, Fair Housing Advertising), which detail the types of advertising prohibited by the Fair Housing Act. The purpose of the HUD guidelines is to assist all advertising media, advertising agencies, and all other persons who use advertising to make, print, or publish or cause to be made, printed, or published advertisements with respect to the sale, rental, or financing of dwellings that are in compliance with the requirements of the Fair Housing Act. HUD published additional guidelines in 1995, which were based on a group of key words determined by HUD to not be discriminatory.

The guidelines also describe the matters that HUD will review in evaluating compliance with the Fair Housing Act in connection with investigations of complaints alleging discriminatory housing practices involving advertising.

The HUD advertising guidelines categorize discriminatory advertising into three groups: (1) advertising that contains words, phrases, symbols, or visual aids that indicate a discriminatory preference or limitation; (2) advertising that selectively uses media, human models, logos, and locations to indicate an illegal preference or limitation; and (3) various types of discriminatory advertising practices condemned by the Fair Housing Act.

Use of Words, Phrases, Symbols, and Visual Aids

HUD regulations prohibit the use of catchwords, phrases, symbols, photographs, and illustrations that convey that dwellings are available or not available to a particular group of persons because of race, color, religion, sex, handicap, familial status, or national origin. The words, phrases, and symbols in the following list typify those most often used in residential real estate advertising to convey either overt or tacit discriminatory preferences or limitations:

- Words descriptive of dwelling, landlord, and tenants: *white private home, colored home, Jewish home, Hispanic residence, adult building*
- Words indicative of race, color, religion, sex, handicap, familial status, or national origin
  - Race: *African American, Caucasian, American Indian*
  - Color: *White, black*
  - Religion: *Protestant, Christian, Catholic, Jewish*
  - National origin: *Mexican American, Puerto Rican, Philippine, Polish, Hungarian, Irish, Italian, African, Hispanic, Chinese, Indian, Latino*
  - Sex: The exclusive use of words in advertisements, including those involving the rental of separate units in a single or multifamily dwelling, stating or tending to imply that the housing being advertised is available to persons of only one sex and not the other, except where the sharing of living areas is involved. This section does not cover advertisements of dwellings used exclusively for dormitory facilities by educational institutions.
  - Handicap: *Blind, deaf, mentally ill, impaired, handicapped, physically fit.* This section does not restrict the inclusion of information about the availability of accessible housing.

— Familial status: *Adults, children, singles, mature persons.* This section does not restrict advertisements of dwellings that are intended and operated for occupancy by older persons and that constitute "housing for older persons."

— Catchwords: Words and phrases used in a discriminatory context should be avoided, for example, *restricted, exclusive, private, integrated, traditional, board approval,* or *membership approval.*

■ Symbols or logotypes that imply or suggest race, color, religion, sex, handicap, familial status, or national origin

■ Colloquialisms: Words or phrases used regionally or locally that imply or suggest race, color, religion, sex, handicap, familial status, or national origin

■ Directions to real estate for sale or rent (use of maps or written instructions). Directions can imply a discriminatory preference, limitation, or exclusion; for example, references to a real estate location made in terms of landmarks that have racial or national origin significance, such as an existing black development or an existing development known for its exclusion of minorities. References to a synagogue, congregation, or parish may also indicate a religious preference.

■ Area description: Names of facilities that cater to a particular racial, national origin, or religious group, such as a country club or private school designations, or names of facilities that are used exclusively by one sex may indicate a preference

Selective Use of Advertising Media or Content

The second general category of unlawful advertising identified in HUD regulations involves the selective use of content or media based on race or other prohibited basis. For example, the selective use of human models in advertisements may have a discriminatory impact. Other examples of this type of discriminatory advertising include the following:

■ Selective geographic advertisements: This may involve the strategic placement of billboards, brochure advertisements distributed within a limited geographic area by hand or in the mail, advertising in particular geographic coverage editions of major metropolitan newspapers or in newspapers of limited circulation that are mainly advertising vehicles for reaching a particular segment of the community, or displays or announcements available only in selected sales offices.

■ Selective use of equal opportunity slogan or logo: This may involve placing the equal opportunity slogan or logo in advertising reaching some geographic areas but not others, or with respect to some properties but not others.

■ Selective use of human models: This regulation covers selective advertising based not only on race but on all of the Fair Housing Act's prohibited bases of discrimination, including sex, handicap, and familial status. The regulations require that human models used in display advertising should be clearly definable as reasonably representing majority and minority groups, both sexes, and, when appropriate, families with children. In addition, models should portray persons in an equal social setting and indicate to the public that the housing is open to all persons, without regard to race, color, religion, sex, handicap, familial status, or national origin.

1995 HUD Memorandum

In January 1995, HUD issued a memorandum on advertising terminology with the purpose of establishing procedures for investigating allegations of discriminatory advertising. The memorandum does not address fair housing issues associated with the publication of advertisements containing human models and does not address liability under the Fair Housing Act for making discriminatory statements.

- Race, color, national origin: Racially neutral terms such as *master bedroom*, *rare find*, and *desirable neighborhood* will not create liability. However, an ad stating "white family home" or "no Irish" would be illegal.
- Religion: Ads that use the legal name of a religious entity or contain a religious symbol, standing alone, may indicate an illegal preference. But if the ads contain a nondiscrimination disclaimer, the act will not be violated. Advertisements containing descriptions of properties, such as "apartment complex with chapel," do not on their face state a preference for persons likely to make use of those facilities and are not violations of the act.
- Sex: The terms *mother-in-law suite* or *bachelor apartment* will not discriminate on the basis of sex because they are commonly used as physical descriptions of housing units. Use of the term *master bedroom* does not constitute a violation of either the sex or race discrimination provisions of the act.
- Handicap: Advertisers may use descriptive terms such as *great view*, *walk-in closet*, and *walk to bus stop* without violating the act. Advertising terms related to the conduct required of residents, such as *non-smoking* or *sober*, do not violate the act. Advertisements containing descriptions of accessibility features are lawful, for instance, *wheelchair ramp*.
- Familial status: Advertisers may not limit the number or ages of children but may use terms to describe the property or services and facilities, such as *two bedroom*, *no bicycles allowed*, *family room*, or *quiet streets*.

Other Types of Discriminatory Advertising

HUD regulations prohibit the practice of refusing to publish advertisements for the sale or rental of dwellings because of race or other prohibited bases. Such advertisements may not be subject to different charges or terms.

According to the HUD guidelines, all advertising of residential real estate for sale or rent should contain an equal housing opportunity logotype, statement, or slogan (see Figure 6.4) as a means of educating the homeseeking public that the property is available to all persons, regardless of race, color, religion, sex, handicap, familial status, or national origin. The choice of logotype, statement, or slogan will depend on the type of media used and, in space advertising, on the size of the advertisement.

Note:

HUD has published tables to serve as a guide with respect to the size of the logotype in display advertising. At no time should the size of the logotype be smaller than ½ inch by ½ inch in size, and it is not required in advertising of less than four column inches. In any other advertisements, if other logotypes are used, then the Equal Housing Opportunity logo should be of a size at least equal to the largest of the other logotypes. Alternatively, when no other logotypes are used, 3 to 5% of an advertisement may be devoted to an equal housing opportunity statement.

The equal housing opportunity statement is as follows:

> We are pledged to the letter and spirit of U.S. Policy for the achievement of equal housing opportunity throughout the Nation. We encourage and support an affirmative advertising and marketing program in which there are no barriers to obtaining housing because of race, color, religion, sex, handicap, familial status, or national origin.

FIGURE 6.4: The Equal Housing Opportunity Logotype and Slogan

HUD Publisher's Notice

All publishers should publish at the beginning of the real estate advertising section the HUD Publisher's Notice, a notice that all real estate advertised therein is subject to the federal Fair Housing Act, which makes it illegal to advertise any preference, limitation, or discrimination because of race, color, religion, sex, handicap, familial status, or national origin. The notice should state that the publisher will not knowingly accept any advertising for real estate that violates the law. All persons are thereby informed that all dwellings advertised are available on an equal opportunity basis.

Publishers will not intentionally accept discriminatory ads, because if they do, they may be held liable for violating the Fair Housing Act. The first appellate decision to review the merits of a human models case was handed down in 1991 in *Ragin v. The New York Times Co.*, a case brought by plaintiffs who alleged that the Sunday *New York Times* had a 20-year record of publishing housing ads that featured "thousands of human models of whom virtually none were black," except for those black models who were used to depict service employees or homeseekers interested in units in predominantly black neighborhoods. Given the "ordinary reader" concept, the court ruled that the allegations were sufficient to enable them to prove "that the *Times* has published, and continues to publish, some discriminatory ads."

If a human model ad or any other advertising campaign, such as one using words or phrases that express a preference, limitation, or discrimination, runs afoul of the Fair Housing Act, then the *New York Times* decision makes clear that liability extends to the newspaper publishing it as well as to the advertiser placing it.

THE FAIR HOUSING POSTER

HUD requires that its fair housing posters be displayed in any place of business where real estate is offered for sale or rent. Following HUD's advertising procedures and using the fair housing slogan and logo keep the public aware of the broker's commitment to equal opportunity.

The secretary of Housing and Urban Development has established regulations with respect to the display of a fair housing poster (see Figure 6.5) by persons subject to Sections 804 through 806 of the Fair Housing Act, 42 USC 3604–3606.

CREATING PROTECTED CLASS–SENSITIVE ADVERTISING

Today, most complaints involving fair housing advertising are based on blatant violations of the Fair Housing Act, such as ads seeking "no children" or "adults only." However, with the increased scrutiny of fair real estate advertising by fair housing organizations, testers, and individual homeseekers, many real estate practitioners are concerned about being charged with housing bias based on the wording in their advertisements. Seemingly harmless words may trigger a complaint. The key to composing advertising that complies with the Fair Housing Act is to describe the property, not the seller, landlord, neighbors, or so-called appropriate buyers or renters.

Creating advertising that is sensitive to the protected classes under the Fair Housing Act is not as difficult as it may seem. Simply review the wording in the ad to see whether anyone might feel excluded by what is being said. Keep in mind that if a person wouldn't pick up the phone to respond to an ad because of exclusionary wording, the ad might generate a complaint. For example, the term "Christian handyman" in an ad for rental housing violated Wisconsin law by expressing illegal preferences on the basis of both sex and religion.

IN PRACTICE   Fair Housing Risk Reduction Tips for Buyer's Agents

When a real estate agent is listing a home and the seller directs the agent to exclude certain buyers based on their race, the decision the agent faces is simple—decline the listing. Fair housing law compliance issues are more complex for the buyer's agent. The following are typical questions that buyers ask:

Is this a safe neighborhood?

What are the crime statistics in the area?

Can you tell me about the quality of the schools?

What is the ethnic composition of the neighborhood?

Can you show me homes in a _____ neighborhood?

The best way to answer such questions is to provide purchasers with information about where they can find the information they seek. There is less liability for brokers and sales associates in being the source of the source of the information and not the source itself.

FIGURE 6.5: Fair Housing Poster

U. S. Department of Housing and Urban Development

**EQUAL HOUSING
OPPORTUNITY**

We Do Business in Accordance With the Federal Fair Housing Law

(The Fair Housing Amendments Act of 1988)

It is illegal to Discriminate Against Any Person Because of Race, Color, Religion, Sex, Handicap, Familial Status, or National Origin

---

■ In the sale or rental of housing or residential lots

■ In advertising the sale or rental of housing

■ In the financing of housing

■ In the provision of real estate brokerage services

■ In the appraisal of housing

■ Blockbusting is also illegal

Anyone who feels he or she has been discriminated against may file a complaint of housing discrimination:
    1-800-669-9777 (Toll Free)
    1-800-927-9275 (TTY)

**U.S. Department of Housing and
Urban Development
Assistant Secretary for Fair Housing and
Equal Opportunity
Washington, D.C. 20410**

Previous editions are obsolete

form HUD-928.1 (2/2003)

PROFESSIONAL ETHICS

Professional conduct involves more than just complying with the law. The Texas Real Estate License Act establishes those activities that are illegal and therefore prohibited. However, merely complying with the letter of the law may not be enough: licensees may perform *legally* yet not *ethically*. *Ethics* refers to a system of *moral* principles, rules, and standards of conduct. These moral principles address two sides of a profession.

■ They establish standards for integrity and competence in dealing with consumers of an industry's services.

■ They define a code of conduct for relations within the industry, among its professionals.

Codes of Ethics

Canons of Professional Ethics and Conduct   The Texas Real Estate Commission has adopted the **Canons of Professional Ethics and Conduct** as part of its Rules. This code of ethics establishes a basis for professional conduct of licensed real estate brokers and salespersons, and has the force and effect of the law (see Figure 6.6). The five canons are as follows:

■ **Fidelity**: The agent's primary duty is to represent the interests of the client.

■ **Integrity**: The agent must be honest and morally sound.

■ **Competency**: The agent must be knowledgeable about national, state, and local issues and conditions.

■ **Consumer Information Form 1-1**: The broker must display a notice concerning the Real Estate Recovery Trust Account (see Chapter 7).

■ **Discriminatory Practices**: The agent may not discriminate based on legally protected classes.

Each applicant for a Texas broker's or salesperson's license pledges to "abide by the provisions of The Real Estate License Act and the Rules of the Texas Real Estate Commission." Furthermore, paragraph 1101.656 of the License Act states that "the commission may suspend or revoke a license, place on probation a person whose license has been suspended, or reprimand a license holder if the license holder violates this chapter [the License Act] or a commission rule." The court case in the In Practice that follows further emphasizes the significance of the Canons of Professional Ethics and Conduct.

IN PRACTICE   A Texas real estate broker was sued for breach of fiduciary duty based on the broker's failure to tell the owner that her listed property had been posted for foreclosure. The broker contended that his conduct was governed exclusively by the listing agreement. The court disagreed stating, "Rules and regulations promulgated within an agency's authority have the force and effect of law" [Kinnard v. Homann, 750 S.W. 2d 30 (1988)].

FIGURE 6.6:   Canons of Professional Ethics and Conduct—Rules of the Texas Real Estate Commission, Chapter 531

Fidelity. A real estate broker or salesperson, while acting as an agent for another, is a fiduciary. Special obligations are imposed when such fiduciary relationships are created. They demand:

(1) that the primary duty of the real estate agent is to represent the interests of the agent's client, and the agent's position, in this respect, should be clear to all parties concerned in a real estate transaction; that, however, the agent, in performing duties to the client, shall treat other parties to a transaction fairly;

(2) that the real estate agent be faithful and observant to trust placed in the agent, and be scrupulous and meticulous in performing the agent's functions;

(3) that the real estate agent place no personal interest above that of the agent's client.

Integrity. A real estate broker or salesperson has a special obligation to exercise integrity in the discharge of the licensee's responsibilities, including employment of prudence and caution so as to avoid misrepresentation, in any ways, by acts of commission or omission.

Competency. It is the obligation of a real estate agent to be knowledgeable as a real estate brokerage practitioner. The agent should:

(1) be informed on market conditions affecting the real estate business and pledged to continuing education in the intricacies involved in marketing real estate for others;

(2) be informed on national, state and local issues and developments in the real estate industry;

(3) exercise judgment and skill in the performance of the work.

Consumer Information Form 1-1.

(a) The Texas Real Estate Commission adopts by reference Consumer Information Form 1-1 approved by the Texas Real Estate Commission in 1991. This document is published by and available from the Texas Real Estate Commission, P.O. Box 12188, Austin, Texas 78711-2188.

(b) Each real estate inspector or active real estate broker licensed by the Texas Real Estate Commission shall display Consumer Information Form 1-1 in a prominent location in each place of business the broker or inspector maintains.

Discriminatory Practices. No real estate licensee shall inquire about, respond to or facilitate inquiries about, or make a disclosure which indicates or is intended to indicate any preference, limitation or discrimination based on the following: race, color, religion, sex, national origin, ancestry, familial status, or handicap of an owner, previous or current occupant, potential purchaser, lessor, or potential lessee of real property. For the purpose of this section, handicap includes a person who had, may have had, has, or may have AIDS, HIV-related illnesses, or HIV infection as defined by the Centers for Disease Control of the United States Public Health Service.

NAR Code of Ethics   The National Association of Realtors® publishes a **Code of Ethics**, along with interpretations of the Code known as *Standards of Practice*. Members of NAR and its affiliated state and local associations are expected to subscribe to this strict code of conduct. (Remember, not all licensees are members of NAR.) Interpretations of the Code establish precedents for a local board to follow in hearings that involve violations of the Code. If a hearing panel finds a REALTOR® in violation of the Code, the member will be assessed a penalty such as a letter of reprimand, a loss of membership in the association, and/or fines up to $5,000. The member may also be required to take an ethics course through the association. If the violation of the Code is also a violation of the Real Estate License Act, the NAR member would additionally be subject to TREC disciplinary proceedings if a complaint were filed with TREC. The NAR Code of Ethics is available on the NAR website: www.realtor.org; choose *Law and Policy*.

Because the real estate business is only as good as its reputation, and reputations are built on sound business practices and fair dealings with clients, all licensees are obligated to conduct themselves in an ethical manner—tell the truth, be up front, live up to promises made, and do more than required.

SUMMARY

The federal regulations regarding equal opportunity in housing are contained principally in two laws: the Civil Rights Act of 1866, which prohibits all racial discrimination; and the federal Fair Housing Act (Title VIII of the Civil Rights Act of 1968, as amended), which prohibits discrimination on the basis of race, color, religion, sex, national origin, handicap, or familial status in the sale or rental of residential property. Discriminatory actions include refusing to deal with an individual or a specific group; changing any terms of a real estate or loan transaction; changing the services offered for any individual or group; making statements or advertisements that indicate discriminatory restrictions; and otherwise attempting to make a dwelling unavailable to any person or group because of race, color, religion, sex, national origin, handicap, or familial status.

In order to avoid a fair housing complaint, today's real estate professional must have an in-depth understanding of the Fair Housing Act and the HUD regulations that further define the law. Agents must be willing to educate both buyers and sellers in the provisions of the law, as well as in the penalties for noncompliance. If, at any time, a seller appears to be considering discriminating against a potential buyer for any reason, the agent should point out that the action would violate the Fair Housing Act. If sellers are unwilling to offer their home to all protected groups on an equal basis, the real estate professional has no choice but to decline or cancel the listing.

Buyer's agents also need to be aware that if their client expresses intent to limit the housing search based on protected-class factors, they too may find themselves involved in litigation. Buyer's agents with an in-depth understanding of fair housing laws will be able to better assist their clients if they encounter discrimination at any point during the home purchasing process, including obtaining financing and property insurance.

Complaints under the federal Fair Housing Act may be reported to and investigated by the Department of Housing and Urban Development or the Texas Workforce Commission Civil Rights Division. Because Texas has passed the Texas Fair Housing Act, which is substantially equivalent to the federal law, most complaints are heard by the Texas Workforce Commission Civil Rights Division or in state district courts. However, complaints under the Civil Rights Act of 1866 must be taken to a federal court.

The Equal Credit Opportunity Act, the Home Mortgage Disclosure Act, and the Community Reinvestment Act contribute to the fair availability of credit. All lenders are defined the same under each act.

The 1988 Fair Housing Amendments Act added familial status and handicap as protected classes and greatly strengthened the enforcement mechanisms. HUD regulations, which went into effect March 12, 1989, further defined discriminatory housing practices and gave a great deal of authoritative material concerning the meaning of the Fair Housing Act. The regulations added a provision that covered obtaining property and hazard insurance and prohibited the refusal to provide such insurance outright based on protected-class factors or subjecting those individuals to different terms or conditions for obtaining coverage. Both the Fair Housing Act and HUD regulations condemn discriminatory lending practices.

Real estate professionals must have an in-depth understanding of the Fair Housing Act's prohibition of discriminatory advertising. All advertising, including newspaper and magazine ads, flyers, radio and television commercials, brochures, and even ads placed in phone books, must comply with fair housing laws. All forms of advertising in any media must not show a preference, limitation, or discrimination directed at the protected classes.

Any discriminatory statements made are illegal under the Fair Housing Act and HUD regulations. Real estate agents should carefully review all ads to ensure that no prohibited words or phrases are included. Remember, it is much safer to describe the property in terms of its physical characteristics than to target people who would be considered appropriate buyers or renters.

A real estate business is only as good as its reputation. Real estate licensees can maintain good reputations by demonstrating good business ability and adhering to an ethical standard of business practices. Compliance with the Texas Real Estate Commission's Canons of Professional Ethics and Conduct is required of all Texas licensees. In addition, many licensees subscribe to a code of ethics as members of professional real estate organizations.

CHAPTER 6 QUESTIONS

1. Which action is permitted under the federal Fair Housing Act?
   a. Advertising property for sale only to a special group
   b. Refusing to sell a home to a minority individual because of a poor credit history
   c. Telling an individual that an apartment has been rented when in fact it has not
   d. Showing a member of a minority group only those properties located in minority areas

2. Lawsuits relating to the Civil Rights Act of 1866
   a. must be taken directly to a federal court.
   b. are handled by HUD.
   c. are handled by state enforcement agencies.
   d. must be handled by local jurisdiction authority before appealing to federal court.

3. Housing for older persons is exempt from familial status discrimination prohibitions if it is occupied solely by persons this age and older.
   a. 52
   b. 55
   c. 60
   d. 62

4. Which situation is considered discriminatory under the federal Fair Housing Act?
   a. The Penford Club of Metropole City will rent lodging only to graduates of Penford University who are members of this private club.
   b. A Catholic convent provides housing for Catholics only.
   c. The owner of a 20-unit apartment building refuses to rent apartments to women.
   d. An owner refuses to rent the other side of her duplex home to families with children.

5. "I hear *they're* moving in. There goes the neighborhood! Better put your house on the market before values drop!" This is an example of
   a. steering.
   b. redlining.
   c. blockbusting.
   d. channeling.

6. After a broker takes a listing to sell a residence, the owner specifies that he will not sell his home to an Asian family. The broker should do which of the following?
   a. Advertise the property exclusively in non-Asian-language newspapers.
   b. Explain to the owner that the instruction violates federal law and the broker cannot comply with it. If the owner persists, the broker must withdraw from the transaction.
   c. Explain to the owner that the instruction violates federal law. If the owner persists, abide by the principal's instructions to fulfill the agency responsibility of *obedience*.
   d. Require the owner to sign a separate legal document stating the additional instruction as an amendment to the listing agreement.

7. Which statement describes the effect of the Supreme Court's decision in *Jones v. Alfred H. Mayer Company*?
   a. Racial discrimination is prohibited by any party in the sale or rental of real estate.
   b. Sales by individual residential homeowners are exempt from fair housing provisions, provided owners do not use brokers.
   c. Laws against discrimination apply only to federally related transactions.
   d. Persons with disabilities are a protected class.

8. Why is the Civil Rights Act of 1866 unique?
   a. It protects the aged.
   b. It adds welfare recipients as a protected class.
   c. It contains "choose your neighbor" provisions.
   d. It provides no exceptions that would permit racial discrimination.

9. The act of channeling homeseekers to a particular area either to maintain or to change the character of a neighborhood is
   a. blockbusting.
   b. redlining.
   c. steering.
   d. less favorable treatment.

10. A lender's refusal to lend money to potential homeowners attempting to purchase property located in predominantly African American neighborhoods is known as
    a. blockbusting.
    b. redlining.
    c. steering.
    d. qualifying.

11. An exception that allows discrimination in the rental of rooms or units in an owner-occupied building with no more than four units is provided in
    a. the Civil Rights Act of 1964.
    b. the Civil Rights Act of 1866.
    c. *Jones v. Mayer.*
    d. the Fair Housing Act of 1968.

12. The Home Mortgage Disclosure Act requires that lenders disclose the
    a. geographic areas served by the lender.
    b. amount of the loan-related closing costs.
    c. marital status of each applicant.
    d. reason a loan was denied.

13. If a mortgage lender discriminates against a loan applicant on the basis of marital status, it violates what law?
    a. ADA
    b. Civil Rights Act of 1866
    c. ECOA Equal Credit Opportunity Act
    d. Fair Housing Act

14. The Community Reinvestment Act (CRA) requires that lenders
    a. maintain a branch office in each geographic area where loans are made.
    b. reinvest at least 90% of their loan proceeds in properties located within the communities they serve.
    c. make loans within the communities from which they derive their deposits.
    d. report the race, sex, and income of applicants, the type of loan desired, property location by census tract, and whether the application was approved, denied, or withdrawn.

15. The federal Fair Housing Act of 1988 added as protected groups
    a. families with children and persons with handicaps.
    b. senior citizens and persons with handicaps.
    c. single parents and those older than 65.
    d. persons unemployed and having a disability.

16. A real estate broker wants to achieve racial balance in residential housing. As an office policy, he requires that salespersons show prospective buyers from racial or ethnic minority groups only properties that are in areas of town where few members of their groups currently live. Which statement is *TRUE* regarding the broker's policy?
    a. While the policy may appear to constitute blockbusting, the practice is legal.
    b. Because the effect of the policy is discriminatory, it constitutes illegal steering regardless of the broker's intentions.
    c. The broker's policy constitutes redlining.
    d. While the broker's policy may appear to constitute steering, the practice is legal.

17. The famous "separate but equal" doctrine is from which of the following Supreme Court decisions?
    a. *Jones v. Mayer*
    b. *Shelley v. Kraemer*
    c. *Plessy v. Ferguson*
    d. *Brown v. the Board of Education*

18. Sex was added as a protected class by the
    a. 1988 Fair Housing Amendments Act.
    b. 1968 Fair Housing Act.
    c. 1974 Housing and Community Development Act.
    d. Civil Rights Act of 1964.

19. The definition of the term *handicap* includes all of the following *EXCEPT*
    a. former drug addicts.
    b. alcoholics.
    c. persons who test positive for HIV infection.
    d. current illegal drug users.

20. The 1995 HUD memorandum on advertising prohibited which of the following terms?
    a. Bachelor apartment
    b. Master bedroom
    c. Both of these
    d. Neither of these

21. The key to composing advertising that complies with the federal Fair Housing Act is to describe
    a. the seller.
    b. the landlord.
    c. appropriate buyers or renters.
    d. the property.

Detailed rationales for the end-of-chapter review questions are available online at www.dearborn.com through the *Instructor Resource Guides* link.

CHAPTER

7

Texas Real Estate License Act

■ **LEARNING OBJECTIVES**   *When you have completed this chapter, you will be able to*

- **identify** the purpose of licensing laws, the activities that require a license, the situations that may not require a license, and the types of license categories;
- **describe** the membership and the scope of authority of the Texas Real Estate Commission (TREC) and the Texas Real Estate Broker-Lawyer Committee;
- **distinguish** the general and education requirements for real estate broker and salesperson licensing and the procedures for receiving or renewing an active or an inactive license;
- **explain** the purpose and operation of the real estate recovery trust account;
- **identify** the reasons for which a license may be suspended or revoked, the manner in which the commission may investigate a licensee, and the disciplinary actions available to TREC; and
- **define** the following *key terms:*

apprentice inspector	party	salesperson annual education (SAE)
ARELLO	professional inspector	subagent
broker	real estate inspector	Texas Real Estate Broker-Lawyer Committee
core real estate course	real estate recovery trust account	
intermediary		Texas Real Estate Commission (TREC)
mandatory continuing education (MCE)	residential rental locator	
	salesperson	Texas Real Estate Research Center
nonresident broker		

OVERVIEW

In Texas, broker and salesperson license applicants are required to pass an examination designed to test their knowledge of real estate principles and laws. Foremost among these laws is the *Real Estate License Act*, which sets forth strict operating restrictions for licensees and penalties for noncompliance.

Chapter 1101 of the Texas Occupations Code, better known as the *Real Estate License Act*, is reproduced in its entirety in this chapter. The license law analysis form that precedes the end-of-chapter questions will help students learn the requirements of state law. The form can be used as a study device while reading through the state law or as a testing device after studying the license law.

REAL ESTATE LICENSE LAWS IN ALL STATES

All states, the District of Columbia, and Canadian provinces have enacted real estate license laws that regulate the activities of real estate brokers and salespersons. Details vary from state to state, but in many states the main provisions are similar and are based on the so-called pattern law recommended by the License Law Committee of the National Association of REALTORS®. In addition, **ARELLO**—the Association of Real Estate License Law Officials—promotes uniform policies and standards in the fields of license law administration and enforcement.

Purposes of the License Law

Although a fee is charged for real estate licenses, the primary purpose of the license law is not to raise revenue. The purposes of the law are to protect the public from dishonest or incompetent brokers or salespersons, prescribe certain minimum standards and qualifications for licensing brokers and salespersons, maintain high standards in the real estate profession, and protect licensed brokers and salespersons from unfair or improper competition.

The Texas Real Estate Commission

Administration of the Texas Real Estate License Act (TRELA) is vested in the **Texas Real Estate Commission (TREC)**, which by statute is composed of nine members. Three are members of the public who may have no affiliation with real estate brokerage, and six are real estate broker-members. The commissioners are appointed by the governor with confirmation by the state senate. The governor of Texas appoints the TREC chair.

The Sunset Act

Texas law provides for a periodic review of each state agency, commission, and board to evaluate its purpose, efficiency, and need. This review is performed by a statutory agency known as the *Sunset Commission*, which recommends retaining or abolishing the state entity under review. The Real Estate Commission has been reviewed four times under the *Sunset Act* and has received approval for retention each time. Its last review was in 2007; the next one will be in 2019.

BASIC PROVISIONS OF THE TEXAS REAL ESTATE LICENSE ACT

Definitions of Broker and Salesperson

A licensed real estate *broker* is authorized to operate a real estate brokerage business. A real estate **salesperson** with an active license is sponsored by and responsible to a licensed broker for the purposes of performing real estate brokerage transactions.

Licensing Procedure

All states require that an applicant for either the broker's or salesperson's license pass an examination to demonstrate knowledge of real estate principles and practices. In addition to the examination, Texas licensing requirements relate to age, citizenship, education, apprenticeship, and residency. Application forms, sources of acceptable real estate education, an exam study outline, practice exam questions, and information related to the activities of the Texas Real Estate Commission can be obtained from the TREC website. Information regarding license application procedures can also be obtained by calling TREC at 512-936-3864 or by writing the Commission at P.O. Box 12188, Austin, TX 78711-2188.

WEBLINK @ www.trec.texas.gov

Members of the real estate profession should be committed to promoting the profession and maintaining and improving its standards. This is best done by carefully adhering to licensing and fair housing laws, pledging to comply with the Texas Real Estate Commission's Canons of Professional Ethics and Conduct (see Chapter 6), and taking advantage of every opportunity to expand professional knowledge and ability.

The licenses or registration certificates issued to qualified individuals and business entities are legal permits to operate a real estate brokerage business as described and permitted by state law. In Texas, a license is required to sell, purchase, rent, lease, auction, or exchange real estate for others and for compensation. Real estate licenses are issued for definite terms and must be renewed within specified time limits. Each license is a personal right and terminates on death of the licensee or dissolution of the business entity. While a license or registration certificate is in effect, the activities of each licensed person or entity are subject to control of TREC as prescribed by the Real Estate License Act. For this reason, every licensed person must be thoroughly familiar with the act.

Certain persons are exempt from the license law. Usually these are owners dealing with their own property; trustees, executors, receivers, and others operating under court orders; public officials; and Texas attorneys at law.

Real Estate Brokers Do Not Give Legal Advice

Texas law prohibits nonmembers of the state bar from practicing law in the state. Although the legal rights and contractual obligations of the parties to a real estate transaction are the broker's fundamental concerns, it is not the broker's responsibility to offer legal advice. In fact, the License Act authorizes the Texas Real Estate Commission to suspend or revoke a broker's or salesperson's license for the unlawful practice of law. To ensure valid sales contracts, licensees should advise sellers and buyers to secure legal counsel if they do not understand the provisions of the various contract forms that the act requires licensees to use.

THE REAL ESTATE LICENSE ACT (TRELA)

As discussed in Chapter 1, the first law to regulate brokerage in Texas was the Texas Real Estate Dealers Act, passed in 1939. The law that currently regulates real estate in *Texas is The Real Estate License Act (TRELA)*, Article 6573a of Vernon's Texas Civil Statutes, passed by the Texas Legislature in 1949 and codified as Title 7, Occupations Code, Chapter 1101 in June 2003. The License Act can be changed or amended only by action of the state legislature and with the governor's signature. It has been amended in almost every biennial session of the Texas Legislature, most recently in 2011.

The Real Estate License Act is administered by TREC, which is authorized to pass rules to interpret, define, and enforce the act's provisions. The *Rules of the Texas Real Estate Commission* may be amended by the commission and are subject to review by the legislature. As discussed in Chapter 1, the Rules expand on the law and have the effect of law; however, they are not "the law." A copy of the Rules may be obtained from the TREC website. In addition, the TREC website has a "question and answer" section from the Enforcement Division, which can provide interpretations for many questions left unanswered by the License Act itself.

Reproduction in full of The Real Estate License Act on the following pages is intended to help applicants study the law. Some headings have been added by the author, and some parts are emphasized in bold or italic type. This act must be interpreted by legal counsel as applied to each person or case.

WEBLINK @ www.trec.texas.gov/questions/faq-enf.asp

An *Analysis Form* is provided at the end of this chapter. Completing it as you read the License Act may increase your comprehension and retention of the details of the license law.

TEXAS OCCUPATIONS CODE
TITLE 7. PRACTICES AND PROFESSIONS RELATED TO REAL PROPERTY AND HOUSING
SUBTITLE A. PROFESSIONS RELATED TO REAL ESTATE

CHAPTER 1101. REAL ESTATE BROKERS AND SALESPERSONS
THE REAL ESTATE LICENSE ACT (TRELA)
EFFECTIVE SEPTEMBER 1, 2011 AND JANUARY 1, 2012

Subchapter A. General Provisions

§ 1101.001. Short Title

This chapter may be cited as **The Real Estate License Act.**

§ 1101.002. Definitions

In this chapter:

(1) **"Broker":**

(A) means a person who, in exchange for a commission or other valuable consideration or with the expectation of receiving a commission or other valuable consideration, performs for another person one of the following acts:

(i) sells, exchanges, purchases, or leases real estate;

(ii) offers to sell, exchange, purchase, or lease real estate;

(iii) negotiates or attempts to negotiate the listing, sale, exchange, purchase, or lease of real estate;

(iv) lists or offers, attempts, or agrees to list real estate for sale, lease, or exchange;

(v) auctions or offers, attempts, or agrees to auction real estate;

(vi) deals in options on real estate, including buying, selling, or offering to buy or sell options on real estate;

(vii) aids or offers or attempts to aid in locating or obtaining real estate for purchase or lease;

(viii) procures or assists in procuring a prospect to effect the sale, exchange, or lease of real estate;

(ix) procures or assists in procuring property to effect the sale, exchange, or lease of real estate;

(x) controls the acceptance or deposit of rent from a resident of a single-family residential real property unit; or

(xi) provides a written analysis, opinion, or conclusion relating to the estimated price of real property if the analysis, opinion, or conclusion:

(a) is not referred to as an appraisal;

(b) is provided in the ordinary course of the person's business; and

(c) is related to the actual or potential management, acquisition, disposition, or encumbrance of an interest in real property; and

(B) includes a person who:

(i) is employed by or for an owner of real estate to sell any portion of the real estate; or

(ii) engages in the business of charging an advance fee or contracting to collect a fee under a contract that requires the person primarily to promote the sale of real estate by:

(a) listing the real estate in a publication primarily used for listing real estate; or

(b) referring information about the real estate to brokers.

(1-a) **"Business entity"** means a "domestic entity" or a "foreign entity" as those terms are defined by Section 1.002, Business Organizations Code.

(2) **"Certificate holder"** means a person registered under Subchapter K.

(3) **"Commission"** means the Texas Real Estate Commission.

(4) **"License holder"** means a broker or salesperson licensed under this chapter.

(5) **"Real estate"** means any interest in real property, including a leasehold, located in or outside this state. The term does not include an interest given as security for the performance of an obligation.

(6) **"Residential rental locator"** means a person who offers for consideration to locate a unit in an apartment complex for lease to a prospective tenant. The term does not include an owner who offers to locate a unit in the owner's complex.

(7) **"Salesperson"** means a person who is associated with a licensed broker for the purpose of performing an act described by Subdivision (1).

(8) **"Subagent"** means a license holder who:

 (A) represents a principal through cooperation with and the consent of a broker representing the principal; and

 (B) is not sponsored by or associated with the principal's broker.

(Revised, S.B. 747, 2011.)

§ 1101.003. Core Real Estate Courses

(a) For purposes of this chapter, **"core real estate courses"** include:

 (1) **agency law**, which includes the following topics:

  (A) the relationship between a principal and an agent;

  (B) an agent's authority;

  (C) the termination of an agent's authority;

  (D) an agent's duties, including fiduciary duties;

  (E) employment law;

  (F) deceptive trade practices;

  (G) listing or buying representation procedures; and

  (H) the disclosure of agency;

 (2) **contract law**, which includes the following topics:

  (A) elements of a contract;

  (B) offer and acceptance;

  (C) statute of frauds;

  (D) remedies for breach, including specific performance;

  (E) unauthorized practice of law;

  (F) commission rules relating to use of adopted forms; and

  (G) owner disclosure requirements;

 (3) **principles of real estate**, which includes:

  (A) an overview of:

   (i) licensing as a broker or salesperson;

   (ii) ethics of practice as a license holder;

   (iii) titles to and conveyance of real estate;

   (iv) legal descriptions;

   (v) deeds, encumbrances, and liens;

   (vi) distinctions between personal and real property;

   (vii) appraisal;

   (viii) finance and regulations;

   (ix) closing procedures; and

   (x) real estate mathematics; and

  (B) at least three hours of classroom instruction on federal, state, and local laws relating to housing discrimination, housing credit discrimination, and community reinvestment;

 (4) **property management**, which includes the following topics:

  (A) the role of a property manager;

  (B) landlord policies;

  (C) operational guidelines;

  (D) leases;

  (E) lease negotiations;

  (F) tenant relations;

  (G) maintenance;

  (H) reports;

(I) habitability laws; and

(J) the Fair Housing Act (42 U.S.C. Section 3601 et seq.);

(5) **real estate appraisal**, which includes the following topics:

(A) the central purposes and functions of an appraisal;

(B) social and economic determinants of the value of real estate;

(C) appraisal case studies;

(D) cost, market data, and income approaches to value estimates of real estate;

(E) final correlations; and

(F) reporting;

(6) **real estate brokerage**, which includes the following topics:

(A) agency law;

(B) planning and organization;

(C) operational policies and procedures;

(D) recruitment, selection, and training of personnel;

(E) records and control; and

(F) real estate firm analysis and expansion criteria;

(7) **real estate finance**, which includes the following topics:

(A) monetary systems;

(B) primary and secondary money markets;

(C) sources of mortgage loans;

(D) federal government programs;

(E) loan applications, processes, and procedures;

(F) closing costs;

(G) alternative financial instruments;

(H) equal credit opportunity laws;

(I) community reinvestment laws, including the Community Reinvestment Act of 1977 (12 U.S.C. Section 2901 et seq.); and

(J) state housing agencies, including the Texas Department of Housing and Community Affairs;

(8) **real estate investment**, which includes the following topics:

(A) real estate investment characteristics;

(B) techniques of investment analysis;

(C) the time value of money;

(D) discounted and nondiscounted investment criteria;

(E) leverage;

(F) tax shelters, depreciation; and

(G) applications to property tax;

(9) **real estate law**, which includes the following topics:

(A) legal concepts of real estate;

(B) land description;

(C) real property rights and estates in land;

(D) contracts;

(E) conveyances;

(F) encumbrances;

(G) foreclosures;

(H) recording procedures; and

(I) evidence of titles;

(10) **real estate marketing**, which includes the following topics:
    (A) real estate professionalism and ethics;
    (B) characteristics of successful salespersons;
    (C) time management;
    (D) psychology of marketing;
    (E) listing procedures;
    (F) advertising;
    (G) negotiating and closing;
    (H) financing; and
    (I) Subchapter E, Chapter 17, Business & Commerce Code; and
(11) **real estate mathematics**, which includes the following topics:
    (A) basic arithmetic skills and review of mathematical logic;
    (B) percentages;
    (C) interest;
    (D) the time value of money;
    (E) depreciation;
    (F) amortization;
    (G) proration; and
    (H) estimation of closing statements.
(b) The commission may designate a course as an equivalent of a course listed in Subsection (a).
(c) The commission by rule may prescribe:
    (1) the content of the core real estate courses listed in Subsection (a); and
    (2) the title and content of additional core real estate courses.

§ 1101.004. Acting as Broker or Salesperson

A person acts as a broker or salesperson under this chapter if the person, with the expectation of receiving valuable consideration, directly or indirectly performs or offers, attempts, or agrees to perform for another person any act described by Section 1101.002(1), as a part of a transaction or as an entire transaction.

§ 1101.005. Applicability of Chapter [Exemptions]

This chapter does not apply to:
    (1) an attorney licensed in this state;
    (2) an attorney-in-fact authorized under a power of attorney to conduct a real estate transaction;
    (3) a public official while engaged in official duties;
    (4) an auctioneer licensed under Chapter 1802 while conducting the sale of real estate by auction if the auctioneer does not perform another act of a broker or salesperson;
    (5) a person conducting a real estate transaction under a court order or the authority of a will or written trust instrument;
    (6) a person employed by an owner in the sale of structures and land on which structures are located if the structures are erected by the owner in the course of the owner's business;
    (7) an on-site manager of an apartment complex;
    (8) an owner or the owner's employee who leases the owner's improved or unimproved real estate; or

(9) a transaction involving:
　(A) the sale, lease, or transfer of a mineral or mining interest in real property;
　(B) the sale, lease, or transfer of a cemetery lot;
　(C) the lease or management of a hotel or motel; or
　(D) the sale of real property under a power of sale conferred by a deed of trust or other contract lien. **(Revised, S.B. 747, 2011.)**

§ 1101.0055. Nonapplicability of Law Governing Cancellation of Certain Transactions

A service contract that a license holder enters into for services governed by this chapter is not a good or service governed by Chapter 39, Business and Commerce Code.

§ 1101.006. Application of Sunset Act

The Texas Real Estate Commission is subject to Chapter 325, Government Code (Texas Sunset Act). Unless continued in existence as provided by that chapter, the commission is abolished and this chapter, Chapter 1102 and Chapter 1303 of this code, and Chapter 221, Property Code, expire September 1, 2019.

§ 1101.007. Compliance with Sunset Recommendations

(a) The commission shall:
　(1) comply with and implement the management action recommendations regarding the commission adopted by the Sunset Advisory Commission on January 10, 2007, as a result of its review of the commission; and
　(2) report to the Sunset Advisory Commission not later than November 1, 2008, the information the Sunset Advisory Commission requires regarding the commission's implementation of the recommendations under Subdivision (1).
(b) This section expires June 1, 2009.

IN PRACTICE   Subchapter A contains the official definitions of most terms used in the act. Of particular importance are the definitions of broker and salesperson because they specifically describe those activities for which licensure is required. The act makes no distinction between the types of activities that each is permitted to practice. The reason for the separate classification of licensure is to place the responsibility for the salesperson's actions on the broker. Property, real property, and real estate all have the same meaning when used in the License Act. Valuable consideration is defined to include money, gifts of merchandise having a retail value greater than $50, rent bonuses, and discounts (Rule 535.20(a)).

Section 1101.003 describes 11 core courses and their content. In addition, Promulgated Contract Forms and Residential Inspection for Real Estate Agents have both been established by TREC rule.

Section 1101.005 lists the exemptions from licensing requirements. The Rules further clarify that licensure is not required of the following:

- Those who buy and sell real property only for their own account, even if buying property to resell it

- Attorneys licensed in Texas. However, a licensee may not share a commission with an attorney; the attorney must be paid by the buyer or seller.

- Auctioneers when auctioning real estate. however, auctioneers may not show property, prepare offers, or negotiate contracts unless licensed as brokers or salespersons.

- Trade associations that provide an electronic listing service for members but do not receive compensation when real estate is sold

- Those who perform secretarial, clerical, or administrative tasks, as long as they do not solicit business for brokers or hold themselves out as authorized to act as real estate brokers or salespersons. Unlicensed persons may act as hosts or hostesses at a property being offered for sale by the broker, provided they do not engage in any activity for which a license is required (see Chapter 5 for more details about unlicensed personal assistants).

SUBCHAPTER B. TEXAS REAL ESTATE COMMISSION

§ 1101.051. Commission Membership

(a) The Texas Real Estate Commission consists of nine members appointed by the governor with the advice and consent of the senate as follows:

(1) six members who have been engaged in the brokerage business as licensed brokers as their major occupation for the five years preceding appointment; and

(2) three members who represent the public.

(b) Each member of the commission must be a qualified voter.

(c) Appointments to the commission shall be made without regard to the race, color, disability, sex, religion, age, or national origin of the appointee.

§ 1101.052. Public Member Eligibility

A person is not eligible for appointment as a public member of the commission if the person or the person's spouse:

(1) is registered, certified, or licensed by an occupational regulatory agency in the real estate industry;

(2) is employed by or participates in the management of a business entity or other organization regulated by the commission or receiving funds from the commission;

(3) owns or controls, directly or indirectly, more than a 10% interest in a business entity or other organization regulated by the commission or receiving funds from the commission; or

(4) uses or receives a substantial amount of tangible goods, services, or funds from the commission, other than compensation or reimbursement authorized by law for commission membership, attendance, or expenses.

§ 1101.053. Membership and Employee Restrictions

(a) In this section, "Texas trade association" means a cooperative and voluntarily joined statewide association of business or professional competitors in this state designed to assist its members and its industry or profession in dealing with mutual business or professional problems and in promoting their common interest.

(b) A person may not be a member of the commission and may not be a commission employee employed in a "bona fide executive, administrative, or professional capacity," as that phrase is used for purposes of establishing an exemption to the overtime provisions of the federal Fair Labor Standards Act of 1938 (29 U.S.C. Section 201 et seq.) if:

(1) the person is an officer, employee, or paid consultant of a Texas trade association in the real estate industry; or

(2) the person's spouse is an officer, manager, or paid consultant of a Texas trade association in the real estate industry.

(c) A person may not serve as a commission member or act as the general counsel to the commission if the person is required to register as a lobbyist under Chapter 305, Government Code, because of the person's activities for compensation on behalf of a profession related to the operation of the commission.

§ 1101.054. Official Oath; Bond

Not later than the 15th day after the date of appointment, each appointee must:

(1) take the constitutional oath of office; and

(2) execute a bond payable to the governor in the amount of $10,000, conditioned on the faithful performance of the member's duties.

§ 1101.055. Terms; Vacancy

(a) Commission members serve staggered six-year terms, with the terms of three members expiring January 31 of each odd-numbered year.

(b) If a vacancy occurs during a member's term, the governor shall appoint a person to fill the unexpired term.

§ 1101.056. Officers

(a) The governor shall designate a commission member who is a licensed broker as presiding officer. The presiding officer serves in that capacity at the pleasure of the governor.

(b) At a regular meeting in February of each year, the commission shall elect an assistant presiding officer and secretary from its membership.

§ 1101.057. Grounds for Removal

(a) It is a ground for removal from the commission that a member:

(1) does not have at the time of appointment the qualifications required by Section 1101.051(a) or (b) or 1101.052;

(2) does not maintain during service on the commission the qualifications required by Section 1101.051(a) or (b) or 1101.052;

(3) is ineligible for membership under Section 1101.053;

(4) cannot discharge the member's duties for a substantial part of the member's term; or

(5) is absent from more than half of the regularly scheduled commission meetings that the member is eligible to attend during each calendar year, unless the absence is excused by majority vote of the commission.

(b) The validity of an action of the commission is not affected by the fact that it is taken when a ground for removal of a commission member exists.

(c) If the administrator has knowledge that a potential ground for removal exists, the administrator shall notify the presiding officer of the commission of the potential ground. The presiding officer shall then notify the governor and the attorney general that a potential ground for removal exists. If the potential ground for removal involves the presiding officer, the administrator shall notify the next highest ranking officer of the commission, who shall then notify the governor and the attorney general that a potential ground for removal exists.

§ 1101.058. Per Diem; Reimbursement

A commission member is entitled to receive:
  (1) $75 for each day the member performs the member's official duties; and
  (2) reimbursement for actual and necessary expenses incurred in performing the member's official duties.

§ 1101.059. Training

(a) A person who is appointed to and qualifies for office as a member of the commission may not vote, deliberate, or be counted as a member in attendance at a meeting of the commission until the person completes a training program that complies with this section.

(b) The training program must provide the person with information regarding:
  (1) this chapter and other laws regulated by the commission;
  (2) the programs, functions, rules, and budget of the commission;
  (3) the results of the most recent formal audit of the commission;
  (4) the requirements of laws relating to open meetings, public information, administrative procedure, and conflicts of interest; and
  (5) any applicable ethics policies adopted by the commission or the Texas Ethics Commission.

(c) A person appointed to the commission is entitled to reimbursement for the travel expenses incurred in attending the training program regardless of whether the attendance at the program occurs before or after the person qualifies for office. **(Revised, S.B. 1000, 2011.)**

IN PRACTICE Subchapter B establishes the composition of the Texas Real Estate Commission, which oversees the administration of The Real Estate License Act. Additionally, it states the eligibility requirements for commissioners, the length of membership terms, the grounds for removal of a commission member, and the contents of a training program for new commission members. S.B. 1000 (2011) awarded self-directed and semi-independent status to TREC and the Texas Appraiser Licensing and Certification Board. This permits the agencies to keep the licensing fees they receive and requires them to cover their operating expenses without state appropriations.

SUBCHAPTER C. ADMINISTRATOR AND OTHER COMMISSION PERSONNEL

§ 1101.101. Administrator and Other Personnel

(a) The commission shall appoint an administrator.
(b) The commission may designate a subordinate officer as assistant administrator to act for the administrator in the administrator's absence.
(c) The commission may employ other subordinate officers and employees necessary to administer and enforce this chapter and Chapter 1102, including a general counsel, attorneys, investigators, and support staff.
(d) The commission shall determine the salaries of the administrator, officers, and employees of the commission.
(Revised, S.B. 1000, 2011.)

§ 1101.102. Division of Responsibilities

The commission shall develop and implement policies that clearly separate the policymaking responsibilities of the commission and the management responsibilities of the administrator and the staff of the commission.

§ 1101.103. Code of Ethics; Standards of Conduct

Each member, officer, employee, and agent of the commission is subject to the code of ethics and standards of conduct imposed by Chapter 572, Government Code.

§1101.104. Qualifications and Standards of Conduct Information

The commission shall provide, as often as necessary, to its members and employees information regarding their:
(1) qualifications for office or employment under this chapter and Chapter 1102; and
(2) responsibilities under applicable laws relating to standards of conduct for state officers or employees.

§ 1101.105. Career Ladder Program; Performance Evaluations

(a) The administrator or the administrator's designee shall develop an intra-agency career ladder program. The program must require intra-agency postings of all nonentry level positions concurrently with any public posting.
(b) The administrator or the administrator's designee shall develop a system of annual performance evaluations. All merit pay for commission employees must be based on the system established under this subsection.

§ 1101.106. Equal Employment Opportunity Policy; Report

(a) The administrator or the administrator's designee shall prepare and maintain a written policy statements to ensure implementation of an equal employment opportunity program under which all personnel transactions are made without regard to race, color, disability, sex, religion, age, or national origin. The policy statement must include:

(1) personnel policies, including policies relating to recruitment, evaluation, selection, appointment, training, and promotion of personnel;

(2) a comprehensive analysis of the commission workforce that meets federal and state guidelines;

(3) procedures by which a determination can be made of significant underuse in the commission workforce of all persons for whom federal or state guidelines encourage a more equitable balance; and

(4) reasonable methods to appropriately address those areas of underuse.

(b) A policy statement prepared under Subsection (a) must:

(1) cover an annual period;

(2) be updated at least annually; and

(3) be filed with the governor.

(c) The governor shall deliver a biennial report to the legislature based on the information received under Subsection (b). The report may be made separately or as a part of other biennial reports made to the legislature.

IN PRACTICE Subchapter C provides for the employment of personnel for the day-to-day administration of the License Act. Chapter 1102 of the Texas Occupations Code, referred to in a 1101.101(c), is the law that regulates real estate inspectors and establishes the educational and examination requirements for licensing of **professional inspectors**, **real estate inspectors** (who are under the indirect supervision of a professional inspector), and **apprentice inspectors** (who are under the direct supervision of a professional inspector). Disciplinary proceedings and enforcement provisions are included, along with the stipulation that all inspectors are required to use a standard report form. Inspectors are prohibited by law from doing the following:

- Accepting an assignment for real property inspection if the employment or a fee is contingent on reporting a specific, predetermined condition of the property

- Acting in a manner that is dishonest or fraudulent or involves deceit or misrepresentation

- Acting in the dual capacity of inspector and undisclosed principal, broker, or salesperson

- Performing repairs or maintenance in connection with a real estate inspection under an earnest money contract, lease, or exchange of real property

The full text of the inspectors law may be obtained at the TREC website: www.trec.texas. gov; choose "Forms, Laws, and Contracts" and "Real Estate License Act."

SUBCHAPTER D. COMMISSION POWERS AND DUTIES

§ 1101.151. General Powers and Duties of Commission

(a) The commission shall:

(1) administer this chapter and Chapter 1102;

(2) adopt rules and establish standards relating to permissible forms of advertising by a license holder acting as a residential rental locator;

(3) maintain a registry of certificate holders; and

(4) design and adopt a seal.

(b) The commission may:

(1) adopt and enforce rules necessary to administer this chapter and Chapter 1102; and

(2) establish standards of conduct and ethics for persons licensed under this chapter and Chapter 1102 to:

(A) fulfill the purposes of this chapter and Chapter 1102; and

(B) ensure compliance with this chapter and Chapter 1102.

§ 1101.152. Fees

(a) The commission shall adopt rules to charge and collect fees in amounts reasonable and necessary to cover the costs of administering this chapter, including a fee for:

(1) filing an original application for a broker license;

(2) annual renewal of a broker license;

(3) filing an original application for a salesperson license;

(4) annual renewal of a salesperson license;

(5) annual registration;

(6) filing an application for a license examination;

(7) filing a request for a branch office license;

(8) filing a request for a change of place of business, change of name, return to active status, or change of sponsoring broker;

(9) filing a request to replace a lost or destroyed license or certificate of registration;

(10) filing an application for approval of an education program under Subchapter G;

(11) annual operation of an education program under Subchapter G;

(12) filing an application for approval of an instructor of core real estate courses;

(13) transcript evaluation;

(14) preparing a license or registration history;

(15) filing an application for a moral character determination; and

(16) conducting a criminal history check for issuing or renewing a license.

(b) The commission shall adopt rules to set and collect fees in amounts reasonable and necessary to cover the costs of implementing the continuing education requirements for license holders, including a fee for:

(1) an application for approval of a continuing education provider;

(2) an application for approval of a continuing education course of study;

(3) an application for approval of an instructor of continuing education courses; and

(4) attendance at a program to train instructors of a continuing education course prescribed under Section 1101.455.

(c) Notwithstanding Subsection (a), if the commission issues an original inactive salesperson license under Section 1101.363(b) to a salesperson who is not sponsored by a licensed broker and the salesperson is subsequently sponsored by a licensed broker, the commission may not charge:

(1) the salesperson a fee for filing a request to place the salesperson license on active status; or

(2) the broker a fee for filing a request to sponsor a salesperson.

§ 1101.153. Fee Increase

(a) The fee for filing an original application for an individual broker license and the fee for annual renewal of an individual broker license is the amount of the fee set by the commission under Section 1101.152 and a fee increase of $200.

(b) Of each fee increase collected under Subsection (a):

(1) $50 shall be transmitted to Texas A&M University for deposit in a separate banking account that may be appropriated only to support, maintain, and carry out the purposes, objectives, and duties of the Texas Real Estate Research Center;

(2) $50 shall be deposited to the credit of the foundation school fund; and

(3) $100 shall be deposited to the credit of the general revenue fund.

§ 1101.154. Additional Fee: Texas Real Estate Research Center

(a) The fee for the issuance or renewal of a:

(1) broker license is the amount of the fee set under Sections 1101.152 and 1101.153 and an additional $20 fee;

(2) salesperson license is the amount of the fee set under Section 1101.152 and an additional $20 fee; and

(3) certificate of registration is the amount of the fee set under Section 1101.152 and an additional $20 fee.

(b) The commission shall transmit quarterly the additional fees collected under Subsection (a) to Texas A&M University for deposit in a separate banking account that may be appropriated only to support, maintain, and carry out the purposes, objectives, and duties of the Texas Real Estate Research Center.

§ 1101.155. Rules Relating to Contract Forms

(a) The commission may adopt rules in the public's best interest that require license holders to use contract forms prepared by the Texas Real Estate Broker-Lawyer Committee and adopted by the commission.

(b) The commission may not prohibit a license holder from using for the sale, exchange, option, or lease of an interest in real property a contract form that is:

(1) prepared by the property owner; or

(2) prepared by an attorney and required by the property owner.

(c) A listing contract form adopted by the commission that relates to the contractual obligations between a seller of real estate and a license holder acting as an agent for the seller must include:

(1) a provision informing the parties to the contract that real estate commissions are negotiable; and

(2) a provision explaining the availability of Texas coastal natural hazards information important to coastal residents, if that information is appropriate.

§ 1101.156. Rules Restricting Advertising or Competitive Bidding

(a) The commission may not adopt a rule restricting advertising or competitive bidding by a person regulated by the commission except to prohibit a false, misleading, or deceptive practice by the person.

(b) The commission may not include in rules to prohibit false, misleading, or deceptive practices by a person regulated by the commission a rule that:

(1) restricts the use of any advertising medium;

(2) restricts the person's personal appearance or use of the person's voice in an advertisement;

(3) relates to the size or duration of an advertisement used by the person; or

(4) restricts the person's advertisement under a trade name.

§ 1101.157. Subpoena Authority

(a) The commission may request and, if necessary, compel by subpoena:

(1) the attendance of witnesses for examination under oath; and

(2) the production for inspection and copying of records, documents, and other evidence relevant to the investigation of an alleged violation of this chapter.

(b) A subpoena may be issued throughout the state and may be served by any person designated by the commission.

(c) If a person fails to comply with a subpoena issued under this section, the commission, acting through the attorney general, may file suit to enforce the subpoena in a district court in Travis County or in the county in which a hearing conducted by the commission may be held.

(d) The court shall order compliance with the subpoena if the court finds that good cause exists to issue the subpoena.

§ 1101.158. Advisory Committees

(a) The commission may appoint advisory committees to perform the advisory functions assigned to the committees by the commission. An advisory committee under this section is subject to Section 2110, Government Code.

(b) A member of an advisory committee who is not a member of the commission may not receive compensation for service on the committee. The member may receive reimbursement for actual and necessary expenses incurred in performing committee functions as provided by Section 2110.004, Government Code.

(c) A member of an advisory committee serves at the will of the commission.

(d) An advisory committee may hold a meeting by telephone conference call or other video or broadcast technology.

(e) Advisory committee meetings are subject to Chapter 551, Government Code.

§ 1101.159. Use of Technology

The commission shall implement a policy requiring the commission to use appropriate technological solutions to improve the commission's ability to perform its functions. The policy must ensure that the public is able to interact with the commission on the internet.

§ 1101.160. Negotiated Rulemaking and Alternative Dispute Resolution Procedures

(a) The commission shall develop and implement a policy to encourage the use of:

> (1) negotiated rulemaking procedures under Chapter 2008, Government Code, for the adoption of commission rules; and
>
> (2) appropriate alternative dispute resolution procedures under Chapter 2009, Government Code, to assist in the resolution of internal and external disputes under the commission's jurisdiction.

(b) The commission's procedures relating to alternative dispute resolution must conform, to the extent possible, to any model guidelines issued by the State Office of Administrative Hearings for the use of alternative dispute resolution by state agencies.

(c) The commission shall designate a trained person to:

> (1) coordinate the implementation of the policy adopted under Subsection (a);
>
> (2) serve as a resource for any training needed to implement the procedures for negotiated rulemaking or alternative dispute resolution; and
>
> (3) collect data concerning the effectiveness of those procedures, as implemented by the commission.

§1101.161. Gifts, Grants, and Donations

The commission may solicit and accept a gift, grant, donation, or other item of value from any source to pay for any activity under this chapter or Chapter 1102 or 1103.

(Added, S.B. 747, 2011.)

IN PRACTICE Subchapter D outlines the duties of the Texas Real Estate Commission, among them to adopt and enforce rules necessary to administer the License Act and to establish standards of conduct and ethics for persons licensed under the act. The rules adopted by TREC are quite extensive and have the net effect of law on licensees.

TRELA Section 1101.152 lists the fees that can be charged by TREC, and Rule 535.101 specifies the amount for each fee, as set by TREC. Section 1101.154 provides for the collection of fees to support the Texas Real Estate Research Center (now the Real Estate Center) at Texas A&M University.

SUBCHAPTER E. PUBLIC INTEREST INFORMATION AND COMPLAINT PROCEDURES

§ 1101.201. Public Interest Information

(a) The commission shall prepare information of public interest describing the functions of the commission.

(b) The commission shall make the information available to the public and appropriate state agencies.

§ 1101.202. Complaints

(a) The commission by rule shall establish methods by which consumers and service recipients are notified of the name, mailing address, and telephone number of the commission for the purpose of directing a complaint to the commission. The commission may provide for that notice:

(1) on each application for a license or certificate of registration or written contract for services of a person regulated under this chapter or Chapter 1102;

(2) on a sign prominently displayed in the place of business of each person regulated under this chapter or Chapter 1102;

(3) in a bill for services provided by a person regulated under this chapter or Chapter 1102;

(4) in conjunction with the notice required by Section 1101.615; or

(5) to be prominently displayed on the internet website of a person regulated under this chapter or Chapter 1102.

(b) The commission shall provide to a person who files a complaint with the commission relating to a license holder and to the license holder against whom the complaint is filed:

(1) an explanation of the remedies that are available to the person under this chapter; and

(2) information about appropriate state or local agencies or officials with whom the person may file a complaint.

§ 1101.203. Complaint Information

(a) The commission shall maintain a system to promptly and efficiently act on complaints filed with the commission. The commission shall maintain a file on each complaint. The file must include:

(1) information relating to the parties to the complaint;

(2) the subject matter of the complaint;

(3) a summary of the results of the review or investigation of the complaint; and

(4) the disposition of the complaint.

(b) The commission shall make information available describing its procedures for complaint investigation and resolution.

(c) The commission shall periodically notify the parties to the complaint of the status of the complaint until final disposition, unless the notice would jeopardize an undercover investigation authorized under Section 1101.204.

§ 1101.204. Complaint Investigation and Disposition

(a) The commission or commission staff may file a complaint and conduct an investigation as necessary to enforce this chapter, Chapter 1102, or a rule adopted under those chapters.

(b) The commission shall investigate the actions and records of a license holder if:

(1) a person submits a signed, written complaint; and

(2) the complaint and any evidence presented with the complaint provide reasonable cause for an investigation.

(c) The commission may not conduct an investigation of a person licensed under this chapter or Chapter 1102 in connection with a complaint submitted later than the fourth anniversary of the date of the incident that is the subject of the complaint.

(d) The commission shall promptly provide a written notice to a person licensed under this chapter or Chapter 1102 who is the subject of an investigation unless after deliberation the commission decides against notification.

(e) Notwithstanding any other provision of this chapter, an undercover or covert investigation may not be conducted unless the commission expressly authorizes the investigation after considering the circumstances and determining that the investigation is necessary to implement this chapter.

(f) An investigation or other action against a person licensed under this chapter or Chapter 1102 may not be initiated on the basis of an anonymous complaint.

(g) Repealed, 2007.

(h) The commission shall ensure that the commission gives priority to the investigation of a complaint filed by a consumer and an enforcement case resulting from the consumer complaint. The commission shall assign priorities and investigate complaints using a risk-based approach based on the:

   (1) degree of potential harm to a consumer;

   (2) potential for immediate harm to a consumer;

   (3) overall severity of the allegations in the complaint;

   (4) number of license holders potentially involved in the complaint;

   (5) previous complaint history of the license holder; and

   (6) number of potential violations in the complaint.

§ 1101.205. Complaint Investigation of Certificate Holder

The commission shall investigate a signed complaint received by the commission that relates to an act of a certificate holder or a person required to hold a certificate under Subchapter K.

§ 1101.206. Public Participation

(a) The commission shall develop and implement policies that provide the public with a reasonable opportunity to appear before the commission and to speak on any issue under the commission's jurisdiction.

(b) The commission shall prepare and maintain a written plan that describes how a person who does not speak English or who has a physical, mental, or developmental disability may be provided reasonable access to the commission's programs.

IN PRACTICE   Subchapter E establishes the procedures for notifying the public about filing complaints. In addition, it outlines the action taken by the commission when a written complaint is filed against a licensee or certificate holder. The statute of limitations for investigating a complaint is four years.

SUBCHAPTER F. TEXAS REAL ESTATE BROKER-LAWYER COMMITTEE

§ 1101.251. Definition of Committee

In this subchapter, "committee" means the Texas Real Estate Broker-Lawyer Committee.

§ 1101.252. Committee Membership

(a) The Texas Real Estate Broker-Lawyer Committee consists of 13 members appointed as follows:
    (1) six members appointed by the commission;
    (2) six members of the State Bar of Texas appointed by the president of the state bar; and
    (3) one public member appointed by the governor.
(b) Appointments to the committee shall be made without regard to the race, creed, sex, religion, or national origin of the appointee.

§ 1101.253. Terms; Vacancies

(a) Committee members serve staggered six-year terms, with the terms of two commission appointees and two State Bar of Texas appointees expiring every two years and the term of the public member expiring every six years.
(b) A committee member shall hold office until the member's successor is appointed.
(c) If a vacancy occurs during a member's term, the entity making the original appointment shall appoint a person to fill the unexpired term.

§ 1101.254. Powers and Duties

(a) In addition to other delegated powers and duties, the committee shall draft and revise contract forms that are capable of being standardized to expedite real estate transactions and minimize controversy.
(b) The contract forms must contain safeguards adequate to protect the principals in the transaction.

IN PRACTICE   Subchapter F provides for the creation of the Texas Real Estate Broker-Lawyer Committee. It outlines the duties of the committee for drafting and revising standardized contract forms to be used by licensees. *6 years term*

SUBCHAPTER G. ACCREDITATION AND APPROVAL OF REAL ESTATE EDUCATIONAL PROGRAMS AND COURSES OF STUDY

§ 1101.301. Accreditation of Programs and Courses of Study

(a) The commission, as necessary for the administration of this chapter and Chapter 1102, may:
    (1) establish standards for the accreditation of educational programs or courses of study in real estate and real estate inspection conducted in this state, excluding programs and courses offered by accredited colleges and universities;
    (2) establish by rule reasonable criteria for the approval of real estate and real estate inspection courses; and

(3) inspect and accredit real estate and real estate inspection educational programs or courses of study.

(b) The commission shall determine whether a real estate or real estate inspection course satisfies the requirements of this chapter and Chapter 1102.

(c) In establishing accreditation standards for an educational program under Subsection (a), the commission shall adopt rules setting an examination passage rate benchmark for each category of license issued by the commission under this chapter or Chapter 1102. The benchmark must be based on the average percentage of examinees that pass the licensing exam on the first attempt. A program must meet or exceed the benchmark for each license category before the commission may renew the program's accreditation for the license category.

(d) The commission may deny an application for accreditation if the applicant owns or controls, or has previously owned or controlled, an educational program or course of study for which accreditation was revoked.

(Revised, S.B. 747, 2011.)

§ 1101.302. Bond Required

(a) In this section, "educational institution" means a school, excluding an accredited college or university, authorized by the commission under this chapter to offer a real estate or real estate inspection educational program or course of study.

(b) An educational institution shall maintain a corporate surety bond or other security acceptable to the commission that is:

    (1) in the amount of $20,000;

    (2) payable to the commission; and

    (3) for the benefit of a party who suffers damages caused by the failure of the institution to fulfill obligations related to the commission's approval.

§ 1101.303. Approval of Continuing Education Provider or Course of Study

(a) If the commission determines that an applicant for approval as a continuing education provider satisfies the requirements of this subchapter or Section 1102.205 and any rule adopted under this subchapter or Section 1102.205, the commission may authorize the applicant to offer continuing education for a two-year period.

(b) If the commission determines that an applicant for approval of a continuing education course of study satisfies the requirements of this subchapter or Section 1102.205 and any rule adopted under this subchapter or Section 1102.205, the commission may authorize the applicant to offer the course of study for a two-year period.

§ 1101.304. Examination Passage Rate Data

(a) The commission shall adopt rules regarding the collection and publication of data relating to examination passage rates for graduates of accredited educational programs.

(b) Rules adopted under this section must provide for a method to:

    (1) calculate the examination passage rate;

(2) collect the relevant data from the examination administrator or the accredited program; and

(3) post the examination passage rate data on the commission's internet website, in a manner aggregated by educational program and by license group.

(c) In determining the educational program a graduate is affiliated with for purposes of this section, the educational program is the program the graduate last attended.

§ 1101.305. Review Committee

(a) The commission may appoint a committee to review the performance of an educational program performing below the standards set by the commission under Section 1101.301. The committee shall consist of:

(1) at least one commission member;

(2) at least one member of the commission staff;

(3) individuals licensed under this chapter or Chapter 1102; and

(4) a representative from the Texas Real Estate Research Center.

(b) A committee formed under this section shall review and evaluate any factor causing an educational program's poor performance and report findings and recommendations to improve performance to the program and to the commission.

(c) A committee formed under this section may not revoke the accreditation of an educational program. The commission may temporarily suspend a program in the same manner as a license under Subchapter N.

SUBCHAPTER H. LICENSE REQUIREMENTS

§ 1101.351. License Required

(a) Unless a person holds a license issued under this chapter, the person may not:

(1) act as or represent that the person is a broker or salesperson; or

(2) act as a residential rental locator.

(a-1) Unless a business entity holds a license issued under this chapter, the business entity may not act as a broker.

(b) An applicant for a broker or salesperson license may not act as a broker or salesperson until the person receives the license evidencing that authority.

(c) A licensed salesperson may not act or attempt to act as a broker or salesperson unless the salesperson is associated with a licensed broker and is acting for that broker.

(Revised, S.B. 747, 2011.)

§ 1101.352. License Application

(a) Each applicant for a broker or salesperson license must submit an application on a form prescribed by the commission.

(b) Each applicant for a broker or salesperson license must disclose in the license application whether the applicant has:

(1) entered a plea of guilty or nolo contendere to a felony; or

(2) been convicted of a felony and the time for appeal has elapsed or the judgment or conviction has been affirmed on appeal.

(c) The disclosure under Subsection (b) must be provided even if an order has granted community supervision suspending the imposition of the sentence.

(d) At the time an application is submitted under Subsection (a), each applicant shall provide the commission with the applicant's current mailing address and telephone number, and email address if available. The applicant shall notify the commission of any change in the applicant's mailing or email address or telephone number during the time the application is pending.
(**Revised, S.B. 747, 2011.**)

§ 1101.3521. Criminal History Record Information Requirement for License

(a) The commission shall require that an applicant for a license or renewal of an unexpired license submit a complete and legible set of fingerprints, on a form prescribed by the commission, to the commission or to the Department of Public Safety for the purpose of obtaining criminal history record information from the Department of Public Safety and the Federal Bureau of Investigation.

(b) The commission shall refuse to issue a license to or renew the license of a person who does not comply with the requirement of Subsection (a).

(c) The commission shall conduct a criminal history check of each applicant for a license or renewal of a license using information:

(1) provided by the individual under this section; and

(2) made available to the commission by the Department of Public Safety, the Federal Bureau of Investigation, and any other criminal justice agency under Chapter 411, Government Code.

(d) The commission may:

(1) enter into an agreement with the Department of Public Safety to administer a criminal history check required under this section; and

(2) authorize the Department of Public Safety to collect from each applicant the costs incurred by the department in conducting the criminal history check.

§ 1101.353. Moral Character Determination

(a) If before applying for a license under this chapter a person requests that the commission determine whether the person's moral character complies with the commission's moral character requirements for licensing under this chapter and pays the fee prescribed by Section 1101.152, the commission shall make its determination of the person's moral character.

(b) Not later than the 30th day after the date the commission makes its determination, the commission shall notify the person of the determination.

(c) If a person applies for a license after receiving notice of a determination, the commission may conduct a supplemental moral character determination of the person. The supplemental determination may cover only the period after the date the person requests a moral character determination under this section.

(d) The commission may issue a provisional moral character determination. The commission by rule shall adopt reasonable terms for issuing a provisional moral character determination.

§ 1101.354. General Eligibility Requirements

To be eligible to receive a license under this chapter, a person must:
(1) at the time of application:
(A) be at least 18 years of age;
(B) be a citizen of the United States or a lawfully admitted alien; and
(C) be a resident of this state;
(2) satisfy the commission as to the applicant's honesty, trustworthiness, and integrity;
(3) demonstrate competence based on an examination under Subchapter I;
(4) complete the required courses of study, including any required core real estate courses prescribed under this chapter; and
(5) complete at least:
(A) three classroom hours of course work on federal, state, and local laws governing housing discrimination, housing credit discrimination, and community reinvestment; or
(B) three semester hours of course work on constitutional law.

§ 1101.355. Additional General Eligibility Requirements for Business Entities

(a) To be eligible for a license under this chapter, a business entity must:
(1) designate one of its managing officers as its agent for purposes of this chapter; and
(2) provide proof that the entity maintains errors and omissions insurance with a minimum annual limit of $1 million for each occurrence if the designated agent owns less than 10% of the business entity.
(b) A business entity may not act as a broker unless the entity's designated agent is a licensed broker in active status and good standing according to the commission's records.
(c) A business entity that receives compensation on behalf of a license holder must be licensed as a broker under this chapter.
(Revised, S.B. 747, 2011.)

All salesperson and broker license applicants must be fingerprinted and submit to a criminal history check.

IN PRACTICE   Senate Bill 747 amended the License Act to require licensure of all business entities, other than sole proprietorships, that engage in real estate brokerage for compensation. Before the act was amended, a partnership did not need to be licensed as long as the general partner was licensed as a broker. Under the amendment, a licensed business entity must also have E&O insurance if the designated broker owns less than 10% of the business entity. Under TREC Rule 535.50, a designated broker of a licensed business entity must be an "individual holding an active Texas real estate broker license designated by a business entity licensed by the commission to act on its behalf. The designated broker must be an officer of a corporation, a manager of a limited liability company or a general partner of a partnership." This means that the designated broker of a business entity may not be another business entity; the designated broker must be a licensed individual.

§ 1101.356. Broker License: Experience and Education Requirements

(a) An applicant for a broker license must provide to the commission satisfactory evidence that the applicant:

(1) has had at least four years of active experience in this state as a license holder during the 60 months preceding the date the application is filed;

(2) has successfully completed at least 60 semester hours, or equivalent classroom hours, of postsecondary education, including:

(A) at least 18 semester hours or equivalent classroom hours of core real estate courses, two semester hours of which must be real estate brokerage; and

(B) at least 42 hours of core real estate courses or related courses accepted by the commission.

(b-1) The commission by rule shall establish what constitutes active experience for purposes of this section and Section 1101.357.

(b) Subsection (a) does not apply to an applicant who, at the time of application, is licensed as a real estate broker by another state that has license requirements comparable to the requirements of this state.
(Revised, S.B. 747, 2011; effective January 1, 2012.)

§ 1101.357. Broker License: Alternate Experience Requirements for Certain Applicants

An applicant for a broker license who does not satisfy the experience requirements of Section 1101.356 must provide to the commission satisfactory evidence that:

(1) the applicant:

(A) is a licensed real estate broker in another state;

(B) has had at least four years of active experience in that state as a licensed real estate broker or salesperson during the 60 months preceding the date the application is filed; and

(C) has satisfied the educational requirements prescribed by Section 1101.356; or

(2) the applicant was licensed in this state as a broker in the year preceding the date the application is filed.
(Revised, S.B. 747, 2011; effective September 1, 2012.)

§ 1101.358. Salesperson License: Education Requirements

(a) An applicant for a salesperson license must provide to the commission satisfactory evidence that the applicant has completed at least 12 semester hours, or equivalent classroom hours, of postsecondary education, consisting of:

(1) at least four semester hours of core real estate courses on principles of real estate; and

(2) at least two semester hours of each of the following core real estate courses:

(A) agency law;

(B) contract law;

(C) contract forms and addendums; and

(D) real estate finance.

(b) The commission shall waive the education requirements of Subsection (a) if the applicant has been licensed in this state as a broker or salesperson within the six months preceding the date the application is filed.

(c) If an applicant for a salesperson license was licensed as a salesperson within the six months preceding the date the application is filed and the license was issued under the conditions prescribed by Section 1101.454, the commission shall require the applicant to provide the evidence of successful completion of education requirements that would have been required if the license had been maintained without interruption during the preceding six months.
(Revised, S.B. 747, 2011; effective September 1, 2012.)

§ 1101.359. Alternate Education Requirements for Certain License Holders

An applicant for a broker license who is not subject to the education requirements of Section 1101.356(a)(2) and an applicant for a salesperson license who is not subject to the education requirements of Section 1101.358 or 1101.454 must provide to the commission satisfactory evidence that the applicant has completed the number of classroom hours of continuing education that would have been required for a timely renewal under Section 1101.455 during the two years preceding the date the application is filed.

§ 1101.360. Eligibility Requirements for Certain Nonresident Applicants

(a) A resident of another state who is not a licensed real estate broker and who was formerly licensed in this state as a broker or salesperson may apply for a license under this chapter not later than the first anniversary of the date of the expiration of the former license.

(b) A nonresident applicant is subject to the same license requirements as a resident. The commission may refuse to issue a license to a nonresident applicant for the same reasons that it may refuse to issue a license to a resident applicant.

(c) A nonresident applicant must submit with the application an irrevocable consent to a legal action against the applicant in the court of any county in this state in which a cause of action may arise or in which the plaintiff may reside. The action may be commenced by service of process or pleading authorized by the laws of this state or by delivery of process on the administrator or assistant administrator of the commission. The consent must:

    (1) stipulate that the service of process or pleading is valid and binding in all courts as if personal service had been made on the nonresident in this state;

    (2) be acknowledged; and

    (3) if made by a corporation, be authenticated by its seal.

(d) A service of process or pleading served on the commission under this section shall be by duplicate copies. One copy shall be filed in the commission's office, and the other copy shall be forwarded by registered mail to the last known principal address recorded in the commission's records for the nonresident against whom the process or pleading is directed.

(e) A default judgment in an action commenced as provided by this section may not be granted:

(1) unless the commission certifies that a copy of the process or pleading was mailed to the defendant as provided by Subsection (d); and

(2) until the 21st day after the date the process or pleading is mailed to the defendant.

§ 1101.361. Additional Eligibility Requirements for Certain Nonresident Applicants

(a) Notwithstanding Section 1101.360, a nonresident applicant for a license who resides in a municipality whose boundary is contiguous at any point with the boundary of a municipality in this state is eligible to be licensed under this chapter in the same manner as a resident of this state if the nonresident has been a resident of that municipality for at least the 60 days preceding the date the application is filed.

(b) A person licensed under this section shall maintain at all times a place of business in the municipality in which the person resides or in the municipality in this state that is contiguous to the municipality in which the person resides. The place of business must meet all the requirements of Section 1101.552. A place of business located in the municipality in which the person resides is considered to be in this state.

(c) A person licensed under this section may not maintain a place of business at another location in this state unless the person complies with Section 1101.356 or 1101.357.

§ 1101.362. Waiver of License Requirements: Previous License Holders

The commission by rule may waive some or all of the requirements for a license under this chapter for an applicant who was licensed under this chapter within the six years preceding the date the application is filed.

§ 1101.363. Issuance of License

(a) The commission shall issue an appropriate license to an applicant who meets the requirements for a license.

(b) The commission may issue an inactive salesperson license to a person who applies for a salesperson license and satisfies all requirements for the license. The person may not act as a salesperson unless the person is sponsored by a licensed broker who has notified the commission as required by Section 1101.367(b). Notwithstanding Section 1101.367(b), the licensed broker is not required to pay the fee required by that subsection.

(c) A license remains in effect for the period prescribed by the commission if the license holder complies with this chapter and pays the appropriate renewal fees.

§ 1101.364. Denial of License

(a) The commission shall immediately give written notice to the applicant of the commission's denial of a license.

(b) A person whose license application is denied under this section is entitled to a hearing under Section 1101.657.

§ 1101.365. Probationary License

(a) The commission may issue a probationary license.

(b) The commission by rule shall adopt reasonable terms for issuing a probationary license.

§1101.366. Inactive License: Broker

(a) The commission may place on inactive status the license of a broker if the broker:

> (1) is not acting as a broker;
>
> (2) is not sponsoring a salesperson; and
>
> (3) submits a written application to the commission before the expiration date of the broker's license.

(b) The commission may place on inactive status the license of a broker whose license has expired if the broker applies for inactive status on a form prescribed by the commission not later than the first anniversary of the expiration date of the broker's license.

(c) A broker applying for inactive status shall terminate the broker's association with each salesperson sponsored by the broker by giving written notice to each salesperson before the 30th day preceding the date the broker applies for inactive status.

(d) A broker on inactive status:

> (1) may not perform any activity regulated under this chapter; and
>
> (2) must pay annual renewal fees.

(e) The commission shall maintain a list of each broker whose license is on inactive status.

(f) The commission shall remove a broker's license from inactive status if the broker:

> (1) submits an application to the commission;
>
> (2) pays the required fee; and
>
> (3) submits proof of attending at least 15 classroom hours of continuing education as specified by Section 1101.455 during the two years preceding the date the application under Subdivision (1) is filed.

§1101.367. Inactive License: Salesperson

(a) When the association of a salesperson with the salesperson's sponsoring broker terminates, the broker shall immediately return the salesperson license to the commission. A salesperson license returned under this subsection is inactive.

(b) The commission may remove a salesperson license from inactive status under Subsection (a) if, before the expiration date of the salesperson license, a licensed broker files a request with the commission advising the commission that the broker assumes sponsorship of the salesperson, accompanied by the appropriate fee.

(c) As a condition of returning to active status, an inactive salesperson whose license is not subject to the education requirements of Section 1101.454 must provide to the commission proof of attending at least 15 hours of continuing education as specified by Section 1101.455 during the two years preceding the date the application to return to active status is filed.

(Revised, S.B. 747, 2011.)

IN PRACTICE **License requirements** Subchapter H establishes the general and educational requirements for obtaining a real estate broker's or salesperson's license. Other than a sole proprietorship, a business entity that receives compensation on behalf of a licensee must be licensed as a broker and must have a designated agent who is an active licensed individual broker. Section 1101.3521 requires that all applicants for a license or renewal submit a set of fingerprints to the commission or to the Texas Department of Public Safety (DPS). Then the DPS and the Federal Bureau of Investigation will provide criminal history record information to the commission. In practice, license renewals require an updated background check but not fingerprinting. An applicant who has been convicted of a felony or a misdemeanor should obtain a provisional moral character determination before license application as outlined in Section 1101.353. Rules 535.52 and 541.1 list criminal offenses that demonstrate inability to represent the interest of another with honesty, trustworthiness, and integrity; among those are:

- a plea of guilty or nolo contendere to or a conviction of any offense listed in Rule 541.1 [a list of 15 specific offenses];

- failing to satisfactorily complete any term or condition of parole, supervised release, probation, or community supervision;

- providing false or misleading information to the commission;

- disciplinary action taken against, or the surrender of, any other professional or occupational license or registration, in this or any other state;

- engaging in activities for which a license or registration is required without having the legal authorization to do so, in this or any other state;

- violating any provision of the Real Estate License Act;

- violating any of the Rules of the Real Estate Commission;

- failing to pay a judgment (including any court-ordered costs, fees, penalties, or damages), that is not otherwise discharged in bankruptcy.

TREC Rules for defining *active experience* require an applicant to obtain 3,600 points of documented experience before taking the broker license exam. Different types of transactions conducted while licensed as a salesperson are worth a specified number of points (e.g., each closed sale counts as 300 points). An applicant documents points on a Qualifying Experience Report form submitted to TREC.

S.B. 747 (2011) revised the education/experience requirements for both salesperson and broker applicants. Prior to September 1, 2012, a salesperson license requires 14 semester hours, or equivalent classroom hours of postsecondary education, including: at least 4 semester hours of core real estate principles, 2 semester hours of agency law, 2 semester hours of contract law, 2 semester hours of an additional core real estate course, and 4 semester hours of core or related courses. Effective September 1, 2012, the required 12 semester hours consist of all prescribed real estate core courses. Although the number of required education hours for broker license did not change, the experience requirement increased from 2 years of active experience during the 36 months prior to application to 4 years of active experience during the 60 months before application, effective for applications on or after January 1, 2012. S.B. 747 required TREC to establish active experience requirements for broker applicants after January 1, 2012.

After education and/or experience requirements have been met, a prospective licensee must submit an application to TREC, along with copies of education verification and the appropriate fees. Unless a salesperson applicant submits a broker's sponsorship form along with the initial application, the license received after passing the examination will be an inactive license. To begin the practice of real estate, a new inactive licensee must obtain a sponsoring broker and submit a broker's sponsorship form.

Section 1101.360 provides for the licensing of a **nonresident broker**. Texas does not accept a real estate license issued by any other state. Therefore, all persons desiring to practice real estate in Texas must satisfy all of the requirements of Subchapter H of this act, whether they are applying for nonresident licensure or are relocating a real estate brokerage practice to Texas after being licensed in another state. Rule 535.57(b) does authorize the commission to waive the national portion of the license exam if the applicant has an equivalent license in another state and has passed a comparable national exam.

License renewal   Each real estate license expires on the date shown on the face of the license certificate issued to the licensee. The licensee has the responsibility to apply for renewal of a license by making proper application, paying the fee set by the commission, and completing required education within the time periods required by the act. A renewal application is timely filed if it is postmarked on or before the expiration date of the license.

Inactive license   Sections 1101.366–.367 describe the procedures for obtaining an inactive license, along with the procedures for reactivation. The license of a salesperson immediately becomes inactive upon each of the following circumstances: (1) the death of the sponsoring broker; (2) the expiration, suspension, revocation, or inactivation of the sponsoring broker's license; (3) the dissolution or forfeiture of charter or the loss of the license of the person designated as the broker, if the sponsoring broker is a business entity; or (4) broker notification in writing to the commission that the broker no longer sponsors the salesperson. Termination of sponsorship must be in writing—whether from a broker to a salesperson or from a salesperson to a broker. In addition, TREC requires the broker to "immediately return the salesperson's license or copy thereof . . . or otherwise notify the commission in writing that the sponsorship has ended" (Rule 535.121). Until a new sponsorship form for the salesperson is mailed or delivered to TREC and **Mandatory Continuing Education (MCE)** requirements are met, the salesperson's license is inactive. If a licensee has allowed his license to lapse, Section 1101.362 permits TREC to waive some or all of the education and/or examination requirements by rule for persons licensed in Texas within the previous six years; Rules 535.55-535.57 limit this period to two years.

SUBCHAPTER I. EXAMINATIONS

§ 1101.401. Examination Required

(a) The competency requirement prescribed under Section 1101.354(3) shall be established by an examination prepared or contracted for by the commission.

(b) The commission shall determine the time and place in the state for offering the examination.

(c) The examination must be of sufficient scope in the judgment of the commission to determine whether a person is competent to act as a broker or salesperson in a manner that will protect the public.

(d) The examination for a salesperson license must be less exacting and less stringent than the broker examination.

(e) The commission shall provide each applicant with study material and references on which the examination is based.

(f) An applicant must satisfy the examination requirement not later than one year after the date the license application is filed.
(**Revised, S.B. 747, 2011.**)

§ 1101.402. Waiver of Examination

The commission shall waive the examination requirement for an applicant for:

     (1) a broker license if:

          (A) the applicant was previously licensed in this state as a broker; and

(B) the application is filed before the first anniversary of the expiration date of that license; and

(2) a salesperson license if:

(A) the applicant was previously licensed in this state as a broker or salesperson; and

(B) the application is filed before the first anniversary of the expiration date of that license.

§ 1101.403. Administration of Examination; Testing Service

(a) The commission shall administer any examination required by this chapter or Chapter 1102 unless the commission enters into an agreement with a testing service to administer the examination.

(b) The commission may accept an examination administered by a testing service if the commission retains the authority to establish the scope and type of the examination.

(c) The commission may negotiate an agreement with a testing service relating to examination development, scheduling, site arrangements, administration, grading, reporting, and analysis.

(d) The commission may require a testing service to:

(1) correspond directly with license applicants regarding the administration of the examination;

(2) collect fees directly from applicants for administering the examination; or

(3) administer the examination at specific locations and specified frequencies.

The commission shall adopt rules and standards as necessary to implement this section.

§ 1101.404. Examination Results

(a) Not later than the 30th day after the date an examination is administered, the commission shall notify each examinee of the results of the examination. If an examination is graded or reviewed by a national testing service, the commission shall notify each examinee of the results of the examination not later than the 14th day after the date the commission receives the results from the testing service.

(b) If the notice of the results of an examination graded or reviewed by a national testing service will be delayed for more than 90 days after the examination date, the commission shall notify each examinee of the reason for the delay before the 90th day.

(c) If requested in writing by a person who fails an examination, the commission shall provide to the person an analysis of the person's performance on the examination.

§ 1101.405. Reexamination

An applicant who fails an examination may apply for reexamination by filing a request accompanied by the proper fee.

IN PRACTICE Subchapter I sets out the provisions for determining the competency of the license applicant. The applicant must satisfy the examination requirement within one year from the date the application is filed (§ 1101.401(f)). According to the Rules of the Texas Real Estate Commission, the examinee must show a photo ID at the exam site and will be permitted to use a silent, electronic, nonprogrammable, pocket-sized calculator without an alphabetic keyboard or communication capabilities.

Contents of salesperson and broker examinations are confidential. Obtaining or attempting to obtain specific questions or answers, removing or attempting to remove questions or answers from an examination site, or providing or attempting to provide examination questions or answers to another person (whether an individual or a school) is grounds for disapproval of a pending application.

SUBCHAPTER J. LICENSE RENEWAL

§ 1101.451. License Expiration and Renewal

(a) The commission may issue or renew a license for a period not to exceed 24 months.

(b) The commission by rule may adopt a system under which licenses expire on various dates during the year. The commission shall adjust the date for payment of the renewal fees accordingly.

(c) For a year in which the license expiration date is changed, renewal fees payable shall be prorated on a monthly basis so that each license holder pays only that portion of the fee that is allocable to the number of months during which the license is valid. On renewal of the license on the new expiration date, the total renewal fee is payable.

(d) Except as provided by Subsection (e), a renewal fee for a license under this chapter may not exceed, calculated on an annual basis, the amount of the sum of the fees established under Sections 1101.152, 1101.154, and 1101.603.

(e) A person whose license has been expired for 90 days or less may renew the license by paying to the commission a fee equal to 1½ times the required renewal fee. If a license has been expired for more than 90 days but less than six months, the person may renew the license by paying to the commission a fee equal to two times the required renewal fee.

(f) If a person's license has been expired for six months or longer, the person may not renew the license. The person may obtain a new license by submitting to reexamination and complying with the requirements and procedures for obtaining an original license.
(Revised, S.B. 747, 2011.)

§ 1101.452. Information Required for License Renewal

(a) To renew an active license that is not subject to the education requirements of Section 1101.454, the license holder must provide to the commission proof of compliance with the continuing education requirements of Section 1101.455.

(b) Each applicant for the renewal of a license must disclose in the license application whether the applicant has:

    (1) entered a plea of guilty or nolo contendere to a felony; or

    (2) been convicted of a felony and the time for appeal has elapsed or the judgment or conviction has been affirmed on appeal.

(c) The disclosure under Subsection (b) must be provided even if an order has granted community supervision suspending the imposition of the sentence.
(Revised, S.B. 747, 2011.)

A renewal notice is emailed 60–90 days before expiration of the current license; it is mailed if the licensee has no email address on file. Unexpired licenses may be renewed with a credit or debit card on the TREC website. If a renewal form is downloaded from the TREC website and mailed with a check or money order, a $20 processing fee must be included. It is a licensee's responsibility to know the license expiration date, to complete required SAE or MCE courses, to ensure that TREC has a correct email address on file, and to make a timely renewal.

§ 1101.4521. Criminal History Record Information for Renewal

An applicant for the renewal of an unexpired license must comply with the criminal history record check requirements of Section 1101.3521.

§ 1101.453. Additional Renewal Requirements for Business Entities

(a) To renew a license under this chapter, a business entity must:
(1) designate one of its managing officers as its agent for purposes of this chapter; and
(2) provide proof that the entity maintains errors and omissions insurance with a minimum annual limit of $1 million for each occurrence if the designated agent owns less than 10% of the business entity.
(b) A business entity may not act as a broker unless the entity's designated agent is a licensed broker in active status and good standing according to the commission's records.
(Revised, S.B. 747, 2011.)

§ 1101.454. Salesperson License Renewal [Salesperson Annual Education—SAE]

(a) An applicant applying for the first renewal of a salesperson license must provide to the commission satisfactory evidence of completion of at least 18 semester hours, or equivalent classroom hours, of core real estate courses.
(b) The commission may not waive the requirements for renewal under this section.
(Revised, S.B. 747, 2011.)

§ 1101.455. Continuing Education Requirements [Mandatory Continuing Education—MCE]

(a) In this section, "property tax consulting laws and legal issues" includes the Tax Code, preparation of property tax reports, the unauthorized practice of law, agency law, tax law, law relating to property tax or property assessment, deceptive trade practices, contract forms and addendums, and other legal topics approved by the commission.
(b) A license holder who is not subject to the education requirements of Section 1101.454 must attend during the term of the current license at least 15 classroom hours of continuing education courses approved by the commission.
(Revised, S.B. 747, 2011.)
(c) The commission by rule may:
(1) prescribe the title, content, and duration of continuing education courses that a license holder must attend to renew a license; and
(2) approve as a substitute for the classroom attendance required by Subsection (b):
(A) relevant educational experience; and
(B) correspondence courses.
(d) In addition, the commission may approve supervised video instruction as a course that may be applied toward satisfaction of the

classroom hours of continuing education courses required by Subsection (b).

(e) At least six of the continuing education hours required by Subsection (b) must cover the following legal topics:

(1) commission rules;

(2) fair housing laws;

(3) Property Code issues, including landlord-tenant law;

(4) agency law;

(5) antitrust laws;

(6) Subchapter E, Chapter 17, Business & Commerce Code;

(7) disclosures to buyers, landlords, tenants, and sellers;

(8) current contract and addendum forms;

(9) unauthorized practice of law;

(10) case studies involving violations of laws and regulations;

(11) current Federal Housing Administration and U.S. Department of Veterans Affairs regulations;

(12) tax laws;

(13) property tax consulting laws and legal issues; or

(14) other legal topics approved by the commission.

(f) The remaining nine hours may be devoted to other real estate-related topics approved by the commission.

(g) The commission may consider courses equivalent to those described by Subsections (e) and (f) for continuing education credit.

(h) The commission shall automatically approve the following courses as courses that satisfy the mandatory continuing education requirements of Subsection (f):

(1) core real estate courses; and

(2) real estate-related courses approved by the State Bar of Texas for minimum continuing legal education participatory credit.

(i) The commission may not require an examination for a course under this section unless the course is a correspondence course or a course offered by an alternative delivery system, including delivery by computer.

(j) Daily classroom course segments must be at least one hour and not more than 10 hours.

(k) Notwithstanding the number of hours required by Subsection (e), a member of the legislature licensed under this chapter is only required to complete three hours of continuing education on the legal topics under Subsection (e).

(l) An online course offered under this section may not be completed in less than 24 hours.

§ 1101.456. Exemption from Continuing Education Requirements for Certain Brokers

Notwithstanding any other provision of this chapter, a broker who, before October 31, 1991, qualified under former Section 7A(f), The Real Estate License Act (Article 6573a, Vernon's Texas Civil Statutes), as added by Section 1.041, Chapter 553, Acts of the 72nd Legislature, Regular Session, 1991, for an exemption from continuing education requirements is not required to comply with the mandatory continuing education requirements of this subchapter to renew the broker's license.

§ 1101.457. Deferral of Continuing Education Requirements

(a) The commission by rule may establish procedures under which an applicant may have the applicant's license issued, renewed, or returned to active status before the applicant completes continuing education requirements.

(b) The commission may require an applicant under this section to:

(1) pay a fee, not to exceed $200, in addition to any fee for late renewal of a license under this chapter; and

(2) complete the required continuing education not later than the 60th day after the date the license is issued, renewed, or returned to active status.

§ 1101.458. Additional Education Requirements for Certain License Holders.

(a) A broker who sponsors a salesperson, or a license holder who supervises another license holder, must attend during the term of the current license at least six classroom hours of broker responsibility education courses approved by the commission.

(b) The commission by rule shall prescribe the title, content, and duration of broker responsibility education courses required under this section.

(c) Broker responsibility education course hours may be used to satisfy the hours described by Section 1101.455(f).

(d) This section does not apply to a broker who is exempt from continuing education requirements under Section 1101.456.

(Added, S.B. 747, 2011.)

IN PRACTICE   Subchapter J stipulates license renewal requirements and procedures. Although TREC sends a reminder notice, failure to receive a license renewal notice does not relieve a licensee of the obligation to submit a timely renewal. However, if a licensee does let a license expire, Rule 535.93 permits renewal of a license that has been expired for less than six months. Additional fees are charged (from 1½ to 2 times the normal renewal fee) as specified in Rule 535.101. To renew a license on active status without any lapse in licensure, a salesperson must also submit a form on which a broker certifies sponsorship for the "expired" time period. This subchapter also provides that a person may not renew a license that has been expired for six months or longer without meeting the requirements for obtaining an original license and retaking the state examination. However, Rules 535.55-.57 establish specific conditions under which education, experience, and/or examination requirements may be waived for up to two years.

All licensees who have been fingerprinted for TREC are required to pay a fee for another background check with each subsequent renewal or application. An applicant who is in default on a Texas Guaranteed Student Loan Corporation repayment agreement [Rule 535.95(d)] and a person who has failed to pay child support for six months or more (H.B. 1674, 2011) may be prevented from getting a license or renewing one.

Subchapter J provides for the completion of salesperson annual education (SAE) courses for all salesperson licensees and mandatory continuing education (MCE) courses for some brokers and all salespersons as prerequisites for license renewal. If, upon initial licensure, a salesperson licensee does not have at least 18 semester hours (270 classroom hours) of core courses, the new licensee must obtain the remaining hours as SAE during the two-year initial license period, effective for renewals on or after September 1, 2012. Renewals prior to that date require completion of at least 18 semester hours, including 14 semester hours of core courses, during the first year of licensure. Documentation of SAE hours must be submitted to TREC at least 10 business days in advance of online license renewal.

MCE renewal hours become effective after a salesperson completes all SAE hours. Persons affected by MCE requirements must complete 15 classroom hours every two years prior to license renewal. At least six hours must be in nonelective legal topics: a three-hour legal update course and a three-hour legal ethics course (Rule 535.91). Core real estate courses and continuing legal education courses are accepted for elective MCE credit, as well as some professional designation courses, such as the GRI or ABR [Rule 535.92(k-l)]. Credit for an online MCE course will be awarded when the course requirements are met but not earlier than 24 hours after a student starts the course. For licenses renewed on or after September 1, 2012, a broker who sponsors a salesperson, the designated broker of a licensed business entity, or a broker or salesperson who supervises another licensee must attend at least six hours of broker responsibility education every two years, which may be used to meet MCE requirements.

Under the provisions of Rule 535.92(g), if MCE hours have not been completed by the expiration date for license renewal, TREC will renew a current license in an active status but require the licensee to pay a $200 deferral fee and complete MCE hours within 60 days after the effective date of the new license. If a licensee fails to timely pay the deferral fee or fails to complete the MCE requirements within 15 days after the 60-day period, the license will be placed on inactive status. To reactivate the license, the licensee must pay a $250 late-reporting fee, pay the original $200 deferral fee, complete the MCE requirements, certify that the licensee has not engaged in real estate brokerage activity, and pay the appropriate license reactivation fee.

Figure 7.1 summarizes prelicensing and license-renewal requirements.

SUBCHAPTER K. CERTIFICATE REQUIREMENTS

§ 1101.501. Certificate Required

A person may not sell, buy, lease, or transfer an easement or right-of-way for another, for compensation or with the expectation of receiving compensation, for use in connection with telecommunication, utility, railroad, or pipeline service unless the person:
(1) holds a license issued under this chapter; or
(2) holds a certificate of registration issued under this subchapter.

§ 1101.502. Eligibility Requirements for Certificate

(a) To be eligible to receive a certificate of registration or a renewal certificate under this subchapter, a person must be:
(1) at least 18 years of age; and
(2) a citizen of the United States or a lawfully admitted alien.
(b) To be eligible to receive a certificate of registration or a renewal certificate under this subchapter, a business entity must designate as its agent one of its managing officers who is registered under this subchapter.
(Revised S.B. 747, 2011.)

§ 1101.503. Issuance of Certificate

(a) The commission shall issue a certificate of registration to an applicant who meets the requirements for a certificate of registration.

(b) The certificate remains in effect for the period prescribed by the commission if the certificate holder complies with this chapter and pays the appropriate renewal fees.

§ 1101.504. Certificate Expiration

The duration, expiration, and renewal of a certificate of registration are subject to the same provisions as are applicable under Section 1101.451 to the duration, expiration, and renewal of a license.

§ 1101.5041. Criminal History Record Information Requirement for Certificate.

An applicant for an original certificate of registration or renewal of a certificate of registration must comply with the criminal history record check requirements of Section 1101.3521.
(Added, S.B. 747, 2011.)

§ 1101.505. Denial of Certificate

The denial of a certificate of registration is subject to the same provisions as are applicable under Section 1101.364 to the denial of a license.

§ 1101.506. Change of Address

Not later than the 10th day after the date a certificate holder moves its place of business from a previously designated address, the holder shall:
(1) notify the commission of the move; and
(2) obtain a new certificate of registration that reflects the address of the new place of business.

§ 1101.507. Display of Certificate

A certificate holder shall prominently display at all times the holder's certificate of registration in the holder's place of business.

IN PRACTICE   Subchapter K requires a *right-of-way agent* to register with the Texas Real Estate Commission unless the person is licensed as a real estate broker or salesperson. A right-of-way agent is a person who sells, buys, leases, or transfers an easement or right-of-way for another for compensation.

SUBCHAPTER L. PRACTICE BY A LICENSE HOLDER

§ 1101.551. Definitions

In this subchapter:
(1) **"Intermediary"** means a broker who is employed to negotiate a transaction between the parties to a transaction and for that purpose may act as an agent of the parties.
(2) **"Party"** means a prospective buyer, seller, landlord, or tenant or an authorized representative of a buyer, seller, landlord, or tenant, including a trustee, guardian, executor, administrator, receiver, or attorney-in-fact. The term does not include a license holder who represents a party.

Licensees are required to provide a mailing address, phone number, and email address to TREC and to report any change in the listed contact information within 10 days after the change occurs. No fee is charged for a change of mailing address.

§ 1101.552. Fixed Office Required; Change of Address; Branch Offices

(a) A resident broker shall maintain a fixed office in this state. The address of the office shall be designated on the broker's license.

(b) Not later than the 10th day after the date a broker moves from the address designated on the broker's license, the broker shall submit an application, accompanied by the appropriate fee, for a license that designates the new location of the broker's office. The commission shall issue a license that designates the new location if the new location complies with the requirements of this section.

(c) A broker who maintains more than one place of business in this state shall obtain a branch office license for each additional office maintained by the broker by submitting an application, accompanied by the appropriate fee.

(d) A nonresident licensed broker is not required to maintain a place of business in this state.

(e) A license holder shall provide the commission with the license holder's current mailing address and telephone number, and email address if available. A license holder shall notify the commission of a change in the license holder's mailing or email address or telephone number.

(Revised, S.B. 747, 2011.)

§ 1101.553. Display of License

A residential rental locator shall prominently display in a place accessible to clients and prospective clients:

(1) the locator's license;

(2) a statement that the locator is licensed by the commission; and

(3) the name, mailing address, and telephone number of the commission as provided by Section 1101.202(a).

§ 1101.554. Copy of Salesperson License

The commission shall deliver or mail a copy of each salesperson license to the broker with whom the salesperson is associated.

(Revised, S.B. 747, 2011.)

§ 1101.555. Notice to Buyer Regarding Abstract or Title Policy

When an offer to purchase real estate in this state is signed, a license holder shall advise each buyer, in writing, that the buyer should:

(1) have the abstract covering the real estate that is the subject of the contract examined by an attorney chosen by the buyer; or

(2) be provided with or obtain a title insurance policy.

§ 1101.556. Disclosure of Certain Information Relating to Occupants

Notwithstanding other law, a license holder is not required to inquire about, disclose, or release information relating to whether:

(1) a previous or current occupant of real property had, may have had, has, or may have AIDS, an HIV-related illness, or an HIV infection as defined by the Centers for Disease Control and Prevention of the United States Public Health Service; or

(2) a death occurred on a property by natural causes, suicide, or accident unrelated to the condition of the property.

§ 1101.557. Acting as Agent; Regulation of Certain Transactions

(a) A broker who represents a party in a real estate transaction or who lists real estate for sale under an exclusive agreement for a party is that party's agent.

(b) A broker described by Subsection (a):

(1) may not instruct another broker to directly or indirectly violate Section 1101.652(b)(22);

(2) must inform the party if the broker receives material information related to a transaction to list, buy, sell, or lease the party's real estate, including the receipt of an offer by the broker; and

(3) shall, at a minimum, answer the party's questions and present any offer to or from the party.

(c) For the purposes of this section:

(1) a license holder who has the authority to bind a party to a lease or sale under a power of attorney or a property management agreement is also a party to the lease or sale;

(2) an inquiry to a person described by Section 1101.005(6) about contract terms or forms required by the person's employer does not violate Section 1101.652(b)(22) if the person does not have the authority to bind the employer to the contract; and

(3) the sole delivery of an offer to a party does not violate Section 1001.652(b)(22) if:

(A) the party's broker consents to the delivery;

(B) a copy of the offer is sent to the party's broker, unless a governmental agency using a sealed bid process does not allow a copy to be sent; and

(C) the person delivering the offer does not engage in another activity that directly or indirectly violates Section 1101.652(b)(22).

§1101.558. Representation Disclosure

(a) In this section, "substantive dialogue" means a meeting or written communication that involves a substantive discussion relating to specific real property. The term does not include:

(1) a meeting that occurs at a property that is held open for any prospective buyer or tenant; or

(2) a meeting or written communication that occurs after the parties to a real estate transaction have signed a contract to sell, buy, or lease the real property concerned.

(b) A license holder who represents a party in a proposed real estate transaction shall disclose, orally or in writing, that representation at the time of the license holder's first contact with:

(1) another party to the transaction; or

(2) another license holder who represents another party to the transaction.

(c) A license holder shall provide to a party to a real estate transaction at the time of the first substantive dialogue with the party the written statement prescribed by Subsection (d) unless:

    (1) the proposed transaction is for a residential lease for not more than one year and a sale is not being considered; or

    (2) the license holder meets with a party who is represented by another license holder.

(d) The written statement required by Subsection (c) must be printed in a format that uses at least 10-point type and read as follows:

"Before working with a real estate broker, you should know that the duties of a broker depend on whom the broker represents. If you are a prospective seller or landlord (owner) or a prospective buyer or tenant (buyer), you should know that the broker who lists the property for sale or lease is the owner's agent. A broker who acts as a subagent represents the owner in cooperation with the listing broker. A broker who acts as a buyer's agent represents the buyer. A broker may act as an intermediary between the parties if the parties consent in writing. A broker can assist you in locating a property, preparing a contract or lease, or obtaining financing without representing you. A broker is obligated by law to treat you honestly.

"IF THE BROKER REPRESENTS THE OWNER: The broker becomes the owner's agent by entering into an agreement with the owner, usually through a written listing agreement, or by agreeing to act as a subagent by accepting an offer of subagency from the listing broker. A subagent may work in a different real estate office. A listing broker or subagent can assist the buyer but does not represent the buyer and must place the interests of the owner first. The buyer should not tell the owner's agent anything the buyer would not want the owner to know because an owner's agent must disclose to the owner any material information known to the agent.

"IF THE BROKER REPRESENTS THE BUYER: The broker becomes the buyer's agent by entering into an agreement to represent the buyer, usually through a written buyer representation agreement. A buyer's agent can assist the owner but does not represent the owner and must place the interests of the buyer first. The owner should not tell a buyer's agent anything the owner would not want the buyer to know because a buyer's agent must disclose to the buyer any material information known to the agent.

"IF THE BROKER ACTS AS AN INTERMEDIARY: A broker may act as an intermediary between the parties if the broker complies with The Texas Real Estate License Act. The broker must obtain the written consent of each party to the transaction to act as an intermediary. The written consent must state who will pay the broker and, in conspicuous bold or underlined print, set forth the broker's obligations as an intermediary. The broker is required to treat each party honestly and fairly and to comply with The Texas Real Estate License Act. A broker who acts as an intermediary in a transaction: (1) shall treat all parties honestly; (2) may not disclose that the owner will accept a price less than the asking price unless authorized in writing to do so by the owner; (3) may not disclose that the buyer will pay a price greater than the price submitted in a written offer unless authorized in writing to do so by the buyer; and (4) may not disclose any confidential information or any information that a party specifically instructs the broker in writing not to disclose unless authorized in writing to disclose the information or required to do so by The Texas Real Estate License Act or a court order or if the information materially relates to the condition of the property. With the parties' consent, a broker acting as an intermediary between the parties may appoint a person who is licensed under The Texas Real Estate License Act and associated with the broker to communicate with and carry

out instructions of one party and another person who is licensed under that Act and associated with the broker to communicate with and carry out instructions of the other party.

"If you choose to have a broker represent you, you should enter into a written agreement with the broker that clearly establishes the broker's obligations and your obligations. The agreement should state how and by whom the broker will be paid. You have the right to choose the type of representation, if any, you wish to receive. Your payment of a fee to a broker does not necessarily establish that the broker represents you. If you have any questions regarding the duties and responsibilities of the broker, you should resolve those questions before proceeding."

(e) The license holder may substitute "buyer" for "tenant" and "seller" for "landlord" as appropriate in the written statement prescribed by Subsection (d).

§ 1101.559. Broker Acting as Intermediary

(a) A broker may act as an intermediary between parties to a real estate transaction if:

(1) the broker obtains written consent from each party for the broker to act as an intermediary in the transaction; and

(2) the written consent of the parties states the source of any expected compensation to the broker.

(b) A written listing agreement to represent a seller or landlord or a written agreement to represent a buyer or tenant that authorizes a broker to act as an intermediary in a real estate transaction is sufficient to establish written consent of the party to the transaction if the written agreement specifies in conspicuous bold or underlined print the conduct that is prohibited under Section 1101.651(d).

(c) An intermediary shall act fairly and impartially. Appointment by a broker acting as an intermediary of an associated license holder under Section 1101.560 to communicate with, carry out the instructions of, and provide opinions and advice to the parties to whom that associated license holder is appointed is a fair and impartial act.

§ 1101.560. Associated License Holder Acting as Intermediary

(a) A broker who complies with the written consent requirements of Section 1101.559 may appoint:

(1) a license holder associated with the broker to communicate with and carry out instructions of one party to a real estate transaction; and

(2) another license holder associated with the broker to communicate with and carry out instructions of any other party to the transaction.

(b) A license holder may be appointed under this section only if:

(1) the written consent of the parties under Section 1101.559 authorizes the broker to make the appointment; and

(2) the broker provides written notice of the appointment to all parties involved in the real estate transaction.

(c) A license holder appointed under this section may provide opinions and advice during negotiations to the party to whom the license holder is appointed.

§ 1101.561. Duties of Intermediary Prevail

(a) The duties of a license holder acting as an intermediary under this subchapter supersede the duties of a license holder established under any other law, including common law.

(b) A broker must agree to act as an intermediary under this subchapter if the broker agrees to represent in a transaction:

(1) a buyer or tenant; and

(2) a seller or landlord.

IN PRACTICE   Subchapter L describes requirements for a broker's maintaining a fixed office address and mandates title notice and property disclosures. In addition, it defines the agency relationships that may exist between brokers and buyers, sellers, landlords, or tenants, as described in Chapter 5.

SUBCHAPTER M. REAL ESTATE RECOVERY TRUST ACCOUNT

§ 1101.601. Real Estate Recovery Trust Account

(a) The commission shall maintain a real estate **recovery trust account** to reimburse aggrieved persons who suffer actual damages caused by an act described by Section 1101.602 committed by:

(1) a license holder;

(2) a certificate holder; or

(3) a person who does not hold a license or certificate and who is an employee or agent of a license or certificate holder.

(b) The license or certificate holder must have held the license or certificate at the time the act was committed.

§ 1101.602. Entitlement to Reimbursement

An aggrieved person is entitled to reimbursement from the trust account if a person described by Section 1101.601 engages in conduct described by Section 1101.652(a)(3) or (b) or 1101.653(1), (2), (3), or (4).

§ 1101.603. Payments into Trust Account

(a) In addition to other fees required by this chapter, an applicant for an original license must pay a fee of $10.

(b) In addition to other fees required by this chapter, an applicant for an original certificate of registration or renewal certificate must pay a fee of $50.

(c) The commission shall deposit to the credit of the trust account:

(1) fees collected under Subsections (a) and (b); and

(2) an administrative penalty collected under Subchapter O for a violation by a person licensed as a broker or salesperson.

(d) An administrative penalty collected under Subchapter O for a violation by a person who is not licensed under this chapter or Chapter 1102 shall be deposited to the credit of the trust account or the real estate inspection recovery fund, as determined by the commission.

(e) On a determination by the commission at any time that the balance in the trust account is less than $1 million, each license holder at the next license renewal must pay, in addition to the renewal fee, a fee that is equal to the lesser of $10 or a pro rata share of the amount necessary to obtain a balance in the trust account of $1.7 million. The commission shall deposit the additional fee to the credit of the trust account.

(f) To ensure the availability of a sufficient amount to pay anticipated claims on the trust account, the commission by rule may provide for the collection of assessments at different times and under conditions other than those specified by this chapter.

§ 1101.604. Management of Trust Account

(a) The commission shall hold money credited to the trust account in trust to carry out the purpose of the trust account.

(b) Money credited to the trust account may be invested in the same manner as money of the Employees Retirement System of Texas, except that an investment may not be made that would impair the liquidity necessary to make payments from the trust account as required by this subchapter.

(c) Interest from the investments shall be deposited to the credit of the trust account.

(d) If the balance in the trust account on December 31 of a year is more than the greater of $3.5 million or the total amount of claims paid from the trust account during the preceding four fiscal years, the commission shall transfer the excess amount of money in the trust account to the credit of the general revenue fund.

§ 1101.605. Deadline for Action; Notice to Commission

(a) An action for a judgment that may result in an order for payment from the trust account may not be brought after the second anniversary of the date the cause of action accrues.

(b) When an aggrieved person brings an action for a judgment that may result in an order for payment from the trust account, the license or certificate holder against whom the action is brought shall notify the commission in writing of the action.

§ 1101.606. Claim for Payment from Trust Account

(a) Except as provided by Subsection (c), an aggrieved person who obtains a court judgment against a license or certificate holder for an act described by Section 1101.602 may, after final judgment is entered, execution returned nulla bona, and a judgment lien perfected, file a verified claim in the court that entered the judgment.

(b) After the 20th day after the date the aggrieved person gives written notice of the claim to the commission and judgment debtor, the person may apply to the court that entered the judgment for an order for payment from the trust account of the amount unpaid on the judgment. The court shall proceed promptly on the application.

(c) If an aggrieved person is precluded by action of a bankruptcy court from executing a judgment or perfecting a judgment lien as required by Subsection (a), the person shall verify to the commission that the person has made a good faith effort to protect the judgment from being discharged in bankruptcy.

(d) The commission by rule may prescribe the actions necessary for an aggrieved person to demonstrate that the person has made a good faith effort under Subsection (c) to protect a judgment from being discharged in bankruptcy.

§ 1101.607. Issues at Hearing

At the hearing on the application for payment from the trust account, the aggrieved person must show:

(1) that the judgment is based on facts allowing recovery under this subchapter;

(2) that the person is not:

(A) the spouse of the judgment debtor or the personal representative of the spouse; or

(B) a license or certificate holder who is seeking to recover compensation, including a commission, in the real estate transaction that is the subject of the application for payment;

(3) that, according to the best information available, the judgment debtor does not have sufficient attachable assets in this or another state to satisfy the judgment;

(4) the amount that may be realized from the sale of assets liable to be sold or applied to satisfy the judgment; and

(5) the balance remaining due on the judgment after application of the amount under Subdivision (4).

§ 1101.608. Commission Response

(a) On receipt of notice under Section 1101.606 and the scheduling of a hearing, the commission may notify the attorney general of the commission's desire to enter an appearance, file a response, appear at a hearing, defend the action, or take any other action the commission considers appropriate.

(b) The commission and the attorney general may act under Subsection (a) only to:

(1) protect the trust account from spurious or unjust claims; or

(2) ensure compliance with the requirements for recovery under this subchapter.

(c) The commission may relitigate in the hearing any material and relevant issue that was determined in the action that resulted in the judgment in favor of the aggrieved person.

§ 1101.609. Court Order for Payment

The court shall order the commission to pay from the trust account the amount the court finds payable on the claim under this subchapter if at a hearing the court is satisfied:

(1) of the truth of each matter the aggrieved person is required by Section 1101.607 to show; and

(2) that the aggrieved person has satisfied each requirement of Sections 1101.606 and 1101.607.

§ 1101.610. Payment Limits; Attorney's Fees

(a) Payments from the trust account for claims, including attorney's fees, interest, and court costs, arising out of a single transaction may not exceed a total of $50,000, regardless of the number of claimants.

(b) Payments from the trust account for claims based on judgments against a single license or certificate holder may not exceed a total of $100,000 until the license or certificate holder has reimbursed the trust account for all amounts paid.

(c) If the court finds that the total amount of claims against a license or certificate holder exceeds the limitations in this section, the court shall proportionately reduce the amount payable on each claim.

(d) A person receiving payment from the trust account is entitled to receive reasonable attorney's fees in the amount determined by the court, subject to the limitations prescribed by this section.

§ 1101.611. Application of Judgment Recovery

An aggrieved person who receives a recovery on a judgment against a single defendant before receiving a payment from the trust account must apply the recovery first to actual damages.

§ 1101.612. Subrogation

(a) The commission is subrogated to all rights of a judgment creditor to the extent of an amount paid from the trust account, and the judgment creditor shall assign to the commission all right, title, and interest in the judgment up to that amount.

(b) The commission has priority for repayment from any subsequent recovery on the judgment.

(c) The commission shall deposit any amount recovered on the judgment to the credit of the trust account.

§ 1101.613. Effect on Disciplinary Proceedings

(a) This subchapter does not limit the commission's authority to take disciplinary action against a license or certificate holder for a violation of this chapter or a commission rule.

(b) A license or certificate holder's repayment of all amounts owed to the trust account does not affect another disciplinary proceeding brought under this chapter.

§ 1101.614. Waiver of Rights

An aggrieved person who does not comply with this subchapter waives the person's rights under this subchapter.

§ 1101.615. Notice to Consumers and Service Recipients

(a) Each license and certificate holder shall provide notice to consumers and service recipients of the availability of payment from the trust account for aggrieved persons:

(1) in conjunction with the notice required by Section 1101.202;

(2) on a written contract for the license or certificate holder's services;

(3) on a brochure that the license or certificate holder distributes;

(4) on a sign prominently displayed in the license or certificate holder's place of business;

(5) in a bill or receipt for the license or certificate holder's services; or

(6) in a prominent display on the internet website of a person regulated under this chapter.

(b) The notice must include:
(1) the commission's name, mailing address, and telephone number; and
(2) any other information required by commission rule.

IN PRACTICE   Subchapter M provides for a real estate recovery trust account. This fund is to be used to reimburse members of the public who have been financially injured or damaged by the actions of a real estate broker or salesperson, a certificate holder, or an employee or agent of a licensee. A person desiring to benefit from the trust account first must obtain a final money judgment against the offending licensee. Then to receive payment from the recovery trust account, the person must follow very specific requirements, including making a good faith effort to protect the judgment from being discharged in bankruptcy. The commission, upon making a payment from the trust account, may revoke the license of the offending licensee until the recovery trust account has been reimbursed, plus interest (§ 1101.655). License and certificate holders must inform the public of the availability of payment from the real estate recovery trust account.

SUBCHAPTER N. PROHIBITED PRACTICES AND DISCIPLINARY PROCEEDINGS

§ 1101.651. Certain Practices Prohibited

(a) A licensed broker may not pay a commission to or otherwise compensate a person directly or indirectly for performing an act of a broker unless the person is:
(1) a license holder; or
(2) a real estate broker licensed in another state who does not conduct in this state any of the negotiations for which the commission or other compensation is paid.

(b) A salesperson may not accept compensation for a real estate transaction from a person other than the broker with whom the salesperson is associated or was associated when the salesperson earned the compensation.

(c) A salesperson may not pay a commission to a person except through the broker with whom the salesperson is associated at that time.

(d) A broker and any broker or salesperson appointed under Section 1101.560 who acts as an intermediary under Subchapter L may not:
(1) disclose to the buyer or tenant that the seller or landlord will accept a price less than the asking price, unless otherwise instructed in a separate writing by the seller or landlord;
(2) disclose to the seller or landlord that the buyer or tenant will pay a price greater than the price submitted in a written offer to the seller or landlord, unless otherwise instructed in a separate writing by the buyer or tenant;
(3) disclose any confidential information or any information a party specifically instructs the broker or salesperson in writing not to disclose, unless:
(A) the broker or salesperson is otherwise instructed in a separate writing by the respective party;
(B) the broker or salesperson is required to disclose the information by this chapter or a court order; or

Licensees who hold more than a 10% interest in a property (or who are a trustee or beneficiary, or whose spouse, parent or child is a beneficiary of a trust) will be considered owners and must disclose in writing their license status when dealing with their own property. A *person related within the first degree by consanguinity* means a license holder's parent or child (Rule 535.144).

(C) the information materially relates to the condition of the property;

(4) treat a party to a transaction dishonestly; or

(5) violate this chapter.

§ 1101.652. Grounds for Suspension or Revocation of License

(a) The commission may suspend or revoke a license issued under this chapter or take other disciplinary action authorized by this chapter if the license holder:

(1) enters a plea of guilty or nolo contendere to or is convicted of a felony or a criminal offense involving fraud, and the time for appeal has elapsed or the judgment or conviction has been affirmed on appeal, without regard to an order granting community supervision that suspends the imposition of the sentence;

(2) procures or attempts to procure a license under this chapter for the license holder or a salesperson by fraud, misrepresentation, or deceit or by making a material misstatement of fact in an application for a license;

(3) engages in misrepresentation, dishonesty, or fraud when selling, buying, trading, or leasing real property in the name of:

(A) the license holder;

(B) the license holder's spouse; or

(C) a person related to the license holder within the first degree by consanguinity;

(4) fails to honor, within a reasonable time, a check issued to the commission after the commission has sent by certified mail a request for payment to the license holder's last known business address according to commission records;

(5) fails or refuses to produce on request, for inspection by the commission or a commission representative, a document, book, or record that is in the license holder's possession and relates to a real estate transaction conducted by the license holder;

(6) fails to provide, within a reasonable time, information requested by the commission that relates to a formal or informal complaint to the commission that would indicate a violation of this chapter;

(7) fails to surrender to the owner, without just cause, a document or instrument that is requested by the owner and that is in the license holder's possession;

(8) fails to use a contract form required by the commission under Section 1101.155;

(9) fails to notify the commission, not later than the 30th day after the date of a final conviction or the entry of a plea of guilty or nolo contendere, that the person has been convicted of or entered a plea of guilty or nolo contendere to a felony or a criminal offense involving fraud; or

(10) disregards or violates this chapter.

(b) The commission may suspend or revoke a license issued under this chapter or take other disciplinary action authorized by this chapter if the license holder, while acting as a broker or salesperson:

(1) acts negligently or incompetently;

> A real estate broker is responsible for acts and conduct performed by a real estate salesperson associated with or acting for the broker (Rule 535.2).

Although not a part of TRELA, three additional laws set forth prohibitions that relate to real estate promotional practices: the National Do Not Call Registry, the CAN-SPAM Act, and the Junk Fax Prevention Act. They are discussed in Chapter 13.

(2) engages in conduct that is dishonest or in bad faith or that demonstrates untrustworthiness;

(3) makes a material misrepresentation to a potential buyer concerning a significant defect, including a latent structural defect, known to the license holder that would be a significant factor to a reasonable and prudent buyer in making a decision to purchase real property;

(4) fails to disclose to a potential buyer a defect described by Subdivision (3) that is known to the license holder;

(5) makes a false promise that is likely to influence a person to enter into an agreement when the license holder is unable or does not intend to keep the promise;

(6) pursues a continued and flagrant course of misrepresentation or makes false promises through an agent or salesperson, through advertising, or otherwise;

(7) fails to make clear to all parties to a real estate transaction the party for whom the license holder is acting;

(8) receives compensation from more than one party to a real estate transaction without the full knowledge and consent of all parties to the transaction;

(9) fails within a reasonable time to properly account for or remit money that is received by the license holder and that belongs to another person;

(10) commingles money that belongs to another person with the license holder's own money;

(11) pays a commission or a fee to or divides a commission or a fee with a person other than a license holder or a real estate broker or salesperson licensed in another state for compensation for services as a real estate agent;

(12) fails to specify a definite termination date that is not subject to prior notice in a contract, other than a contract to perform property management services, in which the license holder agrees to perform services for which a license is required under this chapter;

(13) accepts, receives, or charges an undisclosed commission, rebate, or direct profit on an expenditure made for a principal;

(14) solicits, sells, or offers for sale real property by means of a lottery;

(15) solicits, sells, or offers for sale real property by means of a deceptive practice;

(16) acts in a dual capacity as broker and undisclosed principal in a real estate transaction;

(17) guarantees or authorizes or permits a person to guarantee that future profits will result from a resale of real property;

(18) places a sign on real property offering the real property for sale or lease without obtaining the written consent of the owner of the real property or the owner's authorized agent;

(19) offers to sell or lease real property without the knowledge and consent of the owner of the real property or the owner's authorized agent;

(20) offers to sell or lease real property on terms other than those authorized by the owner of the real property or the owner's authorized agent;

(21) induces or attempts to induce a party to a contract of sale or lease to break the contract for the purpose of substituting a new contract;

(22) negotiates or attempts to negotiate the sale, exchange, or lease of real property with an owner, landlord, buyer, or tenant with knowledge that that person is a party to an outstanding written contract that grants exclusive agency to another broker in connection with the transaction;

(23) publishes or causes to be published an advertisement, including an advertisement by newspaper, radio, television, the internet, or display, that misleads or is likely to deceive the public, tends to create a misleading impression, or fails to identify the person causing the advertisement to be published as a licensed broker or agent;

(24) withholds from or inserts into a statement of account or invoice a statement that the license holder knows makes the statement of account or invoice inaccurate in a material way;

(25) publishes or circulates an unjustified or unwarranted threat of a legal proceeding or other action;

(26) establishes an association by employment or otherwise with a person other than a license holder if the person is expected or required to act as a license holder;

(27) aids, abets, or conspires with another person to circumvent this chapter;

(28) fails or refuses to provide, on request, a copy of a document relating to a real estate transaction to a person who signed the document;

(29) fails to advise a buyer in writing before the closing of a real estate transaction that the buyer should:

(A) have the abstract covering the real estate that is the subject of the contract examined by an attorney chosen by the buyer; or

(B) be provided with or obtain a title insurance policy;

(30) fails to deposit, within a reasonable time, money the license holder receives as escrow agent in a real estate transaction:

(A) in trust with a title company authorized to do business in this state; or

(B) in a custodial, trust, or escrow account maintained for that purpose in a banking institution authorized to do business in this state;

(31) disburses money deposited in a custodial, trust, or escrow account, as provided in Subdivision (30), before the completion or termination of the real estate transaction;

(32) discriminates against an owner, potential buyer, landlord, or potential tenant on the basis of race, color, religion, sex, disability, familial status, national origin, or ancestry, including directing a prospective buyer or tenant interested in equivalent properties to a different area based on the race, color, religion, sex, disability,

familial status, national origin, or ancestry of the potential owner or tenant; or

(33) disregards or violates this chapter.

§ 1101.653. Grounds for Suspension or Revocation of Certificate

The commission may suspend or revoke a certificate of registration issued under this chapter if the certificate holder:

(1) engages in dishonest dealing, fraud, unlawful discrimination, or a deceptive act;

(2) makes a misrepresentation;

(3) acts in bad faith;

(4) demonstrates untrustworthiness;

(5) fails to honor, within a reasonable time, a check issued to the commission after the commission has mailed a request for payment to the certificate holder's last known address according to the commission's records;

(6) fails to provide to a party to a transaction a written notice prescribed by the commission that:

(A) must be given before the party is obligated to sell, buy, lease, or transfer a right-of-way or easement; and

(B) contains:

(i) the name of the certificate holder;

(ii) the certificate number;

(iii) the name of the person the certificate holder represents;

(iv) a statement advising the party that the party may seek representation from a lawyer or broker in the transaction; and

(v) a statement generally advising the party that the right-of-way or easement may affect the value of the property; or

(7) disregards or violates this chapter or a commission rule relating to certificate holders.

§ 1101.654. Suspension or Revocation of License or Certificate for Unauthorized Practice of Law

(a) The commission shall suspend or revoke the license or certificate of registration of a license or certificate holder who is not a licensed attorney in this state and who, for consideration, a reward, or a pecuniary benefit, present or anticipated, direct or indirect, or in connection with the person's employment, agency, or fiduciary relationship as a license or certificate holder:

(1) drafts an instrument, other than a form described by Section 1101.155, that transfers or otherwise affects an interest in real property; or

(2) advises a person regarding the validity or legal sufficiency of an instrument or the validity of title to real property.

(b) Notwithstanding any other law, a license or certificate holder who completes a contract form for the sale, exchange, option, or lease of an interest in real property incidental to acting as a broker is not engaged in the unauthorized or illegal practice of law in this state if the form was:

(1) adopted by the commission for the type of transaction for which the form is used;

(2) prepared by an attorney licensed in this state and approved by the attorney for the type of transaction for which the form is used; or

(3) prepared by the property owner or by an attorney and required by the property owner.

§ 1101.655. Revocation of License or Certificate for Claim on Account

(a) The commission may revoke a license, approval, or registration issued under this chapter or Chapter 1102 if the commission makes a payment from the real estate recovery trust account to satisfy all or part of a judgment against the license or registration holder.

(b) The commission may probate an order revoking a license under this section.

(c) A person is not eligible for a license or certificate until the person has repaid in full the amount paid from the account for the person, plus interest at the legal rate.

§ 1101.656. Additional Disciplinary Authority of Commission

(a) In addition to any other authority under this chapter, the commission may suspend or revoke a license, place on probation a person whose license has been suspended, or reprimand a license holder if the license holder violates this chapter or a commission rule.

(b) The commission may probate a suspension, revocation, or cancellation of a license under reasonable terms determined by the commission.

(c) The commission may require a license holder whose license suspension or revocation is probated to:

(1) report regularly to the commission on matters that are the basis of the probation;

(2) limit practice to an area prescribed by the commission; or

(3) continue to renew professional education until the license holder attains a degree of skill satisfactory to the commission in the area that is the basis of the probation.

§ 1101.6561. Suspension or Revocation of Educational Program Accreditation

The commission may suspend or revoke an accreditation issued under Subchapter G or take any other disciplinary action authorized by this chapter if the provider of an educational program or course of study violates this chapter or a rule adopted under this chapter.
(Added, S.B. 747, 2011.)

§ 1101.657. Hearing

(a) If the commission proposes to deny, suspend, or revoke a person's license or certificate of registration, the person is entitled to a hearing conducted by the State Office of Administrative Hearings.

(b) A hearing under this section is governed by the contested case procedures under Chapter 2001, Government Code.

§ 1101.658. Appeal

(a) A person aggrieved by a ruling, order, or decision under this sub-chapter is entitled to appeal to a district court in the county in which the administrative hearing was held.

(b) An appeal is governed by the procedures under Chapter 2001, Government Code.

§ 1101.659. Refund

(a) Subject to Subsection (b), the commission may order a person regulated by the commission to pay a refund to a consumer as provided in an agreement resulting from an informal settlement conference or an enforcement order instead of or in addition to imposing an administrative penalty or other sanctions.

(b) The amount of a refund ordered as provided in an agreement resulting from an informal settlement conference or an enforcement order may not exceed the amount the consumer paid to the person for a service or accommodation regulated by this commission. The commission may not require payment of other damages or estimate harm in a refund order.

§ 1101.660. Informal Proceedings

(a) The commission by rule shall adopt procedures governing informal disposition of a contested case.

(b) Rules adopted under this section must:

    (1) provide the complainant and the license holder, certificate holder, or regulated entity an opportunity to be heard; and

    (2) require the presence of:

        (A) a public member of the commission for a case involving a consumer complaint; and

        (B) at least two staff members of the commission with experience in the regulatory area that is the subject of the proceeding.

§ 1101.661. Final Order

The commission may issue a final order in a proceeding under this sub-chapter or Subchapter O regarding a person whose license has expired during the course of an investigation or administrative proceeding.

§ 1101.662. Temporary Suspension

(a) The presiding officer of the commission shall appoint a disciplinary panel consisting of three commission members to determine whether a person's license to practice under this chapter should be temporarily suspended.

(b) If the disciplinary panel determines from the information presented to the panel that a person licensed to practice under this chapter would, by the person's continued practice, constitute a continuing threat to the public welfare, the panel shall temporarily suspend the license of that person.

(c) A license may be suspended under this section without notice or hearing on the complaint if:

    (1) institution of proceedings for a hearing before the commission is initiated simultaneously with the temporary suspension; and

(2) a hearing is held under Chapter 2001, Government Code, and this chapter as soon as possible.

(d) Notwithstanding Chapter 551, Government Code, the disciplinary panel may hold a meeting by telephone conference call if immediate action is required and convening the panel at one location is inconvenient for any member of the panel.

IN PRACTICE Subchapter N lists possible actions by a licensee that can result in the revocation or suspension of a broker's or salesperson's license or right-of-way agent's certificate of registration. Violation of other state laws could also result in license revocation; for example, upon court order TREC must suspend a real estate license based on nonpayment of awarded child support three or more months in arrears, and TREC may not renew or reissue a license until the court or appropriate agency orders otherwise. TREC Rules further explain the following practices:

■ A licensed broker may not pay a commission to or otherwise compensate a person directly or indirectly for performing an act of a broker unless the person is licensed in Texas or licensed as a broker in another state. This means that a broker or salesperson cannot pay or share a commission with an attorney unless the attorney is also licensed as a broker or salesperson. If the broker is licensed out of state, all negotiations physically conducted within Texas must be handled by Texas licensees. Payment of referral fees to out-of-state brokers would be authorized under this Rule. (TRELA 1101.651(a); Rule 535.131(a))

■ An unlicensed person may share in the income earned by a real estate broker if the person engages in no acts for which a license is required and does not lead the public to believe that the person is in the real estate brokerage business. This Rule would apply to a broker's sharing his commission with a buyer or a seller in a transaction. (Rule 535.147(b))

■ A person may not assign to another licensee a personal service contract to which the person is a party and which obligates the person to perform acts for which a license is required without first obtaining the written consent of the other parties to the contract. A listing agreement is a contract for personal service of a licensee; therefore, it cannot be assigned without consent. (Rule 535.141(k))

■ Unless a different time to deposit earnest money is expressly agreed upon in writing by the principals to a transaction, the deposit is to be placed in a trust account maintained for that purpose or in trust with a title company *within a reasonable time*, defined by the Rules as *by the close of business of the second working day after execution of the contract*. If the earnest money check is dishonored by the bank on which it was drawn, the broker shall immediately notify all parties to the transaction. (Rule 535.159(i) and (k))

■ *Nonresident brokers* acting as real estate agents in Texas who accept money as escrow agents must deposit the money in a Texas banking institution or Texas title company. (Rule 535.159(d))

■ Disclosure of licensed status when acquiring or disposing of property as a principal may be in a sales or rental agreement or by disclosure in any other written form given before entering into any sales or rental contract. However, if an advertisement fails to identify the person placing it as a licensed broker or agent, the commission may suspend or revoke a license. (TRELA i 1101.652(a)(3) and (b)(23); Rule 535.144(b))

■ The term *advertisement* includes, but is not limited to, all publications, radio or television broadcasts, all electronic media including email, text messages, social networking websites, and the internet, business stationery, business cards, signs and billboards. Because a listing may be solicited and accepted only in a broker's name, any advertisements concerning listings must clearly and conspicuously contain the name of the broker and must not mislead or deceive the public. TREC has adopted extensive advertising regulations; see Rule 535.154 for more details.

■ Because landlord-tenant law permits automatic extensions on leases, the requirement for a definite termination date does not apply to leases (§ 1101.652(b)(12)).

■ Section 1101.654 defines the *unauthorized practice of law* by a license or certificate holder.

■ If a person has had a payment made from the Recovery Trust Account on her behalf and has had her license revoked, that person is not eligible for a real estate license until the full amount has been repaid, plus interest (§ 1101.655(c)).

If a licensee or certificate holder violates any provision of the License Act, § 1101.657 and § 1101.658 address the hearings and appeals processes, with Rules 533.3 through 533.40 providing specific procedures to be followed. Hearings are conducted by the State Office of Administrative Hearings. The commission may order a licensee or certificate holder to pay a refund to a consumer instead of or in addition to any other penalty or sanction described in Subchapters O and P. The amount of the refund may not exceed the amount that the consumer actually paid to the person for a service or accommodation.

SUBCHAPTER O. ADMINISTRATIVE PENALTY

§ 1101.701. Imposition of Administrative Penalty

(a) The commission may impose an administrative penalty on a person who violates this chapter or a rule adopted or order issued by the commission under this chapter.
(b) The commission shall periodically review the commission's enforcement procedures and ensure that administrative penalty and disciplinary proceedings are combined into a single enforcement procedure.
(c) The commission may combine a proceeding to impose an administrative penalty with another disciplinary proceeding, including a proceeding to suspend or revoke a license.

§ 1101.7015. Delegation of Administrator's Authority

The commission may authorize the administrator to delegate to another commission employee the administrator's authority to act under this subchapter.

§ 1101.702. Amount of Penalty

(a) The amount of an administrative penalty may not exceed $5,000 for each violation. Each day a violation continues or occurs may be considered a separate violation for purposes of imposing a penalty.
(b) In determining the amount of the penalty, the administrator shall consider:
　(1) the seriousness of the violation, including the nature, circumstances, extent, and gravity of the prohibited acts;
　(2) the history of previous violations;
　(3) the amount necessary to deter a future violation;
　(4) efforts to correct the violation; and
　(5) any other matter that justice may require.

(c) The commission by rule shall adopt a schedule of administrative penalties based on the criteria listed in Subsection (b) for violations subject to an administrative penalty under this section to ensure that the amount of a penalty imposed is appropriate to the violation. The rules adopted under this subsection must provide authority for the commission to suspend or revoke a license in addition to or instead of imposing an administrative penalty.

§ 1101.703. Notice of Violation and Penalty

(a) If, after investigation of a possible violation and the facts relating to that violation, the administrator determines that a violation has occurred, the administrator may issue a notice of violation stating:

(1) a brief summary of the alleged violation;

(2) the administrator's recommendation on the imposition of the administrative penalty or another disciplinary sanction, including a recommendation of the amount of the penalty; and

(3) that the respondent has the right to a hearing to contest the alleged violation, the recommended penalty, or both.

§ 1101.704. Penalty to Be Paid or Hearing Requested

(a) Not later than the 20th day after the date the person receives the notice under Section 1101.703, the person may:

(1) accept the administrator's determination, including the recommended administrative penalty; or

(2) request in writing a hearing on the occurrence of the violation, the amount of the penalty, or both.

(b) If the person accepts the administrator's determination, or fails to respond in a timely manner to the notice, the commission by order shall approve the determination and order payment of the recommended penalty or impose the recommended sanction.

§ 1101.705. Hearing; Decision

(a) If the person requests a hearing, the administrator shall set a hearing and give notice of the hearing to the person.

(b) An administrative law judge of the State Office of Administrative Hearings shall conduct the hearing. The administrative law judge shall:

(1) make findings of fact and conclusions of law; and

(2) promptly issue to the commission a proposal for decision regarding the occurrence of the violation and the amount of any proposed administrative penalty.

(c) Based on the findings of fact, conclusions of law, and proposal for decision of the administrative law judge, the commission by order may determine that:

(1) a violation occurred and impose an administrative penalty; or

(2) a violation did not occur.

(d) A proceeding under this section is subject to Chapter 2001, Government Code.

(e) The notice of the commission's order given to the person under Chapter 2001, Government Code, must include a statement of the person's right to judicial review of the order.

§ 1101.706. Notice of Order

The administrator shall give notice of the commission's order to the person. The notice must:

(1) include the findings of fact and conclusions of law, separately stated;

(2) state the amount of any penalty imposed;

(3) inform the person of the person's right to judicial review of the order; and

(4) include other information required by law.

§ 1101.707. Options Following Decision: Pay or Appeal

(a) Not later than the 30th day after the date the commission the order; and The not the person shall:

(1) pay the administrative penalty; or

(2) file a petition for judicial review contesting the occurrence of the violation, the amount of the penalty, or both.

(b) Within the 30-day period prescribed by Subsection (a), a person who files a petition for judicial review may:

(1) stay enforcement of the penalty by:

(A) paying the penalty to the court for placement in an escrow account; or

(B) giving the court a supersedes bond in a form approved by the court that:

(i) is for the amount of the penalty; and

(ii) is effective until judicial review of the order is final; or

(2) request the court to stay enforcement by:

(A) filing with the court an affidavit of the person stating that the person is financially unable to pay the penalty and is financially unable to give the supersedes as bond; and

(B) giving a copy of the affidavit to the administrator by certified mail.

(c) If the administrator receives a copy of an affidavit under Subsection (b)(2), the administrator may file with the court, within five days after the date the copy is received, a contest to the affidavit.

(d) The court shall hold a hearing on the facts alleged in the affidavit as soon as practicable and shall stay the enforcement of the penalty on finding that the alleged facts are true. The person who files an affidavit has the burden of proving that the person is financially unable to pay the penalty and to give a supersedeas bond.

§ 1101.708. Collection of Penalty

If the person does not pay the administrative penalty and the enforcement of the penalty is not stayed, the administrator may refer the matter to the attorney general for collection of the penalty.

§ 1101.7085. Determination by Court

(a) If the court sustains the determination that a violation occurred, the court may uphold or reduce the amount of the administrative penalty and order the person to pay the full or reduced amount of the penalty.

(b) If the court does not sustain the finding that a violation occurred, the court shall order that a penalty is not owed.

§ 1101.709. Remittance of Penalty and Interest

(a) If after judicial review the administrative penalty is reduced or is not upheld by the court, the court shall remit the appropriate amount, plus accrued interest, to the person if the person paid the penalty.

(b) The interest accrues at the rate charged on loans to depository institutions by the New York Federal Reserve Bank.

(c) The interest shall be paid for the period beginning on the date the penalty is paid and ending on the date the penalty is remitted.

(d) If the person gave a supersedes bond and the penalty is not upheld by the court, the court shall order, when the court's judgment becomes final, the release of the bond.

(e) If the person gave a supersedes bond and the amount of the penalty is reduced, the court shall order the release of the bond after the person pays the reduced amount.

§ 1101.710. Administrative Procedure

A proceeding under this subchapter is subject to Chapter 2001, Government Code.

SUBCHAPTER P. OTHER PENALTIES AND ENFORCEMENT PROVISIONS

§ 1101.751. Injunctive Action Brought by Commission

(a) In addition to any other action authorized by law, the commission may bring an action in its name to enjoin a violation of this chapter or a commission rule.

(b) To obtain an injunction under this section, the commission is not required to allege or prove that:

    (1) an adequate remedy at law does not exist; or

    (2) substantial or irreparable damage would result from the continued violation.

§ 1101.752. Additional Injunctive Authority

(a) In addition to any other action authorized by law, the commission, acting through the attorney general, may bring an action to abate a violation or enjoin a violation or potential violation of this chapter or a commission rule if the commission determines that a person has violated or is about to violate this chapter.

(b) The action shall be brought in the name of the state in the district court in the county in which:

    (1) the violation occurred or is about to occur; or

    (2) the defendant resides.

(c) An injunctive action may be brought to abate or temporarily or permanently enjoin an act or to enforce this chapter.

(d) The commission is not required to give a bond in an action under Subsection (a), and court costs may not be recovered from the commission.

(e) If the commission determines that a person has violated or is about to violate this chapter, the attorney general or the county attorney or district attorney in the county in which the violation has occurred or is about to occur or in the county of the defendant's residence may bring an action in the name of the state in the district court of the county to abate or temporarily or permanently enjoin the violation or to enforce this chapter. The plaintiff in an action under this subsection is not required to give a bond, and court costs may not be recovered from the plaintiff.

§ 1101.753. Civil Penalty for Certain Violations by Broker, Salesperson, or Certificate Holder

(a) In addition to injunctive relief under Sections 1101.751 and 1101.752, a person who receives a commission or other consideration as a result of acting as a broker or salesperson without holding a license or certificate of registration under this chapter is liable to the state for a civil penalty of not less than the amount of money received or more than three times the amount of money received.

(b) The commission may recover the civil penalty, court costs, and reasonable attorney's fees on behalf of the state.

(c) The commission is not required to give a bond in an action under this section, and court costs may not be recovered from the commission.

§ 1101.754. Private Cause of Action for Certain Violations by Broker, Salesperson, or Certificate Holder

(a) A person who receives a commission or other consideration as a result of acting as a broker or salesperson without holding a license or certificate of registration under this chapter is liable to an aggrieved person for a penalty of not less than the amount of money received or more than three times the amount of money received.

(b) The aggrieved person may file suit to recover a penalty under this section.

§ 1101.755. Appeal Bond Exemption

The commission is not required to give an appeal bond in an action to enforce this chapter.

§ 1101.756. General Criminal Penalty

(a) A person commits an offense if the person willfully violates or fails to comply with this chapter or a commission order.

(b) An offense under this section is a Class A misdemeanor.

§ 1101.757. Criminal Penalty for Certain Violations by Residential Rental Locator

(a) A person commits an offense if the person engages in business as a residential rental locator in this state without a license issued under this chapter.

(b) An offense under this section is a Class A misdemeanor.

§ 1101.758. Criminal Penalty for Certain Violations by Broker, Salesperson, or Certificate Holder

(a) A person commits an offense if the person acts as a broker or salesperson without holding a license under this chapter or engages in an activity for which a certificate of registration is required under this chapter without holding a certificate.

(b) An offense under this section is a Class A misdemeanor.

Prosecution for fraud in a real estate transaction can be either in the county where the property is located or in the county where the fraud was committed (S.B. 485, 2011).

§ 1101.759. Cease and Desist Order

(a) If it appears to the commission that a person is violating this chapter or Chapter 1102 or a rule adopted under this chapter or Chapter 1102, the commission, after notice and opportunity for a hearing, may issue a cease and desist order prohibiting the person from engaging in the activity.

(b) A violation of an order under this section constitutes grounds for imposing an administrative penalty under Subchapter O.

IN PRACTICE Subchapters O and P address penalties for violating the provisions of the Real Estate License Act—both for licensees and nonlicensees. Subchapter O outlines the procedures for TREC to assess an administrative penalty against anyone who violates the License Act or a TREC rule, and that penalty may be as much as $5,000 for each day a violation occurred. The complete Schedule of Administrative Penalties is set forth in Rule 535.191. The commission may suspend or revoke a license or take other disciplinary action in addition to or instead of imposing an administrative penalty.

Subchapter P, Section 1101.753 provides that an unlicensed person who receives a commission or other consideration for performing acts requiring a license is liable to the state for a civil penalty of not less than the amount of money received or more than three times the amount of money received. In addition, an aggrieved person may file a suit to recover a like amount. Timely renewal of a real estate license is crucial to a licensee's avoiding charges under these Subchapters.

Sections 1101.756–.758 stipulate that a violation of the License Act by an unlicensed person is a Class A misdemeanor. It is punishable by up to a $4,000 fine or imprisonment for a term not to exceed one year or both.

SUMMARY OF TRELA ENFORCEMENT PROVISIONS A person may file a complaint with TREC against a real estate licensee if the person believes the licensee has violated The Real Estate License Act (TRELA). The commission will generally investigate the allegations by interviewing the parties and witnesses and gathering relevant information. If TREC determines that the facts revealed in the investigation do not warrant disciplinary action but, if not corrected, could lead to further complaints and ultimately to potential disciplinary action, TREC may simply issue an advisory letter to the licensee. However, if TREC intends to initiate disciplinary proceedings, it will notify the licensee. After a hearing or other settlement procedure, the commission will render a decision. If the evidence establishes a violation of the Real Estate License Act, the commission may impose disciplinary action, which may include a reprimand, suspension of the license, revocation of the license, probation of the license, an administrative penalty, or a combination of possible actions. In addition, TREC can order a licensee to pay a refund to a consumer, may issue a cease and desist order, may seek an injunction, and may recover civil penalties on behalf of the state. If TREC's investigation indicates that a person has engaged in *unlicensed* activity, the commission may impose an administrative penalty, issue a cease and desist order, file a complaint with the appropriate law enforcement official, or take other necessary action—the outcome of which could be a fine and possible imprisonment for a Class A misdemeanor. Beyond TREC's disciplinary authority, the licensee may be subject to a lawsuit brought by an aggrieved person. Because licensees are responsible to clients, customers, and the public at large for upholding the law and maintaining high ethical standards, a thorough knowledge of the License Act is imperative to avoid sanctions for its violation.

SUBCHAPTER Q. GENERAL PROVISIONS RELATING TO LIABILITY ISSUES

§ 1101.801. Effect of Disciplinary Action on Liability

Disciplinary action taken against a person under Section 1101.652 does not relieve the person from civil or criminal liability.

§ 1101.802. Liability Relating to HIV Infection or AIDS

Notwithstanding Section 1101.801, a person is not civilly or criminally liable because the person failed to inquire about, make a disclosure relating to, or release information relating to whether a previous or current occupant of real property had, may have had, has, or may have AIDS, an HIV-related illness, or HIV infection as defined by the Centers for Disease Control and Prevention of the United States Public Health Service.

§ 1101.803. General Liability of Broker

A licensed broker is liable to the commission, the public, and the broker's clients for any conduct engaged in under this chapter by the broker or by a salesperson associated with or acting for the broker.

§ 1101.804. Liability for Providing Certain Information

A license holder or nonprofit real estate board or association that provides information about real property sales prices or the terms of a sale for the purpose of facilitating the listing, selling, leasing, financing, or appraisal of real property is not liable to another person for providing that information unless the disclosure of that information is specifically prohibited by statute.

§ 1101.805. Liability for Misrepresentation or Concealment

(a) In this section, "party" has the meaning assigned by Section 1101.551.
(b) This section prevails over any other law, including common law.
(c) This section does not diminish a broker's responsibility for the acts or omissions of a salesperson associated with or acting for the broker.
(d) A party is not liable for a misrepresentation or a concealment of a material fact made by a license holder in a real estate transaction unless the party:
    (1) knew of the falsity of the misrepresentation or concealment; and
    (2) failed to disclose the party's knowledge of the falsity of the misrepresentation or concealment.
(e) A license holder is not liable for a misrepresentation or a concealment of a material fact made by a party to a real estate transaction unless the license holder:
    (1) knew of the falsity of the misrepresentation or concealment; and
    (2) failed to disclose the license holder's knowledge of the falsity of the misrepresentation or concealment.

(f) A party or a license holder is not liable for a misrepresentation or a concealment of a material fact made by a subagent in a real estate transaction unless the party or license holder:

(1) knew of the falsity of the misrepresentation or concealment; and

(2) failed to disclose the party's or license holder's knowledge of the falsity of the misrepresentation or concealment.

§ 1101.806. Liability for Payment of Compensation or Commission

(a) This section does not:

(1) apply to an agreement to share compensation among license holders; or

(2) limit a cause of action among brokers for interference with business relationships.

(b) A person may not maintain an action to collect compensation for an act as a broker or salesperson that is performed in this state unless the person alleges and proves that the person was:

(1) a license holder at the time the act was commenced; or

(2) an attorney licensed in any state.

(c) A person may not maintain an action in this state to recover a commission for the sale or purchase of real estate unless the promise or agreement on which the action is based, or a memorandum, is in writing and signed by the party against whom the action is brought or by a person authorized by that party to sign the document.

(d) A license holder who fails to advise a buyer as provided by Section 1101.555 may not receive payment of or recover any commission agreed to be paid on the sale.

> A licensee is required to obtain the consent of the licensee's principal before paying a portion of the licensee's fee to a party the licensee does not represent.

IN PRACTICE Subchapter Q addresses a real estate agent's liability regarding a variety of disclosure topics—among them AIDS, sales price in a competitive market analysis, and misrepresentation or concealment by a buyer, seller, or subagent. It also addresses the broker's responsibility for the acts or omissions of a salesperson acting for the broker. Section 1101.806 (b–d) is the source for the "three requirements for compensation" listed in Chapter 5.

SUMMARY

The Texas Real Estate License Act was enacted by the Texas Legislature to protect the public from dishonest brokers, salespersons, and registrants; prescribe certain licensing and registration standards; maintain high standards in the real estate profession; and protect licensed brokers from unfair or improper competition. The act stipulates who must be licensed or registered and who is exempt from licensing or registration; sets forth certain operating standards to which brokers, salespersons, and registrants must adhere; creates certain licensing and registration procedures and requirements; and prescribes penalties for violations of the act and procedures for hearings. It is imperative that prospective brokers, salespersons, and registrants fully understand the Texas Real Estate License Act.

FIGURE 7.1:   Education Requirements for Salesperson and Broker Licenses

Requirements for an Active Salesperson License Effective September 1, 2012	First Salesperson Renewal (SAE) Effective September 1, 2012	Requirements for an Active Broker License Effective January 1, 2012	Mandatory Continuing Education (MCE)
12 semester hours (180 classroom hours) 4 semester hours (60 classroom hours) of Principles of Real Estate 2 semester hours (30 classroom hours) of Law of Agency 2 semester hours (30 classroom hours) of Law of Contracts 2 semester hours (30 classroom hours) of Contract Forms and Addendums 2 semester hours (30 classroom hours) of Real Estate Finance	6 semester hours (90 classroom hours) of core* real estate courses during the 2-year initial license period Must have a total of 18 semester hours (270 classroom hours) in core real estate courses An applicant may complete all 18 semester hours (270 classroom hours) required for prelicense and SAE prior to applying for a license. In that event, the new licensee would be subject to MCE for the first renewal.	60 semester hours (900 classroom hours); a bachelor's degree counts toward all related† education requirements (up to 42 semester hours) 18 semester hours (270 classroom hours) minimum of core* real estate courses, 2 semester hours of which must be real estate brokerage Four-year apprenticeship required (four of the last five years)	All brokers and salespersons who have completed salesperson annual education (SAE) courses must complete 15 hours of MCE during the license renewal period. Nonelective courses include a three-hour legal update course and a three-hour legal ethics course. On or after September 1, 2012, a license renewal requires a broker responsibility course of at least six classroom hours for a broker who sponsors a salesperson or a broker or salesperson who supervises another licensee. (Exemptions apply to some brokers.) The designated broker of a licensed business entity must also take the mandatory continuing education course.

Notes:

One semester hour equals 15 classroom hours.

Salesperson education requirements before September 1, 2012: 14 semester hours, or equivalent classroom hours of postsecondary education, including at least 4 semester hours of core real estate principles, 2 semester hours of agency law, 2 semester hours of contract law, 2 semester hours of an additional core real estate course, and 4 semester hours of core or related courses.

SAE requirements prior to September 1, 2012: 4 semester hours (60 classroom hours) in the first year of licensure; a total of 18 hours, 14 of which must be in core real estate courses

Broker experience requirements prior to January 1, 2012: two years of active experience during the 36 months prior to application

*Core real estate courses—Principles, Agency, Appraisal, Law, Finance, Marketing, Mathematics, Brokerage, Property Management, Investments, Promulgated Contract Forms (Contract Forms and Addendums), Residential Inspection for Real Estate Agents, Law of Contracts.

†Related courses—An extensive list of approved related courses is available on the TREC website: www.trec.texas.gov (choose Education; R. E. Related Courses). Among the courses are Business Math, Government, Economics, and Marketing.

ANALYSIS FORM: TEXAS REAL ESTATE LICENSE ACT

Instructions: After studying the Texas Real Estate License Act, carefully complete the following worksheet. The information will be invaluable in preparation for the state license examination and in future real estate activities.

1. When was the Texas Real Estate License Act originally passed? _____

2. When was it last amended? _____

3. What are the requirements for licensure in Texas?

	For Broker's License	For Salesperson's License
a. Minimum age	_____	_____
b. Length of residence	_____	_____
c. Apprenticeship (years)	_____	_____
d. Education	_____	_____
e. Examination required?	_____	_____
f. Amount of payment into recovery trust account	_____	_____

4. From the following list of real estate activities, check those that require a Texas real estate license or registration.

_____ auction

_____ sell

_____ exchange

_____ purchase

_____ rent

_____ owner who performs the above for himself or herself

_____ owner's employee who performs the above for owners

_____ lease

_____ assist in procuring prospects

_____ assist in finding listings

_____ appraise

_____ collect rents

_____ mortgage

_____ build

_____ survey

_____ repair

_____ serve as a hostess at an open house

_____ trade

_____ garden

_____ buy

_____ buy easements

_____ inspect property condition

_____ locate renters

5. State the definition of *broker* as given by state law. Know this definition and be able to list the activities that it includes.
_____
_____

6. State the definition of *salesperson* as given by state law. Learn this definition.
_____
_____

7. What persons or transactions are *exempt* from licensure in Texas?
_____
_____

8. Examine Sections 1101.651 and 1101.652 of the act. Then list at least nine reasons why the Texas Real Estate Commission may discipline a broker or a salesperson, refuse to issue a license, or revoke or suspend a license.

1. _____

2. _____

3. _____

4. _____

5. _____

6. _____

7. _____

8. _____

9. _____

9. Acting as a broker or salesperson without first obtaining a license is a Class _____ misdemeanor, which is punishable by _____ .

10. The Texas Real Estate Commission consists of how many members?

_____

How long are their terms? _____

11. What are the requirements in regard to a broker's maintaining an office?

_____

_____

12. What provisions and/or requirements are made for the discharge or termination of employment of a real estate salesperson by a broker?

_____

_____

13. What constitutes the unauthorized practice of law by a licensee?

_____

_____

14. What is the Real Estate Recovery Trust Account?

_____

_____

What are the dollar limits on claims?

_____

_____

When is it used?

_____

_____

15. What is the composition of the Broker-Lawyer Committee?

_____

_____

What is its purpose?

_____

_____

16. Sections 1101.454 and 1101.455 outline the requirements for continuing education for licensees. What are the requirements for Salesperson Annual Education (SAE)?

_____

_____

What are the requirements for Mandatory Continuing Education (MCE)?

_____

_____

CHAPTER 7 QUESTIONS

1. It is unlawful for persons to act in the capacity of or represent themselves as real estate brokers without first
   a. registering with the Texas Real Estate Commission.
   b. obtaining a license from the Texas Securities Commission.
   c. obtaining a license from the Texas Real Estate Commission.
   d. obtaining an office in an area zoned commercial.

2. It is unlawful for a person to act as a real estate salesperson unless
   a. such person is acting as the agent of the property owner.
   b. such person is legally associated with a licensed Texas real estate broker.
   c. the property owner or the prospective buyer gives such person a written statement acknowledging the unlicensed status of such person.
   d. such person is employed in a clerical capacity by a licensed real estate broker.

3. A real estate salesperson may
   a. accept compensation only from the broker under whom the salesperson is or was licensed.
   b. pay a compensation only from the broker under whom the sales
   c. accept compensation from any licensed real estate broker.
   d. split the commission with any licensed attorney.

4. A real estate broker's license is *NOT* required of a person who
   a. agrees to negotiate a trade for another for a fee.
   b. offers to list real estate for sale.
   c. attempts to negotiate the rental of real estate for another in exchange for one month's rent.
   d. advertises and leases his own properties.

5. Persons required to hold a license under the License Act include
   a. on-site managers of apartment complexes.
   b. real estate brokers operating out of their home.
   c. those employed by a builder in the regular course of their business.
   d. lawyers licensed in Texas.

6. The Texas Real Estate Commission is composed of
   a. nine members elected by the public in the general election.
   b. six members appointed by the lieutenant governor.
   c. nine real estate brokers appointed by the governor.
   d. nine members, six of whom are brokers and three of whom are lay members, each appointed by the governor with senate approval.

7. The Real Estate Center at Texas A&M University is funded by
   a. $20 from brokers and $17.50 from salespersons, to be paid with a license renewal.
   b. $20 from brokers and salespersons, each time a license is issued or renewed.
   c. $10 of each application fee for brokers and salespersons.
   d. a fee not to exceed $15 from each broker and salesperson annually.

8. An applicant for a Texas real estate license must be
   a. at least 18 years old and a legal resident of Texas at the time of filing the application, or be a legally admitted alien.
   b. either 18 years old or have the disabilities of minority removed.
   c. either 18 years of age or be married.
   d. at least 21 years old and a resident of Texas for six months before filing the application.

9. Under the inspector licensing laws, the inspector

    a. may use any report form drawn up by the inspection firm or its attorney.

    b. must use a report form prescribed by TREC.

    c. may act as both inspector and real estate salesperson in a transaction.

    d. may act as both inspector and repairperson in a transaction.

10. Which statement is *TRUE* of payment that is made from the real estate recovery trust account?

    a. The license is revoked automatically and a new one will not be issued until the trust account has been reimbursed, with interest.

    b. The license will be revoked if the trust account is not reimbursed within six months, with interest.

    c. The license may be revoked if payment is made from the recovery trust account.

    d. The license is suspended immediately but will be reissued upon reimbursement of the trust account, with interest.

11. License renewal fees are set by

    a. TREC rule.

    b. statute.

    c. the Texas Legislature in January of each year.

    d. the commission each year based on budgetary needs.

12. A broker or salesperson who fails to give the statutory title notice to the buyer at or before closing

    a. will have the license suspended without reinstatement for two years.

    b. may have the license suspended or revoked and cannot collect a commission on the subject sale.

    c. is required to show cause as to why such disclosure was not made.

    d. must forfeit the entire commission on the subject transaction but in so doing is absolved of any other liability.

13. A licensee who draws an earnest money contract instead of using a form promulgated for a specific purpose

    a. will have her license revoked or suspended.

    b. may have his license revoked or suspended.

    c. is acting in the best interest of the seller if no commission is charged.

    d. may do so provided proper disclosure is made to all parties.

14. A licensee must use the earnest money contract forms, addenda, and leases promulgated by the commission unless

    a. the forms do not fit the circumstances of the transaction.

    b. the agent is offering legal advice to the parties.

    c. an attorney prepares the forms and the property owner requires their use.

    d. the agent secures special permission from TREC.

15. To collect a commission through litigation, the seller's broker is *NOT* required to prove

    a. being duly licensed at the time the services were commenced.

    b. the seller signed a written agreement to pay the fee.

    c. the required title notice was provided to the buyer.

    d. the buyer was aware of the commission amount.

16. The License Act provides for

    a. a broker to act as an intermediary solely with the written consent of the buyer.

    b. a minimum of 15 classroom hours as a prerequisite to license renewal every two years after SAE requirements have been met.

    c. definite liability if a licensee fails to disclose that an owner has AIDS.

    d. a 10-year limit within which core courses taken at a college or approved proprietary school can be counted toward license requirements.

Detailed rationales for the end-of-chapter review questions are available online at www.dearborn.com through the *Instructor Resource Guides* link.

CHAPTER 8

Interests in Real Estate

■ **LEARNING OBJECTIVES**

When you have completed this chapter, you will be able to

- **identify** the limitations on ownership rights that are imposed by government action;
- **describe** the various estates in land and the rights and limitations they convey;
- **list** the nine lien rights that are foreclosable against Texas homesteads;
- **explain** concepts related to encumbrances, including the creation and termination of easements;
- **distinguish** among the surface and groundwater rights in Texas; and
- **define** the following *key terms*:

allodial system	escheat	life estate
defeasible fee estate	estate in land	littoral rights
determinable fee estate	fee simple	police power
easement	fee simple subject to a condition subsequent	prior appropriation
easement appurtenant		remainder interest
easement by implication	feudal system	restriction
easement by necessity	freehold estate	reversionary interest
easement by prescription	grantee	right-of-way
easement in gross	grantor	riparian rights
eminent domain	groundwater rights	taxation
encroachment	homestead	
encumbrance	license	

OVERVIEW

Ownership of a parcel of real estate is not necessarily absolute; it is dependent on the type of interest a person holds in the property. For example, one may own real property forever and be able to pass it on to heirs or this ownership may exist only as long as the owner lives. Real estate ownership may be restricted to exist only as long as the owner uses it for one specific purpose; likewise, it may be restricted to exist only as long as the owner *refrains from* using it for a specific purpose. In addition, the interest in real estate a person possesses may be reduced by the interests others possess in the property.

This chapter discusses the various interests in real estate and how they affect ownership and use. Government rights, encumbrances, water rights, and other interests of parties who do not own the property are also addressed.

HISTORICAL BACKGROUND

According to old English common law, the government or king held title to all lands under what was known as the **feudal system** of ownership. Through a series of social reforms in the 17th century, however, the feudal system evolved into the **allodial system** of ownership. Land held in the United States is under the allodial system. As firmly established by the Bill of Rights of the U.S. Constitution, property is owned by individual citizens.

GOVERNMENT POWERS

The four government powers can be remembered as **PETE**: **P**olice Power, **E**minent Domain, **T**axation, and **E**scheat.

Individual ownership rights are subject to certain powers, or rights, held by federal, state, and local governments. Because they are intended to promote the general welfare of the community, these limitations on the ownership of real estate supersede the individual's rights. Such government rights include the following:

■ **Police power**: This is the power vested in a state to establish legislation to preserve order; to protect the public health, safety, and morals; and to promote the general welfare. There is no federal police power—it exists in this manner on a state level only. A state's police power is passed on to municipalities and counties through legislation called *enabling acts*. The use and enjoyment of property is subject to restrictions authorized by such legislation, including environmental protection laws and zoning and building ordinances that regulate the use, size, location, and construction of real estate (see Chapter 24). For example, some cities, through their police powers, require owners of vacant buildings to register those buildings with the city.

■ **Eminent domain**: The power of a government or public entity such as a utility or railroad company to take private property for a *public use* is *eminent domain*. Land in Texas cannot be condemned for private use. The governmental entity or private entity granted the power of eminent domain determines the location and the amount of land that is needed; however, it cannot legally condemn more property than is reasonably required to serve the public use. Some examples of acquisitions under eminent domain are for highways, public buildings, airports, parks, street-widening projects, and utility services.

A city or county may acquire and pay for water rights through the condemnation process—if it can prove it has developed a water conservation plan, has made a good faith effort to obtain alternative water supplies, and can show the need for the water rights.

Before a governmental or private entity begins negotiating with a property owner to acquire real property by eminent domain, a landowner must be given the "Landowner's Bill of Rights," a written statement of legal rights and options in eminent domain proceedings. The entity proposing to take a property for public use must initially make a good faith offer to acquire the real property through direct negotiation and purchase from the owner. If the parties cannot agree on the amount of compensation, the entity may begin a *condemnation suit*, the legal process for the taking of private property. The court appoints three special commissioners to determine the amount of money to be awarded as adequate compensation to the landowner. Adequate compensation includes the market value of the property and certain damages, if any, to the remaining property. Either party may object to the award and may ask for a trial by judge or jury. Under some circumstances, if private property was condemned by a governmental entity and the purpose for which the property was acquired is canceled or the "public use" has not been initiated within 10 years of acquisition, the property owner may be entitled to repurchase the property at the price received from the entity that acquired the property through eminent domain (S.B. 18, 2011).

There are some limitations on government powers, too. A landowner is entitled to compensation from the state when a state law or regulation reduces all or a portion of the value of a tract by 25% or more through the process of inverse condemnation.

■ **Taxation**: Taxation is a charge on real estate to raise funds to meet the public needs of a government (see Chapter 11).

■ **Escheat**: Although escheat actually is not a limitation on ownership, Texas law provides for ownership of real estate to revert, or escheat, to the state when an owner dies and leaves no heirs and no will disposing of the real estate. Additionally, the property of an owner who has been absent for seven years and whose whereabouts are unknown will escheat to the state if there are no heirs or will. Escheat occurs only when a property becomes ownerless. The Texas General Land Office manages escheated property, and proceeds from its sale or lease are deposited into the Foundation School Fund.

IN PRACTICE   The U.S. Supreme Court ruling in *Kelo et al. v. City of New London et al.* (2005) allows the taking of private property by eminent domain for economic development purposes. In opposition to this decision, the Texas Legislature has reaffirmed limitations on the use of the power of eminent domain in Texas by prohibiting the taking of private property for economic development or enhancement of tax revenues, with certain limited exceptions. A 2009 constitutional amendment further safeguards private property rights; it provides that no property shall be taken, damaged, or destroyed unless the taking is

■ for public ownership, use, and enjoyment by the State, a political subdivision of the state, the public at large, or an entity granted the power of eminent domain or

■ for the elimination of urban blight on a particular parcel of property.

For more information about eminent domain, read the "Landowner's Bill of Rights," which is available at the Office of the Attorney General: www.oag.texas.gov.

ESTATES IN LAND

The degree, quantity, nature, and extent of interest that a person has in real property is an **estate in land**. In the United States, estates in land are unique. Our present rights and interests in land are complete and free of state domination (except for the state's right to taxation, police power, and eminent domain, as previously mentioned).

Estates in land are divided into two major classifications: *freehold estates* and *leasehold estates* (those involving tenants). The freehold estates are illustrated in Figure 8.1. Leaseholds are covered in Chapter 21.

FIGURE 8.1: Freehold Estates

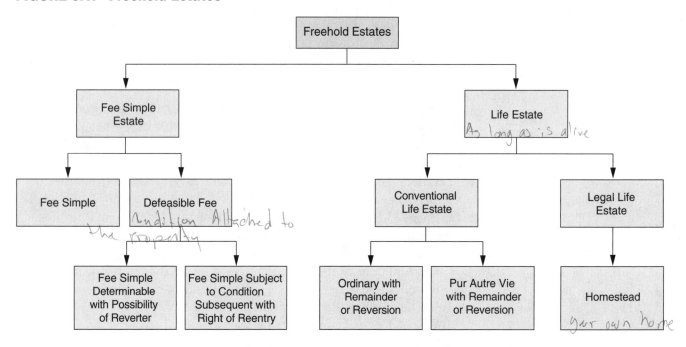

Freehold Estates

- Fee Simple Estate
  - Fee Simple
  - Defeasible Fee — *Condition Attached to the property*
    - Fee Simple Determinable with Possibility of Reverter
    - Fee Simple Subject to Condition Subsequent with Right of Reentry
- Life Estate — *As long as is alive*
  - Conventional Life Estate
    - Ordinary with Remainder or Reversion
    - Pur Autre Vie with Remainder or Reversion
  - Legal Life Estate
    - Homestead — *your own home*

Freehold estates are *estates of indeterminable length*, such as those existing for a lifetime or forever. These include

- fee simple estates,
- defeasible fee estates,
- conventional life estates, and
- legal life estates.

Fee simple and defeasible fee estates continue for an indefinite period and are inheritable by the heirs of the owner. **Life estates** terminate upon the death of the person on whose life they are based.

> **Fee simple**: Complete ownership
>
> **Defeasible fee**: A fee simple that may be defeated on the occurrence or nonoccurrence of a specified event

Fee Simple Estate

An estate in **fee simple** is the *highest type of interest in real estate recognized by law*. In Texas, a transfer of title or an interest in real property conveys a fee simple estate unless otherwise expressed. A fee simple estate is one in which the holder is entitled to all rights incident to the property (complete ownership). There is no time limit on its existence—it is said to run forever. Because this estate is of unlimited duration, on the death of its owner, it passes to the heirs or as provided in the owner's will. The fee simple estate is subject, however, to the governmental powers previously explained. The terms *fee*, *fee simple*, and *fee simple absolute* are basically the same. Such an estate can be freely *devised* (passed by a will) to a designated person known as the *devisee*.

Defeasible Fee Estate

A **defeasible fee estate**, also called a *fee simple defeasible* or a *qualified fee*, is an estate in which the holder has a fee simple title that may be divested on the occurrence or nonoccurrence of a specified event. There are two categories of defeasible fee estates: *fee simple determinable and fee simple subject to a condition subsequent.*

A **determinable fee estate**, sometimes referred to as a *fee on conditional limitation*, is a defeasible fee estate that may be inherited. However, this estate *will be determined* (come to an end) *immediately on the occurrence of a designated event*, the time of such occurrence being uncertain. In other words, the condition or event that will terminate the estate may be one that is certain to happen, but the time of its happening is uncertain. Such an estate also may be based on an uncertain condition or event.

When a parcel of real estate is conveyed and the deed specifically states that the land is granted so long as it is used for certain purposes (for example, as a schoolhouse or a church), the estate conveyed is a *determinable fee*. The words *so long as, until, while,* or *during* are the key to the creation of this estate. If the specified purpose ceases, title will revert (go back) to the original grantor or the heirs or to some specified third person (or that person's heirs). The person to whom such title will revert holds a future, or contingent, interest as long as the determinable fee is in effect. This future interest is called a *possibility of reverter*, and its holder is called a *remainderman*.

FOR EXAMPLE A grant of land from an owner to her church "so long as the land is used only for religious purposes" is a determinable fee estate. If the church uses the land for a nonreligious purpose, title will revert automatically to the previous owner (or the heirs or successors).

A **fee simple subject to a condition subsequent**, the second type of defeasible fee estate, is similar to a determinable fee in that a grantor conveys a parcel of real estate subject to a condition of ownership, but it differs in the way the estate will terminate on violation of this condition. In a determinable fee, title to the subject property reverts back to the original owner immediately and automatically. In contrast, in a fee simple subject to a condition subsequent, the estate does not automatically end on the occurrence or nonoccurrence of a stipulated condition.

Grantors reserve for themselves only the right of reentry to the property. The estate does not actually terminate until the grantors go to court to assert this right. The court orders a return of title to the previous owners, who can recover rent, profits, and damages for the period after the occurrence of the condition subsequent. The following terms are commonly used to establish a fee simple subject to a condition subsequent: *on the condition that, provided that,* or *if.*

FOR EXAMPLE A grant of land "on the condition that" there be no sales of alcohol on the premises is a fee simple subject to a condition subsequent. If alcohol is sold on the property, the former owner has the right to reacquire full ownership. It will be

Defeasible Fee Estates
- **Determinable Fee**: Automatically ends
- **Fee Simple Subject to a Condition Subsequent**: Grantor must go to court to assert right of reentry

A **grantor** gives title to a **grantee**. To remember which party gives and which one receives: The "or" gives to the "ee."

necessary for the grantor (or the grantor's heirs or successors) to go to court to assert that right, however.

Conventional Life Estates

A conventional life estate is a freehold estate limited in duration to the life of the owner or the life of some other designated person or persons. Unlike other freehold estates, a life estate is not inheritable. It passes to future owners according to the provisions of the life estate.

A conventional life estate is established by a deed from an owner of a fee simple estate to an individual who is called the *life tenant*. Life tenants have full enjoyment of ownership for the duration of their life. When a life tenant dies, the estate ends and its ownership passes to another designated individual or returns to the previous owner (see Figures 8.2 and 8.3).

FIGURE 8.2: Remainder Interest

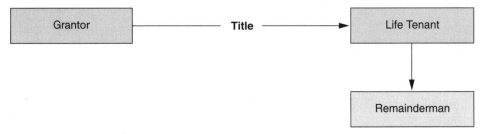

FIGURE 8.3: Reversionary Interest

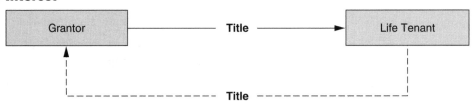

FOR EXAMPLE *A*, who has fee simple title, conveys a life estate to B for B's lifetime. B is the life tenant. On B's death, the life estate terminates. Subsequent ownership of the property would be determined by the provisions of the deed.

A *pur autre vie* life estate is created when the grantor conveys property to the life tenant *for the life of another*, and the estate ends with the death of that third party. A pur autre vie life estate may be inherited by the life tenant's heirs, but only until the death of the person against whose life the estate is measured. A life estate pur autre vie is often created for a physically or mentally incapacitated person as an incentive for someone to care for that person.

FOR EXAMPLE *A*, who owns a fee simple estate, conveys a life estate in the property to *B*, a niece and private nurse, as life tenant for the duration of the life of *D*, *A*'s elderly aunt. *B* is the life tenant, but the measuring life is *D*'s. On *D*'s death, the life estate ends and subsequent ownership is determined by the deed. If *B* should die while *D* is still alive, *B*'s heirs may inherit the life estate. However, when *D* dies, the heirs' estate ends.

Remainder and Reversion   When creating a life estate, the original fee simple owner also must consider the future ownership of the property after the death of the life estate owner. The holder of the future interest will ultimately be the owner of a fee simple estate and is commonly called the *remainderman*. The future interest may take one of two forms:

- **Remainder interest**: When the deed or will that creates the life estate names a third party (or parties) to whom title will pass on the death of the life estate owner, then such third party is said to own the remainder interest or estate (see Figure 8.2). The remainder interest is a nonpossessory estate—a *future* interest.

- **Reversionary interest**: When the creator of a life estate (the original fee simple owner) does not convey the remainder interest to a third party (or parties), then on the death of the life estate owner full ownership reverts to the original fee simple owner—or if that person is deceased, to the heirs or devisees set forth in the fee simple owner's will. This interest or estate is called a *reversion* (see Figure 8.3).

> A *remainder interest* passes to a named third party. A *reversionary interest* reverts to the grantor or heirs.

A life tenant is entitled to the rights of ownership. The life tenant can enjoy both possession and the ordinary use and profits arising from ownership, just as though the individual were a fee owner. A life tenant's rights are not absolute, however. She can enjoy the rights of the land but cannot encroach on those of the remainderman. For example, a life tenant cannot destroy a building or allow it to deteriorate, and a life tenant cannot remove oil, gas, or minerals without the remainderman's permission. In other words, the life tenant cannot perform any acts that would permanently injure the land or property. In legal terms, this injury is known as *waste*. If waste occurs, those who will eventually own the property can bring legal action against the life tenant for the damages or seek an injunction.

A life estate ownership may be sold, mortgaged, or leased; but the life interest will always terminate on the death of the person against whose life the estate is measured. Therefore, the value of a life estate is considerably less than that of a fee simple estate. If a life estate is mortgaged, a lender generally will require a credit life insurance policy that would pay the loan balance on the death of the person against whose life the estate is measured.

Legal Life Estates

Homestead   Whereas the conventional life estate is created by agreement of the parties, a legal life estate is created by operation of law. Created by the Texas Constitution, **homestead** is a legal life estate in *land that is owned and occupied as the family home*. The purpose of the Texas homestead law is to protect the family against eviction by general creditors and to protect spouses by requiring that both husband and wife join in executing any deed conveying homestead property or in any document creating a voluntary lien on the homestead property. A family can have only one homestead at any one time, and occupancy automatically creates the homestead—no filing is required.

> If a *homestead tax exemption* is filed with the appraisal district, that property is automatically designated as the homestead unless a voluntary designation of another property is recorded in the county records.

The Texas homestead right is constitutional and therefore *cannot be waived* through any contractual agreement or change in state law. The homestead law includes the following requirements: (1) Every *head of a family* and every *single person* may hold a homestead. (2) The family or householder must occupy or intend to *occupy the premises as a home*. (3) The head of the family or householder must *own or lease the property*. The rights to occupy the homestead and protect it from

> **Homestead Limits**
> - Urban: 10 acres
> - Rural: 200 acres (family)

forced sale continue for the life of the husband and wife and their survivor(s) and for minor children until they reach age 18. If a homestead property is sold, the proceeds of the sale are exempt from creditors for a period of six months after the sale, allowing time for the purchase of another homestead property.

In Texas, a homestead may be either urban or rural but not both. A *rural homestead* is limited to 200 acres for a family and 100 acres for a single person, regardless of the value of the land or improvements on the land; the designated acreage must include the owner's home. An *urban homestead—that is, in a city, town, or village—* is limited to a lot (or contiguous lots) not to exceed 10 acres. There is no limit on the value of the improvements on the lot or on any improvements subsequently built. The urban homestead may include both a home and a place of business for the head of the family or for the single householder, provided the total of both homestead claims does not exceed 10 acres.

The homestead may be selected from the separate property of either spouse or from the community property (see Chapter 9). In either case, any documents conveying or encumbering the homestead property must be signed by both husband and wife. If the homestead is selected from the separate property of a spouse and that spouse dies, the surviving spouse obtains a conditional life estate in that homestead. This can be troublesome if the decedent has children by a prior marriage and they desire to sell the separate property used as the homestead. Unless the surviving spouse leaves the homestead voluntarily or agrees to a settlement, the decedent's children will be unable to sell the property until the surviving spouse dies.

Homestead rights in property may be terminated by death, sale of the property, or abandonment. *Abandonment* has been defined as the discontinuance of use of the property coupled with an intention not to use it again as a home; the intention of the householder is a key factor. Sometimes a notice or declaration of abandonment is filed or recorded to confirm the release of homestead.

Homestead Protection Exemptions   In Texas, the homestead is exempt from forced sale by creditors for payment of most debts. However, there are a few lien rights that have been determined to be foreclosable against Texas homesteads.

- Taxes on the property
- Purchase money mortgages
- Mechanics' and materialmen's claims for the cost of improvements on the homestead property
- A homeowners association assessment lien, if certain filing requirements have been met
- An owelty lien, including a loan against the homestead to settle property claims in cases of divorce or death
- Refinance of a lien against a homestead, including a federal tax lien
- Home equity loans for any purpose, which will be discussed in Chapter 16
- Reverse mortgages, under which advances against a home's equity are provided to a borrower who is 62 years old or older
- Conversion and refinance of a personal property lien secured by a manufactured home to a lien on real property, including the refinance of the purchase price of the home and the land and the cost of installing the home on the land

Legal Life Estate
- Created by statute
- Homestead: Legal life estate in land owned and occupied as the family home
- Protects families against eviction by general creditors
- Protects spouses by requiring signatures

A valid lien for labor or material on a homestead improvement (constr improvements or repairing or renovating existing improvements) mus on a written contract, consented to by both spouses and acknowledged a before the work was performed or the materials delivered. Additional requirements provide that (a) the contract for the work and material must not be signed until five days after loan application; (b) the owner may rescind the contract up to three days after signing; and (c) the contract must be signed at the office of a third-party lender, an attorney, or a title company.

IN PRACTICE   Under the provisions of the federal Bankruptcy Abuse Prevention and Consumer Protection Act of 2005, a debtor must have lived in Texas for two years before filing bankruptcy to qualify to use the Texas homestead exemption limits. If the debtor has owned the home for more than 1,215 days (3 years plus 120 days) and there was no criminal conduct or attempt to defraud a creditor, the Texas homestead exemptions remain intact, as they do in every situation if the homestead is the "principal residence of a family farmer." However, homestead exemptions for a debtor who has acquired the homestead within 1,215 days will be limited to $125,000 plus the value of a previous homestead owned by the debtor within Texas during that period. A debtor who has engaged in criminal conduct or attempted to defraud creditors may not exempt *more than* $125,000—in some cases, it could be less.

ENCUMBRANCES

Encumbrances
■ Liens
■ Restrictions
■ Easements
■ Licenses
■ Encroachments

A claim, charge, or liability that attaches to and is binding on real estate is an **encumbrance.** It is a right or an interest held by a party who is not the fee owner of the property. An encumbrance is anything that affects the title to or use of the property. An encumbrance may lessen the value or obstruct the use of the property, but it does not necessarily prevent a transfer of title.

Encumbrances may be divided into two general classifications:
■ Liens (usually monetary), which affect the title
■ Encumbrances, which affect the use of the property, such as restrictions, easements, licenses, and encroachments

Liens

A claim against property that provides security for repayment of a debt or obligation of the property owner is a *lien*. If the obligation is not repaid, the lienholder, or creditor, has the right to have it paid from the proceeds of the sale of the debtor's property unless such property is exempt under the homestead laws. Real estate taxes, mortgages and trust deeds, judgments, and mechanics' liens (for people who have furnished labor or materials in the construction or repair of real estate) are possible liens against an owner's real estate. Liens are discussed in detail in Chapter 11.

Restrictions

Private agreements placed in the public record that affect the use of land are deed **restrictions,** or *restrictive covenants.* Deed restrictions typically would be imposed by a developer or subdivider to maintain specific standards in a subdivision. They would be listed in the original development plans for the subdivision filed in the public record and included in the seller's deed to the buyer. Restrictive covenants normally cover such things as lot size, building lines, type of architecture, and uses to which the property may be put.

Easements

A right acquired by one party to use the land of another party for a special purpose is an **easement**. Although this is the common definition of *easement*, a party also may have an easement right in the air above a parcel of real estate.

Because an easement is a right to *use* land, it is classified as an interest in real estate, but it is not an estate in land. The holder of an easement has only a right; he does not have an estate or ownership interest in the land over which the easement exists. An easement may be either appurtenant or in gross (see Figure 8.4).

FIGURE 8.4:   Easement Appurtenant and Easement in Gross

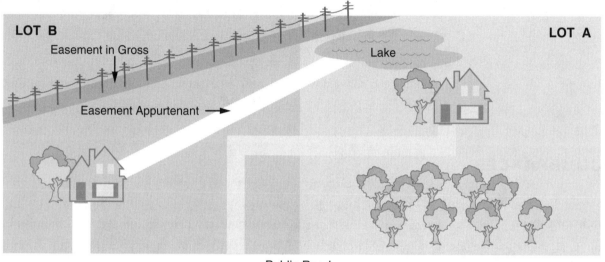

The owner of Lot B has an appurtenant easement across Lot A to gain access to the lake. Lot B is dominant and Lot A is servient. The utility company has an easement in gross across both parcels of land for its power lines. Note that Lot A also has an appurtenant easement across Lot B for its driveway. Lot A is dominant and Lot B is servient.

Dominan Acomanent

Easement Appurtenant   An easement that is *annexed to the ownership and used for the benefit of another's parcel of land* is an **easement appurtenant**. For example, if A and B own adjacent properties in a resort community and only A's property borders the lake, A may grant B a **right-of-way** across A's property to the lake. A right-of-way is the right acquired through accepted usage or contract to *pass over* a designated portion of the property of another.

For an easement appurtenant to exist, there must be two adjacent tracts of land owned by different parties. The tract over which the access easement runs is known as the *servient tenement*; the tract that is to benefit from the easement is known as the *dominant tenement*.

An easement appurtenant is considered part of the dominant tenement; if the dominant tenement is conveyed to another party, the easement passes with the title. In legal terms it is said that the easement *runs with the land*. However, ownership of the land over which an easement actually passes is retained by the servient tenement. As a rule, the dominant estate owner has the duty to maintain the easement.

Public Road

The owner of Lot B has an appurtenant easement across Lot A to gain access to the lake. Lot B is dominant and Lot A is servient. The utility company has an easement in gross across both parcels of land for its power lines. Note that Lot A also has an appurtenant easement across Lot B for its driveway. Lot A is dominant and Lot B is servient.

A *party wall easement*, another example of an easement appurtenant, is an exterior wall of a building that straddles the boundary line between two owners' lots, with half of the wall on each lot. The lot owners own the half of the wall that is on their individual lot, have an easement right in the other half of the wall for support of their building, and must pay half the expenses to build and maintain the wall. A written party-wall agreement should be used to create these easement rights.

Easement in Gross   A *mere personal interest* in or right to use the land of another is an **easement in gross**. Such an easement is not appurtenant to any ownership estate in land. Examples of easements in gross are the easement rights a railroad has in its right-of-way or the right-of-way for gas, electricity, and telephone lines. A person employed to acquire or sell easements or rights-of-way for others must be either licensed as a real estate broker or salesperson or registered with TREC. Commercial easements in gross may be assigned or conveyed and may be inherited. However, personal easements in gross usually are not assignable and terminate on the death of the easement owner.

Creating an Easement   To create an easement, there must be *two separate parties* because it is impossible for the owner of a parcel of property to have an easement over her own land. Easements commonly are created by written agreement between the parties establishing the easement right. Easements also may be created by *express grant* in a deed from the owner of the property over which the easement will run or by *express reservation* by the grantor in a deed of conveyance reserving an easement over the sold land. Three other ways that an easement can be created are *easement by necessity, easement by prescription, and easement by implication.*

Easement by Necessity   When an owner sells part of the land that has no access to a street or public way except over the seller's remaining land, an **easement by necessity** arises because all owners have rights of ingress to and egress from their land—they cannot be landlocked. However, some parcels are already landlocked, and being landlocked does not by itself create a right to an easement by necessity. Two factors must be established through the courts:

■   Both parcels must at one time have been part of a single unit.
■   There must be an absolute necessity for the easement, and the necessity must have existed as of the severance of the two estates.

County commissioners are authorized under certain circumstances to condemn easements for landlocked property owners in rural areas.

Easement by Prescription   When the claimant has made use of another's land for a certain period as defined by state law, an **easement by prescription** is acquired, which limits the landowner's use of the property. In Texas, this *prescriptive period* is 10 years. The claimant's use must have been continuous, exclusive, and without the owner's approval. Additionally, the use must be visible, open, and notorious, so that the owner readily could learn of it.

Through the concept of *tacking*, a party not in possession of real property for the entire required statutory period may successfully establish a claim for an easement by prescription. Successive periods of continuous and uninterrupted occupation by different parties may be tacked on, or combined, to reach the prescriptive period. To tack on one person's possession to that of another, the parties must be *successors in interest*, such as an ancestor and an heir, a landlord and a tenant, or a seller and a buyer.

F O R   E X A M P L E   For the past 12 years, F has driven his car across J's front yard several times a day to reach his garage from a more comfortable angle. F has an easement by prescription.

For 15 years, L has driven across J's front yard two or three times a year to reach her property when she's in a hurry. She does not have an easement by prescription because her use was not continuous.

For 6 years, E parked his car on J's property, next to J's garage. Five years ago, E sold his house to N, who continued to park his car next to J's garage. Last year, N acquired an easement by prescription through tacking.

Easement by Implication   An **easement by implication** arises when the parties' actions may imply that they intend to create an easement. For example, a person acquiring mineral rights on a property also acquires an implied easement to enter the property for the purpose of removing the minerals.

Terminating an Easement   Easements may be terminated by any of the following four events:

- Failure of purpose (when the purpose for which the easement was created no longer exists)
- Merger (when the owner of either the dominant or the servient tenement becomes the owner of the other)
- Release (when the dominant estate gives up the right to use the easement)
- Abandonment (when the dominant estate stops using the easement)

License

A *personal privilege to enter the land of another for a specific purpose* is a **license**. A license is *not* an estate in land; it is a personal privilege or right of the party to whom it is given. A license differs from an easement in that *it can be terminated or canceled by the licensor* (the person who granted the license). If permission to use another's property is given orally or informally, it generally will be considered a license rather than a personal easement in gross. A license ceases on the death of either party and is revoked by the sale of the land by the licensor. Examples of license include permission to park in a neighbor's driveway and the privileges that are granted by the purchase of a ticket for the theater or a sports event.

A property owner who wishes to limit access to the land may do so by posting a No Trespassing sign, enclosing the property with a fence, or marking trees or posts with "purple marks." Notice is not given by the "purple marks" unless signs outlining the meaning of the purple marks are placed at each vehicle entry point on the property (Section 30.03, Penal Code).

Encroachments

When a building (or some portion of it) or a fence or a driveway *illegally extends beyond the land of its owner* and covers some land of an adjoining owner or a street or alley, an **encroachment** occurs. Encroachments usually are disclosed by a physical inspection of the property or by an improvement survey, which shows the location of all improvements located on a property and whether they extend over the lot lines. Note that encroachments usually are not disclosed by the title evidence normally provided in a real estate sale unless a survey is submitted while the examination is being made. If the building on a lot or the limbs of a tree encroach on neighboring land, the neighbor may be able to recover damages or secure removal of the portion that encroaches. Encroachments existing for more than 10 years may give rise to easements by prescription.

IN PRACTICE   Because an undisclosed encroachment could render a title unmarketable, its existence should be noted in a listing agreement, and the sales contract governing the transaction should be made subject to the existence of the particular disclosed encroachment.

WATER RIGHTS

One of the interests that may attach to the ownership of real estate is the right to use adjacent bodies of water. Because the existence of a water supply directly affects the value of land, it is important that agents understand water rights. The ownership of water and the land adjacent to it is determined by either the doctrines of riparian and littoral rights or the doctrine of prior appropriation.

Surface Water Rights

Riparian Rights   Although Texas generally subscribes to the English common law doctrine of riparian rights, its use today has been diminished by statute. Under common law, **riparian rights** were granted to owners of land located along the course of a river or stream. The owners had the right to use the water for domestic purposes, provided they did not interrupt or alter the flow of the water or contaminate the water. Land acquired under Mexican land grants did not carry riparian rights. However, land patented into private ownership from the Republic of Texas and from the State of Texas before July 1, 1895, carries riparian rights. Land granted after that date does not and is subject to the Texas prior appropriation doctrine discussed later in this chapter. Since 1969, however, a riparian owner's right to use water has been limited by a state permit for the maximum actual water put to beneficial use without waste.

The law in Texas after 1895 provided that water in every river, stream, lake, canyon, ravine, and watershed is the property of the State of Texas unless a riparian owner can prove otherwise. Furthermore, the State of Texas classifies streams as being *navigable* or *nonnavigable*. An owner of land that borders a nonnavigable waterway may own the land under the water to the exact center of the waterway. Land adjoining navigable rivers usually is owned to the mean vegetation line, with the state holding title to the remaining land (see Figure 8.5). Navigable waters are considered public highways over which the public has an easement or right to travel.

FIGURE 8.5: Riparian Rights

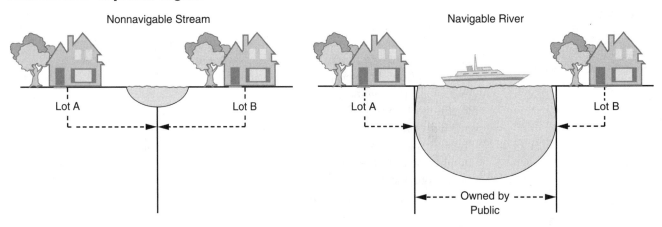

Riparian refers to rivers, streams, and similar waterways. Littoral refers to lakes, oceans, and similar bodies of water.

The terms *navigable* and *nonnavigable* are very significant. In practice, it is sometimes surprising to find that a certain stream is classified as *navigable*. In dealing with property abutting or crossed by a stream, the stream's classification must be determined from an official source. Not only does this question affect boundary lines, it also affects mineral rights and royalties because the State of Texas owns these interests in navigable streams. However, in certain unusual situations, private ownership of the bed of a navigable river is recognized (see *Selkirk v. Standley*, 683 SW 2nd 793, 1985).

Littoral Rights Closely related to riparian rights are the **littoral rights** of owners whose land borders on closed bodies of water, such as large, navigable lakes, and on oceans. Riparian and littoral rights are appurtenant (attached) to the land and cannot be retained when the property is sold. The right to use the water belongs to whoever owns the bordering land. Owners with littoral rights may enjoy unrestricted use of available water for domestic purposes but own the land adjacent to the water only up to the mean vegetation line (see Figure 8.6). All land below this point is owned by the government or other public authority, such as the Lower Colorado River Authority or various water districts.

FIGURE 8.6: Littoral Rights

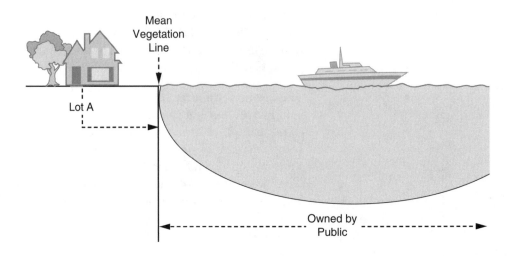

Where land adjoins streams or rivers, an owner is entitled to all *accretions*, increases in the land resulting from the deposit of soil by the natural action of the water. *Alluvion* is the term used for the land so created. Conversely, an owner may lose land through *erosion*, the gradual and imperceptible wearing away of the land caused by flowing water or other natural forces. This is contrasted to *avulsion*, the sudden removal of soil by an act of nature. A riparian owner generally does not lose title to land lost by avulsion—the boundary lines stay the same no matter how much soil is lost—whereas a riparian owner loses title to any land washed away by erosion or the changing of a river's course over a period of time.

Prior Appropriation   Under **prior appropriation**, *the right to use* any water, with the exception of limited domestic use, is controlled by the state rather than by the adjacent landowner. To secure water rights, a person must show a beneficial use for the water, such as crop irrigation, and file for and obtain a permit from the Texas Commission on Environmental Quality (TCEQ). The priority of the water right usually is determined by the oldest recorded permit date, subject to the adjudication of these rights by the state. After they are granted, water rights may be perfected through the legal processes prescribed by the state. When the water right is perfected, it generally becomes attached to the land of the person holding the permit. Issuance of a water permit does not grant access to the water source, however. All access rights-of-way over the land of another (easements) must be obtained from the property owner. TCEQ is authorized to cancel a state surface water right if it has not been used for a period of 10 years unless the non-use was the result of a water conservation plan submitted by the water right holder.

> With prior authorization from TCEQ, the beds and banks of any flowing natural stream in the state may be used to import water into Texas from another U.S. state.

Groundwater

Groundwater is water under the earth's surface below the saturation point. In Texas, groundwater provides for approximately 60% of the state's water needs. One of the sources of groundwater is the series of 9 major and 21 minor *aquifers*—underground geologic formations that contain a usable supply of water. Together these aquifers underlie approximately 76% of the state's surface area. A map of the "Major Aquifers of Texas" is available at the Texas Water Department Board's website.

WEBLINK @ www.twdb.texas.gov/mapping/maps.asp

Texas landowners own the groundwater below the surface of their land as real property (S.B. 332, 2011) and are entitled to drill for and remove groundwater below the surface. Since 1903, Texas has adhered to the *rule of capture* regarding **groundwater rights**; it gives landowners the right to pump as much groundwater as they choose without being held liable for damage to others. However, landowners may not maliciously take water for the sole purpose of injuring a neighbor nor may the landowner waste it. Landowners are liable for the subsidence (sinking) on another's land if it is caused by the negligent withdrawal of groundwater. A groundwater conservation district may facilitate management of groundwater by requiring owners or operators of water wells to report the amount of water withdrawn and by regulating well spacing.

Open Beach Law

A constitutional amendment passed by Texas voters in 2009 further protects the public's unrestricted right to use and the right of ingress and egress from a public beach, granting a permanent public easement along the Gulf of Mexico.

Texas's "open beach" law reserves to the public the perpetual right to use the public beaches. This right has been acquired by "prescription, dedication or presumption," as specified in Sections 61.016 and 61.017, Natural Resources Code. This easement extends from the line of mean low tide to the line of vegetation (see Figure 8.7). This means that even though fee simple title to a lot belongs to an individual, no structure is permitted to be built within the easement. In some circumstances, as a result of coastal erosion or storm events, an entire lot can be located within the easement, in which case its owner must share its use with the public. If a structure is located on the public beach, the owner could be forced to remove it, incurring all costs of removal. Because of this severe limitation on use, the Natural Resources Code, Section 61.025, requires that sellers provide to buyers a statutory notice relating to this easement. Failure to do so is, by statute, a violation of the Texas Deceptive Trade Practices Act; therefore, the notice is included in applicable TREC contract forms.

FIGURE 8.7: Line of Vegetation

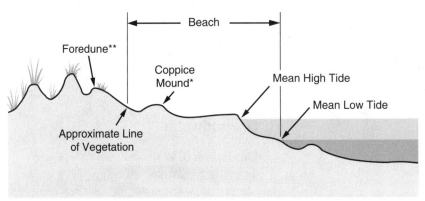

* Coppice Mounds: initial stages of dune growth that may become vegetated.
** Foredune: first clearly vegetated dune formations landward of the water.

Source: Government Land Office, *Dune Manual*, 2003.

In some areas of the Texas coast, structures damaged by storms have become a public health and safety issue, and their existence has prevented or delayed projects that could reduce damage from future storms. After Hurricane Ike in 2008, coastal communities have been required to have plans for disaster avoidance and remediation in critical erosion areas, including a building setback line that will accommodate a shoreline retreat.

IN PRACTICE In most cases, the owner of littoral property on the Texas coast may construct a pier on adjacent costal public land and "associated appurtenances" (such as a boat ramp or boat house) without first obtaining an easement from the School Land Board. However, both the pier and appurtenances must ultimately be registered with the Board.

SUMMARY

An estate is the degree, quantity, nature, and extent of interest a person holds in land. The several types of estates are distinguished according to the degree of interest held. Freehold estates are estates of indeterminate length. Nonfreehold estates are those for which the length can be determined accurately. These are called *leasehold estates*, and they concern tenants.

Freehold estates are further divided into estates of inheritance and life estates. Estates of inheritance include fee simple and defeasible fee estates. There are two types of life estates: conventional life estates, which are created by acts of the parties, and legal life estates, which are created by law. Homestead gives rise to the legal life estate in Texas.

Encumbrances against real estate may be in the form of liens, deed restrictions, easements, licenses, and encroachments. A lien is a monetary encumbrance that affects the title. An easement is the right acquired by one person to use another's real estate. Easements are classified as interests in real estate but are not estates in land. Easements appurtenant involve two separately owned tracts. The tract benefited is the dominant tenement; the tract that is subject to the easement is the servient tenement. An easement in gross is a personal right, such as that granted to utility companies to maintain poles, wires, and pipelines.

Easements may be created by agreement, express grant, reservation in a deed, implication, necessity, or prescription. They can be terminated when the purpose of the easement no longer exists, by merger of both interests, by release, or by an intention to abandon the easement.

A license is permission to enter another's property for a specific purpose. A license usually is created orally, is of a temporary nature, and can be revoked.

An encroachment exists when an improvement on one property illegally extends beyond the land of its owner and covers some land of an adjoining owner.

Ownership of land encompasses not only the land itself but also the right to use the water on or adjacent to it. Surface water rights include riparian, littoral, and prior appropriation rights. Texas generally subscribes to the common law doctrine of riparian rights, which may permit the owner of land adjacent to a nonnavigable stream to use the water for domestic purposes and to hold ownership of the stream to its midpoint. Littoral rights are held by owners of land bordering large lakes and oceans and include rights to use the water and ownership of the land up to the mean vegetation line. In most circumstances, water use is decided by the doctrine of prior appropriation, under which water belongs to the state and is allocated to users who have obtained permits. Groundwater ownership adheres to the rule of capture. A Texas landowner does not own the water beneath the land—just the rights to drill for and remove water that is found.

CHAPTER 8 QUESTIONS

1. Passage of title of real property to the State of Texas in the absence of heirs is called
   a. police power.
   b. escheat.
   c. prior appropriation.
   d. eminent domain.

2. The right of a government body to take ownership of real estate for public use is called
   a. escheat.
   b. eminent domain.
   c. police power.
   d. reversion.

3. Randy has constructed a fence that extends one foot over his lot line onto the property of a neighbor. The fence is an example of a(n)
   a. license.
   b. encroachment.
   c. easement by necessity.
   d. easement by prescription.

4. A Texas homeowner may be allowed certain protection from judgments of creditors as a result of the state
   a. homestead laws.
   b. police power rights.
   c. lien laws.
   d. equal credit laws.

5. A purchaser of real estate learned that his ownership rights will continue forever and that no other person claims to be the owner or has any ownership control over the property. This person owns a
   a. fee simple interest.
   b. life estate.
   c. determinable fee estate.
   d. defeasible fee estate.

6. Kenneth has permission from Antonio to hike on Antonio's land during the autumn months. Kenneth has a(n)
   a. easement by necessity.
   b. easement by prescription.
   c. license.
   d. restriction.

7. Which is NOT true under the Texas homestead law?
   a. A single person may hold a homestead.
   b. The homestead may be either urban or rural.
   c. The homestead is exempt from forced sale by creditors, with a few exceptions.
   d. Homestead rights in property may be terminated by the death of a spouse.

8. Janet owned the fee simple title to a vacant lot adjacent to a hospital and was persuaded to make a gift of the lot to the hospital. She wanted to have some control over its use, so her attorney prepared her deed to convey ownership of the lot to the hospital "so long as it is used for hospital purposes." After completion of the gift, the hospital will own a
   a. fee simple estate.
   b. determinable fee estate.
   c. leasehold estate.
   d. reversionary interest.

9. If the owner of real estate in Texas does not take action to force removal of an encroachment before 10 years have passed, then the encroachment may continue through a(n)
   a. easement by necessity.
   b. license.
   c. easement by prescription.
   d. right by prior appropriation.

10. Peter's driveway is regularly used by his neighbor to reach a garage located on the neighbor's property. Title to the neighbor's real estate includes an easement appurtenant that gives him the driveway right. Peter's property is called the
    a. leasehold tenement.
    b. license tenement.
    c. dominant tenement.
    d. servient tenement.

11. A father conveys ownership of his residence to his son but reserves for himself a life estate in the residence. The interest the son owns during the father's lifetime is
   a. pur autre vie.
   b. a remainder.
   c. reversionary.
   d. a life tenancy.

12. Which *BEST* describes a conventional life estate?
   a. An estate conveyed to A for the life of Z, and on Z's death to B
   b. An estate held by A and B in joint tenancy with right of survivorship
   c. A fee simple estate
   d. An estate in which there is no time limit on its existence

13. In Texas, for which claim may a residence *NOT* be subject to forced sale?
   a. The owner has not paid annual real estate taxes.
   b. Payments for a mortgage used to buy the residence are in arrears.
   c. The owner is six months behind on car payments.
   d. A mechanic has filed a claim for payment for improvements made to the residence.

14. Encumbrances on real estate
   a. may include liens, easements, and deed restrictions.
   b. make it impossible to sell the encumbered property.
   c. cannot affect the transfer of title.
   d. must all be removed before the title can be transferred.

15. If a grantor must go to court to assert the right of reentry to a property after a condition in the deed has been violated, the estate is a
   a. fee simple subject to a condition subsequent.
   b. determinable fee.
   c. fee simple.
   d. terminating estate.

16. Under riparian rights, Bert, owner of land located along the course of a nonnavigable stream,
   a. may own the land under the water to the exact center of the waterway.
   b. has the right to use the water for any purpose, so long as he does not pollute it.
   c. may dam the stream for irrigation purposes.
   d. has no water rights because the stream is state property.

17. When a homeowner who is entitled by Texas law to a homestead exemption is sued by creditors, the general creditors
   a. can have the court sell the home and apply the full proceeds of the sale to the debts.
   b. usually have no right to have the debtor's home sold.
   c. can force the debtor to sell the home to pay them.
   d. can have the sheriff serve an eviction notice.

18. An urban homestead is limited to a lot or lots not to exceed
   a. $10,000 in value.
   b. $100,000 in value.
   c. 1 acre.
   d. 10 acres.

Detailed rationales for the end-of-chapter review questions are available online at www.dearborn.com through the *Instructor Resource Guides* link.

CHAPTER 9

How Home Ownership Is Held

■ **LEARNING OBJECTIVES** *When you have completed this chapter, you will be able to*

■ **identify** the four basic forms of co-ownership and explain how each is created and terminated;

■ **describe** the ways in which various business organizations may own property;

■ **explain** the common business entities through which real estate brokerages are organized; state the filing requirements and the License Act/TREC Rules governing each;

■ **distinguish** among cooperative ownership, condominium ownership, and time-share ownership; and

■ **define** the following *key terms*:

beneficiary	general partnership	severalty
common elements	joint tenancy	sole proprietorship
community property	limited liability company	syndicate
community property right	(LLC)	tenancy in common
of survivorship	limited partnership	time-sharing
condominium	partition	trust
cooperative	partnership	trustee
co-ownership	right of survivorship	trustor
corporation	separate property	undivided interest
deed in trust		

OVERVIEW

Purchasers can consider many different forms of ownership before taking title to a parcel of real estate. The choice of ownership form will affect such matters as the owner's legal right to sell the real estate without the consent of others, the owner's right to choose who will own the property after his death, and the rights of creditors in the future. The choice in many cases also will have tax implications, both in terms of a possible gift tax and in terms of future income and estate taxes.

This chapter discusses the many basic forms of real estate ownership available to individuals and business entities. The cooperative and condominium forms of ownership also are addressed.

FORMS OF OWNERSHIP

In Texas, a fee simple estate in land may be held by one owner or by two or more co-owners under one of three forms of ownership:

1. In **severalty**, which means that title is held by one owner
2. In **co-ownership**, where title is held by two or more persons or two or more legal entities
3. In **trust**, where title is held by a third person for the benefit of another (or others), called the *beneficiary* (or *beneficiaries*)

The form by which property is owned is important to the real estate broker for two reasons: First, the form of ownership existing when a property is sold determines who must sign the various documents involved (listing contract, sales contract, and deed). Second, the purchaser must determine in what form he wishes to take title. For example, if one purchaser is taking title in his name alone, it is tenancy in severalty; two or more purchasers might take title as tenants in common or as joint tenants. Married purchasers' choices are governed by state laws. Texas law provides for married couples to own real estate under community property laws.

Forms of ownership are controlled by the laws of the state in which the land is located. When questions about these forms are raised by the parties to a transaction, the real estate broker should recommend that the parties seek legal advice.

OWNERSHIP IN SEVERALTY

When title to real estate is *vested in* (presently owned by) one entity, that person or organization is said to own the property *in severalty*, as the *sole owner*. The root word is *sever*, which means "individually" or "severed from others." A property title that reads "jointly and severally" literally means "collectively and individually." Businesses (partnerships, corporations, and limited liability companies) usually hold title to property in severalty with all real and personal property owned by the business. Texas has special laws that affect title held in severalty by either a husband or a wife. These laws are covered later in this chapter in the section titled "Community Property Rights."

CO-OWNERSHIP

When title to one parcel of real estate is vested in two or more persons or organizations, those parties are said to be *co-owners*, or *concurrent owners*, of the property. Concurrent ownership means that the property is owned by two or more owners at the same time, each sharing in the right to use, occupy, and possess each part of the property, but not exclusively. The forms of co-ownership most commonly recognized in Texas are (1) tenancy in common, (2) joint tenancy, and (3) community property. Each of these has unique legal characteristics and will be discussed separately.

Tenancy in Common

A **tenancy in common**, which is owned by two or more people or organizations, has two important characteristics. *First*, the ownership interest of a tenant in common is an **undivided interest**; there is a *unity of possession* among the co-owners, or *cotenants*. A tenant in common may hold, for example, a one-half or one-third interest in a property, but the physical property is not divided into a specific half or third. Ownership shares among the cotenants in a tenancy in common do not have to be equal. For example, if there were three cotenants, one person could have one-half interest with each of the remaining two cotenants having one-fourth interest. However, if no fractional interest is stated in the deed creating the tenancy in common, ownership shares are equal. Thus, if five people hold title, each owns an undivided one-fifth interest.

The *second* important characteristic of a tenancy in common is that each owner holds an *undivided fractional interest* in severalty and can sell, convey, mortgage, or transfer that interest without the consent of the other cotenants. However, cotenants do have a duty to protect and preserve the property against waste. A party committing waste is responsible to the other cotenants for damages. Cotenants are also responsible for the payment of a common debt, such as the mortgage and property taxes, contributing proportionately according to their undivided interest. On the death of a cotenant, the deceased's undivided interest passes to heirs or devisees (recipients by will) according to the will. If there is no will, this interest passes to the next of kin according to the Texas Probate Code. The interest of a deceased tenant in common does not pass to another tenant in common unless the surviving cotenant is an heir, devisee, or purchaser (see Figure 9.1). In Texas, the spouse of a married tenant in common generally is required to sign a deed to a purchaser to release her rights. Both husband and wife *must* sign the deed if the property held in a tenancy in common is homestead property.

When two or more people acquire title to a parcel of real estate and the deed of conveyance does not stipulate the character of the tenancy created, by operation of law the grantees usually acquire title as tenants in common. However, in Texas a conveyance made to a husband and wife with no further explanation creates a community property interest.

FIGURE 9.1: Tenancy in Common

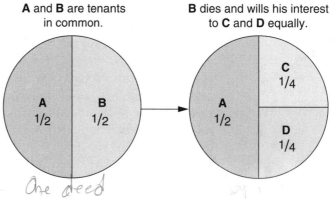

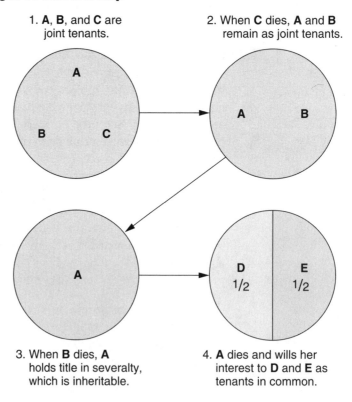

Joint Tenancy

Joint tenancy is the ownership of real estate by two or more people, typically with the **right of survivorship** (see Figure 9.2). A right of survivorship in the joint tenancy must be agreed to in writing between the joint owners. As each successive joint tenant dies, the surviving joint tenants acquire the interest of the deceased joint tenant. The last survivor takes title in severalty; on this person's death, the property goes to the heirs.

FIGURE 9.2: Joint Tenancy with Right of Survivorship

Creating Joint Tenancies   Because the law presumes a tenancy in common relationship if two or more unmarried people hold an interest in property, a joint tenancy relationship must be created by a signed, written agreement of the joint owners. The agreement must specifically state the intention to create a joint tenancy with right of survivorship, and the grantees in a deed must be identified explicitly as joint tenants with right of survivorship. For example, typical wording in a conveyance creating a joint tenancy is "to A and B as joint tenants and to the survivor of them, his or her heirs and assigns." Particularly in community real estate, a property owner should consult an attorney before creating a joint tenancy with rights of survivorship in Texas.

A joint tenancy with right of survivorship may be used by people who share a business and want the property to pass to the surviving business members to keep the company running. It also may be used when family members want property to pass to remaining immediate family members without its being diluted in various estates. As with tenants in common, joint tenants may sell, convey, mortgage, or transfer their undivided interests without consent of the other cotenants. They are responsible for protecting and preserving the property and for payment of a proportionate share of common debt.

Common law dictates that four *unities* are required to create a joint tenancy: unity of *time*, unity of *title*, unity of *interest*, and unity of *possession*. These four unities are present when title is acquired by *one deed, executed and delivered at one time and conveying equal interests to all the grantees who hold undivided possession of the property as joint tenants.*

Terminating Joint Tenancies   A joint tenancy is destroyed when any one of the four essential unities of joint tenancy is terminated. Thus, although a joint tenant is free to convey his interest in the jointly held property, doing so will destroy the unity of interest and, in turn the joint tenancy. For example, if A, B, and C hold title as joint tenants and A conveys her interest to D, then D will own an undivided one-third interest in severalty as a tenant in common with B and C, who will continue to own their undivided two-thirds interest as joint tenants (see Figure 9.3). Joint tenancies also may be terminated by operation of law, as in bankruptcy or foreclosure sale proceedings.

FIGURE 9.3:   Combination of Tenancies

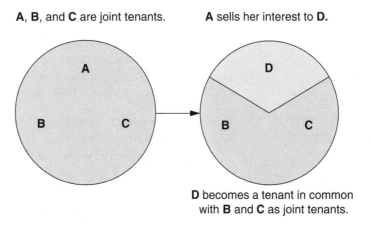

D becomes a tenant in common
with **B** and **C** as joint tenants.

Termination of Co-Ownership by Partition Suit

Tenants in common or joint tenants who wish to terminate their co-ownership of real estate may file a suit in court to **partition** the land. The right of partition is a legal way to dissolve a co-ownership when the parties do not voluntarily agree to its termination. If the court determines that the land cannot actually be divided into parts *of equal value*, not size, it will order the real estate sold and divide the proceeds of the sale among the co-owners according to their fractional interests.

Community Property Rights

Texas community property laws are based on the concept that a husband and wife, rather than merging into one entity, are equal partners. The laws apply to all Texas citizens even if their marriage occurred in another state or country. Under community property laws, any property acquired during a marriage (either formal or common law) is considered obtained by mutual effort. The concept originated in Spanish law and has been adopted by only nine states (Arizona, California, Idaho, Louisiana, Nevada, New Mexico, Texas, Washington, and Wisconsin). The states' community property laws vary widely but they all recognize two kinds of property: separate property and community property.

Separate property is property owned solely by either spouse before the marriage or acquired by gift or inheritance after the marriage. Such separate property also includes any property purchased with separate funds after the marriage, proceeds from the sale of separate property, settlement or judgment proceeds for personal injury, or property separated during marriage by a written contract signed by both spouses (*contractual separate property*). Normally, any income earned from separate property is community property, such as interest on a separate property savings account or rental income from a separate property real estate investment. However, contractual separate property agreements and gifts to spouses may provide that future earnings and income arising from the partitioned property be the separate property of the owning spouse. Property classified as sole and separate can be mortgaged or conveyed by the owning spouse without the signature of the non-owning spouse, unless such property is homestead property.

Even though property is separate property, an equitable interest exists for the nonowning spouse under certain circumstances, among them (1) there was an enhancement in the value of the separate property from community property funds during the marriage, (2) community property funds were used to discharge all or part of the mortgage on the separate property, or (3) community property funds were used to reduce unsecured debt incurred by the separate estate. Generally, the equitable interest created is proportionate to the amount of payments made from community funds versus separate funds. Should a marriage terminate, the court is required to impose an equitable lien on community or separate property to secure the claim for reimbursement.

Community property consists of all other property, real and personal, acquired by either spouse during the marriage. In addition, if both spouses agree, all or part of their separate property can be converted to community property. In addition to statutorily prescribed language, the written agreement must identify the property being converted, specify that the property is being converted to community property, and be signed by both spouses. Certain employee benefits, such as a *deferred benefit retirement plan* or a *stock option plan*, may have both separate and community property interests.

Any conveyance or encumbrance of community property requires the signatures of both spouses, unless one spouse is the manager of that particular piece of community property. Although community property in Texas *may* be conveyed by a managing spouse alone, many attorneys and title companies require the signatures of both spouses "pro forma" ("for form") because of the possibility of commingling

Separate Property

Includes property acquired during marriage
- by gift,
- by inheritance,
- by purchase from separate funds,
- by sale of separate property,
- by settlement or judgment for personal injury, or
- by written contract with a spouse.

In Texas, most property acquired by either spouse during marriage is *community property*. Additionally, income earned from separate property is generally community property.

separate and community property funds. *Homestead rights can be conveyed only by the joint deed of husband and wife*, even if the homestead is the separate property of one spouse and title is held by that one spouse as sole owner.

On the death of one spouse who leaves no will, the survivor inherits all community property, *if* the surviving children and descendants are common to both spouses. Otherwise, the surviving spouse retains one-half interest in community property and the other half is distributed to the children of the deceased (see Chapter 17).

A **community property right of survivorship** provides for the existence of a community property estate with a right of survivorship. It differs from a joint tenancy in the parties' responsibilities for debts: in a joint tenancy, each party is liable for the *proportional* share of debts; in community property, both spouses may be jointly and severally liable for *all* community debts. Upon the death of one spouse, probate is eliminated, and all interest in the property goes automatically to the surviving spouse.

The agreement to create the community property right of survivorship must
- be in writing;
- be signed by both spouses;
- describe the community property subject to the agreement; and
- contain a phrase that demonstrates the intent, such as "with right of survivorship," "will become the property of the survivor," or "shall pass to the surviving spouse."

Revocation of a community property right of survivorship agreement requires a written instrument signed by both spouses or signed by one spouse and delivered to the other spouse.

IN PRACTICE Because neither the community property right of survivorship agreement nor the revocation agreement must be filed in the county clerk's office, community property estates with rights of survivorship are not widely accepted by Texas mortgage lenders or title insurance companies and are, therefore, discouraged.

Co-ownership examples are as follows:
- A deed conveys title to A and B (who are not a married couple). If the intention of the parties is not stated, ownership as tenants in common is created. If A dies, her one-half interest will pass to her heirs or according to her will.
- A deed conveying title of one-third to C and two-thirds to D (who are not a married couple) creates a tenancy in common, with each owner having the fractional interest specified.
- A deed to H and W as husband and wife creates community property.
- A written joint tenancy agreement and a conveyance of real estate to two people (not husband and wife) by such wording as "to Y and Z, as joint tenants with right of survivorship" creates a joint tenancy ownership. Upon the death of Y, title to the property passes to Z by right of survivorship.
- M and spouse hold title to an undivided one-half interest in real estate as community property, and S and spouse hold title to the other undivided one-half with a community property right of survivorship. The relationship among the owners of the two half interests is that of tenants in common. In this example, a combination of interests exists in one parcel of real estate.

TRUSTS

The principal or capital placed in a trust is its *corpus*.

A *trust* is a device by which one person transfers ownership of property to someone else to hold or manage for the benefit of a third party. Perhaps a grandfather wishes to ensure the college education of his granddaughter, so he transfers his oil field into a trust through a **deed in trust**. He instructs the grandchild's mother to use its income to pay for the grandchild's college tuition. In this case, the grandfather is the **trustor**—the person who creates the trust. The granddaughter is the **beneficiary**—the person who benefits from the trust; she holds a personal property interest. The mother is the **trustee**—the party who holds legal title to the trust property (the oil field) and is entrusted with carrying out the trustor's instructions regarding the purpose of the trust (manage the trust assets and pay college tuition). The trustee is a *fiduciary*, who acts in confidence, trust, or responsibility in the management of property for the beneficiary. An individual, corporation, or any other legal entity, such as a trust company, can be the trustee. The trustee's power and authority are limited by the terms of the trust agreement, will, or deed in trust. Figure 9.4 illustrates the relationship of parties to a trust.

FIGURE 9.4:   Trust Ownership

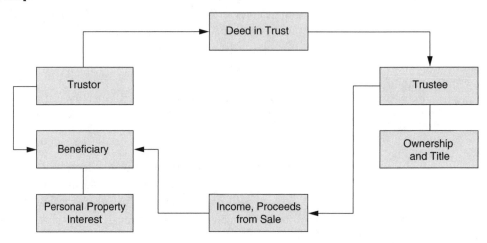

The trustee's duties may include the care and investment of the trust assets to produce an income. After paying the trust's operating expenses and trustee's fees, the income is paid to or used for the benefit of the beneficiary. The trust may continue for the beneficiary's lifetime, or the assets may be distributed when the beneficiary reaches a certain age or when other conditions are met.

Real estate can be owned under living trusts, testamentary trusts, and land trusts. In addition, real estate may be held by a number of people in a *real estate investment trust (REIT)*, discussed in Chapter 25.

Living and Testamentary Trusts

Trust ownership of property is becoming increasingly more popular. It permits property owners to provide for their own financial care and/or that of their families; it is a tax and estate planning tool. Trusts may be created by agreement during a property owner's lifetime (living or *inter vivos*) or established by will after that person's death (testamentary).

Trusts

■ Living: Created during a person's lifetime to manage assets while alive and after death

■ Testamentary: Established by will after death

■ Land: Real estate is the only asset; beneficiaries are not included in public records

A *revocable living trust* is basically a will substitute, and it can be changed or revoked at any time. While still living, the trustor places titles to real estate, securities, and other assets into a trust. Homestead real property can be transferred into a revocable living trust without affecting the homestead protection as long as the grantor is also a beneficiary and is occupying and using the property as a primary residence.

A trust document outlines instructions for managing the assets and distributing them both during the trustor's life and after death. The trustor can act as trustee, retaining the right to control and use the assets for the rest of his life; the trustor can also be the beneficiary of the trust, receiving the income and other benefits of the trust assets for as long as he is alive. The trust document can name one or more other persons as beneficiaries upon the trustor's death. Among the advantages of the revocable living trust are

- avoidance of probate for distribution of trust assets after death,
- privacy about the details of the estate since the administration of the trust would not be part of a probate hearing, and
- taxation at individual income tax rates if a trustor is also the trustee of the revocable living trust.

Irrevocable living trusts cannot be amended or revoked once they are executed. The assets placed into an irrevocable trust are permanently removed from a grantor's estate and transferred to the trust. Income taxes on assets in the trust are paid by the trust at a higher tax rate than on an individual return.

FOR EXAMPLE   Jack, a successful business executive, has a son (Carl) who is a well-known musician. Because Carl has little interest in financial matters, Jack irrevocably transferred certain securities and real estate to XYZ Trust Company to be administered by the company with the income going to Carl for life. On Carl's death, the property is to go into the music scholarship fund at a nearby university.

Land Trusts

Real estate is the only asset in a land trust, and the owner (trustor) is generally the beneficiary. One of the distinguishing characteristics of a land trust is that the public records do not indicate the beneficiary's identity. A land trust agreement is executed by the trustor and the trustee. Under this agreement, the trustee has a *real property* interest, yet deals with the property only on the beneficiary's written direction. Although the beneficial interest in the trust real estate is considered to be *personal property*, the beneficiary retains management and control of the property through the trustee and has the right of possession, as well as the right to any income or proceeds from its sale.

A land trust generally continues for a definite term, such as 20 years. If the beneficiary does not extend the trust term when it expires, the trustee usually is obligated to sell the real estate and distribute the net proceeds to the beneficiary. Land trusts are normally used for speculative holding purposes and are popular among multiple owners who seek protection against the effects of divorce, judgments, or bankruptcy of the other owners.

Anyone who might consider setting up a trust should seek expert financial and legal counsel because trusts are very complex, with not only advantages but also serious disadvantages under some circumstances.

OWNERSHIP OF REAL ESTATE BY BUSINESSES

By Sole Proprietorships

A **sole proprietorship** exists when a single individual operates a business, owns all the assets, and assumes personal liability for all debts. It is the simplest form of business organization. A sole proprietorship may have employees, but only one person controls the business.

The sole owner has the opportunity to operate independently and to make all decisions related to the operation of the company, for example, deciding which properties to purchase as investments and how much to pay for them. In exchange for complete control, the sole owner assumes the risks for all assets owned, whether used in the business or personally owned. If a business owner has unpaid debts, creditors can go after the business owner's personal assets, such as a personal checking account. Also, all profits and losses from a sole proprietorship are reported directly on the sole owner's personal income tax return.

A sole proprietorship is frequently used in real estate brokerage. An individual proprietor may run a brokerage company if he has a valid broker's license. If the business is operated under a name other than that of the licensed broker, the Rules of the Texas Real Estate Commission require the broker to notify the Commission in writing within 30 days of adopting an "assumed name," such as *Alicia Bennett, doing business as ABC Realty* (or Alicia Bennett, DBA ABC Realty). (See Rule 535.154(c).) Additionally, an Assumed Name Certificate, indicating the name under which business is to be conducted, must be filed with the county clerk in each county where business premises will be maintained. The owner of a sole proprietorship is not required to register the *business* with the Secretary of State.

By Business Organizations

Ownership by a business organization makes it possible for many people to hold an interest in the same parcel of real estate—combining their cash and sharing the risks. Investors may be organized to finance a real estate project in various ways. Some methods provide for the real estate to be owned by the entity itself; others provide for direct ownership of the real estate by the investors. Business organizations may be categorized as partnerships, corporations, limited liability companies, or real estate investment trusts (REITs) and are organized under the Texas Business Organizations Code. (REITs will be discussed in Chapter 25.) The purchase or sale of real estate by any business organization involves complex legal questions, and legal counsel usually is required.

Partnerships

An association of two or more people who operate a business as co-owners and share in the business's profits and losses is a **partnership**. The agreement between partners may be oral or written, and title may be held in the names of the individual partners (as tenants in common or as joint tenants) or in the name of the partnership (as owners in severalty).

Sole Proprietorship
- Operated by a single individual
- Owner assumes all risks and gets all profits

DBA: "doing business as"
- Used to identify a business name other than that of the person under whom the business is registered
- Also called an assumed name

Partnerships
- General: All partners are liable for all losses
- Limited: General partners and limited partners; limited partners are obligated to the extent of their investment
- Limited Liability: Partners are not personally liable in most cases

FOR EXAMPLE   A partnership decides to sell some of its real property holdings. If the partners hold the property as tenants in common, the signature of each partner will be required. If the property is held in the name of the partnership, only one signature will be required to convey the real estate.

There are two kinds of partnerships, general and limited. In a **general partnership** all partners participate to some extent in the operation and management of the business and may be held jointly and severally (together and separately; personally) liable for all business losses and obligations. A **limited partnership** includes general partners as well as limited partners. The general partner or partners run the business; however, the limited partners do not participate in the management. Each general partner can be held liable for business losses and obligations, but the liability of the limited partners is limited to the extent of their individual investment. The limited partnership is a popular method of organizing investors in a real estate project. Profits and losses on partnership income are *passed through* to the individuals' income tax returns; the partnership itself does not pay taxes on its income.

Partnerships, whether general or limited, may be continued after the death, withdrawal, or bankruptcy of one of the partners as long as the majority-in-interest partners agree to continue the partnership and as long as there is at least one limited partner remaining in a limited partnership.

A *limited liability partnership* (LLP) is managed like a general partnership, but a partner is not personally liable to any person, including a partner, for any obligation of the partnership unless the obligation relates to an action or omission or arises under a contract or commitment entered into while the partnership is an LLP (S.B. 748, 2011).

IN PRACTICE   A general partnership is required to file an Assumed Name Certificate for each name that the business will use. It must be filed with the county clerk in each county in which business premises will be maintained. A general partnership is not required to register with the secretary of state.

Limited partnerships and limited liability partnerships are required to register the *business* with the secretary of state and must file an Assumed Name Certificate only if the business is to be identified by a name other than that on file with the secretary of state.

Corporations

Corporations
- Ownership in severalty
- Owned by stockholders
- Liability limited to amount of investment
- Double taxation

A **corporation** is an artificial person, or legal entity, created under the authority of the laws of the state from which it receives its charter. Because a corporation is a legal entity, real estate ownership by a corporation is an *ownership in severalty*. A corporation is managed and operated by its *board of directors*. A corporation's charter sets forth the powers of the corporation, including its right to buy and sell real estate after passage of a resolution to that effect by its board of directors. Some charters permit a corporation to purchase real estate for any purpose; others limit such purchases to land needed to fulfill the entity's corporate purpose. A licensee should ask for a copy of the corporate resolution authorizing a sale before listing a property. However, a deed signed by an officer of the corporation is prima facie evidence that a resolution of the board of directors was adopted.

As a legal entity, a corporation exists in perpetuity until it is formally dissolved. The death of one of the officers or directors does not affect title to property that is owned by the corporation. Individuals participate, or invest, in a corporation by purchasing stock. Because stock is *personal property*, stockholders do not have a direct ownership interest in real estate owned by a corporation. The stockholders' liability for the corporation's losses usually is limited to the amount of their individual investment. Officers and directors of corporations have limited liability when they rely on information, opinions, reports, and statements prepared by the corporation or other professional counsel and there is no evidence of fraud.

One of the main disadvantages of corporate ownership of income property is that the profits are subject to double taxation unless organized as an S corporation. As a legal entity, a corporation must pay a franchise tax, file an income tax return, and pay tax on profits. In addition, the remaining profits distributed to stockholders as dividends are taxed again as part of the stockholders' individual incomes.

An *S corporation*, once called a *subchapter S corporation*, is a corporation that has elected to be treated more like a partnership for tax purposes, avoiding the double taxation feature of corporate ownership. Profits and losses are passed through to each stockholder for reporting on an individual personal tax return. Although there is no limitation on the amount of corporate income for an S corporation, the number of shareholders is limited to 75. Its basic disadvantage is that aggregate losses that may be passed through to individual shareholders may equal only the amount of cash each shareholder paid for the stock plus any loans made to the company.

Limited Liability Companies

LLCs
- Limited liability of a corporation
- Tax advantages of a partnership

A **limited liability company (LLC)** is a hybrid business entity with the combined characteristics and benefits of both limited partnerships and S corporations. The owners of an LLC, called *members*, enjoy the pass-through tax advantages of a partnership and the limited liability offered by a corporate form of ownership (S.B. 323, 2011). Neither members nor managers are liable for company debts, obligations, or liabilities. Unlike an S corporation, an LLC places no restriction on the number of shareholders who take part. A membership interest in an LLC is considered personal property, and a member has no interest in specific company property.

A Series LLC is a new form of LLC permitting one or more series (units) to be established within a master LLC (S.B. 1442, 2009). Each unit has its own members and may be managed separately from the master LLC and the other units. Some of the key features of the Series LLC form of ownership include each unit's (1) having its own assets and liabilities, (2) being responsible for its own debts and obligations, and (3) conducting part of the business of the master LLC or conducting wholly different businesses, if desired. Members of one series have no rights to the assets or income of any other series; each series operates essentially as a separate LLC within the master LLC. In general, creditors of one series may only reach the assets of that series. As long as separate records are maintained for a particular series, the members of the series are protected from personal liability for the debts and obligations of the master LLC or the series, as with a regularly formed LLC.

IN PRACTICE   All corporations and limited liability companies doing business in Texas must be registered with the secretary of state. If business is to be transacted under a name other than the one filed with the secretary of state, the corporation or limited liability company must file an Assumed Name Certificate with both the secretary of state and the county clerk in each county in which the business has a registered or principal office.

If a real estate brokerage is organized as a partnership, corporation, or limited liability company, the Rules of the Commission require that an officer, manager, or general partner who is an active Texas real estate broker be designated to act for it. The business entity would be required to obtain a broker's license in the name of the business entity and to maintain errors and omissions insurance with a minimum annual limit of $1 million if the designated broker owns less than 10% of the entity (S.B. 747, 2011; Rule 535.53).

Business Franchise Taxes   The Texas franchise tax, or margins tax, is a privilege tax imposed on each taxable entity chartered/organized in Texas or doing business in Texas. It applies to all entities that enjoy liability protection: limited partnerships, limited liability partnerships, corporations, LLCs, professional associations, and business trusts. General partnerships that are solely owned by individuals and sole proprietorships are not subject to the tax. Also among other exclusions, businesses with $1 million or less in total revenue are exempt (H.B. 500, 2013).

In October 2012, the Texas Supreme Court ruled that the application of higher state franchise tax rates for certain businesses does not violate the Texas Constitution's equal and uniform clause.

Syndicates

Generally speaking, a **syndicate** is a *joining together of two or more people or firms to make and operate a real estate investment.* A syndicate is not in itself a legal entity; however, it may be organized into a number of ownership forms, including co-ownership (tenancy in common, joint tenancy), partnership, trust, or corporation. Real estate syndicates and other complex business arrangements will be discussed in Chapter 25.

IN PRACTICE   Property investment and ownership by a business entity may affect the recognition, treatment, and carryover of ordinary income and losses and capital gains and losses. Therefore, legal and tax advice should be sought to determine the best form of business ownership for a particular situation.

COOPERATIVE AND CONDOMINIUM OWNERSHIP

Prompted by the urge to "own a part of the land" and certain tax advantages that accrue to ownership, cooperatives and condominiums were created, in many instances in buildings that originated as apartment rental units.

Cooperative Ownership

Cooperative

Purchaser has
- stock ownership (personal property) and
- a proprietary lease.

The cooperative was the first form of individual ownership within multiunit buildings. Under the usual **cooperative** arrangement, title to land and building is held by the cooperative, which is a type of corporation. The building management sets a price for each apartment in the building. Each purchaser of an apartment in the building receives stock in the cooperative upon paying the agreed price for the apartment. The purchaser then becomes a stockholder of the cooperative and, *by virtue of that stock ownership, receives a proprietary lease* to the apartment for the life of the cooperative.

The cooperative building's real estate taxes are assessed against the cooperative as the owner. The mortgage is signed by the cooperative, creating one lien on the entire parcel of real estate. Taxes, mortgage interest and principal, and operating and maintenance expenses on the property are shared by the tenants/shareholders in the form of monthly assessments similar to rent.

Thus, even though the cooperative tenants/owners do not actually own an interest in real estate (they own stock, which is *personal property*), for all practical purposes they control the property through their stock ownership and their voice in the management of the cooperative. Bylaws may provide that an administrative board must approve each prospective purchaser of an apartment lease.

FOR EXAMPLE   In a highly publicized incident, former President Richard Nixon's attempt to move into an exclusive Manhattan cooperative apartment building was blocked by the cooperative's board. In refusing to allow the controversial ex-president to purchase shares, the board cited the unwanted publicity and media attention other tenants would suffer.

One disadvantage of cooperative ownership is the possibility that if enough owners/occupants fail to make prompt payment of their monthly assessments, the cooperative might be forced to default. The entire property could be ordered sold by court order in a foreclosure suit. Such a sale usually would destroy the interests of all occupants/shareholders, even those who paid their assessments regularly. Another disadvantage is that some cooperatives provide that tenants/owners can sell their interest back to the cooperative only at the original purchase price, so that the cooperative gains any profits made on the resale. These limitations have diminished the appeal of this form of ownership and resulted in greater preference for the condominium form of ownership.

Condominium Ownership

The **condominium** form of ownership of apartment buildings has gained increasing popularity in Texas, particularly in urban areas. The condominium form of ownership typically is used for residential buildings. However, it also is used for commercial property, office buildings, or multiuse buildings that contain offices and shops as well as residential units. A condominium in Texas may be created on lands owned in fee simple or held under a lease. Under the *Texas Uniform Condominium Act*, the owner of each apartment or unit holds a *fee simple title* to the unit (sometimes referred to as *owning from carpet to ceiling and paint to paint*) and also a specified share of the indivisible parts of the building and land, known as the **common elements** (see Figure 9.5). The individual unit owners in a condominium own these common elements together as *tenants in common*. The condominium legal documents usually stipulate that there is *no right to partition*.

FIGURE 9.5: Condominium Ownership

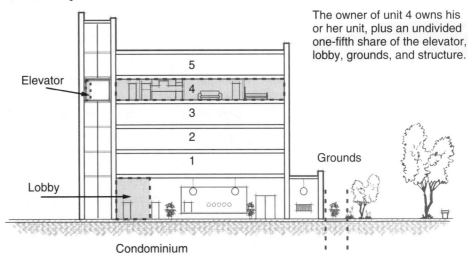

The owner of unit 4 owns his or her unit, plus an undivided one-fifth share of the elevator, lobby, grounds, and structure.

Ownership of a condominium generally breaks down into four subcategories. These are

1. full ownership of the airspace within the unit bounded by the surfaces of the floors, ceilings, and walls;
2. pro rata ownership of the limited common elements (such as bearing walls, porch, balcony, patio, and stairs that serve only the unit);
3. pro rata ownership of the general common elements (land, foundation, roof, pool, driveways, structure, clubhouse, and other items existing for common use); and
4. pro rata ownership in the homeowners association.

Creation of a Condominium   To create a condominium (or *horizontal property regime*, as they are sometimes called), a condominium declaration and a condominium regime plat are recorded in the county in which the real estate is located. The condominium declaration sets out the rights and obligations of each unit owner.

The plat subdivides the land and building into apartment units, describes each apartment by unit number, and assigns a fractional share of the common elements to each unit; the minimum number of units in a condominium is four. Texas law provides that the boundaries of the fee simple units are the interior surfaces of the perimeter walls, floors, and ceilings. In the event of settling, rising or lateral movement, or substantial reconstruction of the building, the law states that the existing physical boundaries shall be conclusively presumed to be the actual boundaries.

Condominium owners have the following:
- Fee simple title to a unit
- Pro rata ownership of limited and general common elements
- Pro rata ownership of the homeowners' association

Ownership After the property is established as a condominium, each unit becomes a separate parcel of real estate that may be dealt with like any other parcel of real property. A condominium unit is owned in fee simple and may be held by one or more people in any type of ownership or tenancy that is recognized by state law.

Before a condo unit can be sold, whether as a new unit from the developer or a resale from another individual, a prospective buyer must receive several documents from the seller. If the buyer does not receive the required disclosures prior to signing a purchase contract, the buyer may cancel the contract before the sixth day after the date the buyer receives the required disclosures. All payments made before cancellation must be refunded to the buyer.

Real estate taxes are assessed and collected on each unit as an individual property, and condominium unit owners should insure their own unit. Default in the payment of taxes or a mortgage loan by one unit owner may result in a foreclosure sale of that unit but does not affect the ownership of the other unit owners.

Operation and Administration The condominium property generally is administered by an association of unit owners according to the bylaws set forth in the declaration. The association may be governed by a board of directors or other official entity, it may manage the property on its own, or it may engage a professional property manager to perform this function.

Acting through its board of directors or other officers, the association must enforce any rules it adopts regarding the operation and use of the property. The association is responsible for the maintenance, repair, cleaning, and sanitation of the common elements and structural portions of the property. It also must maintain fire and extended-coverage insurance, as well as liability insurance, for these portions of the property. Expenses incurred in fulfilling these responsibilities are paid for by the unit owners in the form of monthly *assessments*, collected by the owners association. Such fees are assessed to each unit owner and are due periodically, depending on the provisions of the bylaws. If such assessments are not paid, the association usually has the option to seek a court-ordered judgment to have the property sold to cover the outstanding amount. Texas courts have held that this is an enforceable lien against the homestead, provided the condominium documents were filed properly prior to the creation of the homestead.

Termination of Condominium Ownership If a condominium declaration provides for termination of condominium ownership, most or all of the unit owners must be party to a revocation agreement filed in the public record in the county where the property is located. All unit owners then would become tenants in common, each owning an undivided interest in the entire property that is equal to the percentage of ownership in the common elements previously held.

Familiarity with the *Texas Uniform Condominium Act* is essential. Condominium ownership should not be confused with townhouse ownership, which typically includes fee simple ownership of the land beneath it. In a condominium interest, the land is held as part of the general common elements.

Time-Share
- Fee simple interest or a license
- Right to use for a fixed or variable time period

Time-Share Ownership   Time-sharing (sometimes referred to as a *vacation ownership interest* or a *vacation ownership plan*) is a variation of condominium ownership that permits multiple purchasers to buy undivided interests in the same piece of real estate—usually a unit of a resort hotel or development—with a right to use the facility for a fixed or variable time period. In most cases, the time-share interest is a fee simple title interest, but it can be merely a right to use (a license). In the latter case, the right terminates after a specified time. Time-sharing enables a person to own a share in a vacation home in a desirable location for a fraction of the cost of full ownership. Year-round maintenance and other common expenses are prorated among the unit owners.

Some time-share programs allow for a rotation system in which the tenant in common can occupy the unit at different times of the year in different years. Other programs sell only specific months or weeks of the year. For example, 12 individuals could own equal, undivided interests in one condominium unit, with each owner entitled to use the premises for a specified month out of each year. Most time-share contracts allow owners of interests in one property to exchange time at their vacation sites for time at other properties around the world.

Another newer time-share program—the vacation club—is an organization that may own units in multiple resorts in different locations. Members of a vacation club generally receive an annual allotment of vacation points based on the size of real estate interest purchased, for example, 100 points or 210 points. Each vacation accommodation has a vacation point value that is determined by the type of room and the timing of the stay—weekends and peak seasons use more points than less busy times of the year.

More than 4.7 million American households owned at least one time-share at the end of 2007.

Before a developer can sell or offer to sell a time-share interest in Texas, a developer must register the time-share plan with the Texas Real Estate Commission. If the salesperson selling a time-share is not an employee of either the builder of the project or the owner of the time-share interest, the salesperson must be licensed by TREC as a broker or salesperson. An extensive time-share disclosure statement must be given to a prospective purchaser of a time-share interest prior to the purchaser's signing a contract. The buyer must be given such information as the number of time-share interests available, the existing and proposed amenities, the procedures for scheduling a reservation, and current and anticipated fees and assessments to be paid by time-share buyers. Purchasers of time-share interests are protected against a developer's failure to meet the terms and conditions of the time-share disclosure statement. Prior to the release of funds escrowed for each time-share interest, the developer must provide TREC with satisfactory evidence that the time-share interest is free and clear of any claims of the developer, a lender, a judgment creditor, or any other person having an interest in or lien or encumbrance against the time-share interest. If any entity has an interest in the property, that interest would be subordinate to the rights of the owners of the time-share interests.

In addition to the time-share disclosure statement, each purchase contract must contain a statutorily prescribed "Purchaser's Right to Cancel." A purchase contract may be canceled before the sixth day after the date the purchaser signs and receives a copy of the purchase contract or receives a required time-share disclosure statement, whichever is later. The purchaser cannot waive this right of cancellation. Cancellation is without penalty and all payments made by the purchaser must be refunded. A developer or seller who violates the time-share act is guilty of a Class A misdemeanor.

IN PRACTICE   Because the Texas Real Estate Commission regulates the sale of time-share interests, the Texas Timeshare Act and the TREC Rules applicable to time-shares may be accessed through the "Forms, Laws, and Contracts" tab at the TREC website.

WEBLINK @ www.trec.texas.gov

SUMMARY

Sole ownership, or ownership in severalty, indicates that title is held by one person or entity. Title to real estate can be held concurrently by more than one person, called *co-ownership*, in several ways. In Texas, the most common forms of co-ownership are tenancy in common and community property.

Under tenancy in common, each party holds an undivided interest in severalty. Individual owners may sell, mortgage, convey, or transfer their own interest. On the death of one cotenant, that cotenant's interest passes to the heirs or according to the will. When two or more parties hold title to real estate, they will hold title as tenants in common unless there is an expressed intention otherwise or the conveyance is to a husband and wife. Joint tenancy with a right of survivorship involves two or more owners with the right of survivorship. The intention to establish a joint tenancy with a right of survivorship must be stated clearly in an agreement between the parties. Under common law, joint tenancy has four unities: time, title, interest, and possession.

Community property pertains to land owned by husband and wife and acquired by joint efforts during a marriage. Each spouse owns one-half of all community property. Properties acquired by a spouse before the marriage and through bequests, inheritance, gifts, or agreements after the marriage are deemed separate property. Additionally, property purchased from separate funds and money received from the sale of separate property are considered separate property. A community property right of survivorship agreement eliminates probate.

Real estate ownership also may be held in trust. In creating a trust, title to the property is conveyed by a trustor to a trustee, who holds title to the property and manages it for the benefit of a beneficiary. Trust forms include a living trust (which may be revocable or irrevocable), a testamentary trust, and a land trust.

Business ownership of real estate may take several different forms. In a sole proprietorship, a single individual operates a business, owns all the assets, and assumes personal liability for all debts. A partnership is an association of two or more people who operate a business and share in its profits and losses. General partners may be personally liable for all business losses. Limited partnerships and limited liability partnerships protect personal assets of limited partners. A corporation is a legal entity and it holds title to real estate in severalty. Individuals purchase stock in the corporation, with liability for corporation losses limited to the amount of each person's investment. A limited liability company combines the pass-through tax advantages of a limited partnership with the limited liability offered by an S corporation. A syndicate is an association of two or more people or firms to make a real estate investment.

Cooperative ownership of apartment buildings indicates title in one entity: the cooperative. Each purchaser receives stock in the cooperative along with a long-term proprietary lease to an apartment unit. The cooperative pays taxes, mortgage payments, and all operating expenses. Under condominium ownership, each owner holds fee simple title to the unit plus a share of the common elements. Each owner receives an individual tax bill and may mortgage the unit as desired. Expenses for operating the building are collected by an owners' association through monthly assessments.

Time-sharing, a variation of condominium ownership, enables multiple purchasers to own a share in real estate or at least the right to use it for a certain part of each year. Time-share developers must register with TREC; and salespersons must be licensed by TREC as a broker or a salesperson, unless they are employees of the builder or the owner of a time-share interest.

CHAPTER 9 QUESTIONS

1. Which *BEST* describes ownership of a time-share?

    a. The purchaser owns a right to use the facilities in a specified project(s) for a specified length of time for a specified number of years.

    b. Two or more purchasers become members of a business organization and receive a proprietary lease to a condominium for the life of the corporation.

    c. Two or more people or firms join together to make and operate a real estate investment.

    d. An association of two or more people operates a business as co-owners and share in the business profits and losses.

2. Howard and Tinker purchased a parcel of real estate. The seller's deed received at the closing conveyed the property "to Howard Evers and Tinker Chance" without further explanation. Thus Howard and Tinker

    a. are joint tenants.

    b. are tenants in common.

    c. hold community property rights.

    d. hold equal shares in a land trust.

3. Martin, Eduardo, and Shari are joint tenants owning a tract of land. Shari conveys her interest to Sandra. After the conveyance, which relationship exists?

    a. Martin, Eduardo, and Sandra are joint tenants.

    b. Martin, Eduardo, and Sandra are all tenants in common.

    c. Martin, Eduardo, and Shari are all tenants in common.

    d. Martin and Eduardo are joint tenants; Sandra is a tenant in common.

4. The four unities of time, title, interest, and possession are associated with which of the following?

    a. Community property right of survivorship

    b. Ownership in severalty

    c. Tenancy in common

    d. Joint tenancy

5. A purchaser under the cooperative form of ownership receives

    a. stock in the corporation and a proprietary lease.

    b. ownership of the airspace within the unit and a prorated portion of the common elements.

    c. the advantage of not having ownership interest destroyed by default of other occupants/shareholders.

    d. the statutory right to sell his interest back to the cooperative at the current market price.

6. Ownership of real property by one person without the ownership participation of others is called

    a. joint tenancy.

    b. severalty.

    c. solety.

    d. condominium.

7. The term *right of survivorship* is closely associated with a

    a. corporation.

    b. trust.

    c. joint tenancy.

    d. tenancy in common.

8. Because a corporation is a legal entity (an artificial person), real estate owned by it is owned in

    a. joint tenancy.

    b. partnership.

    c. severalty.

    d. survivorship tenancy.

9. Anthony and Anita purchased a block of apartment buildings in Houston and, for business reasons, took ownership to the real estate under a land trust, as permitted in Texas. Under this ownership arrangement,

    a. their identities will not appear in the public records.

    b. they will be unable to control the property or personally participate in the building's management.

    c. the land trust exists in perpetuity.

    d. legal title is held by the beneficiaries.

10. In a trust, title is vested in the
    a. trustee.
    b. trustor.
    c. beneficiary.
    d. vestee.

11. A property is owned by Fran, Gwen, and Hal as tenants in common. When Gwen dies, to whom will her interest pass?
    a. Fran and Hal equally
    b. Gwen's heirs
    c. Fran and Hal in joint tenancy
    d. The state, by the law of escheat

12. Gayle and Sam are engaged to be married. Any real estate that either owns at the time of marriage will remain that spouse's property in severalty, and property acquired after the wedding belongs to both of them equally. The form of ownership upon their marriage will be
    a. joint tenancy.
    b. cooperative.
    c. community property.
    d. tenancy in common.

13. Harold owns a fee simple title to unit 12 and 5% of the common elements. What does Harold own?
    a. A cooperative
    b. A condominium
    c. A townhouse
    d. A land trust

14. A legal arrangement whereby title to property is held for the benefit of a beneficiary is a
    a. trust.
    b. limited partnership.
    c. general partnership.
    d. corporation.

15. Under community property, the co-owners
    a. are spouses.
    b. must own equal interests in all real and personal property.
    c. inherit the deceased spouse's one-half interest upon the death of one co-owner.
    d. are joint tenants with right of survivorship.

16. A condominium is created when
    a. the owner or developer files a declaration of condominium and a condominium regime plat in the public record.
    b. a condominium owners association is established.
    c. all unit owners file documents in the public records asserting their decision.
    d. the construction of the improvements is completed.

17. Which is TRUE of a joint tenancy?
    a. A joint tenant may not sell her ownership share.
    b. The conveyance must specifically state the intention to create a joint tenancy.
    c. Joint tenants need not hold an equal interest in the property.
    d. The death of one joint tenant destroys the joint tenancy relationship of other parties.

18. A married couple is selling their homestead, owned as community property. For the deed conveying the property to be valid, who must sign it?
    a. The husband
    b. The wife
    c. Both husband and wife
    d. Only the managing spouse

19. The term *separate property* is MOST closely associated with which of the following?
    a. Joint tenancy
    b. Tenancy in common
    c. Community property
    d. Partnership

20. An advantage for organizing a business as a limited liability company is its
    a. taxation as a corporation.
    b. ability to designate a proportional interest in the real property to each member.
    c. limits on the liability of members for company debts or other obligations.
    d. ability to operate without registering with the state.

21. Which is generally classified as community property?
    a. Settlement proceeds for personal injury
    b. Income earned from separate property
    c. Inheritance after the marriage
    d. Proceeds from the sale of separate property after the marriage

22. Under a sole proprietorship form of business,
    a. the owner works alone, without employees.
    b. the owner is subject to double taxation.
    c. the owner's personal assets are protected from the claims of business creditors.
    d. the owner assumes personal liability for all debts.

23. When a business is organized as a partnership,
    a. title must be held in the name of the partnership.
    b. limited partners are jointly and severally responsible for all business debts.
    c. general partners are jointly and severally responsible for all business debts.
    d. the partnership automatically terminates upon the death of one partner

Detailed rationales for the end-of-chapter review questions are available online at www.dearborn.com through the *Instructor Resource Guides* link.

CHAPTER

10

Legal Descriptions

When you have completed this chapter, you will be able to

■ **identify** the three methods used to describe real estate;

■ **explain** how to read a metes-and-bounds survey description, how to divide a section of land, and how to calculate the acreage in a tract of land;

■ **describe** how a survey is prepared and how a datum and a benchmark relate to that process;

■ **distinguish** the various units of land measurement; and

■ **define** the following *key terms:*

air lot	monument	subdivision plat
base line	point (place) of beginning	survey
benchmark	principal meridian	township line
datum	range	township square
legal description	rectangular survey system	township tier
metes and bounds	section	

OVERVIEW

People often refer to real estate by its street address, such as "1546 East Main Street." While that is usually enough for the average person to find a particular building, it is not precise enough to be used on documents affecting the ownership of land. Deeds, sales contracts, and other documents require that property be identified by a *legally sufficient* description.

This chapter explains how land is identified and measured and discusses the three forms of legal description used in the United States. Although one of these forms, the rectangular survey system, is not used in Texas, it is discussed because all states surrounding Texas use this method of legal description.

LEGAL DESCRIPTIONS

A **legal description** is *an exact way of describing real estate in a contract, deed, mortgage, or other document that will be accepted by a court of law.* It is generally ascertained through a **survey**—*the process of precisely determining the area, dimensions, and location of a piece of land.* The courts have usually held that a description of the real estate in question is sufficient from a legal standpoint if a competent surveyor can locate it. Most state courts accept a street address as being sufficient to identify a parcel of real estate but not to serve as a legal description. Therefore, the legal description in a deed or mortgage may be followed by the words *commonly known as* and the street address.

An accurate description of the land being conveyed is an essential element of a valid real estate sales contract and of a deed. The real estate must be identifiable from the wording of the contract or deed and with reference to only the documents named in the contract or deed. Because the average parcel of land has been conveyed and transferred many times in the past, its description in a deed, mortgage, or other instrument should be the same as that used in a previous instrument of conveyance. Discrepancies, errors, and legal problems can be avoided or minimized if this practice is followed in drawing up subsequent conveyances.

METHODS OF DESCRIBING REAL ESTATE IN TEXAS

Three basic methods are used to describe real estate in the United States: (1) *metes and bounds*, (2) *rectangular (government) survey*, and (3) *recorded subdivision plat* (lot and block). Figure 10.4 shows which states use metes and bounds and which states use the rectangular survey method for describing property. A fourth method, usable under limited conditions, is *by reference to a previously recorded document.* However, it is essential with this method that no partial sales or subsequent acquisitions have occurred since the date of the referenced document.

Land in Texas has been under the sovereignty of the king of Spain, the Republic of Mexico, the Republic of Texas, and, since 1845, the State of Texas. The original grants from these sovereignties identified the land by metes-and-bounds descriptions, which give the distances and directions of the boundaries of the tract of land. During the sovereignty of the Republic of Texas (1836–1845) and after the formation of the State of Texas, the term *section* was used to designate a unit of land in surveying and laying out the state's public lands.

Metes and Bounds

The **metes-and-bounds** description is the oldest type of legal description. In it, the surveyor describes the perimeter of the subject property in terms of *distance, direction,* and *boundaries.* The description generally starts at a section corner or some other permanent reference marker established by the original surveyor of record—for example, "Beginning at a brass cap common to the northwest corner of Section 13 and the northeast corner of Section 14, BS&F-8 survey, Randall County, Texas . . ." From this point, the surveyor sets out the distance and direction to reach the **point (place) of beginning** (POB) for a particular parcel. The point may be represented by a post, a tree, an iron pipe, a rod, or some other clearly identifiable object. The description in the example above continues, "thence S 85° E, 1320' to an iron rod marking the *point of beginning.*"

The bearing (angular direction) of most boundary lines is northbound or southbound, with the variance from due north or due south measured in degrees, minutes, and seconds to the east or west; for example, S 85° E. Due north and due south are 0°; due east and due west are 90° (see Figure 10.1). Therefore, in the example in the previous paragraph, the property being described begins 1,320 feet southeast of the corner of Sections 13 and 14 on a line that runs at an 85° angle—5° south of due east. The legal description proceeds from the POB, generally *clockwise,* around the boundaries of the tract by reference to directions and linear measurements (measured in feet to the nearest one-hundredth of a foot). The next bearing continues from the POB and starts the description of the parcel in question—"thence 90° E, 1320'; thence S 20° W, 660'; thence to the point of beginning." In other words, from the POB head due east for 1,320 feet; from that point, go southwest at a 20° angle for 660 feet; from that point, go straight back to the POB. The parcel described forms a triangle (see Figure 10.2). A metes-and-bounds description always ends at the POB so that the tract being described is fully enclosed (the survey "closes").

> Land in the original 13 colonies, plus Hawaii, Maine, Vermont, Tennessee, Kentucky, Texas, West Virginia, and parts of Ohio were surveyed with the metes-and-bounds system.

FIGURE 10.1: Metes-and-Bounds Bearings

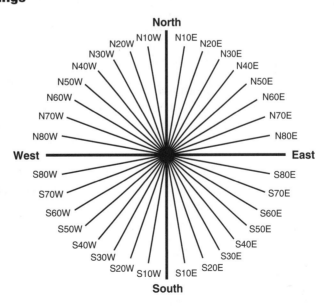

FIGURE 10.2: Survey Sketch

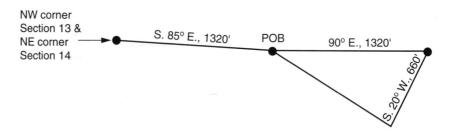

In some instances, **monuments** are used to establish real estate boundaries, corners, or points where directions change. Monuments are sometimes natural objects, such as trees, streams, or piles of stones; but they are generally man-made objects, such as iron pipes, posts, or stakes. Although court action may be required to resolve discrepancies in descriptions containing monuments, the following rules generally apply:

- The actual distance between monuments takes precedence over linear measurements set forth in the description if the two measurements differ (measurements often include the words *more or less*).
- Natural objects take precedence over man-made monuments.

> A possible problem with natural monuments is that they are not necessarily permanent—trees may die, streams may change course, and stones may be moved.

An example of a metes-and-bounds description containing references to monuments (pictured in Figure 10.3) follows:

> Beginning at the intersection of the east line of Jones Road and the south line of Skull Drive; thence East along the south line of Skull Drive 200 feet to a 1/2" rebar; thence South 15° East 216.5 feet, more or less, to the center of Red Skull Creek; thence Northwesterly along the center line of said creek to its intersection with the east line of Jones Road; thence North 105 feet, more or less, along the east line of Jones Road to the place of beginning.

When used to describe property within a town or city, a metes-and-bounds description may begin as follows:

> Beginning at a point on the Southerly side of Kent Street, 100 feet Easterly from the corner formed by the intersection of the Southerly side of Kent Street and the Easterly side of Broadway; thence . . .

In this description, the POB is given by reference to the corner intersection. The *description must close by returning to the POB*. The reference point of the street intersection is not included in the land described but is the point of beginning, sometimes called the *point of commencement* (POC), of this description.

Metes-and-bounds descriptions are highly complicated and should be handled with extreme care. When they include compass directions of the various lines and concave or convex curved lines, they can be difficult to understand. In such cases, the advice of a surveyor should be sought.

FIGURE 10.3: Metes-and-Bounds Tract

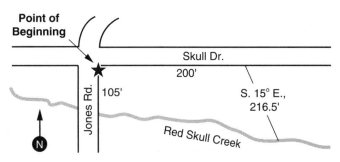

Rectangular (Government) Survey System

With the exception of "section" measurements, the rectangular survey system is not used in Texas.

In 1785, Congress established the **rectangular survey system**, sometimes called the *government survey method*, to standardize the description of land acquired by the federal government. The system is based on sets of two intersecting lines: principal meridians and base lines. The **principal meridians** run north and south, and the **base lines** run east and west. Both are located by reference to degrees of longitude and latitude. Each principal meridian has a name or number and is crossed by a base line. These lines are pictured in Figure 10.4. Each principal meridian and its corresponding base line are used to survey a definite area of land, indicated on the map by boundary lines.

FIGURE 10.4: Public Land Survey

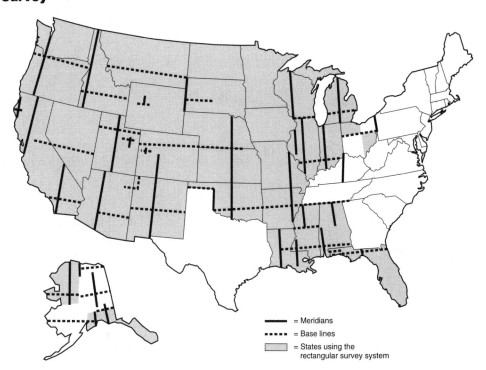

The directions of township lines and range lines may be easily remembered by thinking of the words this way:

Township lines

Range lines

Ranges   The land on either side of a principal meridian is divided into *six-mile-wide strips* by lines that run north and south, parallel to the meridian. These north-south strips of land are called **ranges** and are designated by consecutive numbers east or west of the principal meridian. For example, Range 3 East is a strip of land between 12 and 18 miles east of its principal meridian.

Township Tiers   Lines running east and west parallel to the base line and six miles apart are referred to as **township lines** and form *strips* of land called township tiers. These **township tiers** are designated by consecutive numbers north or south of the base line. For instance, the strip of land between 6 and 12 miles north of a base line is Township 2 North.

Township Squares   When the horizontal township lines and the vertical range lines intersect, they form **township squares**, which are the basic units of the rectangular survey system (see Figure 10.5). Theoretically, townships are 6 miles square and contain 36 square miles (23,040 acres). Each township is given a legal description by using

- the designation of the township strip in which the township is located,
- the designation of the range strip, and
- the name or number of the principal meridian for that area.

For example, a township described as Township 3 North, Range 4 East of the Indian Meridian is in the third strip, or tier, north of the base line. This strip (or tier) designates the township number and direction. The township is also located in the fourth range strip (those running north and south) east of the Indian Meridian. Reference is made to the Indian Meridian because the land being described was surveyed from that meridian. This description is abbreviated as *T3N, R4E Indian Meridian*.

FIGURE 10.5: Rectangular Survey System

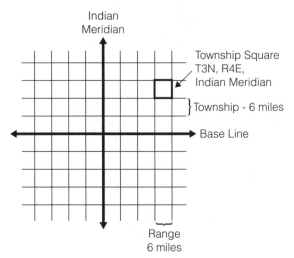

Sections   Each township contains 36 **sections**. Each section is one square mile, or 640 acres, with 43,560 square feet in each acre. Sections are numbered 1 through 36, as shown in Figure 10.6. Section 1 is always in the northeast, or upper-right, corner; Section 36 is in the southeast, or lower-right, corner. By law each section number 16 has been set aside for school purposes and is referred to as a *school section*. The sale or rental proceeds from this land originally were available

Memory Tip

An acre of land contains 43,560 square feet: 4 people driving down I-35 at 60 miles per hour.

for township school use. As previously mentioned, the word *section* is used in descriptions of some Texas land.

FIGURE 10.6: Sections in a Township

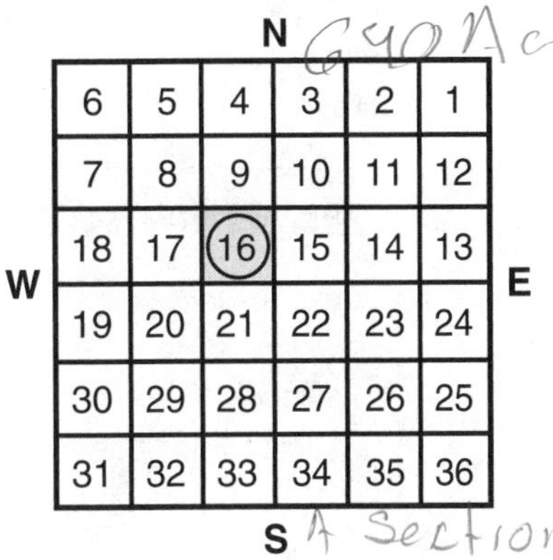

#16 is always the School *640 Acres* *A Section 1 mile square*

6	5	4	3	2	1
7	8	9	10	11	12
18	17	(16)	15	14	13
19	20	21	22	23	24
30	29	28	27	26	25
31	32	33	34	35	36

Sections (see Figure 10.7) may be divided into halves (320 acres) or quarters (160 acres). The southeast quarter of a section, which is a 160-acre tract, is abbreviated SE¼. Quarter-sections can be divided into quarters or halves, and such parts can be further divided by quarters. The SE¼ of SE¼ of SE¼ of Section 1 is a 10-acre square in the lower-right corner of Section 1; the acreage would be calculated as ¼ × ¼× ¼ × 640 = 10 acres. Sometimes this description is written without the word of: SE¼, SE¼, SE¼, Section 1. It is possible to combine portions of a section, such as: NE¼ of SW¼ and N½ of NW¼ of SE¼ of Section 1. Notice that because *and* is in this description, there are two parcels, and the total area is 60 acres [(¼ × ¼ × 640) + (½ × ¼ × ¼ × 640)].

FIGURE 10.7: Divisions of a Section

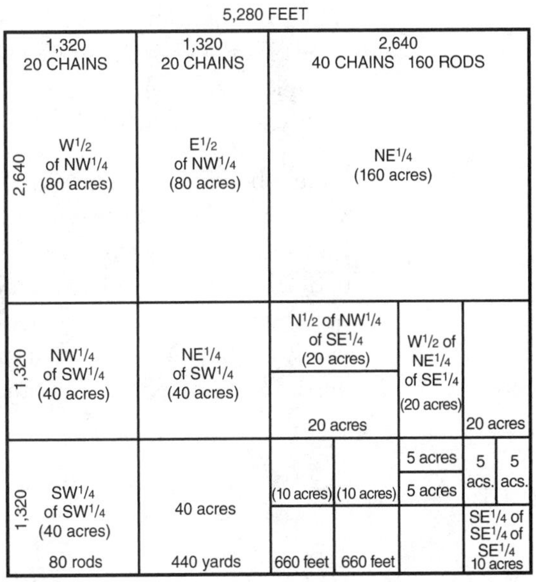

5,280 FEET			
1,320 20 CHAINS	1,320 20 CHAINS	2,640 40 CHAINS 160 RODS	
W½ of NW¼ (80 acres) 2,640	E½ of NW¼ (80 acres)	NE¼ (160 acres)	
NW¼ of SW¼ (40 acres) 1,320	NE¼ of SW¼ (40 acres)	N½ of NW¼ of SE¼ (20 acres) / 20 acres	W½ of NE¼ of SE¼ (20 acres) / 20 acres
SW¼ of SW¼ (40 acres) 1,320 / 80 rods	40 acres / 440 yards	(10 acres) / 660 feet (10 acres) / 660 feet	5 acres / 5 acres 5 acs. / 5 acs. / SE¼ of SE¼ of SE¼ 10 acres

IN PRACTICE   Texas uses the "section" measurement in rural legal descriptions; otherwise, the rectangular survey system is not used in Texas. In some counties (primarily those bordering adjacent states), some legal descriptions have the appearance of using the rectangular survey system. However, the township and range description (TWP 3N, R 3E, Section 22, Deaf Smith County) is completed with "as described by metes and bounds as follows . . ." In reality, because most sections in Texas are not exactly 1 mile square, each section does not equal exactly 640 acres. Most sections are actually larger than 640 acres.

MATH CONCEPTS

Calculate the number of acres and square feet in the following land description:
N½, NW¼, NE¼ of Section 12, Block 9, BS&F Survey, Potter County, Texas.

1 section = 640 acres × ¼ × ¼ × ½ = 20 acres

20 acres × 43,560 square feet per acre = 871,200 square feet

Recorded Subdivision Plat

The third method of land description is by *lot and block number*, referring to a **subdivision plat** placed in the public records of the county where the land is located.

The first step in subdividing land is the preparation of a *subdivision plat* by a licensed surveyor, as illustrated in Figure 10.8. On this plat, the land is divided into blocks and lots; and streets or access roads for public use are indicated. The blocks and lots are assigned numbers or letters. Lot sizes and street details must be indicated completely and must comply with all local ordinances and requirements. When properly signed and approved, the subdivision plat may be recorded in the county in which the land is located if all taxes (current and delinquent) have been paid. Once filed, the subdivision plat becomes part of the legal description. In Texas, it is a misdemeanor to describe a tract by lot and block if the subdivision plat has not been recorded in the county where the property is located.

In describing a lot from a recorded subdivision plat, the lot and block number, name or number of the subdivision, and name of the county and state are used. For example: "Lots 2, 3, and 4 in Block 5 of L. Robinson's Subdivision, City of Austin, Travis County, Texas."

Some subdivided lands are further divided by a later resubdivision. For example, if Alan Roswell bought two full blocks of John Welch's subdivision and resubdivided this land into different-sized lots, then Roswell might convey as follows: "Lot 1 in Block A of Roswell's resubdivision of Blocks 2 and 3 of John Welch's Hometown Subdivision, City of Austin, Travis County, Texas." Cities and counties can specify the smallest tract that may be conveyed without having a subdivision plat prepared, approved, and recorded.

FIGURE 10.8: Subdivision Plat Map

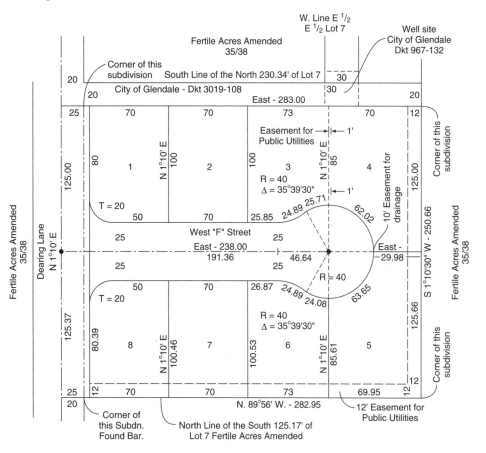

Surveying—Preparation and Use of a Survey

Land is surveyed on a flat-plane basis: an acre of land is an acre of land regardless of the height of hills or mountains on it.

A licensed surveyor is trained and authorized to locate a given parcel of land and to determine its legal description. The surveyor does this by preparing a survey, which sets forth the legal description of the property, and a *survey sketch*, which shows the location and dimensions of the parcel. When a survey also shows the location, size, and shape of improvements located on the lot, it is called an *improvement survey*. Improvement surveys reflect buildings, fences, sidewalks, pools, and other structures situated on the parcel, as well as any conflicting boundary evidence or visible encroachments, easements, and underground utilities. Surveys are required in many real estate transactions, for example:

- Conveying a portion of a given tract of land
- Conveying real estate as security for a mortgage loan
- Showing the location of new construction
- Locating roads and highways
- Determining the legal description of the land on which a particular building is located

Legal descriptions should not be changed, altered, or combined without adequate information from a competent authority such as a licensed surveyor or title attorney. To avoid ambiguity, legal descriptions *must* include the name of the county and state in which the land is located.

IN PRACTICE   Once they are recorded, legal descriptions affect title to real estate. Therefore, they should be prepared only by a licensed surveyor or a real estate attorney. Further, when a real estate agent prepares listing agreements or contracts, legal descriptions should be copied with care. For example, a legal description that is worded incorrectly in a sales contract may obligate the seller to convey (or the buyer to purchase) more or less land than intended. Title problems can arise for the buyer when seeking to convey the property at a future date. Even if the contract can be corrected before the sale is closed, the licensee risks losing a commission and might be held liable for damages suffered by an injured party because of an improperly worded legal description.

To become licensed as a registered professional land surveyor in Texas, an applicant for registration must have a bachelor's degree and at least two years' experience as a surveyor-in-training working under a registered or licensed surveyor. The surveyor-in-training certificate is valid for no longer than eight years.

MEASURING ELEVATIONS

Just as surface rights must be identified, surveyed, and described, so must rights to the property above the earth's surface. Recall from Chapter 2 that *land* includes the space above the earth's surface. In the same way that land may be measured and divided into parcels, the air itself may be divided. The owner of a parcel of land may subdivide the air above the land into **air lots**, which are composed of airspace within specific boundaries located over a parcel of land. This type of description is found in titles to tall buildings located on air rights (generally over railroad tracks) and in legal descriptions for condominiums.

Datum   A point, line, or surface from which elevations are measured or indicated is a **datum**. For the purpose of the United States Geological Survey (USGS), *datum* is defined as the mean sea level at New York harbor. Surveyors would use a datum in determining the height of a structure or establishing the grade of a street.

Virtually all large cities have established a local official datum that is used in place of the U.S. Geological Survey datum. For instance, the city of Austin has two local datum markers. One is in a brass plate at the old post office building at Seventh and Lavaca streets. The other is in the relocated post office building at Seventh and Colorado streets. These datum points have been used for reference in Austin for all surveys since the early 1900s.

Benchmarks   To aid surveyors, **benchmarks**, permanent reference markers such as an iron post or brass plate embedded in a sidewalk, have been established throughout the United States (see Figure 10.9). Cities with local datums also have designated local benchmarks, which are given official status when assigned a permanent identifying number. Local benchmarks simplify surveyors' work, for each benchmark has its own recognized official elevation, or datum, and measurements may be based on them rather than on the basic benchmark, which may be miles away. For example, the top of a fire hydrant, a local benchmark near Amarillo College in Amarillo, Texas, has a datum reference of 3,681.58 feet, which serves as a vertical reference point for surveys in the area.

FIGURE 10.9: Benchmark

Legal Description of a Condominium Interest. As discussed in Chapter 9, the Texas Uniform Condominium Act requires that a licensed surveyor prepare a condominium regime plat showing the elevations of floor and ceiling surfaces and the boundaries of a condominium apartment with reference to an official datum. A unit's floor, for instance, might be 60 feet above the datum, and its ceiling, 69 feet. Typically, a separate plat is prepared for each floor in the condominium building.

The following is an example of a legal description for a condominium unit that includes a fractional share of the common elements of the building and land:

UNIT 15 as delineated on survey of the following described parcel of real estate (hereinafter referred to as Development Parcel): The north 99 feet of the west 1/2 of Block 4 (except that part, if any, taken and used for street), in Sutton's Division Number 5, a subdivision out of the City of Austin, Travis County, Texas, according to a plat thereof of record in Book 45, at page 125 of the Plat Records of Travis County, Texas, which survey is attached as Exhibit A to Declaration made by Travis Bank and Trust Company as Trustee under Trust No. 1250, said declaration being of record in Volume 4506 at page 1325 of the Deed Records of Travis County, Texas, together with an undivided 5% interest in said Development Parcel (excepting from said Development Parcel all the property and space comprising all the units thereof as defined and set forth in said Declaration and Survey).

Subsurface rights can be legally described in the same manner as air rights. However, they are measured *below* the datum rather than above it. Subsurface rights are used not only for coal mining, petroleum drilling, and utility line location but also for multistory buildings that have several floors below ground level.

UNDERSTANDING LAND UNITS AND MEASUREMENTS

It is important to know and understand land units and measurements because they are an integral part of legal descriptions. Some commonly used measurements are listed in Figure 10.10.

FIGURE 10.10: Units of Land Measurement

vara	33⅓ inches (by Texas statute)
rod	16.5 feet; 5.5 yards
chain	66 feet; 4 rods; 100 links
mile	5,280 feet; 1,760 yards; 320 rods
sq. mile	640 acres (5,280 × 5,280 = 27,878,400 ÷ 43,560)
acre	43,560 sq. feet; 160 sq. rods
section	640 acres
sq. foot	144 sq. inches
sq. yard	9 sq. feet
cu. yard	27 cu. feet

Carpeting , floor , concret [handwritten]

MATH CONCEPTS

Land Acquisition Costs

To calculate the cost of purchasing land, use the same unit in which the cost is given. Costs quoted per square foot must be multiplied by the proper number of square feet; costs quoted per acre must be multiplied by the proper number of acres; et cetera.

To calculate the cost of a three-acre parcel of land at $1.10 per square foot, convert the acreage to square feet before multiplying:

43,560 square feet per acre × 3 acres = 130,680 square feet

130,680 square feet × $1.10 per square foot = $143,748

To calculate the cost of a 17,500 square-foot parcel of land at $60,000 per acre, convert the cost per acre into the cost per square foot before multiplying by the number of square feet in the parcel:

$60,000 per acre ÷ 43,560 square feet per acre = $1.38 (rounded)

per square foot

17,500 square feet × $1.38 per square foot = $24,150

SUMMARY

A legal description is a precise method of identifying a parcel of land. Documents affecting or conveying interests in real estate must contain an accurate legal description of the property involved, and the description should be the same as the one used in previous documents. The three methods of describing land used in the United States are (1) metes and bounds, (2) rectangular (government) survey, and (3) recorded subdivision plat.

Including Texas, 20 states (and parts of Ohio) use metes-and-bounds descriptions rather than the rectangular survey system used in the remaining 30 states. In a metes-and-bounds description, the actual location of monuments takes precedence over the written linear measurement in a document. When property is being described by metes and bounds, the description always must enclose a tract of land; that is, the boundary line must end where it started, at the point of beginning.

Sections are measurements used in some Texas land descriptions. A section consists of 640 acres, more or less, and can be divided into quarter-sections (160 acres), quarter of quarter-sections (40 acres), et cetera.

Land in every state can be subdivided into lots and blocks by means of a recorded subdivision plat. An approved subdivision plat is filed for record in the county clerk's office of the county in which the land is located. The plat shows the division into blocks; gives the size, location, and designation of lots; and specifies the location and size of streets to be dedicated to public use. It is possible to resubdivide portions of a previously recorded subdivision. By referring to a subdivision plat, the legal description of a building site in a town or city can be given by lot, block, and subdivision.

The services of licensed surveyors are necessary in the conduct of the real estate business. A survey is the usual method of certifying the legal description of a certain parcel of land. A survey sketch shows the location and dimensions of a parcel. A survey that also shows the location, size, and shape of the improvements located on a lot is referred to as an *improvement survey*. Improvement surveys customarily are required in the purchase of real estate when a mortgage or new construction is involved.

Air lots, condominium descriptions, and other measurements of vertical elevations may be computed from the U.S. Geological Survey datum, which is the mean sea level in New York harbor. Most large cities have established a local datum or elevation. Brass plates and other benchmarks are placed at intervals within an area and reflect official elevations.

CHAPTER 10 QUESTIONS

1. What is the legal description of the shaded area in the following diagram?

    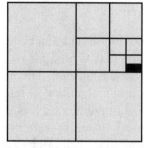

    a. S½ of the SE¼ of the NE¼
    b. S½ of the SE¼ of the SE¼ of the NE¼
    c. SE¼ of the SE¼ of the NE¼
    d. NE¼ of the SE¼

2. The N½ of the SW¼ of a section contains
    a. 40 acres.
    b. 20 acres.
    c. 160 acres.
    d. 80 acres.

3. A street address identifying a parcel of real estate is
    a. generally by itself an adequate legal description.
    b. not an adequate legal description.
    c. the same as a recorded plat description.
    d. the basic monument used in a metes-and-bounds legal description.

4. A system of describing real estate that uses feet, degrees, and natural markers as monuments is the
    a. rectangular survey.
    b. metes-and-bounds survey.
    c. government survey.
    d. recorded subdivision plat.

5. A portion of airspace within specific boundaries located over a parcel of land is called a(n)
    a. elevated parcel.
    b. vertical description.
    c. air lot.
    d. datum.

6. In a metes-and-bounds description,
    a. linear measurements take precedence over the position of monuments.
    b. the measurements given in the recorded description take precedence over the actual distance between monuments.
    c. the actual distance between monuments takes precedence over linear measurements set forth in a description.
    d. man-made monuments take precedence over natural monuments.

7. A map of a subdivision that has been recorded in the office of the county clerk is called a
    a. rectangular survey plat.
    b. metes-and-bounds description.
    c. recorded subdivision plat.
    d. subdivision survey.

8. A survey showing the location, size, and shape of buildings located on a lot, in addition to the legal description, is called a(n)
    a. survey sketch.
    b. improvement survey.
    c. complete and accurate survey.
    d. surveyor's survey.

9. John purchased a one-acre parcel from Sarah for $2.15 per square foot. What was the selling price of the parcel?
    a. $344
    b. $774
    c. $1,376
    d. $93,654

10. If a farm described as "the NW¼ of the SE¼ of Section 10" sold for $1,500 an acre, what would the total sales price be?
    a. $15,000
    b. $30,000
    c. $45,000
    d. $60,000

11. The following metes-and-bounds description contains a major error. After reading the description, check the statement that accurately describes the error.

    A tract of land located in Travis County, Texas, described as follows: Beginning at the intersection of the east line of Jones Road and the south line of Skull Drive; thence East along the south line of Skull Drive 200 feet; thence South 15° East 216.5 feet, more or less, to the center of Red Skull Creek; thence Northwesterly along the center line of said creek to its intersection with the east line of Jones Road; thence North 105 feet, more or less, along the east line of Jones Road.

    a. The use of *more or less* makes the description inadequate.
    b. Red Skull Creek is not a proper monument.
    c. The description is incomplete because it does not enclose a parcel of land by returning to the point of beginning.
    d. The linear measurements between monuments are inaccurate.

12. An acre contains
    a. 160 square feet.
    b. 43,560 square feet.
    c. 640 square feet.
    d. 5,280 square feet.

13. How many acres does the following tract contain?

    Beginning at the NW corner of the SW¼, thence South along the west line to the SW corner of the section, then East along the south line of the section 2,640 feet, more or less, to the SE corner of the said SW¼, then in a straight line to the POB.

    a. 100 acres
    b. 160 acres
    c. 90 acres
    d. 80 acres

14. A datum is
    a. used in the description of an air lot.
    b. the basic unit of the rectangular survey system.
    c. the description of a subdivision recorded in the county clerk's office.
    d. a legal description by which property can be definitely located.

15. Which shaded area depicts the NE¼ of the SE¼ of the SW¼?

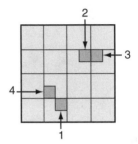

    a. Area 1
    b. Area 2
    c. Area 3
    d. Area 4

16. A vara is
    a. 33⅓ inches.
    b. 16.5 feet.
    c. a measurement used for rectangular surveys.
    d. a measurement used for reporting elevation.

17. A legal description for a parcel of real estate to be conveyed should be prepared by a(n)
    a. developer of the subdivision.
    b. county tax appraiser.
    c. attorney or licensed surveyor.
    d. attorney only.

18. A section of land contains
    a. 160 acres.
    b. 320 acres.
    c. 640 acres.
    d. 43,560 square feet.

FIGURE 10.11:   **Plat of Mesquite Manor Subdivision**

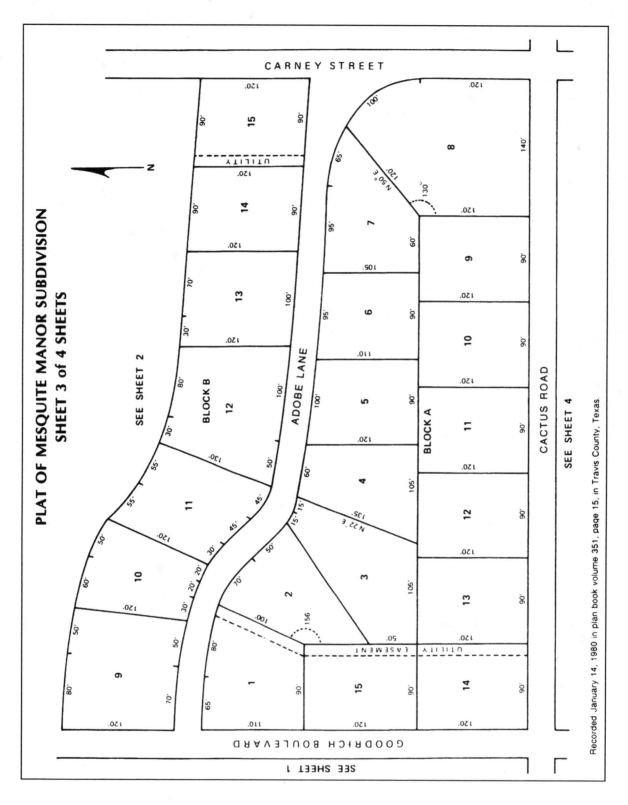

Answer questions 19 to 21 by referring to the plat map for Mesquite Subdivision, shown in Figure 10.11.

19. Which lot has the most frontage on Adobe Lane?
    a. Lot 10, Block B
    b. Lot 11, Block B
    c. Lot 1, Block A
    d. Lot 2, Block A

20. "Beginning at the intersection of the east line of Goodrich Boulevard and the south line of Adobe Lane and running South along the east line of Goodrich Boulevard a distance of 230 feet; thence East parallel to the north line of Cactus Road a distance of 195 feet; thence Northeasterly on a course N 22° E a distance of 135 feet; and thence Northwesterly along the south line of Adobe Lane to the point of beginning." Which lots are described here?
    a. Lots 13, 14, and 15, Block A
    b. Lots 9, 10, and 11, Block B
    c. Lots 1, 2, 3, and 15, Block A
    d. Lots 7, 8, and 9, Block A

21. How many lots on the plat have easements?
    a. Two
    b. Three
    c. Four
    d. Five

22. What is the legal description of the shaded area in the following diagram?

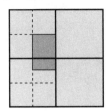

    a. SW¼ of the NE¼ and the N½ of the SE¼ of the SW¼
    b. N½ of the NE¼ of the SW¼ and the SE¼ of the NW¼
    c. SW¼ of the SE¼ of the NW¼ and the N½ of the NE¼ of the SW¼
    d. S½ of the SW¼ of the NE¼ and the NE¼ of the NW¼ of the SE¼

23. Terri purchased 4.5 acres of land for $78,400. An adjoining owner wants to purchase a strip of her land measuring 150 feet by 100 feet. What should this strip cost the adjoining owner if Terri sells it for the same price per square foot she originally paid for it?
    a. $3,000
    b. $6,000
    c. $7,800
    d. $9,400

Detailed rationales for the end-of-chapter review questions are available online at www.dearborn.com through the *Instructor Resource Guides* link.

CHAPTER

11

Real Estate Taxes and Other Liens

■ **LEARNING OBJECTIVES**   *When you have completed this chapter, you will be able to*

■ **distinguish** between specific and general liens, voluntary and involuntary liens, statutory and equitable liens and give examples of each;

■ **describe** the key components in each of the four phases of the annual tax levy process, as well as the steps for levying special assessments;

■ **identify** the process through which real estate taxes become delinquent and/ or become a lien, the enforcement options, and the equitable and statutory rights of redemption;

■ **explain** the various types of liens other than taxes and how they are prioritized to satisfy unpaid debts; and

■ **define** the following *key terms*:

ad valorem tax	involuntary lien	statutory right of
appraisal review board	IRS tax lien	redemption
assessment roll	judgment	subcontractor
attachment	lien	subordination agreement
equitable lien	mechanic's lien	surety bail bond lien
equitable right of	mortgage (purchase	tax lien
redemption	money) lien	tax sale
estate taxes	priority	Uniform Commercial
federal judgment lien	security agreement	Code
financing statement	special assessment	vendee's lien
general contractor	specific lien	vendor's lien
general lien	statutory lien	voluntary lien
inheritance taxes		wage lien

OVERVIEW

As discussed in previous chapters, ownership interests in real estate can be diminished by the interests of others. Specifically, taxing bodies, creditors, and courts can lessen an ownership interest by making a claim—called a *lien*—against property to secure payment of taxes, debts, and other obligations.

This chapter discusses the nature of liens, focusing on real estate tax liens, which affect every owner of real estate. In addition, the chapter describes liens other than taxes that involve real and personal property.

LIENS

> All liens are encumbrances, but not all encumbrances are liens.

A **lien** is a charge against property that provides security for a debt. It is an encumbrance that represents an interest in ownership; it does not constitute ownership in the property. The interest gives the lienholder the right to force the sale of or confiscate the property if the owner defaults on the debt, subject to the Texas homestead laws. Liens distinguish themselves from other encumbrances because, although they attach to the property, they do so because of a debt. Other encumbrances may be physical in nature, such as the easements and encroachments discussed in Chapter 8.

The lien created by a deed of trust is enforced through the power-of-sale provisions in that document, which permit the trustee to sell the subject property for the benefit of the beneficiary. This is a public sale, called a *nonjudicial foreclosure sale*, and is not conducted under the supervision of any court. Otherwise, liens are enforced by court order. A creditor must institute a legal action for the court to sell the real estate in question for full or partial satisfaction of the debt.

> The four ways of creating a lien may be remembered by the acronym **VISE**: **V**oluntary, **I**nvoluntary, **S**tatutory, and **E**quitable.

A lien may be voluntary or involuntary. A **voluntary lien** is created by the lienee's action, such as taking out a mortgage loan. An **involuntary lien** is created by law and is either statutory or equitable. A **statutory lien** is created by statute; federal tax liens, ad valorem tax liens, judgment liens, and mechanics' and materialmen's liens are statutory liens. An **equitable lien** arises out of common law. A vendor's lien or a vendee's lien is an involuntary, equitable lien on the debtor's property. In contrast, a real estate tax lien is an involuntary, statutory lien; that is, it is created by statute without any action by the property owner.

Liens may be further classified as to the property they affect. **General liens** usually affect all of a debtor's property, both real and personal, and include judgments, estate and inheritance taxes, debts of a deceased person, Internal Revenue Service taxes, and federal judgment liens. **Specific liens** usually are secured by a particular parcel of real estate and affect only that property. These include mechanics' liens, mortgages, taxes, special assessments, vendors' liens, vendees' liens, and surety bail bond liens. Figure 11.1 categorizes the types of liens to be discussed in this chapter.

FIGURE 11.1: Real Estate–Related Liens

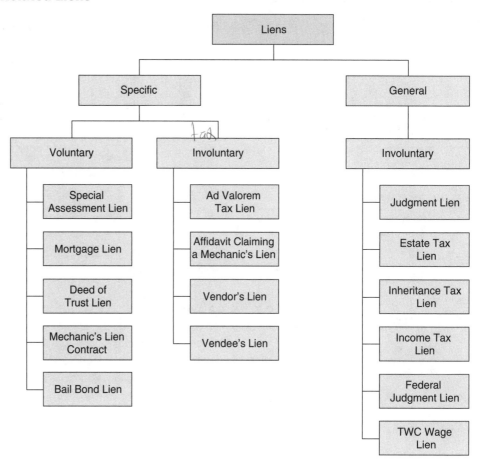

Effect of Liens on Title

The priority of a real estate tax lien prevails, even if a debt, lien, future interest, or other encumbrance existed before the attachment of the tax lien.

Although the fee simple estate held by a typical real estate owner can be reduced in value by the lien and encumbrance rights of others, the owner still is free to convey title to a willing purchaser. This purchaser, however, will buy the property subject to any liens and encumbrances of the seller. This is because, after they are properly established, liens will *run with the land*; that is, they will bind successive owners if steps are not taken to clear them.

Remember, specific liens attach to property, not to the property owner. Thus, although a purchaser who buys real estate under a delinquent specific lien is not responsible for payment of the debt secured by the lien, he risks losing the property if the creditor takes court action to enforce payment of the lien.

Priority of Liens   Real estate taxes and special assessments generally take **priority** over all other liens. This means that if the property goes through a court sale to satisfy unpaid debts or obligations, outstanding real estate taxes and special assessments are the *first* to be paid from the proceeds. The remainder is used to pay other outstanding liens in the order of their priority, which (with the exception of mechanics' liens and TWC wage liens, discussed later in this chapter) are established from the date of their recording in public records of the county where the property is located (see Figure 11.2). Finally, **IRS tax liens** do not have a specific priority; they are general liens but usually attach only to the taxpayer's equity interest in her property.

FIGURE 11.2: Priority of Liens

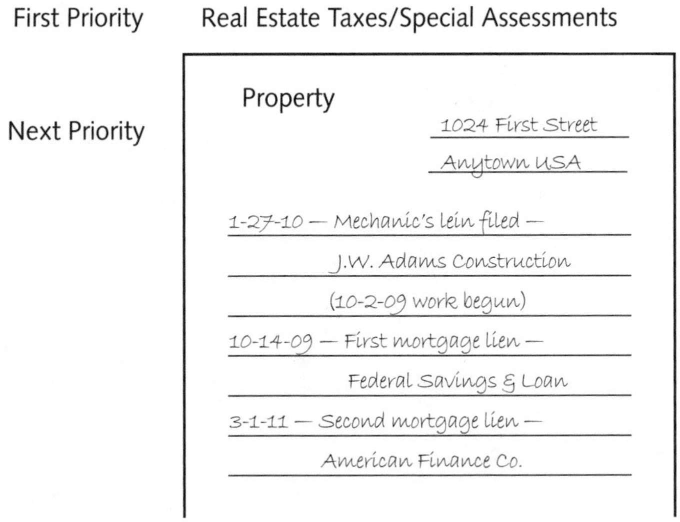

First Priority   Real Estate Taxes/Special Assessments

Next Priority

Property

1024 First Street

Anytown USA

1-27-10 — Mechanic's lein filed —

J.W. Adams Construction

(10-2-09 work begun)

10-14-09 — First mortgage lien —

Federal Savings & Loan

3-1-11 — Second mortgage lien —

American Finance Co.

F O R   E X A M P L E   Smith Estate is sold to satisfy a judgment resulting from a mechanic's lien ($25,000) for work begun on February 7, 2009, subject to a first mortgage lien ($295,000) recorded January 22, 2008, and to this year's outstanding real estate taxes ($10,000). If Smith Estate is sold at the foreclosure sale for $390,000, the proceeds of the sale will be distributed in the following order:

1. $10,000 to the taxing bodies for this year's outstanding real estate taxes

2. $295,000 to the mortgage lender for the entire amount of the mortgage loan outstanding as of the date of the sale

3. $25,000 to the creditor named in the judgment lien

4. $60,000 to the foreclosed landowner (the proceeds remaining after paying the first three items)

However, if Smith Estate sold for $310,000, the proceeds would be distributed as follows:

- $10,000 to the taxing bodies for this year's outstanding real estate taxes

- $295,000 to the mortgage lender for the entire amount of the mortgage loan outstanding as of the date of the sale

- $5,000 to the creditor named in the judgment lien

- $0 to the foreclosed landowner

Although the creditor is not repaid in full, this outcome is considered fair because the creditor's interest arose later than the other and the creditor *should have known* about the lien interests ahead of it and of the risk involved.

Subordination agreements are written agreements between lienholders to change the priority of mortgage, judgment, and other liens. For example, a landowner might agree to sell a parcel of land to a developer whose purpose is to build an apartment complex. To allow the developer to obtain a construction loan with a first-lien position, the landowner would have to agree to a subordination agreement and accept a second-lien position if full purchase price for the lot is not received. Priority and recording of liens will be discussed further in Chapter 18.

TAX LIENS

As discussed in Chapter 8, ownership of real estate is subject to certain government powers. One of these powers is the right of state and local governments to impose **tax liens** for the support of their governmental functions. Because the location of real estate is permanently fixed, the government can levy taxes with high confidence that the taxes will be collected. The annual taxes levied on real estate usually have priority over other previously recorded liens and may be enforced by the court sale of real estate free of such other liens.

Real estate taxes can be divided into two types: (1) **ad valorem** (according to value) **tax** and (2) **special assessment**, or *improvement tax*. Both taxes are levied against specific parcels of property and automatically become liens on those properties.

Ad Valorem Tax

The ad valorem tax is levied on real estate by various governmental agencies and municipalities such as cities, towns, villages, and counties. Other taxing bodies are public school districts or boards (including junior and community colleges), drainage districts, hospital districts, water districts, and sanitary districts, as well as municipal authorities operating recreational preserves such as forest preserves and parks. Ad valorem taxes are levied for the *general support or operation* of the government agency authorized to impose the levy. These taxes are called *ad valorem* because the amount of the tax is *calculated on the appraised value of the property being taxed*. Ad valorem taxes are specific, involuntary statutory liens.

Under Texas law, public or nonprofit property is not subject to taxation. For example, property owned by cities, various municipal organizations (such as schools, parks, playgrounds), the state and federal governments, religious corporations, hospitals, or educational institutions are tax exempt, provided they are for charity and nonprofit. However, if the property is not used for tax-exempt purposes, it is subject to taxation.

The annual tax levy process has four phases:

1. Property valuation
2. A protest period
3. Tax rate adoption
4. Tax collection

Property Valuation   Between January 1 and April 30, the appraisal district in each county processes applications for tax exemptions, agricultural appraisals, other tax relief, and property renditions (reports from owners of real or personal property, usually businesses, to a taxing entity to indicate property owned on January 1). The appraisal district also makes value determinations—tax appraisals—for all taxable property within its boundaries. A notice of appraised value on a single-family residence homestead must be delivered by April 1 of each year (or as soon thereafter as practicable). For all other properties, the deadline for delivery is May 1. Appraisal district property tax records are available online; they reflect the current appraised value, sales history, building characteristics, land value, legal description, and taxes on each property taxed in the district. (Search for the appropriate county's Appraisal District; then choose Property Search, by name or tax account number.) For occupant safety, an appraisal district may not post on the internet a photograph, sketch, or floor plan of a residential property.

An *exemption* removes part of the value of a home from taxation and thus lowers the tax bill. Some general comments about three exemptions from ad valorem real estate taxes are made here, but for specific data, consult local county, city, and school tax assessors because the state law permits great latitude in this matter.

1. **Homestead.** Texas law grants a homestead tax exemption of $15,000 off a home's taxable value for school district taxes. Other taxing districts may also allow for optional homestead tax exemptions of varying amounts. To qualify for a general homestead exemption, the homeowner must
   — own and live in the property as a principal residence on January 1 of the tax year,
   — submit a *homestead exemption application* form to the appraisal district office between January 1 and April 30 the tax year—ideally, within the first year of ownership (the form is available online at www.window.texas.gov; choose *property tax forms*, then *exemptions*); and
   — submit a copy of the homeowner's driver's license (or state-issued ID) and vehicle registration receipt, showing the same address as the property for which the exemption is requested (H.B. 252, 2011).

   If a homeowner moves from the home for a period of less than two years, the homeowner can still receive an exemption as long as she intends to return and does not establish another principal residence. An absence for military service or a stay in a facility providing services related to health, infirmity, or aging, however, may extend the two-year limitation. In addition, renting part of a home or using part of it for a business does not disqualify the rest of the home from the homestead tax exemption. As discussed in Chapter 2, the owner of a manufactured home is entitled to obtain a homestead tax exemption regardless of whether he has elected to treat the home as real property or personal property and regardless of whether the home is listed on the tax rolls with the real property to which it is attached or separately.

2. **Age 65 or older.** A person qualifies for an age-65 exemption as of January 1 of the year age 65 is reached. The age-65 age exemption is automatic if the homeowner provided a birth date on the original homestead exemption application. To reduce the home's value for school taxes, school districts are *required* to grant a $10,000 age exemption, in addition to the $15,000 homestead exemption. Other taxing authorities or districts may *elect* to grant tax reductions to property owners older than 65.

   Once the age-65 exemption is in place, senior homeowners qualify for other benefits, as follows:
   — Tax ceiling freeze—The homeowner's property has a tax ceiling for calculation of school taxes; the school taxes cannot increase as long as the homeowner owns and lives in the home and does not "improve" the home other than routine maintenance and repairs. (A county, city, or community college district has the option to freeze taxes.)
   — Portability of tax freezes—If another home is purchased anywhere in Texas, tax freezes for school taxes are portable to a new residence at a dollar amount proportional to the old tax freeze value. For example, if the school tax ceiling on the old home is $100 but would be $400

If a homestead property is rendered uninhabitable by a casualty or by wind or water damage, the homestead tax exemption can be continued for up to two years while building a replacement. Construction must begin within one year, and the owner must intend to return to the property as a principal residence.

The Texas Department of Public Safety provides copies of driver's license or other identification records to each appraisal district to assist in the determination of both homestead and age-65 exemptions.

without the freeze, the new school tax ceiling would be 25% of the amount that would otherwise be collected without the over-65 freeze ($100/$400 = 25%). (To transfer a county, city, or community college district tax ceiling, the homeowner must move to another home in the same taxing unit.)

— Installment payments—Tax payments on the primary residence may be made in four equal installments, without penalty or interest.

— Tax deferral—If a homeowner age 65 or older owes delinquent taxes on the home he lives in, the homeowner may defer the payment of taxes for as long as he owns and lives in the home. A tax deferral only postpones the tax liability; it does not cancel it. Any existing tax, penalty, interest, or attorney fees at the time of the deferral are preserved and continue to accrue interest at a rate of 8% until paid off. Any new taxes that come due do not incur the penalty but do incur interest at the 8% rate. When the homeowner or the surviving spouse sells the home or moves from it, all accumulated taxes and interest must be paid within 181 days.

— Surviving-spouse benefit—The surviving spouse of an individual receiving the age-65 exemption is entitled to that exemption for the same property if the surviving spouse is age 55 or older when the deceased spouse dies and if the surviving spouse owns the home and lives in it.

3. **Disability status.** School districts are required to grant a $10,000 exemption to persons having a physical or other recognized disability; it is optional for other taxing authorities. The taxpayer may be required to provide documentation of disability. A taxpayer cannot obtain both an age-65 exemption and the disability exemption at the same time. Disabled homeowners have other benefits similar to those provided to age-65 homeowners: a tax ceiling freeze, portability of tax freezes, installment payments, and tax deferral. The transfer of tax-reduction benefits to the surviving spouse of a disabled homeowner is determined by each appraisal district. Additional tax exemptions accrue to a disabled Texas veteran or the surviving spouse or child of a disabled veteran. A totally disabled veteran may receive an exemption of 100% of the appraised value of the veteran's residence homestead.

IN PRACTICE   The real estate licensee must determine from official sources the basis for the ad valorem taxes. For example, taxes assessed against the subject property may be substantially less than normal because of the benefit of a particular tax exemption. However, the new owner may not qualify for a continuation of the exemption. A licensee who fails to determine this status might incur considerable liability from a surprised—and disgruntled—buyer.

Tax Appraisal   Real estate is valued, or appraised, for tax purposes by appraisal districts in each county. Texas law provides for property to be reappraised *at least* every three years. The tax appraisal must be 100% of a property's market value, based solely on its value as a residential homestead regardless of the property's highest and best use; and the land must be appraised separately from the building. For instance, if a residential property is located where its best use would be as a site for an office building, it still must be appraised as a residence.

Any increase in appraised value of a residence homestead is capped at the lesser of the most recent market value *or* 110% of the value for the preceding tax year, plus improvements to the property. Appraisal districts must maintain both the market value and capped value in their records.

To save time and money, the appraisal district uses *mass appraisal* to appraise large numbers of properties, following generally accepted appraisal practices. In a mass appraisal, the district first collects detailed descriptions of each taxable property in the district. It then classifies properties according to a variety of factors, such as size, use, and construction type.

Using data from recent property sales, the district appraises the value of typical properties in each class. Whether one property is comparable to another must be determined by similarities in location, lot size, improvements, age, condition, access, amenities, views, income, operating expenses, occupancy, and the existence of easements, deed restrictions, or other factors that affect marketability. Unless the number of sales is insufficient to do an adequate market analysis, a sale is considered a comparable sale only if it occurred within 24 months of the date of the tax appraisal. S.B. 1256 (2013) amended the tax code to provide that for counties with a population of more than 150,000, the sale is considered to be a comparable sale if it occurred within 36 months of the tax appraisal, regardless of the number of comparable properties sold during that period. In appraising residence homesteads, though, appraisers must consider foreclosure sales within the past three years. For properties without recent sales data, such as oil leases or utility companies, the appraisal district uses the income or cost approaches. These methods ask questions such as "What would an investor pay for this property based on its income?" or "How much would it cost to replace the property?" (Appraisal methods will be discussed in greater detail in Chapter 14.) After the tax appraisals have been completed, the appraisal district sends out a *notice of appraised value* to each property owner.

Alternate methods of valuation are available for property that is used for agriculture. They are productivity valuations rather than market valuations. A property owner must apply for the special valuations and qualify by meeting the conditions in the paragraphs that follow.

Agricultural use valuation. To qualify for an agricultural use valuation, Article 8, Section 1-d, of the Texas Constitution requires 50% of a landowner's income to be from farming or ranching. Such property is appraised based on its agricultural value rather than its market value. If the property is sold or its use is changed, the land is subject to a maximum three-year rollback lien to recover the difference between taxes based on the special valuation and taxes at market value plus interest at 7% for each year. Very few landowners apply for the "1-d" because of the agricultural-use income requirements.

> A constitutional amendment passed by Texas voters in November 2011 provides for a 100% exemption to an unremarried surviving spouse of a totally disabled veteran (SJR 14, 2011).

Open space valuation. To qualify for open space land appraisal, the land must have been used for agriculture for five of the previous seven years. Agriculture includes farming, ranching, timber production, and wildlife management. The primary source of income does not have to be farming. If the use of the subject property is changed, the land is subject to a maximum five-year tax rollback lien to recover the difference between taxes based on the special valuation and taxes at market value plus interest at 7% for each year. The owner who changes the use of the land is responsible for the rollback tax.

Protest Period   The protest period generally begins after the appraisal district has sent out appraisal notices. Property owners who claim that errors were made in appraising their property or in allowing exemptions may present their objections and supporting documentation to the district appraiser's office for review. Most appraisal districts will informally review a tax protest and try to resolve the taxpayer's concerns.

Two or more adjoining appraisal review boards may form one consolidated ARB, which is more likely to occur in less populated counties.

However, if the property owner is not satisfied with the determination of the appraiser's office, the taxpayer may file a *written* protest with the appraisal district by the later of two events: (1) before May 31 or (2) within 30 days after the appraised value was *mailed* by the appraisal district. In return, the property owner would receive a notice of the date, time, and place for a hearing before an **appraisal review board** (ARB), an impartial panel of citizens who are authorized to resolve disputes between taxpayers and the appraisal district and who must be independent from the employees and directors of the appraisal district. Upon request and prior to the hearing on a protest, the chief appraiser will provide the property owner with a copy of any written material that will be offered or submitted to the ARB at the hearing. Likewise, the property owner is required to give any written evidence to the chief appraiser at or before the hearing. Generally, information regarding sales prices and property descriptions held by an appraisal district is confidential. Therefore, written evidence obtained for a protest must remain confidential in the possession of the property owner or the owner's agent. If a protesting property owner submits a recent independent certified appraisal as evidence of property value, the protest must be determined in favor of the property owner unless the appraisal district can disprove that value.

In a county having a population of 500,000 or more, an appraisal district with an internet website must have in place a system for electronic filing of protests claiming excessive or unequal value on residence homesteads. The system must provide for the electronic delivery of pre-hearing information, including comparable sales, and settlement offers. Any settlement reached through electronic communications will be final and binding on both parties. If the property owner rejects a settlement offer made electronically, the protest would then be heard by the ARB. The availability for electronic filing of protests does not extend to unusually complex property appraisals. Chief appraisers are required to provide notice of the availability of agreement forms authorizing an electronic communication between the appraisal district and a property owner or designated property tax agent (H.B. 3216, 2011). The electronic filing process must be implemented by year 2013 for counties with 250,000 or fewer people.

ARB hearings begin around May 1 and are generally complete by July 20. A protesting taxpayer or a designated agent is entitled to one postponement of the ARB hearing if the owner or agent shows good cause for postponement (S.B. 1546, 2011). In taxpayer protests, the ARB listens to both the chief appraiser and the taxpayer (or someone authorized in writing to appear on his behalf) and determines whether the appraisal district has acted properly. Among others, the protest issues that an ARB can consider include the following:

- Is the proposed value of the property too high when compared with sales of similar properties in the area?
- Is the property valued unequally compared with other properties in the area?
- Did the chief appraiser deny an exemption or agricultural appraisal?

Licensed attorneys may serve as arbitrators; and with required training and registration, real estate brokers and salespersons, real estate appraisers, and certified public accountants may also serve.

A property owner is entitled to appeal an order of the ARB to the district court in the county in which the property is located or to submit the dispute to binding arbitration. To qualify for binding arbitration, the property must have an appraisal of $1 million or less or be a residential homestead. A property owner who elects to proceed with binding arbitration would pay a $500 arbitration deposit that would be forfeited if the appraisal district won. Or a property owner may request an expedited arbitration, which would provide up to an hour of argument and testimony for each party to the dispute at a cost of only $250. If a property's appraised value for a particular year is lowered as the result of a protest or appeal, the appraisal district cannot raise the property value in the next year unless the increase is reasonably supported by substantial evidence presented by the appraisal district.

IN PRACTICE   A property owner may appeal an ARB order to the State Office of Administrative Hearings (SOAH) rather than to the state district court in the county in which the property is located in certain Texas cities. The cities include Austin, Beaumont, Corpus Christi, El Paso, Fort Worth, Houston, Lubbock, Lufkin, McAllen, Midland, San Antonio, Tyler, and Wichita Falls (H.B. 316, 2013). The property involved may be real or personal (other than industrial property) that was appraised at more than $1 million.

A real estate broker, salesperson, or appraiser may perform property tax consulting services for single-family residences, farms, and ranches. The requirements for registering as a property tax consultant include approved education courses and a competency exam. To designate a tax consultant as an agent in a property tax matter, a property owner must file a required form with the appraisal district in which the property is located—unless the agent is an attorney, mortgage lender, or employee of the property owner.

Property Tax Basics is available online at the Texas Comptroller of Public Accounts website. It provides detailed discussions of the property appraisal, protest filing, tax rate adoption, and tax collection phases of the annual tax levy process.

Several bills, including H.B. 385, were enacted by the Texas Legislature in 2013 that amended the Texas Tax Code regarding local appraisal review boards and property tax appraisal. A document entitled Texas Property Law Changes 2013 is available at the Texas Comptroller of Public Accounts website. It provides a detailed summary of many of the changes to the tax code on the above-referenced subject matter.

WEBLINK @
www.window.texas.gov/taxinfo/proptax/
www.window.state.tx.us/taxinfo/proptax/laws/96-669_2013.pdf

Tax Rate Adoption   Once the ARB approves the appraisal records, the appraisal district gives each taxing unit a list of taxable property known as a *certified appraisal roll*. Each property in Texas is subject to taxation by two or more taxing units: a county and a school district, along with others such as city, hospital, community college, water, or other taxing districts. In August or September, each taxing unit adopts a budget. (See Figure 11.3.) They decide what services they will provide during the next year and how much money will be needed. A budget must include an estimate of all expenditures for the year and indicate the amount of income expected from all fees, revenue sharing, and other sources. The net amount remaining to be raised from real estate taxes is determined from these figures.

The next step is *appropriation*, the action taken by each taxing body that authorizes the expenditure of funds and provides for the sources of such monies. Appropriation generally involves the adoption of an ordinance or the passage of a law setting forth the specifics of the proposed taxation.

FIGURE 11.3: Calculating a Real Estate Tax Rate

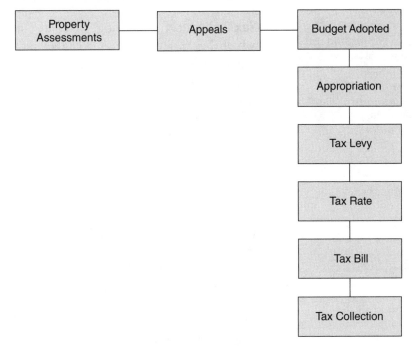

The amount to be raised from the general real estate tax then is imposed on property owners through a *tax levy* (the formal action taken to impose the tax) by a vote of the taxing district's governing body

The *tax rate* for each individual taxing unit is computed separately. To arrive at a tax rate, the total monies to be raised from real estate taxes for the coming fiscal year are divided by the total appraisal of all applicable real and personal property located within the jurisdiction of the taxing body.

FOR EXAMPLE   A taxing district's budget indicates that $275,000 must be raised from tax revenues, and the appraisal roll of all taxable real and personal property within this district equals $15,000,000. The tax is computed thus:

$275,000 ÷ $15,000,000 = $0.01833

The tax rate is expressed in dollars per $100 of value. Therefore, the tax rate computed in the foregoing example would be expressed as $1.833 per $100 of assessed value. Then a property owner's tax bill is computed by applying the tax rate to the taxable value of the property.

FOR EXAMPLE   If a property is appraised for tax purposes at $90,000 with no exemptions and a tax rate of $1.833 per $100, the tax will be computed as follows:

$90,000 × ($1.833 | $100) = $1,649.70

IN PRACTICE Tax bills must include a comparison, expressed as a percentage increase or decrease, between the current tax year's figures and the fifth tax year before the current tax year for (1) the appraised value of the property and (2) the amount of taxes imposed on the property; and they must show a percentage comparison of the tax data for each of the preceding five tax years. Beginning with the 2012 tax year, each county tax assessor-collector must post on its website a five-year history of tax rates for each taxing entity in the county (H.B. 2338, 2011).

> Taxes on homestead and certain small business properties that were damaged in a declared disaster may be paid in four installments.

Tax Collection Real estate taxes are paid *in arrears*—at the end of the period for which they are levied (that is, not in advance). The ad valorem real estate tax becomes a lien on January 1 of the year of the tax. For example, taxes for 2011 became a lien on January 1, 2011. Tax collection begins around October 1 when tax bills generally are mailed to property owners or to lenders on properties with loans. One tax bill may incorporate all real estate taxes levied by the various taxing districts. However, in some areas separate bills are prepared by each taxing district.

By state law, the annual tax is payable on or after October 1 of the year of the tax, but provision may be made at the option of the taxing district or governing body that when half of the tax is paid by November 30, the balance may be paid without penalty on or before June 30 of the next year. Discounts may be allowed by local option for taxes paid in advance: 3% discount if paid by October 31, 2% if paid by November 30, and 1% if paid by December 31. Most property owners pay their property taxes before the end of the year so they can deduct the payments from their federal income taxes. Taxes are payable in cash, check, money order, credit card, or electronic funds transfer and are considered timely if sent by regular first-class mail and postmarked on or before the due date. School boards may adopt policies permitting work contracts through which taxpayers perform services for the district in lieu of paying taxes.

The delinquency date for annual taxes is February 1 of the year following the tax year (2011 taxes are delinquent as of February 1, 2012). Penalties and interest are added after the delinquency date, and taxing units may impose an additional penalty on July 1 for legal costs on unpaid taxes.

IN PRACTICE Beginning in 2012, a tax office may offer a paperless, electronic tax bill. A taxpayer has the option to continue to receive a paper tax bill or to receive it electronically (H.B. 843, 2011).

Enforcement of Tax Liens To be enforceable, real estate taxes must be valid; that is, they must be (1) levied properly, (2) used for a legal purpose, and (3) applied equitably to all affected property. Tax liens generally are given priority over all other liens against a property, and they are not extinguished in a mortgage foreclosure.

> A mortgage foreclosure does not clear tax liens on the property.

If real estate taxes become delinquent, the tax collector will send at least one *delinquent tax notice*. Some tax collectors will allow a taxpayer to pay delinquent taxes in installments that can last up to 36 months. However, if the taxes are not paid *or* if an installment agreement is not entered into or the agreement is defaulted, the tax collector's last resort is to take a delinquent taxpayer to court to foreclose on the tax lien. After a court has rendered judgment for the tax, penalties, and interest and ordered the property to be sold, a **tax sale** is held pursuant to a published notice.

The sale is conducted by the sheriff or constable at a public sale. The purchaser must pay at least the amount of delinquent tax, penalty, interest, and attorney's fee or the appraised value of the property, whichever is less. All unpaid taxes, including the current year's taxes, can be recovered from the proceeds of the sale with all property and interest accrued to the date of the sale. If the property sells for more than the minimum bid, the delinquent taxpayer is generally entitled to the amount of excess proceeds.

Under Texas law, the successful bidder receives a deed from the sheriff or constable conducting the sale. The deed conveys all right, title, and interest of the defaulted taxpayer, including the defendant's right to the use and possession of the property. The deed, however, is subject to the property owner's right of redemption. Under what is known as an **equitable right of redemption**, the delinquent taxpayer can redeem the property at any time *prior* to the tax sale by paying the delinquent taxes plus interest and charges (court costs or attorney fees). In addition to the equitable right of redemption, Texas law provides for a period of redemption *after* the tax sale during which the defaulted owner may redeem the property by paying the amount paid at the tax sale, plus interest and other charges. This is known as the **statutory right of redemption**. Under this redemption right, if the property is the residence homestead of the defaulted taxpayer or a mineral interest or if it is designated for agricultural use, the owner may redeem the property within two years after the purchaser's deed was recorded (for other properties, the redemption period is limited to six months). Redemption is illustrated in Figure 11.4.

FIGURE 11.4: Ad Valorem Tax Time Line

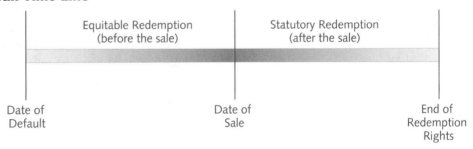

The cost of the statutory right of redemption is an additional 25% of the purchase price if redeemed during the first year and 50% if redeemed during the second year as long as the property is redeemed from a third-party purchaser. If a defaulted taxpayer wishes to redeem the real property but cannot find the purchaser or cannot reach an agreement with the purchaser, the taxpayer may redeem the real property within the statutory period by paying the required amount to the assessor-collector of the county in which the property was sold. The assessor-collector would then pay the money received to the purchaser.

As noted, only the right, title, and interest of the defaulted taxpayer are conveyed to the purchaser at a tax sale. Property that is not sold at a tax sale due to a lack of bidders is "struck off," or sold to a taxing unit that is a party to the judgment. This taxing unit takes title to the property (as trustee) for the use and benefit of itself and all other taxing units that established tax liens in the suit. One or more of the taxing units may use the property for its own benefit; if the trustee taxing unit does not resell the property within six months after the expiration of the redemption period, any taxing unit that is entitled to receive proceeds from the sale may force a *public* sale of the property. A *private* sale of the property is allowed—but only by the trustee-taxing unit.

IN PRACTICE In Texas, property that is a residence homestead, a mineral interest, or designated for agricultural use may be redeemed during the two-year period following a sale of land because of a tax lien. A property sold after foreclosure of a homeowners association assessment lien may be redeemed no later than 180 days after written notice of the sale is mailed to the owner. There is no right of redemption if the foreclosure sale is made pursuant to a nonjudicial deed-of-trust enforcement of a mortgage loan or a judicial enforcement of a vendor's lien.

A property owner who owes delinquent ad valorem property taxes may consent to a third-party's paying the taxes and assuming the taxing authority's preexisting lien on the property. Texas law requires specific disclosures to the property owner, loan servicer, and first-lien holder and strict procedures upon foreclosure of the transferred tax lien. Property tax lenders must be licensed by the state (S.B. 762, 2011).

Excess proceeds from a tax sale are deposited with the county clerk, and the former property owner can retain an attorney to petition the court for them. The delinquent taxpayer may, however, transfer or assign his interest in any excess proceeds to a third party. However, the transferee must pay at least 80% of the amount of the excess proceeds claim to the delinquent taxpayer and may not receive from the court more than 125% of the amount paid for the assignment or transfer.

Special Assessment (Improvement Tax)

Special assessments are taxes levied on real estate that require property owners to pay for improvements that benefit the real estate they own. These taxes often are levied to pay for such improvements as streets, alleys, street lighting, curbs, and similar items and are enforced in the same manner as general real estate taxes. Special assessments are always specific and statutory; however, they can be either voluntary or involuntary liens. When property owners petition the local government to install a public improvement for which the owners agree to pay, such as a sidewalk or paved alley, the assessment lien is voluntary. However, improvements initiated by a public agency create involuntary liens, such as extension of water lines to a new subdivision.

The following steps are taken to achieve the *specific improvements*:

> A homestead may not be subjected to a forced sale for nonpayment of a public improvement district assessment, according to a Texas Attorney General Opinion (June 2001).

1. Property owners may petition for an improvement; or a proper legislative authority, such as the city council or board of trustees, may initiate the proposal for an improvement.
2. Notices are given to the owners of the property affected, and hearings are held.
3. After the preliminary legal steps are taken, the legislative body authorized by statute to act in such cases adopts an *ordinance* that details the nature of the improvement, its cost, and a description of the area to be assessed.
4. The **assessment roll** spreads the assessment over the various parcels of real estate that will benefit, and hearings are held to *confirm the roll*. The amount of the assessment for each parcel usually is determined by one of the two following criteria: (1) estimated benefit each tract will receive by reason of the assessment or (2) front footage. Regardless of the basis used, the assessment usually varies from parcel to parcel because all will not benefit equally from the improvement.

5. The assessment becomes a lien on the land assessed.
6. Once the improvement is completed, a *warrant* is issued by the proper authority, often the clerk of the court that approved the roll. This warrant gives the local collector the authority to issue special assessment bills and begin collection.

In Texas, an assessment becomes a *lien* after the confirmation of the roll. As a rule, special assessments are due and payable in equal annual installments over a period of 5 to 10 years. Interest is charged each property owner on the total amount of his assessment. The first installment generally becomes due during the year after confirmation. The bill will include yearly interest on the entire assessment. As subsequent installments are billed in following years, each bill will include a year's interest on the unpaid balance. Property owners have the right to prepay any or all installments and thus avoid the interest charges.

IN PRACTICE   Although real property taxes on a personal residence are deductible items for income tax purposes, special assessment taxes are not. The annual interest charged in connection with special real estate assessments is deductible, however.

Utility District Tax

The purpose of a utility district is to provide water, sewer, drainage, and/or flood control protection facilities or services for properties located outside the boundaries of a town or city, although it is possible for a utility district to be located in whole or in part within the boundaries of a municipality. Some examples of utility districts are water control districts, underground water conservation districts, municipal utility districts (MUDs), and drainage districts. A utility district is generally created by a property developer, the utilities are paid for by bonds, and the bonds are retired by the levying of taxes. Unpaid taxes can result in the creation of a lien. If property being sold is located within a utility district, Section 49.452 of the Texas Water Code requires the seller to furnish to the buyer a statutory notice relating to the tax rate, bonded indebtedness, or standby fee of the district prior to final execution of the contract.

LIENS OTHER THAN TAXES

Aside from real estate tax and special assessment liens, other types of liens also may be charged against real property, either voluntarily or involuntarily. These include mortgage liens, mechanics' liens, judgments, estate and inheritance tax liens, vendors' liens, vendees' liens, surety bail bond liens, TWC wage liens, IRS tax liens, federal judgment liens, and Uniform Commercial Code (UCC) liens.

Mortgage (Deed of Trust or Purchase Money) Liens

In general, a **mortgage** or **purchase money lien** is a voluntary, specific lien on real estate given to a lender by a borrower as security for a mortgage loan. It becomes a lien on real property when the mortgage funds are disbursed. The lender then files or records the mortgage or deed of trust in the office of the county clerk where the property is located.

Mortgage lenders generally require a preferred lien, referred to as a *first mortgage lien*; this means that no other major liens against the property (aside from real estate taxes) take priority over the mortgage lien. Even a discharge of debts in bankruptcy does not eliminate a mortgage lien. The mortgage lien may still be foreclosed so the lender can attempt to recover the debt. Mortgages and mortgage liens are discussed in detail in Chapter 15, "Real Estate Financing Principles."

Mechanics' Liens

A **mechanic's lien** is a specific lien that gives security to persons or companies that perform labor or furnish material to improve real property. It is based on the *enhancement of value theory*—because the labor performed and material furnished enhanced the value, the property should be security for payment. A mechanic's lien is available to contractors, subcontractors, architects, engineers, surveyors, laborers, and other providers. Mechanics' liens come in two types: an Affidavit Claiming a Mechanic's Lien is an involuntary lien and a Mechanic's Lien Contract creates a voluntary lien.

> In an economic downturn, it becomes more prevalent for builders and homeowners to sell homes without paying the contractors or subcontractors.

To be entitled to an *Affidavit Claiming a Mechanic's Lien*, the provider must have worked under contract (express or implied) with the owner or the owner's authorized representative. For example, a property owner usually hires a **general contractor** to perform a particular construction job and pays all construction fees and expenses to this person. The general contractor in turn hires a number of **subcontractors** to actually furnish the materials and perform the labor. A mechanic's lien is filed when the general contractor has not been fully paid by the property owner or when the general contractor has been paid but has not paid the subcontractors or suppliers of materials. In the latter instance, payment in full to the general contractor will not necessarily free a property owner from the lien rights of unknown, unpaid suppliers and laborers. *A person claiming a mechanic's lien must file a notice of lien in the public records of the county where the property is located and within a limited time after the work has been completed.* Subcontractors generally are required to serve a landowner with personal notice of their individual lien claims.

Even though the claimant's notice of lien may be filed within a specified period after the work is completed, a mechanic's lien usually takes effect (establishes priority) from the time labor was performed or the material was supplied in whole or in part. As shown in Figure 11.2, a mechanic's lien may take priority over previously recorded liens such as mortgages. Enforcement of an Affidavit Claiming a Mechanic's Lien is by a foreclosure suit and a court order to have the sheriff sell the real estate to satisfy the claimant.

A mechanic's lien may be a voluntary lien when it is created contractually under a *Mechanic's Lien Contract*, which is commonly used for new construction and for improvements to homesteads. If the property to be subject to the lien is a homestead, both spouses must sign a contract prior to any work being performed or any materials being delivered. As discussed in Chapter 8, additional requirements provide that (a) the contract for the work and material must not be signed until five days after loan application; (b) the owner may rescind the contract up to three days after signing; and (c) the contract must be signed at the office of a third-party lender, an attorney, or a title company. A Mechanic's Lien Contract normally contains a provision for nonjudicial foreclosure like that contained in a mortgage lien. There is no right of redemption after foreclosure of a mechanic's lien. *A purchaser of property that has been recently constructed, altered, or repaired should be cautious about possible unrecorded mechanics' liens against such property.*

Homeowner Protection   To protect against unknown liens by subcontractors who might not have been paid by the general contractor, the property owner is required by the Texas Property Code to withhold a *10% retainage* of the total construction bill for 30 days following the completion of work. Failure to do so may subject the owner to additional liability to subcontractors. In addition, an original contractor must give a *"final bills paid affidavit"* to a property owner on receipt of the final payment for completed construction. On a residential homestead construction project in excess of $5,000, a contractor must deposit trust funds received from the owner into an escrow account at a financial institution and account for deposits and disbursements. Because mechanic's lien statutes are very complex, always refer questions to an attorney.

Judgments

A **judgment** is a *decree issued by a court*. When the decree provides for the awarding of money and sets forth the amount of money owed by the debtor to the creditor, the judgment is referred to as a money judgment. The county clerk then prepares an "abstract" of the judgment, a short summary of the judgment telling who sued whom and won and how much money is owed under the judgment. The county clerk certifies the *abstract of judgment* and records it in the real property records creating a lien.

A judgment becomes a *general, involuntary, statutory lien on both real and personal property* owned by the debtor, including real and personal property acquired after the judgment is recorded. Judgment liens do not attach to homestead property in Texas unless a mechanic's lien has been perfected on the property in accordance with the law or unless another exemption from forced sale by creditors applies. Therefore, if a judgment lien has been filed against an owner of homestead property and no exemptions from forced sale apply, the judgment debtor may, at any time, file an affidavit that serves as a release of a judgment lien as to the homestead property. Specific notice requirements must be met, and the affidavit and evidence of notices must be filed with the county clerk of the county in which the homestead is located. If nonhomestead community property is owned in the sole name of the husband, the wife's community property interest can be made subject to a judgment lien against the wife; the reverse is also true.

A judgment takes its priority as a lien on the debtor's property from the date the abstract of judgment is recorded in the real property records in the county in which the property is located. An abstract of judgment creates a lien only against property located within the county or counties in which the abstract is recorded. Therefore, when a creditor wishes to extend the lien coverage, the abstract must be recorded in other counties where the debtor owns property. For a creditor to pursue collection on the judgment, the court must issue a legal document called a *writ of execution* directing the sheriff to seize and sell as much of the debtor's nonexempt real or personal property as is necessary to pay the debt and the expenses of the sale. When property encumbered by an abstract of judgment lien is sold to satisfy the debt, or when the judgment is paid in full by the debtor, the debtor should demand from the judgment holder a legal document known as a *release of judgment*. The release should then be recorded in the real property records in the county where the property is located.

In most cases, an abstract of judgment lien is valid for 10 years; if the judgment lienholder has attempted to enforce the judgment through an execution, it may

> A child support lien rendered by a court is a judgment lien that attaches to all real and personal property owned or later acquired by a defaulting parent.

be extended for an additional 10-year period. If an abstract of judgment has not been extended within the 10-year period, it becomes dormant and is no longer a valid lien. However, a dormant judgment may be renewed if an action is brought before the second anniversary of the date that the judgment became dormant. The exception to a judgment's continuing for 10 years is a judgment in favor of the federal government or a federal government agency or a state or a state agency (including a university or college, other than a public junior or community college). In this case, a judgment continues for 20 years and may be renewed for one additional 20-year period by filing a renewed abstract of judgment before the expiration of the original 20-year period.

IN PRACTICE As discussed in Chapter 8, homestead real property is generally protected against forced sale by creditors to satisfy debts, including judgments. In addition, Chapter 42 of the Property Code provides for a number of personal property exemptions, not to exceed an aggregate fair market value of $60,000 for a family or $30,000 for a single adult. Some examples of exempt personal property are

- a Bible or other book containing sacred religious literature or writing (not to be included in the aggregate limits);
- home furnishings, including family heirlooms;
- provisions for consumption;
- tools, equipment, and books used in a trade or profession (including boats and motor vehicles);
- wearing apparel;
- jewelry (with limitations);
- two firearms;
- athletic and sporting equipment, including bicycles;
- a motor vehicle for each adult who holds a driver's license
- farm animals (with limitations);
- household pets; and
- certain assets held in retirement plans.

Attachments To prevent a debtor from conveying title to unsecured real estate (realty that is not mortgaged or is similarly unencumbered) while a court suit is being decided, a creditor may seek a writ of **attachment** by which the court retains custody of the property until the suit is concluded. To obtain an attachment, a creditor first must post with the court a surety bond or deposit sufficient to cover any possible loss or damage the debtor may sustain during the period the court has custody of the property, in case the judgment is not awarded to the creditor.

Lis Pendens A judgment or other decree affecting real estate is rendered at the conclusion of a lawsuit. Generally, there is a considerable time lag between the filing of a lawsuit and the rendering of a judgment. Therefore, when a suit is filed that affects title to a specific parcel of real estate, a notice known as a *lis pendens* (Latin for "litigation pending") is recorded. A lis pendens is not a lien but rather a *notice of a possible future lien*. Recording of the lis pendens gives notice to all interested parties, such as prospective purchasers and lenders, and establishes a priority for the later lien, which is dated back to the date the lis pendens was filed for record and indexed in the public record, available for public access (S.B. 1187, 2011).

Estate and Inheritance Tax Liens

Federal **estate taxes** and state **inheritance taxes** (as well as the debts of deceased persons) are *general, statutory, involuntary liens* that encumber a deceased person's real and personal property. These are normally paid or cleared in probate court proceedings. Probate and issues of inheritance will be discussed in Chapter 17.

Vendors' Liens

In Texas, the seller (vendor) has, by statute, a **vendor's lien** when he has not received in cash the full purchase price from the buyer (vendee) of the real estate. A vendor's lien is a claim on the real estate and is used only as security for the purchase money debt. This is a *specific, equitable, involuntary lien* for the amount of unpaid balance due the seller. If the sale is not vendor-financed, the seller assigns the vendor's lien to the third-party lender. The vendor's lien is usually reserved in the deed; but even if it is not, Texas law imposes one. Recording the grantor's deed creates a vendor's lien, which then is valid against the grantee, spouse, heirs, and devisees and subsequent creditors and purchasers. A seller enforces a vendor's lien by filing suit to have the real estate to pay the amount due.

Vendees' Liens

A **vendee's lien** is a *buyer's claim* against a seller's property in the event that the seller failed to deliver title. This usually occurs when property is purchased under an installment contract or contract for deed and the seller fails to deliver title after all other terms of the contract have been satisfied. A vendee's lien is a *specific, equitable, involuntary lien* for any money paid plus the value of any improvements made to the property by the buyer. It arises because of the doctrine or theory of *equitable title* in favor of the buyer.

Surety Bail Bond Lien

A real estate owner charged with a crime requiring a trial may choose to put up real estate instead of cash as surety for bail. In Texas, the execution and recording of such a **surety bail bond lien** creates a legal requirement that the owner of surety provide assurance of a net worth at least twice the amount of the sum of the bail. This voluntary lien is enforceable by the sheriff or other court officer if the accused person does not appear in court as required. A surety bail bond lien cannot be levied against a homestead property.

TWC Wage Lien

A **wage lien** attaches to all real and personal property belonging to an employer who owes back wages to an employee, as determined and ordered by the Texas Workforce Commission. The wage lien is given "superiority" status and, except for ad valorem tax liens, takes priority over all other liens, including previously recorded liens. The effect is that a wage lien will take priority over a lender's purchase money deed of trust lien and would not be extinguished by a lender's foreclosure.

A wage lien should not attach to homestead property because the homestead exemption is a constitutional protection. However, if a wage lien appears in a property title search, always refer it to the attorney and the title company involved in the transaction.

IRS Tax Lien

An IRS (Internal Revenue Service) tax lien results from a person's failure to pay any portion of federal IRS taxes owed, such as income and withholding taxes. A federal tax lien is a *general, statutory, involuntary lien* on the taxpayer's equity interest in all real and personal property owned by the delinquent taxpayer. A federal tax lien is effective for 10 years unless renewed by refiling.

Federal Judgment Liens

Federal judgment liens are liens in favor of the federal government or any department or entity of the federal government for such debts as unpaid student loans and deficiencies on government-insured or government-guaranteed loans. A federal judgment lien becomes a lien on all property of the judgment debtor upon the government's recording a certified copy of the judgment or an abstract of judgment in the county in which a debtor owns real property. The lien is effective for 20 years and applies to all judgments entered on or after May 21, 1981. The judgment lien may be extended once for an additional 20 years by filing a notice of renewal in the county clerk's records. Federal judgment liens are *general, statutory, involuntary liens.*

UNIFORM COMMERCIAL CODE

The **Uniform Commercial Code** (UCC) is a body of law that attempts to codify and make uniform throughout the country all laws relating to commercial transactions. The main relevance of the UCC to real property is in the area of personal property and fixtures. Section 9 of the Texas Business and Commerce Code is the Texas version of the UCC as it applies to pledging personal property or fixtures to secure a loan or credit purchase.

To create a security interest in personal property, including personal property that will become fixtures, the Texas code requires the use of a **security agreement**, which must contain a complete description of the items against which the lien applies. A short notice of this agreement, called a **financing statement**, which includes the legal description of the real estate involved, must be filed in the county clerk's office in the county in which the property is located. The recording of the financing statement constitutes notice to subsequent purchasers and mortgagees of the security interest in personal property and fixtures on the real estate. Many mortgagees require the signing and recording of a financing statement when the mortgaged premises include personal property or readily removable fixtures (such as washers and dryers) as part of the security for the mortgage debt. If the financing statement has been recorded properly, on the borrower's default the creditor could repossess the personal property and remove it from the property.

SUMMARY

Liens are claims, or charges, of creditors or tax officials against the real and personal property of a debtor. A lien is a type of encumbrance. Liens are either general, covering all real and personal property of a debtor/owner, or specific, covering only the specific parcel of real estate described in the mortgage, tax bill, building or repair contract, or other document.

The priority of liens generally is determined by the order in which they are placed in the public record of the county in which the debtor's property is located. Exceptions are IRS tax liens, real estate tax liens, TWC wage liens, and mechanics tax lie

Real estate taxes are levied annually by local taxing authorities. Tax liens generally have priority over other liens. Payments are required before stated dates, after which penalties accrue. An owner may lose title to property for nonpayment of taxes because such tax-delinquent property can be sold at a tax sale. Texas allows a maximum two-year period during which a defaulted owner can redeem the real estate after a tax sale on residential homestead, mineral interest, or agricultural property.

Special assessment taxes are levied on real estate that benefits from improvements, such as new sidewalks, curbs, or paving, to cover the cost of these improvements. Assessments usually are payable annually over a five-year or 10-year period, together with interest due on the balance of the assessment each year.

Mortgage (deed of trust or purchase money) liens are voluntary, specific liens given to lenders to secure payment for mortgage loans. Mechanics' liens protect general contractors, subcontractors, material suppliers, architects, engineers, and surveyors whose work enhances the value of real estate.

A judgment is a court decree obtained by a creditor, usually for a monetary award from a debtor. The abstract of judgment lien can be enforced by issuance of a writ of execution and sale by the sheriff to pay the judgment amount and costs.

Attachment is a means of preventing a defendant from conveying the real estate before completion of a suit in which a judgment is sought. Lis pendens is a recorded notice of a lawsuit that is awaiting trial in court and may result in a judgment that will affect title to a parcel of real estate.

Federal estate taxes and state inheritance taxes are general liens against a deceased owner's property. They usually are paid or cleared in probate court proceedings.

Vendors' liens and vendees' liens are claims against a specific parcel of real estate. A vendor's lien is a seller's claim against a purchaser who has not paid the entire purchase price in cash. A vendee's lien is a purchaser's claim against a seller who has not conveyed title under the terms of an installment contract.

TWC wage liens are general liens on the property of an employer who, as determined by the Texas Workforce Commission, owes back wages to an employee. They take priority over all other liens except ad valorem tax liens.

Internal Revenue Service tax liens are general liens against the property of a person who is delinquent in payment of IRS taxes. Federal judgment liens are general liens resulting from attempts to collect debts owed to the federal government.

Under the Uniform Commercial Code, a security agreement describes all personal property against which a UCC lien is to be filed. A financing statement is recorded in the county clerk's office giving notice to purchasers and mortgagees of the security interests in personal property and fixtures on the specific parcel of real estate.

CHAPTER 11 QUESTIONS

1. Which *BEST* refers to the type of lien that affects all real and personal property of a debtor?
   a. Specific lien
   b. Involuntary lien
   c. General lien
   d. Statutory lien

2. Working under a written agreement, a general contractor built a room addition on Tom and Harriet's homestead property. The general contractor completed the work several weeks ago but still has not been paid. In this situation, the contractor is entitled to a mechanic's lien. Which of the following is correct concerning his lien?
   a. It is a general lien.
   b. It is an involuntary lien.
   c. Foreclosure on the lien would normally be through nonjudicial procedures.
   d. The general contractor cannot file a notice of lien because he failed to withhold the 10% retainage for 30 days.

3. In Texas, after homestead real estate has been sold by the state or county to satisfy a delinquent real estate tax lien, the owner usually has a right to
   a. be paid for any improvement made during ownership.
   b. remain in possession indefinitely.
   c. redeem the property from sale within a two-year period.
   d. have the sale canceled.

4. Donny sold Ernest a parcel of real estate. Title has passed, but to date Ernest has not paid the purchase price in full as originally agreed. If Donny does not receive payment, which of the following is he entitled to enforce?
   a. Vendee's lien
   b. Lis pendens
   c. Vendor's
   d. Judgment

5. *Priority of liens* refers to which of the following?
   a. The order in which a debtor assumes responsibility for payment of obligations
   b. The order in which liens will be paid if property is sold by court order to satisfy a debt
   c. The fact that mortgage liens will always be paid before mechanics' liens if property is sold by court order to satisfy a debt
   d. The fact that specific liens have a greater priority than general liens

6. Which is a lien on real estate to secure payment for specific municipal improvements to a parcel of real estate?
   a. Mechanics' lien
   b. Special assessment
   c. Ad valorem lien
   d. Utility lien

7. Which entities do *NOT* levy ad valorem real estate taxes?
   a. Counties
   b. Texas Legislature
   c. Cities
   d. Hospital districts

8. A specific parcel of real estate is appraised for tax purposes at $80,000 market value. The tax rate for the county in which the property is located is $1.50 per $100 of value. The tax bill will be
   a. $1,000.
   b. $1,100.
   c. $1,200.
   d. $1,400.

9. Which tax is used to distribute the cost of public services among real estate owners?
   a. Personal property tax
   b. Sales tax
   c. Real property tax
   d. Special assessment

10. A mechanic's lien claim arises when, on the owner's order, a general contractor has performed work or provided material to improve a parcel of real estate but has not been paid. Such a contractor has a right to
    a. tear out the work.
    b. file a notice of nonresponsibility.
    c. record a notice of the lien and file a court suit within the time required by state law.
    d. have the owner's personal property sold to satisfy the lien.

11. Which is (are) considered a lien on real estate?
    a. Easements running with the land
    b. Unpaid mortgage loans
    c. An attachment
    d. An encroachment

12. A mortgage lien and a judgment lien have which of the following characteristics in common?
    a. Both are general liens.
    b. Both are involuntary liens.
    c. Both are voluntary liens.
    d. Both may involve a debtor-creditor relationship.

13. Which is classified as a general lien?
    a. Vendor's lien
    b. Judgment lien
    c. Real estate tax lien
    d. Mechanic's lien

14. Which lien usually is given higher priority?
    a. A mortgage dated last year
    b. The current real estate tax
    c. A mechanic's lien for work started before the mortgage was made
    d. A judgment rendered yesterday

15. The right of a defaulted taxpayer to recover the property before its sale for unpaid taxes is the
    a. statutory right of reinstatement.
    b. equitable right of appeal.
    c. statutory right of redemption.
    d. equitable right of redemption.

16. Which statement MOST accurately describes special assessment liens?
    a. They are general liens.
    b. They are paid on a monthly basis.
    c. They take priority over mechanics' liens.
    d. They cannot be prepaid in full without penalty.

17. Which is a voluntary, specific lien?
    a. Judgment lien
    b. Mortgage lien
    c. Vendor's lien
    d. Federal judgment lien

18. General contractor Kim is suing homeowner Bob for nonpayment for services; suit will be filed in the next few weeks. Recently Kim learned that Bob has listed his property with a local real estate broker for sale. In this instance, which of the following probably will be used by Kim and her attorneys to protect her interest?
    a. Notice of responsibility
    b. Lis pendens
    c. Vendee's lien
    d. Vendor's lien

19. To give notice of a security interest in personal property items, a lienholder must record a
    a. security agreement.
    b. financing statement.
    c. vendor's lien.
    d. quitclaim deed.

20. Which is a specific, involuntary, statutory lien?
    a. Real estate tax lien
    b. Income tax lien
    c. Estate tax lien
    d. Judgment lien

21. Which entity would probably be subject to real estate taxes?
    a. Public hospital
    b. Golf course operated by the city's park department
    c. Community church
    d. Apartment building

Detailed rationales for the end-of-chapter review questions are available online at www.dearborn.com through the *Instructor Resource Guides* link.

CHAPTER 12

Real Estate Contracts

■ LEARNING OBJECTIVES   *When you have completed this chapter, you will be able to*

- **distinguish** among express and implied contracts; bilateral and unilateral contracts; executed and executory contracts; and valid, void, voidable, and unenforceable contracts;
- **identify** the requirements for a valid contract and the statute of limitations for contract enforcement;
- **explain** how contracts may be discharged and the remedies available to a nondefaulting party;
- **describe** the differences between *promulgated* and *approved* forms and the requirements for their use;
- **discuss** the provisions of the Texas promulgated contract, a broker's avoiding the *unauthorized practice of law*, and the computation of time;
- **identify** the purpose and procedures for a buyer's getting a property condition inspection;
- **distinguish** between the option contract and a contract for deed, including the characteristics of each; and
- **define** the following *key terms*:

agreement in writing and signed	equitable title	option
assignment	escrow agreement	specific performance
bilateral contract	executed contract	statute of limitations
breach	executory contract	Texas Real Estate Broker-Lawyer Committee
competent parties	express contract	unenforceable contract
consideration	implied contract	unilateral contract
contract	legality of object	valid contract
contract for deed	liquidated damages	void contract
counteroffer	novation	voidable contract
earnest money deposit	offer and acceptance	

OVERVIEW

"Get it in writing" is a phrase commonly used to warn one party to an agreement to protect her interests by entering into a written contract with the other party, outlining the rights and obligations of both. The real estate business makes use of many different types of contracts, including listing agreements, leases, and sales contracts. Brokers and salespersons must understand the content and uses of such agreements and must be able to explain them to buyers and sellers.

This chapter first deals with the legal principles governing contracts in general. Then it examines some of the special types of contracts used in the real estate business.

CONTRACTS

Brokers and salespersons use many types of contracts and agreements in the course of their business to carry out their responsibilities to sellers, buyers, and the general public. Among these are listing agreements, buyer representation agreements, sales contracts, option agreements, installment contracts, leases, and escrow agreements.

Before studying these specific types of contracts, students first must understand *contract law*, the general body of law that governs the operation of such agreements. The following discussion provides an introduction to that portion of the law.

CONTRACT DEFINED

A contract is a voluntary, legally enforceable promise between two competent parties to perform some legal act in exchange for consideration.

A **contract** is a voluntary agreement between legally competent parties to perform or refrain from performing some legal act, supported by legal consideration. In essence, a contract is an enforceable promise that must be performed and for which, if a breach of promise occurs, the law provides a remedy. Depending on the situation and the nature or language of the agreement, a contract may be (1) express or implied; (2) unilateral or bilateral; (3) executory or executed; and (4) valid, unenforceable, voidable, or void. These terms are used to describe the type, status, and legal effect of a contract and are discussed in the sections that follow.

Express and Implied Contracts

Depending on how a contract is created, it may be express or implied. In an **express contract** the parties state the terms and show their intentions in words. An express contract may be oral or written. In an **implied contract**, the agreement of the parties is demonstrated by their acts and conduct.

IN PRACTICE   In the typical agency relationships, a listing agreement is an express contract between the seller and the broker, and a buyer representation agreement is an express contract between the buyer and the broker. Both contracts name the broker as the fiduciary representative of the principal. However, the courts have held that under certain situations a broker also may have an implied contract to represent the opposing principal in the transaction. For example, a broker took a listing for a residence and showed it to several potential purchasers, one of whom requested that a physical inspection of the property be made. The broker complied but mistakenly hired an unqualified person to make the inspection. The interested party bought the property, discovered a serious physical defect, and sued the broker. The court ruled that, although the broker was the agent of the seller, in complying with the buyer's request, by implication he had accepted an agency agreement to represent the purchaser. By hiring an inspector who was not competent to do the job, the broker violated his duty to the purchaser under this implied agreement.

Bilateral and Unilateral Contracts

- *Bi-* means "two"—a *bilateral contract* must have two promises.
- *Uni-* means "one"—a *unilateral contract* has only one promise

According to the nature of the agreement made, contracts also may be classified as either bilateral or unilateral. In a **bilateral contract**, both parties promise to do something; one promise is given in exchange for another. A real estate sales contract is a bilateral contract because the seller promises to sell a parcel of real estate and deliver title to the property to the buyer, who promises to pay a certain sum of money for the property. The courts today interpret most real estate contracts to be bilateral, that is, an exchange of promises.

Alternatively, a **unilateral contract** is a one-sided agreement whereby one party makes a promise in order to induce a second party to do something. The second party is not legally obligated to act; however, if the second party does comply, the first party is obligated to keep the promise. An offer of a reward is an example of a unilateral contract. For example, if a person runs a newspaper ad offering a reward for the return of a lost pet, that person is promising to pay if the act of returning the pet is fulfilled. A contract giving one party the option or right to purchase at specified terms also is an example of a unilateral contract because the seller cannot compel the buyer to perform; the unilateral option agreement is discussed later in this chapter.

Executory and Executed Contracts

A contract may be classified as either executory or executed, depending on whether the agreement is partially or completely performed. An executory contract exists when something remains to be done by one or both parties; that is, the agreement is partially performed. When a real estate sales contract is negotiated and signed by both parties, it is an **executory** agreement. There are still obligations to be met by both parties—payment of the purchase price to the seller and delivery of the deed to the purchaser, among others. When all parties have fulfilled all promises in the agreement, the contract is considered fully **executed**. Once closing and funding have occurred, the real estate sales contract is an executed agreement—the purchase price is paid, the deed is delivered, and the purchaser has possession of the property.

Validity of Contracts

A contract can be described as valid, void, voidable, or unenforceable, depending on the circumstances. These contracts are summarized in Figure 12.1.

A **valid contract** complies with all the essential elements and is binding and enforceable on both parties. (The essential elements of a contract are discussed later in this chapter.)

A **void contract** has no legal force or effect because it does not meet the essential elements of a contract. For example, one essential condition for a contract to be valid is that it be for a legal purpose. Thus, a "contract" to commit a crime is void; it is not a contract at all.

A **voidable contract** seems on the surface to be valid but may be rescinded, or disaffirmed, by the party who might be injured if the contract were to be enforced (in some cases, this might be both parties). For example, a contract entered into with a minor or one in which fraud can be proven is usually voidable. A minor generally is permitted to disaffirm a real estate contract while underage (a minor) or within a reasonable time after reaching legal age. A voidable contract will be considered by the courts to be a valid contract if the party who has the option to disaffirm the agreement does not do so within a prescribed period.

FIGURE 12.1: Legal Effects of Contract

Type of Contract	Legal Effect	Example
Valid	Binding and enforceable on both parties	Agreement complying with essentials of a valid contract
Void	No legal effect	Contract for an illegal purpose
Voidable	Valid, but may be disaffirmed by one party	Contract with a minor
Unenforceable	Valid between the parties, but neither may force performance	Certain oral agreements

An **unenforceable contract** has all the elements of a valid contract; however, neither party can sue the other to force performance. For example, an oral listing agreement is unenforceable. A broker who takes an oral listing risks being unable to sue a seller if the broker sells the seller's property but is not paid a commission as promised. Unenforceable contracts are said to be "valid as between the parties," because after the agreement is fully executed or performed and both parties are satisfied, neither would have reason to initiate a lawsuit to force performance.

Essential Elements for a Valid Contract

A contract establishes the interest of the purchasers and their right to enforce that interest by court action. Thus, it prevents the seller from selling the property to another person who might offer a higher price. The signed contractual agreement also obligates the buyer to complete the transaction according to the terms agreed on in the contract. The five essential elements for a valid and enforceable contract in Texas are described in the following.

Offer and acceptance are not present if *misrepresentation*, *fraud*, *undue influence*, or *duress* are involved.

- **Competent parties**: The buyer and the seller must be of legal age and free from a mental handicap that would make them incompetent. In Texas, people are considered to be of legal age if they are at least 18 years old, or are married, or have had their minority status removed by a court. Contracts with the mentally infirm can be either void or voidable; they are void if the person has been adjudicated to be incompetent. To make a valid contract, a fiduciary, a corporate officer, or an agent must have legal authority given by a written document.

- **Offer and acceptance**: This requirement, also called mutual assent, means that a "meeting of the minds" must occur. Offer and acceptance are technical legal terms. Courts look to the objective intent of the parties to determine whether they meant to enter into a binding agreement. The agreement terms must be fairly definite and understood by both parties.

Offer and acceptance requires that a contract be entered into as the free and voluntary act of each party. Contracts signed by a person under duress (use of force), menace (threat of violence), or undue influence or as a result of misrepresentation or fraud are voidable (may be canceled) by the injured party or by a court. Extreme care should be taken when one or more of the parties to a contract is elderly, sick, in great distress, or under the influence of drugs or alcohol.

- **Consideration**: Consideration is an act or a promise that is offered by one party to induce another to enter into a contract; it is that which is given in exchange for something from another. Even though the sales price is stated in the contract to purchase real property and earnest money is received, the actual consideration that supports the contract is the mutual exchange of promises by buyer and seller to legally obligate themselves to do something they were not legally required to do before; that is, the seller agrees to sell a property for a certain price, and the buyer agrees to pay that price to buy the described property (John W. Reilly, *The Language of Real Estate*).

> If a license holder, who has authority to bind a party to a lease or sale under a power of attorney or a property management agreement, executes the agreement, that license holder is also considered a party to the lease or sale.

For example, Bob promises to pay Alice $75,000 for her house, the promise would not serve as consideration unless Alice has made a promise to do something in return, such as tender the deed to her house.

Consideration must be "good and valuable" between the parties. The courts do not inquire into the adequacy of consideration. Adequate consideration ranges from as little as a promise of "love and affection" to a substantial sum of money. Anything that has been bargained for and exchanged is legally sufficient to satisfy the requirement for consideration. The only requirements are that the parties agree and that no undue influence or fraud has occurred.

- **Legality of object**: To be valid, a contract must not contemplate a purpose that is illegal or against public policy.
- **Agreement in writing and signed**: The Texas statute of frauds requires that contracts for the sale of real estate and leases for more than one year be in writing to be enforceable. The statute provides the following requirements to prevent fraudulent proof of a fictitious oral contract:
  - the signature of the party to be charged is required;
  - a spouse's signature must be included when necessary to release marital rights, such as community property and homestead rights;
  - an agent may sign for a principal if the agent has proper written authority, such as a power of attorney; and
  - when sellers are co-owners, all co-owners must sign.

The *Uniform Electronic Transactions Act* (UETA) and the Uniform Real Property Electronic Recording Act of 2005 permit electronic records and electronic signatures in electronic transactions to be legally enforceable, so long as both parties to a transaction agree to conduct the transaction electronically. Furthermore, either party may withdraw consent to conduct a transaction electronically at any time. The laws provide that if there is a law or other requirement that a document be an original, on paper, in writing, signed, witnessed, or acknowledged, then a document in electronic form satisfies those requirements. If the law requires a signature, an electronic signature satisfies the law. An electronic signature is an electronic sound, symbol, or process attached to a record and executed or adopted by a person with the intent to sign the record. An electronic record is received when (1) it enters an information processing system that the recipient has designated and (2) it is in a form capable of being processed by that system.

A county clerk is authorized to receive, index, store, archive, and transmit electronic documents and to provide access to documents and information by electronic means. However, if a nonoriginal paper document (one that has been faxed, emailed, or copied) is presented to a county clerk for recording, it must contain, or be attached as an exhibit to a document that contains, original signatures that are acknowledged or sworn to before a notary.

Accurate Description of the Property   In addition to the five elements for all contracts as listed, a real estate sales contract must contain an accurate legal description of the property being conveyed. The test that most courts use is whether the subject property can be identified with reasonable certainty.

Performance of Contract

Each party to a contract has certain rights and duties to fulfill. The question of when a contract must be performed is an important factor. Many contracts call for a specific time at which or by which the agreed acts must be completely performed. When a contract does not specify a date or time frame for performance, the acts it requires must be performed within a "reasonable time." Most activities related to Texas real estate contracts must be performed within a "reasonable time."

However, some contract forms provide that "time is of the essence." This means that the contract must be performed within the time limit specified and that any party who has not performed on time is liable for breach of contract. Of the promulgated contract forms required for use by licensees, only five state that "time is of the essence": the "Termination Option" paragraph (paragraph 23) of the sales contracts, the "Addendum for Sale of Other Property by Buyer," the "Third Party Financing Addendum for Credit Approval," the "Addendum for 'Back-Up' Contract," and the "Short Sale Addendum."

If contract terms are vague and one party sues the other based on one of these terms, the courts will make the presumption that the document is a valid contract. The courts will apply the *four corners doctrine* and make every effort to enforce it by determining the intent of the parties from within the "four corners" of the contract itself, with all provisions considered together in the original context.

Furthermore, the *parol evidence* rule prevents the admission into court of any prior or simultaneous oral or written agreements that contradict the terms of the written contract. If, for example, the buyer and the seller orally agree that the seller will pay the appraisal fee but the final written contract states that the buyer will pay, then the written contract prevails.

IN PRACTICE   The courts generally interpret the agreement against the party who prepared it. For example, a broker is responsible for preparing all listing agreements for the firm. If there were any doubt as to whether a listing agreement was an exclusive agency or an exclusive right to sell, the courts probably would construe it to be an exclusive agency, thus ruling against the broker who prepared the document.

Assignment and Novation

Often, after entering into a contract, one party may want to withdraw without actually terminating the agreement. This may be accomplished through either assignment or novation.

Assignment refers to a transfer of rights and/or duties under a contract. The purchase of a home on assumption or subject to an existing loan is an assignment. The duty of loan repayment may be delegated to the purchaser but the original obligor remains secondarily liable for the amount of the loan balance, unless specifically released from this responsibility. A contract that requires some personal quality or unique ability of one of the parties may not be assigned. Examples of such a contract are an owner-financed sale, which may not be assigned without express permission from the seller, and a listing agreement, which is a personal service contract. Most contracts include a clause that either permits or forbids assignment.

Novation, or the substitution of a new contract for an existing agreement with the intent of extinguishing the old contract, is another way to perform a contract. The new agreement may be between the same parties, or a new party may be substituted for either (the latter case is novation of the parties). The parties' intent must be to discharge the old obligation. The new agreement must be supported by consideration and must conform to all the essential elements of a valid contract. For example, a novation would occur if a buyer fell behind on payments and the lender modified the note terms to reflect a new payback arrangement. The courts determine whether or not a novation has occurred.

Assignment = substitution of parties

Novation = substitution of contracts

Discharge of Contract

A contract may be *completely performed*, with all terms carried out, or it may be *breached* (broken) if one party defaults. In addition, a contract may be *discharged* by other methods. These include the following:

- *Partial performance of the terms* along with a written acceptance by the person for whom acts have not been done or to whom money has not been paid
- *Substantial performance*, in which one party has substantially performed the contract but does not complete all the details exactly as the contract requires. Such performance—for example, under construction contracts—may be sufficient to force payment, with certain adjustments for damages suffered by the other party.
- *Impossibility of performance*, in which an act required by the contract cannot be accomplished legally
- *Mutual agreement* of the parties to cancel
- *Operation of law*, as in the voiding of a contract by a minor, or as a result of fraud or the expiration of the statute of limitations or as a result of a contract's being altered without the written consent of all parties involved

Default—Breach of Contract   A **breach** of contract is a violation of any of the terms or conditions of a contract without legal excuse, as when a seller breaches a sales contract by not delivering title to the buyer under the conditions stated in the agreement. If either party breaches, or defaults, the defaulting party assumes certain burdens and the nondefaulting party has certain rights.

If one of the parties defaults on a real estate sales contract, the nondefaulting party may

- sue for **specific performance** to force the defaulting party to carry out the terms of the contract and/or seek such other relief as may be provided by law (such as, submit to arbitration or mediation, seek an injunction, or sue for compensatory damages); or
- terminate the contract and receive the earnest money, releasing both parties from the contract (see Figure 12.3, paragraph 15).

If a damaged buyer gets the earnest money back or a damaged seller accepts the earnest money as **liquidated damages**, all parties are released from further obligations under the contract. In the event that the defaulting party wrongfully fails or refuses to sign a release to permit the title company to disburse the earnest money to the damaged party, the defaulting party will be liable to the other party for liquidated damages in an amount equal to the sum of (1) three times the amount of the earnest money, (2) the earnest money, (3) reasonable attorney's fees, and (4) all costs of suit.

Statute of Limitations The **statute of limitations** allows a specific time limit during which parties to a contract may bring legal suit to enforce their rights. Any party who does not take steps to enforce his rights within this time may lose those rights. Under Texas law, any action for the specific performance of a contract for the conveyance of real property must be commenced within four years from the date of the breach. A suit brought for a DTPA violation must be begun within two years from the date a buyer could reasonably have discovered the deceptive act. A party who intends to file a claim for payment from the real estate recovery fund must file an action within two years from the date a cause of action a cruise.

CONTRACTS USED IN THE REAL ESTATE BUSINESS

As mentioned earlier, the types of written agreements most commonly used by brokers and salespersons are listing agreements, buyer representation agreements, real estate sales contracts, option agreements, contracts for deed, leases, and escrow agreements.

Sales Contracts

In some cases, execution of a contract may refer solely to the act of signing it. In others, it refers to the complete performance of all terms by all parties.

The sales contract is the most important document in the transfer of real estate because it sets forth all details of the agreement between a buyer and a seller and establishes their legal rights and obligations. It is even more important than the deed because the sales contract dictates *the content of the deed.*

Offer and Acceptance One of the essential elements of a valid sales contract is a meeting of the minds whereby the buyer and the seller agree on the terms of the sale. This is usually accomplished through the process of offer and acceptance.

A broker lists an owner's real estate for sale at the price and conditions set by the owner. A prospective buyer, who wants to purchase the property at those terms or at some other terms, is found and a contract is signed by the prospective buyer. Because of the fiduciary duty of the agent to the principal, the broker should promptly communicate the receipt of the offer and present it to the seller. At this point, the contract is an *offer.* If the seller agrees to the offer *exactly as it was made* and signs (executes) the contract, the offer has been accepted. After appropriate *notification of acceptance* is given (explained in the next paragraph), the contract is *valid*. The licensee would then deliver a fully signed copy of the contract to the buyer, although it is not a requirement for validity of the contract.

An acceptance must not change or qualify the terms of an offer. If it does, the modification becomes a counteroffer, which voids the original offer.

Any attempt by the seller to change the terms proposed by the buyer creates a **counteroffer.** The buyer is relieved of the original offer because the seller has, in effect, rejected it; the original offer is void. The buyer can accept the seller's counteroffer or reject it and, if desired, make another counteroffer. Any change in the last offer made results in a counteroffer, until one party finally agrees to the other party's last offer and both parties initial all changes and sign (execute) the final contract. Then acceptance must be communicated as detailed below. An offer or counteroffer *may be withdrawn at any time before it has been accepted* (even if the person making the offer or counteroffer agreed to keep the offer open for a set period of time). In addition, an offer is not considered accepted until the person making the offer has been notified of the other party's acceptance. In a transaction involving subagency, notification of contract acceptance must be given directly to the buyer after seller acceptance because the buyer has no agent; but notification of acceptance to the seller can be given to the seller's broker or the salesperson working for the seller. In a buyer brokerage transaction, notification of acceptance is complete when the other party's agent has been notified. The real estate broker or salesperson must transmit all offers, acceptances, or other responses as soon as possible to avoid questions that might arise regarding whether an acceptance, rejection, or counteroffer has effectively taken place. Notification of contract acceptance may be made orally, with written confirmation recommended to avoid future disputes. The *effective date* of the contract is the date on which the communication of acceptance was made. Notifications between the parties after contract acceptance (for such items as inspection and repair reports) must be in writing and may be mailed, hand delivered, or transmitted by fax or electronic submission.

A counteroffer is created by
■ offeree's rejection or
■ offeror's revocation.

IN PRACTICE   There are three items of special importance regarding offer and acceptance:

- According to the TREC Enforcement Division, all contract offers that are delivered to the seller's agent must be presented to the seller—unless the seller has specifically instructed the listing broker not to bring offers below a certain price or the seller has a binding contract on the property and has instructed the agent in writing not to bring additional offers.

- If a broker receives more than one offer before presentation of a contract to the seller, all offers must be presented to the seller at the same meeting unless the seller instructed the broker otherwise. All offers should be presented promptly and no offer has priority over another. The agent representing each potential buyer should be notified that multiple offers have been received; however, the listing agent must keep the terms and conditions of the other offers confidential.

- Although a real estate broker and an escrow agent may sign agreements on the contract form, they are not parties to the contract, with one exception. A broker who has the authority to bind a party to a lease or sale under a power of attorney or property management agreement is also a party to the contract.

As discussed in Chapter 5, the *minimum services requirement* of the License Act dictates that a limited service broker (1) must inform the client if material information related to the transaction is received by the broker, (2) must answer the client's questions and present any offer to or from the client, and (3) may not instruct another broker to negotiate directly with the client.

Equitable Title   A buyer who signs a contract to purchase real estate does not receive fee title to the land; only a deed can convey fee title. However, after both buyer and seller have signed a sales contract, the buyer acquires an interest in the land known as **equitable title**. Acquisition of equitable title may give the buyer an insurable interest in the property. If the parties decide not to go through with the purchase and sale and if the contract has been recorded, the buyer will be required to give the seller a quitclaim deed to release the buyer's equitable interest in the land.

Destruction of Premises   Once both parties sign the sales contract, who bears the loss of any damage to, or destruction of, the property by fire or other casualty prior to closing? The contract forms promulgated by the Texas Real Estate Commission place this risk of loss on the seller, who would probably be aided by insurance proceeds. If the seller does not repair the property, the purchaser may terminate the contract or accept the damaged property and an assignment of the insurance proceeds.

Earnest Money Deposits   It is customary for a purchaser to put down a cash deposit when making an offer to purchase real estate. This cash deposit, commonly called an **earnest money deposit**, gives evidence of the purchaser's intent to carry out the terms of the contract. Earnest money is not required to have a valid contract, but a reasonable amount of earnest money helps to ensure a closing. Earnest money does not fulfill the requirement for consideration in a contract.

The amount of the deposit is a matter to be agreed on by the parties, although the selling broker may be asked to suggest an amount. Under the terms of many listing agreements, a real estate broker is required to obtain a reasonable amount as earnest money. Generally the deposit should be sufficient to discourage the buyer from defaulting, to compensate the seller for taking the property off the market, and to cover any expenses the seller and broker might incur if the buyer defaults.

Until an offer is accepted and notification is given to the other party, the earnest money check is not deposited. After the offer is accepted, the broker must deposit the earnest money by the close of business of the second working day after execution of the contract. The buyer may not get a refund of the money until the transaction is closed, the buyer terminates the contract under the option provision, or the seller defaults on the contract. *Under no circumstances does the earnest money belong to the broker.*

Generally, a title insurance company or similar institution holds the earnest money. If the broker holds it, it must be in a special *trust*, or *escrow*, *account*. This money cannot be *commingled*, or mixed, with a broker's personal funds. Likewise, a broker may not use such funds for personal use, an illegal act known as *conversion*. A broker does not need a special escrow account for each earnest money deposit received; one such account into which all such funds are deposited is sufficient. A broker must maintain full, complete, and accurate records of all earnest money deposits; otherwise, a broker's license may be suspended or revoked for failure to account properly for such deposits.

Computation of Time   In computing a period of time prescribed or allowed for negotiating a contract or for meeting a contract obligation, the period generally begins on the day after the act, event, or default in controversy. It concludes on the last day of the computed period. Calendar days, not business days, are used. For example, if the last day to exercise a contract option were Saturday, December 25, the buyer would not have the right to exercise the option after that date.

Promulgated Contract Forms   The Texas Real Estate License Act provides for the establishment of the **Texas Real Estate Broker-Lawyer Committee**. The purpose of this special committee is the drafting and revising of standard contract forms to be used by real estate licensees because most real estate transactions are basically similar in nature. Once the Broker-Lawyer Committee has drafted the forms, the Texas Real Estate Commission has the option of approving or promulgating the forms for use by brokers and their salespersons. A licensee *may* use a form that has been "approved" by the commission. Once a contract form or addendum has been "promulgated" by the commission, though, it *must* be used by a licensee for that particular contract situation. There are four exceptions to this requirement (Rule 537.11(a)):

- Transactions in which the licensee is functioning solely as a principal, not as an agent
- Transactions in which an agency of the U.S. government requires a different form to be used
- Transactions for which a contract form has been prepared by the property owner or prepared by an attorney and required by the property owner
- Transactions for which no standard contract form has been promulgated by the Texas Real Estate Commission, and the licensee uses a form prepared by an attorney-at-law licensed by this state and approved by the attorney for the particular kind of transactions involved or prepared by the Texas Real Estate Broker-Lawyer Committee and made available for trial use by licensees with the consent of the commission

As public records, the promulgated contract forms are available to any person. However, TREC contract forms are intended for use only by licensed real estate brokers or salespersons who are trained in their correct use. Mistakes in the use of a form may result in financial loss or a contract that is unenforceable. A notice on TREC's website advises nonlicensees who obtain the forms for use in a real estate transaction to contact a real estate licensee or an attorney for assistance.

Broker's Authority   Section 1101.654 of the License Act limits the broker's authority to prepare contracts for clients and customers. A licensed real estate broker is not authorized to practice law—that is, to give legal advice or to prepare legal documents such as deeds and mortgages. However, the broker may fill in TREC-approved and promulgated forms or other forms permitted by TREC Rules, as discussed. Rule 537.11 (d-h) further clarifies the broker's authority:

> A licensee may not undertake to draw or prepare documents fixing and defining the legal rights of the principals to a transaction. In negotiating real estate transactions, the licensee may fill in forms for such transactions, using exclusively forms which have been approved and promulgated by the commission or such forms as are otherwise permitted by these rules. When filling in a form authorized for use by this section, the licensee may only fill in the blanks provided and may

The Non-Realty Items Addendum is approved by TREC, for voluntary use, to convey personal property related to a real estate transaction.

not add to or strike matter from such form, except that licensees shall add factual statements and business details desired by the principals and shall strike only such matter as is desired by the principals and as is necessary to conform the instrument to the intent of the parties. A licensee *may not add to a promulgated contract form factual statements or business details for which a contract addendum, lease, or other form has been promulgated by the commission for mandatory use. Nothing in this section shall be deemed to prevent the licensee from explaining to the principals the meaning of the factual statements and business details contained in the said instrument so long as the licensee does not offer or give legal advice.*

IN PRACTICE If a licensee fills in the blanks of a promulgated contract form, that does not constitute the unauthorized practice of law—provided the forms are used correctly. Notice that the rule cited in the previous section prohibits a licensee from paraphrasing provisions contained in a promulgated addendum or lease and inserting such into the base contract. This means that the licensee must use the appropriate promulgated addendum or lease form or one that is required by a party to the contract.

Sample Real Estate Sales Contract

As shown in Figure 12.2, the commission has promulgated 6 earnest money contract forms, 17 special conditions addenda and forms, and 2 temporary leases. Figure 12.3 is an example of the real estate contract most frequently used in Texas. Study the sample contract and the corresponding summary of each clause provided. A HUD-1 closing statement for the transaction represented by this contract is located in Chapter 20 (Figure 20.4).

A real estate broker or agent may not receive a fee for referring a buyer or seller to a home warranty company. To do so is a violation of the Real Estate Settlement Procedures Act (RESPA).

1. *Parties*—identifies the seller and the buyer, as well as establishing the intent to sell and to buy
2. *Property*—sets forth the legal description and thus identifies the property to be sold by this contract; lists fixtures, improvements, and accessories that are a part of the property, as well as those to be excluded
3. *Sales Price*—establishes the cash down, loan amount, and sales price
4. *Financing*—stipulates the source of borrowed funds; details of the financing are specified in an addendum to the contract—for example, Third Party Financing Addendum for Credit Approval, Loan Assumption Addendum, or Seller Financing Addendum
5. *Earnest Money*—specifies the amount of earnest money and identifies the escrow agent
6. *Title Policy and Survey*—identifies which party is to pay for the title policy; notes the exceptions to title if a title policy is furnished; stipulates requirements for a title commitment; provides survey options; specifies procedures for a buyer to object to documents required in this paragraph; and includes required notices to buyer
7. *Property Condition*—specifies a buyer's right to have the property inspected; provides for the seller's disclosure of property condition and lead-based paint and hazards; specifies any limitations on the buyer's acceptance of property condition; establishes procedures for completion of repairs; includes an environmental notice to the buyer; and presents the residential service contract/home warranty option
8. *Brokers' Fees*—notes that payments of brokers' fees are contained in separate written agreements

9. *Closing*—establishes the target date for closing of the sale and identifies buyer and seller responsibilities at closing; contains seller representations regarding liens, assessments, and security interests
10. *Possession*—specifies when the buyer may take possession of the property
11. *Special Provisions*—clarifies any business details of the sale not covered by the provisions of the printed earned money contract form and not included in another TREC form; cannot include items that may constitute unauthorized practice of law
12. *Settlement and Other Expenses*—identifies which party is to pay a specific expense at closing
13. *Prorations*—specifies which items are to be prorated and fixes the timing of such proration *through* the day of closing; permits tax prorations to account for a change in exemptions; and provides for an adjustment of the tax proration after closing, when necessary
14. *Casualty Loss*—specifies the seller's responsibility for a casualty loss before closing and the buyer's options
15. *Default*—specifies the remedies available to each party in the event the other party breaches the contractual agreements
16. *Mediation*—encourages peaceable resolution of disputes through mediation
17. *Attorney's Fees*—specifies how the expenses of litigation are to be paid
18. *Escrow*—specifies the conditions under which the escrow agent agrees to be the holder of the earnest money and stipulates how such money is to be handled in the event the transaction does not close
19. *Representation*—provides for the contract to survive closing, for a remedy if seller representations are untrue, and for the seller to continue to show the property
20. *Federal Tax Requirements*—outlines the procedures for the buyer to follow if the seller is a "foreign person," as defined by applicable law
21. *Notices*—state requirements for delivery of notices affecting the contract
22. *Agreement of Parties*—clarifies the understanding that no other agreements are to be relied on and identifies any TREC addenda or other forms to be a part of the contract
23. *Termination Option*—provides the buyer with an unrestricted right to terminate the contract for a specified fee within a specified number of days after the effective date (if an option fee is paid to the seller)
24. *Consult an Attorney*—provides notice to both parties that real estate licensees cannot give legal advice and advises both parties to seek legal counsel for advice; an agent may not discourage a principal to a real estate transaction from employing a lawyer; includes *Date of Final Acceptance* (establishing the *effective date* of the contract) and the signature block

At the bottom of the contract negotiated between the buyer and the seller are the broker information, option fee receipt, and contract and earnest money receipt paragraphs. The broker information section specifies the brokers involved in the transaction and the fee to be paid to the "other broker" by the listing broker. The broker information section is merely informational and is not part of the contract between the parties or a separate contract between the brokers; therefore, licensees should print and not sign their names in this section.

The Third Party Financing Addendum for Credit Approval in Figure 12.4 is one of the three addenda promulgated to expand the "financing" paragraph, ¶4, of the contract, providing conditions under which the buyer agrees to obtain financing.

FIGURE 12.2: Forms Promulgated by the Texas Real Estate Commission

Contract Forms (Abbreviated Titles)
- One to Four Family Residential Contract (Resale)
- Unimproved Property
- New Home, Incomplete Construction
- New Home, Completed Construction
- Farm and Ranch
- Residential Condominium Contract

Special Conditions Addenda and Forms
- Sale of Other Property by Buyer Addendum
- Back-up Contract Addendum
- Release of Liability Addendum and/or Restoration of VA Entitlement
- Seller Financing Addendum
- Environmental Assessment Addendum
- Condominium Resale Certificate
- Coastal Area Property Addendum
- Property Located Seaward of the Gulf Intracoastal Waterway Addendum
- Property Subject to Membership in an Owners' Association Addendum
- Subdivision Information, including Resale Certificate for Property Subject to Membership in an Owners' Association
- Notice of Buyer's Termination of Contract
- Amendment to Contract
- Loan Assumption Addendum
- Third Party Financing Addendum for Credit Approval
- Reservation of Oil, Gas, and Other Minerals Addendum
- Short Sale Addendum
- Addendum for property in a propane gas system service area

Temporary Residential Lease Forms
- Seller's Lease
- Buyer's Lease

Property Condition   Although ¶7.D.(1) of the One to Four Family Residential Contract in Figure 12.3 allows a buyer to "As Is" with no stipulations for repairs or treatments, in most cases, it is not a wise decision to do so because most buyers are not experts in home construction. For example, most buyers would not be able to identify "a roof covering that is not appropriate for the slope of the roof" or "the absence of fireblocking at the attic penetration of the chimney flue." So what is a buyer to do? Paragraph 7.A. of the One to Four Family Residential Contract permits a buyer to have the property inspected by a TREC-licensed inspector or other licensed contractor, such as a plumber or an electrician.

So how does the inspection process work? The buyer selects the inspector or inspectors—not the real estate agent—and the buyer pays for any inspections. The inspector is hired to complete an inspection and, using a standard report form, issues an inspection report within three days unless otherwise agreed in writing (Rule 535.222). It is essential, though, that the inspection report be issued before the time frame allowed in Paragraph 23, Termination Option. The *Property Inspection Report* is a written opinion as to the condition of the improvements to real property, including structural items, electrical items, heating and air-conditioning systems, plumbing systems, appliances, and other equipment. In each category, the inspector notes any deficiencies in systems and components, with a deficiency defined as *a condition that, in the inspector's reasonable opinion, adversely and materially affects the performance of a system or component or constitutes a hazard to life, limb, or property as defined in the TREC Rules.* (TREC Rule 535.227(a)(4)). General deficiencies include, but are not limited to, inoperability, material distress, water penetration, damage, deterioration, missing parts, and unsuitable installation. In addition, the buyer may wish to employ one or more other licensed inspectors to conduct hydrostatic or static tests or inspections for structural soundness, termites, radon, lead-based paint, asbestos, and more.

After receiving the inspectors' reports, the buyer must then decide what to do with the information. Items identified in an inspection report do not obligate any party to make repairs or take other action: the buyer is not required to request that the seller take any action and the seller is not obligated to do any repairs. When deficiencies are reported, it is the buyer's responsibility to determine whether to terminate the contract under the Termination Option paragraph, obtain further evaluations, request that the seller make all or some of the necessary repairs at the seller's expense, make the repairs himself, or simply "live with" the reported deficiencies. Property inspections are not exhaustive inspections of the structure, systems, or components and they may not reveal all deficiencies. However, real estate inspections help to reduce some of the risk involved in purchasing a home and, at the very least, give the buyer a greater understanding of the condition of the property before closing on it.

Two additional decisions must be made by the buyer when the contract is prepared: to get or not to get a *residential service contract* and to ask or not to ask the seller to pay for it. A residential service contract is a home warranty to maintain, repair, or replace all or any part of the appliances, structural components, electrical, plumbing, heating, or air-conditioning systems of residential property. Paragraph 7.H. of the One to Four Family Residential Contract stipulates that a buyer may purchase a service contract and then may request that the seller reimburse him or her at closing for the cost of the warranty—or some portion of it. Because there are various companies authorized to write the service contracts, a buyer should evaluate the coverage and cost of each before purchasing one.

IN PRACTICE   Rule 535.148 prohibits a licensee from receiving an undisclosed fee or payment from a service provider. With respect to residential service companies, a licensee may not contract or agree to represent one service company exclusively. A licensee may receive a fee for providing advertising and other services on behalf of a residential service company. The licensee must disclose such payments to the client, using TREC Form RSC-1, Disclosure of Relationship with Residential Service Company. The disclosure is not attached to the contract as an addendum but should be retained in the broker's transaction records.

The licensing of both inspectors and residential service companies is regulated by TREC. The applicable laws and rules, along with the Property Inspection Report and a list of residential service company licensees, are available on the TREC website: www.trec.texas.gov.

FIGURE 12.3: Residential Sales Contract

12-05 -2011

PROMULGATED BY THE TEXAS REAL ESTATE COMMISSION (TREC)
ONE TO FOUR FAMILY RESIDENTIAL CONTRACT (RESALE)
NOTICE: Not For Use For Condominium Transactions

1. PARTIES: The parties to this contract are _John Iuro and wife, Joanne Iuro_
(Seller) and _Blake Redemann and wife, Connie Redemann_ (Buyer). Seller agrees to sell and convey to Buyer and Buyer agrees to buy from Seller the Property defined below.

2. PROPERTY:
  A. LAND: Lot ___15___ Block___7___, _Cedar Oaks_
  Addition, City of _Dallas_ , County of _Dallas_ ,
  Texas, known as _3040 North Racine 75340_
  (address/zip code), or as described on attached exhibit.
  B. IMPROVEMENTS: The house, garage and all other fixtures and improvements attached to the above-described real property, including without limitation, the following **permanently installed and built-in items,** if any: all equipment and appliances, valances, screens, shutters, awnings, wall-to-wall carpeting, mirrors, ceiling fans, attic fans, mail boxes, television antennas and satellite dish system and equipment, mounts and brackets for televisions and speakers, heating and air-conditioning units, security and fire detection equipment, wiring, plumbing and lighting fixtures, chandeliers, water softener system, kitchen equipment, garage door openers, cleaning equipment, shrubbery, landscaping, outdoor cooking equipment, and all other property owned by Seller and attached to the above described real property.
  C. ACCESSORIES: The following described related accessories, if any: window air conditioning units, stove, fireplace screens, curtains and rods, blinds, window shades, draperies and rods, door keys, mailbox keys, above ground pool, swimming pool equipment and maintenance accessories, artificial fireplace logs, and controls for: (i) satellite dish systems, (ii) garage doors, (iii) entry gates, and (iv) other improvements and accessories.
  D. EXCLUSIONS: The following improvements and accessories will be retained by Seller and must be removed prior to delivery of possession:___N/A___
  _____.

The land, improvements and accessories are collectively referred to as the "Property".

3. SALES PRICE:
  A. Cash portion of Sales Price payable by Buyer at closing............................ $ _50,000.00_
  B. Sum of all financing described below (excluding any loan funding
  fee or mortgage insurance premium)... $ _165,000.00_
  C. Sales Price (Sum of A and B)... $ _215,000.00_

4. FINANCING: The portion of Sales Price not payable in cash will be paid as follows: (Check applicable boxes below)
  ☒ A. THIRD PARTY FINANCING: One or more third party mortgage loans in the total amount of $ _165,000.00_ (excluding any loan funding fee or mortgage insurance premium).
    (1) Property Approval: If the Property does not satisfy the lenders' underwriting requirements for the loan(s) (including, but not limited to appraisal, insurability and lender required repairs), Buyer may terminate this contract by giving notice to Seller prior to closing and the earnest money will be refunded to Buyer.
    (2) Credit Approval: (Check one box only)
      ☒ (a) This contract is subject to Buyer being approved for the financing described in the attached Third Party Financing Addendum for Credit Approval.
      ❑ (b) This contract is not subject to Buyer being approved for financing and does not involve FHA or VA financing.
  ❑ B. ASSUMPTION: The assumption of the unpaid principal balance of one or more promissory notes described in the attached TREC Loan Assumption Addendum.
  ❑ C. SELLER FINANCING: A promissory note from Buyer to Seller of $_____,
  secured by vendor's and deed of trust liens, and containing the terms and conditions described in the attached TREC Seller Financing Addendum. If an owner policy of title insurance is furnished, Buyer shall furnish Seller with a mortgagee policy of title insurance.

Initialed for identification by Buyer_____ _____ and Seller _____ _____   TREC NO. 20-11

FIGURE 12.3: Residential Sales Contract (continued)

Contract Concerning _____3040 North Racine 75340_____Page 2 of 9   12-05 -2011
(Address of Property)

5. EARNEST MONEY: Upon execution of this contract by all parties, Buyer shall deposit $__15,000.00_____ as earnest money with __ABC Title Co._____, as escrow agent, at _____1234 Settlement Street, Dallas, TX 75340_____ (address). Buyer shall deposit additional earnest money of $_____ with escrow agent within _____ days after the effective date of this contract. If Buyer fails to deposit the earnest money as required by this contract, Buyer will be in default.

6. TITLE POLICY AND SURVEY:
   A. TITLE POLICY: Seller shall furnish to Buyer at ☒ Seller's ☐ Buyer's expense an owner policy of title insurance (Title Policy) issued by ___ABC Title Co._____ (Title Company) in the amount of the Sales Price, dated at or after closing, insuring Buyer against loss under the provisions of the Title Policy, subject to the promulgated exclusions (including existing building and zoning ordinances) and the following exceptions:
      (1) Restrictive covenants common to the platted subdivision in which the Property is located.
      (2) The standard printed exception for standby fees, taxes and assessments.
      (3) Liens created as part of the financing described in Paragraph 4.
      (4) Utility easements created by the dedication deed or plat of the subdivision in which the Property is located.
      (5) Reservations or exceptions otherwise permitted by this contract or as may be approved by Buyer in writing.
      (6) The standard printed exception as to marital rights.
      (7) The standard printed exception as to waters, tidelands, beaches, streams, and related matters.
      (8) The standard printed exception as to discrepancies, conflicts, shortages in area or boundary lines, encroachments or protrusions, or overlapping improvements. Buyer, at Buyer's expense, may have the exception amended to read, "shortages in area".
   B. COMMITMENT: Within 20 days after the Title Company receives a copy of this contract, Seller shall furnish to Buyer a commitment for title insurance (Commitment) and, at Buyer's expense, legible copies of restrictive covenants and documents evidencing exceptions in the Commitment (Exception Documents) other than the standard printed exceptions. Seller authorizes the Title Company to deliver the Commitment and Exception Documents to Buyer at Buyer's address shown in Paragraph 21. If the Commitment and Exception Documents are not delivered to Buyer within the specified time, the time for delivery will be automatically extended up to 15 days or the Closing Date, whichever is earlier. If, due to factors beyond Seller's control, the Commitment and Exception Documents are not delivered within the time required, Buyer may terminate this contract and the earnest money will be refunded to Buyer.
   C. SURVEY: The survey must be made by a registered professional land surveyor acceptable to the Title Company and Buyer's lender(s). (Check one box only)
      ☐(1) Within _____ days after the effective date of this contract, Seller shall furnish to Buyer and Title Company Seller's existing survey of the Property and a Residential Real Property Affidavit promulgated by the Texas Department of Insurance (T-47 Affidavit). **If Seller fails to furnish the existing survey or affidavit within the time prescribed, Buyer shall obtain a new survey at Seller's expense no later than 3 days prior to Closing Date.** If the existing survey or affidavit is not acceptable to Title Company or Buyer's lender(s), Buyer shall obtain a new survey at ☐Seller's ☐Buyer's expense no later than 3 days prior to Closing Date.
      ☒(2) Within ___3___ days after the effective date of this contract, Buyer shall obtain a new survey at Buyer's expense. Buyer is deemed to receive the survey on the date of actual receipt or the date specified in this paragraph, whichever is earlier.
      ☐(3) Within _____ days after the effective date of this contract, Seller, at Seller's expense shall furnish a new survey to Buyer.
   D. OBJECTIONS: Buyer may object in writing to defects, exceptions, or encumbrances to title: disclosed on the survey other than items 6A(1) through (7) above; disclosed in the Commitment other than items 6A(1) through (8) above; or which prohibit the following use or activity: ___N/A_____
   _____.
   Buyer must object the earlier of (i) the Closing Date or (ii) __10__ days after Buyer receives the Commitment, Exception Documents, and the survey. Buyer's failure to object within the time allowed will constitute a waiver of Buyer's right to object; except that the requirements in Schedule C of the Commitment are not waived by Buyer. Provided Seller is not obligated to incur any expense, Seller shall cure the timely objections of Buyer or any third party

Initialed for identification by Buyer_____ _____ and Seller _____ _____   TREC NO. 20-11

FIGURE 12.3: Residential Sales Contract (continued)

Contract Concerning _____3040 North Racine 75340_____Page 3 of 9   12-05 -2011
(Address of Property)

lender within 15 days after Seller receives the objections and the Closing Date will be extended as necessary. If objections are not cured within such 15 day period, this contract will terminate and the earnest money will be refunded to Buyer unless Buyer waives the objections.

E. TITLE NOTICES:

(1) ABSTRACT OR TITLE POLICY: Broker advises Buyer to have an abstract of title covering the Property examined by an attorney of Buyer's selection, or Buyer should be furnished with or obtain a Title Policy. If a Title Policy is furnished, the Commitment should be promptly reviewed by an attorney of Buyer's choice due to the time limitations on Buyer's right to object.

(2) MEMBERSHIP IN PROPERTY OWNERS ASSOCIATION(S): The Property ☐is ☒is not subject to mandatory membership in a property owners association(s). If the Property is subject to mandatory membership in a property owners association(s), Seller notifies Buyer under §5.012, Texas Property Code, that, as a purchaser of property in the residential community identified in Paragraph 2A in which the Property is located, you are obligated to be a member of the property owners association(s). Restrictive covenants governing the use and occupancy of the Property and all dedicatory instruments governing the establishment, maintenance, or operation of this residential community have been or will be recorded in the Real Property Records of the county in which the Property is located. Copies of the restrictive covenants and dedicatory instruments may be obtained from the county clerk. **You are obligated to pay assessments to the property owners association(s). The amount of the assessments is subject to change. Your failure to pay the assessments could result in enforcement of the association's lien on and the foreclosure of the Property.**
Section 207.003, Property Code, entitles an owner to receive copies of any document that governs the establishment, maintenance, or operation of a subdivision, including, but not limited to, restrictions, bylaws, rules and regulations, and a resale certificate from a property owners' association. A resale certificate contains information including, but not limited to, statements specifying the amount and frequency of regular assessments and the style and cause number of lawsuits to which the property owners' association is a party, other than lawsuits relating to unpaid ad valorem taxes of an individual member of the association.   These documents must be made available to you by the property owners' association or the association's agent on your request.
If Buyer is concerned about these matters, the TREC promulgated Addendum for Property Subject to Mandatory Membership in a Property Owners Association(s) should be used.

(3) STATUTORY TAX DISTRICTS: If the Property is situated in a utility or other statutorily created district providing water, sewer, drainage, or flood control facilities and services, Chapter 49, Texas Water Code, requires Seller to deliver and Buyer to sign the statutory notice relating to the tax rate, bonded indebtedness, or standby fee of the district prior to final execution of this contract.

(4) TIDE WATERS: If the Property abuts the tidally influenced waters of the state, §33.135, Texas Natural Resources Code, requires a notice regarding coastal area property to be included in the contract. An addendum containing the notice promulgated by TREC or required by the parties must be used.

(5) ANNEXATION: If the Property is located outside the limits of a municipality, Seller notifies Buyer under §5.011, Texas Property Code, that the Property may now or later be included in the extraterritorial jurisdiction of a municipality and may now or later be subject to annexation by the municipality. Each municipality maintains a map that depicts its boundaries and extraterritorial jurisdiction. To determine if the Property is located within a municipality's extraterritorial jurisdiction or is likely to be located within a municipality's extraterritorial jurisdiction, contact all municipalities located in the general proximity of the Property for further information.

(6) PROPERTY LOCATED IN A CERTIFICATED SERVICE AREA OF A UTILITY SERVICE PROVIDER: Notice required by §13.257, Water Code: The real property, described in Paragraph 2, that you are about to purchase may be located in a certificated water or sewer service area, which is authorized by law to provide water or sewer service to the properties in the certificated area. If your property is located in a certificated area there may be special costs or charges that you will be required to pay before you can receive water or sewer service.   There may be a period required to construct lines or other facilities necessary to provide water or sewer service to your property. You are advised to determine if the property is in a certificated area and contact the utility service provider

Initialed for identification by Buyer_____ _____ and Seller _____ _____   TREC NO. 20-11

FIGURE 12.3: Residential Sales Contract (continued)

Contract Concerning _____3040 North Racine 75340_____ Page 4 of 9   12-05 -2011
(Address of Property)

to determine the cost that you will be required to pay and the period, if any, that is required to provide water or sewer service to your property. The undersigned Buyer hereby acknowledges receipt of the foregoing notice at or before the execution of a binding contract for the purchase of the real property described in Paragraph 2 or at closing of purchase of the real property.

(7) PUBLIC IMPROVEMENT DISTRICTS: If the Property is in a public improvement district, §5.014, Property Code, requires Seller to notify Buyer as follows: As a purchaser of this parcel of real property you are obligated to pay an assessment to a municipality or county for an improvement project undertaken by a public improvement district under Chapter 372, Local Government Code. The assessment may be due annually or in periodic installments. More information concerning the amount of the assessment and the due dates of that assessment may be obtained from the municipality or county levying the assessment. The amount of the assessments is subject to change. Your failure to pay the assessments could result in a lien on and the foreclosure of your property.

(8) TRANSFER FEES: If the Property is subject to a private transfer fee obligation, §5.205, Property Code, requires Seller to notify Buyer as follows: The private transfer fee obligation may be governed by Chapter 5, Subchapter G of the Texas Property Code.

7. PROPERTY CONDITION:
  A. ACCESS, INSPECTIONS AND UTILITIES: Seller shall permit Buyer and Buyer's agents access to the Property at reasonable times. Buyer may have the Property inspected by inspectors selected by Buyer and licensed by TREC or otherwise permitted by law to make inspections. Seller at Seller's expense shall immediately cause existing utilities to be turned on and shall keep the utilities on during the time this contract is in effect.

  B. SELLER'S DISCLOSURE NOTICE PURSUANT TO §5.008, TEXAS PROPERTY CODE (Notice): (Check one box only)
    ☒ (1) Buyer has received the Notice.
    ❑ (2) Buyer has not received the Notice. Within _____ days after the effective date of this contract, Seller shall deliver the Notice to Buyer. If Buyer does not receive the Notice, Buyer may terminate this contract at any time prior to the closing and the earnest money will be refunded to Buyer. If Seller delivers the Notice, Buyer may terminate this contract for any reason within 7 days after Buyer receives the Notice or prior to the closing, whichever first occurs, and the earnest money will be refunded to Buyer.
    ❑ (3)The Seller is not required to furnish the notice under the Texas Property Code.

  C. SELLER'S DISCLOSURE OF LEAD-BASED PAINT AND LEAD-BASED PAINT HAZARDS is required by Federal law for a residential dwelling constructed prior to 1978.

  D. ACCEPTANCE OF PROPERTY CONDITION: (Check one box only)
    ☒ (1) Buyer accepts the Property in its present condition.
    ❑ (2) Buyer accepts the Property in its present condition provided Seller, at Seller's expense, shall complete the following specific repairs and treatments: _____
    _____.
    (Do not insert general phrases, such as "subject to inspections" that do not identify specific repairs.)

  NOTICE TO BUYER AND SELLER: Buyer's agreement to accept the Property in its present condition under Paragraph 7D(1) or (2) does not preclude Buyer from inspecting the Property under Paragraph 7A, from negotiating repairs or treatments in a subsequent amendment, or from terminating this contract during the Option Period, if any.

  E. LENDER REQUIRED REPAIRS AND TREATMENTS: Unless otherwise agreed in writing, neither party is obligated to pay for lender required repairs, which includes treatment for wood destroying insects. If the parties do not agree to pay for the lender required repairs or treatments, this contract will terminate and the earnest money will be refunded to Buyer. If the cost of lender required repairs and treatments exceeds 5% of the Sales Price, Buyer may terminate this contract and the earnest money will be refunded to Buyer.

  F. COMPLETION OF REPAIRS AND TREATMENTS: Unless otherwise agreed in writing, Seller shall complete all agreed repairs and treatments prior to the Closing Date. All required permits must be obtained, and repairs and treatments must be performed by persons who are licensed or otherwise authorized by law to provide such repairs or treatments. At Buyer's election, any transferable warranties received by Seller with respect to the repairs and treatments will be transferred to Buyer at Buyer's expense. If Seller fails to complete any agreed repairs and treatments prior to the Closing Date, Buyer may exercise remedies under Paragraph 15 or extend the Closing Date up to 15 days if necessary for Seller to complete the repairs and treatments.

  G. ENVIRONMENTAL MATTERS: Buyer is advised that the presence of wetlands, toxic

Initialed for identification by Buyer_____ _____ and Seller _____ _____   TREC NO. 20-11

FIGURE 12.3: Residential Sales Contract (continued)

Contract Concerning __3040 North Racine 75340__ _____ Page 5 of 9   12-05 -2011
(Address of Property)

substances, including asbestos and wastes or other environmental hazards, or the presence of a threatened or endangered species or its habitat may affect Buyer's intended use of the Property. If Buyer is concerned about these matters, an addendum promulgated by TREC or required by the parties should be used.

H. RESIDENTIAL SERVICE CONTRACTS: Buyer may purchase a residential service contract from a residential service company licensed by TREC. If Buyer purchases a residential service contract, Seller shall reimburse Buyer at closing for the cost of the residential service contract in an amount not exceeding $ _350.00_____. Buyer should review any residential service contract for the scope of coverage, exclusions and limitations. **The purchase of a residential service contract is optional. Similar coverage may be purchased from various companies authorized to do business in Texas.**

8. **BROKERS' FEES:** All obligations of the parties for payment of brokers' fees are contained in separate written agreements.

9. **CLOSING:**

A. The closing of the sale will be on or before _____June 15_____, 20_XX__, or within 7 days after objections made under Paragraph 6D have been cured or waived, whichever date is later (Closing Date). If either party fails to close the sale by the Closing Date, the non-defaulting party may exercise the remedies contained in Paragraph 15.

B. At closing:

(1) Seller shall execute and deliver a general warranty deed conveying title to the Property to Buyer and showing no additional exceptions to those permitted in Paragraph 6 and furnish tax statements or certificates showing no delinquent taxes on the Property.

(2) Buyer shall pay the Sales Price in good funds acceptable to the escrow agent.

(3) Seller and Buyer shall execute and deliver any notices, statements, certificates, affidavits, releases, loan documents and other documents reasonably required for the closing of the sale and the issuance of the Title Policy.

(4) There will be no liens, assessments, or security interests against the Property which will not be satisfied out of the sales proceeds unless securing the payment of any loans assumed by Buyer and assumed loans will not be in default.

(5) If the Property is subject to a lease, Seller shall (i) deliver to Buyer the lease(s) and the move-in condition form signed by the tenant, if any, and (ii) transfer security deposits (as defined under §92.102, Property Code), if any, to Buyer. In such an event, Buyer shall deliver to the tenant a signed statement acknowledging that the Buyer has received the security deposit and is responsible for the return of the security deposit, and specifying the exact dollar amount of the security deposit.

10. **POSSESSION:** Seller shall deliver to Buyer possession of the Property in its present or required condition, ordinary wear and tear excepted: ☒upon closing and funding ☐according to a temporary residential lease form promulgated by TREC or other written lease required by the parties. Any possession by Buyer prior to closing or by Seller after closing which is not authorized by a written lease will establish a tenancy at sufferance relationship between the parties. **Consult your insurance agent prior to change of ownership and possession because insurance coverage may be limited or terminated. The absence of a written lease or appropriate insurance coverage may expose the parties to economic loss.**

11. **SPECIAL PROVISIONS:** (Insert only factual statements and business details applicable to the sale. TREC rules prohibit licensees from adding factual statements or business details for which a contract addendum, lease or other form has been promulgated by TREC for mandatory use.)

Initialed for identification by Buyer_____ _____ and Seller _____ _____   TREC NO. 20-11

FIGURE 12.3: Residential Sales Contract (continued)

Contract Concerning ____3040 North Racine 75340____ Page 6 of 9　12-05 -2011
(Address of Property)

12. SETTLEMENT AND OTHER EXPENSES:
A. The following expenses must be paid at or prior to closing:
(1) Expenses payable by Seller (Seller's Expenses):
(a) Releases of existing liens, including prepayment penalties and recording fees; release of Seller's loan liability; tax statements or certificates; preparation of deed; one-half of escrow fee; and other expenses payable by Seller under this contract.
(b) Seller shall also pay an amount not to exceed $2,475.00 to be applied in the following order: Buyer's Expenses which Buyer is prohibited from paying by FHA, VA, Texas Veterans Land Board or other governmental loan programs, and then to other Buyer's Expenses as allowed by the lender.
(2) Expenses payable by Buyer (Buyer's Expenses): Appraisal fees; loan application fees; adjusted origination charges; credit reports; preparation of loan documents; interest on the notes from date of disbursement to one month prior to dates of first monthly payments; recording fees; copies of easements and restrictions; loan title policy with endorsements required by lender; loan-related inspection fees; photos; amortization schedules; one-half of escrow fee; all prepaid items, including required premiums for flood and hazard insurance, reserve deposits for insurance, ad valorem taxes and special governmental assessments; final compliance inspection; courier fee; repair inspection; underwriting fee; wire transfer fee; expenses incident to any loan; Private Mortgage Insurance Premium (PMI), VA Loan Funding Fee, or FHA Mortgage Insurance Premium (MIP) as required by the lender; and other expenses payable by Buyer under this contract.
B. If any expense exceeds an amount expressly stated in this contract for such expense to be paid by a party, that party may terminate this contract unless the other party agrees to pay such excess. Buyer may not pay charges and fees expressly prohibited by FHA, VA, Texas Veterans Land Board or other governmental loan program regulations.

13. PRORATIONS: Taxes for the current year, interest, maintenance fees, assessments, dues and rents will be prorated through the Closing Date. The tax proration may be calculated taking into consideration any change in exemptions that will affect the current year's taxes. If taxes for the current year vary from the amount prorated at closing, the parties shall adjust the prorations when tax statements for the current year are available. If taxes are not paid at or prior to closing, Buyer shall pay taxes for the current year.

14. CASUALTY LOSS: If any part of the Property is damaged or destroyed by fire or other casualty after the effective date of this contract, Seller shall restore the Property to its previous condition as soon as reasonably possible, but in any event by the Closing Date. If Seller fails to do so due to factors beyond Seller's control, Buyer may (a) terminate this contract and the earnest money will be refunded to Buyer (b) extend the time for performance up to 15 days and the Closing Date will be extended as necessary or (c) accept the Property in its damaged condition with an assignment of insurance proceeds and receive credit from Seller at closing in the amount of the deductible under the insurance policy. Seller's obligations under this paragraph are independent of any other obligations of Seller under this contract.

15. DEFAULT: If Buyer fails to comply with this contract, Buyer will be in default, and Seller may (a) enforce specific performance, seek such other relief as may be provided by law, or both, or (b) terminate this contract and receive the earnest money as liquidated damages, thereby releasing both parties from this contract. If Seller fails to comply with this contract, Seller will be in default and Buyer may (a) enforce specific performance, seek such other relief as may be provided by law, or both, or (b) terminate this contract and receive the earnest money, thereby releasing both parties from this contract.

16. MEDIATION: It is the policy of the State of Texas to encourage resolution of disputes through alternative dispute resolution procedures such as mediation. Any dispute between Seller and Buyer related to this contract which is not resolved through informal discussion ☒will ☐will not be submitted to a mutually acceptable mediation service or provider. The parties to the mediation shall bear the mediation costs equally. This paragraph does not preclude a party from seeking equitable relief from a court of competent jurisdiction.

Initialed for identification by Buyer_____ _____ and Seller _____ _____　TREC NO. 20-11

FIGURE 12.3: Residential Sales Contract (continued)

Contract Concerning _____3040 North Racine 75340_____ Page 7 of 9   12-05 -2011
(Address of Property)

17. **ATTORNEY'S FEES:** A Buyer, Seller, Listing Broker, Other Broker, or escrow agent who prevails in any legal proceeding related to this contract is entitled to recover reasonable attorney's fees and all costs of such proceeding.

18. **ESCROW:**
   A. ESCROW: The escrow agent is not (i) a party to this contract and does not have liability for the performance or nonperformance of any party to this contract, (ii) liable for interest on the earnest money and (iii) liable for the loss of any earnest money caused by the failure of any financial institution in which the earnest money has been deposited unless the financial institution is acting as escrow agent.
   B. EXPENSES: At closing, the earnest money must be applied first to any cash down payment, then to Buyer's Expenses and any excess refunded to Buyer. If no closing occurs, escrow agent may: (i) require a written release of liability of the escrow agent from all parties, (ii) require payment of unpaid expenses incurred on behalf of a party, and (iii) only deduct from the earnest money the amount of unpaid expenses incurred on behalf of the party receiving the earnest money.
   C. DEMAND: Upon termination of this contract, either party or the escrow agent may send a release of earnest money to each party and the parties shall execute counterparts of the release and deliver same to the escrow agent. If either party fails to execute the release, either party may make a written demand to the escrow agent for the earnest money. If only one party makes written demand for the earnest money, escrow agent shall promptly provide a copy of the demand to the other party. If escrow agent does not receive written objection to the demand from the other party within 15 days, escrow agent may disburse the earnest money to the party making demand reduced by the amount of unpaid expenses incurred on behalf of the party receiving the earnest money and escrow agent may pay the same to the creditors. If escrow agent complies with the provisions of this paragraph, each party hereby releases escrow agent from all adverse claims related to the disbursal of the earnest money.
   D. DAMAGES: Any party who wrongfully fails or refuses to sign a release acceptable to the escrow agent within 7 days of receipt of the request will be liable to the other party for liquidated damages in an amount equal to the sum of: (i) three times the amount of the earnest money; (ii) the earnest money; (iii) reasonable attorney's fees; and (iv) all costs of suit.
   E. NOTICES: Escrow agent's notices will be effective when sent in compliance with Paragraph 21. Notice of objection to the demand will be deemed effective upon receipt by escrow agent.

19. **REPRESENTATIONS:** All covenants, representations and warranties in this contract survive closing. If any representation of Seller in this contract is untrue on the Closing Date, Seller will be in default. Unless expressly prohibited by written agreement, Seller may continue to show the Property and receive, negotiate and accept back up offers.

20. **FEDERAL TAX REQUIREMENTS:** If Seller is a "foreign person," as defined by applicable law, or if Seller fails to deliver an affidavit to Buyer that Seller is not a "foreign person," then Buyer shall withhold from the sales proceeds an amount sufficient to comply with applicable tax law and deliver the same to the Internal Revenue Service together with appropriate tax forms. Internal Revenue Service regulations require filing written reports if currency in excess of specified amounts is received in the transaction.

21. **NOTICES:** All notices from one party to the other must be in writing and are effective when mailed to, hand-delivered at, or transmitted by facsimile or electronic transmission as follows:

To Buyer at:	Blake Redemann and	**To Seller at:**	John Iuro and
	Connie Redemann		Joanne Iuro
	7016 Hurst		3040 North Racine
	Amarillo, TX 79109		Dallas, TX 75340
Telephone:	(806) 372-4300	Telephone:	(214) 497-1324
Facsimile:	(806) 372-4301	Facsimile:	(214) 497-2324
E-mail:	bredermann@xyz.net	E-mail:	johniuro@abc.net

Initialed for identification by Buyer_____ _____ and Seller _____ _____   TREC NO. 20-11

FIGURE 12.3: Residential Sales Contract (continued)

Contract Concerning ___3040 North Racine 75340_____ Page 8 of 9   12-05-2011
(Address of Property)

22. AGREEMENT OF PARTIES: This contract contains the entire agreement of the parties and cannot be changed except by their written agreement. Addenda which are a part of this contract are (Check all applicable boxes):

☒ Third Party Financing Addendum for Credit Approval

☐ Seller Financing Addendum

☐ Addendum for Property Subject to Mandatory Membership in a Property Owners Association

☐ Buyer's Temporary Residential Lease

☐ Loan Assumption Addendum

☐ Addendum for Sale of Other Property by Buyer

☐ Addendum for Reservation of Oil, Gas and Other Minerals

☐ Addendum for "Back-Up" Contract

☐ Addendum for Coastal Area Property

☐ Environmental Assessment, Threatened or Endangered Species and Wetlands Addendum

☐ Seller's Temporary Residential Lease

☐ Short Sale Addendum

☐ Addendum for Property Located Seaward of the Gulf Intracoastal Waterway

☐ Addendum for Seller's Disclosure of Information on Lead-based Paint and Lead-based Paint Hazards as Required by Federal Law

☐ Other (list): _____

23. TERMINATION OPTION: For nominal consideration, the receipt of which is hereby acknowledged by Seller, and Buyer's agreement to pay Seller $_100.00_____ (Option Fee) within 2 days after the effective date of this contract, Seller grants Buyer the unrestricted right to terminate this contract by giving notice of termination to Seller within ___10___ days after the effective date of this contract (Option Period). If no dollar amount is stated as the Option Fee or if Buyer fails to pay the Option Fee to Seller within the time prescribed, this paragraph will not be a part of this contract and Buyer shall not have the unrestricted right to terminate this contract. If Buyer gives notice of termination within the time prescribed, the Option Fee will not be refunded; however, any earnest money will be refunded to Buyer. The Option Fee ☐will ☒will not be credited to the Sales Price at closing. **Time is of the essence for this paragraph and strict compliance with the time for performance is required.**

24. CONSULT AN ATTORNEY: TREC rules prohibit real estate licensees from giving legal advice. READ THIS CONTRACT CAREFULLY. If you do not understand the effect of this contract, consult an attorney BEFORE signing.

Buyer's Attorney is: _____

Telephone: (___) _____
Facsimile: (___) _____
E-mail: _____

Seller's Attorney is: _____

Telephone: (___) _____
Facsimile: (___) _____
E-mail: _____

**EXECUTED the _____ day of _____, 20____ (EFFECTIVE DATE).
(BROKER: FILL IN THE DATE OF FINAL ACCEPTANCE.)**

_____ Buyer

_____ Buyer

_____ Seller

_____ Seller

TREC NO. 20-11

FIGURE 12.3: Residential Sales Contract (continued)

Contract Concerning _3040 North Racine 75340_   Page 9 of 9   12-05 -2011
     (Address of Property)

BROKER INFORMATION

	Open Door Real Estate Co. 332324
Other Broker Firm License No.	Listing Broker Firm License No.
represents ☐ Buyer only as Buyer's agent	represents ☒ Seller and Buyer as an intermediary
☐ Seller as Listing Broker's subagent	☐ Seller only as Seller's agent
	Carolyn McMahan (214) 379-4300
Licensed Supervisor of Associate Telephone	Licensed Supervisor of Associate Telephone
	Renee Raymond (214) 379-4300
Associate Telephone	Listing Associate Telephone
	1524 North Spring Drive (214) 379-4309
Other Broker's Address Facsimile	Listing Broker's Office Address Facsimile
	Dallas TX 75340
City State Zip	City State Zip
	rraymond@abc.net
Associate Email Address	Listing Associate's Email Address
	Nancy Nystrom (214) 379-4300
	Selling Associate Telephone
	1524 North Spring Drive (214) 379-4309
	Selling Associate's Office Address Facsimile
	Dallas TX 75340
	City State Zip
	nnystrom@abc.net
	Selling Associate's Email Address

Listing Broker has agreed to pay Other Broker _____N/A_____ of the total sales price when the Listing Broker's fee is received. Escrow agent is authorized and directed to pay other Broker from Listing Broker's fee at closing.

OPTION FEE RECEIPT

Receipt of $___100.00___ (Option Fee) in the form of ___personal check___ is acknowledged.

_____   _____
Seller or Listing Broker   Date

CONTRACT AND EARNEST MONEY RECEIPT

Receipt of ☒Contract and ☒$ ___15,000.00___ Earnest Money in the form of ___personal check___ is acknowledged.

Escrow Agent: _____   Date: _____

By: _____

_____
   Email Address

_____
Address

_____ _____
City   State   Zip

Telephone (_____) _____

Facsimile: (_____) _____

TREC NO. 20-11

FIGURE 12.4: Third Party Financing Addendum

2-10-2014

PROMULGATED BY THE TEXAS REAL ESTATE COMMISSION (TREC)

THIRD PARTY FINANCING ADDENDUM FOR CREDIT APPROVAL
(Not for use with Reverse Mortgage Financing)

TO CONTRACT CONCERNING THE PROPERTY AT

3040 North Racine, Dallas, TX 7530
(Street Address and City)

Buyer shall apply promptly for all financing described below and make every reasonable effort to obtain credit approval for the financing (Credit Approval). Buyer shall furnish all information and documents required by lender for Credit Approval. Credit Approval will be deemed to have been obtained when (1) the terms of the loan(s) described below are available and (2) lender determines that Buyer has satisfied all of lender's requirements related to Buyer's assets, income and credit history. If Buyer cannot obtain Credit Approval, Buyer may give written notice to Seller within 30 days after the effective date of this contract and this contract will terminate and the earnest money will be refunded to Buyer. **If Buyer does not give such notice within the time required, this contract will no longer be subject to Credit Approval. Time is of the essence for this paragraph and strict compliance with the time for performance is required.**

NOTE: Credit Approval does not include approval of lender's underwriting requirements for the Property, as specified in Paragraph 4.A.(1) of the contract.

Each note must be secured by vendor's and deed of trust liens.

CHECK APPLICABLE BOXES:

☑ A. CONVENTIONAL FINANCING:

    ☑ (1) A first mortgage loan in the principal amount of $ 165,000 _____ (excluding any financed PMI premium), due in full in 15 _____ year(s), with interest not to exceed 7 ___% per annum for the first 15 _____year(s) of the loan with Adjusted Origination Charges as shown on Buyer's Good Faith Estimate for the loan not to exceed 2.5 _____ % of the loan.

    ☐ (2) A second mortgage loan in the principal amount of $_____(excluding any financed PMI premium), due in full in _____year(s), with interest not to exceed _____% per annum for the first _____year(s) of the loan with Adjusted Origination Charges as shown on Buyer's Good Faith Estimate for the loan not to exceed _____ % of the loan.

☐ B. TEXAS VETERANS LOAN: A loan(s) from the Texas Veterans Land Board of $_____ for a period in the total amount of _____years at the interest rate established by the Texas Veterans Land Board.

☐ C. FHA INSURED FINANCING: A Section _____ FHA insured loan of not less than $_____ (excluding any financed MIP), amortizable monthly for not less than _____years, with interest not to exceed _____% per annum for the first _____year(s) of the loan with Adjusted Origination Charges as shown on Buyer's Good Faith Estimate for the loan not to exceed _____ % of the loan. As required by HUD-FHA, if FHA valuation is unknown, "*It is expressly agreed that, notwithstanding any other provision of this contract, the purchaser (Buyer) shall not be obligated to complete the purchase of the Property described herein or to incur any penalty by forfeiture of earnest money deposits or otherwise unless the purchaser (Buyer) has been given in accordance with HUD/FHA or VA requirements a written statement issued by the Federal Housing Commissioner, Department of Veterans Affairs, or a Direct Endorsement Lender setting forth the appraised value of the Property of not less than $_____. The purchaser (Buyer) shall have the privilege and option of proceeding with consummation of the contract without regard to the amount of the appraised valuation. The appraised valuation is arrived at to determine the*

Initialed for identification by Buyer____ ____ and Seller_____ ____   TREC NO. 40-6

FIGURE 12.4: Third Party Financing Addendum (continued)

Third Party Financing Condition Addendum Concerning   Page 2 of 2   2-10-2014

3040 North Racine, Dallas, TX 7530
(Address of Property)

maximum mortgage the Department of Housing and Urban Development will insure. HUD does not warrant the value or the condition of the Property. The purchaser (Buyer) should satisfy himself/herself that the price and the condition of the Property are acceptable."

☐ D. VA GUARANTEED FINANCING: A VA guaranteed loan of not less than $_____ (excluding any financed Funding Fee), amortizable monthly for not less than_____years, with interest not to exceed_____% per annum for the first _____year(s) of the loan with Adjusted Origination Charges as shown on Buyer's Good Faith Estimate for the loan not to exceed _____% of the loan.

VA NOTICE TO BUYER: *"It is expressly agreed that, notwithstanding any other provisions of this contract, the Buyer shall not incur any penalty by forfeiture of earnest money or otherwise or be obligated to complete the purchase of the Property described herein, if the contract purchase price or cost exceeds the reasonable value of the Property established by the Department of Veterans Affairs. The Buyer shall, however, have the privilege and option of proceeding with the consummation of this contract without regard to the amount of the reasonable value established by the Department of Veterans Affairs."*

If Buyer elects to complete the purchase at an amount in excess of the reasonable value established by VA, Buyer shall pay such excess amount in cash from a source which Buyer agrees to disclose to the VA and which Buyer represents will not be from borrowed funds except as approved by VA. If VA reasonable value of the Property is less than the Sales Price, Seller may reduce the Sales Price to an amount equal to the VA reasonable value and the sale will be closed at the lower Sales Price with proportionate adjustments to the down payment and the loan amount.

☐ E. USDA GUARANTEED FINANCING: A USDA-guaranteed loan of not less than $_____ (excluding any financed Funding Fee), amortizable monthly for not less than_____years, with interest not to exceed____% per annum for the first ____year(s) of the loan with Adjusted Origination Charges as shown on Buyer's Good Faith Estimate for the loan not to exceed _____% of the loan.

Buyer hereby authorizes any lender to furnish to the Seller or Buyer or their representatives information relating only to the status of Credit Approval of Buyer.

_____   _____
Buyer   Seller

_____   _____
Buyer   Seller

TREC NO. 40-6

Dispute Resolution   When a dispute arises that is related to the promulgated sales contract form, Paragraph 16 of the contract encourages resolution through alternative dispute resolution procedures such as mediation. The buyer and the seller indicate their willingness to submit a dispute to a mutually acceptable mediator by checking a box on the contract form at the time the contract is negotiated. The parties to the mediation bear the mediation costs equally.

In a dispute related to a construction defect in the property purchased, rather than a term or condition of the contract, new home purchasers look to the Residential Construction Liability Act (RCLA) for relief. The RCLA, Chapter 27 of the Property Code, essentially provides that builders/remodelers have a right to repair poor construction before litigation; homeowners can seek only limited damages. Under the RCLA, if a construction defect has not been corrected as required by law or by contract,

- once given proper notice of a construction defect, the contractor may inspect the property;
- within 45 days of the receipt of the notice, the contractor may make an offer of money, an offer of repair, or an offer to cure the construction defect; and
- if the homeowner unreasonably rejects the contractor's settlement offer, damages are limited to the reasonable cost of repairs to cure the construction defect and the reasonable attorney's fees and costs incurred before the offer was rejected. Damages are capped at the purchase price of the home, and triple damages under the DTPA are eliminated unless the court or arbitration tribunal determines that the offer of repair or settlement was not made timely, in writing, and considered to be reasonable.

Option Agreements

An **option** is a unilateral *contract by which an optionor (generally an owner) gives an optionee (a prospective purchaser or lessee) the right to buy or lease the owner's property at a fixed price within a stated period of time.* The optionee must pay an option fee for this option right. The optionee has no other obligation until deciding to either exercise the option right or allow the option right to expire. An option is enforceable by only one party—the optionee.

An option contract is not a sales contract. At the time the option is signed by the parties, the owner does not sell and the optionee does not buy. The parties merely agree that the optionee will have the *right* to buy and the owner will be *obligated* to sell *if* the optionee decides to exercise the right of option.

The option agreement requires that the optionor act only after the optionee gives notice that he elects to exercise the option and buy. If the option is not exercised within the time specified, the optionor's obligation and the optionee's right will expire. The optionee cannot recover the consideration paid for the option right. However, the owner could elect (if desired) to apply the money paid for the option to the purchase price of the real estate if the optionee buys the property. A common real estate option contract is a lease that includes an option for the tenant to purchase the property. Options on commercial real estate frequently are made dependent on the fulfillment of specific conditions, such as obtaining a zoning change or a building permit.

Although it is not considered an option contract, the Texas promulgated residential sales contract provides a termination option that gives the buyer the unrestricted right to terminate the contract within a time frame negotiated between the buyer and the seller (Figure 12.3, ¶23). A buyer may terminate the contract during the option period for any reason. For the termination option to be a part of the sales contract, the buyer must pay an option fee to the seller within two days after the effective date of the contract. The option fee would not be refunded if the buyer were to terminate the contract. However, any earnest money would be refunded. In addition, the buyer and the seller may choose whether or not to credit the option fee to the sales price at closing.

Contracts for Deed (Installment Contracts)

A **contract for deed** (sometimes called a *land contract, executory contract,* an *installment contract,* or a *contract of sale*) is a sales/financing agreement under which the buyer purchases the seller's real estate on time. *Under the Texas Property Code, an executory contract is defined as a contract involving the sale of a residence in which closing occurs more than 180 days after execution. A sale that fits under this definition is subject to SubChapter D of the Texas Property Code which provides a series of complicated procedures with which a seller must comply. Failure to comply with the statutory requirements subjects the executory contract to cancellation, rescission, or refund and the seller to DTPA penalties.*

Under a typical contract for deed, the buyer (called the *vendee*) agrees to give the seller a down payment and pay regular monthly installments of principal and interest over a number of years. The buyer usually also pays real estate taxes, insurance premiums, repairs, and upkeep on the property. The buyer takes possession and gets equitable title to the property, which establishes a homestead shield against the buyer's creditors. Although the buyer obtains possession under the contract, the seller (also known as the *vendor*) retains legal title and generally does not execute and deliver a deed to the buyer until the terms of the contract have been satisfied. This frequently occurs when the buyer has accumulated enough down payment or enough time on a present job to obtain a new mortgage loan—or it may be when the note to the seller has been paid in full.

However, under the Property Code, if electing at any time to convert the contract for deed into recorded, legal title, the purchaser may either
- pay the seller the balance due on the contract for deed; or
- deliver a promissory note to the seller that equals the balance due on the contract for deed, with the same interest rate, due dates, and late fees contained in the contract.

In most cases, the seller would then be required to deliver legal title and to accept the promissory note secured by a deed of trust with a power-of-sale clause. If the contract for deed conveys real property used as the purchaser's residence (excluding the sale of state land, a sale of land by the Veteran's Land Board, or transactions in which the deed is delivered within 180 days), the seller must, before the contract is signed, satisfy many statutory requirements. Among the requirements are
- providing copies of a current survey, a tax certificate, and an insurance policy; and
- disclosing property condition and information about utilities, road maintenance, encumbrances that affect title, and financing terms.

The purchaser has the right to cancel the contract *for any reason* on or before the 14th day after the effective date of the contract. Within 30 days of the execution of the contract for deed, the seller must record the contract and disclosure statements with the county clerk. The seller is further obligated to provide the purchaser with an annual accounting statement that reflects, among other financial details, the amount paid, disbursements for taxes and insurance, and the balance remaining on the contract.

If the purchaser defaults under the terms of the contract, the seller must provide a specific statutory notice and give the purchaser 30 days to cure the default. If the purchaser fails to cure the default within the 30-day period and has paid 40% or more of the amount due or the equivalent of 48 monthly payments, the seller is granted the power to sell the property through a trustee designated by the seller. If the purchaser defaults before paying 40% of the amount due or the equivalent of 48 monthly payments, the seller may enforce the remedy of rescission or of forfeiture and acceleration of the debt. Purchasers in a contract for deed sale should be aware of potential problems, such as the death of the seller before delivery of the deed, the seller's not making payments on a prior mortgage, or the filing of a judgment lien against the seller, which would attach to the subject land. Potential hazards to the seller include the purchaser's leasing the property to another party or possible damage to the property, resulting in a loss of property value if the buyer defaults. Going into an installment contract, the seller should realize that the buyer possibly has credit issues—otherwise, the buyer might prefer a traditional mortgage. A contract for deed can be a useful sales and financing tool but it should never be used in an attempt to defeat a due-on-sale provision in a deed of trust or to hide a transaction from a lender. There is no promulgated contract for deed form in Texas; therefore, it is essential that both parties seek competent legal counsel. Failure to comply with the provisions of the law may subject the seller to a DTPA violation for false, misleading, or deceptive acts or practices. Real estate licensees should not use the promulgated contract forms to create a contract for deed or lease purchase agreement. Doing so is considered an unauthorized practice of law and can be cause for disciplinary action to revoke a salesperson or broker license under the License Act.

> S.B. 1320 (2011) prohibits the execution of a deed in lieu of foreclosure at the time of closing on a contract for deed.

Leases

A lease is a contract in which the owner agrees to give possession of all or part of certain real estate to another person for a specified time in exchange for a rental fee. Leases are discussed in detail in Chapter 21.

Escrow Agreements (as Part of Closing or Settlement)

Escrow is a deposit of funds, a deed, a mortgage, or other instruments by one party for the delivery to another party upon completion of a particular condition or event. An **escrow agreement** states the obligations of each party to a transaction and the duties of the escrow agent, who is a disinterested third party and will not benefit from the contract.

An escrow agreement requires that the seller deposit with the escrow agent the deed and other pertinent documents, such as leases, a survey, and a mortgage payoff letter (if the existing loan is to be paid in full and released of record). It also provides for the buyer to deposit the purchase price and an executed deed of trust and note if he is securing borrowed funds to purchase the property. The escrow agent is authorized to have the title examined; and if it is found to meet the conditions of the escrow agreement, a closing is conducted. Title then passes to the buyer, and the seller receives payment.

In Texas, a title company typically acts as the escrow agent, with the provisions of the promulgated sales contract establishing the escrow agreement in residential transactions (Figure 12.3 ¶18). However, commercial transactions may include a separate set of instructions to the escrow agent that is signed by the contracting parties. Typically, escrow can be used to close real estate sales, mortgage loans, a contract for deed, or a commercial lease. The escrow procedure will be detailed more fully in Chapter 20.

IN PRACTICE Keep in mind that it is always a good idea to get a real estate attorney to review any real estate contract *before* it is signed. Moreover, when it appears that there are unusual matters involved in the transaction, the licensee(s) *must* advise each party to consult a lawyer. A licensee may not employ or pay for the services of a lawyer to represent any principal to a real estate transaction (TREC Rules 537.11 (l)-(m)).

SUMMARY

A contract may be defined as an agreement made by competent parties, with adequate consideration, to take or not take some proper, or legal, action. Contracts may be classified according to whether the parties' intentions are express or are implied by their actions. They also may be classified as bilateral, when both parties have obligated themselves to act, or unilateral, when one party is obligated to perform only if the other party acts. In addition, contracts may be classified according to their legal enforceability as valid, void, voidable, or unenforceable.

Many contracts specify a time for performance. In any case, all contracts must be performed within a reasonable time. An executed contract is one that is fully performed. An executory contract is one that is partially performed.

The essentials of a valid contract are (1) legally competent parties, (2) offer and acceptance, (3) consideration, (4) legality of object, and (5) agreement in writing and signed by the parties. In Texas, a valid real estate contract also must include a legal description for the property.

In a number of circumstances, a contract may be canceled before it is fully performed. Furthermore, in certain types of contracts either party may transfer rights and obligations under the agreement by assignment of the contract or by novation (substitution of a new contract). If either party to a real estate sales contract defaults, several alternative actions are available, among them, to sue for specific performance, submit to mediation, or receive the earnest money, releasing both parties from the contract.

Contracts frequently used in the real estate business include listings, buyer representation agreements, sales contracts, options, contracts for deed, leases, and escrow agreements. A real estate sales contract binds a buyer and a seller to a definite transaction, as described in detail in the contract. The buyer is bound to purchase the property for the amount stated in the agreement. The seller is bound to deliver good and indefeasible title, free from liens and encumbrances (except those allowed by any "subject to" clause of the contract).

Under an option agreement, the optionee purchases from the optionor, for a limited time period, the exclusive right to purchase or lease the optionor's property. For a potential purchaser or lessee, an option is a means of buying time to consider or complete arrangements for a transaction. A contract for deed is a sales/financing agreement under which a buyer purchases a seller's real estate on time; the buyer may take possession of and responsibility for the property but does *not* receive the deed until the terms of the contract are completed.

In closing a real estate transaction through escrow, the seller's deed and the buyer's money are deposited with an escrow agent under an escrow agreement that sets forth the conditions to be met before the sale is consummated. The escrow agent records the deed and performs any other requirements of the escrow agreement, such as accumulating the buyer's funds and writing all of the checks.

CHAPTER 12 QUESTIONS

1. A contract is said to be *bilateral* if
   a. one of the parties is a minor.
   b. only one party to the agreement is bound to act.
   c. all parties to the contract are bound to act.
   d. the contract has yet to be performed.

2. A contract for the sale of real estate that does not state the consideration to be paid for the property and is not signed by the parties is considered
   a. voidable.
   b. executory.
   c. void.
   d. enforceable.

3. Max makes an offer on Robert's house, Robert accepts, and Max is notified of the acceptance. Both parties sign the sales contract. At this point, Max has what type of title to the property?
   a. Equitable
   b. Voidable
   c. Escrow
   d. Recorded

4. A seller gave a listing to several brokers, specifically promising that if one of the brokers found a buyer for the real estate, the seller would then pay a commission to that broker. This offer by the seller is what type of agreement?
   a. Executed
   b. Discharged
   c. Implied
   d. Unilateral

5. In the completion of a promulgated contract form, several words were crossed out and others inserted. To eliminate future controversy as to whether the changes were made before or after the contract was signed, the broker should
   a. write a letter to each party listing the changes.
   b. have each party write a letter to the other approving the changes.
   c. redraw the entire contract.
   d. have both parties initial or sign in the margin near each change.

6. If, after the sales contract is signed, the seller decides *NOT* to sell,
   a. the seller may cancel the contract and retain the buyer's earnest money deposit.
   b. the buyer may institute a suit for specific performance of the contract and/or for money damages.
   c. the buyer may both get his earnest money back and file for specific performance.
   d. the real estate agent forfeits a right to a commission.

7. Under the statute of frauds, contracts for the sale of real estate must be
   a. originated by a real estate broker.
   b. on preprinted forms.
   c. in writing to be enforceable.
   d. accompanied by earnest money deposits.

8. During the period after a real estate sales contract is signed but before title actually passes, the status of the contract is
   a. executed.
   b. executory.
   c. unilateral.
   d. implied.

9. Which is *NOT* one of the elements essential for a valid contract?
   a. Offer and acceptance
   b. Earnest money
   c. Consideration
   d. Competent parties

10. Ramon has a contract to buy property but would rather let his friend Mark buy it instead. If the contract allows, Mark can take over Ramon's contract rights by the process known as
    a. assignment.
    b. subordination.
    c. novation.
    d. mutual consent.

11. Stella makes an offer to purchase certain property listed with broker Sam and leaves a deposit with the broker to show good faith. When the contract is accepted, Sam should
    a. immediately apply the deposit to the listing expenses.
    b. deposit the funds in an escrow account or a title company within two working days.
    c. give the deposit to the seller when the offer is presented.
    d. put the deposit in his checking account.

12. Which BEST describes the contract for deed or installment contract?
    a. A contract to buy land only
    b. A mortgage on land
    c. A means of conveying title immediately while the purchaser pays for the property in installments
    d. A method of selling real estate whereby the purchaser pays for the property in regular installments while the seller retains title to the property

13. When a real estate sales transaction is to be closed through an escrow agent,
    a. the seller and the escrow agent execute a separate escrow agreement.
    b. the buyer's purchase money mortgage and note are deposited with the escrow agent.
    c. one of the parties to the contract is usually appointed as the escrow agent.
    d. the buyer sets forth the obligations of the escrow agent.

14. A contract may be discharged by all EXCEPT which of the following means?
    a. Impossibility of performance
    b. Agreement of the parties
    c. Default by one party
    d. Change in the marital status of one party

15. Broker Kay has found a buyer for Camille's home. The buyer has entered into a real estate sales contract for the property for $1,000 less than the asking price and has deposited $5,000 earnest money with broker Kay. Camille is out of town for the weekend, and Kay has been unable to inform her of the signed offer. At this point, the document is a(n)
    a. voidable contract.
    b. offer.
    c. executory agreement.
    d. implied contract.

16. A suit for specific performance of a real estate contract asks for
    a. money damages.
    b. a deficiency judgment.
    c. conveyance of the property.
    d. a new contract.

17. Caz is selling his home to Burton. After the sales contract has been signed by both parties, but before the title has passed to the buyer, the home is destroyed in a fire. Who is likely to bear the loss?
    a. Caz, the seller
    b. Burton, the buyer
    c. The buyer's mortgage lender
    d. The seller's mortgage lender

18. A broker who uses a client's earnest money deposit for the broker's personal use is guilty of
    a. commutation.
    b. conversion.
    c. cotenancy.
    d. conspiracy.

19. An option-to-purchase agreement
    a. is generally limited to a fixed price within a specified time.
    b. requires option money that is refundable if the buyer does not buy.
    c. binds the buyer only.
    d. binds both buyer and seller.

20. The purchaser of real estate under a contract for deed
    a. generally pays no interest.
    b. is called a vendor.
    c. is not required to pay property taxes for the duration of the contract.
    d. is required to pay taxes and insurance on the property.

21. In Texas, who is authorized to draft deeds, mortgages, deeds of trust, and notes?
    a. A licensed real estate broker
    b. An attorney licensed to practice law
    c. The title company clerk
    d. The mortgage lender

22. Alice and Anne enter into a real estate sales contract. Under the contract's terms, Alice will pay Anne $500 a month for 10 years. Anne will continue to hold legal title to the property. Alice will live in the property and pay all real estate taxes, insurance premiums, and regular upkeep costs. What kind of contract do Alice and Anne have?
    a. Option contract
    b. Contract for mortgage
    c. Unilateral contract
    d. Contract for deed

23. The Franklins offer in writing to purchase a house for $120,000, including its draperies, with the offer to expire on Saturday at noon. The Webers reply in writing on Thursday, accepting the $120,000 offer, but excluding the draperies. On Friday, while the Franklins consider this counteroffer, the Webers decide to accept the original offer, draperies included, and state that in writing. At this point, which statement is *TRUE*?
    a. The Franklins are legally bound to buy the house although they have the right to insist that the draperies be included.
    b. The Franklins are not bound to buy.
    c. The Franklins must buy the house and are not entitled to the draperies.
    d. The Franklins must buy the house but may deduct the value of the draperies from the $120,000.

24. Between June 5 and September 23, Marcus suffered from a mental illness that caused delusions, hallucinations, and loss of memory. On July 1, Marcus signed a contract to purchase a property, with the closing set for October 31. On September 24, Marcus began psychiatric treatment; he was declared completely cured by October 15. Which statement is *TRUE* regarding Marcus's contract?
    a. The contract is voidable.
    b. The contract is void.
    c. The contract lacks offer and acceptance.
    d. The contract is fully valid and enforceable.

Detailed rationales for the end-of-chapter review questions are available online at www.dearborn.com through the *Instructor Resource Guides* link.

CHAPTER 13

Listing Agreements

■ **LEARNING OBJECTIVES** *When you have completed this chapter, you will be able to*

- **distinguish** the different types of listing agreements and their terms;
- **explain** the listing process, the parts of the listing agreement, and the ways in which a listing may be terminated;
- **describe** the required property disclosures, the circumstances under which each one must be given to the buyer, and the ramifications to the seller or the real estate agent for nondisclosure;
- **identify** the limitations on an agent's placing cold calls or sending fax and email advertisements to market real estate; and
- **define** the following *key terms*:

exclusive-agency listing	multiple-listing contract	open listing
exclusive-right-to-sell listing	net listing	Seller's Disclosure Notice

OVERVIEW

A retailer may employ the best salespersons in the business, maintain the most attractive shop in town, and spend thousands of dollars on public relations and advertising to further the company's image, only to go out of business because of an adequate supply of goods on hand to sell. Such is the case in the real estate business. Without a well-stocked inventory of properly priced properties listed to sell, a broker or salesperson is no more than an office clerk without an income. The listing agreement that secures the broker's inventory can take many forms, each with its own rights and responsibilities for seller and agent.

This chapter examines the forms of listing agreements, as well as some factors a broker or salesperson must consider when "taking a listing." The broker, who is a party to the contract, chooses the particular form of listing contract, which is subject to negotiation between the seller and the broker. A multiple listing service (MLS) provides listing contract forms, which may vary from city to city. Or, because the broker is a party to the listing contract, the broker may draft a form for use in his office; but a legal review is certainly recommended to ensure adequate protection for the broker. The student must become familiar with the specific forms supplied by the broker or the local MLS.

LISTING PROPERTY

Every real estate sale involves two parties: the seller and the buyer. The seller furnishes the real estate broker and salesperson with the necessary inventory, the *listing*. How complete and accurately priced this inventory is will determine the broker's ultimate success.

The listing agreement is the contract of employment between a broker and a seller. It creates a special agency relationship between a broker (agent) and a seller (principal, the person for whom the agent works), whereby the agent is authorized to represent the principal's property for sale or lease, solicit offers, and submit the offers to the principal. The agent, however, cannot bind the principal to contracts for sale or lease of the property. Listing agreements in Texas must be in writing to be enforceable and must meet the requirements for a valid real estate contract that were discussed in Chapter 12: competent parties, offer and acceptance, consideration, legality of object, agreement in writing and signed, and an accurate legal description.

The provisions of the Texas Real Estate License Act state that only a broker can act as agent to list, sell, or rent another person's real estate. Throughout this chapter, unless otherwise stated, the terms *broker*, *agent*, and *firm* are intended to include both broker and salesperson. Whereas both have the authority to list, lease, and sell property and to provide other services to a principal, these acts must be done in the name and under the supervision of the broker—*never in the name of the salesperson*.

Listing Agreements

The four forms of listing agreements, or employment contracts, generally used are

- exclusive-right-to-sell listing,
- exclusive-agency listing,
- open listing, and
- net listing.

As discussed in Chapter 5, if the broker is to be able to collect a commission, a listing must be *in writing* and must include the *seller's signed promise to pay the commission.* The broker also must prove that a valid license existed at the time the commission liability arose and that the statutory title notice was given as required. Unless these requirements are met, a broker cannot institute a lawsuit for recovery of commission (Section 1101.806, The Real Estate License Act). Because a listing contract creates a personal obligation for the broker, it is not assignable.

> **Exclusive-Right-to-Sell Listing**
> - One authorized agent
> - Broker receives a commission regardless of who sells the property

Exclusive-Right-to-Sell Listing   In an **exclusive-right-to-sell listing**, one broker is appointed as sole agent of the seller and is given the exclusive right, or authorization, to offer the property in question (see Figure 13.1). Under this form of contract, the seller must pay the broker a commission *regardless of who sells the property* if it is sold while the listing is in effect. In other words, if the seller gives a broker an exclusive-right-to-sell listing but finds a buyer without the broker's assistance, the seller still must pay the broker a commission. This is usually the most popular form of listing agreement among brokers. An example of this form of agreement is reproduced in Figure 13.2.

FIGURE 13.1: Who May Sell a Property and Receive a Commission Under Three Types of Listing Agreements

Open Listing   Exclusive Agency   Exclusive-Right-to-Sell

> **Exclusive-Agency Listing**
> - One authorized agent
> - Broker receives a commission only if the procuring cause
> - Seller retains the right to sell without obligation

Exclusive-Agency Listing   In an **exclusive-agency listing**, *only one broker* is specifically authorized to act as the exclusive agent of the principal; the exclusive agent is entitled to a commission if any other broker sells the property. However, the seller under this form of agreement *retains the right to sell the property himself* without a commission obligation to the broker. In other words, the seller is not obligated to pay a commission to the broker unless the broker has been the procuring cause of the sale. Because most listing contracts taken by real estate agents are exclusive-right-to-sell agreements, the Texas Association of REALTORS® has published an addendum that will convert the exclusive-right-to-sell to an exclusive-agency listing (see Figure 13.3).

FIGURE 13.2: Exclusive-Right-to-Sell Agreement

TEXAS ASSOCIATION OF REALTORS®

RESIDENTIAL REAL ESTATE LISTING AGREEMENT
EXCLUSIVE RIGHT TO SELL

USE OF THIS FORM BY PERSONS WHO ARE NOT MEMBERS OF THE TEXAS ASSOCIATION OF REALTORS® IS NOT AUTHORIZED.
©Texas Association of REALTORS®, Inc. 2014

1. **PARTIES:** The parties to this agreement (this Listing) are:

Seller: _____
_____
   Address: _____
   City, State, Zip: _____
   Phone:_____ Fax: _____
   E-Mail: _____

Broker: _____
   Address: _____
   City, State, Zip: _____
   Phone:_____ Fax: _____
   E-Mail: _____

Seller appoints Broker as Seller's sole and exclusive real estate agent and grants to Broker the exclusive right to sell the Property.

2. **PROPERTY:** "Property" means the land, improvements, and accessories described below, except for any described exclusions.

   A. <u>Land:</u> Lot_____, Block_____, _____
     _____ Addition, City of_____,
     in _____ County, Texas known as _____
     _____ (address/zip code),
     or as described on attached exhibit. *(If Property is a condominium, attach Condominium Addendum.)*

   B. <u>Improvements:</u> The house, garage and all other fixtures and improvements attached to the above-described real property, including without limitation, the following **permanently installed and built-in items,** if any: all equipment and appliances, valances, screens, shutters, awnings, wall-to-wall carpeting, mirrors, ceiling fans, attic fans, mail boxes, television antennas and satellite dish system and equipment, mounts and brackets for televisions and speakers, heating and air-conditioning units, security and fire detection equipment, wiring, plumbing and lighting fixtures, chandeliers, water softener system, kitchen equipment, garage door openers, cleaning equipment, shrubbery, landscaping, outdoor cooking equipment, and all other property owned by Seller and attached to the above-described real property.

   C. <u>Accessories:</u> The following described related accessories, if any: window air conditioning units, stove, fireplace screens, curtains and rods, blinds, window shades, draperies and rods, door keys, mailbox keys, above-ground pool, swimming pool equipment and maintenance accessories, artificial fireplace logs, and controls for: (i) satellite dish systems, (ii) garage doors, (iii) entry gates, and (iv) other improvements and accessories.

FIGURE 13.2: Exclusive-Right-to-Sell Agreement (continued)

Residential Listing concerning_____

D. <u>Exclusions</u>: The following improvements and accessories will be retained by Seller and must be removed prior to delivery of possession: _____
_____.

E. <u>Owners' Association</u>: The property ❑ is ❑ is not subject to mandatory membership in a property owners' association.

3. **LISTING PRICE:** Seller instructs Broker to market the Property at the following price: $_____ (Listing Price). Seller agrees to sell the Property for the Listing Price or any other price acceptable to Seller. Seller will pay all typical closing costs charged to sellers of residential real estate in Texas (seller's typical closing costs are those set forth in the residential contract forms promulgated by the Texas Real Estate Commission).

4. **TERM:**

A. This Listing begins on _____ and ends at 11:59 p.m. on _____.

B. If Seller enters into a binding written contract to sell the Property before the date this Listing begins and the contract is binding on the date this Listing begins, this Listing will not commence and will be void.

5. **BROKER COMPENSATION:**

A. When earned and payable, Seller will pay Broker:

❑ (1) _____% of the sales price.

❑ (2) _____.

B. <u>Earned</u>: Broker's compensation is earned when any one of the following occurs during this Listing:
(1) Seller sells, exchanges, options, agrees to sell, agrees to exchange, or agrees to option the Property to anyone at any price on any terms;
(2) Broker individually or in cooperation with another broker procures a buyer ready, willing, and able to buy the Property at the Listing Price or at any other price acceptable to Seller; or
(3) Seller breaches this Listing.

C. <u>Payable</u>: Once earned, Broker's compensation is payable either during this Listing or after it ends at the earlier of:
(1) the closing and funding of any sale or exchange of all or part of the Property;
(2) Seller's refusal to sell the Property after Broker's compensation has been earned;
(3) Seller's breach of this Listing; or
(4) at such time as otherwise set forth in this Listing.

Broker's compensation is <u>not</u> payable if a sale of the Property does not close or fund as a result of: (i) Seller's failure, without fault of Seller, to deliver to a buyer a deed or a title policy as required by the contract to sell; (ii) loss of ownership due to foreclosure or other legal proceeding; or (iii) Seller's failure to restore the Property, as a result of a casualty loss, to its previous condition by the closing date set forth in a contract for the sale of the Property.

D. <u>Other Compensation</u>:

(1) <u>Breach by Buyer Under a Contract</u>: If Seller collects earnest money, the sales price, or damages by suit, compromise, settlement, or otherwise from a buyer who breaches a contract for the sale of the Property entered into during this Listing, Seller will pay Broker, after deducting attorney's fees

(TAR-1101) 01-01-14   Initialed for Identification by Broker/Associate_____ and Seller_____, _____   Page 2 of 10

FIGURE 13.2: Exclusive-Right-to-Sell Agreement (continued)

Residential Listing concerning_____

and collection expenses, an amount equal to the lesser of one-half of the amount collected after deductions or the amount of the Broker's Compensation stated in Paragraph 5A. Any amount paid under this Paragraph 5D(1) is in addition to any amount that Broker may be entitled to receive for subsequently selling the Property.

(2) <u>Service Providers</u>: If Broker refers Seller or a prospective buyer to a service provider (for example, mover, cable company, telecommunications provider, utility, or contractor) Broker may receive a fee from the service provider for the referral. Any referral fee Broker receives under this Paragraph 5D(2) is in addition to any other compensation Broker may receive under this Listing.

(3) <u>Other Fees and/or Reimbursable Expenses</u>: _____
_____
_____.

E. <u>Protection Period</u>:

(1) "Protection period" means that time starting the day after this Listing ends and continuing for _____ days. "Sell" means any transfer of any fee simple interest in the Property whether by oral or written agreement or option.

(2) Not later than 10 days after this Listing ends, Broker may send Seller written notice specifying the names of persons whose attention was called to the Property during this Listing. If Seller agrees to sell the Property during the protection period to a person named in the notice or to a relative of a person named in the notice, Seller will pay Broker, upon the closing of the sale, the amount Broker would have been entitled to receive if this Listing were still in effect.

(3) This Paragraph 5E survives termination of this Listing. This Paragraph 5E will not apply if:
  (a) Seller agrees to sell the Property during the protection period;
  (b) the Property is exclusively listed with another broker who is a member of the Texas Association of REALTORS® at the time the sale is negotiated; and
  (c) Seller is obligated to pay the other broker a fee for the sale.

F. <u>County</u>: All amounts payable to Broker are to be paid in cash in _____
_____ County, Texas.

G. <u>Escrow Authorization</u>: Seller authorizes, and Broker may so instruct, any escrow or closing agent authorized to close a transaction for the purchase or acquisition of the Property to collect and disburse to Broker all amounts payable to Broker under this Listing.

6. LISTING SERVICES:

❏ A. Broker will file this Listing with one or more Multiple Listing Services (MLS) by the earlier of the time required by MLS rules or 5 days after the date this Listing begins. Seller authorizes Broker to submit information about this Listing and the sale of the Property to the MLS.

Notice: MLS rules require Broker to accurately and timely submit all information the MLS requires for participation including sold data. MLS rules may require that the information be submitted to the MLS throughout the time the Listing is in effect. Subscribers to the MLS may use the information for market evaluation or appraisal purposes. Subscribers are other brokers and other real estate professionals such as appraisers and may include the appraisal district. Any information filed with the MLS becomes the property of the MLS for all purposes. **Submission of information to MLS ensures that persons who use and benefit from the MLS also contribute information.**

FIGURE 13.2: Exclusive-Right-to-Sell Agreement (continued)

Residential Listing concerning_____

❑ B. Seller instructs Broker not to file this Listing with one or more Multiple Listing Service (MLS) until ____ days after the date this Listing begins for the following purpose(s): _____
_____.
(NOTE: Do not check if prohibited by Multiple Listing Service(s).)

❑ C. Broker will not file this Listing with a Multiple Listing Service (MLS) or any other listing service.

Notice: Seller acknowledges and understands that if this option is checked: (1) Seller's Property will not be included in the MLS database available to real estate agents and brokers from other real estate offices who subscribe to and participate in the MLS, and their buyer clients may not be aware that Seller's Property is offered for sale; (2) Seller's Property will not be included in the MLS's download to various real estate Internet sites that are used by the public to search for property listings; and (3) real estate agents, brokers, and members of the public may be unaware of the terms and conditions under which Seller is marketing the Property.

7. ACCESS TO THE PROPERTY:

A. Authorizing Access: Authorizing access to the Property means giving permission to another person to enter the Property, disclosing to the other person any security codes necessary to enter the Property, and lending a key to the other person to enter the Property, directly or through a keybox. To facilitate the showing and sale of the Property, Seller instructs Broker to:
(1) access the Property at reasonable times;
(2) authorize other brokers, their associates, inspectors, appraisers, and contractors to access the Property at reasonable times; and
(3) duplicate keys to facilitate convenient and efficient showings of the Property.

B. Scheduling Companies: Broker may engage the following companies to schedule appointments and to authorize others to access the Property: _____.

C. Keybox: **A keybox is a locked container placed on the Property that holds a key to the Property. A keybox makes it more convenient for brokers, their associates, inspectors, appraisers, and contractors to show, inspect, or repair the Property. The keybox is opened by a special combination, key, or programmed device so that authorized persons may enter the Property, even in Seller's absence. Using a keybox will probably increase the number of showings, but involves risks (for example, unauthorized entry, theft, property damage, or personal injury). Neither the Association of REALTORS® nor MLS requires the use of a keybox.**

(1) Broker ❑ is ❑ is not   authorized to place a keybox on the Property.

(2) If a tenant occupies the Property at any time during this Listing, Seller will furnish Broker a written statement (for example, TAR No. 1411), signed by all tenants, authorizing the use of a keybox or Broker may remove the keybox from the Property.

D. Liability and Indemnification: When authorizing access to the Property, Broker, other brokers, their associates, any keybox provider, or any scheduling company are not responsible for personal injury or property loss to Seller or any other person. Seller assumes all risk of any loss, damage, or injury. **Except for a loss caused by Broker, Seller will indemnify and hold Broker harmless from any claim for personal injury, property damage, or other loss.**

8. COOPERATION WITH OTHER BROKERS: Broker will allow other brokers to show the Property to prospective buyers. Broker will offer to pay the other broker a fee as described below if the other broker procures a buyer that purchases the Property.

FIGURE 13.2: Exclusive-Right-to-Sell Agreement (continued)

Residential Listing concerning_____

    A. <u>MLS Participants:</u> If the other broker is a participant in the MLS in which this Listing is filed, Broker will offer to pay the other broker:
    (1) if the other broker represents the buyer: _____% of the sales price or $_____; and
    (2) if the other broker is a subagent: _____% of the sales price or $_____.

    B. <u>Non-MLS Brokers:</u> If the other broker is not a participant in the MLS in which this Listing is filed, Broker will offer to pay the other broker:
    (1) if the other broker represents the buyer: _____% of the sales price or $_____; and
    (2) if the other broker is a subagent: _____% of the sales price or $_____.

9. INTERMEDIARY: *(Check A or B only.)*

❑ A. <u>Intermediary Status:</u> Broker may show the Property to interested prospective buyers who Broker represents. If a prospective buyer who Broker represents offers to buy the Property, Seller authorizes Broker to act as an intermediary and Broker will notify Seller that Broker will service the parties in accordance with one of the following alternatives.

    (1) If a prospective buyer who Broker represents is serviced by an associate other than the associate servicing Seller under this Listing, Broker may notify Seller that Broker will: (a) appoint the associate then servicing Seller to communicate with, carry out instructions of, and provide opinions and advice during negotiations to Seller; and (b) appoint the associate then servicing the prospective buyer to the prospective buyer for the same purpose.

    (2) If a prospective buyer who Broker represents is serviced by the same associate who is servicing Seller, Broker may notify Seller that Broker will: (a) appoint another associate to communicate with, carry out instructions of, and provide opinions and advice during negotiations to the prospective buyer; and (b) appoint the associate servicing the Seller under this Listing to the Seller for the same purpose.

    (3) Broker may notify Seller that Broker will make no appointments as described under this Paragraph 9A and, in such an event, the associate servicing the parties will act solely as Broker's intermediary representative, who may facilitate the transaction but will not render opinions or advice during negotiations to either party.

❑ B. <u>No Intermediary Status:</u> Seller agrees that Broker will not show the Property to prospective buyers who Broker represents.

Notice: **If Broker acts as an intermediary under Paragraph 9A, Broker and Broker's associates:**
- **may not disclose to the prospective buyer that Seller will accept a price less than the asking price unless otherwise instructed in a separate writing by Seller;**
- **may not disclose to Seller that the prospective buyer will pay a price greater than the price submitted in a written offer to Seller unless otherwise instructed in a separate writing by the prospective buyer;**
- **may not disclose any confidential information or any information Seller or the prospective buyer specifically instructs Broker in writing not to disclose unless otherwise instructed in a separate writing by the respective party or required to disclose the information by the Real Estate License Act or a court order or if the information materially relates to the condition of the property;**
- **may not treat a party to the transaction dishonestly; and**
- **may not violate the Real Estate License Act.**

FIGURE 13.2: Exclusive-Right-to-Sell Agreement (continued)

Residential Listing concerning_____

10. **CONFIDENTIAL INFORMATION:** During this Listing or after it ends, Broker may not knowingly disclose information obtained in confidence from Seller except as authorized by Seller or required by law. Broker may not disclose to Seller any confidential information regarding any other person Broker represents or previously represented except as required by law.

11. **BROKER'S AUTHORITY:**

A. Broker will use reasonable efforts and act diligently to market the Property for sale, procure a buyer, and negotiate the sale of the Property.

B. Broker is authorized to display this Listing on the Internet without limitation unless one of the following is checked:

  ❑   (1)   Seller does not want this Listing to be displayed on the Internet.
  ❑   (2)   Seller does not want the address of the Property to be displayed on the Internet.

  Notice: Seller understands and acknowledges that, if box 11B(1) is selected, consumers who conduct searches for listings on the Internet will not see information about this Listing in response to their search.

C. Broker is authorized to market the Property with the following financing options:

  ❑ (1) Conventional   ❑ (5) Texas Veterans Land Program
  ❑ (2) VA   ❑ (6) Owner Financing
  ❑ (3) FHA   ❑ (7) Other
  ❑ (4) Cash

D. In addition to other authority granted by this Listing, Broker may:
  (1)   advertise the Property by means and methods as Broker determines, including but not limited to creating and placing advertisements with interior and exterior photographic and audio-visual images of the Property and related information in any media and the Internet;
  (2)   place a "For Sale" sign on the Property and remove all other signs offering the Property for sale or lease;
  (3)   furnish comparative marketing and sales information about other properties to prospective buyers;
  (4)   disseminate information about the Property to other brokers and to prospective buyers, including applicable disclosures or notices that Seller is required to make under law or a contract;
  (5)   obtain information from any holder of a note secured by a lien on the Property;
  (6)   accept and deposit earnest money in trust in accordance with a contract for the sale of the Property;
  (7)   disclose the sales price and terms of sale to other brokers, appraisers, or other real estate professionals;
  (8)   in response to inquiries from prospective buyers and other brokers, disclose whether the Seller is considering more than one offer (Broker will not disclose the terms of any competing offer unless specifically instructed by Seller);
  (9)   advertise, during or after this Listing ends, that Broker "sold" the Property; and
  (10) place information about this Listing, the Property, and a transaction for the Property on an electronic transaction platform (typically an Internet-based system where professionals related to the transaction such as title companies, lenders, and others may receive, view, and input information).

E. Broker is not authorized to execute any document in the name of or on behalf of Seller concerning the Property.

FIGURE 13.2: Exclusive-Right-to-Sell Agreement (continued)

Residential Listing concerning_____

12. **SELLER'S REPRESENTATIONS:** Except as provided by Paragraph 15, Seller represents that:
   A. Seller has fee simple title to and peaceable possession of the Property and all its improvements and fixtures, unless rented, and the legal capacity to convey the Property;
   B. Seller is not bound by a listing agreement with another broker for the sale, exchange, or lease of the Property that is or will be in effect during this Listing;
   C. any pool or spa and any required enclosures, fences, gates, and latches comply with all applicable laws and ordinances;
   D. no person or entity has any right to purchase, lease, or acquire the Property by an option, right of refusal, or other agreement;
   E. Seller is current and not delinquent on all loans and all other financial obligations related to the Property, including but not limited to mortgages, home equity loans, home improvement loans, homeowner association fees, and taxes, except_____;
   F. Seller is not aware of any liens or other encumbrances against the Property, except_____ ;
   G. the Property is not subject to the jurisdiction of any court;
   H. all information relating to the Property Seller provides to Broker is true and correct to the best of Seller's knowledge; and
   I. the name of any employer, relocation company, or other entity that provides benefits to Seller when selling the Property is: _____.

13. **SELLER'S ADDITIONAL PROMISES:** Seller agrees to:
   A. cooperate with Broker to facilitate the showing, marketing, and sale of the Property;
   B. not rent or lease the Property during this Listing without Broker's prior written approval;
   C. not negotiate with any prospective buyer who may contact Seller directly, but refer all prospective buyers to Broker;
   D. not enter into a listing agreement with another broker for the sale, exchange, lease, or management of the Property to become effective during this Listing without Broker's prior written approval;
   E. maintain any pool and all required enclosures in compliance with all applicable laws and ordinances;
   F. provide Broker with copies of any leases or rental agreements pertaining to the Property and advise Broker of tenants moving in or out of the Property;
   G. complete any disclosures or notices required by law or a contract to sell the Property; and
   H. amend any applicable notices and disclosures if any material change occurs during this Listing.

14. **LIMITATION OF LIABILITY:**

   A. If the Property is or becomes vacant during this Listing, Seller must notify Seller's casualty insurance company and request a "vacancy clause" to cover the Property. Broker is not responsible for the security of the Property nor for inspecting the Property on any periodic basis.

   B. **Broker is not responsible or liable in any manner for personal injury to any person or for loss or damage to any person's real or personal property resulting from any act or omission not caused by Broker's negligence, including but not limited to injuries or damages caused by:**
      (1) other brokers, their associates, inspectors, appraisers, and contractors who are authorized to access the Property;
      (2) other brokers or their associates who may have information about the Property on their websites;
      (3) acts of third parties (for example, vandalism or theft);
      (4) freezing water pipes;
      (5) a dangerous condition on the Property;
      (6) the Property's non-compliance with any law or ordinance; or
      (7) Seller, negligently or otherwise.

FIGURE 13.2: Exclusive-Right-to-Sell Agreement (continued)

Residential Listing concerning_____

C. **Seller agrees to protect, defend, indemnify, and hold Broker harmless from any damage, costs, attorney's fees, and expenses that:**
   (1) **are caused by Seller, negligently or otherwise;**
   (2) **arise from Seller's failure to disclose any material or relevant information about the Property; or**
   (3) **are caused by Seller giving incorrect information to any person.**

15. **SPECIAL PROVISIONS:**

16. **DEFAULT:** If Seller breaches this Listing, Seller is in default and will be liable to Broker for the amount of the Broker's compensation specified in Paragraph 5A and any other compensation Broker is entitled to receive under this Listing. If a sales price is not determinable in the event of an exchange or breach of this Listing, the Listing Price will be the sales price for purposes of computing compensation. If Broker breaches this Listing, Broker is in default and Seller may exercise any remedy at law.

17. **MEDIATION:** The parties agree to negotiate in good faith in an effort to resolve any dispute related to this Listing that may arise between the parties. If the dispute cannot be resolved by negotiation, the dispute will be submitted to mediation. The parties to the dispute will choose a mutually acceptable mediator and will share the cost of mediation equally.

18. **ATTORNEY'S FEES:** If Seller or Broker is a prevailing party in any legal proceeding brought as a result of a dispute under this Listing or any transaction related to or contemplated by this Listing, such party will be entitled to recover from the non-prevailing party all costs of such proceeding and reasonable attorney's fees.

19. **ADDENDA AND OTHER DOCUMENTS:** Addenda that are part of this Listing and other documents that Seller may need to provide are:
   ☒ A. Information About Brokerage Services;
   ❑ B. Seller Disclosure Notice (§5.008, Texas Property Code);
   ❑ C. Addendum for Seller's Disclosure of Information on Lead-Based Paint and Lead-Based Paint Hazards (required if Property was built before 1978);
   ❑ D. Residential Real Property Affidavit (T-47 Affidavit; related to existing survey);
   ❑ E. MUD, Water District, or Statutory Tax District Disclosure Notice (Chapter 49, Texas Water Code);
   ❑ F. Request for Information from an Owners' Association;
   ❑ G. Request for Mortgage Information;
   ❑ H. Information about Mineral Clauses in Contract Forms;
   ❑ I. Information about On-Site Sewer Facility;
   ❑ J. Information about Property Insurance for a Buyer or Seller;
   ❑ K. Information about Special Flood Hazard Areas;
   ❑ L. Condominium Addendum to Listing;
   ❑ M. Keybox Authorization by Tenant;
   ❑ N. Seller's Authorization to Release and Advertise Certain Information; and
   ❑ O. _____

FIGURE 13.2: Exclusive-Right-to-Sell Agreement (continued)

Residential Listing concerning_____

20. AGREEMENT OF PARTIES:

    A. <u>Entire Agreement</u>: This Listing is the entire agreement of the parties and may not be changed except by written agreement.

    B. <u>Assignability</u>: Neither party may assign this Listing without the written consent of the other party.

    C. <u>Binding Effect</u>: Seller's obligation to pay Broker earned compensation is binding upon Seller and Seller's heirs, administrators, executors, successors, and permitted assignees.

    D. <u>Joint and Several</u>: All Sellers executing this Listing are jointly and severally liable for the performance of all its terms.

    E. <u>Governing Law</u>: Texas law governs the interpretation, validity, performance, and enforcement of this Listing.

    F. <u>Severability</u>: If a court finds any clause in this Listing invalid or unenforceable, the remainder of this Listing will not be affected and all other provisions of this Listing will remain valid and enforceable.

    G. <u>Notices</u>: Notices between the parties must be in writing and are effective when sent to the receiving party's address, fax, or e-mail address specified in Paragraph 1.

21. ADDITIONAL NOTICES:

    A. Broker's compensation or the sharing of compensation between brokers is not fixed, controlled, recommended, suggested, or maintained by the Association of REALTORS®, MLS, or any listing service.

    B. In accordance with fair housing laws and the National Association of REALTORS® Code of Ethics, Broker's services must be provided and the Property must be shown and made available to all persons without regard to race, color, religion, national origin, sex, disability, familial status, sexual orientation, or gender identity. Local ordinances may provide for additional protected classes (for example, creed, status as a student, marital status, or age).

    C. Broker advises Seller to contact any mortgage lender or other lien holder to obtain information regarding payoff amounts for any existing mortgages or liens on the Property.

    D. Broker advises Seller to review the information Broker submits to an MLS or other listing service.

    E. Broker advises Seller to remove or secure jewelry, prescription drugs, other valuables, firearms and any other weapons.

    F. Statutes or ordinances may regulate certain items on the Property (for example, swimming pools and septic systems). Non-compliance with the statutes or ordinances may delay a transaction and may result in fines, penalties, and liability to Seller.

    G. If the Property was built before 1978, Federal law requires the Seller to: (1) provide the buyer with the federally approved pamphlet on lead poisoning prevention; (2) disclose the presence of any known lead-based paint or lead-based paint hazards in the Property; (3) deliver all records and reports to the buyer related to such paint or hazards; and (4) provide the buyer a period up to 10 days to have the Property inspected for such paint or hazards.

FIGURE 13.2: Exclusive-Right-to-Sell Agreement (continued)

    H. Broker cannot give legal advice. **READ THIS LISTING CAREFULLY. If you do not understand the effect of this Listing, consult an attorney BEFORE signing.**

_____   _____

Broker's Printed Name   License No.   Seller's Printed Name

_____   _____

❑ Broker's Signature   Date   Seller's Signature   Date
❑ Broker's Associate's Signature, as an authorized
    agent of Broker

_____   _____

Broker's Associate's Printed Name, if applicable   Seller's Printed Name

         _____

         Seller's Signature   Date

FIGURE 13.3: Addendum for Exclusive Agency

TEXAS ASSOCIATION OF REALTORS®

EXCLUSIVE AGENCY ADDENDUM TO LISTING

USE OF THIS FORM BY PERSONS WHO ARE NOT MEMBERS OF THE TEXAS ASSOCIATION OF REALTORS® IS NOT AUTHORIZED.
©Texas Association of REALTORS®, Inc. 2004

ADDENDUM TO LISTING AGREEMENT BETWEEN THE UNDERSIGNED PARTIES CONCERNING THE PROPERTY AT

_____

A. Definitions:

   (1) "Owner" means the seller or landlord of the above-referenced Property.

   (2) "Excluded Prospect" means a prospective buyer or tenant who:
       (a) has direct communication or negotiations with Owner about the purchase or lease of the Property;
       (b) is procured through Owner's sole efforts; and
       (c) Owner identifies to be an Excluded Prospect as required by Paragraph D.

B. Exclusive Agency: Notwithstanding provisions in the above-referenced listing agreement (the Listing) to the contrary, Owner may sell or lease the Property to an Excluded Prospect if Owner does not use any other real estate broker to market or assist Owner to sell or lease the Property.

C. Broker's Fees: If Owner sells or leases the Property to an Excluded Prospect, Owner will not be obligated to pay the fees due to Broker under Paragraph 5A of the Listing, but Owner will pay Broker, at the time the sale closes or the lease begins, a fee equal to *(check all that apply)*:
   ☐ (1) _____% of the sales price if Owner sells the Property.
   ☐ (2) _____% of the gross rent over the term of the lease if Owner leases the Property.
   ☐ (3) _____.

D. Naming of Excluded Prospects: In order for a person to qualify to be an Excluded Prospect under this Addendum, Owner must send Broker written notice identifying the Excluded Prospect by name, address, and phone. If Broker or any other broker shows the Property to a prospective buyer or tenant before Owner provides written notice to Broker that the prospective buyer or tenant is an Excluded Prospect, then the prospective buyer or tenant is not an Excluded Prospect.

E. Offers from Excluded Prospects: Owner will immediately notify Broker of: (1) Owner's receipt of an offer from an Excluded Prospect; (2) Owner's acceptance of an offer from an Excluded Prospect by providing Broker a copy of the contract or lease; (3) the closing of a contract or lease with an Excluded Prospect; and (4) any termination of such a contract that does not close or a lease that does not commence.

F. Effect on Listing upon Sale or Lease to a Named Exclusion: If Owner enters into a contract to sell or lease the Property to an Excluded Prospect, Broker will have no obligation to provide further services to Owner related to the sale or lease of the Property to an Excluded Prospect and Broker may: (1) terminate the Listing by providing written notice to Owner; or (2) continue to list and market the Property through the date the Listing ends for back-up offers.

G. Advertising: Owner may advertise the Property **only** by: ☐ signs, ☐ newspaper, ☐ Internet, ☐ _____
   _____.

_____   _____
Broker's (Company's) Printed Name   License No.   Seller or Landlord   Date

By:_____   _____
   Broker's Associate's Signature   Date   Seller or Landlord   Date

(TAR-1403) 1-7-04   Page 1 of 1

Open Listing   In an **open listing**, the sellers retain the right to employ any number of brokers to act as their agents. These brokers can act simultaneously, and the seller is obligated to pay a commission only to that broker who successfully produces a ready, willing, and able buyer. A seller who personally sells the property *without the aid of any of the brokers* is not obligated to pay any of them a commission. If a broker was in any way a procuring cause in the transaction, however, that broker may be entitled to a commission. Unless it specifically provides otherwise, a listing contract creates an open listing.

Open Listing
- Multiple agents
- Only the selling agent gets a commission
- Seller retains the right to sell without obligation

Net Listing   A **net listing** is a listing agreement in which the broker's commission is the difference between the sale proceeds and the net amount desired by the owner of the property. The agreement can take the form of an exclusive-right-to-sell, exclusive-agency, or open listing. TREC Rule 535.16(b) states, "A broker may not take net listings unless the principal requires a net listing and the principal appears to be familiar with current market values of real property." Furthermore, the broker must advise the seller as to the broker's opinion of market value.

In a *net listing*, the broker is entitled to any amount exceeding the seller's stated net.

FOR EXAMPLE   A seller explained her situation to her broker: "I want to sell my house, but I don't want to be bothered with percentages and bargaining and offers and counteroffers. I just need to walk out of this deal with $150,000 in my pocket. You sell the place for any price you want and keep anything over $150,000." The broker knows that comparable homes in the area are selling for more than $200,000. What should the broker do about this offer of a net listing?

The broker is obligated under a listing contract to negotiate the best possible transaction for the seller. However, the use of a net listing places an upper limit on the seller's expectancy and places the broker's interest above the seller's interest with reference to obtaining the best possible price. If a net listing is used, the listing agreement must assure the seller of not less than the desired price and limit the broker to a specified maximum commission. If possible, it is recommended that a broker suggest the property be listed for a full sales price that will include the broker's usual commission.

Multiple Listings   **Multiple-listing contracts** are used by those brokers who are members of a multiple-listing organization. Such an organization consists of a group of brokers within an area who agree to pool their listings. The multiple-listing agreement is not actually a separate form of listing; it is, in effect, an *exclusive listing* (either an exclusive right to sell or an exclusive agency) with an additional authority and obligation given to the listing broker *to distribute the listing to other brokers who belong to the multiple listing service (MLS)*. Usually, submission of a listing to this organization carries with it an offer of cooperation and compensation to any cooperating broker who produces a buyer. A cooperating broker who then submits an offer to the listing broker is deemed to have accepted the offer of cooperation according to the terms of that offer. Cooperation can take the form of offers to subagents, buyer agents, or both, at the listing broker's discretion. All offers of cooperation must be accompanied by an offer of compensation; however, the listing broker may offer differing amounts to subagents and to buyer agents. A broker who has entered into a contract to represent a buyer must renounce the offer of subagency (as discussed in Chapter 5).

A *multiple listing service (MLS)* is an arrangement in which brokers share their listings with other brokers in exchange for a share of the commission generated by a transaction.

The contractual obligations among the member brokers of a multiple-listing organization vary widely. Most provide that on sale of the property, *the commission is divided between the listing broker and the cooperating broker.* If a buyer's broker is to be paid by the seller, the listing contract must authorize the listing broker to divide the commission with the buyer's broker.

Most rules of MLSs say that the broker who secures the listing is not only authorized but *obligated* to turn the listing over to the MLS within a definite period of time so that it can be distributed to the other member brokers. The length of time varies as to how long the listing broker can offer the property exclusively without notifying the other member brokers.

A multiple listing offers advantages to broker, seller, and buyer alike. Brokers develop a sizable inventory of properties to be sold and are assured a portion of the commission if they list a property or participate in its sale. Sellers gain because their property is widely marketed through the MLS and because all members of the multiple-listing organization are eligible to sell their property. Buyers benefit because a larger selection of properties is available.

Obtaining Listings

On the first substantive dialogue meeting with the seller, the broker or the salesperson must give the seller a written Information About Brokerage Services form that explains seller representation, subagency, buyer representation, and the intermediary position (see Chapter 5). The broker who lists the property for sale is the owner's agent unless the agent is already employed under a buyer representation agreement with a prospective purchaser. If a prospective purchaser has already been located for the property (as in the case of a For Sale by Owner) and the broker is representing the buyer, a disclosure of buyer representation must be given to the seller at the time of the agent's first contact with the seller. The seller then would have the option to choose intermediary representation or to choose no representation at all.

All legal owners of the listed property or their authorized agents, as well as the listing salesperson and/or broker, should sign the listing agreement. The listing salesperson can sign the contract in the broker's name if so authorized by the broker. If the property being listed is homestead property, both spouses' names and signatures are required, even if the property is the separate property of one spouse.

Information Needed for Listing Agreements When a listing is taken, a listing agent must obtain as much information as possible about the property. This helps ensure that all possible contingencies can be anticipated and provided for, particularly when the listing will be shared with other brokers and salespersons in a multiple-listing arrangement. This information generally includes (where appropriate)

- names and addresses of owners (from the deed);
- legal description of the property (from the deed);
- size of the lot (frontage and depth, from the survey or plat records);
- zoning classification—especially important for vacant land;
- number and sizes of rooms (from accurate measurements taken personally);
- construction and age of the building (from the appraisal district website);
- information relative to the neighborhood—schools, churches, transportation, and so forth (fair housing laws must not be violated);
- current taxes and current tax exemptions (from the appraisal district website);

- existing financing—including present balance, interest, payments, and loan assumability (from the note, deed of trust, and lender);
- utility payments (from owner's records);
- date of occupancy or possession;
- possibility of seller financing; and
- detailed list of personal and real property to be included or excluded.

Because verifiable written information supplied by others can be a broker's defense in a lawsuit involving the Texas Deceptive Trade Practices Act, the agent should verify pertinent information such as legal description, lot size, yearly taxes, and tax exemptions against data in the public records.

IN PRACTICE Some brokers use a separate property profile or information sheet to record many of the foregoing property features. The broker should require that the owner(s) review the property data and sign or initial the completed profile form. Remember all marketing activities for the listed property must comply with federal, state, and local fair housing laws, as well as the License Act and TREC Rules.

Sample Listing Agreement

The sample listing agreement shown in Figure 13.2 is a typical exclusive-right-to-sell agreement. There is no TREC-promulgated listing form; however, the topics that follow are included in most listing agreements.

- *Owner*—The complete legal names of all parties having an ownership interest in the property must be specified. Note the form of co-ownership.
- *Broker or Firm*—The name of the broker entering in the listing contract must be stated clearly and must be the same as the name appearing on the broker's license, whether an individual or a corporate license.
- *Type of Listing*—This form specifies that the agency to be created is an exclusive right to the sell the subject property.
- *Property Description*—The legal description of the property and a statement of fixtures to be included or excluded from the sale must be given.
- *Listing Price*—The listing price is the gross selling price to be quoted to the public. The seller sets the listing price using competitive market data supplied by the agent. The owner should clearly understand that certain sales expenses must be paid at closing. (The competitive market analysis [CMA] is discussed in Chapter 14.)
- *Term*—This section specifies the beginning and ending dates of the listing contract.
- *Brokerage Fee*—The amount of the brokerage fee is negotiated between the owner and the broker.
- *Protection Period*—The protection period establishes the broker's right to a fee, under certain circumstances, if the owner sells the property to one of the broker's prospects.
- *Agency Relationships*—The broker discloses his representation of the seller and the possibility of intermediary status in the future.
- *Broker's Authority*—The owner agrees to permit the broker to submit the property to the MLS, if the broker is a member, and to offer cooperation and compensation to other members of the MLS. Other authorizations may include advertising the property, using a lockbox, placing a yard sign, or disclosing the final sales price to MLS and taxing authorities.

- *Seller Representations*—The owner certifies that no known title defects, adverse claims, or other known defects exist and that the owner has legal capacity to convey the property.
- *Limitation of Liability*—The owner agrees to hold the broker harmless for any loss to the property or any lapse of insurance coverage.
- *Agreement*—The owner acknowledges that the broker will offer the property for sale according to the fair housing laws, that the listing contract has been read and understood, and that the contract is legally binding and cannot be assigned without written approval of the other party.

Termination of Listings

As discussed in Chapter 5, an agency relationship may be terminated for any number of reasons, including

- fulfillment of performance by the broker;
- expiration of the time period stated in the agreement;
- unilateral revocation by the owner or by the broker for just cause, such as abandonment by the broker or noncooperation of the seller for showings (although either party may be liable to the other for damages);
- mutual consent;
- bankruptcy of the seller if title transferred to receiver;
- death or incapacity of either party;
- destruction of the property; and
- a change in property use by outside forces (such as a change in zoning).

Expiration of Listing Period   All listings must specify a definite period during which the broker is to be employed and must have a definite termination date, as provided by the License Act (Section 1101.652(b)(12)). Texas statute prohibits the use of automatic extensions of time in listing agreements.

PROPERTY DISCLOSURES AND NOTICES

A Seller's Disclosure Notice does not have to be given in a transfer by

- court order,
- foreclosure sale,
- bankruptcy,
- a mortgagee or beneficiary,
- a will or trust,
- one co-owner to another,
- one spouse to another,
- a governmental entity, or
- sale of a new residence.

Although the Sellers Disclosure Notice is not required in these types of transfers, common law requires that a seller disclose any known defects.

A seller of real estate must disclose any material fact that would not be discoverable by the purchaser's exercise of ordinary care and diligence or which a reasonable investigation would not uncover. To ensure that buyers have all pertinent facts prior to executing a contract, Texas law requires a seller's written disclosure of property condition and of certain facts about the property. These disclosure notices protect buyers, sellers, and real estate agents alike. They should be prepared when the property is listed. If a broker is not used, a seller still must provide the various applicable disclosures and notices. The most common disclosure notices follow.

Seller's Disclosure Notice   On or before the effective date of a contract for the sale of property, sellers of residential property of not more than one unit must deliver a Seller's Disclosure Notice to the buyer, disclosing latent structural defects or any other known structural defects. The notice is required in almost all residential transactions; the most notable exception being the sale of a new property by a builder. Figure 13.4 shows the Texas Association of REALTORS® (TAR) **Seller's Disclosure Notice**. Licensees who are not TAR members would use a form approved by TREC and available on its website.

FIGURE 13.4: Seller's Disclosure Notice

TEXAS ASSOCIATION OF REALTORS®
SELLER'S DISCLOSURE NOTICE
©Texas Association of REALTORS®, Inc. 2014

Section 5.008, Property Code requires a seller of residential property of not more than one dwelling unit to deliver a Seller's Disclosure Notice to a buyer on or before the effective date of a contract. **This form complies with and contains additional disclosures which exceed the minimum disclosures required by the Code.**

CONCERNING THE PROPERTY AT _____

THIS NOTICE IS A DISCLOSURE OF SELLER'S KNOWLEDGE OF THE CONDITION OF THE PROPERTY AS OF THE DATE SIGNED BY SELLER AND IS NOT A SUBSTITUTE FOR ANY INSPECTIONS OR WARRANTIES THE BUYER MAY WISH TO OBTAIN. IT IS NOT A WARRANTY OF ANY KIND BY SELLER, SELLER'S AGENTS, OR ANY OTHER AGENT.

Seller ❑ is ❑ is not   occupying the Property. If unoccupied (by Seller), how long since Seller has occupied the Property? ❑ _____ or ❑ never occupied the Property

Section 1. The Property has the items marked below: (Mark Yes (Y), No (N), or Unknown (U).)
This notice does not establish the items to be conveyed. The contract will determine which items will & will not convey.

Item	Y	N	U	Item	Y	N	U	Item	Y	N	U
Cable TV Wiring				Liquid Propane Gas:				Pump: ❑ sump ❑ grinder			
Carbon Monoxide Det.				-LP Community (Captive)				Rain Gutters			
Ceiling Fans				-LP on Property				Range/Stove			
Cooktop				Hot Tub				Roof/Attic Vents			
Dishwasher				Intercom System				Sauna			
Disposal				Microwave				Smoke Detector			
Emergency Escape Ladder(s)				Outdoor Grill				Smoke Detector – Hearing Impaired			
Exhaust Fans				Patio/Decking				Spa			
Fences				Plumbing System				Trash Compactor			
Fire Detection Equip.				Pool				TV Antenna			
French Drain				Pool Equipment				Washer/Dryer Hookup			
Gas Fixtures				Pool Maint. Accessories				Window Screens			
Natural Gas Lines				Pool Heater				Public Sewer System			

Item	Y	N	U	Additional Information
Central A/C				❑ electric ❑ gas number of units: ____
Evaporative Coolers				number of units: ____
Wall/Window AC Units				number of units: ____
Attic Fan(s)				if yes, describe: ____
Central Heat				❑ electric ❑ gas number of units: ____
Other Heat				if yes describe: ____
Oven				number of ovens: ____ ❑ electric ❑ gas ❑ other: ____
Fireplace & Chimney				❑ wood ❑ gas logs ❑ mock ❑ other: ____
Carport				❑ attached ❑ not attached
Garage				❑ attached ❑ not attached
Garage Door Openers				number of units: ____ number of remotes: ____
Satellite Dish & Controls				❑ owned ❑ leased from ____
Security System				❑ owned ❑ leased from ____
Water Heater				❑ electric ❑ gas ❑ other: ____ number of units: ____
Water Softener				❑ owned ❑ leased from ____
Underground Lawn Sprinkler				❑ automatic ❑ manual areas covered: ____
Septic / On-Site Sewer Facility				if yes, attach Information About On-Site Sewer Facility (TAR-1407)

FIGURE 13.4: Seller's Disclosure Notice (continued)

Concerning the Property at _____

Water supply provided by: ❏ city ❏ well ❏ MUD ❏ co-op ❏ unknown ❏ other:_____

Was the Property built before 1978? ❏ yes ❏ no ❏ unknown

    (If yes, complete, sign, and attach TAR-1906 concerning lead-based paint hazards).

Roof Type: _____ Age: _____(approximate)

Is there an overlay roof covering on the Property (shingles or roof covering placed over existing shingles or roof covering)? ❏ yes ❏ no ❏ unknown

Are you (Seller) aware of any of the items listed in this Section 1 that are not in working condition, that have defects, or are need of repair? ❏ yes ❏ no   If yes, describe (attach additional sheets if necessary): _____

_____

_____

_____

Section 2. **Are you (Seller) aware of any defects or malfunctions in any of the following?: (Mark Yes (Y) if you are aware and No (N) if you are not aware.)**

Item	Y	N
Basement		
Ceilings		
Doors		
Driveways		
Electrical Systems		
Exterior Walls		

Item	Y	N
Floors		
Foundation / Slab(s)		
Interior Walls		
Lighting Fixtures		
Plumbing Systems		
Roof		

Item	Y	N
Sidewalks		
Walls / Fences		
Windows		
Other Structural Components		

If the answer to any of the items in Section 2 is yes, explain (attach additional sheets if necessary): _____

_____

_____

_____

Section 3. **Are you (Seller) aware of any of the following conditions: (Mark Yes (Y) if you are aware and No (N) if you are not aware.)**

Condition	Y	N
Aluminum Wiring		
Asbestos Components		
Diseased Trees: ❏ oak wilt ❏		
Endangered Species/Habitat on Property		
Fault Lines		
Hazardous or Toxic Waste		
Improper Drainage		
Intermittent or Weather Springs		
Landfill		
Lead-Based Paint or Lead-Based Pt. Hazards		
Encroachments onto the Property		
Improvements encroaching on others' property		
Located in 100-year Floodplain		
Located in Floodway		
Present Flood Ins. Coverage (If yes, attach TAR-1414)		
Previous Flooding into the Structures		
Previous Flooding onto the Property		
Located in Historic District		
Historic Property Designation		
Previous Use of Premises for Manufacture of Methamphetamine		

Condition	Y	N
Previous Foundation Repairs		
Previous Roof Repairs		
Other Structural Repairs		
Radon Gas		
Settling		
Soil Movement		
Subsurface Structure or Pits		
Underground Storage Tanks		
Unplatted Easements		
Unrecorded Easements		
Urea-formaldehyde Insulation		
Water Penetration		
Wetlands on Property		
Wood Rot		
Active infestation of termites or other wood destroying insects (WDI)		
Previous treatment for termites or WDI		
Previous termite or WDI damage repaired		
Previous Fires		
Termite or WDI damage needing repair		
Single Blockable Main Drain in Pool/Hot Tub/Spa*		

FIGURE 13.4: Seller's Disclosure Notice (continued)

Concerning the Property at _____

If the answer to any of the items in Section 3 is yes, explain (attach additional sheets if necessary): _____
_____
_____
_____
_____

    *A single blockable main drain may cause a suction entrapment hazard for an individual.

Section 4. Are you (Seller) aware of any item, equipment, or system in or on the Property that is in need of repair, which has not been previously disclosed in this notice? ❑ yes ❑ no If yes, explain (attach additional sheets if necessary): _____
_____
_____
_____
_____

Section 5.   Are you (Seller) aware of any of the following (Mark Yes (Y) if you are aware. Mark No (N) if you are not aware.)

Y N

❑ ❑   Room additions, structural modifications, or other alterations or repairs made without necessary permits or not in compliance with building codes in effect at the time.

❑ ❑   Homeowners' associations or maintenance fees or assessments. If yes, complete the following:
Name of association:_____
Manager's name: _____ Phone:_____
Fees or assessments are: $_____ per _____ and are: ❑ mandatory ❑ voluntary
Any unpaid fees or assessment for the Property? ❑ yes ($_____) ❑ no
If the Property is in more than one association, provide information about the other associations below or attach information to this notice.

❑ ❑   Any common area (facilities such as pools, tennis courts, walkways, or other) co-owned in undivided interest with others. If yes, complete the following:
Any optional user fees for common facilities charged? ❑ yes ❑ no If yes, describe: _____
_____

❑ ❑   Any notices of violations of deed restrictions or governmental ordinances affecting the condition or use of the Property.

❑ ❑   Any lawsuits or other legal proceedings directly or indirectly affecting the Property. (Includes, but is not limited to: divorce, foreclosure, heirship, bankruptcy, and taxes.)

❑ ❑   Any death on the Property except for those deaths caused by: natural causes, suicide, or accident unrelated to the condition of the Property.

❑ ❑   Any condition on the Property which materially affects the health or safety of an individual.

❑ ❑   Any repairs or treatments, other than routine maintenance, made to the Property to remediate environmental hazards such as asbestos, radon, lead-based paint, urea-formaldehyde, or mold.
If yes, attach any certificates or other documentation identifying the extent of the remediation (for example, certificate of mold remediation or other remediation).

❑ ❑   Any rainwater harvesting system located on the property that is larger than 500 gallons and that uses a public water supply as an auxiliary water source.

❑ ❑   The Property is located in a propane gas system service area owned by a propane distribution system retailer.

FIGURE 13.4: Seller's Disclosure Notice (continued)

Concerning the Property at _____

If the answer to any of the items in Section 5 is yes, explain (attach additional sheets if necessary): _____
_____
_____
_____
_____
_____

Section 6.   Seller ❑ has ❑ has not attached a survey of the Property.

Section 7.   Within the last 4 years, have you (Seller) received any written inspection reports from persons who regularly provide inspections and who are either licensed as inspectors or otherwise permitted by law to perform inspections? ❑ yes ❑ no If yes, attach copies and complete the following:

Inspection Date	Type	Name of Inspector	No. of Pages

Note: A buyer should not rely on the above-cited reports as a reflection of the current condition of the Property. A buyer should obtain inspections from inspectors chosen by the buyer.

Section 8.   Check any tax exemption(s) which you (Seller) currently claim for the Property:
❑ Homestead   ❑ Senior Citizen   ❑ Disabled
❑ Wildlife Management   ❑ Agricultural   ❑ Disabled Veteran
❑ Other:_____   ❑ Unknown

Section 9.   Have you (Seller) ever filed a claim for damage to the Property with any insurance provider? ❑ yes ❑ no

Section 10. Have you (Seller) ever received proceeds for a claim for damage to the Property (for example, an insurance claim or a settlement or award in a legal proceeding) and not used the proceeds to make the repairs for which the claim was made? ❑ yes ❑ no If yes, explain:_____
_____
_____
_____

Section 11. Does the property have working smoke detectors installed in accordance with the smoke detector requirements of Chapter 766 of the Health and Safety Code?* ❑ unknown   ❑ no ❑ yes. If no or unknown, explain. (Attach additional sheets if necessary): _____
_____
_____

*Chapter 766 of the Health and Safety Code requires one-family or two-family dwellings to have working smoke detectors installed in accordance with the requirements of the building code in effect in the area in which the dwelling is located, including performance, location, and power source requirements. If you do not know the building code requirements in effect in your area, you may check unknown above or contact your local building official for more information.

A buyer may require a seller to install smoke detectors for the hearing impaired if: (1) the buyer or a member of the buyer's family who will reside in the dwelling is hearing-impaired; (2) the buyer gives the seller written evidence of the hearing impairment from a licensed physician; and (3) within 10 days after the effective date, the buyer makes a written request for the seller to install smoke detectors for the hearing-impaired and specifies the locations for installation. The parties may agree who will bear the cost of installing the smoke detectors and which brand of smoke detectors to install.

FIGURE 13.4: Seller's Disclosure Notice (continued)

Concerning the Property at _____

Seller acknowledges that the statements in this notice are true to the best of Seller's belief and that no person, including the broker(s), has instructed or influenced Seller to provide inaccurate information or to omit any material information.

_____   ____   _____   ____
Signature of Seller   Date   Signature of Seller   Date

Printed Name: _____   Printed Name: _____

ADDITIONAL NOTICES TO BUYER:

(1) The Texas Department of Public Safety maintains a database that the public may search, at no cost, to determine if registered sex offenders are located in certain zip code areas. To search the database, visit www.txdps.state.tx.us. For information concerning past criminal activity in certain areas or neighborhoods, contact the local police department.

(2) If the property is located in a coastal area that is seaward of the Gulf Intracoastal Waterway or within 1,000 feet of the mean high tide bordering the Gulf of Mexico, the property may be subject to the Open Beaches Act or the Dune Protection Act (Chapter 61 or 63, Natural Resources Code, respectively) and a beachfront construction certificate or dune protection permit may be required for repairs or improvements. Contact the local government with ordinance authority over construction adjacent to public beaches for more information.

(3) If you are basing your offers on square footage, measurements, or boundaries, you should have those items independently measured to verify any reported information.

(4) The following providers currently provide service to the property:

Electric:_____   phone #:_____
Sewer:_____   phone #:_____
Water:_____   phone #:_____
Cable:_____   phone #:_____
Trash:_____   phone #:_____
Natural Gas:_____   phone #:_____
Phone Company:_____   phone #:_____
Propane:_____   phone #:_____

(5) This Seller's Disclosure Notice was completed by Seller as of the date signed. The brokers have relied on this notice as true and correct and have no reason to believe it to be false or inaccurate. YOU ARE ENCOURAGED TO HAVE AN INSPECTOR OF YOUR CHOICE INSPECT THE PROPERTY.

The undersigned Buyer acknowledges receipt of the foregoing notice.

_____   ____   _____   ____
Signature of Buyer   Date   Signature of Buyer   Date
Printed Name: _____   Printed Name: _____

The Seller's Disclosure Notice is usually prepared at the time a property is listed and available online through the MLS or from the listing agent. Sellers are required to mark the form to the best of their knowledge. If information is unknown to the sellers, that fact may be indicated on the notice. The sellers and their agent have no duty to disclose that a death by natural causes, suicide, or accident unrelated to the condition of the property occurred on the property or whether a previous occupant had, may have had, has, or may have AIDS, HIV related illnesses, or HIV infection.

Under Section 62.045(e) of the Code of Criminal Procedure, sellers, builders, and landlords of single-family residential property, as well as the real estate agents in the transaction, are not responsible for obtaining or disclosing information about the location of registered sex offenders. However, real estate agents, sellers, and landlords are not prohibited from doing so. They may, for business purposes or as a matter of policy, choose to provide such information. A listing agent providing such information to prospective buyers is advised to discuss this policy with the seller before taking a listing. Sellers and real estate agents may direct prospects to the Texas Department of Public Safety website, where they may search the Sex Offender Registry. TAR prints this website address in a public information statement on the Seller's Disclosure Notice that it publishes.

If a contract is entered into without the seller's providing the notice, the seller is given a limited time to provide the notice to the buyer. If the seller delivers the notice within the agreed time frame, the buyer may still terminate the contract for any reason within seven days after receiving the notice. If the notice is not received within that time frame, the buyer may terminate the contract any time prior to closing (see Figure 12.3, ¶7.B.(2)).

WEBLINK @ www.txdps.texas.gov

IN PRACTICE Three disclosures were added to the Seller's Disclosure Notice in 2011: (1) disclosure of a single blockable main drain in a residential swimming pool, hot tub, or spa, along with a warning that such a drain may cause a suction entrapment hazard (S.B. 710), (2) disclosure of both natural and liquid propane gas on residential property (H.B. 3389), and (3) disclosure of rainwater harvesting systems connected to a property's public water supply (H.B. 3391). In 2013, H.B. 2781 changed the definition of "rainwater harvesting system" to "any rainwater harvesting system located on the property that is larger than 500 gallons and that uses a public water supply as an auxiliary water source."

An agent should not participate in filling out the required Seller's Disclosure Notice. It should be completed by the seller and signed by the seller. If the agent were to assist in preparing the form and possibly mismark an item or provide false information, the agent could be liable for the misrepresentation.

Lead-Based Paint Exposure to lead from lead-based paint poses a risk to young children. When lead is absorbed into the body, it reportedly can cause damage to the brain and other vital organs, such as the kidneys, nerves, and blood, and can cause behavioral problems, learning disabilities, seizures, and in extreme cases, death. Sellers and landlords of properties built before 1978 must disclose to buyers or tenants any knowledge of lead-based paint or hazards in the property. Houses *exclusively* for the elderly or handicapped (unless there are children living there), houses sold because of foreclosure, and properties that have been inspected and found free of lead-based paint are three of the few exemptions from the disclosure requirements. A TREC-approved Lead-Based Paint Addendum permits sellers or landlords to indicate whether they have

- knowledge of the presence of lead-based paint,
- provided the buyer or tenant with copies of records or reports pertaining to lead-based paint,
- permitted the buyer up to 10 days to have the property inspected for lead-based paint or hazards, and
- provided the buyer or the tenant with a copy of the EPA-approved pamphlet *Protect Your Family from Lead in Your Home*.

Real estate agents share responsibility for ensuring compliance and for three years must retain proof that the appropriate disclosures were made. The federal rules do not require testing, removal, or abatement of lead-based paint—just disclosure. If an inspection is desired, a person certified by the Texas Department of Health as a lead inspector must conduct it.

EPA Renovation, Repair, and Painting (RRP) regulations, effective April 22, 2010, require that renovation or repair work disturbing more than 6 square feet of surface area for interior work or 20 square feet for exterior work be carried out by a trained and certified renovator. A property owner performing the work on a home he occupies does not have to be certified. However, if the property is to be sold or rented, a certified renovator must be used. Owners in violation of RRP rules could be fined from $150 to $37,500 per violation. For more information on lead-based-paint hazards, visit the HUD website.

WEBLINK @ www.hud.gov/offices/lead/

If a promulgated sales contract is used in a transaction, many of these (and other) disclosures are made or referenced (see ¶6 and 7, Figure 12.3).

Notice of Additional Tax Liability   Sellers of vacant land must include in the sales contract a statutorily prescribed disclosure notice regarding possible liability of the purchaser for additional taxes. The buyer is alerted that a change in ownership or a change in the use of the land may not permit the continued use of special appraisal methods that might previously have valued the land at less than its market value. The TREC Farm and Ranch Contract and the Unimproved Property Contract provide for this disclosure. This disclosure requirement does not apply if the sales contract separately allocates responsibility between the seller and the purchaser for any future rollback tax liability. If it is required, however, and if a seller does not make the required disclosure, the seller will be responsible for the additional taxes and interest.

Conditions Under Surface   Unless a seller is obligated to deliver a title commitment to the purchaser, a seller of *unimproved land to be used for residential purposes* must disclose the location of any transportation pipelines for natural gas and related products under the property's surface. If the notice is not received on or before the effective date of the contract, the buyer may terminate the contract for any reason up to seven days after the effective date of the contract.

Notice of Obligations Related to Membership in Property Owners' Association   A seller of residential real estate property that is subject to membership in a property owners association is required to give a prospective purchaser a written notice stating, among other things, that the purchaser would be obligated to be a member of the association and failure to pay association assessment could result in a lien on and the foreclosure of the property. The notice must be delivered to the purchaser before the effective date of the contract; if not, the purchaser may terminate the contract for any reason within the earlier of seven days after the date the purchaser receives the notice or the date of closing. Figure 12.3, ¶6.E.(2) contains this disclosure and a reference to the Promulgated Addendum for Property Subject to Mandatory Membership in a Property Owners Association.

Seller's Disclosure Regarding Potential Annexation   Sellers of property outside the city limits must provide a written notice to a prospective purchaser that the property "may now or later be included in the extraterritorial jurisdiction of a municipality and may now or later be subject to annexation by the municipality." The statutory notice must be given before the effective date of the contract. If not, the buyer may terminate the contract for any reason within seven days after receiving the notice or on the day of closing, whichever is earlier. A buyer who wants more information regarding possible annexation should contact all municipalities located in the general proximity of the property. (See Figure 12.3, ¶ 6.E.(5).)

Addendum for Unimproved Property Located in a Certificated Service Area of a Utility Service Provider   A seller of unimproved property located in a retail utility provider's service area must give written notice to the purchaser before his signing a contract that the extension of water or sewer services might require additional expense to the purchaser and that there might be a delay in the utility's ability to provide the services. If the seller fails to give the notice, the purchaser may terminate the contract and, in some cases, sue the seller for damages and reasonable attorney's fees. TREC promulgated contracts provide this notice in ¶6.E.(6).

Statutory Tax District   As discussed in Chapter 11, a municipal utility district (MUD) is a defined geographic area usually created by a developer to provide utilities, such as water and sewer, outside a municipality. If property being sold is located within a utility district, Section 49.452 of the Texas Water Code requires the seller to furnish to the buyer a statutory notice relating to the tax rate, bonded indebtedness, or standby fee of the district before final execution of the contract. The necessity for this disclosure is included in paragraph 6.E.(3) of the Texas promulgated sales contract. If the seller fails to provide the required notice to the buyer, the statute provides remedies to an injured buyer, including rescission of the contract prior to closing or a set-aside for damages of up to $5,000 after closing. The licensee should obtain the specific form for each district from the county clerk or the district itself for *each* transaction. A seller, purchaser, real estate broker, attorney, or title company would be permitted to use water district taxes as of January 1 of the year the disclosure is made. Information provided by the water district is deemed to be conclusive, eliminating potential liability for the party making the disclosure if the information provided proves to be inaccurate.

Propane Gas System Service Area   If the property is located in a propane gas system service area owned by a distribution system retailer, the seller must give the buyer written notice at or before final execution of the contract or at closing as required by § 141.010, Texas Utilities Code. TREC has promulgated an addendum to provide the appropriate notice required by law. The form notifies the buyer that there may be special costs or charges that a buyer may be required to pay before receiving propane gas service, and that there may be a period of time required to build lines or other facilities necessary to provide gas service to the property.

Gulf Coast Counties   Two TREC-promulgated disclosure addenda reflect the unique circumstances of property located in the Gulf Coast counties.

- The Texas Open Beach Law requires that the Gulf Coast beaches from the mean low tide to the vegetation line remain open to the public, as discussed in Chapter 8. The law requires that a contract for the sale of real property located seaward of the Gulf Intracoastal Waterway must include a prescribed statement regarding open beaches and the possibility that any structure that might become seaward of the vegetation line as a result of natural processes is subject to a lawsuit by the State of Texas for its removal. Before executing the contract, the buyer must also be advised to determine the rate of shore-line erosion in the vicinity of the property. The promulgated Addendum for Property Located Seaward of the Gulf Intracoastal Waterway form contains the statutory notices. If the property is sold without a contract, the seller must deliver the statutory notice to the buyer not later than 10 calendar days prior to closing of the sale. The buyer then must sign a receipt for the notice statement. If the seller fails to include the statement in the contract, the buyer has the option of terminating the contract without liability and getting the earnest money returned. Furthermore, failure to provide the statement either in the contract or by a separate notice constitutes a violation of the Texas Deceptive Trade Practices Act.

- Laws pertaining to wetland areas along the Gulf Coast require that sellers of property that adjoin or share a common boundary with tidally submerged lands must notify buyers about restrictions on the use and development of the property. The promulgated Addendum for Coastal Area Property form contains the statutory notices.

Notice of Obligations Related to Public Improvement District (PID)   The governing body of a municipality or county may undertake an improvement project that benefits a definable part of the community or extraterritorial jurisdiction (ETJ is defined in Chapter 24). A project may include landscaping; erecting fountains, special lighting, and signs; constructing pedestrian malls; or other similar community improvements. Since June 2009, a PID may also help pay for the development, rehabilitation, or expansion of affordable housing. Properties within the PID pay an annual assessment to cover the costs and maintenance of those public improvements. The seller of a single-family residence that is subject to a PID assessment must give written notice of the assessment to a prospective buyer before the effective date of a sales contract. If the notice is not received before his signing the contract, the purchaser may terminate the contract for any reason within seven days after receiving the notice or on the day of closing, whichever is earlier. This notice is included in TREC contracts, ¶6.E.(7).

Mold Remediation Certificate   After mold damage to a property has been remediated, the licensed remediation contractor issues a *certificate of mold remediation*. If a property is sold, a copy of each certificate issued for the property during the five years preceding the sale must be given to the buyer.

Conveyance of Residential Property Encumbered by Lien   If a property being sold has a lien on it and the lien will not be released within 30 days after the sale, a seller must provide (with some exceptions) a notice of lien to the purchaser. Among other disclosures, the seller must identify all lienholders, the specifics of the loan secured by each lien, and the amount of any property taxes that are due. The purchaser must be informed that, if the property is conveyed without the consent of the lienholder, the lienholder could demand full payment on the outstanding balance immediately. The required disclosures must be given to the purchaser and to each lienholder on or before the seventh day before the earlier of the date of closing or the signing of a contract. If not, the purchaser may terminate the contract for any reason on or before the seventh day after the purchaser receives the notice.

Private Transfer Fee Obligation   A seller of real property that may be subject to a private transfer fee must provide written notice of that obligation to a potential purchaser (H.B. 8, 2011).

MARKETING AND PROMOTION

Real estate agents market both themselves and listed properties. Some key elements of online marketing and telemarketing by real estate agents are discussed in the following paragraphs.

Online Marketing   National Association of REALTORS® (NAR) studies have shown that
- over 80% of all properties are sold through an MLS,
- over 90% of all buyers work with real estate professionals,
- over 90% of all buyers use the internet during the process of buying a home, and
- properties listed with real estate agents generally sell for more money than For Sale by Owners (FSBOs).

Therefore, sellers have real incentives for listing with licensed real estate agents and especially those who have a dominant internet presence. Whether to select a real estate agent, to find a home to view with an agent, or to search For Sale by Owners (FSBOs), almost all buyers are using the internet in the purchase of their homes. In fact, an NAR survey indicated that the internet has surpassed the yard sign as the most important marketing tool for reaching consumers.

Online marketing ranges from traditional full-service MLS brokers, with listings on their own websites and on Realtor.com to FSBOs, offering properties online without any assistance from a real estate broker. Somewhere in between the full-service broker and the online FSBO is the discount internet Realtor®, offering a seller the opportunity to list a home as a FSBO for a flat fee based on the services rendered to the seller. Services provided vary from company to company but may include listing with a local MLS and/or on Realtor.com or craigslist.com, providing a comparative market analysis, assisting with contract negotiations, and more. Local MLSs that are affiliated with the National Association of REALTORS® must make their listings available to discount internet REALTORS® under a settlement in 2008 between NAR and the Department of Justice.

Telemarketing   Telephone, fax, and email solicitations are additional promotional and marketing tools for real estate professionals. These media are regulated by both federal and state laws, as summarized in the following paragraphs.

No Call Lists   On January 1, 2002, Texans began registering on the state's *No Call Lists*. The National Do Not Call (DNC) Registry became operational on June 27, 2003. Under each of these programs, consumers have been able to register to have their residential or cell phone numbers removed from telemarketing lists. The Texas no-call list is a combined list consisting of both the Texas registrations and the Texas portion of the national registrations. The no-call lists apply to companies that are trying to "sell" a consumer good or service over the telephone, including text or graphic messages or images to a cell phone number.

Listed below are some key provisions of the law as they relate to real estate agents' placing *cold calls* for marketing purposes.

- Phone numbers remain on the national registry permanently, unless consumers remove their names from the registry (www.donotcall.gov).
- Although cell phone numbers may be registered, they do not have to be included on the registry. FCC regulations prohibit telemarketers from calling a cell phone number with an automatic dialer, which in effect bars most telemarketers from calling consumers on their cell phones without their consent.
- Telemarketers must keep an internal list to register the telephone numbers of consumers who ask to be put on the company's do-not-call list — even if the number is not on the federal DNC list.
- Telemarketers are required to transmit their telephone numbers and, if possible, their names to consumers' caller ID services.
- Prerecorded telemarketing calls (robocalls) are prohibited unless the telemarketer has obtained written permission from consumers who want to receive such calls. Robocalls attempting to sell goods or services are prohibited to consumers whether or not they previously have done business with the seller.

Even though a consumer is registered on the state's No Call List, real estate licensees are allowed to solicit over the telephone (unless they have been asked not to call) if

- the company has an established business relationship (EBR) with a customer—that is, they have been involved in a business transaction within the 18 months prior to the call; or
- the company has received an inquiry from the person within three months of the call; or
- the company has written permission from the consumer; and
- under Texas law, the call is not made by an automated telephone dialing system and the solicitation requires a face-to-face presentation to complete the sales transaction.

> "Do Not Track" legislation has been proposed in Congress to limit how advertisers use internet tracking systems.

FOR EXAMPLE   Louis wants to establish a telemarketing campaign to solicit new listings. Unless a person has previously asked the company not to call, he can contact anyone with whom the company has an established business relationship or from whom the company has received an inquiry or from whom the company has written permission— as long as the call is not made with an automated dialer and the call requires a face-to-face presentation to complete the sales transaction. Otherwise, he cannot call a number that is on the registry.

The Public Utility Commission of Texas has enforcement authority over violations to both the state and federal DNC lists. Calls to consumers registered on the DNC list are subject to fines of up to $11,000 per call, and telemarketing robocalls made without written permission from the consumer are subject to penalties of up to $16,000 per call. For more information, visit the website at www.texasnocall.com.

Junk Fax Prevention Act   The Telephone Consumer Protection Act generally restricts individuals, businesses, and organizations from faxing "unsolicited advertisements." The federal Junk Fax Prevention Act of 2005 grants exceptions for situations in which the organization has a qualifying "established business relationship" (EBR) as defined by the act and

- the fax recipient provided the fax number and previously gave express consent to receive a fax; or
- the fax number was obtained from the recipient's own directory or internet site, unless the recipient noted on such materials that it does not accept unsolicited advertisements; or
- the organization has taken reasonable steps to verify that the recipient consented to have the number listed, if it was obtained from a third-party source.

Additionally, any permissible commercial fax must have an opt-out provision on the first page of the fax, providing a means for the recipient to request removal from the fax distribution list. The liability for sending an unsolicited fax advertisement (one for which an exception has not been granted) is $500 per violation, with possible treble damages.

CAN-SPAM Act   The federal CAN-SPAM Act of 2003 (Controlling the Assault of Non-solicited Pornography and Marketing Act) and the Texas Anti-Spam statute (Texas Business and Commerce Code, Chapter 46) establish requirements for email communications that contain advertising. Neither law prohibits unsolicited commercial email messages, but they do regulate the use of them. Both laws have similar provisions as they relate to the conduct of real estate agents and their marketing activities. They provide that a person may not intentionally transmit a commercial electronic mail message that contains a false, deceptive, or misleading subject line or falsifies routing information. Unsolicited commercial email messages must contain a free opt-out provision with a functioning return email address and a legitimate physical address. If a user opts out, a sender has 3 days to remove the email address from the sender's electronic mailing list under Texas law; 10 days, under federal law. The message must contain clear and conspicuous notice that it is an advertisement or solicitation; Texas law requires *ADV:* as the first four characters in the subject line of the unsolicited commercial email message.

Each violation of the federal CAN-SPAM Act is subject to fines and possible imprisonment. Civil penalties to the state and civil liability to a person injured by a violation of the Texas act are the lesser of $10 for each unlawful message or action or $25,000 for each day an unlawful message is received or an action taken. Furthermore, a violation of the Texas anti-spam statute is considered a violation of the Texas Deceptive Trade Practices Act (DTPA).

IN PRACTICE   Real estate companies or agents who are considering online promotion or telemarketing programs should consult with legal counsel regarding compliance obligations.

SUMMARY

To acquire an inventory of properties to sell, brokers and salespersons must obtain listings. In Texas, listing agreements must be in writing for the broker to collect a commission. The various kinds of listing agreements include open listings, exclusive-agency listings, exclusive-right-to-sell listings, and net listings.

In an open listing, the broker's commission depends on finding a buyer before the property is sold by the seller or another broker. Under an exclusive-agency listing, the broker is given the exclusive right to represent the sellers, but the sellers can avoid paying the broker a commission by selling the property without the broker's help. With an exclusive-right-to-sell listing, the sellers appoint one broker to represent them and must pay that broker a commission regardless of whether it is the broker or the sellers who finds a buyer, as long as the buyer is found within the listing period.

A net listing is based on the net price the sellers will receive if the property is sold. The broker under a net listing may retain as commission any amount over and above the sellers' net. However, it is recommended that a broker suggest the property be listed for a full sales price that would include the broker's commission.

A multiple listing is a subtype of exclusive listing with the additional authority and obligation on the part of the listing broker to distribute the listing to other brokers in the multiple listing organization. This constitutes a unilateral offer of cooperation and compensation.

As an agent of the sellers, a real estate broker is responsible for the disclosure of any material information regarding the property. The many required property disclosures offer protection for buyers, sellers, and real estate agents alike.

Online marketing through the internet has become increasingly essential to an effective property marketing program, both for selling and leasing. Telephone, fax, and email marketing activities are regulated by both federal and state laws.

CHAPTER 13 QUESTIONS

1. Which statement is *TRUE* of a listing contract?

   a. It is an employment contract for the personal and professional services of the broker.

   b. It obligates the seller to convey the property if the broker procures a ready, willing, and able buyer.

   c. It obligates the broker to work diligently for both the seller and the buyer.

   d. It is a TREC-promulgated form.

2. Which statement describes a similarity between an exclusive-agency listing and an exclusive-right-to-sell listing?

   a. Under both types of listings, the sellers retain the right to sell their real estate without the broker's help and without paying the broker a commission.

   b. Both are open listings.

   c. Both give the responsibility of representing the seller to one broker only.

   d. Under both, the seller authorizes only one particular salesperson to show the property.

3. Which statement describes a similarity between an open listing and an exclusive-agency listing?

   a. Under both, the seller avoids paying the broker a commission if the seller sells the property to someone the broker did not procure.

   b. Both listings grant a commission to any licensed broker who finds a buyer for the seller's property.

   c. Both are net listings.

   d. Under both, the broker earns a commission regardless of who sells the property, as long as it is sold within the listing period.

4. A multiple listing

   a. involves more than one parcel of real estate.

   b. is the same as an open listing.

   c. allows the broker to distribute the listing information to other brokers for cooperation and compensation.

   d. allows the broker to offer the property for sale at the highest price possible and retain as the commission any amount over and above the amount requested by the seller.

5. All of the following would terminate an agency relationship *EXCEPT*

   a. expiration of the time period stated in the listing.

   b. death or incapacity of the broker.

   c. nonpayment of the commission by the seller.

   d. destruction of the improvements on the property.

6. A listing contract requiring that all other brokers honor the listing broker's contract but reserves the seller's right to sell directly to a buyer with no commission liability is a(n)

   a. open listing.

   b. exclusive-agency listing.

   c. exclusive-right-to-sell listing.

   d. net listing.

7. A listing agreement that runs for a set period and automatically renews itself for another listing period after the initial period ends is

   a. commonly used in conjunction with a multiple listing.

   b. illegal in Texas.

   c. known as an *open listing*.

   d. a unilateral offer of subagency.

8. The listing price for a property should be determined by the

   a. seller.

   b. salesperson.

   c. broker's competitive market analysis (CMA)

   d. appraised value.

9. All of the following provisions are usually included in listing agreements in Texas, *EXCEPT*

   a. the rate of commission.

   b. the date the agreement commences and the date it terminates.

   c. the minimum earnest money required by the seller.

   d. a protection period.

10. Nick has his property under an exclusive-agency listing with broker Alejandra. If Nick sells his property himself during the term of the listing without using Alejandra's services, he will owe Alejandra

    a. no commission.
    b. the full commission.
    c. a partial commission.
    d. only reimbursement for the broker's costs.

11. A seller lists his residence with a broker and stipulates that he wants to receive $85,000 from the sale but that the broker can sell the residence for as much as possible and keep the difference as a commission. The broker agrees, thus creating a(n)

    a. open listing.
    b. net listing.
    c. exclusive-right-to-sell listing.
    d. exclusive-agency listing.

12. Which statement *BEST* describes the Seller's Disclosure Notice?

    a. Sellers of residential property (single-family or multifamily housing) must provide the disclosure to a buyer.
    b. A buyer must receive a copy of the disclosure on or before the effective date of the contract, or the buyer may terminate the contract for any reason within seven days after receiving the notice.
    c. The seller has a duty to disclose death by natural causes or suicide that occurred on the property.
    d. Only visible structural defects need to be disclosed.

13. A listing taken by a real estate salesperson is an agreement between the seller and the

    a. salesperson.
    b. broker.
    c. salesperson and broker equally.
    d. local multiple listing service.

14. A seller hired Nathan, a broker, under the terms of an open listing. While that listing was still in effect, the seller—without informing Nathan—hired Fred under an exclusive-right-to-sell listing for the same property. If Nathan produces a buyer for the property and the seller accepts that offer, then the seller must pay a

    a. full commission only to Nathan.
    b. full commission only to Fred.
    c. full commission to both Nathan and Fred.
    d. half commission to both Nathan and Fred.

15. Gayle listed her residence with a real estate broker. The broker brought an offer at full price from ready, willing, and able buyers, in accordance with the terms of the listing agreement. However, Gayle changed her mind and rejected the buyer's offer. In this situation, Gayle

    a. must sell the property.
    b. owes a commission to the broker.
    c. is liable to the buyers for specific performance.
    d. is liable to the buyers for compensatory damages.

Detailed rationales for the end-of-chapter review questions are available online at www.dearborn.com through the *Instructor Resource Guides* link.

Real Estate Appraisal

LEARNING OBJECTIVES *When you have completed this chapter, you will be able to*

- **explain** the steps in the appraisal process;
- **identify** the different types, the four characteristics, and the basic principles of value;
- **list** and illustrate the steps taken in the sales comparison approach, cost approach, and income approach to value and the process for reconciling those values;
- **distinguish** a comparative market analysis from an appraisal in pricing a property to be listed;
- **describe** the requirements for becoming a licensed or certified appraiser in Texas; and
- **define** the following *key terms*:

appraisal	functional obsolescence	reconciliation
capitalization rate	gross income multiplier	replacement cost
comparative market analysis	gross rent multiplier	reproduction cost
cost approach	highest and best use	sales comparison approach
depreciation	income approach	substitution
economic life	physical deterioration	value
external obsolescence	plottage value	

OVERVIEW

Real estate is the business of value. Members of the general public informally estimate this value when they buy, sell, or invest in real estate. A formal opinion of value is conducted by an appraiser and serves as a basis for the pricing, financing, insuring, or leasing of real property.

This chapter examines value—what determines it, adds to it, and detracts from it. It also discusses in detail the various methods appraisal professionals use to develop an opinion of value for residential as well as commercial and industrial real estate.

In studying this chapter, the student must be careful not to confuse the job and practices of an appraiser with those of a real estate licensee who, as listing agent, makes an estimate or opinion of price for marketing purposes. Such an estimate is, of necessity and practicality, a very limited and narrow survey of the factors that constitute an objective price of the property.

APPRAISING

An **appraisal** is "the act or process of developing an opinion of value; an opinion of value." Based on education, training, experience, and integrity, the appraiser attempts to project sellers' and buyers' past activities into a current opinion of real estate value. Because of the uniqueness of each property, comparisons of like properties often entail adjustments in arriving at a conclusion. Financial consideration by the layman for similar properties sometimes reflects sentiment, bias, politics, lack of understanding, and other factors not considered by the appraiser. A professional appraiser must remain impartial and objective in the process of developing an opinion of property value.

An appraisal cannot be guaranteed or proven. However, the opinion of value can be substantiated and justified. The final opinion of value is the result of a professional analysis of a considerable quantity of physical and economic facts. An appraisal must not be considered absolute but should be used as a basis of negotiation between parties involved in the property, whatever their interests. Formal appraisal reports are relied on in important decisions made by mortgage lenders, investors, public utilities, government agencies, businesses, and individuals. Home mortgage lenders, for instance, need to know a property's market value so that the loan-to-value ratio (the percentage of value to be loaned) will accurately reflect the property's value as collateral.

While opinions of real estate value are made by appraisal professionals; often the real estate agent must help a seller arrive at a market price for the property without the aid of a formal appraisal report. Thus it is necessary for everyone engaged in the real estate business to command at least a fundamental knowledge of real estate valuation.

The Appraisal Process

The key to an accurate appraisal lies in the methodical collection of accurate and verified data. The appraisal process is an orderly set of procedures used to collect and analyze data to arrive at an ultimate value conclusion. Figure 14.1 outlines the steps an appraiser takes in carrying out an appraisal assignment. The numbers in the following list correspond to the numbers on the diagram.

1. *State the problem*—The kind of value to be estimated must be specified and the valuation approach(es) most valid and reliable for the kind of property under appraisal must be selected. This includes the purpose of the appraisal.
2. *List the data needed and the sources*—Based on the approach(es) the appraiser uses, the types of data needed and the sources to be consulted are listed.
3. *Gather, record, and verify the necessary data—*
   — *General data*: Detailed information concerning the economic, political, and social conditions of the region and/or city; comments on the effects of these data on the subject property must be obtained.
   — *Specific data*: Detailed information about the subject property and improvements including comparative data relating to costs, sales, income, and expenses of similar properties.
   — *Data for each approach*: Depending on the approach(es) used, comparative information relating to sales, income, and expenses and construction costs of comparable properties must be collected. All data should be verified, usually by checking the same information against two different sources. In the case of sales data, one source should be a person directly involved in the transaction.
4. *Determine the highest and best use*—The appraiser determines the most probably use that is legal, physically possible, and financially feasible.
5. *Estimate value by each of the three approaches*—The appraiser uses data collected in step 3 to compute the indicated value by the cost approach, the sales comparison approach, and the income approach.
6. *Report the final opinion of market value*—After the three approaches have been reconciled and an opinion of value reached, the appraiser prepares a formal written report for the client. The statement may be a completed form, a letter, a short summary, or a lengthy written narrative, and it should contain the following information:
   — The opinion of value and the date to which it applies
   — The purpose for which the appraisal was made
   — A description of the neighborhood and the subject property
   — Factual data covering costs, sales, and income and expenses of similar, recently sold properties
   — An analysis and interpretation of the data collected
   — A presentation of one or more of the three approaches to value in enough detail to support the appraiser's final value conclusion
   — Any qualifying conditions
   — Supportive material such as charts, maps, photographs, floor plans, leases, and contracts
   — The certification and signature of the appraiser

It is illegal for a lender to make the payment for an appraisal contingent on an appraiser's producing a specified value—thereby interfering with the appraiser's obligation to provide an independent and impartial opinion of value.

Figure 14.2 is the first three pages of the *Uniform Residential Appraisal Report (URAR)* form required by many government agencies. In addition to the URAR form, all residential appraisals (1–4 units) conducted on or after April 1, 2009, must include a *Market Conditions Addendum*, which is intended to provide the lender/client with a clear and accurate understanding of the market trends and conditions in the neighborhood (see Figure 14.3). As a response to the effect of environmental risks on the value of real estate, *USPAP* requires that licensed and certified appraisers recognize and report environmental conditions as a part of the appraisal report.

FIGURE 14.1: The Appraisal Process

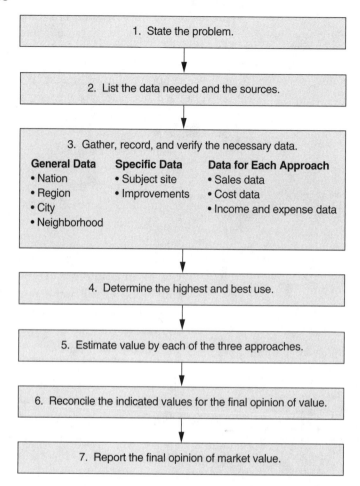

1. State the problem.

2. List the data needed and the sources.

3. Gather, record, and verify the necessary data.

General Data	**Specific Data**	**Data for Each Approach**
• Nation	• Subject site	• Sales data
• Region	• Improvements	• Cost data
• City		• Income and expense data
• Neighborhood		

4. Determine the highest and best use.

5. Estimate value by each of the three approaches.

6. Reconcile the indicated values for the final opinion of value.

7. Report the final opinion of market value.

IN PRACTICE The financial crisis that began in late 2007 brought about a renewed emphasis on "protecting the integrity of the appraisal process when a consumer's home is securing the loan" (Dodd-Frank Act). New appraisal independence requirements ensure that real estate appraisers are free to use their independent professional judgment in assigning home values. They prohibit lenders and brokers from bribing, coercing, extorting, or otherwise inappropriately influencing appraisers to inflate property values. Appraisers may not be selected by mortgage brokers or real estate agents, and a lender's mortgage production staff is prohibited from ordering the appraisal. As a result, by 2011, 70% of all appraisals were conducted through *appraisal management companies* (AMCs). Among other tasks, AMCs recruit and qualify appraisers, verify licensure, receive appraisal orders from lenders, contract with appraisers to perform appraisal assignments, provide completed appraisals to lenders, collect fees from lenders for the appraisals, and reimburse appraisers for services performed. They are also responsible for appraisal review, quality control, and market value dispute resolution. Effective on or after March 1, 2012, with limited exceptions, AMCs operating to manage appraisals on Texas residential properties with fewer than five units must be registered with the TALCB. Exemptions include a person who employs appraisers on an employer-employee basis, a department within a financial institution, and an appraisal firm that employs on an exclusive basis as independent contractors not more than 15 appraisers (H.B. 1146, 2011). H.B. 1146 (2011) also requires appraisal management companies to report separately the various fees charged for an appraisal. Compensation to appraisers must be reasonable and customary and be paid no later than 60 days after completion of the appraisal assignment.

FIGURE 14.2: Uniform Residential Appraisal Report

Uniform Residential Appraisal Report   File

The purpose of this summary appraisal report is to provide the lender/client with an accurate, and adequately supported, opinion of the market value of the subject property.

SUBJECT

Property Address		City		State	Zip Code

Borrower | Owner of Public Record | County

Legal Description

Assessor's Parcel #   Tax Year   R.E. Taxes $

Neighborhood Name   Map Reference   Census Tract

Occupant ☐ Owner ☐ Tenant ☐ Vacant   Special Assessments $ ☐ PUD   HOA $ ☐ per year ☐ per month

Property Rights Appraised ☐ Fee Simple ☐ Leasehold ☐ Other (describe)

Assignment Type ☐ Purchase Transaction ☐ Refinance Transaction ☐ Other (describe)

Lender/Client   Address

Is the subject property currently offered for sale or has it been offered for sale in the twelve months prior to the effective date of this appraisal? ☐ Yes ☐ No

Report data source(s) used, offering price(s), and date(s).

CONTRACT

I ☐ did ☐ did not analyze the contract for sale for the subject purchase transaction. Explain the results of the analysis of the contract for sale or why the analysis was not performed.

Contract Price $ Date of Contract   Is the property seller the owner of public record? ☐ Yes ☐ No Data Source(s)

Is there any financial assistance (loan charges, sale concessions, gift or downpayment assistance, etc.) to be paid by any party on behalf of the borrower? ☐ Yes ☐ No
If Yes, report the total dollar amount and describe the items to be paid.

NEIGHBORHOOD

Note: Race and the racial composition of the neighborhood are not appraisal factors.

Neighborhood Characteristics	One-Unit Housing Trends	One-Unit Housing	Present Land Use %
Location ☐ Urban ☐ Suburban ☐ Rural	Property Values ☐ Increasing ☐ Stable ☐ Declining	PRICE AGE	One-Unit %
Built-Up ☐ Over 75% ☐ 25–75% ☐ Under 25%	Demand/Supply ☐ Shortage ☐ In Balance ☐ Over Supply	$ (000) (yrs)	2-4 Unit %
Growth ☐ Rapid ☐ Stable ☐ Slow	Marketing Time ☐ Under 3 mths ☐ 3–6 mths ☐ Over 6 mths	Low	Multi-Family %
		High	Commercial %
		Pred.	Other %

Neighborhood Boundaries

Neighborhood Description

Market Conditions (including support for the above conclusions)

SITE

Dimensions   Area   Shape   View

Specific Zoning Classification   Zoning Description

Zoning Compliance ☐ Legal ☐ Legal Nonconforming (Grandfathered Use) ☐ No Zoning ☐ Illegal (describe)

Is the highest and best use of the subject property as improved (or as proposed per plans and specifications) the present use? ☐ Yes ☐ No If No, describe

Utilities	Public	Other (describe)		Public	Other (describe)	Off-site Improvements—Type	Public	Private
Electricity	☐	☐	Water	☐	☐	Street	☐	☐
Gas	☐	☐	Sanitary Sewer	☐	☐	Alley	☐	☐

FEMA Special Flood Hazard Area ☐ Yes ☐ No FEMA Flood Zone   FEMA Map #   FEMA Map Date

Are the utilities and off-site improvements typical for the market area? ☐ Yes ☐ No If No, describe

Are there any adverse site conditions or external factors (easements, encroachments, environmental conditions, land uses, etc.)? ☐ Yes ☐ No If Yes, describe

IMPROVEMENTS

General Description	Foundation	Exterior Description materials/condition	Interior materials/condition
Units ☐ One ☐ One with Accessory Unit	☐ Concrete Slab ☐ Crawl Space	Foundation Walls	Floors
# of Stories	☐ Full Basement ☐ Partial Basement	Exterior Walls	Walls
Type ☐ Det. ☐ Att. ☐ S-Det./End Unit	Basement Area sq. ft.	Roof Surface	Trim/Finish
☐ Existing ☐ Proposed ☐ Under Const.	Basement Finish %	Gutters & Downspouts	Bath Floor
Design (Style)	☐ Outside Entry/Exit ☐ Sump Pump	Window Type	Bath Wainscot
Year Built	Evidence of ☐ Infestation	Storm Sash/Insulated	Car Storage ☐ None
Effective Age (Yrs)	☐ Dampness ☐ Settlement	Screens	☐ Driveway # of Cars
Attic ☐ None	Heating ☐ FWA ☐ HWBB ☐ Radiant	Amenities ☐ Woodstove(s) #	Driveway Surface
☐ Drop Stair ☐ Stairs	☐ Other Fuel	☐ Fireplace(s) # ☐ Fence	☐ Garage # of Cars
☐ Floor ☐ Scuttle	Cooling ☐ Central Air Conditioning	☐ Patio/Deck ☐ Porch	☐ Carport # of Cars
☐ Finished ☐ Heated	☐ Individual ☐ Other	☐ Pool ☐ Other	☐ Att. ☐ Det. ☐ Built-in

Appliances ☐ Refrigerator ☐ Range/Oven ☐ Dishwasher ☐ Disposal ☐ Microwave ☐ Washer/Dryer ☐ Other (describe)

Finished area **above** grade contains: Rooms   Bedrooms   Bath(s)   Square Feet of Gross Living Area Above Grade

Additional features (special energy efficient items, etc.)

Describe the condition of the property (including needed repairs, deterioration, renovations, remodeling, etc.).

Are there any physical deficiencies or adverse conditions that affect the livability, soundness, or structural integrity of the property? ☐ Yes ☐ No If Yes, describe

Does the property generally conform to the neighborhood (functional utility, style, condition, use, construction, etc.)? ☐ Yes ☐ No If No, describe

FIGURE 14.2: Uniform Residential Appraisal Report (continued)

Uniform Residential Appraisal Report   File

There are _____ comparable properties currently offered for sale in the subject neighborhood ranging in price from $ _____ to $ _____

There are _____ comparable sales in the subject neighborhood within the past twelve months ranging in sale price from $ _____ to $ _____

FEATURE	SUBJECT	COMPARABLE SALE # 1		COMPARABLE SALE # 2		COMPARABLE SALE # 3	
Address							
Proximity to Subject							
Sale Price	$	$		$		$	
Sale Price/Gross Liv. Area	$ sq. ft.	$ sq. ft.		$ sq. ft.		$ sq. ft.	
Data Source(s)							
Verification Source(s)							
VALUE ADJUSTMENTS	DESCRIPTION	DESCRIPTION	+(-) $ Adjustment	DESCRIPTION	+(-) $ Adjustment	DESCRIPTION	+(-) $ Adjustment
Sale or Financing Concessions							
Date of Sale/Time							
Location							
Leasehold/Fee Simple							
Site							
View							
Design (Style)							
Quality of Construction							
Actual Age							
Condition							
Above Grade	Total Bdrms. Baths	Total Bdrms. Baths		Total Bdrms. Baths		Total Bdrms. Baths	
Room Count							
Gross Living Area	sq. ft.	sq. ft.		sq. ft.		sq. ft.	
Basement & Finished Rooms Below Grade							
Functional Utility							
Heating/Cooling							
Energy Efficient Items							
Garage/Carport							
Porch/Patio/Deck							
Net Adjustment (Total)		☐+ ☐- $		☐+ ☐- $		☐+ ☐- $	
Adjusted Sale Price of Comparables		Net Adj. % Gross Adj. % $		Net Adj. % Gross Adj. % $		Net Adj. % Gross Adj. % $	

I ☐ did ☐ did not research the sale or transfer history of the subject property and comparable sales. If not, explain

My research ☐ did ☐ did not reveal any prior sales or transfers of the subject property for the three years prior to the effective date of this appraisal.

Data source(s)

My research ☐ did ☐ did not reveal any prior sales or transfers of the comparable sales for the year prior to the date of sale of the comparable sale.

Data source(s)

Report the results of the research and analysis of the prior sale or transfer history of the subject property and comparable sales (report additional prior sales on page 3).

ITEM	SUBJECT	COMPARABLE SALE # 1	COMPARABLE SALE # 2	COMPARABLE SALE # 3
Date of Prior Sale/Transfer				
Price of Prior Sale/Transfer				
Data Source(s)				
Effective Date of Data Source(s)				

Analysis of prior sale or transfer history of the subject property and comparable sales

Summary of Sales Comparison Approach

Indicated Value by Sales Comparison Approach $

Indicated Value by: Sales Comparison Approach $ _____ Cost Approach (if developed) $ _____ Income Approach (if developed) $ _____

This appraisal is made ☐ "as is", ☐ subject to completion per plans and specifications on the basis of a hypothetical condition that the improvements have been completed, ☐ subject to the following repairs or alterations on the basis of a hypothetical condition that the repairs or alterations have been completed, or ☐ subject to the following required inspection based on the extraordinary assumption that the condition or deficiency does not require alteration or repair:

Based on a complete visual inspection of the interior and exterior areas of the subject property, defined scope of work, statement of assumptions and limiting conditions, and appraiser's certification, my (our) opinion of the market value, as defined, of the real property that is the subject of this report is $ _____ , as of _____ , which is the date of inspection and the effective date of this appraisal.

FIGURE 14.2: Uniform Residential Appraisal Report (continued)

Uniform Residential Appraisal Report

File #

ADDITIONAL COMMENTS

COST APPROACH TO VALUE (not required by Fannie Mae)

Provide adequate information for the lender/client to replicate the below cost figures and calculations.

Support for the opinion of site value (summary of comparable land sales or other methods for estimating site value)

ESTIMATED ☐ REPRODUCTION OR ☐ REPLACEMENT COST NEW	OPINION OF SITE VALUE ....= $
Source of cost data	Dwelling Sq. Ft. @ $ ....=$
Quality rating from cost service Effective date of cost data	Sq. Ft. @ $ ....=$
Comments on Cost Approach (gross living area calculations, depreciation, etc.)	Garage/Carport Sq. Ft. @ $ ....=$
	Total Estimate of Cost-New ....= $
	Less Physical Functional External
	Depreciation =$( )
	Depreciated Cost of Improvements....................=$
	"As-is" Value of Site Improvements....................=$
Estimated Remaining Economic Life (HUD and VA only) Years	Indicated Value By Cost Approach ....=$

INCOME APPROACH TO VALUE (not required by Fannie Mae)

Estimated Monthly Market Rent $ X Gross Rent Multiplier   = $ Indicated Value by Income Approach

Summary of Income Approach (including support for market rent and GRM)

PROJECT INFORMATION FOR PUDs (if applicable)

Is the developer/builder in control of the Homeowners' Association (HOA)? ☐ Yes ☐ No   Unit type(s) ☐ Detached ☐ Attached

Provide the following information for PUDs ONLY if the developer/builder is in control of the HOA and the subject property is an attached dwelling unit.

Legal name of project

Total number of phases   Total number of units   Total number of units sold

Total number of units rented   Total number of units for sale   Data source(s)

Was the project created by the conversion of an existing building(s) into a PUD? ☐ Yes ☐ No   If Yes, date of conversion

Does the project contain any multi-dwelling units? ☐ Yes ☐ No   Data source(s)

Are the units, common elements, and recreation facilities complete? ☐ Yes ☐ No   If No, describe the status of completion.

Are the common elements leased to or by the Homeowners' Association? ☐ Yes ☐ No   If Yes, describe the rental terms and options.

Describe common elements and recreational facilities

FIGURE 14.3: Market Conditions Addendum

Market Conditions Addendum to the Appraisal Report

File No.

The purpose of this addendum is to provide the lender/client with a clear and accurate understanding of the market trends and conditions prevalent in the subject neighborhood. This is a required addendum for all appraisal reports with an effective date on or after April 1, 2009.

Property Address | City | State | ZIP Code

Borrower

Instructions: The appraiser must use the information required on this form as the basis for his/her conclusions, and must provide support for those conclusions, regarding housing trends and overall market conditions as reported in the Neighborhood section of the appraisal report form. The appraiser must fill in all the information to the extent it is available and reliable and must provide analysis as indicated below. If any required data is unavailable or is considered unreliable, the appraiser must provide an explanation. It is recognized that not all data sources will be able to provide data for the shaded areas below; if it is available, however, the appraiser must include the data in the analysis. If data sources provide the required information as an average instead of the median, the appraiser should report the available figure and identify it as an average. Sales and listings must be properties that compete with the subject property, determined by applying the criteria that would be used by a prospective buyer of the subject property. The appraiser must explain any anomalies in the data, such as seasonal markets, new construction, foreclosures, etc.

MARKET RESEARCH & ANALYSIS

Inventory Analysis	Prior 7–12 Months	Prior 4–6 Months	Current – 3 Months	Overall Trend		
Total # of Comparable Sales (Settled)				☐ Increasing	☐ Stable	☐ Declining
Absorption Rate (Total Sales/Months)				☐ Increasing	☐ Stable	☐ Declining
Total # of Comparable Active Listings				☐ Declining	☐ Stable	☐ Increasing
Months of Housing Supply (Total Listings/Ab.Rate)				☐ Declining	☐ Stable	☐ Increasing
Median Sale & List Price, DOM, Sale/List %	Prior 7–12 Months	Prior 4–6 Months	Current – 3 Months	Overall Trend		
Median Comparable Sale Price				☐ Increasing	☐ Stable	☐ Declining
Median Comparable Sales Days on Market				☐ Declining	☐ Stable	☐ Increasing
Median Comparable List Price				☐ Increasing	☐ Stable	☐ Declining
Median Comparable Listings Days on Market				☐ Declining	☐ Stable	☐ Increasing
Median Sale Price as % of List Price				☐ Increasing	☐ Stable	☐ Declining
Seller-(developer, builder, etc.) paid financial assistance prevalent? ☐ Yes ☐ No				☐ Declining	☐ Stable	☐ Increasing

Explain in detail the seller concessions trends for the past 12 months (e.g., seller contributions increased from 3% to 5%, increasing use of buydowns, closing costs, condo fees, options, etc.).

Are foreclosure sales (REO sales) a factor in the market? ☐ Yes ☐ No If yes, explain (including the trends in listings and sales of foreclosed properties).

Cite data sources for above information.

Summarize the above information as support for your conclusions in the Neighborhood section of the appraisal report form. If you used any additional information, such as an analysis of pending sales and/or expired and withdrawn listings, to formulate your conclusions, provide both an explanation and support for your conclusions.

CONDO/CO-OP PROJECTS

If the subject is a unit in a condominium or cooperative project , complete the following: **Project Name:**

Subject Project Data	Prior 7-12 Months	Prior 4-6 Months	Current – 3 Months	Overall Trend		
Total # of Comparable Sales (Settled)				☐ Increasing	☐ Stable	☐ Declining
Absorption Rate (Total Sales/Months)				☐ Increasing	☐ Stable	☐ Declining
Total # of Active Comparable Listings				☐ Declining	☐ Stable	☐ Increasing
Months of Unit Supply (Total Listings/Ab. Rate)				☐ Declining	☐ Stable	☐ Increasing

Are foreclosure sales (REO sales) a factor in the project? ☐ Yes ☐ No If yes, indicate the number of REO listings and explain the trends in listings and sales of foreclosed properties.

Summarize the above trends and address the impact on the subject unit and project.

APPRAISER

Signature	Signature
Appraiser Name	Supervisory Appraiser Name
Company Name	Company Name
Company Address	Company Address
State License/Certification # State	State License/Certification # State
Email Address	Email Address

Freddie Mac Form 71 March 2009 Page 1 of 1 Fannie Mae Form 1004MC March 2009

VALUE

To have **value** in the real estate market—that is, to have monetary worth based on desirability—a property must have the following four characteristics:

- *Effective Demand*: the need or desire for possession or ownership backed by the financial means to satisfy that need (Note: When the word *demand* is used in economics, *effective demand* is usually assumed.)
- *Utility*: the capacity to satisfy human needs and desires
- *Scarcity*: a finite supply
- *Transferability*: the relative ease with which ownership rights are transferred from one person to another

Market Value

Although a given parcel of real estate may have many different kinds of value at the same time (as illustrated in Figure 14.4), generally the goal of an appraiser is to *develop an opinion of market value*. The market value of a parcel of real estate is the most probable price a property should bring in a competitive and open market under all conditions requisite to a fair sale, with the buyer and the seller each acting prudently and knowledgeably and assuming the price is not affected by undue stimulus. Included in this definition are the following key points:

- Market value is *the most probable price a property should bring—not the average price, highest price, or lowest price.*
- Both buyer and seller are motivated.
- Buyer and seller are *well informed* or *well advised*, with both acting in what they consider their own best interests.
- A reasonable time is allowed for exposure in the *open market*.
- Payment is made in terms of *cash* or its equivalent.
- The price represents the normal consideration for the property sold, unaffected by special financing or sales concessions.

FIGURE 14.4: Kinds of Value

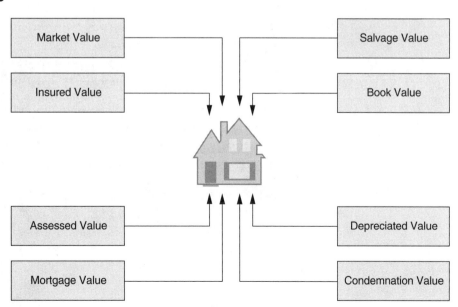

Market Value Versus Market Price Market value is an estimated price based on an analysis of comparable sales and other pertinent market data. *Market price*, on the other hand, is what a property *actually* sells for—its selling price. Theoretically, the ideal market price is the same as the market value; however, sometimes a property may be sold below or above market value, for example, when a seller is forced to sell quickly, when a sale is arranged between relatives, or when buyers are less than fully informed. A transaction in which the parties are dealing from equal bargaining positions is considered an arm's-length transaction. The market price can be taken as accurate evidence of current market value *only* after considering the relationship of the buyer and the seller, the terms and conditions of the market, any financing or sales concessions made by the seller, and the effect of the passage of time since the sale was made.

Market Value Versus Cost It also is important to distinguish between market value and cost. One of the most common errors made in valuing property is the assumption that cost represents market value. Cost and market value may be equal and often are when the improvements on a property are new and represent the highest and best use of the land. More often, however, cost does not equal market value. For example, two homes are identical in every respect except that one is located on a street with heavy traffic and the other is on a quiet residential street. The value of the former may be less than that of the latter, although the cost of each may be exactly the same. Another example would be a situation in which the demand for homes greatly exceeds the available supply to such an extent that buyers actually pay more than it would cost to construct such homes because they want to secure housing without a long delay. In this instance, market value easily could exceed cost.

> *Market value* is a reasonable opinion of a property's value. Market price is the actual selling price of a property. Cost is the original capital outlay for land, labor, materials, and profit.

Basic Principles of Value

A number of economic principles affect the value of real estate. The most important of these principles are defined in the following paragraphs.

Highest and Best Use The most probable use to which a property is suited that will result in its "highest value" is its **highest and best use**. The most probable use must be legal, physically possible, and financially feasible. The highest and best use of a site can change with social, political, and economic forces. For example, a parking lot in a busy downtown area may not maximize the land's profitability to the same extent as an office building.

Substitution The principle of **substitution** states that the maximum value of a property tends to be set by the cost of purchasing an equally desirable and valuable substitute property. For example, if two similar houses were for sale in an area, the one with the lower asking price normally would be purchased first.

Supply and Demand This principle states that the value of a property will increase if the supply decreases and the demand either increases or remains constant—and vice versa. For example, the last lot to be sold in a residential area where the demand for homes is high probably would be worth more than the first lot sold in that area.

Conformity   Maximum value is realized if the use of land conforms to existing neighborhood standards. In single-family residential neighborhoods, for example, buildings should be similar in design, construction, size, and age. For example, the biggest house on the block tends to lose value to its neighbors; it is said to be *overbuilt* for the neighborhood. The reverse is sometimes true for the smallest house on the block. Any decrease in value for large homes or increase in value for small homes would be on a per-square-foot basis.

Externalities   The principle of *externalities* states that influences outside a property may have a positive or negative effect on its value. For example, the federal government's participation in interest rate levels, mortgage loan guarantees, slum clearance, and rehabilitation has a powerful impact on stimulating or retarding supply and demand. At the neighborhood level, even decorative features such as fresh paint, flowers, and plush lawns can enhance property values.

Anticipation   This principle holds that value can increase or decrease in anticipation of some future benefit or detriment affecting the property. For example, the value of a house may be affected by rumors that an adjacent property may be converted to commercial use in the near future.

Increasing and Diminishing Returns   Improvements to land and structures eventually will reach a point at which they no longer have a positive net effect on property values. As long as money spent on improvements produces an increase in income or value, the law of *increasing returns* is applicable. At the point where additional improvements produce no proportionate increase in income or value, the *law of diminishing returns* applies.

Plottage Value   The increased utility and value resulting from the combining or consolidating of adjacent lots into one larger lot is the principle of **plottage value**. For example, two adjacent lots are each valued at $35,000; each one will accommodate a duplex. If the two lots are combined into one lot that will accommodate an eight-unit apartment complex, the land might be worth $90,000. The process of merging the two lots under one owner is known as *assemblage*.

Contribution   The value of any component of a property is measured by the amount it contributes to the value of the whole or the amount its absence detracts from that value. For example, the cost of installing an air-conditioning system and remodeling an older office building may be greater than is justified by the rental increase that may result from the improvement to the property.

Competition   This principle states that excess profits tend to attract competition. For example, the success of a retail store may attract investors to open similar stores in the area. This tends to mean less profit for all stores concerned unless the purchasing power in the area increases substantially.

Change   No physical or economic condition remains constant. Real estate is subject to natural phenomena such as tornadoes, fires, and the routine wear and tear of the elements. The real estate business is also subject to the demands of its market, just as any other business. An appraiser should be knowledgeable about the past and, perhaps, the predictable future effects of natural phenomena and the behavior of the marketplace.

THE THREE APPROACHES TO VALUE

To arrive at an accurate opinion of value, three basic approaches or techniques are traditionally used by appraisers: the sales comparison approach, the cost approach, and the income approach. Each method serves as a check against the others and narrows the range within which the final opinion of value will fall. Each method is generally considered most reliable for specific types of property.

The Sales Comparison Approach

The *sales comparison approach* compares the subject property with recently sold comparable properties and is based on the principle of substitution.

In the **sales comparison approach**, sometimes called the *market data approach*, an *indicated value* is obtained by comparing the subject property (the property under appraisal) with recently sold comparable properties (properties similar to the subject). Because no two parcels of real estate are exactly alike, each comparable property must be compared with the subject property, and the sales prices must be adjusted for any dissimilar features. The principal factors for which adjustments must be made fall into four basic categories:

- *Date of sale*—An adjustment must be made if economic changes occur between the date of sale of the comparable property and the date of the appraisal; as a rule, it is best to use properties that have sold within six months of the appraisal.
- *Location*—An adjustment may be necessary to compensate for locational differences. For example, similar properties might differ in price from neighborhood to neighborhood or even in more desirable locations within the same neighborhood.
- *Physical feature*—Physical features that may cause adjustments include age of building; size of lot; landscaping; construction; number of rooms; square feet of living space; interior and exterior condition; the presence or absence of a garage, fireplace, or air conditioner; and so forth.
- *Terms and conditions of sale*—This consideration becomes important if a sale is not financed by a traditional mortgage.

The sales prices of comparable properties are adjusted by making the features of the comparable properties match those of the subject property.

Short sales and pre-foreclosures are not REOs and could very well be less than arm's-length transactions.

After a careful analysis of the differences between comparable properties and the subject property, the appraiser assigns a dollar value to each difference. On the basis of their knowledge and experience, appraisers estimate dollar adjustments that reflect actual values extracted from the marketplace. The value of a feature present in the subject property but not in the comparable property is *added* to the sales price of the comparable. This presumes that, all other features being equal, a property having a feature (such as a fireplace or a wet bar) not present in the comparable property tends to have a higher market value solely because of this feature. The feature need not be a physical amenity; it may be a locational or an aesthetic feature. Likewise, the value of a feature present in the comparable but not in the subject property is *subtracted from* the sales price of the comparable. The adjusted sales prices of the comparables represent the probable value range of the subject property. From this range, a single market value indication can be reached, the *indicated value by the sales comparison approach*. The sales comparison approach is essential in almost every appraisal of real estate. It is considered the most reliable of the three approaches in appraising residential property, where the amenities (intangible benefits) may be difficult to measure otherwise. An example of the sales comparison approach is shown in Figure 14.5.

IN PRACTICE   According to the TALCB, in an article dated April 2009, a sale labeled *foreclosure* in the MLS is not usually a foreclosure. It is a property that was previously purchased by a financial institution at a foreclosure auction on the courthouse steps and is known as an *REO (real estate owned)*. When the financial institution sells the property to the ultimate purchaser through a real estate broker, the transaction listed in the MLS is an arm's-length transaction. Therefore, REO properties should be included in an appraiser's comparable properties. TALCB investigators concluded that "the existence and volume of REOs in a neighborhood could have a significant impact on market area trends. An appraiser who is not aware of this impact . . . risks producing an appraisal that isn't credible." A similar position was discussed in Chapter 11 relating to tax appraisals: the chief appraiser may not exclude properties sold at a foreclosure sale conducted within the last three years nor properties for which the market values have declined because of a declining economy.

FIGURE 14.5: Sales Comparison Approach to Value

	Subject Property: 155 Potter Dr.	Comparables				
		A	B	C	D	E
Sales price		$118,000	$112,000	$121,000	$116,500	$110,000
Financing concessions	none	none	none	none	none	none
Date of sale		current	current	current	current	current
Location	good	same	inferior +6,500	same	same	same
Age	6 years	same	same	same	same	same
Size of lot	60' × 135'	same	same	larger –5,000	same	larger –5,000
Landscaping	good	same	same	same	same	same
Construction	brick	same	same	same	same	same
Style	ranch	same	same	same	same	same
No. of rooms	6	same	same	same	same	same
No. of bedrooms	3	same	same	same	same	same
No. of baths	1½	same	same	same	same	same
Sq. ft. of living space	1,500	same	same	same	same	same
Other space (basement)	full basement	same	same	same	same	same
Condition—exterior	average	superior –1,500	inferior +1,000	superior –1,500	same	inferior +2,000
Condition—interior	good	same	same	superior –500	same	same
Garage	2-car attached	same	same	same	same	none +5,000
Other improvements	none	none	none	none	none	none
Net adjustments		– 1,500	+ 7,500	– 7,000	-0-	+ 2,000
Adjusted value		$116,500	$119,500	$114,000	$116,500	$112,000

Note: Because comparable D required no adjustment, and comparable A required only one relatively small adjustment, an appraiser would conclude that the indicated market value of the subject is $116,500.

The Cost Approach

The **cost approach** to value is based on the property's reproduction cost. Because most people will not pay more for a property than it would cost to acquire a similar site and erect a similar structure on it, the current reproduction cost of the building plus the value of the land tends to set the upper limit of a property's value. The cost approach is sometimes called *appraisal by summation.*

The cost approach consists of five steps as illustrated in Figure 14.6:

1. Estimate the value of the land as if it were vacant and available to be put to its highest and best use.
2. Estimate the current cost of constructing the building(s) and site improvements.
3. Estimate the amount of accrued depreciation resulting from physical deterioration, functional obsolescence, and/or external obsolescence.
4. Deduct accrued depreciation from the estimated construction cost of a new building(s) and any site improvements.
5. Add the estimated land value to the depreciated cost of the building(s) and site improvements to arrive at the total *indicated value by the cost approach.*

> The *cost approach* calculates the property value based on the improvement's reproduction cost or replacement cost.

FIGURE 14.6: Cost Approach to Value

Land Valuation: Size 60' × 135' @ $450 per front foot		$27,000
Building Valuation: Replacement Cost 1,500 sq. ft. @ $65 per sq. ft. (Includes the combined cost of basic structure, floor coverings, heating and cooling equipment, fixtures, appliances, etc.)		$97,500
Plus site improvements: driveway, walks, landscaping, etc.		+ 4,000
Total Estimated Cost of New Improvements		$101,500
Less Depreciation:		
Physical depreciation		
curable (items of deferred maintenance) roof	$4,000	
incurable (structural deterioration)	5,200	
Functional obsolescence	2,000	
External obsolescence	-0-	
Total Depreciation		−11,200
Depreciated Value of Improvements		$90,300
Indicated Value by Cost Approach		$117,300

Land value (step 1) is most commonly estimated by using the sales comparison approach. That is, the location and improvements of the subject site are compared with those of similar nearby sites and adjustments are made for significant differences.

There are two ways to look at the construction of a building for appraisal purposes (step 2): reproduction cost and replacement cost. **Reproduction cost** is the dollar amount required to construct an exact duplicate of the subject building at current prices. **Replacement cost** of the subject property would be the construction cost at current prices of a property that is not necessarily an exact duplicate but serves the same purpose or function as the original. As an example, this approach permits the installation of less expensive hardwood kitchen cabinets instead of more expensive but outdated enameled steel cabinets. Replacement cost is used more frequently in appraising older structures because it eliminates obsolete features and takes advantage of current construction materials and techniques.

Determining Reproduction or Replacement Cost An appraiser using the cost approach computes the reproduction or replacement cost of a building using one of the following three methods:

- *Square-foot method*—The cost-per-square-foot method of a recently built comparable structure is multiplied by the number of square feet in the subject building. This is the most common method of cost estimation on a residential appraisal (see Figure 14.8). Square-footage measurements are taken from the *exterior* surface of outside walls (brick to brick) for *finished areas* of the dwelling. Finished areas (living areas) include enclosed areas that are suitable for year-round use with walls, floors, and ceilings that are similar to the rest of the house. For some properties, the cost per *cubic foot* of a recently built comparable structure is multiplied by the number of cubic feet in the subject structure.
- *Unit-in-place method*—The replacement cost of a structure is estimated based on the cost per unit of measure of individual building components, including the cost of material, labor, overhead, and profit. For example, insulation might be computed at $0.13 per square foot, drywall at $2.25 per square yard, et cetera. The total in-place cost per unit is multiplied by the number of such units in each building component.
- *Quantity-survey method*—An estimate is made of the quantities of raw materials needed to replace the subject structure (lumber, plaster, brick, etc.), as well as of the current price of such materials and their installation costs. For example, reproduction might be stated as 10,000 ceramic tiles at $3.50 per tile, 1,500 doorknobs at $7.00 each, and so forth. These factors are added to the indirect costs (such as building permit, survey, payroll taxes, builder's profit) to arrive at the total replacement cost of the structure.

Depreciation In a real estate appraisal, **depreciation** refers to any condition that adversely diminishes the value of an improvement to real property; it can be *curable* or *incurable*. As opposed to *incurable depreciation, curable depreciation* is depreciation that can be corrected at an economically feasible cost. Land is not depreciated. Depreciation for tax purposes is discussed in Chapter 25. Depreciation for appraisal purposes can be classified into three types:

- **Physical deterioration** is a loss in value due to wear and tear from use, age, weather, lack of maintenance, or even vandalism. Economically, physical deterioration can be either curable or incurable. *Curable*: A new roof would be a warranted expense on a 40-year-old brick building otherwise in good condition. *Incurable*: Replacing weather-worn siding near the end of a building's economic life may not warrant the financial investment. **Economic life** refers to the period over which a building can be profitably utilized.
- **Functional obsolescence** is caused by a relative loss of building utility. This loss may be due to a deficiency such as a faulty building design, outmoded equipment, or a poorly arranged floor plan. The loss also could be due to an overimprovement (*superadequacy*), such as an in-ground swimming pool in the backyard of a $30,000 house. Functional obsolescence can be curable or incurable. *Curable*: Outmoded plumbing fixtures are usually easily and fairly

inexpensively replaced. *Incurable*: An office building that cannot accommodate a central air-conditioning system has an incurable deficiency.

■ **External obsolescence** is caused by factors not on the subject property (such as environmental, social, or economic forces) and is incurable. Proximity to a nuisance—a polluting factory or a deteriorating neighborhood, for instance—would be an unchangeable factor that could not be cured by the owner of the subject property. This type of depreciation is sometimes called *locational obsolescence* or *economic obsolescence*.

In determining a property's depreciation, most appraisers use the *breakdown method*, in which depreciation is broken down into all three classes, with separate estimates for curable and incurable factors in each class. Depreciation, however, is difficult to measure, and the older the building, the more difficult it is to estimate. Much of functional obsolescence and all of external obsolescence can be evaluated only by analyzing the actions of buyers in the marketplace.

IN PRACTICE   The cost approach is most helpful in the appraisal of special-purpose buildings such as schools, churches, and other public buildings. Such properties are difficult to appraise using other methods because local sales of comparables are seldom available and the properties usually do not generate income.

The Income Approach

The **income approach** to value is based on the premise that the income derived from a property will, to a large extent, influence the value of that property. Residential one-family to four-family properties are usually valued by the gross rent multiplier method, to be discussed later.

The income capitalization approach is used for valuation of income properties such as apartments, offices, and retail and commercial establishments. This approach makes use of both *direct capitalization* and *yield capitalization* methods. The direct capitalization method is the most commonly employed method for most income-producing properties. Figure 14.7 illustrates the steps that an appraiser must go through to develop an indicated value by the direct capitalization method:

1. Estimate annual *potential gross income* (based on market rental rates, not necessarily current rental rates).

2. Based on market experience, deduct an appropriate allowance for vacancy and rent loss to arrive at the *effective gross income*.

3. Based on appropriate operating standards, deduct the annual *operating expenses* of the real estate from the effective gross income to arrive at the annual *net operating income*. Management costs are always included as operating expenses even if the current owner manages the property himself or herself. Mortgage loan payments (including principal and interest), however, are *not* considered operating expenses. For the property to be a viable investment, the net operating income should be sufficient to satisfy the debt service (make the loan payments) and leave some "positive cash flow" income for the owner.

4. Estimate the price a typical investor would pay for the income produced by this particular type and class of property. This is done by estimating the rate of return (or yield) that an investor will demand for the investment of capital in this type of building. This rate of return is called the **capitalization rate** (or "cap" rate) and is determined by comparing the relationship of

The average cap rate for U.S. apartment communities in June 2011 was 6.45%. (*Wall Street Journal*, July 27, 2011)

net income with the sales prices of similar properties that have sold in the current market. For example, a comparable property producing an annual net operating income of $15,000 is sold for $125,000. The capitalization rate is 12% ($15,000 ÷ $125,000). If other comparable properties sold at prices that yielded substantially the same rate, 12% is the rate the appraiser should apply to the subject property.

5. Finally, the property's annual net operating income is divided by the cap rate, resulting in the appraiser's indicated value by the income approach.

FIGURE 14.7: Income Capitalization Approach to Value

Gross Annual Income Estimate		$60,000
(potential rent income plus other income)		
Less vacancy and loss of rent (estimated) @ 5%		– 3,000
Effective Gross Income		$57,000
Expenses:		
Real estate taxes	$9,000	
Insurance	1,000	
Janitor	5,200	
Utilities (electricity, water, gas)	3,600	
Repairs	1,200	
Decorating	1,400	
Replacement of equipment	800	
Maintenance	1,200	
Legal and accounting	600	
Management	3,000	
Total Expenses		$27,000
Annual Net Operating Income		$30,000
Capitalization rate = 10%		
Capitalization of annual net operating income	$\dfrac{\$30{,}000}{0.10}$	

Indicated Value by Income Approach = $300,000

Note: if the annual debt service exceeds $30,000, the property has "negative cash flow," which reduces its value accordingly.

Memory Tip

To calculate value by the income approach, remember the name **IRV**: **i**ncome = **r**ate × **v**alue.

FOR EXAMPLE   If a property has an annual net operating income of $20,000 and the comparable cap rates are 12%, what is the indicated value by the income approach?

Net operating income ÷ capitalization rate = indicated value

$20,000 income ÷ 12% cap rate = $166,700 indicated value by the income approach

This formula and its variations are important in dealing with income property. Variations are as follows:

$$\text{income} = \text{rate} \times \text{value}$$

$$\frac{\text{income}}{\text{rate}} = \text{value}$$

$$\frac{\text{income}}{\text{value}} = \text{rate}$$

Another, and more accurate, method for estimating value by the income capitalization approach can be accomplished by using a yield capitalization method, such as *discounted cash flow analysis*. The application of yield capitalization is beyond the scope of this text.

IN PRACTICE The most difficult step in the income approach to value is determining the appropriate capitalization rate for the property. This rate must be selected to accurately reflect the recapture of the original investment over the building's economic life, give the owner an acceptable rate of return on his investment, and provide for the repayment of borrowed capital. Note that an income property that carries with it a great deal of risk as an investment generally requires a higher rate of return than a property that is considered to be a safer investment.

Gross Rent or Income Multipliers Some properties, such as single-family homes, are not purchased primarily for the income they can produce. As a substitute for a more elaborate income capitalization analysis, the **gross rent multiplier** (GRM) method often is used in appraising such properties. The GRM relates the sales price of a property to its rental income; gross *monthly* income is used for residential property. The gross rent multiplier formula is as follows:

$$\frac{\text{sales price}}{\text{gross monthly rental income}} = \text{gross rent multiplier}$$

For example, if a home recently sold for $97,000 and its gross monthly rental income was $895, the GRM for the property is computed in the following manner:

$$\frac{\$97,000}{\$895} = 108.4 \text{ GRM}$$

To establish an accurate GRM, an appraiser must have recent sales and rental data from properties that are similar to the subject property. The resulting GRM then can be applied to the estimated fair market rental of the subject property to arrive at its market value (see Figure 14.8). The formula is

gross monthly income × GRM = indicated market value

FOR EXAMPLE A residential rental has a gross monthly rental income of $925. The GRM computed for rental properties in the area is 110. Therefore, the indicated market value by the gross rent multiplier method would be $101,750.

$925 gross monthly income × 110 GRM = $101,750 indicated market value

Multipliers

GRM uses gross *monthly* income; it applies primarily to residential properties.

GIM uses *gross annual* income; it applies primarily to industrial and commercial properties.

FIGURE 14.8: Gross Rent Multiplier

Comparable No.	Sales Price	Monthly Rent	GRM
1	$93,600	$650	144
2	78,500	450	174
3	95,500	675	141
4	82,000	565	145
Subject	?	625	?

Note: Based on an analysis of these comparisons, a GRM of 145 seems reasonable for homes in this area. In the opinion of an appraiser, then, the indicated value of the subject property would be $625 × 145, or $90,625.

Gross *annual* income is used in appraising industrial and commercial properties. The ratio used to convert annual income into market value is called a **gross income multiplier** (GIM). The formula to determine a GIM follows:

$$\frac{\text{sales price}}{\text{annual gross income}} = \text{gross income multiplier}$$

Much skill is required to use multipliers accurately because no fixed multiplier is available for all areas or all types of properties. Therefore, many appraisers view the technique simply as a quick, informal way to check the validity of a property value obtained by the other appraisal methods. In fact, GRMs and GIMs have been used less in recent years because this technique not only fails to take into consideration the tax situations of different possible investors but also fails to recognize alternative methods of financing.

Reconciliation

If the three approaches to value are applied to the same property, they normally will produce three separate indications of value. **Reconciliation** is the art of analyzing and effectively weighing the findings from the three approaches. Although each approach may serve as an independent guide to value, whenever possible all three approaches should be used as a check on the final opinion of value. The process of reconciliation is more complicated than simply taking the average of the three indications of value. An average implies that the data and logic applied in each of the approaches are equally valid and reliable and should therefore be given equal weight. In fact, certain approaches are more valid and reliable with certain kinds and ages of properties and certain time periods in the real estate cycle than with others.

For example, in appraising a residence, the income approach is rarely used, and the cost approach is of limited value unless the home is relatively new; therefore, the sales comparison approach usually is given greatest weight in valuing single-family residences. In the appraisal of income or investment property, the income approach normally would be given the greatest weight. In the appraisal of churches, libraries, museums, schools, and other special-use properties where there are few sales and little or no income, the cost approach usually is assigned the greatest weight. From this analysis, or reconciliation, a single opinion of market value is produced.

IN PRACTICE In an effort to reduce costs and speed up loan processing, both Fannie Mae and Freddie Mac (secondary mortgage market entities) are permitting expedited appraisals. Requirements vary, but in some cases they require only that the appraiser first "drive by" the property to determine that a building exists on the property and there are no obvious major problems. Then the appraiser would develop an opinion of value using only the sales comparison approach with appropriate adjustments on three comparable sales. The interior of the building would not be examined unless the appraiser saw a problem during the drive-by appraisal.

PRICING A PROPERTY

A *comparative market analysis* (CMA) is an analysis of market activity among comparable properties; it is not the same as a formal appraisal.

Generally, an appraisal is not conducted on a property until after a contract is received from a buyer. Therefore, initial pricing of the real estate to enable the seller's receiving the highest price in the least amount of time is of primary importance to a listing agent.

It is the responsibility of the broker or salesperson to advise, counsel, and assist in the pricing process, but ultimately it is the seller who must determine a listing price for the property. Because the average seller does not have the background to make an informed decision about a fair market value, the real estate agent prepares a comparative market analysis that can provide guidance to the seller in this process.

Comparative Market Analysis The **comparative market analysis** (CMA), also known as a *competitive market analysis*, is a variation of the sales comparison approach that is prepared by real estate agents to assist sellers and buyers with the determination of listing prices and offering prices. If possible, a CMA should include homes that have sold within the past six months in the same neighborhood as the one being evaluated. Properties should be comparable to the subject property: similar in age, condition, size, amenities, number of rooms, and existing mortgage type. The CMA also includes an analysis of homes currently on the market and homes for which the listings expired before sale. The CMA range of prices for similar sold properties will show a seller what the home probably will sell for and will help an agent decide whether to accept a listing. The licensee must provide the following written statement to the person for whom a market analysis is prepared:

> THIS IS A BROKER PRICE OPINION OR COMPARATIVE MARKET ANALYSIS AND SHOULD NOT BE CONSIDERED AN APPRAISAL. In making any decision that relies upon my work, you should know that I have not followed the guidelines for development of an appraisal or analysis contained in the Uniform Standards of Professional Appraisal Practice of the Appraisal Foundation.

Pricing a home accurately is one of the most important factors in a home's selling. If a home is priced too high, it will generally take longer to sell and the ultimate sales price will likely be lower than if the property were priced correctly when listed. If adequate comparable properties are not available, or if the seller feels the property is unique in some way, a full-scale real estate appraisal may be warranted before listing the property. A broker should reject any listing in which the seller insists on a substantially exaggerated listing price after receiving the CMA or the appraiser's opinion of value.

IN PRACTICE   Although sometimes used synonymously with CMA, a *broker price opinion* (BPO) is more than a CMA but less than a full appraisal. In addition to the data collected for a CMA (both current listings and sold properties), the BPO includes a neighborhood analysis, an estimate of needed repairs, and a *probable selling price* for the property if sold "as is" or "as repaired." Because brokers' fees for preparing a BPO are generally considerably less than the fee for an appraisal, BPOs are frequently used by lending institutions, attorneys, and loss mitigation companies to determine a value to weigh against the options of foreclosure, deed in lieu of foreclosure, short sale, or mortgage modification. The Freddie Mac Broker's Price Opinion form is available at www.freddiemac.com/sell/forms/pdf/1092.pdf.

Seller's Net Return   A major concern of all sellers is how much money they will realize from the sale. Assume that an estimate of value, determined from a CMA, is $155,000. After paying the broker's commission (estimated at 7% in this hypothetical situation) and the other applicable closing costs (estimated at $4,485 for the conventional loan in this illustration), the seller will net $139,665:

$155,000	estimate of value
− 10,850	commission (at 7%)
− 4,485	other closing costs
$139,665	net to seller

More detailed information for calculating closing costs is provided in Chapter 20.

APPRAISAL REGULATIONS

Since 1939, a license has been required to appraise real property for a fee in Texas (unless otherwise exempted by law)—the original requirement was a real estate broker's license. In 1989, as a result of the collapse of many savings and loan associations (which was at least partly due to faulty appraisals), Congress passed the *Financial Institutions Reform, Recovery, and Enforcement Act* (FIRREA) to regulate the appraisal industry nationwide. FIRREA required that a licensed or certified appraiser perform any appraisal used in connection with a federally related transaction of $250,000 and above. *Federally related transactions* are real estate financial transactions that require the services of an appraiser and ones in which a federal financial institution, regulatory agency, or secondary market participant engages. In 1991, the Texas Appraiser Licensing and Certification Board (TALCB) was established to license, certify, and regulate real estate appraisers in Texas and to safeguard the public interest by protecting consumers of real estate services. Effective September 1, 2011, only persons licensed or certified as an appraiser, registered as a temporary out-of-state appraiser, or approved as an appraiser trainee can perform an appraisal of real estate. Unless also licensed or certified by TALCB, a TREC-licensed broker or salesperson can no longer *appraise* property (H.B. 2375; S.B. 747, 2011). All appraisers must adhere to the *Uniform Standards of Professional Appraisal Practice* (USPAP), which set forth the procedures to be followed in developing an appraisal and the manner in which an appraisal is communicated.

FIGURE 14.9: Texas Appraiser Licensing and Certification Board Summary of Requirements

SUMMARY OF REQUIREMENTS
(Effective January 1, 2014)

	CERTIFIED GENERAL Real Estate Appraiser	CERTIFIED RESIDENTIAL Real Estate Appraiser	STATE LICENSED Real Estate Appraiser
EDUCATION	300 hours of AQB required "Core Curriculum" courses and a bachelors degree or higher. In lieu of the required degree Thirty (30) semester credit hours in the following courses; English Composition; Micro Economics; Macro Economics; Finance; Algebra, Geometry or higher mathematics; Statistics; Computer Science; Business or Real Estate Law; and two (2) elective courses in accounting; geography; ageconomics; business management; or real estate. Must include15 hours of the Uniform Standards of Professional Appraisal Practice (USPAP) completed after February 2002.	200 hours of AQB required "Core Curriculum" courses and an Associate degree or higher. In lieu of the required degree, Twenty-one (21) semester credit hours in the following courses; English Composition; Micro Economics; Macro Economics; Finance; Algebra, Geometry or higher mathematics; Statistics; Computer Science; Business or Real Estate Law. Must include 15 hours of the Uniform Standards of Professional Appraisal Practice (USPAP) completed after February 2002.	150 hours of AQB required "Core Curriculum" courses. Must include 15 hours of Uniform Standards of Professional Appraisal Practice (USPAP) completed after February 2002.
EXPERIENCE	3,000 hours of acceptable real estate appraisal experience over a minimum of 30 months (2 1/2 years). A minimum of 1,500 hours must be in non-residential real estate appraising. Experience may be acquired anytime during the appraiser's career when that person had legal authority to perform real estate appraisals. Must comply with the Uniform Standards of Professional Appraisal Practice (USPAP).	2, 500 hours of acceptable real estate appraisal experience over a minimum of 24 months (2 years). Experience may be acquired anytime during the appraiser's career when that person had legal authority to perform real estate appraisals. Must comply with USPAP.	2,000 hours of acceptable real estate appraisal experience over a minimum of 12 months. Experience may be acquired anytime during the appraiser's career when that person had legal authority to perform real estate appraisals. Must comply with USPAP.
EXAM	The National Uniform State Appraiser Examination developed by the Appraiser Qualifications Board (AQB) for general certification examinations. Exam is administered by PSI, a national testing service. Current exam fee: $61. Fee paid directly to PSI. DO NOT submit examination fees to TALCB.	The National Uniform State Appraiser Examination developed by the Appraiser Qualifications Board (AQB) for certified residential examinations. Exam is administered by PSI, a national testing service. Current exam fee: $61. Fee paid directly to PSI. DO NOT submit examination fees to TALCB.	The National Uniform State Appraiser Examination developed by the Appraiser Qualifications Board (AQB) for state licensed examinations. Exam is administered by PSI, a national testing service. Current exam fee: $61. Fee paid directly to PSI. DO NOT submit examination fees to TALCB.
App Fees	$405.00 Application Fee	$355.00 Application Fee	$325.00 Application Fee
COMMENTS	May sit for the examination after ALL educational requirements have been met and eligibility has been established. A person is NOT certified until ALL requirements are met (including experience) and the certification has been issued by the TALCB. Must submit completed Experience Affidavit and Experience Log together with $400 in fees. NOTE: An $80.00 Federal registry Fee will be due after the exam is passed and all requirements are met.	May sit for the examination after ALL educational requirements have been met and eligibility has been established. A person is NOT certified until ALL requirements are met (including experience) and the certification has been issued by the TALCB. Must submit completed Experience Affidavit and Experience Log together with $350 in fees. NOTE: An $80.00 Federal registry Fee will be due after the exam is passed and all requirements are met.	May sit for the examination after ALL educational requirements have been met and eligibility has been established. A person is NOT certified until ALL requirements are met (including experience) and the certification has been issued by the TALCB. Must submit completed Experience Affidavit and Experience Log together with $325 in fees. NOTE: An $80.00 Federal registry Fee will be due after the exam is passed and all requirements are met.
SCOPE OF PRACTICE (§153.8)	May appraise all types of real property without regard to complexity or transaction value for federally related transactions (FRT) and non-federally related transactions (NON-FRT). Must comply with Uniform Standards of Professional Appraisal Practice (USPAP).	May appraise 1-4 unit residential properties without regard to transaction value or complexity of the appraisal for federally related transactions (FRT) and non-federally related transactions (Non-FRT). May associate with a Certified General appraiser, who must sign the report, to appraise non-residential properties. Must comply with USPAP.	May appraise residential 1-4 unit properties when the transaction value is less than $1M (non-complex) or 250K (complex) in both federally related transactions (FRT) and non-federally related transactions (Non-FRT). May associate with a Certified General appraiser, who must sign the report, to appraise nonresidential properties. Must comply with USPAP.

(Revised 01/2014)

Texas law provides for four classifications of state appraiser certifications or licenses, all of which meet Appraiser Qualifications Board (AQB) minimum national standards: Certified General Real Estate Appraiser, Certified Residential Real Estate Appraiser, State Licensed Real Estate Appraiser, and Appraiser Trainee. The appraiser education, experience, and examination requirements, along with the scope of practice for which each classification is permitted, are shown in Figure 14.9. All applicants must meet certain education requirements, including at least 60 classroom hours of specified real estate appraisal courses and 15 classroom hours of *USPAP*. Applicants for Certified General Real Estate Appraiser must have at least a bachelor's degree *or* 30 semester hours of specified general education courses. Applicants for Certified Residential Real Estate Appraiser are required to have at least an associate degree *or* 21 semester hours of specific general education courses. The semester-hour or degree requirements are in addition to mandated classroom hours of real estate appraisal courses. The Appraiser Trainee classification permits a person with no real estate appraisal experience and only 75 hours of qualifying education to enter the real estate appraisal profession and to work toward the requirements to become a State Licensed Real Estate Appraiser.

After licensure, appraisers and trainees must complete 28 classroom hours of Appraiser Continuing Education (ACE) before each two-year license renewal, including the seven-hour *National USPAP Update course.*

IN PRACTICE   Real estate brokers and salespersons may provide a "written analysis, opinion, or conclusion relating to the estimated price of real property if the analysis, opinion, or conclusion is not referred to as an appraisal, is provided in the ordinary course of the person's business, and is related to the actual or potential management, acquisition, disposition, or encumbrance of an interest in real property" (H.B. 2375; S.B. 747, 2011). *USPAP* standards do not apply to the activities of a real estate broker in the normal course of seeking listings or determining a comparative market value for a specific property.

The TALCB is an independent subdivision of TREC. To learn more about the appraiser requirements in Texas, visit the TALCB website.

WEBLINK @
www.talcb.texas.gov
www.appraisalfoundation.org

SUMMARY

Although there are many types of value, the most common objective of a real estate appraisal is to develop an opinion of market value—the most probable sales price of a property. Although appraisals are concerned with values, costs, and prices, it is vital to understand the distinctions among the terms. Value is an estimate of future benefits, cost represents a measure of past expenditures, and price reflects the actual amount of money paid for a property. The value of real estate is influenced by basic economic principles: highest and best use, substitution, supply and demand, conformity, externalities, anticipation, increasing and diminishing returns, plottage, contribution, competition, and change.

A professional appraiser analyzes a property through three approaches to value. In the sales comparison approach, the value of the subject property is compared with the values of others like it that have sold recently. Because no two properties are exactly alike, adjustments must be made to account for differences. With the cost approach, an appraiser calculates the cost of building a similar structure on a similar site. Then he subtracts depreciation (losses in value), which reflects the differences between new properties of this type and the present condition of the subject property. The three types of depreciation typically utilized in the appraisal process are physical deterioration, functional obsolescence, and external obsolescence. The income approach is an analysis based on the relationship between the rate of return that an investor requires and the net operating income that a property produces. A special informal version of the income approach, called the *gross rent multiplier* (GRM), often is used to estimate the value of single-family residential properties that are not usually rented but could be. The GRM is computed by dividing the sales price of a property by its gross monthly rent.

Normally the application of the three approaches will result in three different indications of value. In the process of reconciliation, the validity and reliability of each approach are weighed objectively to arrive at the single best and most supportable conclusion of value. A real estate licensee prepares a comparative market analysis, an abbreviated variation of the sales comparison approach, to assist sellers in pricing property or to assist buyers in determining how much to offer for a property.

CHAPTER 14 QUESTIONS

1. A competitive market analysis
   a. cannot help the seller set a price for the real estate.
   b. is a comparison of recently sold properties that are similar to a seller's parcel of real estate.
   c. is the same as an appraisal.
   d. should not be retained in the property's listing file because of its confidentiality.

2. The elements of value include which of the following?
   a. Anticipation
   b. Scarcity
   c. Competition
   d. Balance

3. Two locations, 457 and 459 Tarpepper Street, are adjacent vacant lots, each worth approximately $50,000. If the owner sells them as a combined parcel, however, they will be worth $120,000. What principle does this illustrate?
   a. Substitution
   b. Plottage
   c. Externalities
   d. Contribution

4. The amount of money a property brings in the marketplace is its
   a. market price.
   b. market value.
   c. intrinsic value.
   d. book value.

5. An appraisal may *NOT* be conducted by
   a. a Texas-licensed appraiser.
   b. an out-of-state appraiser, registered only temporarily in Texas.
   c. an appraiser trainee.
   d. a real estate broker.

6. Howard constructs an eight-bedroom brick house with a tennis court, a greenhouse, and an indoor pool in a neighborhood of modest two-bedroom and three-bedroom frame houses on narrow lots. The value of Howard's house is likely to be affected by what principle?
   a. Conformity
   b. Assemblage
   c. Externalities
   d. Contribution

7. *Reconciliation* refers to which of the following?
   a. Separating the value of the land from the total value of the property to compute depreciation
   b. Analyzing the results obtained by the three approaches to value to determine a final opinion of value
   c. The process by which an appraiser determines the highest and best use for a parcel of land
   d. Averaging the results of the three approaches to determine a final opinion of value

8. One method an appraiser uses to determine a building's replacement cost involves an estimate of the raw materials needed to build the structure, plus labor and indirect costs. This is called the
   a. square-foot method.
   b. quantity-survey method.
   c. cubic-foot method.
   d. unit-in-place method.

9. If a property's annual net income is $37,500 and it is valued at $300,000, what is its capitalization rate?
   a. 12.5%
   b. 10.5%
   c. 15%
   d. 18%

10. An appraiser must determine certain data before value can be computed by the income approach. Which one of the following is NOT required for this process?

   a. Annual net operating income
   b. Capitalization rate
   c. Accrued depreciation
   d. Annual gross income

11. The ceiling, or top limit, of value of an improved parcel of real estate usually is the

   a. sales price paid for a similar property.
   b. cost of buying a lot and erecting a similar building on it.
   c. capitalized value of present net rents.
   d. depreciated value of the building plus the cost of land.

12. An appraiser is asked to determine the value of an existing strip shopping center. Which approach to value will be given the MOST weight?

   a. Cost approach
   b. Sales comparison approach
   c. Income approach
   d. Reproduction approach

13. The market value of a parcel of real estate is

   a. an estimate of the most probable price it should bring.
   b. the amount of money paid for the property.
   c. its value without improvements.
   d. its cost.

14. Capitalization is the process by which annual net operating income is used to

   a. determine cost.
   b. estimate value.
   c. establish depreciation.
   d. determine potential tax value.

15. In the cost approach to value, it is necessary to

   a. determine a dollar value for depreciation.
   b. estimate future expenses and operating costs.
   c. check sales prices of recently sold houses in the area.
   d. reconcile differing value indications.

16. In the sales comparison approach to value, the probable sales price of a building may be estimated by

   a. considering sales of similar properties.
   b. deducting accrued depreciation.
   c. determining construction cost.
   d. computing replacement cost of the structure.

17. Which factor is NOT important in comparing properties under the sales comparison approach to value?

   a. Difference in dates of sale
   b. Difference in financing terms
   c. Difference in appearance and condition
   d. Difference in original cost

18. In the income approach to value,

   a. the reproduction or replacement cost of the building must be computed.
   b. the capitalization rate, or rate of return, must be estimated.
   c. depreciation must be determined.
   d. sales of similar properties must be considered.

19. From the reproduction or replacement cost of the building, an appraiser deducts depreciation, which represents

   a. the remaining useful economic life of the building.
   b. remodeling costs to increase rentals.
   c. loss of value due to any cause.
   d. costs to modernize the building.

20. Which formula is used to determine the capitalization rate of an office building?

   a. Income = rate × value
   b. Value = income ÷ rate
   c. Rate = income ÷ value
   d. Rate = value × income

21. The appraised value of a residence with four bedrooms and one bathroom would probably be reduced because of

   a. external obsolescence.
   b. functional obsolescence.
   c. curable physical deterioration.
   d. incurable physical deterioration.

Detailed rationales for the end-of-chapter review questions are available online at www.dearborn.com through the *Instructor Resource Guides* link.

CHAPTER 15

Real Estate Financing Principles

■ **LEARNING OBJECTIVES**   *When you have completed this chapter, you will be able to*

- **describe** the two theories of mortgage law and the two primary loan instruments executed for a mortgage loan in Texas;
- **identify** the basic provisions of a promissory note and a deed of trust;
- **explain** the procedures involved in a foreclosure, including the right of redemption;
- **distinguish** among the foreclosure-avoidance options; and
- **define** the following *key terms*:

acceleration clause	interest	promissory note
alienation clause	lien theory	redemption
amortized loan	mortgage	release deed
deed in lieu of foreclosure	mortgagee	release of lien
deed of trust	mortgagor	satisfaction of mortgage
defeasance clause	negotiable instrument	short sale
deficiency judgment	nonrecourse note	title theory
foreclosure	power-of-sale clause	trust deed
hypothecation	prepayment penalty	usury

OVERVIEW

Rarely is a parcel of real estate purchased on a cash basis; almost every real estate transaction involves some type of financing. Thus an understanding of real estate financing is of prime importance to the real estate licensee. Usually the buyer in a real estate transaction borrows the major portion of the purchase price by securing a loan and pledging the real property involved as security (collateral) for the loan. This generally is known as a *mortgage loan*.

This chapter explores the principles of mortgage financing through the documents required to establish a valid lien—the promissory note and the deed of trust—and the foreclosure procedures followed if a borrower defaults under the terms of the deed of trust. The sources for mortgage money and some specifics regarding the most common types of loans are discussed in Chapter 16.

MORTGAGE THEORY

Remember

The "*or*" gives to the "*ee*." The *mortgagor* (borrower) gives the mortgage document to the lender. The *mortgagee* (lender) receives the property as security.

The concept of mortgage lending originated in England under Anglo-Saxon law. Originally, a borrower who needed to finance the purchase of land (the **mortgagor**) was forced to convey title to the property to the lender (the **mortgagee**) to ensure payment of the debt. If the obligation was not paid, the mortgagor automatically forfeited the land to the creditor, who was already the legal owner of the property. Through the years, English courts began to acknowledge that a mortgage was only a *security device* and the mortgagor was the true owner of the mortgaged real estate. Under this concept, real estate was merely given as *security* for the payment of a debt, which was represented by a *note*.

United States Mortgage Law

After gaining independence from England, the original 13 colonies adopted the English laws as their basic body of law. From their inception, American courts of equity considered a mortgage a voluntary lien on real estate, given to secure the payment of a debt or the performance of an obligation. Those states, including Texas, that interpret a mortgage purely as a lien on real property are called **lien theory** states. In such states, if a mortgagor defaults, the lender is required to foreclose the lien, offer the property for sale, and apply the funds received from the sale to reduce or extinguish the obligation. The owner, not the lender, has a right to rental income while property is posted for foreclosure. Although many lien theory states allow a statutory redemption period, Texas *law contains no provision for redemption of owner-occupied property foreclosed under a deed of trust.*

Other states recognize a lender as the owner of mortgaged land. This ownership is subject to defeat on full payment of the debt or performance of the obligation. These states are called **title theory** states. Under title theory, a lender has the right to possession of and rents from the mortgaged property on default by the borrower.

SECURITY AND DEBT

Generally, any interest in real estate that may be sold may be pledged as security for a debt. The basic principle of property law—that a person cannot convey greater rights in property than she actually has—applies equally to the right to mortgage. The owner of a fee simple estate can mortgage the fee, and the owner of a leasehold or subleasehold can mortgage that leasehold interest. For example, a large retail corporation renting space in a shopping center may mortgage its leasehold interest to finance some remodeling work.

As discussed in Chapter 9, the owner of a cooperative interest holds a personal property interest, not an interest in real estate. Although a cooperative owner has a leasehold interest, the nature of that leasehold is not generally acceptable to lenders as collateral. Owners of a condominium unit, however, can mortgage their fee simple interest in the condominium unit.

Mortgage Loan Instruments

There are two parts to a mortgage loan—the debt itself and the security for the debt. Therefore, when a property is to be mortgaged, the owner must execute, or sign, two separate instruments:

1. The **promissory note** is the promise, or agreement, to repay the debt in definite installments with interest. The mortgagor executes one or more promissory notes to total the amount of the debt. The note *creates* the debt.
2. The **mortgage** is the document that creates the lien, or conveys the property to the mortgagee as *security* for the debt. The **deed of trust** is the mortgage document generally used in Texas to secure payment of the debt. As backup security, a vendor's lien, a special type of mortgage discussed in Chapter 11, is reserved in the warranty deed conveying title to the buyer. The vendor's lien is held by the seller until paid in full for the property. If third-party financing is obtained, this lien is usually assigned to the lender.

Hypothecation is the pledging of property as security for payment of a loan without giving up possession of the property. A pledge of security—the deed of trust—is not legally effective unless there is a debt to secure. *Both the note and the deed of trust must be executed to create an enforceable mortgage lien.*

PROVISIONS OF THE NOTE

The promissory note (or notes) executed by a borrower (known as the *maker* or *payor*) generally states the lender (payee), the amount of the debt, the time and method of payment, and the rate of interest. It also may refer to, or repeat, several of the clauses that appear in the mortgage document or deed of trust. The note, like the mortgage or deed of trust, should be signed by all parties who have an interest in the property. Where homestead or community property is involved, both spouses have an interest in the property and must sign the note and deed of trust. An exception is community property where one spouse is designated as the manager of that particular piece of community property. Figure 15.1 is an example of a note commonly used with a deed of trust.

FIGURE 15.1: Multi-State Fixed Rate Note

GF No. 123456

NOTE

June 15, 20XX   Dallas   Texas
[Date]   [City]   [State]

3040 North Racine, Dallas, TX 75340
[Property Address]

1. BORROWER'S PROMISE TO PAY

In return for a loan that I have received, I promise to pay U.S. $165,000 (this amount is called "Principal"), plus interest, to the order of the Lender. The Lender is

Thrift Federal Savings

I will make all payments under this Note in the form of cash, check or money order.

I understand that the Lender may transfer this Note. The Lender or anyone who takes this Note by transfer and who is entitled to receive payments under this Note is called the "Note Holder."

2. INTEREST

Interest will be charged on unpaid principal until the full amount of Principal has been paid. I will pay interest at a yearly rate of 7% .

The interest rate required by this Section 2 is the rate I will pay both before and after any default described in Section 6(B) of this Note.

3. PAYMENTS

(A) Time and Place of Payments

I will pay principal and interest by making a payment every month.

I will make my monthly payments on the 1st day of each month beginning on August 1, 20XX. I will make these payments every month until I have paid all of the principal and interest and any other charges described below that I may owe under this Note. Each monthly payment will be applied as of its scheduled due date and will be applied to interest before Principal If, on, July 1, 2026 I still owe amounts under this Note, I will pay those amounts in full on that date, which is called the "Maturity Date."

I will make my monthly payments at the office of the Lender in Dallas, Dallas County, Texas, or a different place if required by the Note Holder.

(B) Amount of Monthly Payments

My monthly payment will be in the amount of U.S. $1,482.00 .

4. BORROWER'S RIGHT TO PREPAY

I have the right to make payments of Principal at any time before they are due. A payment of Principal only is known as a "Prepayment." When I make a Prepayment, I will tell the Note Holder in writing that I am doing so. I may not designate a payment as Prepayment if I have not made all the monthly payments due under the Note.

I may make a full Prepayment or partial Prepayments without paying a Prepayment charge. The Note Holder will use my Prepayments to reduce the amount of Principal that I owe under this Note. However, the Note Holder may apply my Prepayment to the accrued and unpaid interest on the Prepayment amount, before applying my Prepayment to reduce the Principal amount of the Note. If I make a partial Prepayment, there will be no changes in the due date or in the amount of my monthly payment unless the Note Holder agrees in writing to those changes.

FIGURE 15.1: Multi-State Fixed Rate Note (continued)

5. LOAN CHARGES

If a law, which applies to this loan and which sets maximum loan charges, is finally interpreted so that the interest or other loan charges collected or to be collected in connection with this loan exceed the permitted limits, then: (a) any such loan charge shall be reduced by the amount necessary to reduce the charge to the permitted limit; and (b) any sums already collected from me which exceeded permitted limits will be refunded to me. The Note Holder may chose to make this refund by reducing the Principal I owe under this Note or by making a direct payment to me. If a refund reduces Principal, the reduction will be treated as a partial Prepayment.

6. BORROWER'S FAILURE TO PAY AS REQUIRED

(A) Late Charge for Overdue Payments

If the Note Holder has not received the full amount of any monthly payment by the end of fifteen calendar days after the date it is due, I will pay a late charge to the Note Holder. The amount of the charge will be 5.0% of my overdue payment of principal and interest. I will pay this late charge promptly but only once on each late payment.

(B) Default

If I do not pay the full amount of each monthly payment on the date it is due, I will be in default.

(C) Notice of Default

If I am in default, the Note Holder may send me a written notice telling me that I do not pay the overdue amount by a certain date, the Note Holder may require me to pay immediately the full amount of Principal which has not been paid and all the interest that I owe on that amount. That date must be at least 30 days after the date on which the notice is mailed to me or delivered by other means.

(D) No Waiver By Note Holder

Even if, at a time when I am in default, the Note Holder does not require me to pay immediately in full as described above, the Note Holder will still have the right to do so if I am in default at a later time.

(E) Payment of Note Holder's Costs and Expense

If the Note Holder has required me to pay immediately in full as described above, the Note Holder will have the right to be paid back by me for all of its costs and expenses in enforcing this Note to the extent not prohibited by applicable law. Those expenses include, for example, reasonable attorneys' fees.

7. GIVING OF NOTICES

Unless applicable law requires a different method, any notice that must be given to me under this Note will be given by delivering it or by mailing it by first class mail to me at the Property Address above or at a different address if I give the Note Holder a notice of my different address.

Any notice that must be given to the Note Holder under this Note will be given by delivering it or by mailing it by first class mail to the Note Holder at the address stated in Section 3(A) above or at a different address if I am given a notice of that different address.

8. OBLIGATIONS OF PERSONS UNDER THIS NOTE

If more than one person signs this Note, each person is fully and personally obligated to keep all of the promises made in this Note, including the promise to pay the full amount owed. Any person who is a guarantor, surety or endorser of this Note is also obligated to do these things. Any person who takes over these obligations, including the obligations of a guarantor, surety or endorser of this Note, is also obligated to keep all of the promises made in this Note. The Note Holder may enforce its rights under this Note against each person individually or against all of us together. This means that any one of us may be required to pay all of the amounts owed under this Note.

9. WAIVERS

I and any other person who has obligations under this Note waive the rights of Presentment and Notice of Dishonor. "Presentment" means the right to require the Note Holder to demand payment of amounts due. "Notice of Dishonor" means the right to require the Note Holder to give notice to other persons that amounts due have not been paid.

FIGURE 15.1: Multi-State Fixed Rate Note (continued)

10. UNIFORM SECURED NOTE

This Note is a uniform instrument with limited variations in some jurisdictions. In addition to the protections given to the Note Holder under this Note, a Mortgage, Deed of Trust, or Security Deed (the "Security Instrument"), dated the same date as this Note, protects the Note Holder from possible losses which might result if I do not keep the promises which I make in this Note. That Security Instrument describes how and under what conditions I may be required to make immediate payment in full of all amounts I owe under this Note. Some of those conditions are described as follows:

If all or any part of the Property or any Interest in the Property is sold or transferred (or if Borrower is not a natural person and a beneficial interest in Borrower is sold or transferred) without Lender's prior written consent, Lender may require immediate payment in full of all sums secured by this Security Instrument. However, this option shall not be exercised by Lender if such exercise is prohibited by Applicable Law.

If Lender exercises this option, Lender shall give Borrower notice of acceleration. The notice shall provide a period of not less than 30 days from the date the notice is given in accordance with Section 15 within which Borrower must pay all sums secured by this Security Instrument. If Borrower fails to pay these sums prior to the expiration of this period, Lender may invoke any remedies permitted by this Security Instrument without further notice or demand on Borrower.

NOTICE
THIS WRITTEN LOAN AGREEMENT REPRESENTS THE FINAL AGREEMENT BETWEEN THE PARTIES AND MAY NOT BE CONTRADICTED BY EVIDENCE OF PRIOR, CONTEMPORANEOUS, OR SUBSEQUENT ORAL AGREEMENTS OF THE PARTIES.

THERE ARE NO UNWRITTEN ORAL AGREEMENTS BETWEEN THE PARTIES.

WITNESS THE HAND(S) AND SEAL(S) OF THE UNDERSIGNED

_____(Seal)   _____(Seal)
- Borrower   - Borrower

_____(Seal)   _____(Seal)
- Borrower   - Borrower

_____(Seal)   _____(Seal)
- Borrower   - Borrower

_____(Seal)   _____(Seal)
- Borrower   - Borrower

[Sign Original Only]

Page 3 of 3_____ Initials

A note is a **negotiable instrument** like a check or bank draft. The individual who holds the note is called the *payee*. He may transfer the right to receive payment to a third party in one of two ways: by signing the instrument over to the third party *or*, in some cases, by merely delivering the instrument to that person. The transferee, or new holder of the note, is known as a *holder in due course*. Once a loan is closed, the note and mortgage instrument become marketable paper that can be assigned to an entity wishing to purchase that paper for investment purposes.

FOR EXAMPLE   When a loan is sold to Fannie Mae, Freddie Mac, or another secondary mortgage market, as will be discussed in the next chapter, the note is endorsed and signed over to that entity as the holder in due course. Payments on the loan continue to be paid to the original lender or to a designated loan servicer, who passes the funds on to the purchaser in the secondary market.

Interest

The best predictor of real estate mortgage interest rates is the 10-year Treasury bond rate.

A charge for the use of money is called **interest**. A lender charges a borrower a certain percentage of the principal as interest for each year the debt is outstanding. The amount of interest due on any one installment payment date is calculated by computing the total yearly interest, based on the unpaid balance, and dividing that figure by the number of payments made each year. For example, if the current outstanding loan balance is $50,000 with interest at the rate of 12% per annum and constant monthly payments of $617.40, the interest and principal due on the next payment would be computed as follows:

Step 1: $50,000 loan balance × 0.12 = $6,000 annual interest

Step 2: $6,000 annual interest ÷ 12 = $500.00 month's interest

Step 3: $617.40 P&I payment − 500.00 interest = $117.40 month's principal reduction

The monthly mortgage payment (P&I) remains the same from the first payment until the last payment on a fixed-rate note. This is called a monthly direct reduction, **amortized loan**. The interest on monthly amortized loans sold to Fannie Mae and Freddie Mac is calculated on a 30-day month/360-day year basis; that is, annual interest divided by 360 days equals the daily interest charge. Ginnie Mae requires a 365-day year interest computation; annual interest divided by 365 days equals the daily interest charge.

Interest may be due either at the end of each payment period (known as payment *in arrears*) or at the beginning of each payment period (payment in *advance*). Whether interest is charged in arrears or in advance is specified in the note. In practice, the distinction becomes important if the property is sold before the debt is repaid in full, as discussed in Chapter 20. Most residential notes specify that interest is paid in arrears; when a note payment is made, it includes interest for the prior month. For example, May's payment includes interest for the use of the borrowed money in April.

IN PRACTICE   As discussed in Chapter 4, interest payments made under a mortgage loan on the taxpayer's residence are deductible for federal income tax purposes. This deduction in effect reduces the borrower's total cost of housing for the year. Under most types of amortized loans, the borrower pays mostly interest in the early years of the loan, and thus the borrower's tax liability will be reduced even more for these years than in the later years of the loan.

Usury   The maximum rate of interest that may be charged on mortgage loans is set by state law. Charging interest in excess of this rate is called **usury**, and lenders are penalized for making usurious loans. Usury laws were enacted to protect borrowers from unscrupulous lenders that charge unreasonably high interest rates.

Under Texas state law, the maximum rate of interest is determined by the buyer's use of the property. The parties to a written contract that is primarily for personal, family, household, or agricultural use may agree to any rate of interest that does not exceed 18% per year. This ceiling may be raised if a floating index calculated by the Federal Reserve Board and published by the Consumer Credit Commissioner in the *Texas Register* exceeds 18% per year. In that event, the new usury ceiling is 24% per year, but the rate will "float" between 18 and 24%, based on the published index.

For credit extended for business, commercial, investment, or similar-purpose loans, the maximum interest rate may rise, via the floating index, to 28% per year. A lender that makes usurious loans in Texas is subject to substantial penalties, which may include a forfeiture of all principal and interest, as well as reasonable attorney fees and other costs.

Money available for borrowing is a commodity subject to the economic laws of supply and demand, and lenders are in business to make money by lending money and charging interest. When plenty of money is available, interest rates become fairly low. When money is scarce, interest rates go up. Because both lenders and consumers want to earn a fair return on their money, they invest their funds where they will yield the highest rate of interest. Banks, wanting the deposits of consumers, will raise interest rates paid to depositors to compete with higher yielding alternative investments. They then will raise interest rates charged to borrowers for home and consumer loans. The usury laws protect the consumer against unreasonably high interest rates, but they also free lenders to make loans at economically viable interest rates.

IN PRACTICE   Texas usury rates were established during a time of high interest rates. Because current rates are much lower than the usury limits, the usury law has little significance in today's lending market.

Prepayment

When a loan is paid in installments over a long term, the total interest paid by the borrower can be a larger amount of money than the loan principal. If such a loan is paid off ahead of its full term, the lender will collect less interest than planned. For this reason, during the first three to five years of the loan, some mortgage notes require that the borrower pay a **prepayment penalty** against the unearned portion of the interest for payments made ahead of schedule. The Good-Faith Estimate (GFE) given to a borrower at the time of loan application and the HUD-1 Settlement Statement given at closing must state whether or not a mortgage has a prepayment penalty. If there is one, some lenders allow the borrower to pay off 20% of the original loan in any one year without paying a premium; but if the loan is paid off in full, the borrower may be charged a prepayment penalty on the principal paid in excess of the 20% allowance.

Under Texas law, a prepayment penalty is prohibited on a loan on residential homestead property if the note has an interest rate of 12% or more and on a federally related mortgage loan—one insured by FHA or guaranteed by VA. Usury statutes permit parties to a commercial loan to agree to a prepayment charge.

IN PRACTICE   Under the federal Dodd-Frank Act and new rules amending Regulation Z adopted by the Consumer Financial Protection Bureau (CPFB), effective as of January 2014, a secured residential mortgage loan may not include a prepayment penalty unless the penalty is otherwise permitted by law and the annual percentage rate (APR) cannot increase after closing; it meets the definition of a "qualified mortgage" as defined in the rule; and it is not a higher-priced mortgage loan. (See Chapter 16 for a detailed discussion of the new definition of a qualified mortgage.) A higher-priced mortgage loan is one with an APR that exceeds the average prime offer rate by 1.5 or more percentage points for first-lien loans or by 3.5 or more percentage points for subordinate lien loans. Therefore, subprime loans and adjustable-rate loans cannot include prepayment penalties.

If a loan meets the three requirements described above, a prepayment penalty may only apply during the first three years after consummation of the loan. The penalty may not exceed 2% of the outstanding loan balance during the first two years, and 1% in the third year. After three years, there can be no prepayment penalty. If a lender offers an applicant a loan with a prepayment penalty, it must also offer the applicant a no-prepayment-penalty loan.

PROVISIONS OF THE MORTGAGE DOCUMENT (OR DEED OF TRUST)

Deeds of Trust

The *borrower* is the *trustor*.

The neutral *third party* is the *trustee*.

The *lender* is the *beneficiary*.

In Texas, lenders prefer to use a three-party security instrument known as a *deed of trust*, or **trust deed**, rather than a *regular two-party mortgage* document. The three parties involved in the deed of trust mortgage transaction are the borrower (the *mortgagor, trustor,* or *grantor*), the lender (the *mortgagee* or *beneficiary*), and a neutral third party (the *trustee*). A deed of trust conditionally conveys the real estate as security for the loan to the trustee, who acquires a *mortgage lien* on the real estate. The title remains in trust until the loan is paid off. The trustee is limited to carrying out the duties as directed by the beneficiary, or lender. The wording of the conveyance in the deed of trust sets forth actions that the trustee may take if the borrower defaults under any of the terms. Usually the lender chooses the trustee (who is generally an employee of the lender) and reserves the right to substitute trustees in the event of death or dismissal. Because Texas is a lien theory state, the borrower (rather than the lender) is considered the owner of the property. See Figures 15.2 and 15.3 for a comparison of mortgages and deeds of trust. In Texas and other states where deeds of trust generally are preferred, foreclosure procedures for defaulted deeds of trust are usually simpler and speedier than those for regular mortgages.

FIGURE 15.2: Mortgages

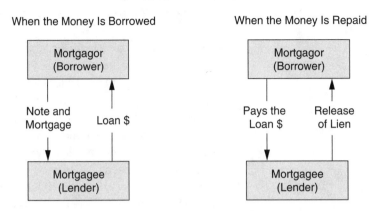

Mortgage —Two Parties

FIGURE 15.3: Deeds of Trust

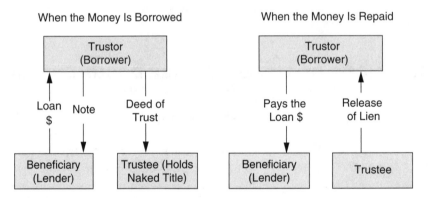

Deed of Trust—Three Parties

The deed of trust refers to the terms of the note and clearly establishes that the conveyance of land is security for the debt. It identifies the lender and the trustee as well as the borrower. It includes an accurate legal description of the property and sets forth the obligations of the borrower and the rights of the lender. All parties who have an interest in the real estate should sign it. Deeds of trust provisions can vary significantly; an attorney should be consulted for specific interpretations.

Figure 15.4 shows the first three pages of the Texas Single Family Fannie Mae/ Freddie Mac Deed of Trust. As other key paragraphs from the deed of trust are discussed on the following pages, the appropriate sections will be included. The full Texas deed of trust form is available online at www.freddiemac.com/uniform/ unifsecurity.html.

FIGURE 15.4: Deed of Trust

After Recording Return To:
<u>Blake and Connie Redemann</u>
<u>3040 N. Racine</u>
<u>Dallas, TX 75340</u>
_____

_____ [Space Above This Line For Recording Data] _____

DEED OF TRUST

DEFINITIONS

Words used in multiple sections of this document are defined below and other words are defined in Sections 3, 11, 13, 18, 20 and 21. Certain rules regarding the usage of words used in this document are also provided in Section 16.

(A) "Security Instrument" means this document, which is dated<u>   June 15, 20XX   </u>, together with all Riders to this document.

(B) "Borrower" is <u> Blake Redemann and wife Connie Redemann </u>. Borrower is the grantor under this Security Instrument.

(C) "Lender" is _____<u>Thrift Federal Savings</u>_____. Lender is a federally chartered savings and loan association organized and existing under the laws of <u> the United States of America</u>. Lender's address is <u>567 Lender's Place, Dallas, TX 75240</u>. Lender is the beneficiary under this Security Instrument.

(D) "Trustee" is _____<u>Samuel Smith</u>_____. Trustee's address is <u>567 Lender's Place, Dallas, TX 75240</u>.

(E) "Note" means the promissory note signed by Borrower and dated <u>June 15, 20XX</u>. The Note states that Borrower owes Lender <u>One Hundred Sixty-Five Thousand Dollars</u><u>(U.S. $165,000.00)</u> plus interest. Borrower has promised to pay this debt in regular Periodic Payments and to pay the debt in full not later than <u>July 1, 20XX</u>.

(F) "Property" means the property that is described below under the heading "Transfer of Rights in the Property."

(G) "Loan" means the debt evidenced by the Note, plus interest, any prepayment charges and late charges due under the Note, and all sums due under this Security Instrument, plus interest.

TEXAS-SingleFamily-**Fannie Mae/Freddie Mac UNIFORM INSTRUMENT**   Form 3044 1/01 (page 1 of 17 pages)

FIGURE 15.4: Deed of Trust (continued)

(H) **"Riders"** means all Riders to this Security Instrument that are executed by Borrower. The following Riders are to be executed by Borrower [check box as applicable]:

❑ Adjustable Rate Rider   ❑ Condominium Rider   ❑ Second Home Rider
❑ Balloon Rider   ❑ Planned Unit Development Rider   ❑ Other(s) [specify] _____
❑ 1-4 Family Rider   ❑ Biweekly Payment Rider

(I) **"Applicable Law"** means all controlling applicable federal, state and local statutes, regulations, ordinances and administrative rules and orders (that have the effect of law) as well as all applicable final, non-appealable judicial opinions.

(J) **"Community Association Dues, Fees, and Assessments"** means all dues, fees, assessments and other charges that are imposed on Borrower or the Property by a condominium association, homeowners association or similar organization.

(K) **"Electronic Funds Transfer"** means any transfer of funds, other than a transaction originated by check, draft, or similar paper instrument, which is initiated through an electronic terminal, telephonic instrument, computer, or magnetic tape so as to order, instruct, or authorize a financial institution to debit or credit an account. Such term includes, but is not limited to, point-of-sale transfers, automated teller machine transactions, transfers initiated by telephone, wire transfers, and automated clearinghouse transfers.

(L) **"Escrow Items"** means those items that are described in Section 3.

(M) **"Miscellaneous Proceeds"** means any compensation, settlement, award of damages, or proceeds paid by any third party (other than insurance proceeds paid under the coverages described in Section 5) for: (i) damage to, or destruction of, the Property; (ii) condemnation or other taking of all or any part of the Property; (iii) conveyance in lieu of condemnation; or (iv) misrepresentations of, or omissions as to, the value and/or condition of the Property.

(N) **"Mortgage Insurance"** means insurance protecting Lender against the nonpayment of, or default on, the Loan.

(O) **"Periodic Payment"** means the regularly scheduled amount due for (i) principal and interest under the Note, plus (ii) any amounts under Section 3 of this Security Instrument.

(P) **"RESPA"** means the Real Estate Settlement Procedures Act (12 U.S.C. §2601 et seq.) and its implementing regulation, Regulation X (24 C.F.R. Part 3500), as they might be amended from time to time, or any additional or successor legislation or regulation that governs the same subject matter. As used in this Security Instrument, "RESPA" refers to all requirements and restrictions that are imposed in regard to a "federally related mortgage loan" even if the Loan does not qualify as a "federally related mortgage loan" under RESPA.

(Q) **"Successor in Interest of Borrower"** means any party that has taken title to the Property, whether or not that party has assumed Borrower's obligations under the Note and/or this Security Instrument.

TRANSFER OF RIGHTS IN THE PROPERTY

This Security Instrument secures to Lender: (i) the repayment of the Loan, and all renewals, extensions and modifications of the Note; and (ii) the performance of Borrower's covenants and agreements under this Security Instrument and the Note. For this purpose, Borrower irrevocably grants and conveys to Trustee, in trust,

FIGURE 15.4: Deed of Trust (continued)

with power of sale, the following described property located in the
_____County_____ **of** _____**Dallas**_____ **:**
      [Type of Recording Jurisdiction]   **[Name of Recording Jurisdiction]**

Lot 10, Block 5, Sometime Addition, an addition to the City of Dallas, Dallas County, Texas, according to the map or plat thereof recorded in Volume 9999, Page 1111, deed records of Dallas County, Texas.

     which currently has the address of _____3040 North Racine_____
                                                [Street]
_____Dallas_____ , Texas _____75340_____ ("Property Address"):
         [City]   [Zip Code]

     TOGETHER WITH all the improvements now or hereafter erected on the property, and all easements, appurtenances, and fixtures now or hereafter a part of the property. All replacements and additions shall also be covered by this Security Instrument. All of the foregoing is referred to in this Security Instrument as the "Property."

     BORROWER COVENANTS that Borrower is lawfully seised of the estate hereby conveyed and has the right to grant and convey the Property and that the Property is unencumbered, except for encumbrances of record. Borrower warrants and will defend generally the title to the Property against all claims and demands, subject to any encumbrances of record.

     THIS SECURITY INSTRUMENT combines uniform covenants for national use and non-uniform covenants with limited variations by jurisdiction to constitute a uniform security instrument covering real property.

     UNIFORM COVENANTS. Borrower and Lender covenant and agree as follows:
     1. Payment of Principal, Interest, Escrow Items, Prepayment Charges, and Late Charges.
Borrower shall pay when due the principal of, and interest on, the debt evidenced by the Note and any prepayment charges and late charges due under the Note. Borrower shall also pay funds for Escrow Items pursuant to Section 3. Payments due under the Note and this Security Instrument shall be made in U.S. currency. However, if any check or other instrument received by Lender as payment under the Note or this Security Instrument is returned to Lender unpaid, Lender may require that any or all subsequent payments due under the Note and this Security Instrument be made in one or more of the following forms, as selected by Lender: (a) cash; (b) money order; (c) certified check, bank check, treasurer's check or cashier's check, provided any such check is drawn upon an institution whose deposits are insured by a federal agency, instrumentality, or entity; or (d) Electronic Funds Transfer.

Duties of the Mortgagor or Trustor

The borrower is required to fulfill many obligations. Usually these include
- payment of the debt in accordance with the terms of the note;
- payment of all real estate taxes on the property given as security;
- maintenance of adequate insurance to protect the lender if the property is destroyed or damaged by fire, windstorm, or other hazard;
- maintenance of the property in good repair at all times; and
- not introducing hazardous material (as defined by the EPA) to the property.

Failure to meet any of these obligations can result in a borrower's default on the note. When this happens, the trust deed may provide for a grace period (30 days on the Fannie Mae/Freddie Mac deed of trust) during which the borrower can meet the obligation and cure the default. Otherwise, the lender has the right to foreclose on the deed of trust and collect on the note. The most frequent cause of default is the borrower's failure to meet monthly installments.

Provisions for Default

The provisions of deeds of trust include an **acceleration clause** to assist the lender in foreclosure (¶22). The terms of both the note and deed of trust allow the borrower to amortize the debt in regular payments over a period of years. If a borrower defaults, both documents give the lender the right to accelerate the maturity of the debt—to declare the unpaid balance of the debt due and payable *immediately*. Without the acceleration clause, the lender would have to sue the borrower every time a payment was in default.

Other clauses in the deed of trust enable the lender to take care of the property in the event of the borrower's negligence or default. If the borrower does not pay taxes or insurance premiums or make necessary repairs on the property, the lender may step in and do so to protect its security (the real estate). Any money advanced by the lender to cure such defaults is either added to the unpaid debt or declared immediately due and payable from the borrower.

> **22. Acceleration; Remedies.**   Lender shall give notice to Borrower prior to acceleration following Borrower's breach of any convenant or agreement in this Security Instrument (but not prior to acceleration under Section 18 unless Applicable Law provides otherwise). The notice shall specify: (a) the default; (b)the action required to cure the default; (c) a date, not less than 30 days from the date, the notice is given to Borrower, by which the default must be cured; and (d) that failure to cure the default on or before the date specified in the notice will result in acceleration of the sums secured by this Security Instrument and sale of the Property. The notice shall further inform Borrower of the right to reinstate after acceleration and the right to bring a court action to assert the non-existence of a default or any other defense of Borrower to acceleration and sale. If the default is not cured on or before the date specified in the notice, Lender at its option may require immediate payment in full of all sums secured by this Security Instrument without further demand and may invoke the power of sale and any other remedies permitted by Applicable Law. Lender shall be entitled to collect all expenses incurred in pursuing the remedies provided in this Section 22, including, but not limited to, reasonable attorneys' fees and costs of title evidence. For the

purposes of this Section 22, the term "Lender" includes any holder of the Note who is entitled to receive payments under the Note.

Power-of-sale clause. If Lender invokes the power of sale, Lender or Trustee shall give notice of the time, place and terms of sale by posting and filing the notice at least 21 days prior to sale as provided by Applicable Law. Lender shall mail a copy of the notice to Borrower in the manner prescribed by Applicable Law. Sale shall be made at public venue. The sale must begin at the time stated in the notice of sale or not later than three hours after that time and between the hours of 10 a.m. and 4 p.m. on the first Tuesday of the month. Borrower authorizes Trustee to sell the Property to the highest bidder for cash in one or more parcels and in any order Trustee determines. Lender or its designee may purchase the Property at any sale.

Trustee shall deliver to the purchaser Trustee's deed conveying indefeasible title to the Property with covenants of general warranty from Borrower. Borrower covenants and agrees to defend generally the purchaser's title to the Property against all claims and demands. The recitals in the Trustee's deed shall be prima facie evidence of the truth of the statements made therein. Trustee shall apply the proceeds of the sale in the following order: (a) to all expenses of the sale, including, but not limited to, reasonable Trustee's and attorneys' fees; (b) to all sums secured by this Security Instrument; and (c) any excess to the person or persons legally entitled to it.

If the Property is sold pursuant to this Section 22, Borrower or any person holding possession of the Property through Borrower shall immediately surrender possession of the Property to the purchaser at that sale. If possession is not surrendered, Borrower or such person shall be a tenant at sufferance and may be removed by writ of possession or other court proceeding.

Assignment of the Mortgage

As mentioned previously, a note is a negotiable instrument; it may be sold to a third party, or holder in due course. When a note is sold to a third party, the mortgagee endorses the note to the third party and executes an *assignment of deed of trust*. This assignment must be recorded. On payment in full, or satisfaction of the debt, the assignee who holds the note and deed of trust is required to sign the release, or satisfaction, of lien as discussed in the following section. In the event of a foreclosure, the assignee (not the original mortgagee) is required to file the suit.

When a lender sells a loan to an investor, the lender is under no obligation to notify the borrower *unless* the servicing rights are also sold. When servicing rights are sold, the federal Real Estate Settlement Procedures Act (RESPA) requires that the loan servicer inform the mortgagor in writing 15 days prior to the transfer of servicing and furnish address and telephone contact information for the new servicer. The new loan servicer must notify the buyer in writing within 30 days after the transfer to comply with the Truth in Lending Act.

Release of the Deed of Trust Lien

Under certain circumstances, if a mortgagee does not issue a release of lien in a timely manner, a title insurance company affidavit can function as a release of lien.

When all mortgage loan payments have been made and the note is paid in full, the mortgagor wants the public record to show that the debt has been paid and the lien released. By the provisions of the **defeasance clause** in the regular mortgage document, when the note has been fully paid the mortgagee is required to execute a **release of lien**, or **satisfaction of mortgage**. This document reconveys to the mortgagor (borrower) all interest in the real estate that was conveyed to the mortgagee (lender) by the original recorded mortgage lien document. Remember that this interest is a lien interest and not a title interest. When a real estate loan secured by a deed of trust has been repaid, the beneficiary (lender) requests in writing that the trustee reconvey the property to the grantor (borrower) (¶23). The trustee then executes a release of lien and delivers a **release deed**, sometimes called a *deed of reconveyance*, to the trustor conveying the same rights and powers that the trustee was given under the trust deed. The release deed should be acknowledged and recorded in the county clerk's records in the county where the property is located to show that the lien has been removed from the property. If a mortgage or deed of trust has been transferred by a recorded assignment, the release must be executed by the assignee mortgagee.

> **23. Release.** Upon payment of all sums secured by this Security Instrument, Lender shall provide a release of this Security Instrument to Borrower or Borrower's designated agent in accordance with Applicable Law. Borrower shall pay any recordation costs. Lender may charge Borrower a fee for releasing this Security Instrument, but only if the fee is paid to a third party for services rendered and the charging of the fee is permitted under Applicable Law.

Tax and Insurance Reserves

Many lenders require that borrowers provide a reserve fund, called an *escrow account*, to make future payments for real estate taxes, property insurance premiums, and, when applicable, homeowner's dues and mortgage insurance premiums. In some instances, such as loans on manufactured housing and certain jumbo nonconforming loans with above-market interest rates, escrow accounts are required by Regulation Z of the Truth in Lending Act. RESPA limits the amount of tax and insurance reserves that a lender may require. When the mortgage or deed of trust loan is made, the borrower starts the escrow account by depositing funds to cover the amount of year-to-date unpaid real estate taxes, including the month of closing and two months' tax reserve. If a new insurance policy has been purchased, the insurance premium reserve will be started with the deposit of two months of the annual insurance premium liability. An aggregate adjustment will then be made to the initial escrow amount collected to ensure that at least once each year the escrow account does not exceed two times the monthly escrow payment. The monthly loan payments required of the borrower will include *principal* and *interest* and one month's *tax* and *insurance* reserves (PITI) plus mortgage insurance, if required on the borrower's loan.

Buying "Subject to" or Assuming a Seller's Loan Secured by a Mortgage or Deed of Trust

A person who purchases real estate that has an outstanding loan on it secured by a mortgage or deed of trust may take the property subject to the mortgage or may assume it and agree to pay the debt. This technical distinction becomes important if the buyer defaults and the mortgage or deed of trust is foreclosed.

When the property is sold *subject to* the mortgage or deed of trust, the courts hold that the purchaser is not personally obligated to pay the debt in full. The purchaser has bought the real estate knowing that she must make the loan payments and that on default, the lender will foreclose and the property will be sold to pay the debt. If the sale does not pay off the entire debt, the purchaser is not liable for the difference. However, the original borrower might still have some liability for that difference.

In contrast, when the grantee not only purchases the property but *assumes and agrees to pay* the seller's debt, the grantee becomes personally obligated for the payment of the *entire debt*. If the deed of trust or mortgage is foreclosed and the sale does not bring enough money to pay the debt in full, a deficiency judgment against the assumer may be obtained for the unpaid balance of the note. Unless the lender agrees to the assumption and a release of liability is given to the original borrower, the original borrower also will be liable for the unpaid balance. When a mortgage loan is assumed, most lending institutions charge a transfer fee to the purchaser to cover the costs of changing their records.

FOR EXAMPLE   Jane is being transferred out of town. When she bought her house, interest rates were very low; but rates have risen dramatically since that time. Buyers may be attracted by the prospect of *assuming* her mortgage to retain a more favorable interest rate, thereby saving money.

Alienation Clause   Frequently, when a real estate loan is made, the lender wishes to prevent some future purchaser of the property from being able to assume that loan, particularly at its old rate of interest. For this reason, most lenders include an **alienation clause** (also known as a *resale clause* or *due-on-sale clause*) in the note and deed of trust (¶18). An alienation clause provides that, on the sale of the property by the original borrower to a buyer who wants to assume the loan, the lender has the choice of either declaring the entire loan balance immediately due and payable or permitting the buyer to assume the loan at current market interest rates. This operates much like the acceleration clause that allows the lender to demand payment of the note in full if the provisions of the note or deed of trust are breached. Most conventional loans sold to Fannie Mae and Freddie Mac are not assumable and, therefore, have a due-on-sale clause in the deed of trust. Since FHA and VA loans are assumable, they do not contain due-on-sale clauses.

> **Alienation (due-on-sale) clause.** If all or any part of the Property or any Interest in the Property is sold or transferred (or if Borrower is not a natural person and a beneficial interest in Borrower is sold or transferred) without Lender's prior written consent, Lender may require immediate payment in full of all sums secured by this Security Instrument. However, this option shall not be exercised by Lender if such exercise is prohibited by Applicable Law.

If Lender exercises this option, Lender shall give Borrower notice of acceleration. The notice shall provide a period of not less than 30 days from the date the notice is given in accordance with Section 15 within which Borrower must pay all sums secured by this Security Instrument. If Borrower fails to pay these sums prior to the expiration of this period, Lender may invoke any remedies permitted by this Security Instrument without further notice or demand on Borrower.

Deed of Trust to Secure Assumption

As shown earlier, a deed of trust is an instrument used to tie the payment of a note to a piece of property in such a manner that a default on the note or the deed of trust permits the holder thereof to foreclose and regain legal title to the encumbered property. The *deed of trust to secure assumption* is a document developed to protect the seller who allows someone to assume the loan. If the buyer subsequently defaults in payment of the note assumed, the seller has the obligation to pay the delinquent sums to the original lender. The seller may then demand reimbursement from the buyer; if not repaid, the seller may foreclose under the power-of-sale clause in the deed of trust to secure assumption.

From the buyer's perspective, however, the deed of trust to secure assumption may create problems in obtaining a subsequent second lien on the property. For example, a prospective lender on a second lien note may require the subordination of the deed of trust to secure assumption as a condition of making the second lien loan. Some lenders perceive the deed of trust to secure assumption as a lien on the property; others, merely the granting of the right of foreclosure to another party. Therefore, sellers and buyers should consult a competent attorney if an assumption of loan is involved.

Recording Mortgages and Deeds of Trust

Although the deed of trust is normally recorded, it does not have to be recorded to be valid. However, recording the deed of trust in the county clerk's office where the real estate is located gives constructive notice to the world of the borrower's obligations and establishes the lien's priority. Promissory notes are not recorded.

First and Second Mortgages or Deeds of Trust

Mortgages and other liens normally have priority in the order in which they have been recorded. A mortgage or deed of trust on land that has no prior mortgage lien on it is a *first mortgage* or *first deed of trust*. If the owner of this land later executes another loan on the same property, for additional funds, the new loan becomes a *second mortgage (deed of trust)*, or *junior lien*, when recorded. The second lien is subject to the first lien; the first has prior claim to the value of the land pledged as security. If a first lien is being foreclosed under the power-of-sale provisions of a deed of trust, a second-lien holder would be required to purchase the first lien to preserve its interest in the property. Otherwise, the balance on the second lien would be forfeited because a power-of-sale foreclosure extinguishes all liens that are inferior to the one being foreclosed. Furthermore, in most cases the first-lien holder has no obligation to give notice of a nonjudicial foreclosure to a junior-lien holder. Therefore, not only does foreclosure of a first lien cut off a junior lien, but a foreclosure can happen without the junior-lien holder's having an opportunity to preserve its lien interest. Because second loans represent a greater risk to the lender, they usually are issued at higher interest rates.

The priority of mortgage or deed of trust liens may be changed by the execution of a *subordination agreement*, in which the first lender subordinates his lien to that of the second lender, as discussed in Chapter 11. To be valid, such an agreement must be signed by both lenders.

FORECLOSURE

If a borrower defaults in making payments or fulfilling any of the obligations in the deed of trust, the lender can enforce her rights through foreclosure. **Foreclosure** is a legal procedure whereby the property that is pledged as security in the mortgage document or deed of trust is sold to satisfy the debt. The foreclosure procedure brings the rights of all parties to a conclusion and passes title in the subject property to either the person holding the deed of trust or a third party who purchases the real estate at a *foreclosure sale*. Property thus sold is *free of the mortgage and all junior liens*—but not unpaid taxes.

Methods of Foreclosure

The two general types of foreclosure proceedings recognized in Texas are judicial and nonjudicial foreclosure.

Judicial Foreclosure for Home Equity, Reverse Mortgage, Vendors', and Homeowners Association Assessment Liens.   A judicial foreclosure proceeding provides that the property pledged as security may be sold by court order after the mortgagee gives sufficient public notice. On a borrower's default, the lender may *accelerate* the due date of all remaining monthly payments. The lender's attorney must then file suit and obtain a judgment ordering foreclosure of the lien. A public sale is advertised and held, and the real estate is sold to the highest bidder. The Texas Supreme Court has promulgated rules of civil procedure for expedited judicial foreclosure proceedings.

Nonjudicial Foreclosure (for a Deed of Trust Lien)   Texas allows nonjudicial foreclosure procedures through the **power-of-sale clause** contained in the deed of trust (see "Provisions for Default" on the previous pages). This provision allows the trustee to conduct a foreclosure sale without going through court proceedings. It simplifies and expedites foreclosure and eliminates costly court fees. A lender generally will not start the preforeclosure process until the homeowner misses two or more payments. The lender first must give a demand notice, which is usually accompanied by a notice of intent to accelerate the debt. A homeowner then has at least 20 days to cure the default before the lender can accelerate the debt through the *acceleration clause* and give notice that acceleration has occurred. If a Fannie Mae/Freddie Mac note and deed of trust were used, the defaulting property owner must be allowed 30 days to cure the default before the lender can accelerate the note. Finally, if the homeowner does not make the payments that are in default, the lender requests the trustee to sell the property.

The trustee must give written notice of the proposed sale at least 21 days preceding the date of the sale by (1) filing it with the county clerk of each county in which the property is located, (2) sending it by certified mail to each debtor obligated to pay the debt, *and* (3) posting it at the courthouse door in the county in which the property is located or posting it on an electronic display such as an electronic kiosk, electronic bulletin board, or the county's public internet site. The notice must state the date of the sale, the earliest time that the sale will occur (it may not be started more than three hours after the stated time), and the location for the sale. Traditionally, foreclosure sales have been conducted at a designated door at the county courthouse. However, a county commissioners court may designate an area other than the courthouse for conducting the sales. The designated area must be within reasonable proximity to the county courthouse and in a location as accessible to the public as the courthouse door.

Foreclosure sales occur on the first Tuesday of each month between the hours of 10:00 am and 4:00 pm. They are public auctions conducted by trustees named in the deeds of trust. A successful bidder at a sale is required to pay the purchase price, generally in cash, "without delay" or within a timeframe agreed upon by the purchaser and the trustee if the purchaser requests additional time. The deed executed by the trustee, a trustee's deed, *conveys whatever title the borrower had*; the title passes "as is" but free of the former defaulted debt. There are no warranties, but it is possible to procure a title insurance policy. Sale, foreclosure, or seizure of property under a mortgage, deed of trust, or other contract lien (including a property owners' assessment lien) on real property or personal property that is a dwelling owned by a military servicemember is prohibited during a military servicemember's period of active duty or during the nine months after the servicemember leaves the military. A notice relating to relief available to certain members of the military must be included in a notice of default (H.B. 1127; S.B. 101, 2011).

Redemption

Texas recognizes the *equitable right of* **redemption** before a mortgage foreclosure sale (¶19). If, after default but *before the foreclosure sale*, the borrower or any other person who has an interest in the real estate (such as another creditor) pays the lender the amount in default, plus costs, the debt usually will be reinstated. However, in some cases, the person who redeems may be required to repay the accelerated loan in full. If a person other than the mortgagor or trustor redeems the real estate, the borrower becomes responsible to that person for the amount of the redemption.

Although a defaulted borrower may redeem the property at any time before the sale, Texas law contains *no* provisions for *statutory redemption* of property after a sale to satisfy a home equity lien or a power-of-sale clause in a deed of trust. Following a foreclosure and sale, the deed will be executed and delivered to the purchaser by the officer conducting the sale.

However, as discussed in Chapter 11, if the foreclosure sale is held to satisfy a tax lien on a residence, Texas does have a two-year statutory redemption period on homestead property (six months on nonhomestead property). Or if foreclosure occurs on a homeowners association assessment lien and the property is purchased by the association at the sale, there is a 90-day statutory period for redemption.

> **19. Borrower's Right to Reinstate After Acceleration.** If Borrower meets certain conditions, Borrower shall have the right to have enforcement of this Security Instrument discontinued at any time prior to the earliest of: (a) five days before sale of the Property pursuant to any power of sale contained in this Security Instrument;

(b) such other period as Applicable Law might specify for the termination of Borrower's right to reinstate; or (c) entry of a judgment enforcing this Security Instrument. Those conditions are that Borrower: (a) pays Lender all sums which then would be due under this Security Instrument and the Note as if no acceleration had occurred; (b) cures any default of any other covenants or agreements; (c) pays all expenses incurred in enforcing this Security Instrument, including, but not limited to, reasonable attorneys' fees, property inspection and valuation fees, and other fees incurred for the purpose of protecting Lender's interest in the Property and rights under this Security Instrument; and (d) takes such action as Lender may reasonably require to assure that Lender's interest in the Property and rights under this Security Instrument, and Borrower's obligation to pay the sums secured by this Security Instrument, shall continue unchanged. Lender may require that Borrower pay such reinstatement sums and expenses in one or more of the following forms, as selected by Lender: (a) cash; (b) money order; (c) certified check, bank check, treasurer's check or cashier's check, provided any such check is drawn upon an institution whose deposits are insured by a federal agency, instrumentality or entity; or (d) Electronic Funds Transfer. Upon reinstatement by Borrower, this Security Instrument and obligations secured hereby shall remain fully effective as if no acceleration had occurred. However, this right to reinstate shall not apply in the case of acceleration under Section 18.

Deficiency Judgment

If the foreclosure sale of real estate securing a deed of trust does not produce enough money to pay the loan balance in full, all expenses of sale, and accrued unpaid interest, the lender may be entitled to a *personal judgment* against the borrower for the unpaid balance. Such a judgment is called a **deficiency judgment**. It may also be obtained against any endorsers or guarantors of the note and any owners of the mortgaged property who may have assumed the debt by written agreement. Lenders may often pursue a deficiency judgment to ensure their ability to collect on a federal guarantee or mortgage insurance related to the loan. Deficiency judgments must be sought within two years after the foreclosure sale. If the foreclosure sales price exceeds the amount needed for principal, interest, attorneys' fees, and other expenses, any surplus funds are paid to the borrower.

If, however, the lender had agreed to a **nonrecourse note** and mortgage, the lender would not be able to seek a deficiency judgment against the purchaser but would be limited to foreclosing and taking possession of the real estate. Equity loans and reverse-annuity mortgages are made without recourse to the borrower.

Foreclosure Avoidance

Risk of redefault is 30–40 percent for loans with principal reductions around 20 percent—but only 12 percent for those with 50 percent principal reductions.

Borrowers and lenders both benefit when foreclosure proceedings can be avoided. Lenders save the tens of thousands of dollars lost on the average foreclosure, and borrowers get to keep their homes and avoid potentially disastrous personal and financial consequences. The federal government has established programs to help responsible homeowners avoid foreclosure when they fall behind in their payments.

The key foreclosure-avoidance options are discussed in the paragraphs that follow.

Mortgage Modification   In a mortgage modification, a lender changes the basic terms of a mortgage to make the payments more affordable. Most mortgage modification programs require the lender or mortgage servicer to adjust loan terms so the borrower's housing expense ratio on the first-mortgage is no more than 31% of gross monthly income. Delinquent loans or loans at risk of becoming delinquent are most commonly modified by reducing the interest rate and/or increasing the loan term to a point that the borrower can meet the 31% requirement. Loan terms can be extended out as far as 40 years. If a rate reduction and an increase in loan term do not provide enough assistance for the borrower, other loan modification options are available.

Forbearance   If a borrower has experienced a verifiable loss of income or an increase in living expenses, a forbearance arrangement with the mortgage company could work in one of several ways, including the following:

- Allowing a borrower to pay less than the full amount of the payment owed each month or even pay nothing, depending on the borrowers situation. The borrower would resume making full monthly payments when he or she has recovered from the cause of the default. The missed payments and late fees could be paid in a lump sum at some specified date in the future or the borrower's monthly payments may be increased over an extended period of time to permit gradual repayment of the amount in arrears.

Some loan refinance and modification programs are set to expire December 31, 2015. However, these deadlines may be extended.

- Reducing the loan principal by an amount that would enable the borrower to make the payments. If a servicer reduced the principal by $20,000, that amount would be subtracted from the loan amount used to calculate the monthly mortgage payment. The borrower would make the new lower payments monthly, and the $20,000 would be due when the loan is paid off, with or without interest, in a balloon payment.

Forgiveness   A portion of the debt could be forgiven; the principal balance on the loan could be reduced by the loan servicer and written off the books. The borrower would make payments on the new loan amount.

Mortgage Refinance   In a mortgage refinance, a lender negotiates a new loan with the borrower to make the payments more affordable—both for the short-term and the long-term stability of a loan. The most common reasons for refinancing are to achieve a reduction in interest rate or to change an adjustable-rate loan to a fixed-rate loan. Refinancing an existing mortgage may not be possible if a homeowner has made more than one late payment during the year. Homeowners who have been behind in payments or who need a principal reduction would generally go through a mortgage modification program rather than refinancing.

Short Sale   If a loan modification or refinance is not possible, a **short sale** may enable a quick private sale of the property. In a short sale transaction, the lender accepts less than the balance due on the mortgage loan. For example, if the borrower has a loan balance of $120,000 but the home's value has declined to $100,000, the borrower would be short $20,000, not including the real estate commission and closing costs. If a sales contract involves a short sale of the property, the TREC promulgated addendum shown in Figure 15.5 must be attached; note that *time is of the essence.*

FIGURE 15.5: Short Sale Addendum

PROMULGATED BY THE TEXAS REAL ESTATE COMMISSION (TREC)   12-05-11

SHORT SALE ADDENDUM

ADDENDUM TO CONTRACT CONCERNING THE PROPERTY AT

_____
(Street Address and City)

A. This contract involves a "short sale" of the Property. As used in this Addendum, "short sale" means that:

  (1) Seller's net proceeds at closing will be insufficient to pay the balance of Seller's mortgage loan; and

  (2) Seller requires:
    (a) the consent of the lienholder to sell the Property pursuant to this contract; and
    (b) the lienholder's agreement to:
      (i) accept Seller's net proceeds in full satisfaction of Seller's liability under the mortgage loan; and
      (ii) provide Seller an executed release of lien against the Property in a recordable format.

B. As used in this Addendum, "Seller's net proceeds" means the Sales Price less Seller's Expenses under Paragraph 12 of the contract and Seller's obligation to pay any brokerage fees.

C. The contract to which this Addendum is attached is binding upon execution by the parties and the earnest money and the Option Fee must be paid as provided in the contract. The contract is contingent on the satisfaction of Seller's requirements under Paragraph A(2) of this Addendum (Lienholder's Consent and Agreement). Seller shall apply promptly for and make every reasonable effort to obtain Lienholder's Consent and Agreement, and shall furnish all information and documents required by the lienholder. Except as provided by this Addendum, neither party is required to perform under the contract while it is contingent upon obtaining Lienholder's Consent and Agreement.

D. If Seller does not notify Buyer that Seller has obtained Lienholder's Consent and Agreement on or before _____, this contract terminates and the earnest money will be refunded to Buyer. Seller must notify Buyer immediately if Lienholder's Consent and Agreement is obtained. For purposes of performance, the effective date of the contract changes to the date Seller provides Buyer notice of the Lienholder's Consent and Agreement (Amended Effective Date).

E. This contract will terminate and the earnest money will be refunded to Buyer if the Lienholder refuses or withdraws its Consent and Agreement prior to closing and funding. Seller shall promptly notify Buyer of any lienholder's refusal to provide or withdrawal of a Lienholder's Consent and Agreement.

F. If Buyer has the unrestricted right to terminate this contract, the time for giving notice of termination begins on the effective date of the contract, continues after the Amended Effective Date and ends upon the expiration of Buyer's unrestricted right to terminate the contract under Paragraph 23.

G. For the purposes of this Addendum, time is of the essence. Strict compliance with the times for performance stated in this Addendum is required.

H. Seller authorizes any lienholder to furnish to Buyer or Buyer's representatives information relating to the status of the request for a Lienholder's Consent and Agreement.

I. If there is more than one lienholder or loan secured by the Property, this Addendum applies to each lienholder.

_____   _____
Buyer   Seller

_____   _____
Buyer   Seller

TREC NO. 45-1

In general, to qualify for a short sale, certain conditions must exist: the home's market value is less than the unpaid balance on the loan; the mortgage is in or near default status; the seller has encountered extenuating circumstances that create a hardship, such as losing a job; and/or the seller has no assets with which to pay the shorted difference. A short sale will show up on the borrower's credit report as a pre-foreclosure that has been redeemed; the drop in the FICO score may be identical to a foreclosure. FICO scores will be discussed in Chapter 16, *Application for Credit*.

Deed in Lieu of Foreclosure   If a home loan cannot be modified and a short sale does not occur, the borrower can still avoid foreclosure by giving the keys to the lender through a **deed in lieu of foreclosure**. With a deed in lieu of foreclosure, a defaulting borrower negotiates with a lender to transfer voluntarily the property's title to the lender, thus eliminating costly foreclosure proceedings. This is sometimes called a *friendly foreclosure* because it is by agreement rather than by civil action; however, the drop in the FICO score may be identical to a foreclosure. To the lender, the major disadvantage of this default settlement is that the lender takes the real estate subject to all junior liens, whereas a power-of-sale foreclosure eliminates all such liens. (Foreclosure of a vendor's lien does not extinguish junior liens, however, unless those lienholders were named in the foreclosure suit.) By accepting a deed in lieu of foreclosure, the lender may lose any rights pertaining to FHA or private mortgage insurance or VA guarantees, unless a prearrangement agreement is reached with the mortgage insurer/guarantor.

Mortgage Forgiveness and Debt Cancellation   Usually, if a lender agrees to forgive any part of the debt or accept a deed in lieu of foreclosure, the borrower could owe federal income taxes on the amount forgiven. The Mortgage Forgiveness Debt Relief Act of 2007 generally allows taxpayers to exclude from income any debt reduced through mortgage restructuring or debt forgiven in connection with a short sale, deed in lieu of foreclosure, or foreclosure of a principal residence. This provision applies to debt forgiven through December 31, 2013, with a maximum of $2 million in forgiven debt ($1 million if married filing separately). In addition, forgiveness of debts discharged through bankruptcy is excluded from taxable income. However, the amount of debt forgiven on second homes, rental property, business property, credit cards, or car loans is taxable income. Although the December 31, 2013, debt forgiveness deadline has passed, as of this writing, there is a bill currently pending in Congress that would extend the deadline for two more years until December 31, 2016.

Fannie Mae's Deed-for-Lease Program (D4L) allows eligible borrowers facing foreclosure to stay in their primary residences, transferring their property to the lender through a deed in lieu of foreclosure and signing a lease for up to one year. Freddie Mac requires the foreclosure process to be completed before allowing the former homeowners month-to-month leases while the property is shown to potential buyers.

IN PRACTICE   As just discussed, if a homeowner experiences a financial crisis, there are many options available before a lender's foreclosing on the property. In addition, there is *time* to work out options to foreclosure. Therefore, as soon as the homeowner realizes there is a problem or even a potential problem, the first contact should be with the lender. With the average cost of a foreclosure to a lender in the tens of thousands of dollars, lenders really don't want the property back. The homeowner should open all mail from the lender and respond to it. Notices from the lender will offer good information about various foreclosure avoidance options and the availability of free housing counseling through Hope Now (an alliance between counselors, mortgage companies, and investors) or other non-profit programs. A counselor should help a homeowner understand the law and the options available, organize his finances, and compile an intake package for his lender or loan servicer. The counselor should recommend the best available course of action for the homeowner based on such information as the current loan amount, the loan-to-value ratio, and the borrower's FICO score and credit history. Early options would include selling a second car, a vacation home, or other assets. From there, loan modification or refinancing may be an option. When payment adjustments are not enough, selling is another way to stop foreclosure. Deed in lieu of foreclosure and short sale both still give the homeowner the opportunity to leave the property without going through the foreclosure process, but they should be reserved only for situations in which counselors, lenders, and the homeowner see no other options. The most important advice a real estate professional can give to a client or customer is to seek a solution early: call the Hope Now hotline (at 888-995-HOPE) or check government housing agency websites.

Licensed real estate agents who assist consumers in obtaining short sales from their lenders or servicers do not have to comply with the MARS Rule—unless they engage in misrepresentation while assisting a consumer.

To protect distressed homeowners from scams related to foreclosure, the Federal Trade Commission (FTC) issued the Mortgage Assistance Relief Services (MARS) Rule, effective January 31, 2011. Private mortgage assistance relief services are no longer allowed to charge up-front fees. The MARS Rule created a total ban on collecting any fees—including appraisal, application, and processing fees—until the homeowner has signed a written agreement with the lender that includes the desired relief. If the homeowner rejects the lender's written offer, there are no fees payable to the mortgage assistance relief service. Chapter 21 of the Texas Business and Commerce Code provides for the regulation of certain Texas residential mortgage foreclosure consulting services, requiring, among other things, written contracts for services, a statutorily prescribed disclosure notice, and restrictions against compensation being paid until the contract has been fully performed.

However, there is really no need for distressed homeowners to employ private companies for mortgage relief services. Foreclosure prevention counseling services are provided free of charge by nonprofit housing counseling agencies working in partnership with the federal government. Free counseling agencies can be found online at www.hud.gov or reached by phone at 800-569-4287.

WEBLINK @

www.knowyouroptions.com
www.hud.gov/foreclosure
www.youtube.com/freddiemac (*Get the Facts on Foreclosure*)

SUMMARY

Mortgage and deed of trust loans provide the principal sources of financing for real estate operations. Mortgage loans involve a borrower, called the *mortgagor*, and a lender, the *mortgagee*. Deed of trust loans involve a third party, called the *trustee*, in addition to the borrower (in this case the *trustor*) and the lender (the *beneficiary*).

States that recognize the lender as the owner of mortgaged property are known as *title theory states*. Others recognize the borrower as the owner of mortgaged property and are known as *lien theory states*. Texas is a lien theory state.

A borrower of funds for the purchase of a home is required to execute a note, agreeing to repay the debt, and a mortgage or deed of trust, placing a lien on the real estate to secure the note. The deed of trust is normally recorded in the public records to give notice to the world of the lender's interest.

The note sets the rate of interest at which the loan is made and that the mortgagor or trustor must pay as a charge for borrowing the money. Charging more than the maximum interest rate allowed by state statute is called *usury* and is illegal. The mortgage document or deed of trust secures the debt and sets forth the obligations of the borrower and the rights of the lender. Payment in full of the note by its terms entitles the borrower to a release, or satisfaction, of lien, which is recorded to clear the lien from the public records. Default by the borrower may result in acceleration of payments, a foreclosure sale, and loss of title. To avoid foreclosure, however, the borrower can pursue loan modification or loan refinance programs to try to keep the home. Short sale and deed in lieu of foreclosure options allow the borrower to sell or give up the property without having to go through foreclosure proceedings.

CHAPTER 15 QUESTIONS

1. A promissory note
   a. is a negotiable instrument.
   b. may not be sold by the lender to a third party.
   c. is recorded in the county clerk's records.
   d. is security for the loan.

2. The person who obtains a real estate loan and signs a mortgage (deed of trust) is called the
   a. trustee.
   b. beneficiary.
   c. mortgagee.
   d. mortgagor.

3. The Escalantes sold their farmland to the Crawfords but retained the rights to and ownership of all coal and other minerals in the land. The Crawfords obtained a mortgage loan from their bank and executed a mortgage to the bank as security. Which statement is *TRUE* regarding this transaction?
   a. The Crawfords' mortgage covers the land and the minerals.
   b. The Crawfords' mortgage covers the land but not the minerals.
   c. The Crawfords' mortgage covers only the minerals.
   d. If the Crawfords default, the bank automatically acquires the mineral rights.

4. The lender under a deed of trust is known as the
   a. trustor.
   b. trustee.
   c. beneficiary.
   d. vendee.

5. A borrower obtains a $76,000 mortgage loan at 11½% interest. If the monthly payments of $785 are credited first on interest and then on principal, what will the balance of the principal be after the borrower makes the first payment?
   a. $75,215.00
   b. $75,943.33
   c. $75,543.66
   d. $75,305.28

6. A mortgage or deed of trust document requires that the mortgagor perform certain duties. Which of the following is *NOT* one of these?
   a. Maintain the property in good condition at all times.
   b. Obtain the mortgagee's permission before renting a room to a boarder.
   c. Maintain adequate insurance on the property.
   d. Forbear from disposing of hazardous waste on the property.

7. Which is *NOT* a necessary element of a deed of trust mortgage?
   a. Consideration
   b. Signature of trustee
   c. Legal capacity of parties
   d. Written document

8. A state law provides that lenders cannot charge more than 18% interest on a loan. This law is called
   a. a truth-in-lending law.
   b. a usury law.
   c. the statute of frauds.
   d. RESPA.

9. Before the foreclosure sale, a defaulting borrower seeks to pay off the debt plus any accrued interest and costs under the right of
   a. equitable redemption.
   b. statutory redemption.
   c. hypothecation.
   d. defeasance.

10. The clause in a note that gives the lender the right to have all future installments become due on default is the
    a. escalation clause.
    b. defeasance clause.
    c. alienation clause.
    d. acceleration clause.

11. What document is given to the trustor when the deed of trust debt is completely repaid?
    a. Satisfaction of mortgage
    b. Defeasance certificate
    c. Deed of trust
    d. Release deed

12. Which allows a mortgagee to proceed to a foreclosure sale without having to go to court first?
    a. Waiver of redemption right
    b. Power of sale
    c. Alienation clause
    d. Acceleration clause

13. Pledging property for a loan without giving up possession is *BEST* described as
    a. hypothecation.
    b. alienation.
    c. novation.
    d. defeasance.

14. The provisions of a nonjudicial foreclosure include all the following *EXCEPT*
    a. written notice must be posted at the courthouse at least 21 days before the sale.
    b. homestead property owners must be given 45 days to cure the default before notice of sale is given.
    c. notice of the proposed sale must be sent to each debtor at least 21 days before the sale.
    d. notice of the sale must state where the sale will take place.

15. In a foreclosure through a power-of-sale clause, who actually conducts the foreclosure?
    a. Mortgagee
    b. Mortgagor
    c. Trustee
    d. Trustor

16. The borrower under a deed of trust is known as the
    a. trustor.
    b. trustee.
    c. beneficiary.
    d. vendee.

17. A homeowner wants to sell his house to someone who will assume his loan. If the lender wants to prevent the assumption, which clause in the deed of trust would the lender invoke?
    a. Escalation clause
    b. Defeasance clause
    c. Acceleration clause
    d. Alienation clause

Detailed rationales for the end-of-chapter review questions are available online at www.dearborn.com through the *Instructor Resource Guides* link.

CHAPTER

16

Real Estate Financing Practice

■ **LEARNING OBJECTIVES** *When you have completed this chapter, you will be able to*

- ■ **describe** the various primary sources of mortgage money, the loan application process, and the payment plans available to real estate purchasers;
- ■ **explain** the provisions of and qualifications for conventional, FHA, VA, agricultural, and Texas loan programs;
- ■ **distinguish** among the various types of *creative financing* techniques that address borrowers' different needs;
- ■ **identify** the mechanisms used by the Federal Reserve System ("the Fed") to control the economy and the entities that participate in the secondary mortgage market;
- ■ **review** legislation affecting real estate financing and activities that would be classified as predatory lending or mortgage fraud; and
- ■ **define** the following *key terms*:

adjustable-rate mortgage	FHA loan	Rural Development (RD)
automated underwriting	flexible-payment loan	sale-and-leaseback
balloon payment	Freddie Mac	secondary mortgage
biweekly payment plan	fully amortized loan	market
blanket mortgage	Ginnie Mae	shared-appreciation
buydown mortgage	loan origination fee	mortgage
computerized loan	loan-to-value ratio	term loan
origination (CLO)	mortgage-backed	Texas Department
construction loan	securities	of Housing and
contract for deed	open-end mortgage	Community Affairs
conventional loan	package mortgage	(TDHCA)
discount points	primary mortgage market	Texas Veterans Land
equity loan	private mortgage	Board
Fannie Mae	insurance	trigger terms
Farmer Mac	purchase money	VA loan
Farm Service Agency	mortgage	warehousing agency
Federal Reserve System	Regulation Z	wraparound loan
(the "Fed")	reverse mortgage	

OVERVIEW

Without mortgage loans, the American dream of owning a home would be possible for very few people. Through programs of the Department of Housing and Urban Development (HUD), the U.S. Department of Veterans Affairs (VA), and agencies such as Ginnie Mae, the federal government has assisted the American citizen by providing affordable housing money.

This chapter explores the alternative types of financing and payment plans. The chapter also examines the various primary and secondary sources for mortgage money and looks at the role of the federal government in real estate financing.

SOURCES OF REAL ESTATE FINANCING—THE PRIMARY MORTGAGE MARKET

The funds used to finance the purchase of real estate come from a variety of sources in the **primary mortgage market**—lenders who supply funds to borrowers as an investment. Mortgage loans generally are made by institutional lenders such as savings associations, commercial banks, state savings banks, insurance companies, mortgage banking companies, mortgage brokers, and credit unions.

There are government sources of real estate financing as well. Many local government bodies issue interest-bearing certificates, called *bond issues*, to finance real estate projects and community improvements. In Texas, the Department of Housing and Community Affairs and regional or local housing authorities have the authority to make mortgages and temporary loans to assist people with low or moderate incomes.

The Texas version of the national Secure and Fair Enforcement Mortgage Licensing Act of 2008 (the SAFE Act) and implementing rules as passed by the Texas Legislature in 2009 (Texas Finance Code Chapter 180 and 7 Texas Administrative Code Chapters 80 and 81) require residential mortgage loan originators who accept loan applications or make, transact, or negotiate mortgage loans to be enrolled in the Nationwide Mortgage Licensing System and Registry (NMLS) and to be licensed by the state through the NMLS. Residential mortgage loan originators who are employed by depository institutions are required only to register through the federal NMLS system. Final rules issued by HUD clarify that governmental entities, government employees, and employees of "bona fide" nonprofits are exempt from licensing and registration. If, in addition to a real estate sales commission, a real estate agent receives a fee for taking an application or offering to negotiate terms of a residential mortgage loan, the agent must be licensed under SAFE. If, however, all compensation from the transaction is in the form of a real estate sales commission, licensing under SAFE is not required. Among the statutory exemptions to SAFE licensing are individuals working with or on behalf of an immediate family member and the owner of real property who makes no more than five mortgage loans in a consecutive 12-month period to purchasers of his properties.

Savings Associations

Savings associations (also called savings and loan associations or S&Ls) specialize in long-term residential loans. All savings associations must be chartered either by the federal government or by the state in which they are located. The principal function of a savings association has been to promote thrift and home ownership. Generally real estate–related assets are the main source of investment for savings associations: residential mortgage loans, residential construction loans, home equity loans, and **mortgage-backed securities**. Traditionally savings associations are the most flexible of all the lending institutions in regard to their mortgage lending procedures. Savings associations participate in conventional, FHA-insured, and VA-guaranteed loans.

Commercial Banks

Commercial banks are an important source of real estate financing. Historically, bank loan departments have handled such short-term loans as construction, home improvement, and manufactured housing loans. However, commercial banks are also originating an increasing number of conventional, FHA, and VA home mortgages. Like the savings associations, banks must be chartered by the state or federal government.

Savings Banks

Savings banks operate like savings associations. They issue no stock and are mutually owned by their investors, the depositors themselves. Although savings banks do offer limited checking account privileges, they are primarily savings institutions and are highly active in the mortgage market, investing in loans secured by income property as well as residential real estate. In addition, because savings banks usually seek low-risk loan investments, they often prefer to originate FHA-insured or VA-guaranteed loans.

Insurance Companies

Insurance companies amass large sums of money from the premiums paid by their policyholders. Although a certain portion of this money is held in reserve to satisfy claims and cover operating expenses, much of it is invested in profit-earning enterprises such as long-term real estate loans that finance commercial and industrial properties. They also invest in residential mortgage and deed of trust loans by purchasing large blocks of government-backed (FHA-insured and VA-guaranteed) loans from Fannie Mae and other agencies that warehouse such loans for resale in the *secondary mortgage market* (discussed later in this chapter). In addition, many insurance companies seek to ensure further the safety of their investments by insisting on equity positions (known as *equity kickers*) in many projects they finance. They may require a partnership arrangement with a project developer or subdivider as a condition for making a loan.

Mortgage Banking Companies

Mortgage banking companies use money borrowed from other institutions and/or funds of their own to make real estate loans. They make loans in the name of the mortgage banker with the intention of selling them to investors either on a loan-by-loan basis or pooled together as a security. Many mortgage bankers will sell only the loans and retain the servicing, which includes collecting PITI payments and disbursing and accounting for those funds. They charge a fee for loan servicing, usually 0.25%, and they retain any late charges paid by the borrower. Other mortgage bankers will retain servicing until a certain volume is reached to optimize its value for a sale to another loan servicer. A mortgage banking company is generally organized as a stock company or as a wholly owned subsidiary of a bank or savings association.

Mortgage Brokers

Mortgage brokers are not lenders but are often instrumental in obtaining financing. Mortgage brokers are individuals who act as intermediaries to bring borrowers and lenders together. They locate potential borrowers, process preliminary loan applications, and submit the applications to lenders for final approval. The loans are generally closed in the name of the lender, not the mortgage broker. Frequently they work with or for mortgage banking companies in these activities. They do not service loans once they are made. Many mortgage brokers are also real estate brokers who offer these financing services in addition to their regular brokerage activities; however, full disclosure must be made to all parties to the transaction.

Credit Unions

Credit unions are cooperative organizations in which members place money in savings accounts, usually at higher interest rates than other savings institutions offer. In the past, most credit unions made only short-term consumer and home improvement loans, but in recent years they have branched out into originating longer-term first and second mortgage and deed of trust loans. They generally sell their long-term loans in the secondary market.

APPLICATION FOR CREDIT

Prequalification and Preapproval

The "calculator" section on many real estate websites, such as Fannie Mae's *www. homepath.com*, can help a buyer or agent determine how much house a purchaser can buy and what the maximum qualifying payment would be, less monthly taxes and insurance premiums.

All mortgage lenders require that prospective borrowers file an application for credit that provides the lender with the basic information needed to evaluate the acceptability of the proposed loan. Residential lenders are required to use the Uniform Residential Loan Application for *all* loans (FHA, VA, FSA, and conventional) secured by one-family to four-family properties (see Figure 16.1). The application includes information regarding the purpose of the loan, the amount, the rate of interest, and the proposed terms of repayment. This is considered a preliminary offer of a loan agreement; final terms may require lengthy negotiations. In some cases a borrower may want to be prequalified or preapproved for a loan prior to making an offer on a home. When an applicant is *prequalified* for a loan, the lender has estimated the maximum loan for which the applicant could qualify—using the borrower's account of earnings, outstanding debt, and savings. When an applicant is *preapproved*, however, the lender has verified income, debt, and savings and has run a thorough credit check, permitting the lender to quote a specific maximum loan amount and to assert that it would advance a loan under the terms and conditions existing at the time of loan application.

Before approving a loan, the lender must qualify the buyer, the title, and the property. Within the application, a prospective borrower must submit personal information to the lender, including employment, earnings, assets, and financial obligations. Details of the real estate that will be the security for the loan must be provided, including legal description, improvements, title, survey, and taxes. For loans on income property or those made to corporations, additional information is required, such as financial and operating statements, schedules of leases and tenants, and balance sheets.

The lender carefully investigates the application information, studying credit reports and an appraisal of the property before deciding whether to grant the loan. Some lenders issue a written *loan commitment*, which creates a contract to make a loan and sets forth the details. Under some circumstances, lenders charge a fee for this commitment.

IN PRACTICE   Although lenders compute loan qualifying ratios for prospective homebuyers, "credit scoring" has become a major factor in lending decision making. FICO (formerly Fair, Isaac and Company) created a system for reducing the loan application creditworthiness elements into one number, a FICO score. Five factors account for the majority of a FICO credit score: the borrower's payment history, amounts owed, length of credit history, types of credit used, and number of new credit applications or queries. To learn more about the specific elements evaluated within these five categories, visit the FICO website: www.myfico.com; choose Education; then What's In Your FICO Score.

FIGURE 16.1: Uniform Residential Loan Application

Uniform Residential Loan Application

This application is designed to be completed by the applicant(s) with the Lender's assistance. Applicants should complete this form as "Borrower" or "Co-Borrower," as applicable. Co-Borrower information must also be provided (and the appropriate box checked) when ☐ the income or assets of a person other than the Borrower (including the Borrower's spouse) will be used as a basis for loan qualification or ☐ the income or assets of the Borrower's spouse or other person who has community property rights pursuant to state law will not be used as a basis for loan qualification, but his or her liabilities must be considered because the spouse or other person has community property rights pursuant to applicable law and Borrower resides in a community property state, the security property is located in a community property state, or the Borrower is relying on other property located in a community property state as a basis for repayment of the loan.

If this is an application for joint credit, Borrower and Co-Borrower each agree that we intend to apply for joint credit (sign below):

Borrower _____ Co-Borrower _____

I. TYPE OF MORTGAGE AND TERMS OF LOAN

Mortgage Applied for:	☐ VA ☒ Conventional ☐ Other (explain): ☐ FHA ☐ USDA/Rural Housing Service	Agency Case Number	Lender Case Number DEMOCNV

Amount $ 80,000.00	Interest Rate 7.375 %	No. of Months 360	Amortization Type: ☒ Fixed Rate ☐ GPM	☐ Other (explain): ☐ ARM (type):

II. PROPERTY INFORMATION AND PURPOSE OF LOAN

Subject Property Address (street, city, state & ZIP) **1456 House TEXAS** — No. of Units **1**

Legal Description of Subject Property (attach description if necessary) — Year Built **1994**

Purpose of Loan ☒ Purchase ☐ Construction ☐ Other (explain): ☐ Refinance ☐ Construction-Permanent | Property will be: ☒ Primary Residence ☐ Secondary Residence ☐ Investment

Complete this line if construction or construction-permanent loan.

Year Lot Acquired	Original Cost $	Amount Existing Liens $	(a) Present Value of Lot $	(b) Cost of Improvements $	Total (a + b) $

Complete this line if this is a refinance loan.

Year Acquired	Original Cost $	Amount Existing Liens $	Purpose of Refinance	Describe Improvements ☐ made ☐ to be made Cost $

Title will be held in what Name(s) **JOHN DOE AND JANE DOE** | Manner in which Title will be held **TENANTS IN COMMON** | Estate will be held in: ☒ Fee Simple ☐ Leasehold (show expiration date)

Source of Down Payment, Settlement Charges, and/or Subordinate Financing (explain)

III. BORROWER INFORMATION

	Borrower	Co-Borrower
Name	JOHN DOE	JANE DOE
Social Security Number	123-45-6789	
Home Phone	806-355-0000	
DOB / Yrs. School		
Marital	☒ Married ☐ Unmarried ☐ Separated	☒ Married ☐ Unmarried ☐ Separated
Dependents	no. 2 ages 8, 6	no. 2 ages 8, 6
Present Address	☒ Own ☐ Rent 5.00 No. Yrs. 1234 ANY STREET, AMARILLO, TEXAS 79177	☒ Own ☐ Rent 5.00 No. Yrs. 1234 ANY STREET, AMARILLO, TEXAS 79177

Mailing Address, if different from Present Address

If residing at present address for less than two years, complete the following:

Former Address (street, city, state, ZIP) ☐ Own ☐ Rent ___ No. Yrs. | Former Address ☐ Own ☐ Rent ___ No. Yrs.

IV. EMPLOYMENT INFORMATION

	Borrower	Co-Borrower
Name & Address of Employer	MASON AND HANGER PO BOX 30020 AMARILLO, TEXAS 79177 ☐ Self Employed	AMARILLO I S D 7200 I-40 WEST AMARILLO, TEXAS 79106 ☐ Self Employed
Yrs. on this job	7.00	5.00
Yrs. employed in this line of work/profession	7.00	5.00
Position/Title/Type of Business	SECURITY COURIER GOVT	TEACHER EDUCATION
Business Phone	806-477-000	

If employed in current position for less than two years or if currently employed in more than one position, complete the following:

FIGURE 16.1: Uniform Residential Loan Application (continued)

Borrower			IV. EMPLOYMENT INFORMATION (cont'd)		Co-Borrower	
Name & Address of Employer	☐ Self Employed	Dates (from – to)	Name & Address of Employer	☐ Self Employed	Dates (from – to)	
		Monthly Income $			Monthly Income $	
Position/Title/Type of Business		Business Phone (incl. area code)	Position/Title/Type of Business		Business Phone (incl. area code)	
Name & Address of Employer	☐ Self Employed	Dates (from – to)	Name & Address of Employer	☐ Self Employed	Dates (from – to)	
		Monthly Income $			Monthly Income $	
Position/Title/Type of Business		Business Phone (incl. area code)	Position/Title/Type of Business		Business Phone (incl. area code)	

V. MONTHLY INCOME AND COMBINED   HOUSING EXPENSE INFORMATION

Gross Monthly Income	Borrower	Co-Borrower	Total	Combined Monthly Housing Expense	Present	Proposed
Base Empl. Income*	$ 3800.00	$ 2200.00	$ 6000.00	Rent	$	
Overtime				First Mortgage (P&I)	1666.00	$ 552.54
Bonuses				Other Financing (P&I)		
Commissions				Hazard Insurance		75.00
Dividends/Interest				Real Estate Taxes		166.67
Net Rental Income				Mortgage Insurance		
Other (before completing, see the notice in "describe other income," below)				Homeowner Assn. Dues		
				Other:		
Total	$ 3800.00	$ 2200.00	$ 6000.00	Total	$ 1666.00	$ 794.21

*   Self Employed Borrower(s) may be required to provide additional   documentation such as tax returns and financial statements.

Describe Other Income

Notice: Alimony, child support, or separate maintenance income need not be revealed if the Borrower (B) or Co-Borrower (C) does not choose to have it considered for repaying this loan.

B/C		Monthly Amount
		$

VI. ASSETS AND LIABILITIES

This Statement and any applicable supporting schedules may be completed jointly by both married and unmarried Co-Borrowers if their assets and liabilities are sufficiently joined so that the Statement can be meaningfully and fairly presented on a combined basis; otherwise, separate Statements and Schedules are required. If the Co-Borrower section was completed about a non-applicant spouse or other person, this Statement and supporting schedules must be completed about that spouse or other person also.

Completed ☒ Jointly ☐ Not Jointly

ASSETS	Cash or Market Value	Liabilities and Pledged Assets. List the creditor's name, address, and account number for all outstanding debts, including automobile loans, revolving charge accounts, real estate loans, alimony, child support, stock pledges, etc. Use continuation sheet, if necessary. Indicate by (*) those liabilities, which will be satisfied upon sale of real estate owned or upon refinancing of the subject property.		
Description				
Cash deposit toward purchase held by: Stewart Title Co.	$			
List checking and savings accounts below		LIABILITIES	Monthly Payment & Months Left to Pay	Unpaid Balance
Name and address of Bank, S&L, or Credit Union FIRST STATE BANK HAPPY, TEXAS PO BOX 7855 AMARILLO, TEXAS 79114-7865 222222222 5000.00		Name and address of Company MBNA AMERICA PO BOX 15019 WILMINGTON, DE	$ Payment/Months	$
Acct. no. 111111111 $ 1000.00		Acct. no.	80 / 63	5000.00
Name and address of Bank, S&L, or Credit Union AETNA 401K		Name and address of Company	$ Payment/Months	$
Acct. no. 555555555 $ 20,000.00		Acct. no.	526 / 19	10000.00
Name and address of Bank, S&L, or Credit Union		Name and address of Company	$ Payment/Months	$
Acct. no. $		Acct. no.	219 / 46	10000.00

FIGURE 16.1: Uniform Residential Loan Application (continued)

VI. ASSETS AND LIABILITIES (cont'd)				
Name and address of Bank, S&L, or Credit Union		Name and address of Company	$ Payment/Months	$
Acct. no.	$	Acct. no.		
Stocks & Bonds (Company name/ number & description) MASSACHUSETTS MUTUAL	$ 10000.00	Name and address of Company	$ Payment/Months	$
		Acct. no.		
Life insurance net cash value Face amount: $	$	Name and address of Company	$ Payment/Months	$
Subtotal Liquid Assets	$ 36000.00			
Real estate owned (enter market value from schedule of real estate owned)	$			
Vested interest in retirement fund	$			
Net worth of business(es) owned (attach financial statement)	$	Acct. no.		
Automobiles owned (make and year) CAR 1 CAR 2	$ 20000.00 35000.00	Alimony/Child Support/Separate Maintenance Payments Owed to:	$	
Other Assets (itemize) PERSONAL PROPERTY	$ 50000.00	Job-Related Expense (child care, union dues, etc.)	$	
		Total Monthly Payments	$ 825	
Total Assets a.	$ 141000.00	Net Worth (a minus b) ▶ $	Total Liabilities b.	$ 25000.00

Schedule of Real Estate Owned (If additional properties are owned, use continuation sheet.)

Property Address (enter S if sold, PS if pending sale or R if rental being held for income) ▼	Type of Property	Present Market Value	Amount of Mortgages & Liens	Gross Rental Income	Mortgage Payments	Insurance, Maintenance, Taxes & Misc.	Net Rental Income
		$	$	$	$	$	$
Totals		$	$	$	$	$	$

List any additional names under which credit has previously been received and indicate appropriate creditor name(s) and account number(s):

Alternate Name	Creditor Name	Account Number

VII. DETAILS OF TRANSACTION			VIII. DECLARATIONS				
a.	Purchase price	$	If you answer "Yes" to any questions a through i, please use continuation sheet for explanation.	Borrower		Co-Borrower	
				Yes No		Yes No	
b.	Alterations, improvements, repairs		a. Are there any outstanding judgments against you?	☐ ☐		☐ ☐	
c.	Land (if acquired separately)		b. Have you been declared bankrupt within the past 7 years?	☐ ☐		☐ ☐	
d.	Refinance (incl. debts to be paid off)		c. Have you had property foreclosed upon or given title or deed in lieu thereof in the last 7 years?	☐ ☐		☐ ☐	
e.	Estimated prepaid items		d. Are you a party to a lawsuit?	☐ ☐		☐ ☐	
f.	Estimated closing costs		e. Have you directly or indirectly been obligated on any loan which resulted in foreclosure, transfer of title in lieu of foreclosure, or judgment?	☐ ☐		☐ ☐	
g.	PMI, MIP, Funding Fee						
h.	Discount (if Borrower will pay)		(This would include such loans as home mortgage loans, SBA loans, home improvement loans, educational loans, manufactured (mobile) home loans, any mortgage, financial obligation, bond, or loan guarantee. If "Yes," provide details, including date, name, and address of Lender, FHA or VA case number, if any, and reasons for the action.)				
i.	Total costs (add items a through h)						

FIGURE 16.1: Uniform Residential Loan Application (continued)

VII. DETAILS OF TRANSACTION	VIII. DECLARATIONS

VIII. DECLARATIONS

	Borrower		Co-Borrower	
If you answer "Yes" to any question a through I, please use continuation sheet for explanation.	Yes	No	Yes	No

VII. DETAILS OF TRANSACTION:
- j. Subordinate financing
- k. Borrower's closing costs paid by Seller
- l. Other Credits (explain)
- m. Loan amount (exclude PMI, MIP, Funding Fee financed)
- n. PMI, MIP, Funding Fee financed
- o. Loan amount (add m & n)
- p. Cash from/to Borrower (subtract j, k, l & o from i)

VIII. DECLARATIONS:
- f. Are you presently delinquent or in default on any Federal debt or any other loan, mortgage, financial obligation, bond, or loan guarantee? ☐ ☐ ☐ ☐
- g. Are you obligated to pay alimony, child support, or separate maintenance? ☐ ☐ ☐ ☐
- h. Is any part of the down payment borrowed? ☐ ☐ ☐ ☐
- i. Are you a co-maker or endorser on a note? ☐ ☐ ☐ ☐
- j. Are you a U.S. citizen? ☐ ☐ ☐ ☐
- k. Are you a permanent resident alien? ☐ ☐ ☐ ☐
- l. Do you intend to occupy the property as your primary residence? ☐ ☐ ☐ ☐ If "Yes," complete question m below.
- m. Have you had an ownership interest in a property in the last three years? ☐ ☐ ☐ ☐
  - (1) What type of property did you own—principal residence (PR), second home (SH), or investment property (IP)?
  - (2) How did you hold title to the home— by yourself (S), jointly with your spouse or jointly with another person (O)?

IX. ACKNOWLEDGEMENT AND AGREEMENT

Each of the undersigned specifically represents to Lender and to Lender's actual or potential agents, brokers, processors, attorneys, insurers, servicers, successors and assigns and agrees and acknowledges that: (1) the information provided in this application is true and correct as of the date set forth opposite my signature and that any intentional or negligent misrepresentation of this information contained in this application may result in civil liability, including monetary damages, to any person who may suffer any loss due to reliance upon any misrepresentation that I have made on this application, and/or in criminal penalties including, but not limited to, fine or imprisonment or both under the provisions of Title 18, United States Code, Sec. 1001, et seq.; (2) the loan requested pursuant to this application (the "Loan") will be secured by a mortgage or deed of trust on the property described in this application; (3) the property will not be used for any illegal or prohibited purpose or use; (4) all statements made in this application are made for the purpose of obtaining a residential mortgage loan; (5) the property will be occupied as indicated in this application; (6) the Lender, its servicers, successors or assigns may retain the original and/or an electronic record of this application, whether or not the Loan is approved; (7) the Lender and its agents, brokers, insurers, servicers, successors, and assigns may continuously rely on the information contained in the application, and I am obligated to amend and/or supplement the information provided in this application if any of the material facts that I have represented herein should change prior to closing of the Loan; (8) in the event that my payments on the Loan become delinquent, the Lender, its servicers, successors or assigns may, in addition to any other rights and remedies that it may have relating to such delinquency, report my name and account information to one or more consumer reporting agencies; (9) ownership of the Loan and/or administration of the Loan account may be transferred with such notice as may be required by law; (10) neither Lender nor its agents, brokers, insurers, servicers, successors or assigns has made any representation or warranty, express or implied, to me regarding the property or the condition or value of the property; and (11) my transmission of this application as an "electronic record" containing my "electronic signature," as those terms are defined in applicable federal and/or state laws (excluding audio and video recordings), or my facsimile transmission of this application containing a facsimile of my signature, shall be as effective, enforceable and valid as if a paper version of this application were delivered containing my original written signature.

Acknowledgement. Each of the undersigned hereby acknowledges that any owner of the Loan, its servicers, successors and assigns, may verify or reverify any information contained in this application or obtain any information or data relating to the Loan, for any legitimate business purpose through any source, including a source named in this application or a consumer reporting agency.

Borrower's Signature X	Date	Co-Borrower's Signature X	Date

X. INFORMATION FOR GOVERNMENT MONITORING PURPOSES

The following information is requested by the Federal Government for certain types of loans related to a dwelling in order to monitor the lender's compliance with equal credit opportunity, fair housing and home mortgage disclosure laws. You are not required to furnish this information, but are encouraged to do so. The law provides that a lender may not discriminate either on the basis of this information, or on whether you choose to furnish it. If you furnish the information, please provide both ethnicity and race. For race, you may check more than one designation. If you do not furnish ethnicity, race, or sex, under Federal regulations, this lender is required to note the information on the basis of visual observation and surname if you have made this application in person. If you do not wish to furnish the information, please check the box below. (Lender must review the above material to assure that the disclosures satisfy all requirements to which the lender is subject under applicable state law for the particular type of loan applied for.)

BORROWER ☐ I do not wish to furnish this information	CO-BORROWER ☐ I do not wish to furnish this information
Ethnicity: ☐ Hispanic or Latino ☐ Not Hispanic or Latino	Ethnicity: ☐ Hispanic or Latino ☐ Not Hispanic or Latino
Race: ☐ American Indian or Alaska Native ☐ Asian ☐ Black or African American ☐ Native Hawaiian or Other Pacific Islander ☐ White	Race: ☐ American Indian or Alaska Native ☐ Asian ☐ Black or African American ☐ Native Hawaiian or Other Pacific Islander ☐ White
Sex: ☐ Female ☐ Male	Sex: ☐ Female ☐ Male

To be Completed by Loan Originator:
This information was provided:
☐ In a face-to-face interview
☐ In a telephone interview
☐ By the applicant and submitted by fax or mail
☐ By the applicant and submitted via e-mail or the Internet

Loan Originator's Signature X	Date
Loan Originator's Name (print or type)	Loan Originator Identifier	Loan Originator's Phone Number (including area code)
Loan Origination Company's Name	Loan Origination Company Identifier	Loan Origination Company's Address

In mid-2011, FHA reported that loans with 10% down and FICO scores from 620 to 679 had an 8.6% default rate; scores from 580 to 619 had a 19.6% default rate.

History has shown that the higher the credit score, the less likely it is that the borrower will default on a loan. The range on FICO scores is 300–850. FHA normally requires a minimum score of 580; prospective borrowers with scores under 500 are not eligible for FHA loans. Fannie Mae and Freddie Mac look for at least 620 but may charge a higher rate of interest or a higher down payment if the score is under 660. Before applying for a mortgage loan, borrowers should check the accuracy of their credit score. Consumers can obtain one free credit report each year from all three major credit-reporting bureaus at www.annualcreditreport.com; however, free credit reports do not contain FICO scores. If an applicant is rejected for a loan based on a credit score or approved for a loan with a higher rate than one provided to best customers, a lender must provide the consumer with the credit score, explain the factors that adversely affected the score, and indicate the range of possible scores (Dodd-Frank Act).

Computerized Loan Origination and Automated Underwriting

A **computerized loan origination (CLO)** system is an electronic network for handling loan applications through remote computer terminals linked to several lenders' computers. With a CLO system, a real estate broker or salesperson can call up a menu of mortgage lenders, interest rates, and loan terms, then help a buyer select a lender and apply for a loan right from the brokerage office. Keep in mind that the SAFE Act requires a person who takes a loan application, negotiates terms, or discusses rates or terms to be licensed as a residential mortgage loan originator.

If appropriately licensed, the real estate agent may assist the applicant in answering the on-screen questions and in understanding the services offered. The broker in whose office the terminal is located may earn fees of up to one half percent of the loan amount. The *borrower*, not the mortgage broker or lender, *must pay the fee*. The fee amount may be financed, however. While multiple lenders may be represented on an office's CLO computer, consumers must be informed that other lenders are available. A CLO system enhances an applicant's ability to comparison shop for a loan. One-stop shopping real estate services are regulated by RESPA, which is discussed in Chapter 20.

Automated underwriting is the process of electronically evaluating a loan application and subsequently providing a recommendation for or against loan approval. It has become the primary method for making loan decisions and has shortened the loan approval process from weeks to minutes. Even complex or difficult mortgages can be processed in less than 72 hours. Through such programs as Freddie Mac's *Loan Prospector* and Fannie Mae's *Desktop Underwriter*, lenders evaluate the borrower's income, assets, and debt-to-income ratios. The computer models determine the borrower's likelihood of defaulting on the mortgage loan and thus determine the amount of income, credit history, and other documentation required by the lender. Automated underwriting has lowered the cost of loan processing for lenders and created homeowners from borrowers who might not have been approved through the traditional manual underwriting procedures.

Real estate agents should advise borrowers not to take on additional debt between the time of loan application and the date of closing. If a borrower discloses or a lender discovers additional debt and/or reduced income after the initial underwriting decision was made, lenders may be required to resubmit a loan for underwriting (Fannie Mae, August 2010).

IN PRACTICE   Online mortgage lenders are putting even more loan choices into buyers' hands. Because buyers may research lenders' websites, it benefits a licensee to stay informed about the latest internet resources.

PAYMENT PLANS

Although most mortgage and deed of trust loans are *fully amortized loans,* other payment plans may be more appropriate under certain circumstances—such as the interest-only payment, the flexible payment, and the balloon payment. These payment plans are illustrated in Figure 16.2.

FIGURE 16.2: Payment Plans

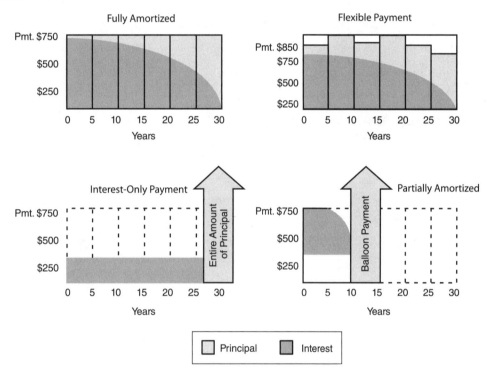

Fully Amortized Payment

The mortgagor's equity increases with each monthly principal payment, as well as through appreciation in the property's value.

In a **fully amortized loan** payment plan, the mortgagor pays a *constant amount,* usually monthly. The mortgagee credits each payment first to the interest owed; mortgage interest is generally paid in arrears, that is, interest is paid for the use of money during the prior month. The balance is then applied to reduce the principal amount over a term of years. Although the amount of each principal and interest payment is the same, the portion applied toward repayment of the principal grows; and the interest due declines as the unpaid balance of the loan is reduced. At the end of the term (usually 15 or 30 years, but occasionally even 40 years), the full amount of the principal and all interest due is reduced to zero. Such loans also are called *direct reduction loans.*

MATH CONCEPTS

Calculating a House Payment or Loan Amount

Calculating a house payment. Start by finding the appropriate interest rate in Figure 16.3. Then follow that row over to the column for the appropriate loan term. This number is the *interest rate factor* required each month **to amortize a $1,000 loan**. To calculate the principal and interest (P&I) payment, multiply the interest rate factor by the number of 1,000s in the total loan.

For example, if the interest rate is 5½% for a term of 30 years, the interest rate factor is 5.68. If the total loan is $100,000, the loan contains 100 thousands. Therefore, 100 × 5.68 = $568 P&I only.

Calculating a mortgage loan amount. Divide the P&I payment that a buyer can qualify for based on income by the appropriate interest rate factor and multiply by $1,000.

For example, if a homebuyer makes $2,272 gross income each month and the loan company uses a 25% housing expense ratio, what is the maximum loan (5½%, 30 years) for which the buyer can qualify?

$2,272 × .25 = $568 maximum payment

$568 ÷ 5.68 per $1,000 rate factor = $100,000 maximum loan

FIGURE 16.3: Mortgage Factor Chart

Interest Rate	Term 15 Years	Term 30 Years	Interest Rate	Term 15 Years	Term 30 Years
5	7.91	5.37	6 ⅝	8.78	6.40
5 ⅛	7.97	5.44	6 ¾	8.85	6.49
5 ¼	8.04	5.52	6 ⅞	8.92	6.57
5 ⅜	8.10	5.60	7	8.98	6.65
5 ½	8.17	5.68	7 ⅛	9.06	6.74
5 ⅝	8.24	5.76	7 ¼	9.12	6.82
5 ¾	8.30	5.84	7 ⅜	9.20	6.91
5 ⅞	8.37	5.92	7 ½	9.27	6.99
6	8.44	6.00	7 ⅝	9.34	7.08
6 ⅛	8.51	6.08	7 ¾	9.41	7.16
6 ¼	8.57	6.16	7 ⅞	9.48	7.25
6 ⅜	8.64	6.24	8	9.56	7.34
6 ½	8.71	6.32			

MATH CONCEPTS

Amortizing a Loan

The monthly principal and interest (P&I) payment on a $100,000 loan at 6% amortized over 30 years is $600 (see Figure 16.3: $100,000 ÷ $1,000 × $6.00). To determine the principal balance remaining after the first payment, (1) calculate the interest portion of the payment, (2) deduct that amount from the P&I payment, and (3) subtract the resulting principal reduction from the principal balance.

To compute one month's interest, use the formula $I = P \times R \times T$, where

    I = Interest

    P = Principal

    R = Rate

    T = Time

    $100,000 × 0.06 × \frac{1}{12}$ = $500 interest

To compute the principal portion of the payment:

    $600 − $500 = $100 applied to the principal

The principal balance used to calculate the next month's payment is $99,900.

    $100,000 − $100 = $99,900

Most amortized mortgage and deed of trust loans are paid in monthly installments. If the borrower wishes to pay off the loan more quickly and reduce the total interest costs, he may

- pay additional amounts that are applied directly to the principal (with the consent of the lender) or

- negotiate a **biweekly payment plan** that calls for 26 half-month payments a year (reducing the principal balance approximately twice each month and resulting in one full month's additional payment each year).

Interest-Only Payment

A mortgagor may choose an interest-only loan, or **term loan**, that calls for periodic payments of interest, with the principal to be *paid in full at the end of the loan term*. A Fannie-Mae-backed interest-only loan requires a 30% down payment, at least a 720 credit score, and a 24-month cash cushion. Term loans are generally used for home improvement loans, second mortgages, and investor loans rather than for residential first mortgage loans.

Flexible Payment

The mortgagor may elect to take advantage of a **flexible-payment loan**, generally used to enable younger buyers and buyers in times of high interest rates to purchase real estate. Under this plan, a mortgagor makes lower monthly payments for the first few years of the loan (typically the first five years) and larger payments for the remainder of the term, when the mortgagor's income is expected to increase.

Balloon Payment

When a mortgage or deed of trust loan requires periodic payments that will not fully amortize the amount of the loan by the time the final payment is due, the final payment is larger than the others. This is called a **balloon payment**, and this type of loan is a *partially amortized loan*. For example, the payments on a loan made for $80,000 at 11½% interest may be computed on a 30-year amortization schedule but paid over a 20-year term, with a final balloon payment due at the end of the 20th year. In this case, each monthly payment would be $792.24 (the amount taken from a 30-year amortization schedule), with a final balloon payment of $56,340 (the amount of principal still owing after 20 years). It is presumed that if the payments are made promptly, the lender will extend the balloon payment for another limited term. The lender, however, is not legally obligated to grant this extension and can require payment in full when the note is due. A balloon payment is frequently used in seller-financing transactions.

CONVENTIONAL, FHA, AND VA LOANS

Most first mortgage or deed of trust loans advanced for residential purposes are 15-year to 30-year fully amortized loans classified as conventional, FHA, or VA loans. These are discussed in detail in the following subsections.

Conventional Loans

The conforming loan limit for 2013 was $417,000.

A **conventional loan** is one that is not underwritten by a federal agency. It may be "conforming" or "nonconforming." Most conventional loans are *conforming* loans, meeting Fannie Mae and Freddie Mac guidelines so they can easily be sold in the secondary market. The conforming loan limit for 2013 was $417,000. Loans are *nonconforming* if they do not meet Fannie Mae/Freddie Mac guidelines—they may exceed the conforming loan limit or buyers may lack sufficient credit or collateral. Nonconforming loans can be made by any lender to be held in its own portfolio or sold to a private mortgage packager.

High down payment = *Low* LTV and *low* lender risk

Borrower qualifications for most conventional loans are somewhat more stringent than for FHA or VA loans. A buyer's maximum house payment (PITI) for a conventional loan is generally 25 to 28% of gross monthly income (the housing-expense or front-end ratio). Total debts cannot exceed 33 to 36% (the total-debt or back-end ratio), which includes the house payment, all installment and revolving account payments, and child support. Depending on a borrower's credit score, cash reserves, and residual income, higher ratios may be allowed. Because loan underwriting guidelines can vary, check with a local lender for its particular requirements. A conventional loan calculator is available at www.realtor.com.

Loan terms—such as minimum credit scores required, interest rate charged, and the necessity for mortgage insurance—are based on a **loan-to-value ratio (LTV)**, the ratio of debt to value of the property. Historically, the LTV on a conventional loan has been 80% of the value of the property or less, which requires a 20% or more down payment. Currently, the maximum LTV for most conventional loans is 95% (a 5% down payment); VA guarantees loans up to 100% of value (no down payment); FHA insures loans up to 96.5% (a 3.5% down payment) in its 203(b) program. The LTV is calculated by dividing the amount of the loan by the value of the property, which is the lesser amount of sales price or appraisal.

MATH CONCEPTS

Determining LTV

If a property has a sales price of $105,000 and an appraised value of $100,000, secured by an $80,000 loan, the LTV is 80%: $80,000 (loan) ÷ $100,000 (lesser of sales price or appraisal) = 80%.

Mortgage insurance premiums for conventional and FHA loans and funding fees for VA loans are tax deductible for some homebuyers.

Private Mortgage Insurance   Historically, Fannie Mae records indicate that loans on which a borrower has made a 3% down payment (a 97% LTV) are foreclosed four times more often than loans with a 10% down payment (a 90% LTV). The more money a homeowner has invested in the property, the more likely it is that he will do everything possible to keep the loan payments current and avoid foreclosure. To insure a lender against borrower default and loss due to foreclosure, **private mortgage insurance** (PMI) is required on high LTV loans for which the borrower has invested less than 20%, that is, on loans with LTVs over 80%. Mortgage insurance is purchased from a private mortgage insurance company when the loan is closed.

PMI insures a certain percentage of a loan, usually 25 to 30%, which limits the lender's exposure to only 70 to 75% in the event of a default. On all loans sold to Fannie Mae and Freddie Mac and on all other conventional loans if closed after July 29, 1999, borrowers must be sent an annual notice that states the borrower may cancel the PMI when the loan balance is 80% or less of the *original value* of the property. (Texas law requires notification when the loan-to-*current value* reaches 80%.) Depending on the size of the mortgage and the risk, automatic cancellation is required when the loan reaches 77 to 78% of the original property value.

A **point** is 1 percent of the *loan amount—not* 1 percent of the purchase price.

Discount Points   From a borrower's point of view, a deed of trust loan is a means of financing an expenditure; from a lender's point of view, it is an investment. To continually replenish their supplies of funds, lending institutions will often sell the loans to investors instead of holding them for the full term. However, the interest rate that a lender charges for a loan might be less than the *yield* (true rate of return) an investor demands. To make up the difference, the lender charges the borrower **discount points**.

FOR EXAMPLE   An investor is offered two loans—one made at an interest rate of 10% and the other at 10½%. If both loans were offered to an investor at the same price, the investor would choose the 10½% loan.

Discount points, then, represent the percentage by which the face amount of a mortgage loan is discounted, or reduced, when it is sold to an investor to make its interest rate yield competitive in the current money market. Without this discount, an investor would not be interested in the lower-rate loan.

As a general rule of thumb, each point of discount raises the effective yield by ⅛, of 1%; the actual amount depends on the term and type of loan obtained. For the borrower, one discount point equals 1% of the loan amount and is charged as prepaid interest at closing. Buyers and sellers negotiate to determine the portion of the points to be paid by each party.

MATH CONCEPTS

Calculating Discount Points

A house sells for $100,000, and the borrower seeks an 80% LTV loan. Each point charged on the $80,000 loan would be $800 ($80,000 x 0.01). If the lender charges 3 discount points, the total discount points due to the lender at closing would be $2,400 ($80,000 × 0.03). The lender's yield would be increased by an estimated ⅜ (⅛,% × 3 points).

Loan Origination Fee   A **loan origination fee** is a charge made by the lender for the expense involved in taking the loan application and processing and closing the loan. The loan origination fee is usually 1% of the loan amount, but the amount can vary with the complexity of the transaction and the supply and demand forces for mortgage money. A loan origination fee is not prepaid interest and is, therefore, collected in addition to any discount points charged on the loan.

FHA-Insured Loans

The Federal Housing Administration (FHA), which operates under the Department of Housing and Urban Development (HUD), neither builds homes nor lends money itself. The common term **FHA loan** refers to a loan that is *insured* by the agency. An FHA-approved appraiser must appraise the house and confirm that the property meets HUD's minimum property standards.

Section 203(b) Loans   The most popular FHA program is Title II, Section 203(b), which provides fixed-interest rate loans for 10 to 40 years on one-family to four-family residences.

Down Payment Calculation   Borrowers with 580 or higher credit scores are eligible for maximum financing through FHA. The maximum FHA-insured loan is 96.5% of the lesser of either (1) the appraiser's estimate of value or (2) the contract price for the property minus any required adjustments. Therefore, the minimum down payment requirement is 3.5% (100% – 96.5%). Borrowers with credit scores between 500 and 579 are limited to 90% LTV, which requires a 10% down payment. Borrowers with credit scores of less than 500 are not eligible for FHA financing. Currently, FHA permits down payment assistance from a limited number of sources, including community redevelopment programs. FHA single-family loans must include a consumer disclosure (within three days after loan application) that compares the costs of an FHA loan with that of a conventional loan. The down payment requirement for a mortgage with an original principal balance above $625,500 is 5%.

Maximum loan calculation notes:

■ The maximum FHA loan amount is established by regions. The maximum mortgage amounts for 2013 were at least $271,050 in all areas, which was 65% of the $417,000 Fannie Mae conforming loan. For 2014, the new national-ceiling loan limit for the very highest cost areas was reduced from $729,750 to $625,500.

- For homes less than one-year-old that were not built to FHA standards and do not carry a 10-year warranty plan, the loan ratio is 90% of the appraised value or selling price, whichever is less.
- If the contract purchase price of a property exceeds the FHA-appraised value, the buyer may pay the difference in cash as part of the down payment or opt out of the contract. The lender must base the loan on the lesser of the sales price or the appraised value.

Mortgage Insurance   In addition to paying interest, the borrower is charged a *one-time mortgage insurance premium* for the FHA insurance and a *monthly mortgage insurance premium*. The rate for the one-time, up-front mortgage insurance premium (UFMIP) is 1.75% of the loan amount. The UFMIP premium may be paid at closing by the borrower or by someone else but typically is added to the loan amount. Starting April 1, 2013, FHA annual mortgage insurance premiums increased from 1.25% of the loan amount to 1.35%. (A previous increase on April 1, 2012, raised the MIP from 1.15 to 1.25.) Starting June 1, 2013, for loans above $625,500, premium costs increased to 1.55% of the loan amount.

Effective June 3, 2013, FHA requires most FHA borrowers to continue paying annual premiums for the life of their mortgage loan—not just until homeowners build equity of 22% in their homes. Based on original principal amount, one of the two plans listed below apply:

- For all mortgages regardless of their amortization terms, any mortgage involving an original principal (excluding financed UFMIP) less than or equal to 90% LTV, the annual MIP will be assessed until the end of the mortgage term or for the first 11 years of the mortgage term, whichever occurs first.
- For any mortgage involving an original principal with an LTV greater than 90%, FHA will assess the annual MIP until the end of the mortgage term or for the first 30 years of the term, whichever occurs first. (FHA Mortgage Letter 2013-04, January 31, 2013)

Other FHA Loans   Title I FHA loans are granted for home improvements and repairs and for the purchase of manufactured homes. Title II FHA loans are granted for the construction or purchase of a home. They may also be obtained to refinance an existing mortgage debt. In addition to the 203(b) program previously discussed, major Title II FHA programs include the following:

- Disaster Victims Mortgage Insurance Program, Section 203(h), for homeowners in a presidentially designated disaster area
- Rehabilitation Loan Insurance Program, Section 203(k), for rehabilitation or purchase and rehabilitation of property; a streamlined version is designed for "as is" fixer-uppers, allowing borrowers to roll the cost of nonstructural major repairs into their mortgages
- Adjustable Rate Mortgage Insurance Program, Section 251, for loans that adjust annually based on a cost-of-funds index
- Home Equity Conversion Mortgage (HECM) Insurance Program (Reverse Mortgage), Section 255, for borrowers who are at least 62 years of age to convert the equity in their homes into a monthly stream of income or a line of credit
- Energy-Efficient Mortgage Program (EEM) for homes with energy improvements

> In the appraisal of properties for FHA loans, appraisers are required to adjust comparable sales to reflect sales concessions.

FHA Loan Qualifying   To qualify for an FHA-insured loan, the buyer must have a housing-expense ratio (including PITI, MIP, and homeowners' dues, if any) of no more than 31% of gross monthly income. The buyer's total-debt ratio cannot exceed 43% of gross monthly income; included in this amount must be the house payment, installment accounts (10 or more months remaining), all revolving accounts, and child support payments. FHA qualifying procedures are more lenient than those for conventional or VA loans. Effective April 1, 2013, transactions where the borrower has a credit score below 620 and the debt-to-income ratio exceeds 43.00% must be manually underwritten. (HUD Mortgagee Letter 2013-05)

Discount Points   The lender of an FHA-insured loan can charge discount points in addition to a *loan origination fee*. The payment of points is a matter of negotiation between the seller and the buyer. Sellers may contribute up to 6% of the sales price toward normal closing costs, prepaid expenses, and discount points. However, if the seller pays more than 6%, the lender is to treat such payments as *sales concessions*, and the price of the property for purposes of the loan will have to be reduced.

Assumption Rules   The assumption rules for FHA-insured loans vary, depending on the date that the loan was originated.

- FHA-insured loans originated prior to December 1986 generally have no restrictions on their assumption; the seller remains liable until the loan is paid off unless released by the lender or FHA.
- FHA-insured loans originated between December 1, 1986, and December 15, 1989, are fully assumable after 12 months; a creditworthiness review of the person proposing to assume is required. The seller remains liable for five years unless released by the lender or FHA.
- FHA-insured loans originated December 15, 1989, and thereafter require that the buyer/assumptor live in the house as a primary residence. These loans are not assumable without complete buyer qualification; the seller is released of all liability.

IN PRACTICE   As described, many FHA reforms were implemented in 2013. Check with a local lender for current FHA underwriting requirements. For more information, visit the HUD website.

WEBLINK @ www.hud.gov/buying/index.cfm

VA-Guaranteed (GI) Loans

The U.S. Department of Veterans Affairs (VA) is authorized to guarantee loans to purchase or construct homes for eligible veterans and their spouses (including the unremarried spouse of a veteran whose death was service-related or the spouse of a serviceperson missing in action or a prisoner of war). The VA also guarantees loans to purchase manufactured homes and land on which to place them. A veteran who meets any of the time-in-service criteria shown in Figure 16.4 is eligible for a VA loan. VA-guaranteed loans assist veterans in financing the purchase of homes with little or no down payments. Residential property must be owner-occupied.

Like the term *FHA loan*, *VA loan* is something of a misnomer. The VA normally does not lend money; it guarantees loans made by lending institutions approved by the agency. Therefore, the term **VA loan** refers to a loan that is not made by the agency, but *guaranteed by it*.

Maximum Loan and Guaranty   There is no VA limit on the amount of loan a veteran can obtain; the limit is determined by the lender. The VA simply limits the amount of loan it will guarantee in the event that a veteran defaults on the loan. Because most lenders want to participate in the secondary market and because Ginnie Mae (the secondary market for most VA loans) requires at least a 25% guaranty, the lenders will generally base the maximum VA loan amount on VA's guaranty.

To determine the portion of a mortgage loan that the VA will guarantee, the veteran must apply for a *certificate of eligibility*. *Eligibility* is the veteran's entitlement to VA home loan benefits under the law, based on military service. A certificate of eligibility does not guarantee that the veteran will get a loan; it simply reflects the available *entitlement*, which is the maximum amount the VA will guarantee. Each veteran receives $36,000 of basic home loan *entitlement*, provided the service requirements shown in Figure 16.4 are met. However, the specific amount of loan that would be guaranteed is based on the loan amount and prior use of the entitlement for another VA loan. For example, the VA will guarantee up to 50% of a loan of $45,000 or less; $22,500 on a loan between $45,001 and $56,250; up to 40% of a loan between $56,251 and $90,000; and $36,000 on a loan between $90,001 and $144,000. The maximum guaranty for loans between $144,001 and $417,000 is 25% of the conforming loan limit ($417,000). Therefore, the maximum guaranty for 2011 was $104,250 (25% × $417,000). For individuals with full eligibility, no down payment was required for a loan up to $417,000 in 2011.

FIGURE 16.4: VA Requirements for Eligibility

Period of Service	Dates	Minimum Service
WW II	9/16/40–7/25/47	90 days
Peacetime	7/26/47–6/26/50	181 days
Korean War	6/27/50–1/31/55	90 days
Post–Korean Era	2/1/55–8/4/64	181 days
Vietnam War	8/5/64–5/7/75	90 days
Post-Vietnam Era	5/8/75–9/7/80	181 days
Enlisted Personnel	after 9/7/80	24 months
Commissioned Officers	after 10/16/81	24 months
Persian Gulf War	after 8/2/90	24 months
If on active duty		90 days, wartime 181 days, peacetime
Reserves and National Guard	after 10/28/92	6 years

FOR EXAMPLE   On a $95,000 VA loan, $36,000 is the amount of the guaranty—the maximum amount the lender would receive from the VA if a foreclosure sale did not bring enough to cover the outstanding balance. Therefore, if the $95,000 loan were in default, the property could sell at foreclosure for as little as $59,000 ($95,000 – $36,000), and the lender would recoup the full value of the loan (disregarding the costs of foreclosure).

VA Loan Qualifying   Two methods must be employed to determine a veteran's ability to qualify for a loan—*debt-to-income ratio* and *residual income*. The combined total of monthly debts shall not exceed 41% of the veteran-borrower's gross monthly income; debts include the house payment, all installment accounts, all revolving accounts, minimum payments on paid-out revolving accounts, child support, and child care. *Residual income* is defined as the amount of monthly income remaining after all the debts listed above, income tax, Social Security tax, and maintenance and utilities are deducted. A regional chart showing residual incomes based on family size and loan amounts can be obtained from a local lender.

Appraisal and Closing   After an appraisal is conducted by a VA-approved appraiser, the VA issues a *Notice of Value* (NOV) for the property being purchased, stating its current market value. The NOV places a ceiling on the amount of a VA loan allowed for the property. If the purchase price is greater than the amount cited in the NOV, the veteran may withdraw from the contract without penalty and have the earnest money refunded or pay the difference in cash at closing.

VA regulations limit the fees that the veteran can pay to obtain a loan. The veteran can pay reasonable and customary amounts for VA "Itemized Fees and Charges," plus up to 1% as a flat charge by the lender as an origination fee to cover expenses that are not included in the itemized fees, plus reasonable discount points. A veteran is permitted to pay fees such as recording fees, a credit report, a survey, and most appraisal fees. A veteran is not permitted to pay directly certain other expenses of closing, such as loan closing or settlement fees, document preparation fees, or loan application fees; the lender is reimbursed for those fees by the 1% flat charge paid by the veteran. Either the veteran or the seller may pay any discount points, but they may not be financed in the loan.

In order to defray the cost of administering the VA home loan program, each veteran must pay a funding fee to the VA at closing. The amount of the funding fee varies depending on *regular* or *reserve* military status, amount of down payment, and whether it is a first or subsequent use of VA financing. For example, a *regular* military veteran making no down payment and using the VA loan program for the first time would pay a funding fee of 2.15%. Generally, the funding fee can be added to the loan amount. Funding fee rates are subject to change.

Assumption Rules   VA-guaranteed loans can be assumed by purchasers who do not qualify as veterans, and the balance of the veteran's entitlement will still be available for a new VA-guaranteed loan. However, if the seller-veteran wishes to have the full guaranty entitlement reinstated, an assumption must be by another qualified veteran who agrees to substitute his eligibility, or the old loan must be paid off. The assumption rules for VA-guaranteed loans vary, depending on the date that the loan was originated.

- Loans made prior to March 1, 1988—The veteran-seller can sell on assumption without prior approval from the VA and remain liable for loan repayment or require the purchaser to be approved by the VA and obtain a release from further liability on the loan.
- Loans made after March 1, 1988—The assumption borrower must have prior approval from the VA or the loan holder. The original veteran is given a release of liability. However, this procedure does not restore the veteran's entitlement to be used on another loan.

For more information on VA loans, visit the VA website.

WEBLINK @ www.homeloans.va.gov

Figure 16.5 is a comparison of conventional, FHA, and VA loan programs. The regulations and requirements of all home loan programs change occasionally. Check with local lenders for current information regarding any proposed loan.

FIGURE 16.5: Comparison of Loan Programs

Conventional	Federal Housing Administration	U.S. Department of Veterans Affairs
1. Financing is available to veterans and nonveterans.	1. Financing is available to veterans and nonveterans.	1. Financing available only to veterans and certain unremarried widows and widowers.
2. Financing for one-family to four-family dwellings; owner-occupied or investor loans.	2. Financing programs are for owner-occupied (one-family to four-family), residential dwellings.	2. Financing is limited to owner-occupied residential (one- to four-family) dwellings; must sign occupancy certificate.
3. Generally requires a larger down payment than FHA or VA.	3. Requires a larger down payment than VA.	3. Normally does not require down payment.
4. Requires appraisal by a licensed or certified appraiser.	4. Requires appraisal by an FHA-approved appraiser.	4. VA issues a Notice of Value (NOV) based on an appraisal by a VA-approved appraiser.
5. Maximum loan based on the lesser of the contract sales price or the appraised value; buyer may pay in cash the amount exceeding appraised value.	5. FHA valuation sets the maximum loan FHA will insure but does not limit the sales price; buyer may pay in cash the amount exceeding appraised value.	5. The VA loan may not exceed the appraised value of the home; buyer may pay in cash the amount exceeding appraised value.
6. No prepayment penalty if interest is 12% or more.	6. No prepayment penalty.	6. No prepayment penalty.
7. On foreclosure, the lender receives the amount of insurance coverage and sells the property.	7. On default, foreclosure, and claim, the FHA lender usually gets U.S. debentures.	7. Following default, foreclosure, and claim, the lender usually receives cash (if VA elects to take the house).
8. Insures loans over 80% LTV with private mortgage insurance (PMI), payable by buyer in cash or added to the note.	8. Insures the loan by way of mutual mortgage insurance; UFMIP payable at closing by buyer or seller; annual MIP paid monthly in the house payment.	8. Guarantees loans according to each veteran's personal entitlement.
9. Second-lien financing is permitted concurrently with first lien as long as minimum down payment requirements are met.	9. No secondary financing is permitted until after closing.	9. Secondary financing is permitted in exceptional cases.
10. Buyer may pay loan origination fee and discount points.	10. Buyer may pay loan origination fee and discount points.	10. Buyer may pay discount points but cannot finance them in the loan. Buyer may pay up to 1% as a flat charge origination fee to the lender. A funding fee must be paid to the VA in addition to other fees; it may be paid by the seller or buyer; if paid by the buyer, it may be paid in cash or added to the note.
11. Loans are generally nonassumable; a lender may permit assumption with a qualified assumptor.	11. Loans made prior to 12/1/86 are fully assumable; seller remains liable until the loan is paid off. Loans made between 12/1/86 and 12/15/89 are fully assumable after 12 months on owner-occupied loans; seller remains liable for 5 years. Loans made since 12/15/89 require prior approval of assumptor; seller is released from liability.	11. VA loan can be assumed without VA approval for loans made prior to 3/1/88; otherwise, approval is required. For loans originated after 3/1/88, release of liability is automatic if VA approves the assumption.

Agricultural Loan Programs

Two programs under the U.S. Department of Agriculture (USDA)—the Farm Service Agency and Rural Development—provide loans to farmers and/or homeowners in rural areas. Both programs were a part of the former Farmers Home Administration (FmHA).

The Farm Service Agency   The Farm Service Agency (FSA) offers both direct and guaranteed loans to purchase farmland and to construct or repair buildings and other fixtures. Using government funds, direct farm loans are made and serviced by the FSA. *Guaranteed* farm loans are made and serviced by local lenders and guaranteed by the FSA in the event of the borrower's default. For more information, visit the FSA website and select "Farm Loan Program."

WEBLINK @ www.fsa.usda.gov

Rural Development   Rural Development (RD) provides both direct and guaranteed loans for the purchase or construction of single-family homes, repair of existing homes, and the development of affordable rental housing. Under its Guaranteed Rural Housing program, RD targets very-low-income to moderate-income applicants in rural communities with populations of 10,000 or less (up to 20,000 under some circumstances). The home loans have *no down payment, no monthly mortgage insurance,* and *no loan limits.* The maximum loan amount is determined by the applicant's repayment ability, with income qualifying ratios of 29%/41%. Effective October 1, 2013, there is a guaranty fee of 2% of the loan amount (which can be added to the loan) and an annual fee of 0.4% of the unpaid principal balance, with authorization for RD to raise the fees to 3.5% and 0.5%, respectively. For more information, visit the RD website.

WEBLINK @ www.rurdev.usda.gov/HSF-About_Guaranteed_Loans.html

TEXAS LOAN PROGRAMS

Department of Housing and Community Affairs

Two programs are available through the **Texas Department of Housing and Community Affairs (TDHCA)** to finance the acquisition, construction, or rehabilitation of housing that meets the needs of very-low-income to moderate-income persons and families. By generating funds through bond issues, the Housing Finance Division helps lower-income working families buy homes through programs such as the following:

1. The *Texas First-Time Homebuyer Program* channels below-market interest rate mortgage money through participating Texas lending institutions to very-low-income to moderate-income Texas residents who are purchasing their first home or who have not owned a home in the past three years. Loans may be made only on a homebuyer's principal residence. To be eligible for a mortgage loan, a homebuyer must have an income of not more than 115% of area median family income or 140% of area median family income in targeted areas. The First-Time Homebuyer Program is also authorized to offer down payment and closing cost assistance.

2. The Texas "Bootstrap" Loan Program makes loans in amounts up to $45,000 to very-low-income families. The program is a self-help construction

program, which requires borrowers to provide at least 65% of the labor that is necessary to construct or rehabilitate the home being purchased. A portion of the 65% personal labor requirement can be contributed by nonpaid help from friends, family, or other volunteers. Loans from other funds may be combined with the "Bootstrap" loan, but the total of all loans cannot exceed $90,000.

For more information about these programs and others available through the TDHCA, call 800-525-0657; or visit their website.

WEBLINK @ www.tdhca.texas.gov/overview.htm

Texas Veterans Loan Programs

The **Texas Veterans Land Board** (VLB), a division of the General Land Office of Texas, administers three programs to assist Texas veterans in purchasing a principal residence and/or land and in financing home improvements. A veteran may participate in all loan programs simultaneously but may have only one loan in each of the three programs at one time. To qualify as a *Texas veteran*, a loan applicant must

- have served no fewer than 90 cumulative days of active duty service or active duty training in the Army, Navy, Air Force, Marine Corps, Coast Guard, U.S. Public Health Service, or recognized reserve component (unless discharged sooner due to a service-connected disability);
- have completed all required active duty training in the National Guard or Reserve;
- not have been dishonorably discharged;
- be a bona fide resident of Texas at the time of application; live in Texas with the intent to remain in Texas; this may include a Texas resident serving on active military duty outside of Texas;
- have repaid a previous VLB loan in the specific loan program for which the veteran is applying; or
- be the unmarried, surviving spouse of a Texas veteran who is missing in action, who died in the line of duty, or who died from a service-connected cause; the veteran's home of record must have been Texas at the time of entry into the military, or the veteran must have been a legal resident of Texas at the time of death.

Veterans Housing Assistance Program   The Veterans Housing Assistance Program (VHAP) provides funds to purchase a primary residence in Texas. The veteran must occupy the property within 60 days of closing and must live in the home as a principal residence for a period of three years from the date of closing. Properties that are eligible include single-family residences, condos, owner-occupied two- to four-family units (if constructed at least five years prior to closing), and some manufactured and modular homes. Although the VLB has set no limit on the amount of acreage bought with the home, lenders may have a maximum number of acres they will finance. All new-construction homes must be Energy-Star certified.

There is no maximum or minimum sales price restriction with this program; however, the VLB can only loan a maximum of $325,000 toward the purchase of a home. The VLB works with participating lenders to originate, process, close, and service the loans that may be underwritten as fixed-rate conventional, FHA, or

VA notes. The down payment, if any, will be based on the loan type. Subject to VLB guidelines, the down payment can be obtained as a gift from a relative, domestic partner, fiancée, or a grant from an employer or a public agency. The interest rate on a Housing Assistance loan is determined by the VLB and is, in most cases, lower than other forms of financing. A rate discount is available for veterans with a 30% or more service connected disability rating and for qualified unmarried surviving spouses. The base rate and discounts change weekly and are published each Friday after 5:00 pm on the VLB website.

Although no discount points are allowed, lenders may charge reasonable and customary fees, including a 1% origination fee and actual amounts for an appraisal, title insurance, credit report, and other closing costs. A 1% participation fee may also be charged by the lender, but this fee cannot be financed as part of the principal loan amount with an FHA or VA loan. The seller may pay all or part of the fees on behalf of the buyer, subject to specific loan underwriting guidelines.

Veterans Land Program   The Veterans Land Program offers eligible Texas veterans the opportunity to buy at least one acre of land and finance the purchase up to $80,000 over a 30-year term with a minimum of 5% down. If the purchase price of the land is more than $80,000, the veteran must pay the difference at closing from the veteran's own funds. The land must meet specific VLB criteria, including its being wholly located in Texas and having legal access to a public road. The veteran does not have to live on the land. The VLB originates all land loans, not private lenders. Applications are available online; allow 45–60 days to close.

Veterans Home Improvement Program   The Veterans Home Improvement Program (VHIP) will lend eligible Texas veterans up to $25,000 for up to 20 years to make substantial improvements to their existing primary residence. A veteran must get a minimum of two bids on the improvements to be made, and a general contractor must complete all work. The FHA-insured loan is originated directly through the VLB and requires no down payment. It is secured by a deed of trust, using the veteran's home as collateral. The VLB must be in a first- or second-lien position, and the veteran must occupy the home as a primary residence for at least three years from the date of completion of the home improvements. VHIP loans are closed at a title company or an attorney's office and funded in full within four days after closing.

IN PRACTICE   The Texas VLB waives the interest on VHAP loans for Texas reservists and national guard troops called to active duty. The monthly payment includes principal and escrow funds only. The waiver continues for three months after deactivation and the interest never has to be repaid. A land loan is frozen during activation and no payments are due until three months after deactivation.

Veterans can locate real estate professionals in their areas of the state by searching the Broker Registry on the VLB website. Licensed real estate agents who have completed VLB training may be listed in the Broker Registry and may link the VLB website to their own. To obtain up-to-date information about the Broker Registry or VLB programs, including interest rates and discounts, call 800-252-8387 or visit the website.

WEBLINK @ www.glo.texas.gov/vlb

OTHER FINANCING TECHNIQUES

Some special-purpose financing techniques have been created to meet special needs of borrowers. To avoid unexpected results, both the licensee and borrower must understand the long-term effect of any loan being considered.

Adjustable-Rate Mortgages (ARMs)

Current rates for the LIBOR or Treasury indices are available under "Interest Rates" at *www.moneycafe.com.*

Adjustable-rate mortgages (ARMs) are originated at one rate of interest, with the rate fluctuating up or down during the loan term based on a specified economic indicator. Because the interest may change, so may the mortgagor's loan payments. The amount of interest-rate adjustment is governed by the movement of an index that is beyond the control of the lender—such as the constant-maturity Treasury rate or the London interbank offered rate (LIBOR). Details of how, when, and how much the interest rate will change are included in the note. A *convertible feature* on most ARMs allows a borrower to convert to a fixed-rate loan during specified periods of the loan.

FOR EXAMPLE   An adjustable-rate loan starts at 6% a year, which is lower than a fixed-rate loan available at that time. The note states that the lender may adjust that rate no more often than once a year (the *adjustment period*) and that each year's new note rate will be the One-Year Constant-Maturity Treasury Rate (the *index*) plus 1.6% (the *margin*), with a *periodic rate cap* of 2% each year. In other words, with an initial 6% rate, the second year interest rate could not exceed 8% even if the index plus the margin exceeded that amount. The *aggregate rate cap* stated in the note provides for no more than a 5% increase/decrease over the 30-year term of the loan. Thus, the 6% loan could go no higher than 11%, no matter what happened to the lender's cost of money. And unless the loan terms stipulated a specific floor for the interest rate, it could go as low as 1%.

In times of rising interest rates, ARMs allow the lender to keep a loan profitable over the length of its term; in times of falling interest rates, the mortgagor can take advantage of lower mortgage rates without refinancing the loan. Lenders favor loans that do not have fixed interest rates—because with fixed-rate loans, they are making long-term loans based on short-term deposits. Even if a traditional fixed-rate loan is available, some borrowers choose the flexible-rate loan because the initial rate is generally lower and the borrower may believe there is a greater chance for long-term rates to decrease rather than increase. For ARMs with initial periods of five years or less, Fannie Mae requires a borrower to qualify at the greater of the note rate plus 2% or the fully indexed rate—11% in the example above.

Buydown Mortgages

With a **buydown mortgage**, the interest rate starts well below the market rate. The lender charges a buydown fee, which pays a portion of the mortgage loan interest in advance for the purpose of temporarily reducing the interest rate. The buydown fee is like a loan discount fee in that it increases the lender's yield on a loan, Typical buydown arrangements provide for a reduced interest rate over the first one to two years of the loan term and generally do not involve deferred interest or negative amortization.

FOR EXAMPLE A homebuilder wishes to stimulate sales by offering a lower-than-market rate. Or a first-time homebuyer may have difficulty qualifying for a loan at the prevailing rates, and relatives or the sellers want to help the buyer qualify. If the loan market interest rate is 6%, a "2-1" buydown would result in first-year loan payments at 4% interest (6% minus 2%); the second year, at 5%; the third and subsequent years, at 6%.

Purchase Money Mortgages (Deeds of Trust)

A **purchase money mortgage** is a note and deed of trust *created at the time of purchase*. The term is used in two ways: First, it may refer to any security instrument originated at the time of sale. More often, it refers to the instrument given by the purchaser to a seller who "takes back" a note for part or all of the purchase price. It may be a first or a junior lien, depending on whether prior mortgage liens exist. In the event of a foreclosure, a purchase money deed of trust is valid against the homestead.

FOR EXAMPLE A buyer wants to purchase a property for $200,000. He has $40,000 for a down payment and agrees to assume the existing mortgage of $100,000. The owner agrees to take back a purchase money second mortgage in the amount of $60,000. At closing, the buyer will execute a note and deed of trust in favor of the owner and the seller will transfer the title.

Equity Loans

A home equity loan may be used as a tool to enable a homebuyer to close on a new home before a previous home has sold and closed—as long as the buyer can qualify for the payments on all loans advanced against both properties.

In an **equity loan**, the lender agrees to make a loan based on the amount of equity in a borrower's home. It allows the homeowner to use the funds that accumulate from rising home prices and/or the first-loan paydown. Equity loans are popular as a source of funds for home improvement, college expenses, new business start-ups, and additional real estate investment.

Texas equity loans have many protective restrictions for homeowners, only a few of which are given here.

- The maximum loan-to-value ratio is 80%, less any existing liens on the subject property; closing costs cannot exceed 3%; and no negative amortization can occur.
- A decrease in market value cannot trigger loan acceleration, and prepayment penalties are prohibited.
- In the event of default on the equity loan, the lender must pursue a judicial foreclosure; and the loan is nonrecourse (there is no personal liability beyond the homestead property).
- Only one equity loan can be in place at a time; only one equity loan can be made in a given year, except in the case of a declared emergency.
- An equity loan cannot be closed sooner than 12 days after loan application, and the owner has a 3-day right of rescission after the credit has been extended.
- If the lender fails to comply with any of the detailed technical requirements for making an equity loan, the lender will forfeit all principal and interest on that loan.
- If the terms of the agreement were negotiated in Spanish, a summary of those terms and other pertinent information must be provided to the debtor in Spanish.

- The home equity loan may not be secured by homestead property that is designated for agricultural use as of the date of closing.

Home Equity Line of Credit Borrowers can use equity in a home to establish a *home equity line of credit (HELOC)*. The line of credit is set up as an open-end account in which the borrower may request advances, repay money, and reborrow money if desired. A few of the stipulations attached to the HELOC loans are as follows:

- Advances of up to 50% of the fair market value of the home are permitted but the maximum principal amount on all loans against the property may not exceed 80% of the fair market value of the home on the date the line of credit was established.
- Each advance must be at least $4,000.
- A lender may charge a fee for the line of credit loan only at the time the loan is initially established—not with additional advances or payments. Closing costs cannot exceed 3% of the entire loan amount.

Reverse Mortgages

Reverse mortgages enable homeowners who are 62 years old or older to borrow against the equity in their homes. The loan amount depends on the borrower's age, current interest rates, and the value of the home. The home does not have to be owned free and clear to qualify for a reverse mortgage. Loan proceeds can be used for any purpose and can be taken out as a lump sum, fixed monthly payment, line of credit, or a combination. In addition, a reverse mortgage can be used to refinance a home equity loan. The loan balance of the reverse mortgage increases as funds are advanced from the lender and as interest and other charges accrue. No repayment will be due on the funds advanced until

- the property is sold;
- the borrowers move from the home for longer than 12 months without prior approval from the lender;
- all borrowers have died; or
- the borrower defaults on any of the terms of the deed of trust, commits fraud in connection with the loan, or fails to maintain the priority of the lender's lien.

The average life of an FHA HECM loan is under 8 years.

Homeowners with reverse mortgages must continue to pay homeowners insurance premiums, real estate property taxes, homeowners' association dues, and maintenance expenses. The lender cannot require repayment from any asset other than the home, and the obligation to repay the loan is limited to the market value of the home without recourse for personal liability against the owner.

One of the most popular reverse mortgages is the FHA *home equity conversion mortgage* (HECM). There are currently two "traditional" HECM loan options, the HECM Standard (one option consolidated by HUD from the original "standard" and "saver" products), and the HECM for Purchase, where a buyer can purchase a home and obtain a reverse mortgage at the same time. In addition, in 2014, several lenders have made other HECM loan options available such as the HECM Choice, the HECM Fixed Advantage, and the HECM Fixed Fourtune. Under new HUD rules implemented in September 2013 for FHA HECM loans, borrowers are restricted on the amounts accessible to them at closing and during the first year after closing.

In November 2013, Texans voted in favor of Proposition 5 to amend Article16, section 50 of the Texas Constitution to authorize reverse mortgage loans for purchase of a residence homestead. Proposition 5 provided as follows: "The constitutional amendment to authorize the making of a reverse mortgage loan for the purchase of homestead property and to amend lender disclosures and other requirements in connection with a reverse mortgage loan." Prior to the constitutional amendment, Texans were unable to obtain an HECM for Purchase, although other HECM option were available so long as the mortgage was not used for the purchase of a home.

IN PRACTICE   Married couples interested in taking out a reverse mortgage loan should make sure that both names are on the loan, or they risk having to repay or refinance the loan if the signing spouse passes away or is unable to remain in the home. According to current HUD policy, if the surviving spouse wants to keep the home, the spouse must purchase it for at least the lesser of the mortgage balance or 95% of the current appraised value.

However, according to HUD Mortgagee letter 2014-07, for loans originated on or after August 4, 2014, a surviving spouse may stay in the home without having to immediately repay or refinance the loan so long as the surviving spouse meets certain criteria. Keep in mind that this new HUD policy only applies to loans originated on or after the effective date.

To obtain up-to-date information about FHA HECM loans, visit the HUD website.

Shared-Appreciation Mortgages (SAMs, Deeds of Trust)

With a **shared-appreciation mortgage** (SAM), the lender originates a deed of trust loan at a favorable interest rate (several points below the current rate) in return for a guaranteed share of the gain (if any) the borrower realizes when the property is sold. SAMs are primarily made to developers of large real estate projects. In some instances, they are also used in exchange for a lender's writedown of loan principal when a property is refinanced; refinancing borrowers share profits with the lender when the property is sold.

Package Mortgages (Deeds of Trust)

A **package mortgage** includes not only the real estate but also all personal property and appliances installed on the premises. In recent years, this kind of loan has been used extensively to finance furnished condominium units. Package loans usually include personal property, such as furniture, drapes, and kitchen appliances, as part of the sales price of the home. A package deed of trust may serve as a security agreement on the personal property and fixtures to be placed in or attached to the real property. Otherwise, as described in Chapter 11, the Texas Business and Commerce Code governs the pledging of personal property, with a UCC financing statement to secure the loan.

Blanket Mortgages (Deeds of Trust)

A **blanket mortgage** or deed of trust pledges *more than one parcel or lot*. It is usually used to finance subdivision developments; however, it can finance the purchase of improved properties or consolidate loans as well. A blanket loan usually includes a *partial release clause* that permits the borrower to obtain the release of any one lot or parcel from the lien by paying a specified amount of the loan. The lender issues a partial release for each parcel as it is released from the mortgage lien. The release includes a provision that the lien will continue to cover all unreleased lots.

Wraparound Loan

A **wraparound loan** enables a borrower to obtain additional financing from a second lender *without paying off the first loan*. The second lender gives the borrower a new, increased loan at a higher interest rate and assumes payment of the existing loan. The total amount of the new loan includes the existing loan as well as the additional funds needed by the borrower. The borrower makes payments to the new lender on the larger loan, and the new lender makes payments on the original loan out of the borrower's payments. The buyer should require a protective clause in the loan documents granting him or her the right to make payments directly to the original lender in the event of a potential default on the original loan by the second lender.

F O R   E X A M P L E   A buyer purchases a property for $100,000 with $15,000 down. The seller, acting as a lender, gives the buyer a wraparound note for $85,000 at 13%, and the buyer makes payments of $920.83 to the seller. The seller continues to make payments of $438.79 to the original lender on his $50,000 mortgage at 10%—and realizes a net monthly income of $482.04 ($920.83 – $438.79).

A due-on-sale clause (alienation clause) in the original deed of trust generally prevents a sale with a wraparound loan; therefore, it is not used often.

Open-End Mortgages (Deeds of Trust)

An **open-end mortgage** or deed of trust loan secures a note executed by the borrower to the lender, as well as any future advances of funds made by the lender to the borrower. The interest rate on the initial amount borrowed is fixed, but interest on future advances may be at the market rate then in effect. Often a less costly alternative to a home improvement loan, this financing technique allows the borrower to "open" the mortgage or deed of trust to increase the debt to its original amount, or the amount stated in the note, after the debt has been reduced by payments over a period of time. The mortgage usually states the maximum amount that can be secured, the terms and conditions under which the loan can be opened, and the provisions for repayment.

Construction Loans

A **construction loan** is made to *finance the construction of improvements* on real estate (homes, apartments, and office buildings). Under a construction loan, the lender commits the full amount of the loan but disburses the funds, known as *draws*, throughout the construction period. Draws are made to the general contractor or the owner for that part of the construction work that has been completed since the previous payment. Before each payment, the lender inspects the work. The general contractor must provide the lender with adequate waivers releasing all mechanics' lien rights for the work covered by the payments.

Although interest is charged only on the amount disbursed, this kind of loan generally bears a higher-than-market interest rate because of the risks to the lender, such as the inadequate release of mechanics' liens, possible delays in construction, or the financial failure of the contractor. Construction loans are generally *short-term* or *interim financing*. The ultimate buyer/borrower is expected to arrange for a permanent loan, also known as a *takeout loan*, that will repay or "take out" the construction financing lender when the work is completed.

Sale and Leaseback

Sale-and-leaseback arrangements are used to finance large commercial or industrial properties. The land and the building, usually used by the seller for business purposes, are sold to an investor, such as an insurance company. The buyer/investor then leases the real estate back to the seller, who continues to conduct business on the property as a tenant. The buyer/investor becomes the lessor, and the original owner becomes the lessee. This enables a business firm that has money invested in a plant to free that money so it can be used as working capital.

Contract for Deed (Installment Contract)

As discussed in Chapter 12, a **contract for deed** can be effectively used when mortgage financing is unavailable or too expensive or when the purchaser has insufficient down payment funds. Title to property purchased on a contract for deed normally does not transfer to the purchaser until the full price has been paid.

The Texas Veterans Land Board sells land through its Veterans Land Program with a contract for deed.

IN PRACTICE When complex financing situations exist, a real estate broker should advise parties to consult with legal and tax experts.

GOVERNMENT INFLUENCE IN MORTGAGE LENDING

In addition to the FHA-insured and VA-guaranteed loan programs and the USDA agricultural loan programs, the federal government plays a major role in mortgage lending through the Federal Reserve System, as well as its secondary market activities.

Federal Reserve System

The **Federal Reserve System (the "Fed")**, the nation's central bank, operates to maintain sound credit conditions, help counteract inflationary and deflationary trends, and create a favorable economic climate. The Federal Reserve System divides the country into 12 federal reserve districts, each served by a federal reserve bank. All nationally chartered banks must join the Federal Reserve and purchase stock in its district reserve banks. The Fed regulates the flow of money and interest rates in the marketplace indirectly by controlling *reserve requirements* and *discount rates* for member banks and by its *open market operations*.

Reserve The Federal Reserve requires that each member bank keep a certain amount of its assets on hand as reserve funds, unavailable for loans or any other use. This requirement not only protects customer deposits but also provides a means of manipulating the flow of cash in the money market.

In setting its reserve requirements, the Federal Reserve in effect establishes the amount of money that member banks can use to make loans. When the reserve requirement is increased and the amount of money available for lending decreases, interest rates rise. By causing interest rates to rise, the government can slow down an overactive economy, limiting the number of loans that would have been directed toward major purchases of goods and services. The opposite is also true: By decreasing the reserve requirements and causing the amount of money circulated in the marketplace to rise, the Fed can encourage more lending and interest rates drop.

Since October 2008, the Fed has had the authority to pay banks interest on their reserves in excess of the requirement. By raising or lowering those interest rates, the Fed can control the release of money from banks to businesses and consumers. For example, when the Fed offers a higher interest rate than businesses are willing to pay, the banks will retain their excess reserves and earn the higher interest rates offered by the Fed, limiting the amount of money going into the marketplace and tightening the reins on an expanding economy.

Discount Rates   Federal Reserve member banks are permitted to borrow money from the district reserve banks to maintain their liquidity but not to expand their lending operations. The interest rate charged by the district banks for the use of this money is called the *discount rate*. This rate is the basis on which banks determine the percentage rate of interest they will charge their loan customers. The *prime rate*, the short-term interest rate charged to a bank's largest, most creditworthy customers, is strongly influenced by the Fed's discount rate. In turn, the primate rate is often the basis for determining a bank's interest rates on other loans, including mortgages. In theory, when the Federal Reserve discount rate is high, bank interest rates are high, fewer loans will be made, and less money will circulate in the marketplace. Conversely, a lower discount rate results in lower interest rates, more bank loans, and more money in circulation.

Open Market Operations   The Fed's open market operations encompass the movement of cash into or out of the commercial banks through the buying or selling of government bonds. When the Fed buys bonds, the banks receive an influx of cash that can be used to make more loans and thus lift the economy.

IN PRACTICE   The Fed activities of the late 2000s illustrate its role in counteracting potential deflationary trends and working to create a favorable economic climate. Between December 2006 and March 2009, banks' reserve requirements decreased from 10% to 3%. In spring 2008, the *federal funds* rate, the interest rate banks charge each other for loans, was 2%; by December 2008, it was reduced to between 0 and 0.25%, where it is today. In November 2008, the Fed bought up $1.25 trillion of mortgage-backed securities and by fall 2009 had bought up $300 billion of Treasury securities. By decreasing the reserve requirement, lowering the discount rate, and buying securities, the Fed increased the amount of money in circulation, thereby helping banks to loan money and consumers to make purchases—providing an atmosphere for economic recovery.

The Secondary Market

In addition to the *primary mortgage market*, where loans are originated, there is a **secondary mortgage market**. Here, loans are bought and sold after they have been closed and funded by a primary mortgage market lender. Lenders routinely sell loans to avoid interest rate risks and to realize profits on the sales. Selling the loans they have originated to secondary market entities enables lenders to recoup their capital to continue making mortgage loans. When a loan is sold, the original lender may retain the servicing (collecting the payments from the borrower and disbursing monies) or the servicing may be sold too. The *loan servicer* passes the payments along to the investor who purchased the loan and collects a servicing fee from the investor. Effective September 1, 2011, residential mortgage loan servicers are required to register with the Texas Department of Savings and Mortgage Lending unless they are already regulated by other state or federal laws (S.B. 17, 2011).

Loans are eligible for sale to the secondary market only when the collateral, borrower, and documentation meet certain requirements to provide a degree of safety for the investors. **Warehousing agencies** purchase a number of mortgage loans and assemble them into packages called *pools*. Securities that represent shares in these pooled mortgages are then sold to investors. Because real estate mortgage loans are traded on the stock exchanges as mortgage-backed securities, interest rates and loan discount rates are sensitive to the pressures of the markets and can change daily. The major secondary market entities are discussed in the following paragraphs.

Fannie Mae Fannie Mae is a government-sponsored enterprise (GSE) chartered by Congress as a private corporation. It was placed into conservatorship with the Federal Housing Finance Agency (FHFA) in September 2008. Its mission is to increase the availability and affordability of homes for low-, moderate-, and middle-income Americans. To accomplish that, it provides a secondary market for conventional, FHA, and VA mortgage loans. Fannie Mae buys individual loans or *pools* of mortgages from a lender in exchange for *mortgage-backed securities*, which the lender may keep or sell. Fannie Mae guarantees payment of all interest and principal to the holder of the securities. For more information, visit the website.

WEBLINK @ www.fanniemae.com

Freddie Mac Freddie Mac is also a GSE chartered by Congress as a private corporation. In September 2008, it too was placed into conservatorship with the FHFA. Freddie Mac has the authority to purchase mortgages, pool them, and sell bonds in the open market with the mortgages as security. Freddie Mac guarantees mortgages in the conventional conforming market. If a borrower stops making payments, Freddie Mac steps in and makes the payments to securities investors.

Fannie Mae and Freddie Mac were created to bring liquidity, stability, and affordability to local mortgage markets by buying loans from lenders, packaging them into securities, and selling them to investors worldwide.

Most lenders use Fannie Mae/Freddie Mac standardized forms and follow the underwriting guidelines issued by those entities so they can sell their mortgages into the agencies' secondary mortgage markets. Their standardized documents include loan applications, credit reports, appraisal forms, notes, and deeds of trust.

WEBLINK @ www.freddiemac.com

Ginnie Mae Chartered as the Government National Mortgage Association (GNMA), Ginnie Mae is a wholly owned corporation within the Department of Housing and Urban Development (HUD). Its goal is to help make affordable housing a reality for low- and moderate-income households. Ginnie Mae does not buy or sell loans or issue mortgage-backed securities. What Ginnie Mae does is guarantee securities issued by private institutions and backed by pools of federally insured or guaranteed loans—mainly FHA, VA, and USDA Rural Development mortgage loans. The *Ginnie Mae pass-through certificate* is a security interest in a pool of mortgages that provides for a monthly "pass-through" of principal and interest payments to investors. Ginnie Mae securities are guaranteed by the full faith and credit of the United States government. Regardless of whether the mortgage payment is made, investors in Ginnie Mae securities will receive full and timely payment of principal as well as interest. For more information about Ginnie Mae, visit its website.

WEBLINK @ www.ginniemae.gov

Farmer Mac   Farmer Mac is another GSE chartered by Congress as a private corporation. It, however, is not in conservatorship. Farmer Mac provides a secondary market for first-mortgage agricultural real estate loans by purchasing USDA guaranteed loans from agricultural mortgage lenders, pooling or bundling those loans, and issuing mortgage-backed securities, increasing the availability of credit for farmers, ranchers, and rural homeowners.

WEBLINK @ www.farmermac.com

Private Mortgage Packagers   *Private mortgage packagers* also purchase and pool mortgages from loan originators selling to the secondary market. Some specialize in areas not serviced by Fannie Mae, Freddie Mac, or Ginnie Mae, such as jumbo loans with balances that exceed limits set by the other secondary markets.

IN PRACTICE   Several proposals have been presented to wind down the operations of Fannie Mae and Freddie Mac, which are in conservatorship. The process is expected to take several years. In the meantime, to discourage unsafe and unsound underwriting practices in the primary mortgage market, mortgage originators and issuers of mortgage securities will be required to retain 5% of the credit risk on each loan unless it is a qualified residential mortgage (QRM). Although the QRM had not been defined at press time, proposed rules include imposing a minimum 20% down payment, stringent debt-to-income ratio requirements, and rigid credit standards.

FINANCING LEGISLATION

The federal government regulates the lending practices of mortgage lenders through several pieces of legislation, among them the Dodd-Frank Act, the Truth in Lending Act (TILA), the Equal Credit Opportunity Act (ECOA), the Community Reinvestment Act, and the Real Estate Settlement Procedures Act (RESPA). Recent consumer protection legislation centers around identity theft, mortgage fraud, and predatory lending issues.

Dodd-Frank Wall Street Reform and Consumer Protection Act of 2010

The Dodd-Frank Act is a very large and multifaceted law created in part to address problems that caused the financial crisis in 2008. Highlights of the legislation (referencing from "A Brief Summary of the Dodd-Frank Wall Street Reform and Consumer Protection Act" on the banking.senate.gov website) relevant to the real estate industry are as follows:

■ Creates the Consumer Financial Protection Bureau (CFPB), an independent agency within the Federal Reserve Board, with authority to protect American consumers from hidden fees and deceptive practices related to obtaining mortgages, credit cards, and other financial products. The Dodd-Frank Act gave the CFPB oversight authority over many of the major federal financial consumer protection laws including RESPA, TILA, and HOEPA, which were assigned previously to a variety of other federal agencies. New rules adopted by the CFPB are addressed below and in other relevant chapters of this book.

■ Ends bailouts of "Too Big to Fail" companies by establishing stricter standards on financial entities, providing additional supervision of the entities, imposing new requirements that make it more difficult for financial entities to get too big, and addressing safe ways for failing financial entities to liquidate.

■ Creates the Financial Stability Oversight Council charged with "identifying and responding to emerging risks through the financial system."

■ Provides transparency and accountability for financial instruments such as derivatives, asset backed securities and hedge funds.

■ Provides for mortgage lending reform by requiring that lenders ensure that a borrower has to ability to repay a home loan, requires additional mortgage disclosures, prohibits prepayment penalties for "not qualified mortgages" and requires a three-year phase out of prepayment penalties for qualified mortgages, prohibits mortgage loan steering and the payment of compensation, including a yield spread premium or YSP, to a mortgage originator "that varies based on the terms of the loan (other than the amount of the principal)," provides for penalties for lenders who violate the provisions of the law including protection from foreclosure for borrowers, and provides addition consumer protections for high-cost mortgages. New Ability to Repay rules adopted by the CPFB under these statutory mandates are detailed below; new rules addressing prepayment penalties are discussed in Chapter 15.

■ Requires the CFPB to adopt rules to establish new disclosures and "a single integrated disclosure" form that must be provided to consumers when applying for and closing on a home loan under TILA and RESPA. The CFPB adopted new rules and forms with an effective date of August 1, 2015. The forms, entitled Loan Estimate, to be provided within three business days after the borrowers submits a loan application, and the Closing Disclosure, to be provided three business days before closing, replace the Good Faith Estimate (GFE) and the HUD-1, respectively. The forms are reproduced and further described in Chapter 20.

Regulation Z (Truth in Lending, TIL)

Regulation Z of the *Truth in Lending Act*, administered by the new Consumer Financial Protection Bureau, requires that credit institutions inform borrowers of the true cost of obtaining credit. Its purpose is to permit borrowers to compare the costs of various lenders and avoid the uninformed use of credit. Regulation Z applies when credit is extended to individuals for personal, family, or household uses and the amount of credit is $50,000 or less, effective July 21, 2011. The Dodd-Frank Act requires this threshold to be adjusted annually beginning December 31, 2011; for 2014, Regulation Z will apply to consumer credit transactions of $53,500 or less. Regardless of the loan amount, however, when a residence secures a credit transaction, *Regulation Z always applies*. The regulation does not apply to business, commercial, or agricultural loans.

Finance charges include:
■ Nominal interest rate
■ Loan origination fees
■ Discount points
■ Finder's fees
■ Servicing fees
■ Mortgage insurance or guaranty fees

APR Regulation Z mandates that the customer be fully informed of all finance charges and the true annual interest rate (annual percentage rate or APR) before a transaction is consummated. In addition to the *nominal interest rate* (the interest rate before finance charges are added), the APR must include the costs that are incurred in a transaction *solely* because there is a loan involved—such as loan origination fees, finders' fees, servicing fees, mortgage insurance or guaranty fees, and points, as well as interest. The lender does not have to include as part of the finance charge such costs as title fees, legal fees, appraisal fees, credit reports, survey fees, and closing expenses because they are incurred whether or not there is a loan involved. In the case of a mortgage loan made to finance the purchase of a dwelling, the Truth-in-Lending (TIL) Disclosure statement shows, among other things, the annual percentage rate (APR), the amount borrowed, the total interest charge, and the total of all principal and interest that will be paid over the full term of the loan.

Creditor   A *creditor*, for purposes of Regulation Z, is any person who extends consumer credit more than 25 times each year or more than 5 times each year if the transactions involve dwellings as security. The credit must be subject to a finance charge or payable in more than four installments by written agreement.

Three-Day Right of Rescission   In most consumer credit transactions covered by Regulation Z, the borrower has three days in which to rescind the transaction by merely notifying the lender. *This right of rescission does not apply to residential first mortgage loans that finance the acquisition or initial construction of a dwelling or to refinancings with the original creditor when no "new money" is advanced.* It does, however, apply to other refinancing options on a home mortgage, to a second lien, or to a home equity loan.

Advertising   Regulation Z provides strict regulation of real estate advertisements that include mortgage financing terms. It applies to advertisements in all media, including newspapers, flyers, signs, billboards, websites, radio, television, and direct mailings. General phrases like "liberal terms available" may be used, and the selling price and APR may be advertised without disclosure of additional financing information. However, if specific **trigger terms** (such as the down payment, number of payments, monthly payment, or dollar amount of the finance charge) are used, the following information must be included as well:

- Amount or percentage of down payment
- Terms of repayment, reflecting repayment obligations over the full term of the loan, including any balloon payment, and
- Annual percentage rate and any increase in the rate after loan closing

Truth-in-lending regulations also specify detailed requirements for print, electronic, and internet advertising, including such prohibitions as using the term "fixed" when a payment can change and using the term "debt elimination" when a program merely replaces one obligation with another.

Recent Additions to TIL Disclosures   After the mortgage industry started to break apart in late 2007, Congress amended several laws that, in part, also amended the Truth in Lending Act. The *Mortgage Disclosure Improvement Act (MDIA)* addressed the timing of disclosures to borrowers on any dwelling and the collection of fees by the lender. The *Home Ownership and Equity Protection Act (HOEPA)* addressed misleading or deceptive mortgage lending practices related to refinancing and home equity mortgages with high interest rates or high fees. The Dodd-Frank Act amended HOEPA to expand the types of loans covered by HOEPA to include purchase money mortgage loans and home equity lines of credit (HELOCs) and to require homeownership counseling for mortgage loans subject to HOEPA. Reverse mortgages, construction loans, loans financed by a Housing Finance Authority, and loans originated under the Rural Development Loan Program are exempt from HOEPA coverage.

The key TIL requirements of **MDIA** include the following.

■ Lenders must provide buyers with good-faith estimates of mortgage loan costs within three business days after receiving a loan application; these are called *early disclosures*.

■ Lenders must wait seven business days after providing early disclosures before closing a loan.

■ Lenders cannot collect fees for appraisals or other expenses until early disclosures are issued.

■ A homebuyer must get a copy of the appraisal at least three business days prior to closing.

■ A lender must reissue a TIL disclosure and wait an additional three business days to close a loan if the APR increases beyond a specified percentage from the initial TIL disclosure.

■ Risky loan features must be disclosed for adjustable-rate mortgages, balloon payments, negative amortizations, and similar arrangements.

■ Under the Dodd-Frank Act and rules adopted by the CPFB for loan applications received on or after August 1, 2015, the TIL early disclosure has been combined with the Good Faith Estimate (GFE) required by RESPA into one document entitled the Loan Estimate form. The Loan Estimate form is discussed in Chapter 20.

The key TIL requirements for high-cost mortgage loans subject to HOEPA, including requirements under the amendments to the rules effective January 10, 2014, are as follows:

■ Lenders must assess the borrower's ability to repay the loan, including verifying income and assets and basing payments on the fully indexed interest rate on adjustable-rate loans.

■ Lenders must provide certain disclosures to borrowers at least three business days before loan closing or account opening on a high-cost mortgage.

■ Lenders may not charge prepayment penalties, or finance points and fees.

■ Lenders must disclose the right of rescission when the new balance on a loan modification exceeds the original balance.

■ Balloon payments are generally banned except under certain circumstances.

■ Late fees may not be more than 4% of the past due payment.

■ Lenders may not advise borrowers to default on a debt so that it may be refinanced by a high-cost mortgage.

■ Lenders must ensure that the borrower has gone through homeownership counseling prior to making a high-cost mortgage loan.

Penalties Regulation Z imposes penalties for noncompliance. A fine of up to $10,000 may be imposed for engaging in an unfair or deceptive practice. The penalty for violation of an administrative order enforcing Regulation Z is $10,000 for each day the violation continues. In addition, on a loan secured by real property, a creditor may be liable to a consumer for twice the amount of the finance charge, for a minimum of $200 and a maximum of $2,000, plus court costs, attorney fees, and any actual damages. Willful violation is a misdemeanor punishable by a fine of up to $5,000 or one year's imprisonment, or both.

The Ability-to-Repay Rule and Qualified Mortgage Standards   The Consumer Financial Protection Bureau (CFPB) issued qualified mortgage and ability to repay rules under Regulation Z effective January 10, 2014. As described previously, the Dodd-Frank Act requires lenders to look at a borrower's financial information and determine the borrower's "ability to repay" a loan before making a mortgage loan, and required the CFPB to adopt rules addressing these requirements. Under the Ability-to Repay rules in Regulation Z, there are eight factors a lender must consider in assessing the financial status of the borrower:

- Income or assets
- Current employment status
- Monthly payments for the mortgage using the highest interest rate that a borrower would have to pay—not a temporary initial low interest rate, and assuming substantially equal fully amortized payments
- Monthly payments for other simultaneous loans secured by the property
- Mortgage-related obligations such as property taxes, insurance and HOA fees
- Debt obligations, including alimony and child support
- Monthly debt-to-income ratio
- Credit history

Home equity lines of credit, time-share plans, reverse mortgages, and temporary loans are not subject to the Ability-to-Repay rule.

The Ability-to-Repay rule presumes a lender has met the ability-to-repay requirements if the loan is considered a qualified mortgage (QM). A qualified mortgage is defined in the rule as follows:

- It cannot be an interest-only loan, a negative amortization loan, or a balloon loan [a balloon loan may be permitted in a rural or underserved area] and it cannot have a loan term longer than 30 years.
- The creditor must verify income and assets (prohibits "no-doc" loans).
- The debt-to-income ratio cannot exceed 43%.
- Upfront points and fees cannot exceed 3% of the loan amount for loans of $100,000 or greater.
- Monthly payments must be calculated based on the highest payment that will apply in the first five years of the loan.
- Full documentation of loans must be preserved by lenders for three years.

The QM rule spells out underwriting standards that lenders must meet to be shielded from litigation. During a transition period that could last up to seven years, loans approved by GSE (Fannie Mae, Freddie Mac) and FHA automated underwriting (AU) systems (even with debt-to-income ratios above 43%) will be considered QM loans.

The Dodd-Frank Act also requires the CFPB to issue a qualified residential mortgage (QRM) rule, which will be based on the requirements of the QM rule summarized above. The QRM rule will determine which securitized mortgages should be exempt from a 5% risk retention requirement on home loans made to consumers. The QRM still has not been defined at the time of this writing.

IN PRACTICE   The new Consumer Financial Protection Bureau (CFPB), an independent agency housed in the Federal Reserve Board, was established to prevent mortgage lenders and other financial service providers from engaging in "unfair, deceptive, or abusive acts or practices." The CFPB inherited some of the regulatory authority previously granted to the Federal Trade Commission (FTC), the Fed, the FDIC, the Comptroller of the Currency, and HUD. The CFPB began operations on July 21, 2011, with a 6- to 18-month implementation period during which regulatory authority for various laws were transferred to the agency and the agency began rulemaking on the numerous statutory mandates of the Dodd-Frank Act. One of the first priorities of the new agency was the creation of a new mortgage disclosure form that combines the Truth-in-Lending Disclosure form and the Good Faith Estimate; the goal is a simpler form that gives a consumer the information needed to pick the best mortgage product. The forms will be required in all transactions beginning August 1, 2015 and are more thoroughly described and reprinted in Chapter 20. The bureau may impose a full range of legal and equitable penalties for violations of the Dodd-Frank Act, including civil penalties ranging from $5,000 to $1 million per day for each violation; civil or criminal enforcement actions may be brought by the Texas attorney general. For more information, visit the Consumer Financial Protection Bureau website.

WEBLINK @ www.consumerfinance.gov

Identity Theft

The Fair and Accurate Credit Transactions Act of 2003 (FACTA)   FACTA, administered by the CFPB, was designed to expand consumer access to credit, enhance the accuracy of consumers' financial information, and help fight identity theft. The primary provisions of the act are as follows:

- Consumers may obtain one free credit report per year from all three major credit-reporting bureaus: Experian, Equifax, and TransUnion. To get a free credit report, consumers can log on to AnnualCreditReport.com or they can call 877-322-8228.
- To help prevent identity theft, merchants may print only the last five digits of a credit card number on a receipt.
- A national system of fraud detection and fraud alerts has been established to make it easier for consumers to report possible identity theft.
- A *disposal rule* requires that reasonable measures be taken to protect against unauthorized access to, or use of, consumer information during record disposal.

Under the FACTA "red flags" rule, financial institutions and certain creditors must develop a written program that identifies and detects the relevant warning signs—or *red flags*—of identity theft. These may include, for example, unusual account activity, fraud alerts on a consumer credit report, or a suspicious address. Each institution's identity theft prevention program must describe appropriate responses that would prevent and mitigate the crime.

WEBLINK @ www.annualcreditreport.com

Security-Freeze Law   Requesting a security freeze allows consumers to lock up their credit reports to protect their credit records from identity thieves who use stolen information to open new accounts in their victims' names. A freeze prevents a credit reporting agency from releasing a credit report or a credit score; and a creditor, such as a credit card company, will not open a new account without a credit check. The Texas Business and Commerce Code requires a consumer reporting agency to place a security freeze on a consumer's credit file within five days after the agency receives an online request or written request sent by certified mail. Each credit reporting agency (Equifax, Experian, and TransUnion) must be contacted separately. If the consumer later wants to apply for a mortgage loan or a credit card, she can lift the freeze for a designated period of time or for an identified requester by again going online or writing to all three agencies. Unless a consumer is a victim of identity theft, the consumer reporting agency can charge a nominal fee for placing a security freeze on a consumer's file or for temporarily lifting a freeze.

WEBLINK @
www.equifax.com
www.experian.com
www.transunion.com

The USA PATRIOT Act   Financial institutions originating mortgages need to comply with a portion of the USA PATRIOT Act that holds them responsible for identifying customers, verifying their identities, keeping records on them, and checking their names against those on a government terrorist list. Additionally, the USA PATRIOT Act requires all financial institutions to establish an anti-money-laundering program.

Predatory Lending/Mortgage Fraud

Predatory Lending   In communities across America, people are losing their homes and their investments because of predatory lending practices. People with lower incomes, senior citizens, and credit-challenged borrowers are most often the targets. HUD has defined predatory lending as lenders, appraisers, mortgage brokers, and home improvement contractors who
- knowingly lend more money than a borrower can afford to repay;
- charge high interest rates to borrowers based on their race or national origin and not on their credit history;
- charge fees for unnecessary or nonexistent products and services;
- pressure borrowers to accept higher-risk loans such as balloon loans, interest-only payments, and steep prepayment penalties;
- use cash-out refinance offerings to target vulnerable borrowers;
- "strip" homeowners' equity from their homes by convincing them to refinance again and again when there is no benefit to them; or
- use high pressure sales tactics to sell home improvements and then finance them at high interest rates.

Both the consumer credit protections in the Texas Finance Code and the Truth in Lending Act afford some protection against unscrupulous and predatory lending practices. Creditors engaged in the business of extending credit for personal, family, or household use are prohibited from advertising a false, misleading, or deceptive statement relating to a rate, term, or condition of a credit transaction or from advertising credit terms that the creditor does not intend to offer to consumers who qualify for them. Effective April 1, 2011, TIL stipulates that loan originators who take an application, assist a consumer in applying or obtaining a loan, or offer to negotiate the terms of a loan
- cannot be compensated on the terms of the loan (interest rate or type of loan),
- cannot receive compensation from both the borrower and the lender, and
- are prohibited from steering borrowers toward loans that are not in the consumer's best interest.

Mortgage Fraud As just discussed, predatory lending is a practice that affects borrowers. Mortgage fraud, on the other hand, affects lenders. There are two distinct types of mortgage fraud: fraud for housing and fraud for profit. According to the FBI, each mortgage fraud scheme contains some type of *material misstatement, misrepresentation, or omission* relating to the property or the potential mortgage.

Fraud for housing involves illegal actions perpetrated solely by the borrower. The motive behind this fraud is simply to acquire and/or maintain ownership of a family's home when they would not otherwise qualify to do so. Borrowers may give false information about their incomes, expenses, or cash available for down payments in order to get a loan.

Fraud for profit involves illegal actions perpetrated by industry insiders. It can take many forms including, but not limited to, equity skimming, property flipping, obtaining loans on fictitious properties, mortgage related identity theft, and intentionally or knowingly making a materially false or misleading written statement in an appraisal of real property. Fraud for profit industry insiders are real estate agents, loan associates, appraisers, escrow officers, attorneys, straw buyers, and many others. The FBI estimates that 80% of all reported fraud losses involve collaboration or collusion by industry insiders. Fraud for profit also includes scams perpetuated by unscrupulous foreclosure rescue businesses and "credit clean-up" services, both of which target vulnerable homeowners or would-be homeowners.

A financial institution or a person may report suspected mortgage fraud without fear of civil liability.

Texas law mandates that all lenders, mortgage bankers, or licensed mortgage brokers require a home loan applicant to sign a statement at closing that all claims to identity, employment, income, and intent to occupy the property as a residence are true and correct. A consumer who intentionally or knowingly makes a materially false or misleading written statement to obtain the property or the mortgage loan may be found guilty of a felony, receiving a fine not to exceed $10,000 and imprisonment for a term of 2 to 99 years. Anyone who suspects that fraudulent activity has been or is about to be committed should notify an authorized governmental agency, such as a local or state law enforcement agency, a prosecuting attorney, or the attorney general. Both Texas and nationwide mortgage fraud task forces have been established to assist local, state, and federal agencies in the investigation and prosecution of mortgage fraud. Mortgage fraud cases can be prosecuted in either the county where the fraud was committed or where the property is located (S.B. 485, 2011).

Federal Equal Credit Opportunity Act

The federal *Equal Credit Opportunity Act* (ECOA), administered by the Consumer Financial Protection Bureau (CFPB), prohibits lenders and others who grant or arrange credit to consumers from discriminating against credit applicants on the basis of race, color, religion, national origin, sex, marital status, age (provided the applicant is of legal age), or dependence on public assistance. In addition, lenders and other creditors must inform all rejected credit applicants, in writing, of the principal reasons why credit was denied or terminated. For more information about the ECOA, refer to Chapter 6.

Real Estate Settlement Procedures Act

The federal *Real Estate Settlement Procedures Act* (RESPA), administered by the CFPB, was created to ensure that the buyer and seller in a residential real estate transaction involving a new first mortgage loan have knowledge of all settlement costs. This important federal law will be discussed in detail in Chapter 20.

Community Reinvestment Act

As discussed in Chapter 6, the *Community Reinvestment Act* (CRA), administered by the CFPB, requires that lenders serve their local communities first—to meet the deposit and credit needs of their low-income moderate-income housing communities and to participate and invest in local community development projects.

Texas Securities Act

The *Texas Securities Act* includes provisions to control and regulate the offering and sale of securities. In some instances, a real estate syndication might actually be selling securities instead of interests in real estate. To protect the public, who may be solicited to participate but may not be sophisticated investors, real estate securities must be registered with state officials and/or with the federal Securities & Exchange Commission when they meet the defined conditions of a public offering. The number of prospects solicited, the total number of investors or participants, the financial background and sophistication of the investors, and the value or price per unit of investment are pertinent facts. Salespersons of such real estate securities may be required to obtain special licenses.

SUMMARY

Home mortgage loans are originated in the primary market—most commonly by savings associations, commercial banks, mortgage banks, or mortgage brokers. Loans through these institutions may be set up as fully amortized loans, interest-only loans, flexible-payment loans, or partially amortized balloon loans.

There are many types of mortgages and deed of trust loans. Conventional loans are not underwritten by a federal agency. Most conventional loans are *conforming*; they meet secondary market guidelines, enabling the lender to sell them once they are originated in the primary market. Unless the borrower puts 20% or more down on the loan, lenders require mortgage insurance, which guarantees the lender against a borrower's default on the loan. FHA loans are insured by the Federal Housing Administration and require both an up-front mortgage insurance premium and a monthly premium. FHA loans generally have more lenient qualifying ratios than conventional loans. VA loans are guaranteed by the U.S. Department of Veterans Affairs and most are no-down-payment loans. VA does not limit the amount of the loan a veteran can obtain; the limit is determined by the lender based on the veteran's eligibility, qualifying ratios, and residual income. Loans through the USDA, particularly the Rural Development loan, provide financing for houses in rural communities. In addition, borrowers in Texas may take advantage of special home-loan programs available through regional and local housing authorities, the Department of Housing and Community Affairs, and the Texas Veterans Land Board.

Other types of real estate financing include adjustable-rate mortgages (ARMs), buydown mortgages, purchase money mortgages, home equity loans, reverse mortgages, shared-appreciation mortgages (SAMs), blanket mortgages, package mortgages, open-end mortgages, wraparound mortgages, construction loans, sale-and-leaseback agreements, and contracts for deed.

The federal government affects interest rates and the availability of money to finance real estate through the Federal Reserve Board's discount rate, reserve requirements, and open market operations. It also participates in the secondary mortgage market, composed of the investors who ultimately purchase and hold the loans as investments. These investors include Fannie Mae, Ginnie Mae, Freddie Mac, and Farmer Mac, as well as insurance companies, investment funds, and pension plans.

Regulation Z, implementing the federal Truth in Lending Act, requires that lenders inform prospective borrowers of the true cost of obtaining credit if they use their homes as security for a loan. The federal Equal Credit Opportunity Act prohibits creditors from discriminating against credit applicants on the basis of race, color, religion, national origin, sex, marital status, age, or dependence on public assistance. The Fair and Accurate Credit Transactions Act of 2003 was designed to expand consumer credit, enhance the accuracy of consumers' financial information, and help fight identity theft. The Real Estate Settlement Procedures Act requires that lenders inform both buyers and sellers in advance of all fees and charges required for the settlement or closing of a residential real estate transaction. Predatory lending and mortgage fraud laws protect borrowers and lenders, respectively, against unscrupulous individuals or businesses. Other important financing legislation includes the Community Reinvestment Act and the Texas Securities Act.

CHAPTER 16 QUESTIONS

1. The Escobars are purchasing a lakefront summer home in a new resort development. The house is completely equipped, and the Escobars have obtained a deed of trust loan that covers the purchase price of the residence, including the furnishings and appliances. This kind of financing is called a(n)
   a. wraparound deed of trust.
   b. package deed of trust.
   c. blanket deed of trust.
   d. unconventional loan.

2. With a fully amortized mortgage or deed of trust loan
   a. each month the total payment is the same, but the allocation to interest is different.
   b. the interest portion of each payment remains the same throughout the entire term of the loan.
   c. periodic payments are made, but the final payment is larger.
   d. the total payment varies each month but a fixed amount is credited toward the principal.

3. What is the primary function of Freddie Mac?
   a. To guarantee mortgages by the full faith and credit of the federal government
   b. To buy and pool blocks of conventional mortgages, selling bonds with such mortgages as security
   c. To act in tandem with Ginnie Mae to provide special assistance in times of tight money
   d. To buy and sell VA and FHA mortgages

4. Fran purchased her home more than 30 years ago. Today, she receives monthly checks from the bank that supplement her income. Fran has MOST likely obtained a(n)
   a. shared-appreciation mortgage.
   b. adjustable-rate mortgage.
   c. reverse mortgage.
   d. package loan.

5. A developer has obtained a large loan to finance the construction of a planned unit development. Which statement is NOT true?
   a. This is a short-term loan, and the developer has arranged for long-term financing to repay it when the construction is completed.
   b. The borrowed money is disbursed in installments, ensuring that all subcontractors and laborers have been paid properly before disbursing each installment of the loan.
   c. The lender inspects the construction that has been completed to date.
   d. The construction loan is called a *takeout loan.*

6. The D'angelos purchased a residence for $95,000. They made a down payment of $15,000 and agreed to assume the seller's existing mortgage, which had a current balance of $23,000. The D'angelos financed the remaining $57,000 of the purchase price by executing a mortgage and note to the seller. This type of loan, by which the seller becomes the mortgagee, is called a
   a. wraparound mortgage.
   b. package mortgage.
   c. balloon note.
   d. purchase money mortgage.

7. When the Federal Reserve Board raises its discount rate, which of the following should happen?
   a. Interest rates will rise.
   b. Interest rates will fall.
   c. The amount of money circulated in the marketplace will increase.
   d. Lenders will be willing to make more mortgage loans.

8. Discount points on a mortgage are computed as a percentage of the
   a. selling price.
   b. amount borrowed.
   c. closing costs.
   d. down payment.

9. Which *BEST* defines the secondary mortgage market?
   a. Lenders who deal exclusively in second mortgages
   b. A market where loans are bought and sold after they have been originated
   c. The major lender of residential mortgages and trust deeds
   d. The major lender of FHA and VA loans

10. Terrence purchased a new residence for $175,000. He made a down payment of $15,000 and obtained a $160,000 mortgage loan. The builder of the house paid the lender 3% of the loan balance for the first year and 2% for the second year. This represented a total savings for Terrence of $8,000. What type of mortgage does this represent?
    a. Wraparound
    b. Package
    c. Blanket
    d. Buydown

11. Funds for FHA-insured loans are usually provided by
    a. the Federal Housing Administration (FHA).
    b. the Federal Deposit Insurance Corporation (FDIC).
    c. approved lending institutions.
    d. Fannie Mae.

12. The federal Equal Credit Opportunity Act prohibits lenders from discriminating against potential borrowers on the basis of all of the following *EXCEPT*
    a. sex.
    b. national origin.
    c. source of income.
    d. amount of income.

13. A charge of three discount points on a $120,000 loan equals
    a. $450.
    b. $3,600.
    c. $4,500.
    d. $36,000.

14. Under the provisions of Regulation Z (the Truth in Lending Act), the annual percentage rate (APR) of a finance charge includes all of the following components *EXCEPT*
    a. discount points paid by borrower.
    b. broker's commission.
    c. loan origination fee.
    d. nominal interest rate.

15. Which is *NOT* a secondary market?
    a. Fannie Mae
    b. Ginnie Mae
    c. FHA
    d. Farmer Mac

16. A developer received a loan that covers five parcels of real estate and provides for the release of the mortgage lien on each parcel when certain payments are made on the loan. This type of loan arrangement is called a
    a. purchase money loan.
    b. blanket loan.
    c. package loan.
    d. wraparound loan.

17. A borrower obtains a $100,000 mortgage loan for 30 years at 7½% interest. If the monthly payments of $699.21 are credited first to interest and then to principal, what will be the balance of the principal after the borrower makes the first payment?
    a. $99,992.14
    b. $99,925.79
    c. $99,379.37
    d. $99,300.79

18. Using Figure 16.3, what is the monthly interest rate factor required to amortize a loan at 6¼% over a term of 15 years?
    a. 8.51
    b. 8.57
    c. 6.16
    d. 6.24

19. Using Figure 16.3, calculate the principal and interest payment necessary to amortize a loan of $135,000 at 7¾% interest over 15 years.
    a. $1,111.85
    b. $1,270.35
    c. $1,279.80
    d. $1,639.16

20. Hellon borrowed $85,000, to be repaid in monthly installments of $509.62 at 6% annual interest. How much of her first month's payment was applied to reducing the principal amount of the loan?

   a. $8.46
   b. $84.62
   c. $4.25
   d. $42.50

21. If a lender agrees to make a loan based on an 80% LTV, what is the amount of the loan if the property appraises for $114,500 and the sales price is $116,900?

   a. $83,200
   b. $91,300
   c. $91,600
   d. $92,900

22. A homeowner needs to refinance her home to avoid foreclosure. Although her monthly income is actually $4,000, she tells the loan officer that her income is $4,800 a month so she can qualify for the loan. She is able to persuade a friend at work to verify the higher amount. This is an example of

   a. mortgage fraud.
   b. predatory lending.
   c. identity theft.
   d. forbearance.

23. For a financial institution, the Red Flag Rule under FACTA includes all of the following practices *EXCEPT*

   a. identifying a suspicious address.
   b. taking planned action upon receiving a consumer credit report containing a fraud alert.
   c. detecting unusual account activity.
   d. pressuring a borrower to accept a high-risk loan.

24. A VA loan

   a. is available to veterans or qualifying spouses only.
   b. is insured by the U.S. Department of Veterans Affairs.
   c. requires a minimum 3.5% down payment.
   d. equals the contract sales price.

25. Which term, when used alone, is acceptable under TIL advertising rules?

   a. Amount of down payment
   b. Number of payments
   c. Monthly payment
   d. Selling price

Detailed rationales for the end-of-chapter review questions are available online at www.dearborn.com through the *Instructor Resource Guides* link.

Transfer of Title

When you have completed this chapter, you will be able to

- **describe** the various requirements for a valid deed;
- **identify** the four fundamental types of deeds, their functions, and their warranties;
- **explain** how property may be transferred through adverse possession and other involuntary means;
- **distinguish** transfers of title by will from transfers by intestate succession, including the disposition of community and separate property in each situation; and
- **define** the following *key terms:*

acknowledgment	formal will	probate
adverse possession	general warranty deed	quitclaim deed
bargain and sale deed	granting clause	special warranty deed
bequest	habendum clause	testate
codicil	heir	testator
decedent	holographic will	title
deed	intestate	trustee's deed
deed in trust	involuntary alienation	voluntary alienation
deed without warranty	jurat	warranty clause
delivery and acceptance	last will and testament	

OVERVIEW

A parcel of real estate may be transferred from one owner to another in a number of different ways. It may be given *voluntarily*, such as by sale or gift, or it may be taken *involuntarily*, by operation of law. It also may be transferred by the living or by will or descent after an owner dies. In every instance, however, a transfer of title to a parcel of real estate is a complex legal procedure involving a number of laws and documents.

This chapter discusses the four methods of title transfer. Also discussed are the various legal documents of conveyance with which the real estate broker or salesperson must be familiar.

TITLE

Title to real estate means the right to or ownership of the land; in addition, it represents the *evidence* of ownership. So the term *title* has two functions: it represents the "bundle of rights" the owner possesses in the real estate, and it denotes the facts that, if proven, would enable a person to recover or retain ownership or possession of a parcel of real estate.

The laws of each state govern real estate transactions for land located within its boundaries. Each state has the authority to pass legislative acts that affect the methods of transferring title or other interests in real estate. Title to real estate may be transferred in Texas by (1) voluntary alienation, (2) involuntary alienation, (3) will, and (4) descent.

VOLUNTARY ALIENATION

Voluntary alienation (transfer) of title may be made by either gift or sale. To transfer title by voluntary alienation during her lifetime, an owner must use some form of deed of conveyance.

A **deed** is a *written instrument by which an owner of real estate intentionally conveys to a purchaser a right, title, or interest in a parcel of real estate.* All deeds must be in writing in accordance with the requirements of the statute of frauds. The owner (who sells or gives the land) is referred to as the *grantor*, and the purchaser (who acquires the title) is called the *grantee*.

Requirements for a Valid Conveyance

The minimum general requirements for an instrument to qualify as a deed in Texas are that it must

The License Act prohibits real estate licensees from drawing up deeds [1101.654(a)(1)].

- name the grantor and grantee,
- state that consideration was given,
- contain a description of the property sufficient to identify it,
- contain words of conveyance,
- be in writing and signed by the grantor or properly authorized agent, and
- be delivered to the grantee or an agent and accepted.

Figure 17.1 is an example of a cash warranty deed used in Texas. Some of the paragraphs in that deed are *required* for a valid deed; others, though not required, are generally expressed in a deed for clarification purposes, when applicable.

Grantor   A grantor must be of sound mind and of lawful age. According to Texas law, a person reaches majority at age 18. A person who is younger than 18 and married is considered to be of legal age to buy and sell real estate even though such person may be divorced before age 18. Majority status can also be obtained by petitioning the court or by serving in the armed forces.

A deed executed by an *infant* (one who has not reached majority) is considered to be *voidable*, not void. The rule is that infants (or minors) can disaffirm, or repudiate, their conveyance of real estate after reaching majority, at which time they have a reasonable period in which to disaffirm. What constitutes a reasonable time varies with the particular case.

A grantor who is capable of understanding the act is generally held to have sufficient mental capacity to execute a deed. A deed executed by a person considered to be mentally incompetent is only *voidable*—it is not void. However, in some states, including Texas, a deed executed by a person who is *judged* legally incompetent is considered to be void. In Texas, legally incompetent people can neither contract nor convey; the court must appoint a guardian.

A grantor's name must be spelled correctly and consistently throughout the deed. If for any reason a grantor's name has been changed from that by which title originally was acquired, the grantor must show both names. It is customary for such a grantor to be described as, for example, "John Smith, now known as Charles Smith"—stating first the name under which the title was acquired.

Grantee   To be valid, a deed must name a grantee in such a way that the grantee is readily identifiable. A deed naming as the grantee a wholly fictitious person—a company that does not exist legally or a society or club that is not properly incorporated—is considered void.

Consideration   To be valid, all deeds must contain a clause acknowledging the grantor's receipt of consideration. When a deed conveys real estate as a gift to a relative, "love and affection" may be sufficient consideration. However, in deeds conveying property as a gift, it is customary in Texas to recite a *nominal* consideration, such as "$10 and other good and valuable consideration." The full dollar amount of consideration is seldom set forth in the deed, except when the instrument is executed by a corporation or trustee or pursuant to court order.

Description of Real Estate   For a deed to be valid, it must contain an accurate legal description of the real estate conveyed.

Reservations and Exceptions ("Subject To" Clauses)   A grantor may *reserve* some right in the land for her own use (minerals, royalties, or easements, for example). A grantor also may place certain restrictions on a grantee's use of the property. For example, a developer may restrict the number of houses that can be built on a one-acre lot in a subdivision. Such restrictions may be stated in the deed or contained in a previously recorded document (such as the subdivider's master deed or plat with restrictive covenants) that is expressly cited in the deed. Many of these deed restrictions have time limits, often including renewal clauses.

In addition to any reservations, a deed should specifically note any encumbrances or limitations that affect the title being conveyed. Such *exceptions* to clear title may include mortgage liens, taxes, restrictions, minerals or mineral leases, and easements that run with the land. For example, a deed may grant title to a grantee "subject to general real estate taxes for the year 2011 and subsequent years."

Granting Clause (Words of Conveyance). A deed of conveyance transfers a present interest in real estate. Therefore, it must contain words that state the grantor's intention to convey the property at this time; an expression of intent to convey at some future time is inadequate. Such words of grant, or conveyance, are contained in the **granting clause**. Depending on the type of deed and the obligations agreed to by the grantor, the wording is generally "convey and warrant," "grant," "grant, bargain, and sell," or "remise, release, and quitclaim."

If more than one grantee is involved, the granting clause should cover the creation of their specific rights in the property. The clause might state, for example, that the grantees will take title as joint tenants or tenants in common. The wording is especially important in creating a joint tenancy.

The granting clause also should indicate what interest in the property is being conveyed by the grantor. Deeds that convey the entire fee simple interest of the grantor usually contain such wording as "to Jacqueline Smith and to her heirs and assigns forever." If the grantor is conveying less than complete interest, such as a life estate to property, the wording must indicate this limitation on the grantee's interest. For example, a deed creating a life estate would convey property "to Jacqueline Smith for the duration of her natural life." See Figure 17.1 for an example of granting and habendum clauses conveying a life estate.

Habendum and Warranty Clauses When it is necessary to define or limit the ownership interest of the grantee (such as a fee simple, defeasible fee, or life estate interest), a **habendum clause** follows the granting clause. The habendum clause begins with the words "to have and to hold." Its provisions must agree with those set down in the granting clause. When a discrepancy between the two clauses exists, the provisions in the granting clause usually are followed. The **warranty clause** states the nature of the grantor's warranties—for example, "forever" in a general warranty deed; "by or through me" in a special warranty deed; "without warranty" in a deed without warranty.

Signature of Grantor To be valid, a deed must be signed by *all grantors* named in the deed. When a grantor's spouse has been named as a grantor, the spouse also must sign the deed to release homestead rights. In Texas, witnesses to the grantor's signature are not necessary and no seal is required, but the signatures must be acknowledged (notarized) to permit recording. If unable to write, grantors may sign their name by *mark*, with two persons other than the notary public as witnesses.

FIGURE 17.1: General Warranty Deed Conveying a Life Estate

CASH WARRANTY DEED

NOTICE OF CONFIDENTIALITY RIGHTS: If you are a natural person, you may remove or strike any or all of the following information from any instrument that transfers an interest in real property before it is filed for record in the public records: Your social security number or your driver's license number.

Date: MAY 29, 20xx

GRANTOR   **Grantor:** JAMES R. ELDER

Grantor's Mailing Address:

4205 PETUNIA
SUNNYSIDE, GRANT COUNTY, TEXAS 79055

GRANTEE   **Grantee:** JOHN Q. YOUNGER, WITH FULL POSSESSION, USE, AND BENEFIT FOR HIS LIFE

Grantee's Mailing Address:

8205 MARIGOLD
SUNNYSIDE, GRANT COUNTY, TEXAS 79055

CONSIDERATION   **Consideration:**   TEN DOLLARS AND OTHER VALUABLE CONSIDERATION

LEGAL DESCRIPTION   **Property (including any improvements):**

LOT 3, BLOCK 12, BLACK ACRE UNIT NO. 15, AN ADDITION TO THE CITY OF SUNNYSIDE, GRANT COUNTY, TEXAS, ACCORDING TO THE RECORDED MAP OR PLAT THEREOF.

Prior Liens:

NONE

RESERVATION AND EXCEPTIONS   **Reservations From and Exceptions To Conveyance and Warranty:**

EASEMENTS, RIGHTS OF WAY, AND PRESCRIPTIVE RIGHTS OF RECORD; ALL PRESENTLY RECORDED RESTRICTIONS, RESERVATIONS, COVENANTS, CONDITIONS, OIL AND GAS LEASES, MINERAL SEVERANCES, AND OTHER INSTRUMENTS, OTHER THAN LIENS AND CONVEYANCES, THAT AFFECT THE PROPERTY; RIGHTS OF ADJOINING OWNERS IN ANY WALLS AND FENCES SITUATED ON A COMMON BOUNDARY; ANY DISCREPANCIES, CONFLICTS, OR SHORTAGES IN AREA OR BOUNDARY LINES; AND ANY ENCROACHMENTS OR OVERLAPPING OF IMPROVEMENTS.

GRANTING CLAUSE   Grantor, for the consideration and subject to the prior liens and the reservations from and exceptions to conveyance and warranty, grants, sells, and conveys to Grantee the property, together with all and singular the rights and appurtenances thereto in any wise belonging, to have and to hold it to Grantee for his life. Grantor binds Grantor and Grantor's heirs, executors, administrators, and successors to warrant and forever defend all and singular

HABENDUM AND WARRANTY CLAUSE   the property to Grantee for his life against every person whomsoever lawfully claiming or to claim the same or any part thereof, except as to the prior liens and the reservations from and exceptions to conveyance and warranty.

When the context requires, singular nouns and pronouns include the plural.

SIGNATURE OF GRANTOR

_____
JAMES R. ELDER

STATE OF TEXAS

COUNTY OF _____

This instrument was acknowledged before me on May 29, 20xx by JAMES R. ELDER.

ACKNOWLEDGMENT (REQUIRED FOR FILING)

_____
NOTARY PUBLIC, STATE OF TEXAS

Warranty Deed
Page 1

Texas law permits a grantor's signature to be signed by an attorney-in-fact act-ing under a power of attorney that has been recorded in the county where the property is located. An *attorney-in-fact* is any person who has been given *power of attorney* (specific written authority) to sign legal instruments for a grantor. Pow-ers of attorney may be *durable* or *non-durable*. In both cases, the grantor must be legally competent when granting the power of attorney. However, if the power of attorney is not made durable, the grantor must also be competent at the time it is used, which often defeats the purpose of the power of attorney. Because the power of attorney terminates on the death of the person granting such authority, adequate evidence must be submitted that the grantor was alive at the time the attorney-in-fact signed the deed. If a party plans to use a power of attorney at clos-ing, a copy of the document should be furnished to the title company for approval in advance of closing.

With the exception of an *owelty deed* to settle property claims in death or divorce, a valid deed does not require a grantee's signature—although some deeds may have a line for it as *proof of acceptance*.

> Transfer of title requires both *delivery and acceptance* of the deed.

Delivery and Acceptance   Title to real estate does not "pass" (transfer) until the deed is actually **delivered** to and **accepted** by the grantee. The grantor may deliver the deed to the grantee personally or through a third party. The effective date of the transfer of title from the grantor and to the grantee is the date of deliv-ery of the deed itself. When a deed is delivered in escrow, the date of delivery is usually the date that the deed was deposited with the escrow agent. Furthermore, delivery and acceptance are generally presumed if a deed has been recorded by the county clerk. Because delivery is a very technical aspect of the validity of a deed, brokers should consult legal counsel when questions arise.

Acknowledgment or Jurat   An **acknowledgment** is a formal declaration before a notary public or other authorized public officer that authenticates signatures on a document for the purpose of recording. It generally states, "This instrument was acknowledged before me on the 16th day of July, 2009, by John Doe." That means that John Doe stood before a notary on that date and acknowledged that the sig-nature on the document was his. The document may not have been signed in front of the notary and may not have been signed that same day, but the signature must be acknowledged in front of the notary. A **jurat** generally says, "SUBSCRIBED AND SWORN TO before me, the undersigned authority, on the 16th day of July, 2009, by John Doe." The notary should ask the person signing the document to swear that the information contained in the document to be notarized is true and correct. Then the document must be signed in the presence of the notary. A document stating, "Subscribed, sworn to, and acknowledged before me" has all the elements of both an acknowledgment and a jurat. It is essential that real estate agents ensure that documents containing an acknowledgment or a jurat are either acknowledged or signed and sworn to in front of a notary. In addition, the person signing the deed or other document must either be known by the notary or must produce sufficient identification to prevent a forgery.

Neither an acknowledgment nor a jurat is essential to the validity of a deed in Texas. However, a deed without either one or the other cannot be recorded and is, therefore, not a satisfactory instrument from a purely practical point of view. Although an unrecorded deed is valid between the grantor and the grantee, it often is not a valid conveyance against subsequent innocent purchasers who do record a deed. To help ensure good title, a grantee always should require that the grantor's signature on a deed be authenticated by an acknowledgment or a jurat.

Execution of Corporate Deeds

Under the law, a corporation is considered a legal entity. For a corporation to convey real estate in Texas, two basic rules must be followed:

- A corporation can convey real estate only by authority granted in its bylaws or on a proper resolution passed by its *board of directors*. If all or a substantial portion of a corporation's real estate is being conveyed, a resolution authorizing the sale usually must be secured from the *stockholders*.
- Deeds to real estate can be *signed only by an authorized officer*. The authority of the officer must be granted by a resolution properly passed by the board of directors, but the signing of a deed by a corporate officer is prima facie evidence of a resolution's existence.

Rules pertaining to religious corporations and not-for-profit corporations vary widely. Because the legal requirements must be followed explicitly, it is advisable to consult an attorney for all corporate conveyances.

Types of Deeds

A *general warranty deed* is the conveyance required by the TREC promulgated sales contract, paragraph 9(B)(1).

Generally, there are four types of deeds that are used in conveying real estate. They are listed and discussed in descending order based on the warranty conveyed.

1. General warranty deed
2. Special warranty deed
3. Deed without warranty (bargain and sale deed)
4. Quitclaim deed

Other instruments affect title to property but do not convey title, including mortgages and deeds of trust (trust deeds). These documents are not intended to convey title but are financing instruments that establish real estate as security for the payment of a debt.

General Warranty Deed

Two basic warranties in Texas:
- Covenant of seisin
- Covenant against encumbrances

General Warranty Deeds   For a purchaser of real estate, a **general warranty deed** (shown in Figures 17.1 and 17.2) provides the *greatest protection* of any deed. It is called a *general warranty deed* or *warranty deed* because certain covenants or warranties legally bind the grantor. In some states, the grantor's warranties are expressly written into the deed itself. In Texas, the warranties usually are implied by the use of certain statutory terms, such as "convey and warrant," "warrant generally," and "grant, bargain, and sell." The five basic implied warranties are as follows:

- *Covenant of seisin*—The grantor warrants that he is the owner of the property and has the right to convey title to it. The grantee may recover damages up to the full purchase price if this covenant is broken.
- *Covenant against encumbrances*—The grantor warrants that the property is free from any liens or encumbrances except those specifically stated in the deed. Encumbrances include such items as mortgages, mechanics' liens, and easements. If this covenant is breached, the grantee may sue for expenses to remove the encumbrance.
- *Covenant of quiet enjoyment*—The grantor guarantees that the grantee's title is good against third parties that might bring court actions to establish

superior title to the property. If the grantee's title is found to be inferior, the grantor is liable for damages.

- *Covenant of further assurance*—The grantor promises to obtain and deliver any instrument needed to make the title good. For example, if the grantor's spouse has failed to sign away homestead rights, the grantor must deliver a quitclaim deed executed by the spouse to clear the title.
- *Covenant of warranty forever*—The grantor guarantees that she will compensate the grantee for the loss sustained if the title fails at any time in the future.

In Texas, the grantor in a deed is not obliged to insert a covenant of warranty of title. However, unless otherwise negated by express language in the deed, the words grant or convey create implied warranties to the grantee and to any heirs and assigns for the first two covenants listed. The last three covenants are derived from language in the deed, such as "warrant and forever defend the grantee against every person lawfully claiming" an interest in the land. Covenants in a general warranty deed are not limited to matters that occurred during the time the grantor owned the property; they extend back to the origin of the title. If possible, a seller should provide no greater warranties than what was received.

Special Warranty Deed

Warrants against defects occurring during the grantor's ownership

Special Warranty Deeds   A conveyance that carries only one covenant is a **special warranty deed**. The grantor warrants only that the property was not encumbered during the time he held title, except as noted in the deed, and that he has done nothing during ownership to cloud or damage the title. Special warranty deeds generally contain the words "remise, release, alienate, and convey" in the granting clause. Any additional warranties to be included must be stated specifically in the deed. A special warranty deed is usually used by fiduciaries such as trustees, executors, and corporations, and sometimes by grantors who have acquired title at tax sales. It is based on the theory that a fiduciary or corporation has no knowledge to warrant against acts of its predecessors in title and does not want the exposure to liability. The full consideration for the property is stated in a special warranty deed.

Deed Without Warranty
- Contains no express warranties
- Implies that the grantor holds title and possession

Deed Without Warranty   The **deed without warranty**, sometimes called a **bargain and sale deed**, uses the words "grant and release" or "grant, bargain, and sell" in the granting clause. A deed without warranty contains no warranties against encumbrances; however, it does imply that the grantor holds title and possession of the property. Without warranties, the grantee has little legal recourse if defects later appear in the title. Figure 17.3 illustrates the deed without warranty.

Quitclaim Deed

No express or implied covenants or warranties; no words of conveyance

Quitclaim Deeds   A **quitclaim deed** provides the grantee with the least protection of any deed. It carries no covenants or warranties and conveys only such interest that the grantor may have when the deed is delivered. If the grantor has no interest, the grantee will acquire nothing, nor will the grantee acquire any right of warranty claim against the grantor. On the other hand, a quitclaim deed *can* convey title as effectively as a warranty deed if the grantor has good title when delivering the deed. However, it provides none of the guarantees that a warranty deed does. Through a quitclaim deed, the grantor only "remises, releases, and quitclaims" interest in the property, if any. A title insurance policy would not be written on a property if it were being conveyed through a quitclaim deed because a quitclaim deed does not have all the protections of the recording statutes. A quitclaim deed frequently is used to cure a title defect, called a *cloud on the title*.

FIGURE 17.2: General Warranty Deed With Vendor's Lien

WARRANTY DEED WITH VENDOR'S LIEN

NOTICE OF CONFIDENTIALITY RIGHTS: If you are a natural person, you may remove or strike any or all of the following information from any instrument that transfers an interest in real property before it is filed for record in the public records: Your social security number or your driver's license number.

Date: MAY 29, 20xx

Grantor: JAMES R. ELDER

Grantor's Mailing Address:

4205 PETUNIA
SUNNYSIDE, GRANT COUNTY, TEXAS 79055

Grantee: JOHN Q. YOUNGER

Grantee's Mailing Address:

8205 MARIGOLD
SUNNYSIDE, GRANT COUNTY, TEXAS 79055

Consideration: TEN DOLLARS AND A NOTE OF EVEN DATE THAT IS IN THE PRINCIPAL AMOUNT OF $80,000.00, IS EXECUTED BY GRANTEE, AND PAYABLE TO THE ORDER OF SUNNYSIDE NATIONAL BANK. THE NOTE IS SECURED BY A VENDOR'S LIEN RETAINED IN FAVOR OF SUNNYSIDE NATIONAL BANK IN THIS DEED AND BY A DEED OF TRUST OF EVEN DATE FROM GRANTEE TO AL L. SMILES, TRUSTEE.

Property (including any improvements):

LOT 3, BLOCK 12, BLACK ACRE UNIT NO. 15, AN ADDITION TO THE CITY OF SUNNYSIDE, GRANT COUNTY, TEXAS, ACCORDING TO THE RECORDED MAP OR PLAT THEREOF.

Prior Liens:

NONE

Reservations From and Exceptions to Conveyance and Warranty:

EASEMENTS, RIGHTS OF WAY AND PRESCRIPTIVE RIGHTS OF RECORD; ALL PRESENTLY RECORDED RESTRICTIONS, RESERVATIONS, COVENANTS, CONDITIONS, OIL AND GAS LEASES, MINERAL SEVERANCES, AND OTHER INSTRUMENTS, OTHER THAN LIENS AND CONVEYANCES, THAT AFFECT THE PROPERTY; RIGHTS OF ADJOINING OWNERS IN ANY WALLS AND FENCES SITUATED ON A COMMON BOUNDARY; ANY DISCREPANCIES, CONFLICTS, OR SHORTAGES IN AREA OR BOUNDARY LINES; AND ANY ENCROACHMENTS OR OVERLAPPING OF IMPROVEMENTS.

Grantor, for the consideration and subject to the prior liens and the reservations from and exceptions to conveyance and warranty, grants, sells, and conveys to Grantee the property, together with all and singular the rights and appurtenances thereto in any wise belonging, to have and to hold it to Grantee, Grantee's heirs, executors, administrators, successors, or assigns forever. Grantor binds Grantor and Grantor's heirs, executors, administrators, and successors to warrant and forever defend all and singular the property to Grantee and Grantee's heirs, executors, administrators, successors, and assigns against every person whomsoever lawfully claiming or to claim the same or any part thereof, except as to the prior liens and the reservations from and exceptions to conveyance and warranty.

Grantor transfers the vendor's lien against and superior title to the property to SUNNYSIDE NATIONAL BANK. The vendor's lien against and superior title to the property are retained until each note described is fully paid according to its terms, at which time this deed shall become absolute.

When the context requires, singular nouns and pronouns include the plural.

_____
JAMES R. ELDER

STATE OF TEXAS

COUNTY OF _____

This instrument was acknowledged before me on May 29, 20xx by JAMES R. ELDER.

_____
NOTARY PUBLIC, STATE OF TEXAS

Warranty Deed With Vendor's Lien
Page 1

FIGURE 17.3: Deed Without Warranty (Bargain and Sale Deed)

DEED WITHOUT WARRANTY

NOTICE OF CONFIDENTIALITY RIGHTS: If you are a natural person, you may remove or strike any or all of the following information from any instrument that transfers an interest in real property before it is filed for record in the public records: Your social security number or your driver's license number.

Date: MAY 29, 20xx

Grantor: JAMES R. ELDER

Grantor's Mailing Address:

4205 PETUNIA
SUNNYSIDE, GRANT COUNTY, TEXAS 79055

Grantee: JOHN Q. YOUNGER

Grantee's Mailing Address:

8205 MARIGOLD
SUNNYSIDE, GRANT COUNTY, TEXAS 79055

Consideration: TEN DOLLARS AND OTHER VALUABLE CONSIDERATION

Property (including any improvements):

LOT 3, BLOCK 12, BLACK ACRE UNIT NO. 15, AN ADDITION TO THE CITY OF SUNNYSIDE, GRANT COUNTY, TEXAS, ACCORDING TO THE RECORDED MAP OR PLAT THEREOF.

Prior Liens:

NONE

Reservations From and Exceptions To Conveyance:

EASEMENTS, RIGHTS OF WAY, AND PRESCRIPTIVE RIGHTS OF RECORD; ALL PRESENTLY RECORDED RESTRICTIONS, RESERVATIONS, COVENANTS, CONDITIONS, OIL AND GAS LEASES, MINERAL SEVERANCES, AND OTHER INSTRUMENTS, OTHER THAN LIENS AND CONVEYANCES, THAT AFFECT THE PROPERTY; RIGHTS OF ADJOINING OWNERS IN ANY WALLS AND FENCES SITUATED ON A COMMON BOUNDARY; ANY DISCREPANCIES, CONFLICTS, OR SHORTAGES IN AREA OR BOUNDARY LINES; AND ANY ENCROACHMENTS OR OVERLAPPING OF IMPROVEMENTS.

Grantor, for the consideration and subject to the prior liens and the reservations from and exceptions to conveyance, conveys to Grantee the property without express or implied warranty, and all warranties that might arise by common law and the warranties in Section 5.023 of the Texas Property Code (or its successor) are excluded.

When the context requires, singular nouns and pronouns include the plural.

_____
JAMES R. ELDER

STATE OF TEXAS

COUNTY OF _____

This instrument was acknowledged before me on May 29, 20xx by JAMES R. ELDER.

_____
NOTARY PUBLIC, STATE OF TEXAS

Deed Without Warranty
Page 1

For example, it might convey an easement, it might reconvey equitable title back to a seller, or it might divide property in a divorce proceeding. If the name of the grantee is misspelled on a warranty deed placed in the public record, a quitclaim deed with the correct spelling might be executed to the grantee to perfect the title. A quitclaim deed is also used when a grantor allegedly has *inherited* property but is not certain that the decedent's title was valid. A warranty deed in such an instance could carry with it obligations of warranty, whereas a quitclaim deed would convey only the grantor's interest.

Special-purpose Deeds   Generally, all deeds are one of the four types previously discussed. There are several *special circumstances* for which one of the four deed forms would be used; their titles describe their function.

- A **deed in trust** is a method of *delivering* a deed into a trust from a *trustor* to a *trustee*—until some future event that would cause the trustee to deliver the deed to the *beneficiary/grantee*. A deed in trust is usually a general warranty deed or a special warranty deed.
- A **trustee's deed** is used when a trustee named in a will, trust agreement, or deed of trust (mortgage document) sells or conveys property out of the trust; it is generally a special warranty deed.
- A deed executed pursuant to court order, a sheriff's deed, an executor's deed, and an administrator's deed, among others, are signed and delivered by court order or through another directive. They are generally special warranty deeds. *Full consideration* is usually stated in these deeds; and by Texas statute, the party executing the deed may be entitled to a sales fee or commission based on a percentage of the full consideration.

> A *deed in trust* conveys property into a trust and should not be confused with a *deed of trust*, which is a security instrument for a loan, not a deed.

INVOLUNTARY ALIENATION

In addition to voluntary alienation by gift or sale as just discussed, title to property can be transferred by **involuntary alienation**—that is, without the owner's consent (see Figure 17.4). Such transfers usually are carried out by operation of law and include several concepts studied earlier in this text: *escheat, eminent domain, tax or mortgage foreclosure,* and *erosion.*

Adverse possession is another means of involuntary transfer. An owner who does not use her land or does not inspect it for a number of years may lose title to another person who has some claim to the land, takes possession, and uses the land. If the property owner does not file a suit or otherwise remove the trespasser within a prescribed period, the adverse possessor receives "full title, precluding all claims"—he acquires fee simple title. The intent of the adverse possession laws is not to legally *steal* someone's property but rather to clear up boundary and title disputes. The possession of the claimant must be open, notorious, hostile, and uninterrupted for a period of 3, 5, 10, or 25 years as set by Texas state law and summarized in Figure 17.5.

> **Adverse Possession**
>
> The acquiring of full title to real property owned by someone else by open, notorious, hostile, and continuous possession for a statutory period

FIGURE 17.4: Involuntary Alienation

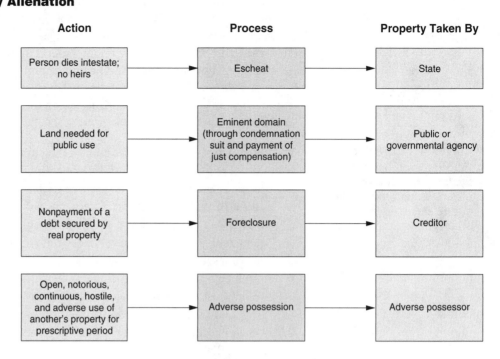

FIGURE 17.5: Adverse Possession

3-Year Statute	5-Year Statute	10-Year Statute	25-Year Statute
Requirements:			
Have title or color of title Possess a general or special warranty deed	Cultivate, use, or enjoy the property Pay taxes Register a deed (a quitclaim deed does not suffice)	Cultivate, use, or enjoy the property	Have a deed that is recorded in the county Act in good faith
Does not require:	Color of title or chain of title Indefeasible title	A deed or other form of conveyance Payment of taxes	A valid deed; the grantor may not have had legal capacity to sign the deed
Example: *A* sells to *B*, who does not record a deed and lives out of town; the property is vacant. *A* sells to *C*, who does not record a deed, believes he has good title, and moves into the house. More than 3 years later, *B* moves to town and wants his house. *C* can legally claim title under the 3-year adverse possession statute. The adverse possessor must have a deed that appears to be legal title but may not be filed.		**Example:** *Farmer M* knows *Farmer T* is farming a portion of his land; he says nothing because it benefits him. Eleven years later and after having a "disagreement" with *Farmer T*, *Farmer M* files a suit for trespassing. The court awards the property to the "occupant" of the land for the last 10 years, *Farmer T*.	

The *3-year statute* requires that the adverse possessor have title or color of title. *Title* is established by a regular chain of transfers beginning with the original land grant from the government. *Color of title* means a consecutive chain of transfers (which may not be regular) down to the adverse possessor. An irregular chain is one in which an instrument was not recorded or some other defect occurred that was not the result of dishonesty or unfairness. The adverse possessor must be capable of producing a chain of documents that prove in all fairness that title should be in him or her. The *5-year statute* requires that the claimant pay the taxes on the property; cultivate, use, or enjoy the property; and claim the property under a recorded deed. The major difference between the 3-year and 5-year statutes is the requirement of a chain of title from the sovereignty in the 3-year statute. Under the 5-year statute, the adverse possessor is not required to produce a chain of title. The claimant must produce a recorded deed and proof of payment of taxes to support the other elements of adverse possession.

The *10-year statute* is the general adverse possession provision. It requires adverse possession for a 10-year period by one who uses, cultivates, or enjoys the property. A deed or chain of title in support of the claim is not necessary and there is no requirement for payment of taxes by the adverse possessor. The adverse claimant is limited to the acquisition of 160 acres unless there is some type of written memorandum of title that increases the number of acres. A written memorandum of title is any written document reflecting a transfer of title, including a will or sheriff's deed at a tax sale—even a forged deed or quitclaim deed. Finally, the *25-year statute* requires that the adverse possessor have adverse possession of the property for 25 years, be in good faith, and have a recorded deed that purports to convey title to the claimant. Generally, adverse possession cannot be claimed against public property, minors, the insane, or the imprisoned; however, the 25-year statute runs against title holders who may be minors, insane, or suffering from some other disability. The 25-year statute allows the running of the time period even though the record owner from whom the adverse possessor received the property may have been under a legal disability at the time. Although this provision is used infrequently, the 25-year period is the absolute bar against claims of others.

> The adverse possessor acquires the mineral interest of the surface owner at the time the adverse possession begins, according to Texas case law.

Through the principle of *tacking*, successive periods of adverse possession can be combined by successive adverse possessors, thus enabling a person who is not in possession for the entire required time to establish a valid claim.

The principle of adverse possession recognizes that the use of land is an important function of its ownership. If a property owner discovers a use that might later be claimed as adverse possession, the property owner should give permission to use the land and file the permission document with the county clerk. Permission stops adverse possession. A claimant who cannot prove title through adverse possession may acquire an easement by prescription (see Chapter 8).

When a transaction involves the possibility of title by adverse possession, the parties should seek competent legal counsel. To protect a landowner from having to bear the cost of litigation in an adverse possession suit, the record landowner *must* be awarded costs and reasonable attorney's fees if the court finds that the adverse claimant made a claim that was groundless and made in bad faith. If the record landowner prevails but the claim was not found to be groundless and made in bad faith, the landowner *may* be awarded costs and attorney's fees.

ESTATE OWNERSHIP

The type of estate and the way that an estate is held influences how and to what degree it can be transferred. As detailed in Chapter 8, freehold estates are estates of indeterminate length and can be divided into estates of inheritance and life estates. Estates of inheritance include fee simple and defeasible fee estates. There are two types of life estates: conventional life estates, which are created by acts of the parties, and legal life estates, which are created by law.

As detailed in Chapter 9, sole ownership, or ownership in severalty, indicates that title is held by one person or entity. Title to real estate can be held concurrently by more than one person, called *co-ownership*, in several ways. In Texas, the most common forms of co-ownership are tenancy in common and community property.

Under tenancy in common, each party holds an undivided interest in severalty. Individual owners may sell, mortgage, convey, or transfer their own interest. On the death of one cotenant, that cotenant's interest passes to the heirs or according to the will. When two or more parties hold title to real estate, they will hold title as tenants in common unless there is an expressed intention otherwise or the conveyance is to a husband and wife. Joint tenancy involves two or more owners normally with the right of survivorship. The intention to establish a joint tenancy with a right of survivorship must be stated clearly in an agreement between the parties. Under common law, joint tenancy has four unities: time, title, interest, and possession.

Community property pertains to land owned by husband and wife and acquired by joint efforts during a marriage. Each spouse owns one-half of all community property. Properties acquired by a spouse before the marriage and through bequests, inheritance, gifts, or agreements after the marriage are deemed separate property. Additionally, property purchased from separate funds and money received from the sale of separate property are considered separate property. A community property right of survivorship agreement eliminates probate.

Real estate ownership also may be held in trust. In creating a trust, title to the property is conveyed by a trustor to a trustee, who holds title to the property and manages it for the benefit of a beneficiary. Trust forms include a living trust (which may be revocable or irrevocable), a testamentary trust, and a land trust.

TRANSFER OF A DECEDENT'S PROPERTY

When a person dies **intestate** (without having left a valid will), the decedent's real estate and personal property pass to the heirs according to the *statute of descent and distribution*. In effect, the state makes a will for the **decedent**, the person who has died. In contrast, a person who dies **testate** has prepared a will indicating how property will be disposed of after her death.

Testator: a person who makes a will

Devise: gift of real property by will

Bequest or *legacy*: gift of personal property by will

Transfer of Title by Will

A **last will and testament** is an instrument made by an owner to voluntarily convey title to the owner's property after death. A will takes effect only after the death of the decedent; until that time, any property covered by the will can be conveyed by the owner and can thus be removed from the owner's estate. In Texas, a surviving spouse automatically owns one-half of the couple's community property acquired during the marriage and a will is not necessary to protect that interest. Because a person who has died and left a will is said to have *died testate*, a party who makes a will is known as a **testator**. The gift of real property by will is known as a devise, and a person who receives real property by will is known as a *devisee*. In addition, a gift of personal property is known as a *legacy* or **bequest**; the person receiving the personal property is known as a *legatee*.

A will differs from a deed in that a deed conveys a present interest in real estate during the lifetime of the grantor, whereas a will conveys no interest in the property until after the death of the testator. To be valid, a deed *must* be delivered during the grantor's lifetime. In contrast, the parties named in a will have no rights or interests as long as the testator is still alive; they acquire interest or title only after the owner's death.

Legal Requirements for Making a Will   The legal capacity to make a will is given by Texas law to every person who is of sound mind and is 18 years of age *or* who is lawfully married or a member of maritime services, the U.S. armed forces, or auxiliaries *or* who has obtained majority status by petitioning the court.

Requirements for a Valid Formal Will
■ Legal age
■ Sound mind
■ Proper wording
■ No undue influence
■ Signed
■ Witnessed

The testator must be of *sound mind* at the time of executing the will. There are no rigid tests to determine the capacity to make a will. Usually the courts hold that the testator must have sufficient mental capacity to understand the nature and extent of the property, the identity of the natural heirs, and the fact that execution of the will means that the property passes to those named in the will at the testator's death. The courts also hold that the drawing of a will must be a voluntary act, free of any undue influence by other people. A will that was made by someone who had previously been declared mentally incompetent by the courts would be void. Because a will must be valid to convey title to real estate effectively, it must be executed and prepared in accordance with the laws of the state where the real estate is located. In Texas a **formal**, or witnessed, **will** must be in writing and signed by the testator in the presence of two or more credible witnesses above the age of 14 who will subscribe their names as witnesses. The witnesses should be persons not named as devisees or legatees in the will. The testator may modify the executed will by means of a **codicil**, which must be in the same form as the will it amends. A will may be revoked at any time prior to the death of the testator. Texas law also recognizes a **holographic will**—one that is wholly in the handwriting of the maker. The document must indicate that the decedent intended the writing to be the last will and testament. Witnesses to the execution of the will are not required.

Legally, a decedent's title to real estate immediately passes either to the persons named in the will or to the heirs by descent. However, the will must be probated if there is a dispute among the devisees.

Probate Proceedings

Probate is a legal process by which a court determines the validity of a will and establishes the assets of a decedent and who will inherit those assets. Probate proceedings take place in the county where the deceased resided, if the decedent had a fixed place of residence in Texas or, if not, then either in the county where his principal estate was located or in the county where he died (S.B. 1198, 2011). To initiate probate proceedings, the custodian of the will, an heir, or another interested party must petition the court. The court then holds a hearing to determine the validity of the will and/or the order of descent, should no valid will exist. If the will is upheld, the property is distributed according to the will's provisions; and if the decedent owned real estate in another county, a certified copy of the probate would be recorded in that county also. If the court declares that the will is invalid or if the will is not probated within four years after the date of death, any property owned by the decedent passes by the laws of descent.

FOR EXAMPLE   A widow is selling a house that was owned as community property with her late husband, who died five years ago. During the title search, the title company discovers that her husband had left a will but it had not been probated. It is too late to probate the will, which left all property to her, and now the property passes one-half to the surviving spouse and the other half to the children of the deceased spouse from a prior marriage. The moral of the story: A will that is not probated may be no will at all.

After the heirs are established, the court appoints an *administrator* (an *administratrix* if a woman) to oversee the administration and distribution of the estate (if no *executor/executrix* was named in a will). The court gives the administrator (if there is no will) or executor (if there is a will) the authority to appraise the assets of the estate and satisfy all debts that are owed by the decedent. Real property specified in a will passes with the debts against it unless the will specifically states that the debt is to be paid from the estate. The administrator or executor is responsible for paying federal estate taxes, state inheritance taxes, and other claims payable against the estate. Then the remaining assets of the estate are distributed according to the provisions of the will or the state law of descent.

IN PRACTICE   A broker entering into a listing agreement with the executor or administrator of an estate in probate should be aware that the amount of commission will be fixed by the court and that such commission is payable only from the proceeds of the sale. The broker will not be able to collect a commission unless the court approves the sale. In addition, the broker should be aware of who owns the property and has the authority to sign the listing agreement. If the previous owner died intestate, it may not be immediately obvious which heirs own the property.

Transfer of Title by Descent (Intestate Succession)

By law, the title to real estate and personal property of an intestate decedent passes to the heirs and will be distributed according to the laws of the state in which the *property* is located. Under the descent statutes, the primary **heirs** of the deceased are the spouse and close blood relatives, such as children, parents, brothers, sisters, aunts, uncles, and, in some cases, first and second cousins. The closeness of the relationship to the decedent determines the specific rights of the heirs. As previously discussed, the relative's right to inherit must be established by proof of heirship during the probate process.

Texas law makes provisions for adopted children. When they have been legally adopted, they usually are considered heirs of the adopting parents but will not be considered heirs of ancestors of the adopting parents. Illegitimate children inherit from the mother but not from the father, unless he has admitted parentage in writing or parentage has been established legally. Of course, if he legally adopts the child, that child will inherit as an adopted child.

Community Property   Community property passes charged with any debts that are against it. Community property passes on the death of one spouse without a will in one of two ways:

- To the surviving spouse, if all surviving children and descendants of the deceased spouse are also children or descendants of the surviving spouse
- One-half to the surviving spouse and one-half to the children or descendants of the deceased spouse if there are any children or descendants of the decedent that are not the children or descendants of the surviving spouse

Separate Property   The *Texas Law of Descent and Distribution* provides that real estate (other than community property) located in Texas and owned as *separate property* by a deceased owner who died intestate is distributed as digested briefly in the scenarios below. Each scenario is illustrated in Figure 17.6. For example, scenario 1 (if the deceased leaves a spouse and children) is shown graphically as one-third of the real property to the surviving spouse for life and two-thirds to the children or their descendants. *Descendants* means living descendants (blood or adopted), however remote, of the deceased.

1. If the deceased leaves a spouse and children or descendants of deceased children, the spouse takes one-third of the real estate for life and the balance is shared equally by the children.
2. If there is no surviving spouse and if the deceased leaves one or more children, the children take the real estate equally among them. If there were descendants of a deceased child, distribution is *per stirpes*; that is, the children receive a proportionate share of their deceased parent's share.
3. When the deceased does not leave children or their descendants but does leave a spouse and parents, brothers, sisters, or descendants of deceased brothers or sisters, the spouse takes one-half of the real estate and the other half passes in *one* of the following ways:
   — To both parents equally
   — Half to the surviving parent and the other half to the brothers and sisters and their descendants
   — All to the surviving parents if there are no living descendants
   — All to the decedent's brothers and sisters or their descendants
4. If the deceased leaves a spouse but no children or descendants of children and no parents or descendants of parents, the spouse takes all of the estate.
5. If the decedent leaves no spouse or descendants (as in the case of an unmarried person), the decedent's entire ownership of real estate passes as indicated in item 3.
6. If none of the foregoing exist, one-half of the real estate passes to the paternal kin and the other half to the maternal kindred. The statute contains detailed instructions for finding heirs by tracing back through maternal and paternal grandparents.
7. If the deceased leaves no surviving spouse and no kindred or heirs, the real estate escheats to the state.

FIGURE 17.6: Descent and Distribution for Separate Property

Scenario	Surviving spouse	Children (including grandchildren) (per stirpes)	Parents and/or Siblings (per stirpes)	State of Texas
1	⅓ real property via life estate	⅔ of real property		
2		All real property		
3	½ real property		½ to parents and/or siblings	
4	All real property			
5			All to parents and/or siblings	
6			½ to maternal kin and ½ to paternal kin	
7				Escheat to state

SUMMARY

Title to real estate is the right to, and evidence of ownership of, the land. It may be transferred in four ways:

■ Voluntary alienation

■ Involuntary alienation

■ Will

■ Descent

The voluntary transfer of an owner's title is made by a deed, executed (signed) by the owner as grantor to the purchaser as grantee. The form and execution of a deed must comply with the statutory requirements of the State of Texas.

The requirements for a valid deed in Texas are a grantor with legal capacity to contract, a readily identifiable grantee, a recital of consideration, a legal description of the property, a granting clause, the signature of the grantor, and delivery and acceptance. To permit recording, the deed should be acknowledged or signed and sworn to in front of a notary public. For purposes of clarification, deeds often include paragraphs to describe exceptions and reservations on the title ("subject to" clauses), limitations on conveyance of a fee simple estate, and habendum and warranty clauses.

The obligation of a grantor is determined by the form of the deed—that is, whether it is a general warranty deed, special warranty deed, deed without warranty, or quitclaim deed. The words of conveyance in the granting clause are important in determining the form of deed. A general warranty deed provides the greatest protection of any deed by binding the grantor to certain covenants or warranties. A special warranty deed warrants only that the grantor has not encumbered the title to the real estate except as stated in the deed. A deed without warranty implies that the grantor holds title but it includes no warranties. A quitclaim deed carries with it no warranties whatsoever and conveys only the interest, *if any*, the grantor possesses in the property.

An owner's title may be transferred without permission by a court action, such as a foreclosure or judgment sale, a tax sale, condemnation under the right of eminent domain, adverse possession, or escheat. Land also may be transferred by the natural forces of water and wind through accretion or erosion.

The real estate of an owner who makes a valid will (who dies testate) passes to the devisees on the death of the testator. The property of an owner who dies without a will (intestate) passes according to the provisions of the law of descent and distribution of the state in which the real estate is located.

CHAPTER 17 QUESTIONS

1. Title to real estate may be transferred during a person's lifetime by which of the following means?
   a. Escheat
   b. Descent
   c. Involuntary alienation
   d. Devise

2. Every deed must be signed by the
   a. grantor.
   b. grantee.
   c. grantor and grantee.
   d. devisee.

3. Alicia, age 15, recently inherited many parcels of real estate from her late father and has decided to sell one of them. If Alicia signed a deed conveying her interest in the property to a purchaser without the signature of her legal guardian, such a conveyance would be
   a. valid.
   b. void.
   c. invalid.
   d. voidable.

4. To voluntarily transfer a right, title, or interest in real estate, an owner may use all the various deeds of conveyance EXCEPT
   a. a sheriff's title,
   b. a warranty deed.
   c. a quitclaim deed.
   d. a deed in trust.

5. Title to an owner's real estate can be transferred at the death of the owner by which one of the following documents?
   a. Special warranty deed
   b. Trustee's deed
   c. Last will and testament
   d. Quitclaim deed

6. Ken signed a deed transferring ownership of a property to Terrence. To provide evidence that Ken's signature was genuine, Ken executed a declaration before a notary. This declaration is known as an
   a. affidavit.
   b. acknowledgment.
   c. affirmation.
   d. estoppel.

7. Matilda inherited acreage in a distant Texas county, never went to see the acreage, and did not use the ground. Harold moved his mobile home onto the land, had a water well drilled, and lived there for 26 years. Harold might become the owner of the land if he has complied with Texas law regarding
   a. adverse possession.
   b. avulsion.
   c. voluntary alienation.
   d. descent and distribution.

8. A grantee receives the greatest protection with what type of deed?
   a. Quitclaim
   b. General warranty
   c. Deed without warranty
   d. Special warranty

9. Alvin executes a deed to Sylvia as grantee, has it acknowledged, and receives payment from Sylvia. Alvin holds the deed, however, and arranges to meet Sylvia the next morning at the courthouse to deliver the deed to her. In this situation at this time,
   a. Sylvia owns the property because she has paid for it.
   b. title to the property will not officially pass until Sylvia has been given the deed the next morning.
   c. title to the property will not pass until Sylvia has received the deed and recorded it the next morning.
   d. Sylvia will own the property when she has signed the deed the next morning.

10. Xavier, a bachelor, died owning real estate that he devised by will to his niece, Annette. In essence, at what point does title pass to his niece?

    a. Immediately upon Xavier's death
    b. After Annette has paid all inheritance taxes
    c. After the executor executes a new deed to the property
    d. When Annette executes a new deed to the property

11. A person who pays for and receives a quitclaim deed

    a. will receive whatever title the grantor possessed in the property.
    b. can force the grantor to make the title good by a suit in court.
    c. receives the greatest protection of any deed.
    d. cannot receive fee simple title.

12. Hap conveys property to Kasey by deed. The deed contains the following: (1) Kasey's name spelled out in full; (2) a statement that Hap has received $10 and Kasey's love and affection; and (3) a statement that the property is conveyed to Kasey "to have and to hold." Which of the following correctly identifies, in order, these three elements of the deed?

    a. Grantee; consideration; granting clause
    b. Grantee; consideration; habendum clause
    c. Grantor; habendum clause; legal description
    d. Grantee; acknowledgment; habendum clause

13. An owner of Texas real estate, who was judged legally incompetent, later made a will during his stay at a nursing home. He died and was survived by a wife and three children. His real estate will pass

    a. to his wife.
    b. to the heirs mentioned in his will.
    c. by the laws of descent and distribution as if no will had been made at all.
    d. to the state.

14. A warranty deed usually implicitly obligates the grantor to the following warranties EXCEPT

    a. seisin.
    b. escheat.
    c. against encumbrances.
    d. further assurance.

15. Entrepreneur Harley is purchasing a large apartment building in a choice urban location. For financial and professional reasons Harley wants to hold the property as beneficiary under a land trust. Which instrument would be used to create this trust?

    a. Trust deed
    b. Deed of trust
    c. Trustee trust
    d. Deed in trust

16. Which is NOT a way in which title to real estate may be transferred by involuntary alienation?

    a. Eminent domain
    b. Escheat
    c. Erosion
    d. Seisin

17. A person who died leaving a valid will is called a(n)

    a. devisee.
    b. testator.
    c. legatee.
    d. intestator.

18. The statute or act that creates the need for a deed to be in writing in order to be enforceable is the

    a. law of descent and distribution.
    b. statute of frauds.
    c. statute of limitations.
    d. Texas Real Estate License Act.

19. An instrument authorizing one person to act for another is called a(n)

    a. power of attorney.
    b. release deed.
    c. quitclaim deed.
    d. acknowledgment.

Detailed rationales for the end-of-chapter review questions are available online at www.dearborn.com through the *Instructor Resource Guides* link.

CHAPTER 18

Title Records

■ **LEARNING OBJECTIVES**   *When you have completed this chapter, you will be able to*

- ■ **explain** the necessity for recording legal documents and the difference between constructive and actual notice;
- ■ **identify** the process and purpose of a title search;
- ■ **describe** the origin of Texas land titles and the two evidences of title commonly used in Texas;
- ■ **distinguish** between lender's and owner's title policies, including covered and excluded risks, and between actual marketable title and good and indefeasible title; and
- ■ **define** the following *key terms:*

abstract of title	evidence of title	priority
actual notice	good and indefeasible	recording
attorney's opinion of title	title	subrogation
chain of title	grantor/grantee indices	suit to quiet title
commitment	league	title insurance
constructive notice	marketable title	title search

OVERVIEW

For the protection of real estate owners, taxing bodies, creditors, and the general public, public records are maintained in every county in Texas. Such records help to establish official ownership, give notice of encumbrances, and establish priority of liens. The placing of documents in the public record is known as **recording**.

This chapter discusses the necessity for recording and the various types of title evidence commonly used in Texas.

PUBLIC RECORDS AND RECORDING

In Texas, public records are maintained by designated officials, as required by state law. These include records maintained by the general land office, county clerks, surveyors, district clerks, county assessor-collectors, county treasurers, city clerks, and clerks of various courts of record. Records involving taxes, special assessments, ordinances, zoning, and building also fall into this category.

The statute of frauds requires that instruments affecting interests in real estate be in writing to be enforceable. Written instruments are required for all transfers of title or interest, whether by deed, mortgage, or lease (unless the lease is for one year or less). In addition to the statute of frauds, the legislature has passed laws that require owners or parties holding interests in real estate to record, or file, in the public records all documents affecting their interests in real estate in order to give *legal, public, and constructive notice* to the world of their interests. These statutory enactments are commonly called recording acts.

Necessity for Recording

Before purchasing a fee simple estate to a parcel of real estate, a prospective buyer wants to be sure that the seller can convey good title to the property. The present owner undoubtedly purchased the interest from a previous owner, so the same question of *kind and condition* of title has been inquired into many times in the past. As long as taxes are paid and liens do not become delinquent, it is expected that a fee simple title will remain marketable.

Texas law provides that a *deed or mortgage is not effective as far as later purchasers are concerned until such documents have been recorded*. Thus the public records should reveal the condition of the title, and a purchaser should be able to rely on a search of the public records.

Recording Acts

To give *notice* to third parties, written documents that affect land *must* be recorded in the county where the land is located.

To give constructive notice under the Texas recording acts, all instruments affecting any estate, right, title, or interest in land *must be recorded in the office of the county clerk in the county where the land is located.* The purpose of this requirement is to give to everyone interested in a property's title notice of the interests of all other parties.

From a practical point of view, the recording acts give legal priority to those interests that are recorded first (first in time is first in priority). However, quitclaim deeds are an exception to *first in time is first in priority* since they convey only the interest held by the grantor at the time of conveyance—and that may be *no interest*. To be *eligible for recording*, an instrument must be drawn and executed in conformity with the provisions of the recording statutes of the state in which the real estate is located. Section 12.001(b) of the Texas Property Code states,

> An instrument conveying real property may not be recorded unless it is signed and acknowledged or sworn to by the grantor in the presence of two or more credible subscribing witnesses or acknowledged or sworn to before and certified by an officer authorized to take acknowledgments of oaths, as applicable.

Most often, instruments for recording are acknowledged or signed and sworn to before a notary. If the document to be recorded is a paper document concerning real or personal property, the paper document must (1) contain original signatures that are acknowledged or sworn to with a jurat or (2) be attached as an exhibit to a paper affidavit that has original signatures acknowledged or sworn to with a jurat. However, an original signature is not required on a document that is being electronically submitted for recording.

Since 1837, all deeds to Texas land must be in English. Deeds made prior to that date may be in Spanish if an English translation is attached. Deeds, mortgages, and deeds of trust must contain a statutorily prescribed "confidentiality notice" on the first page stating that Social Security numbers and driver's license numbers may be removed prior to a document's being filed of record because these instruments are available for review by the public. (Refer to the general warranty deed in Figure 17.1.) The address to which the recorded document is to be returned must be indicated clearly on that document under penalty of law.

The *Uniform Electronic Transactions Act* (2001) and the *Uniform Real Property Electronic Recording Act* (2005) permit a county clerk to receive, index, store, archive, and transmit electronic documents and provide access to documents and information by electronic means. An agent should check with the local county clerk to determine a particular county's processes for electronic notarization and recording of electronic documents.

IN PRACTICE   Confidentiality of a person's Social Security number (SSN), driver's license, and other key identifiers is crucial for protection against identity theft. Because documents filed with a county or district clerk are considered open records, they are available to the public either in the clerk's office or via the internet; many documents currently on file contain key identifiers. An individual may submit a written request to a county or district clerk to redact (remove or blacken) all but the last four numbers of an SSN on a paper or electronically filed document unless another law requires the full SSN to be maintained on the document. The individual must identify the specific documents from which the partial SSN should be redacted. In addition, the preparer of a deed or a deed of trust is no longer permitted to include an individual's SSN on a document to be recorded with the county clerk. However, the county clerk is required to accept a document for filing even if it contains an SSN and has no duty to ensure that an instrument presented for recording does not contain an SSN.

Notice

Anyone who has an interest in a parcel of real estate can take certain steps, called *giving notice*, to ensure that knowledge of the interest is accessible to the public. Through the legal maxim of *caveat emptor*, the courts charge a prospective real estate buyer or mortgagee (lender) with the responsibility of inspecting the property and searching the public records to ascertain the interests of other parties. The two basic types of notice are *constructive notice* and *actual notice*.

Constructive notice is a concept based on the legal presumption that information may be obtained by an individual through diligent inquiry. Properly recording documents in the public record serves as constructive notice to the world of an individual's rights or interest. So does the physical possession of a property. Because the information or evidence is readily available to the world, a prospective purchaser or lender is responsible for discovering the interest.

In contrast, **actual notice** means that not only is the information available but someone has been given the information and actually knows it (see Figure 18.1). After searching the public records and inspected the property, the individual has actual notice. Actual notice is also known as *direct knowledge*. If it can be proved that an individual has actual knowledge of information concerning a parcel of real estate, that person cannot use a lack of constructive notice (such as an unrecorded deed or an owner who is not in possession) to justify a claim.

FIGURE 18.1: Notice

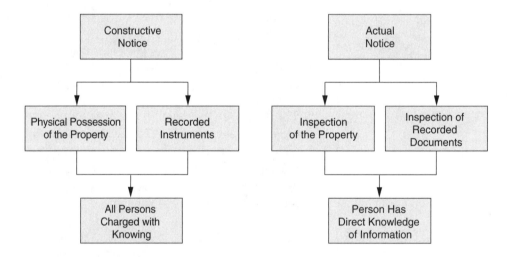

IN PRACTICE   Copies of recorded deeds, powers of attorney, mortgages, and other instruments relating to real property must be maintained in the county clerk's office in the county where the property is located. **Grantor/grantee indices** assist in researching the public records. They are arranged alphabetically and state the specific volume and page on which each instrument is recorded. Because these documents are a matter of public record, anyone can search the property records of any Texas county. Larger Texas counties maintain a searchable computerized database of real property records; many counties are now making these records available at no cost on the internet.

Priority refers to the order of rights in time. Many complicated situations can arise that affect the priority of rights in a parcel of real estate—who recorded first, which party was in possession first, or who had actual or constructive notice. For instance, a purchaser may receive a deed and take possession of the property but not record the deed. By taking possession, a purchaser gives notice that she has an interest in the land. Such a purchaser's rights would be considered superior to the rights of a subsequent purchaser who acquired a deed from the original owner at a later date and recorded the deed but did not inspect the property to determine who was in possession. How the courts rule in any situation depends on the specific facts of the case. These are strictly legal questions that should be referred to lawyers.

FOR EXAMPLE In May, Bob purchased a property from Allen and received a deed. Bob never recorded the deed but began farming operations on the property in June. In November, Allen (who was forgetful) again sold the property, this time to Carol. Carol accepted the deed and promptly recorded it. However, because Carol never inspected the property to see whether someone was in possession, Bob has the superior right to the property even though he never recorded the deed. By taking possession, a purchaser gives constructive notice of an interest in the land. Carol has recourse against Allen for this second sale of the property.

Bill mortgaged his land to Janie, and she failed to record the mortgage. Bill later mortgaged the same land to Edgar, who *knew* of the existence of the earlier mortgage. In this case, Edgar is charged with actual knowledge of the existing mortgage, so his mortgage is a second mortgage, with Janie's mortgage having a prior claim on the property.

Norman gave a dated and notarized warranty deed to Alicia, but she forgot to record it. A week later he gave a quitclaim deed to Jack, who recorded the deed immediately. A month later Alicia recorded the warranty deed. Because Norman had no interest in the property when he gave the quitclaim deed to Jack, Alicia's warranty deed would have priority over Jack's quitclaim deed.

Unrecorded Documents

Certain types of liens are not recorded in the public records. Real estate taxes and special assessments are direct liens on specific parcels of real estate and need not be recorded in the county clerk's office. Other liens, such as inheritance taxes, are placed by statutory authority against all real estate owned by a decedent at the time of death; these liens also are not recorded.

Notice of these liens must be gained from sources other than the county clerk's office. Evidence of the payment of real estate taxes and special assessments can be gathered from paid tax receipts and letters from municipalities. Creative measures are often required to get information about "off the record" liens.

CHAIN OF TITLE

Chain of title is the record of a property's ownership. A search of the grantor-grantee indices reveals a complete line of fee title owners from the original grant (from the sovereignty of the soil) to the most current property owner—linking each owner to the next so that a chain is formed.

Chain of title: linking one owner to the next without a *gap* in the chain

If ownership cannot be traced through an unbroken chain, it is said that there is a *gap* in the chain. In these cases, the cloud on the title makes it necessary to establish ownership by a court action called a **suit to quiet title**. For instance, a suit might be required when a grantor acquired title under one name and conveyed it under another. Or there may be a forged deed in the chain, after which no subsequent grantee would have acquired legal title.

Title Search and Abstract of Title

A **title search** is an examination of all public records in the county to determine who has rights in the property and whether any defects exist in the chain of title. The records of the conveyances of ownership are examined beginning with the present owner. Then the title is traced backward to its origin. A search for title insurance purposes may be traced backward just to the ownership interest that could document a claim through the 25-year statute of adverse possession.

Other public records are examined to identify wills, judicial proceedings, and other encumbrances that may affect title. These include a variety of taxes, special assessments, and other recorded liens.

Abstract of title: a condensed history of documents found in the public records

An **abstract of title** is a condensed history of all the instruments found in the title search that affect a particular parcel of land. A person who prepares this report is called an *abstracter*. The abstracter searches all public records, then summarizes the various events and proceedings that affected the title throughout its history. The report begins with the original grant, then provides a chronological list of recorded instruments. All recorded liens and encumbrances are included, along with their current status.

Origin of Texas Land Titles

While Texas land was under control of the Spanish crown, royal grants of land were made to nobles, generals, explorers, adventurers, and colonists. The originals of these grants, which were signed and authenticated, were called the *protocol* and were made a part of the official record. An authenticated extract of the grant, called a *testimonio*, was given to the owner as evidence of title. While the Republic of Mexico was the sovereign government, colonists called *empresarios* were given grants of land. The best known of these was Stephen F. Austin. The protocols or the *testimonios* have become a part of the archives of the Texas General Land Office and are the basis or source of titles of land described therein.

Land was granted to an individual settler by the Mexican government in a large tract called a **league**. A league consisted of a square, each side being 5,000 varas (a *vara* by Texas statute is 33⅓ inches), or 13,888.89 feet. The area is 4,428.4 acres, or 6.919 square miles. A married colonist was entitled to a league, and a single man was given one-third league, or 1,476 acres. These were known in the records by the name of the colonist—for example, *Walter Scott's League*. Grants or patents from the Republic or the State of Texas are referred to as surveys and are known by the original owner's name—for example, the *Amos Waters Survey*. To identify each survey or league, the General Land Office of Texas has assigned a state abstract number to every grant of land from the Spanish crown, the Mexican government, the Republic of Texas, or the State of Texas. A separate set of numbers is used for each county. A smaller unit of measurement was the *labor* (a Spanish term pronounced la-*bór*), which was 177½ acres.

During the sovereignty of the Republic of Texas and continuing after the formation of the state, settlers were offered tracts of land of 640 acres or fractions thereof. These were surveyed and laid out as square sections.

EVIDENCE OF TITLE

Although the grantor in a general warranty deed warrants that he is the owner of the property and that all encumbrances have been disclosed, a deed is not considered satisfactory evidence of title. It contains no proof of the kind or condition of the grantor's title at the time of conveyance. The grantee needs some assurance that she is actually acquiring ownership and that the title is good and indefeasible. Therefore, an abstract of title and attorney's opinion of title or a title insurance policy would be used to provide **evidence of title**.

Abstract of Title and Attorney's Opinion of Title

If an **attorney's opinion of title** is used to provide *evidence of title*, an *abstracter* is hired to prepare an *abstract of title*. The abstracter concludes with a certificate indicating which records were searched and which records were not searched in preparation of the report. In summarizing a deed in the chain of title, the abstracter might note the recorder's book and page number, the date of the deed, the recording date, the names of the grantor and grantee, a brief description of the property, the type of deed, and any conditions or restrictions contained in the deed.

> **Proof of Good Title**
> - Abstract of title and attorney's opinion
> - Title insurance

Abstracters must exercise due care because they can be liable for negligence for any failure to include or accurately record all pertinent data. An *abstracter does not pass judgment on or guarantee the condition of the title*. Therefore, once the abstract is brought up to date, it is submitted to the buyer's attorney, who must examine the entire abstract. Following this detailed examination, the attorney must evaluate all the facts and prepare a written report for the purchaser on the condition of the ownership. This report, the attorney's opinion of title, should be prepared by an attorney thoroughly familiar with real estate law. The *attorney's opinion of title* does not protect against defects that cannot be discovered from the public records, and mistakes can be made in creating the abstract or the attorney's opinion. Therefore, most lenders require title insurance as satisfactory evidence of title.

Title Insurance

> The most common title insurance policies are
> - *owner's title policy*, insuring the owner has good title, and
> - *mortgagee's title policy*, insuring the lender has a valid lien.

A **title insurance** policy is a contract by which the policyholder is protected from losses arising from defects in the title. Unlike other insurance policies that insure against future losses, title insurance protects the insured from an event that occurred before the policy was issued. A title insurance company determines whether the title is insurable based on a review of the public records. If the title is insurable and a policy is written, a title insurance company agrees, subject to the terms of its policy, to indemnify (that is, to compensate or reimburse) the insured (the owner, mortgagee, or other interest holder) against any losses sustained as a result of defects in the title other than those exceptions listed in the policy. Under the contract, the title insurance company will defend the title at its own expense as well as pay any claims against the property if the title proves to be defective. Title insurance guarantees indemnification (reimbursement) for losses; it does not guarantee continued ownership. When a title company makes a payment to settle a claim covered by a policy, the company acquires by the right of **subrogation** all the remedies and rights of the insured party against anyone responsible for the settled claim. Premiums for title insurance policies are standardized and set by the State Board of Insurance. They are paid only once—when the policies are issued.

Types of Policies   Title companies issue various forms of title insurance policies, the most common of which are the *owner's* title insurance policy (with separate forms for residential and commercial use), the *mortgagee's* title insurance policy, the *leasehold* title insurance policy, and the *certificate of sale* title insurance policy. As the names indicate, each of these policies is issued to insure specific interests. For example, a residential owner's title policy assures the new homeowner that the title is as stated subject only to certain specified exceptions. Title insurance provides for reimbursement up to the purchase price on the owner's policy. Upon sale of the subject property, an owner's policy is automatically converted to a warrantor's policy, which will continue *in perpetuity* at no cost. Because it is the buyer's title that is being insured, the buyer may select the title company.

A mortgagee's title insurance policy assures a lender that it has a valid first lien (or perhaps a second lien) against the property. Reimbursement on the mortgagee's policy is limited to the outstanding loan balance; the lender's coverage decreases as the loan balance decreases. The mortgagee's policy transfers with each sale of the loan note. A leasehold title insurance policy assures a lessee that the lease is valid. A certificate of sale policy is issued to a purchaser in a court sale and ensures the purchaser's interest in property sold under a court order.

IN PRACTICE   An owner's title insurance policy on residential property, if issued to an individual, provides for continuation of coverage in four situations:

- Inheritance of property from the original named insured

- Receipt of title in a dissolution of marriage with the original named insured

- Transfer of title into a living trust by the original named insured

- Transfer of a trust to beneficiaries upon the death of the original named insured

The T-47 Affidavit   The T-47 affidavit requires that the seller, under oath, swear that no easements have been granted on the property and that no material change exists in the structures, fences, structures on adjoining properties, conveyances, or replats.

Title Commitment   In most cases, as soon as a property goes under contract, the real estate agent will deliver a copy of the sales contract to a title company to begin the title search. According to the provisions of the Texas promulgated sales contracts, the seller has 20 days from the date the title company receives the contract to deliver to the buyer a "commitment for title insurance" and deliver, at the buyer's expense, copies of restrictive covenants and documents evidencing exceptions in the commitment other than the standard printed exceptions. If the commitment is not delivered within 20 days, the time for its delivery is automatically extended up to 15 days.

To avoid *practicing law without a license*, refer questions about specific content in a title commitment to the title company or to an attorney.

On completion of the examination, the title company issues a **commitment** to issue a title policy. A commitment for title insurance is not the actual title policy but rather a statement of the terms and conditions on which the title insurance underwriter is willing to issue the title policy. It is the "offer" by the underwriter to enter into a legal contract with the proposed insured under stated conditions. It includes

- the name of the insured party;
- the legal description of the real estate;
- the estate or interest covered;

- a schedule of all exceptions, consisting of encumbrances and defects found in the public records; and
- conditions and stipulations under which the policy is issued.

Thus, a prospective purchaser has the opportunity to examine every outstanding interest against the title to ensure it is consistent with the proposed purchase.

According to the American Land Title Association, one-third of title searches reveals a problem, such as an unpaid contractor or a forgotten tax bill.

Coverage   Exactly which defects the title company will insure against depends on the type of policy it issues and the endorsements requested by the mortgagee. For a partial listing of standard coverage, endorsements, and exclusions, see Figure 18.2. A *standard coverage* policy usually insures against defects that may be found in the public records, forged documents, improperly delivered deeds, and lack of good and indefeasible title. Also covered are liens or encumbrances that were created, attached, filed, or recorded prior to the recording of the deed, such as liens for labor and material that were contracted for by the seller and that have inception before the policy date. "Lack of legal access to and from the property" coverage requires the buyer, the seller, or the agent to prove through a survey or other means that there is access; otherwise, the title company will generally delete the insuring provision covering access to and from the land. A title company *may* accept an existing survey when providing area and boundary coverage, regardless of the age of the survey or the party for whom it was prepared. If an existing survey is used, TREC's promulgated contract forms, ¶6(C)(1), require the seller to provide a T-47 affidavit that nothing has occurred on or around the property that would affect the property's area or boundaries. *Endorsements* may be requested by the lender to cover additional risks (*exceptions*) that may be discovered only through inspection of the property, inquiries of persons in actual possession of the land, or examination of an accurate survey. The company does not agree to insure against any defects in or liens against the title that are found by the title examination and listed in the policy.

FIGURE 18.2: Title Insurance Policy

Standard Coverage	Endorsements	Not Covered (Exclusions)
1. Defects found in public records	1. Property inspection	1. Defects and liens listed in policy
2. Liens or encumbrances on title	2. Rights of parties in possession	2. Unrecorded defects
3. Forged documents	3. Survey coverage	3. Rights of eminent domain
4. Incompetent grantors	4. Unrecorded liens not known of by policyholder	4. Questions of survey
5. Incorrect marital statements	5. EPA lien endorsement	5. Claims arising by reason of bankruptcy or insolvency
6. Improperly delivered deeds	6. Homestead or community property or survivorship rights	
7. Lack of legal access to and from land	7. Guaranty against rollback taxes	
8. Lack of good and indefeasible title		

FOR EXAMPLE   For an additional premium, a purchaser can obtain an endorsement insuring that the boundaries of a property are as shown on a current survey of the property. This endorsement will also insure that any permanent building on the subject property does not overlap property lines or overlap easements that restrict the building of such permanent improvements. It will not insure that a surveyor's calculation of acreage or area is accurate.

An owner's policy usually will *exclude* coverage against unrecorded documents, unrecorded defects of which the policyholder has knowledge, rights of eminent domain, claims arising by reason of bankruptcy or insolvency, and questions of survey.

IN PRACTICE Although by law neither an abstract of title nor a title insurance policy is required to transfer property, the License Act does require that a licensee advise a buyer in writing before closing to have an abstract examined by an attorney or to be provided with or obtain a title insurance policy [1101.652(b)(29)]. That notice is published in paragraph 6(E)(1) of the Texas promulgated sales contract. To safeguard their investment, though, lenders generally require that a title insurance policy be written before advancing funds on a loan. Therefore, paragraph 6(A) of the promulgated contract specifies that a seller must furnish a title policy to a buyer. Contract negotiations determine whether the seller or the buyer bears the expense.

In addition to real property, title insurance can be written on personal property. Such title insurance ensures that a debtor has ownership rights or interest in the property sufficient to transfer the personal property to the lender as collateral. Personal property title insurance can be used to insure against other claims of ownership on personal property or fixtures, such as boats or aircraft or washers, dryers, and refrigerators.

The Title: Marketable or Good and Indefeasible

In most states, title to real property is generally considered satisfactory when it is marketable. A **marketable title** is one that is so free from significant defects that the purchaser can be assured against having to defend the title and would willingly accept it. It is title that is reasonably free from doubt that would affect the market value of the real estate. Although marketable title is not statutorily defined in Texas, generally a marketable title must

- be free from any significant liens and encumbrances,
- disclose no serious defects and not be dependent on doubtful questions of law or fact to prove its validity,
- not expose a purchaser to the hazard of litigation or threaten the quiet enjoyment of the property, and
- convince a reasonably well-informed and prudent person acting on business principles and willful knowledge of the facts and their legal significance that she in turn could sell or mortgage the property at a fair market value.

Practice

Texas title insurance policies insure *good and indefeasible title.*

Title insurance companies in Texas insure **good and indefeasible title**, rather than marketable title. A good and indefeasible title is a title that cannot be defeated by a superior claim, set aside, or made void. It is less than marketable title. However, as noted in Figure 18.2, it insures against defects in the public records, forged documents, incompetent grantors, and more. *Marketable title* is free from any claim—but *good and indefeasible title* insures that, if there is a claim, the claim can be defeated.

SUMMARY

The purpose of the recording acts is to give legal, public, and constructive notice to the world of parties' interests in real estate. The recording provisions have been adopted to create system and order in the transfer of real estate. Without them, it would be virtually impossible to transfer real estate from one party to another. The interests and rights of the various parties in a particular parcel of land must be recorded so that such rights will be legally effective against third parties who do not have knowledge, or notice, of the rights.

Properly recording documents in the public record and physical possession of real estate generally are interpreted as constructive notice of the rights of the person in possession. Actual notice is knowledge acquired directly and personally by an individual.

The purpose of a deed is to transfer a grantor's interest in real estate to a grantee. It does not *prove* that the grantor has any interest at all, even if conveying the interest by means of a warranty deed that carries with it the implied covenants of warranty.

Two forms of title evidence are used in Texas. These are (1) abstract of title and attorney's opinion and (2) owner's title insurance policy.

If a seller provides an abstract of title and attorney's opinion of title as evidence of title, an abstracter first searches the documents that affect title to the subject property and then prepares an abstract with an abstracter's certificate, indicating which records were examined. The attorney for the buyer examines the abstract and issues an opinion of title.

A title insurance policy is a contract by which the policyholder is protected from losses arising from defects in the title. If the title is insurable and a policy is written, a title insurance company agrees to reimburse the insured against any losses sustained as a result of defects in the title other than those exceptions listed in the policy.

Marketable title is generally one that is so free from significant defects that the purchaser can be assured against having to defend the title. Texas title insurance policies insure good and indefeasible title. Should there be a claim against the title, the claim can be defeated.

CHAPTER 18 QUESTIONS

1. An owner's title insurance policy with standard coverage generally covers all *EXCEPT*
   a. forged documents.
   b. rights of parties in possession.
   c. incompetent grantors.
   d. improperly delivered deeds.

2. A mortgagee's title policy protects which parties against loss?
   a. Buyers
   b. Sellers
   c. Lenders
   d. Buyers and lenders

3. Phil bought Larry's house, received a deed, and moved into the residence but neglected to record the document. One week later, Larry died and his heirs in another city, unaware that the property had been sold, conveyed title to Melvin, who recorded the deed. Who owns the property?
   a. Phil
   b. Melvin
   c. Larry's heirs
   d. Both Phil and Melvin

4. Which is a distinguishing characteristic of good and indefeasible title?
   a. It is free from significant liens and encumbrances.
   b. It discloses no serious defects regarding validity.
   c. It convinces a reasonably well-informed and prudent person that he could sell the property.
   d. It cannot be defeated by a superior claim.

5. When the title examination is completed, the title insurance company notifies the buyer in writing of the condition of the title. This notification is called
   a. a chain of title.
   b. commitment for title insurance.
   c. an abstract.
   d. an escrow statement.

6. Albert and Danielle purchased a ranch house near El Paso. To provide evidence of their ownership, they obtained a title insurance policy. The policy
   a. guarantees that they own the property.
   b. will reimburse, up to the amount of the policy, losses that Albert and Danielle sustain as a result of incompetent grantors.
   c. will terminate when they sell the property in the future.
   d. does not guarantee good and indefeasible title.

7. A purchaser went to the county clerk's office to check the records. She found that the seller was the grantee in the last recorded deed and that no mortgage was on record against the property. Thus, the purchaser may assume that
   a. all taxes are paid and no judgments are outstanding.
   b. the seller has good title.
   c. the seller did not mortgage the property.
   d. the seller inherited the property free and clear.

8. An abstract is usually examined by the
   a. broker.
   b. abstract company.
   c. purchaser.
   d. attorney for the purchaser.

9. The person who prepares an abstract of title for a parcel of real estate
   a. writes a brief history of the title after inspecting the county records for documents affecting the title.
   b. ensures the condition of the title.
   c. issues a title insurance policy.
   d. gives an opinion of the status of the title.

10. A purchaser of real estate is charged with knowledge of all recorded documents, as well as with the responsibility to
   a. make improvements on the property.
   b. learn the rights of the parties in possession.
   c. inspect the property after closing.
   d. purchase additional insurance to protect the title.

11. Which statement *BEST* explains why instruments affecting real estate are recorded?

    a. Recording gives constructive notice to the world of the rights and interests in a particular parcel of real estate.
    b. Failing to record will void the transfer.
    c. The instruments must be recorded to comply with the terms of the statute of frauds.
    d. Recording proves the execution of the instrument.

12. When a claim is settled by a title insurance company, the company acquires all rights and claims of the insured against any other person who is responsible for the loss. This is called

    a. escrow.
    b. abstract of title.
    c. subordination.
    d. subrogation.

13. The documents referred to as *title evidence* include

    a. title insurance policies.
    b. general warranty deeds.
    c. quitclaim deeds.
    d. security agreements.

14. Written instruments affecting real estate should be recorded in

    a. the county clerk's office in the county where the real estate is located.
    b. the state auditor's office.
    c. the city tax office.
    d. both state and county tax offices.

15. *Chain of title* refers to which of the following?

    a. A summary or history of all instruments and legal proceedings affecting a specific parcel of land
    b. An instrument that protects the insured parties against errors in the public records and hidden risks, such as forgeries and undisclosed heirs
    c. The succession of conveyances from some starting point whereby the present owner derives title
    d. Documentary proof that title is free of encumbrances

16. The date and time a document was recorded establish

    a. priority.
    b. chain of title.
    c. subrogation.
    d. good and indefeasible title.

17. Kelly sells a portion of her property to Lew. Lew promptly records the deed in the appropriate county office. If Kelly tries to sell the same portion of her property to Melvin, which of the following statements is *TRUE*?

    a. Melvin has been given constructive notice of the prior sale because Lew promptly recorded the deed.
    b. Melvin has been given actual notice of the prior sale because Lew promptly recorded the deed.
    c. Because Melvin's purchase of the portion of Kelly's property is the more recent, it will have priority over Lew's interest, regardless of when Lew recorded the deed.
    d. Because Kelly is selling the property a second time, the courts will request a quitclaim deed from Lew.

Detailed rationales for the end-of-chapter review questions are available online at www.dearborn.com through the *Instructor Resource Guides* link.

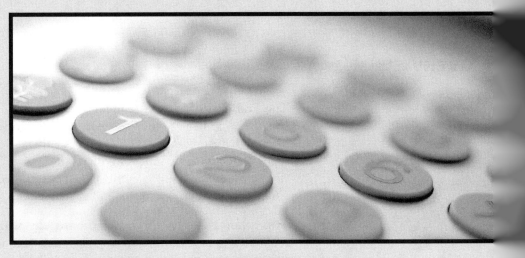

CHAPTER 19

Real Estate Mathematics

OVERVIEW

The *Real Estate License Act* requires that a real estate principles course include instruction in real estate mathematics. The study of real estate mathematics goes beyond that requirement, however, for mathematics plays an important role in the real estate business. Math is involved in nearly every aspect of a typical transaction, from the moment a listing agreement is filled out until the final monies are paid at the closing.

This review is designed to familiarize students with some basic mathematical formulas that are important in day-to-day transactions and that are included on state licensing examinations. Some of this material is covered in detail elsewhere in the text, in which cases reference is made to the appropriate chapter. If you require additional help in working these problems, *Mastering Real Estate Mathematics* can be ordered from Dearborn™ Real Estate Education.

CALCULATORS

Calculators are permitted when taking the state licensing examination. They must be nonprogrammable calculators that are silent, battery-operated, do not have paper-tape printing capabilities, and do not have alphabetic keyboards or communication capabilities. A calculator that will add (+), subtract (−), multiply (×), and divide (÷) is sufficient for licensing examinations. Because calculators are available in many sizes and shapes, choose a calculator that is comfortable for you and allow yourself time to learn to use it correctly before you take the licensing examination. At some point in your profession, you might want to purchase a business or financial calculator with functions for such operations as computing monthly payments, the maximum loan amount for which a buyer can qualify, and the remaining balance on a loan.

Regardless of the calculator you select, follow the user's manual and set the decimal to float or to a minimum of five decimals. This will enable you to arrive at an answer with enough decimals to match multiple-choice answers on exams.

FRACTIONS

$$\frac{7}{8} \quad \begin{array}{l} \text{Numerator} \\ \text{Denominator} \end{array}$$

The denominator shows the number of equal parts in the whole or total. The numerator shows the number of those parts with which you are working. In the example above, the whole or total has been divided into eight equal parts and you have seven of those equal parts.

Proper Fractions The fraction ⅞, is an example of a proper fraction. A proper fraction is one in which the numerator is smaller than the denominator—it is less than a whole, or one.

Improper Fractions

$$\frac{11}{8} \quad \frac{\text{Numerator}}{\text{Denominator}}$$

An improper fraction is one in which the numerator is larger than the denominator—it is more than one.

Mixed Numbers   A mixed number is a whole number plus a fraction—for example, 11½ is a mixed number.

Converting Fractions to Decimals   Fractions will sometimes be used in real estate math problems. These problems are most easily solved when the fractions are converted to decimals. **FORMULA:** *To convert a fraction to a decimal, the numerator is divided by the denominator.* Using the previous three fractions, you can calculate the decimal equivalent:

$$\frac{7}{8} = 7 \div 8 = 0.875$$

$$\frac{11}{8} = 11 \div 8 = 1.375$$

$$11\frac{1}{2} = 1 \div 2 = 0.5 + 11 = 11.5$$

Once fractions have been converted to decimals, other calculations can easily be completed using the calculator.

PERCENTAGES

Many real estate computations are based on the calculation of percentages. A **percent** expresses a portion of a whole; *percent* means "per hundred." The whole or total always represents 100%.

   5% = 5 parts of 100

   75% = 75 parts of 100

   120% = 100 parts of 100 plus 20 parts of another 100

To solve a problem involving percentages, the percentage must be converted to either a decimal or a fraction. **FORMULA:** *To convert a percentage to a decimal, move the decimal two places to the left and drop the percent sign—or divide the number by 100:*

   5% = 0.05

   75% = 0.75

   120% = 1.20

FORMULA: To convert a decimal to a percentage if an answer requires that a number be expressed as a percentage, move the decimal in the number two places to the right and add the percent sign—or multiply the number by 100:

   0.0875 = 8.75% or 8¾%   0.05 = 5%   0.2 = 20%   1.82 = 182%

> Remember: Set the decimal on the calculator to float or to a minimum of five decimal places.

Percentage Formulas   Percentage problems contain three elements: *rate* (percentage), *total*, and *part*. There are three formulas for solving all percentage problems:

$$\text{Total} \times \text{rate} = \text{part}$$

$$\text{Part} \div \text{rate} = \text{total}$$

$$\text{Part} \div \text{total} = \text{rate}$$

A simple way of remembering these formulas is

MULTIPLY when **PART** is the **UNKNOWN**.

DIVIDE when **PART** is the **KNOWN**.

When you divide, always enter **PART** into the calculator **first**.

Another tool to use in place of the three formulas is the T Bar.

	PART	
TOTAL		RATE

The procedure for using the T Bar is as follows:

1. Enter the two known items in the correct places.
2. If the line between the two items is vertical, multiply to solve for the missing item.
3. If the line between the two items is horizontal, divide to solve for the missing item. When you divide, the top (numerator/*Part*) always goes into the calculator first, divided by the bottom (denominator/*Total* or *Rate*).

The following examples show how the formulas and the T Bar can be used to solve percentage problems:

EXAMPLE: There are 200 homes in your prospecting area. If 5% of them sold last year, how many homes sold last year?

200 (total) × 5% (rate) = part
200 × 0.05 = **10 homes (answer)**

or

	PART = ?	
200 (total)		5% = 0.05 (rate)

200 × 0.05 = **10 homes (answer)**

EXAMPLE: A broker received $10,200 for the sale of a house. If the commission rate was 6%, what was the total sales price?

$10,200 (part) ÷ 6% (rate) = sales price (total)
$10,200 ÷ 0.06 = **$170,000 sales price (answer)**

or

	$10,200	
Total = ?		6% = 0.06

$10,200 ÷ 0.06 = **$170,000 sales price (answer)**

E X A M P L E :   If a broker received a $7,700 commission on a $110,000 sale, what was the commission rate?

$7,700 (part) ÷ $110,000 (total) = rate
$7,700 ÷ $110,000 = 0.07 = **7% commission rate**

or

$$\frac{\$7,700}{\$110,000 \quad | \quad Rate = ?}$$

$7,700 ÷ $110,000 = 0.07 = **7% commission rate**

Solving Word Problems

Solving word problems requires careful attention to the following steps:

1. *Read* the problem carefully and completely. Never touch the calculator until you have read the entire problem.
2. *Analyze* the problem to determine what is being asked, which facts are given that *will* be needed to solve for the answer, and which facts are given that *will not* be needed to solve for the answer. Eliminate any information and/or numbers given that are not needed to solve the problem. Take the remaining information and/or numbers and determine which will be needed first, second, et cetera, depending on the number of steps it will take to solve the problem.
3. *Choose* the proper formula(s) and steps needed to solve the problem.
4. *Insert* the known elements and calculate the answer.
5. *Check* your answer to be sure you keyed in the numbers and functions properly on the calculator. Be sure you finished the problem. For example, when the problem asks for the salesperson's share of the commission, do not stop at the broker's share of the commission and mark that answer just because it is one of the choices.

Percentage Problems

Commission   The full commission is a percentage of the sales price unless otherwise stated in the problem. Remember that commission rates charged to clients, commission splits between brokers, and commission splits between the broker and a salesperson are always negotiable.

E X A M P L E :   A seller listed his home for $200,000 and agreed to pay a full commission rate of 5%. The home sold four weeks later for 90% of the list price. The listing broker agreed to give the selling broker 50% of the commission. The listing broker paid the listing salesperson 50% of her share of the commission, and the selling broker paid the selling salesperson 60% of his share of the commission. How much commission did the selling salesperson receive?

Step 1: Calculate the sales price using the formula for part: ***total × rate = part***

$200,000 listing price (total) × 90% (rate) = sales price (part)
$200,000 × 0.9 = $180,000 sales price

Part = ?	
$200,000 (total)	90% = 0.9 (rate)

$200,000 × 0.9 = $180,000 sales price

Step 2: Calculate the full commission using the formula for *part.*

$180,000 (total sales price) × 5% (commission rate) = full commission (part)
$180,000 × 0.05 = $9,000 full commission

Part = ?	
$180,000 (total)	5% = 0.05 (rate)

$180,000 × 0.05 = $9,000 full commission

Step 3: Calculate the selling broker's share using the formula for *part.*

$9,000 full commission (total) × 50% (rate) = selling broker's share (part)
$9,000 × 0.5 = $4,500 selling broker's commission

Part = ?	
$9,000 (total)	50% = 0.50 (rate)

$9,000 × 0.5 = $4,500 selling broker's commission

Step 4: Calculate the selling salesperson's commission using the formula for *part.*

$4,500 selling broker's share (total) × 60% (rate) = selling salesperson (part)
$4,500 × 0.6 = **$2,700 selling salesperson's commission (answer)**

Part = ?	
$4,500 (total)	60% = 0.6 (rate)

$4,500 × 0.6 = **$2,700 selling salesperson's commission (answer)**

Seller's Net   The amount of money left after the real estate commission is deducted from the sales price is called the seller's *net after commission.*

E X A M P L E :   After deducting $5,850 in closing costs and a 5% broker's commission, the sellers received their original cost of $175,000 plus a $4,400 profit. What was the sales price of the property?

Step 1: Calculate the seller's *net after commission*.

$175,000 original cost + $4,400 profit + $5,850 closing costs =
$185,250 net after commission

Step 2: Calculate the *rate after commission*.

100% (total rate) – 5% (commission rate) = 95% rate after commission

Step 3: Calculate the total sales price using the formula for *total*: **part ÷ rate = total**.

$185,250 net after commission (part) ÷ 95% rate after commission =
sales price (total)
$185,250 ÷ 0.95 = **$195,000 sales price (answer)**

$$\frac{\$185{,}250 \text{ net after commission (part)}}{\text{Total} = ? \mid 95\% = 0.95 \text{ rate after commission}}$$

$185,250 ÷ 0.95 = **$195,000 sales price (answer)**

To check the answer, take 5% of the sales price, or,

$195,000 × 0.05 = $9,750

which, if subtracted from the sales price of $195,000, leaves the seller's desired net after commission of $185,250.

PROFIT

A **profit** is made when an item is sold for more than the purchase price. If an item is sold for less than the purchase price, there is a **loss** on the sale. Use the percentage formulas to calculate profit or loss.

E X A M P L E :   A home was listed for $125,000. It sold for $123,200, which resulted in a 10% profit over the original cost. What was the original cost?

Step 1: Calculate the *rate* that the sales price represents.

100% original cost + 10% profit = 110% sales price

Step 2: Calculate the original cost using the formula for *total*: **part ÷ rate = total.**

$123,200 sales price (part) ÷ 110% (rate) = original cost (total)
$123,200 ÷ 1.10 = **$112,000 original cost (answer)**

$$\frac{\$123{,}200 \text{ sales price (part)}}{\text{Original cost (total)} = ? \mid 110\% = 1.10 \text{ (rate)}}$$

$123,200 ÷ 1.10 = **$112,000 original cost (answer)**

Note that in the case of a profit, the "part" is larger than the "total."

INTEREST

Interest is the cost of using money. The amount of interest paid is determined by the agreed annual interest rate, the amount of money borrowed (loan amount) or amount of money still owed (loan balance), and the period of time the money is held. The formulas for percentage calculations also are used for interest computations. For more information about *interest* calculations, see Chapter 16.

Note: Using a calculator with a "%" key, a percentage problem can be computed without moving the decimals "two to the left" or "two to the right." On most calculators, simply enter the first number and depress the appropriate function key; then enter the second number and depress "%." The answer that appears on the calculator is decimally correct. Check the user's manual for instructions on the use of the "%" key on your calculator.

EXAMPLE: What is the annual interest on a $10,000 loan on which the interest rate is 12%?

$10,000 (total) × 12% (rate) = interest (part)
$10,000 × 0.12 = **$1,200 interest (answer)**

or

$$\frac{\text{Part} = ?}{\text{\$10,000 (total)} \mid \text{12\% = 0.12 (rate)}}$$

$10,000 × 0.12 = **$1,200 interest (answer)**

In the preceding problem, the interest was calculated for one year. When interest is not calculated for a full year, the formula must have a "time" factor. Therefore, the following formula is generally used for interest computations:

Principal (total) × rate × time (in months) = interest (part)

EXAMPLE: How much interest would be charged if the loan could be paid off in seven months?

$10,000 × 0.12 × ⁷⁄₁₂ = interest
$10,000 × 0.12 × 0.583333 = **$700 interest (answer)**

or

$$\frac{\text{Part} = ?}{\text{\$10,000 (total)} \mid \text{12\% = 0.12 (annual rate)} \mid \text{⁷⁄₁₂ (time)}}$$

$10,000 × 0.12 × ⁷⁄₁₂ = **$700 interest (answer)**

As explained earlier in this chapter, the percentage calculations illustrated in this section are used to solve most real estate mathematics problems. You can see that both the formula method and the T Bar method yield the same results. Therefore, use the method that makes more sense to you. For the sake of simplicity, the remaining problems in this chapter will be solved using the formula method only. If you prefer the T Bar, just draw the graphic beside each problem.

AMORTIZATION

The process of paying off a loan in equal installments of principal and interest is known as **amortization**. The interest is calculated each month on the remaining loan balance, and "time" is 1 month or $\frac{1}{12}$. The payment is first applied to the accrued interest with the remaining balance applied to reduce the principal (see Chapter 16).

E X A M P L E :   What is the balance after two payments on a loan in the original amount of $150,000 with monthly payments of $1,449.00 at 10% over a 20-year period?

First month:

$150,000 loan (total) × 10% (rate) × $\frac{1}{12}$ (time) = $1,250 interest first month (part)

$1,449.00	total payment
– 1,250.00	interest first month
$ 199.00	principal reduction first month

Second month:

$150,000.00	original loan
– 199.00	first month's reduction
$149,801.00	second month's beginning balance

$149,801.00 loan balance (total) × 10% (rate) × $\frac{1}{12}$ (time) = $1,248.34 interest second month (part)

$1,449.00	total payment
– 1,248.34	interest second month
$ 200.66	principal reduction second month

$149,801.00	second month's beginning balance
– 200.66	second month's reduction
$149,600.34	**balance after second month's payment, beginning of third month (answer)**

LOAN DISCOUNT

The **loan discount** is a method of increasing the lender's yield on a loan without increasing the interest rate. One point equals 1% of the loan amount (see Chapter 16). Use the formula for *Part* to compute a loan discount amount.

E X A M P L E :   The lender will charge a 1-point origination fee and 2½ loan discount points. What will be the total due for points on an $98,000 loan?

$98,000 (total) × 3½% (1% + 2½% rate) = total points (part)

$98,000 × 0.035 = **$3,430 total due for points (answer)**

PROPERTY TAXES AND INSURANCE PREMIUMS

Property taxes and insurance premiums usually are expressed as rates per unit of value. For example, taxes might be computed in a certain county at the rate of $2.50 per $100 of appraised value. An insurance premium on a $65,000 home might be computed at $8.646 per $1,000 of insurable value. Use the formula for *part* to compute taxes or insurance premiums.

E X A M P L E :   A house has been appraised at $90,000 and is taxed at an annual rate of $2.50 per $100 appraised valuation. What is the yearly tax?

$90,000 appraised value (total) × [$2.50 ÷ $100] (rate) = total annual tax (part)
$90,000 × .0250 = **$2,250 total annual tax (answer)**

See Chapter 11 for a further discussion of tax computations.

MEASUREMENTS

Linear   **Linear measurement** is measurement of a line. When the terms per foot, per linear foot, per running foot, or per front foot are used, determine the total length of the object. To measure front footage of a lot, use the street footage. To measure linear feet for a fence, measure the sides to be fenced. If two dimensions are given for a tract of land, the first dimension is the frontage if they are not labeled.

E X A M P L E :   A rectangular lot is 50 feet × 150 feet. The cost to fence this lot is priced per linear/running foot. How many linear/running feet will be used to calculate the price of the fence, assuming the entire lot is to be enclosed in the fence?

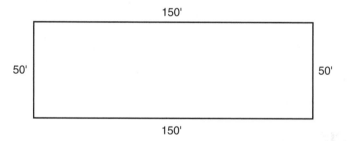

50 feet + 150 feet + 50 feet + 150 feet = **400 linear/running feet (answer)**

E X A M P L E :   A parcel of land that fronts on I-45 in Houston is for sale at $5,000 per front foot. What would it cost to purchase this parcel of land if the dimensions are 150' by 100'?

150 front feet × $5,000 per front foot = **$750,000 cost to purchase (answer)**

Area and volume Area is the two-dimensional surface of an object. Area is quoted in square units (such as feet, yards, or acres). A real estate agent would use this formula to compute the area of a parcel of land or figure the square footage of living area in a house. To *compute the area of a square or rectangular parcel,* use the formula:

area = length × width

E X A M P L E : How many square feet are in a room 15'6"5 × 30'9"?

Step 1: Convert "inches" to a decimal figure by dividing by 12 inches per foot.

6" ÷ 12 = 0.5'   9" ÷ 12 = 0.75'

Step 2: Calculate the area.

15.5' × 30.75' = **476.625 square feet (answer)**

Remember: Area is always expressed in square units.

E X A M P L E : If carpet costs $63 per square yard to install, what would it cost to carpet the room in the previous example?

476.625 square feet ÷ 9 square feet/square yard = 52.958333 square yards
52.958333 square yards × $63 per square yard = **$3,336.37 carpet cost (answer)**

To compute the amount of surface in a triangular-shaped area, use the formula:

area of a triangle = ½ (base × height)

or

area of a triangle = (base × height) ÷ 2

The *base* of a triangle is the bottom, the side on which the triangle rests. The *height* is an imaginary straight line extending from the point of the uppermost angle straight down to the base.

E X A M P L E : How many square feet are contained in a triangular parcel of land that is 400 feet on the base and 200 feet high?

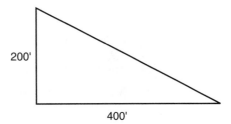

(400' × 200') ÷ 2 = **40,000 square feet (answer)**

E X A M P L E : How many acres are in a three-sided tract of land that is 300' on the base and 400' high?

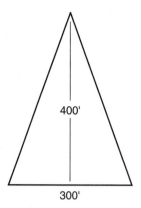

400'

300'

(300' × 400') ÷ 2 = 60,000 square feet ÷ 43,560 sq. ft./acre = **1.377 acres (answer)**

To compute the area of an irregular room, a house, or parcel of land, divide the shape into regular rectangles, squares, or triangles. Next, compute the area of each regular figure and add the areas together to obtain the total area.

E X A M P L E : What is the total square footage of the office building below?

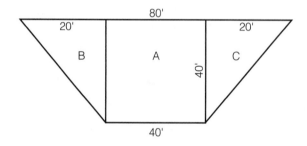

80'

20'   B   A   C   20'

40'

40'

A = 40' = 40' = 1600 sq. ft.
B = 20' = 40' = 2 = 400 sq. ft.
C = 20' = 40' = 2 = 400 sq. ft.
1,600 sq. ft. + 400 sq. ft. + 400 sq. ft. = **2,400 sq. ft. (answer)**

Volume is the space inside a three-dimensional object. It is used, for example, in measuring the interior airspace of a room to determine the required capacity for a heating unit or to calculate the amount of concrete needed on a construction project. *Remember: Volume is always expressed in cubic units.*

The formula for *computing volume* is

volume = length × width × height

E X A M P L E : A building is 500 feet long, 400 feet wide, and 25 feet high. How many cubic feet of space are in this building?

500' × 400' × 25' = **5,000,000 cubic feet (answer)**

E X A M P L E :   How many cubic yards of concrete would it take to build a sidewalk measuring 120' long, 2'6" wide, and 3" thick?

Step 1: Convert inches to feet.

6" = ⁶⁄₁₂' = 0.5'   3" = ³⁄₁₂' = 0.25'

Step 2: Calculate cubic feet and convert to cubic yards.

120' × 2.5' × 0.25' = 75 cubic feet
75 cubic feet ÷ 27 cubic feet/cubic yard = **2.78 cubic yards (answer)**

To compute the volume of a triangular prism, such as the airspace under a gable roof or in an A-frame cabin, use the formula:

volume = ½ (length × width × height)

E X A M P L E :   A building is 40 feet by 25 feet with a 10-foot-high ceiling. The building has a gable roof that is 8 feet high at the tallest point. How many cubic feet are in this structure, including the roof?

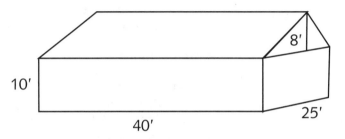

Step 1: Divide the structure into two parts: the rectangular dwelling unit and the triangular prism roof unit.

Dwelling unit: 40' (length) by 25' (width) by 10' (height)
Roof unit: 40' (length) by 25' (width) by 8' (height)

Step 2: Calculate the area of each portion and combine the totals.

40' × 25' × 10' = 10,000 cubic feet
½ (40' × 25' × 8') = 4,000 cubic feet

10,000 cubic feet + 4,000 cubic feet = **14,000 total cubic feet (answer)**

PRORATING

Most closings involve the division of financial responsibility between the buyer and seller for such items as loan interest, taxes, rents, fuel, and utility bills. These allowances are called *prorations.* Prorations are necessary to ensure that expenses are divided fairly between the seller and the buyer. For example, the seller may owe current taxes that have not been billed; the buyer would want this settled at the closing. If the buyer assumes the seller's existing loan, the seller usually owes the buyer for interest from the first of the month *through* the date of closing.

Accrued expense items are items to be prorated that are owed by the seller but eventually will be paid by the buyer (such as interest on an assumed loan or accrued ad valorem property taxes). Therefore, the seller pays the buyer for these expenses at closing.

Prepaid expense items are items to be prorated that have been prepaid by the seller but not fully used up (such as a prepaid insurance policy). The buyer owes the seller for these expenses. *Prepaid income items*, such as rental income, would be prorated and the income for the unused days transferred to the buyer from the seller at closing.

Some general guidelines in computing prorations are listed in the following:

■ The seller owns the property on the day of closing; the seller is charged expenses for that day and gets income for that day. This is called prorating *through* the day of closing, which is a requirement of the Texas promulgated sales contracts.

■ Prorations are based on either a statutory year or a calendar year. A *statutory* or *banker's year* is based on a 360-day year, using 30 days in each month. A *calendar year* is based on a 365-day year, using the actual number of days in each month.

■ The buyer pays the seller for prepaid expense items; the seller pays the buyer for accrued expense items. The party receiving the money "gets the credit"; the party paying the money is "debited."

Proration Steps   When an item is to be prorated, these steps should be followed:

Step 1: The charge must first be broken down into yearly, monthly, and daily amounts, depending on the type of charge. Using a *statutory year*, a total annual charge would be divided by 360 to arrive at a daily charge; a total monthly charge would be divided by 30. Using a *calendar year*, a total annual charge would be divided by 365 to arrive at a daily charge; a total monthly charge would be divided by the actual number of days in the month of closing.

Step 2: The prorated period is calculated using the actual number of months and days, using a *calendar year*, or 30 days per month, using a *statutory year*.

Step 3: The monthly and daily amounts are then multiplied by the number of years, months, and days in the prorated period to determine the accrued or unearned amount to be credited or debited at closing.

Mortgage Interest Proration   Interest on a mortgage loan is collected in arrears; each month's payment includes interest for the prior month. Therefore, if a seller's loan is assumed by the buyer, the seller owes interest for the portion of the month that he owned the property. The interest proration would be a debit to the seller and a credit to the buyer.

E X A M P L E :   A buyer purchases a home for $175,000 and plans to assume the seller's existing loan for $146,750 with monthly payments of $1,449 at 10%. The closing date is set for August 18. Because interest on a mortgage loan is collected in arrears, the August 1 payment covered July's interest. Therefore, the seller has not yet made a payment to cover August's interest, and the seller will owe a portion of the interest to the buyer for the next house payment.

Step 1: The initial step is to calculate the *dollars per day* for the interest on the mortgage. Carry all computations to three decimal places until a final figure is reached, then round off to the nearest penny.

$146,750 (total) × 10% (rate) × $\frac{1}{12}$ = $1,222.916 interest for the month of closing

Using a 30-day month and 360-day **statutory year** (required for computations of prepaid interest on sales to Fannie Mae and Freddie Mac if this were a new loan), divide the monthly charge by 30 to get the daily premium:

$1,222.916 ÷ 30 days = $40.763 daily charge

Step 2: Next, calculate the period for which the seller owes the buyer:

18 days in August *through the day of closing*

Step 3: Finally, multiply the daily interest amount by the number of days to be charged to the seller:

$40.763 daily charge × 18 days = **$733.73 prorated interest,**
using a *statutory year* (answer); a *debit* to the seller and a *credit* to the buyer

Using a **calendar year** (which would normally be used on an assumption's accrued interest computation), the proration would be:

Step 1: Calculate the charge per day (31 days in August):

$1,222.916 ÷ 31 days = $39.448 daily charge

Step 2: Calculate the period: August 1 through August 18 = 18 days

Step 3: Multiply the daily charge by the number of days:

$39.448 × 18 days = $710.06 **prorated interest, using a *calendar year* (answer)**

Tax Proration   Real estate taxes are assessed from January 1 through December 31. Because taxes are usually paid in arrears, the seller will owe the buyer for accrued taxes from January 1 *through* the day of closing. If the current tax bill has not been issued, the proration is generally computed on the previous year's bill.

E X A M P L E :   A sale is to be closed on September 17, and current real estate taxes of $1,200 are to be prorated accordingly.

Step 1: First determine the prorated cost of the real estate tax per month and day; assume a **statutory year**.

$1,200 annual taxes ÷ 12 months = $100 taxes per month
$100 monthly taxes ÷ 30 days = $3.333 taxes per day

Step 2: The accrued period is 8 months and 17 days (January through August = 8 months; September 1 through September 17 = 17 days).

Step 3: Next, multiply the monthly and daily charges by the accrued period and add the totals to determine the prorated real estate tax:

$100 taxes per month × 8 months = $800
$3.333 taxes per day × 17 days = $56.661
$800.00 + 56.661 = $856.661 prorated taxes, using a statutory year (answer)

This amount represents the seller's accrued *earned* tax; it will be *a credit to the buyer and a debit to the seller* on the closing statement.

Another procedure for calculating the proration for the statutory year is this:

Step 1: A tax bill of $1,200 ÷ 360 days = $3.333 per day.

Step 2: January 1 to September 17 runs 257 days (January's 30 days, February's 30 days, etc.).

Step 3: $3.333 × 257 days = $856.58. Note the slight difference in results ($856.66 and $856.58) from rounding.

The following method would be used to compute this proration according to the calendar-year *method*:

Step 1: A tax bill of $1,200 ÷ 365 days = $3.287 per day.

Step 2: The accrued period from January 1 to September 17 runs 260 days (January's 31 days, February's 28 days, etc.).

Step 3: $3.287 × 260 days = $854.62.

For more information about prorations, see Chapter 20.

CHAPTER 19 QUESTIONS

1. If the bank gave John a 90% loan on a house valued at $88,500, how much additional cash must he produce as a down payment if he already had paid $4,500 in earnest money?
   a. $3,500
   b. $4,000
   c. $4,350
   d. $8,850

2. What did the owners originally pay for their home if they sold it for $98,672, which gave them a 12% profit over their original cost?
   a. $86,830
   b. $88,100
   c. $89,700
   d. $110,510

3. Four women pooled their savings and purchased a six-unit apartment building for $350,000. If one person invested $80,000 and two contributed $87,500 each, what percentage of ownership was left for the fourth investor?
   a. 20%
   b. 25%
   c. 27%
   d. 30%

4. Jacob wants to determine the principal amount still owed on his mortgage loan. He knows that the interest portion of his last monthly payment was $391.42. If he is paying interest at the rate of 11½%, what was the outstanding balance of the loan before that last payment was made?
   a. $43,713.00
   b. $40,843.83
   c. $36,427.50
   d. $34,284.70

5. The home at 1358 DeKalb Street is valued at $95,000. The local tax rate is $1.71 per $100. What is the amount of the monthly taxes?
   a. $1,111.50
   b. $926.30
   c. $111.15
   d. $135.38

6. What is the total cost of a driveway 15 feet wide, 40 feet long, and 4 inches thick if the concrete costs $60 per cubic yard and the labor costs $1.25 per square foot?
   a. $527.25
   b. $693.75
   c. $1,194.00
   d. $1,581.75

7. An owner agrees to list his property if he can receive at least $47,300 after paying a 5% broker's commission and paying $1,150 in closing costs. At what price must it sell?
   a. $48,450
   b. $50,815
   c. $50,875
   d. $51,000

8. The Loving Gift Shop pays rent of $600 per month plus 2.5% of gross annual sales in excess of $50,000. What was the average monthly rent last year if gross annual sales were $75,000?
   a. $1,125.00
   b. $756.25
   c. $600.00
   d. $652.08

9. Two brokers split the 6% commission equally on a $73,000 home. The selling salesperson, Saul, was paid 70% of his broker's share. The listing salesperson, Elisha, was paid 30% of her broker's share. How much did Elisha receive?
   a. $657
   b. $4,380
   c. $1,533
   d. $1,314

10. A 100-acre farm is divided into lots for homes. The streets require one-eighth of the whole farm. If there are 140 lots, how many square feet are in each lot?
    a. 43,560
    b. 35,004
    c. 31,114
    d. 27,225

11. How much interest will the seller owe the buyer for a closing date of August 10 if the outstanding loan balance is $43,580? The interest rate on this assumable loan is 10½% and the last payment was paid on August 1. Prorations are to be done *through* the day of closing, using a *statutory year*.
    a. $127.11
    b. $254.22
    c. $508.43
    d. $381.33

12. The buyer has agreed to pay $175,000 for a property. If she makes a 10% down payment, how much will she owe at closing for points if there are 2.5 loan discount points and a 1-point origination fee?
    a. $1,575.00
    b. $3,937.50
    c. $5,512.50
    d. $6,125.00

13. Calculate eight months' interest on a $5,000 interest-only loan at 9½%.
    a. $475.00
    b. $316.67
    c. $237.50
    d. $39.58

14. The Fernandez family has sold their home and closing is set for May 23. If last year's tax bill totaled $1,282 and was paid, how much will the tax proration be? Prorate *through* the day of closing using a *calendar year*.
    a. $498.70
    b. $502.22
    c. $609.98
    d. $613.42

15. What is the monthly net operating income on an investment of $115,000 if the rate of return is 12½%?
    a. $1,150.00
    b. $1,197.92
    c. $7,666.67
    d. $14,375.00

16. What is the interest rate on a $10,000 loan with semiannual interest of $450?
    a. 7%
    b. 9%
    c. 11%
    d. 13.5%

17. An office building produces $68,580 annual net operating income. What price would you pay for this property to show a minimum return of 12% on your investment?
    a. $489,857
    b. $571,500
    c. $685,800
    d. $768,096

18. If a broker received a 6.5% commission that was $5,200, what was the sales price?
    a. $80,400
    b. $80,000
    c. $77,200
    d. $86,600

19. Duc Van earns an annual income of $60,000; Lan earns $2,400 per month. How much can Duc Van and Lan pay monthly for their mortgage payment if the lender uses a 28% qualifying ratio?
    a. $2,072
    b. $1,400
    c. $2,352
    d. $672

20. What percentage of profit would you make if you paid $10,500 for a lot, built a home on the lot at a cost of $93,000, and then sold the house and lot for $134,550?
    a. 13%
    b. 23%
    c. 30%
    d. 45%

21. A fence is being built to enclose a lot 125 feet by 350 feet. How many running feet of fence will it take to enclose the lot?
    a. 475
    b. 600
    c. 825
    d. 950

Detailed rationales for the end-of-chapter review questions are available online at www.dearborn.com through the *Instructor Resource Guides* link.

CHAPTER

Closing the Real Estate Transaction

■ **LEARNING OBJECTIVES**   *When you have completed this chapter, you will be able to*

■ **identify** the documents required from the buyer and the seller as a real estate transaction closes;

■ **describe** RESPA—its purpose, covered transactions, major provisions, and forms required—as well as the related requirements and prohibitions of Regulation Z of the Truth in Lending Act and of the Texas Department of Insurance;

■ **identify** at least six types of expenses incurred by the buyer and/or the seller at closing and who pays each one;

■ **distinguish** between prepaid and accrued expenses and between statutory- and calendar-year proration methods; compute common prorations, referencing the debit and credit distributions; and

■ **define** the following *key terms*:

accrued item	doctrine of relation back	HUD-1 Settlement Statement
closing	escrow	
closing agent	escrow agent	prepaid item
closing statement	Good Faith Estimate (GFE)	prorate
credit		Real Estate Settlement Procedures Act (RESPA)
debit		

OVERVIEW

After securing and servicing a listing, advertising the property, finding and qualifying potential buyers, and negotiating for and obtaining a signed sales contract on the seller's property, a real estate licensee is one step away from receiving a commission. That last step is the real estate closing, a procedure that includes both title and financial considerations.

This chapter discusses both aspects of real estate closing, focusing on the licensee's role in this concluding phase of a real estate transaction. Special emphasis is placed on the computations required to settle all necessary expenses between buyer and seller and between seller and broker; a detailed example of a real estate closing illustrates these computations.

CLOSING THE TRANSACTION—PRECLOSING PROCEDURES

Closing, or settlement, is the consummation of the real estate transaction. It is the time when the title to the real estate is transferred in exchange for payment of the purchase price. In many transactions, it is also the closing of the buyer's loan—the signing of the loan documents and the disbursal of mortgage funds by the lender.

A sales contract is the blueprint for the completion of a real estate transaction. A contract should be complete and should provide for all possibilities to avoid misunderstandings that could delay or even prevent closing of the sale. Before closing, the parties should assure themselves that the various conditions and stipulations of their sales contract have been met and that the closing statement correctly reflects all agreements regarding money.

Buyer's Issues

The buyer will want to ensure that the seller can deliver good title and that the property will be in the promised condition. This involves inspecting

- the commitment for title insurance;
- the seller's deed;
- any documents demonstrating the removal of undesired liens and encumbrances;
- the survey;
- the results of any required inspections, such as termite or structural inspections, or required repairs; and
- any leases if tenants reside on the premises.

Title Evidence The Texas Real Estate License Act requires that a broker advise a purchaser in writing, at or before closing, to have the abstract examined by an attorney or to obtain a title insurance policy. This "advice" is included in Texas promulgated sales contract forms, and the buyer and the buyer's lender want assurance that the seller's title complies with the requirements of the contract. When an abstract of title is used, the buyer's attorney examines it and issues an opinion of title, which sets forth the status of the seller's title. It discloses all liens, encumbrances, easements, conditions, or restrictions that appear on the record and to which the seller's title is subject. When a title insurance policy is used, the buyer receives a title commitment from the title insurance company within 20 days of the contract date, as discussed in Chapter 18. The buyer then has an agreed number of days after receiving the title commitment to object to certain defects, exceptions, or encumbrances to the title. If the objections cannot be cured, the contract will terminate, no closing will occur, and the earnest money will be refunded to the buyer.

There are usually three searches of the public records to check the status of the seller's title. The first (to prepare the title commitment or abstract) shows the status of the seller's title on the date of the sales contract. The second search is made on the day of closing and covers the date when the deed is delivered to the purchaser. A third search is conducted before recording the papers to be sure that nothing affecting the property has been recorded since the last search was made. If title insurance is purchased, the cost of all title searches is included in the cost of both the owner's and mortgagee's title insurance policies.

Releasing Existing Liens   When the purchaser pays cash or obtains a new loan to purchase the property, the seller's existing loan is paid in full and released of record. A payoff amount that is valid through the proposed closing date would be obtained on a *payoff statement* from the lender. Effective since September 1, 2011, and since new rules were adopted by the Finance Commission of Texas, the loan payoff information must be provided on a standard payoff statement form (H.B. 558, 2011).

In a transaction in which the buyer assumes the seller's existing mortgage loan, the buyer will want to know the exact balance of the loan as of the closing date. It is recommended that the buyer obtain an *estoppel certificate* and waiver of acceleration from the lender, stating the exact balance due, the last interest payment made, and the fact that the lender permits the assumption.

For liens that are not released before closing (including mortgage liens, mechanic's liens, and judgment liens), the closing agent must

1. obtain the payoff information from the lienholder,
2. withhold the money from the seller's proceeds,
3. close the transaction,
4. pass title to the buyer, and
5. pay the escrowed money to the lienholder and get a release.

If a property on which a lien exists is to be transferred without paying off the lien within 30 days of the closing and without title insurance, the seller must give the buyer a written notice disclosing the lien and the possible risks to the buyer. The disclosure must be given within seven days before the earlier of the contract effective date or the date of closing. Chapter 13 contains additional details regarding this disclosure.

Survey   An improvement survey gives information about the exact location and dimensions of the land and any improvements on it. In addition, the survey should set out in full any existing easements and encroachments. As discussed in Chapter 18, an existing survey may be used if it is agreed to in the sales contract and if it is acceptable to the lender and title company. In such a case, the seller provides the existing survey and a T-47 area and boundary affidavit to the buyer and the title company.

Checking the Premises   The buyer should inspect the property to determine the interests of any parties in possession or other interests that cannot be determined from inspecting the public record. If a final walk-through has been requested in the purchase contract, it usually occurs on the day of closing or shortly before. At that time, the buyer checks to see that all fixtures and personal property included in the transaction are still present, that no damage has been done to the property, and that any required repairs have been properly completed.

Seller's Issues

Because the seller's main interest is in receiving payment for the property, the seller will want to be sure that the buyer has obtained the necessary financing and has sufficient funds to complete the sale. The seller will also want to be certain that he has complied with all the buyer's inspection and repair requirements so that the transaction can be completed.

CONDUCTING THE CLOSING

Closing is the point at which ownership of a property is transferred in exchange for the selling price.

Generally speaking, the closing of a real estate transaction involves a gathering of interested parties at which the promises made in the *real estate sales contract* are kept, or *executed*; that is, the seller's deed is delivered in exchange for the purchase price. In many sales transactions, two closings actually take place at this time: (1) the closing of the sale and (2) the closing of the buyer's loan—the signing of the loan documents and disbursement of mortgage funds by the lender. A closing that involves all interested parties is often called a *round table close*.

Where Closings Are Held and Who Attends

Closings may be held at a number of locations, including a title company, the buyer's lending institution, an attorney's office, a real estate broker's office, or in front of a notary public. In Texas, the closing usually takes place at a title company. Those attending may include any (not necessarily all) of the following interested parties:

- Buyer
- Seller
- Real estate agent (broker and/or salesperson)
- Attorney(s) for the seller and/or the buyer
- Representatives and/or attorneys for the lending institution(s) involved
- Representative of the title insurance company

Closing Agent   Preparation for closing involves ordering and reviewing an array of documents, such as the title insurance commitment, the survey, the property insurance policy, and the lender's closing instructions. The **closing agent**

- assembles all the documents necessary to finalize the purchaser's loan and the seller's transfer of title;
- prepares the HUD-1 Settlement Statement following the provisions of the contract and the lender's instructions;
- arranges the time and place of closing with all parties; and
- in most cases, conducts the closing.

IN PRACTICE In Texas, title companies are not permitted to prepare legal documents. This is the practice of law and must be done by an attorney, who often is retained by the title company for such purpose.

The Exchange When all parties are satisfied that everything is in order, the exchange is made and the closing agent collects all funds. After the closing, the agent writes all disbursement checks arising from the closing, prepares the final disbursement sheet to prove that money paid in equals money paid out, and transmits the appropriate documents to the county clerk for recording.

Possession of the property is delivered to the buyer on *closing and funding*—when the seller gets the money—or on a date specified in a TREC *temporary residential lease form.* For example, if a closing occurs late in the afternoon, a loan company may not be able to get the funds transmitted to the title company on the day of closing. Thus, possession would be delayed until the next business day (a Monday following a Friday afternoon closing) or longer if there were issues to be resolved after closing.

Closing in Escrow

In an *escrow closing*, a third party coordinates the closing activities on behalf of the buyer and seller.

An **escrow** is a method of closing whereby a disinterested third party is authorized to act as escrow agent and is given the responsibility to coordinate the closing activities. The **escrow agent** also may be called the *escrow holder*. The escrow agent may be an attorney, a title company, a trust company, an escrow company, or the escrow department of a lending institution. Although a real estate brokerage can offer escrow services, a broker cannot be a disinterested party in a transaction from which she expects to collect a commission. Because the escrow agent is placed in a position of great trust, Texas law requires that an escrow agent be licensed by the Texas Department of Insurance and obtain and maintain a surety bond.

The Escrow Procedure

When a transaction will be closed in escrow, the buyer and the seller choose an escrow agent. If a TREC-promulgated sales contract form has been used, the escrow agreement is a part of that contract. The agreement sets forth the details of the transaction and the instructions to the escrow agent. After the contract is signed, the broker turns over the earnest money to the escrow agent, who deposits it in a special trust, or escrow, account. TREC Rules require that the broker deposit the earnest money by the end of the second business day after the contract has been signed by all parties.

Buyers and sellers deposit all pertinent documents with the escrow agent before the specified date of closing. *Sellers* usually deposit
- the deed conveying the property to the buyer,
- title evidence (abstract or title insurance policy),
- the payoff letter (a letter from the mortgagee of the existing mortgage, setting forth the amount needed to pay the loan in full) or an estoppel certificate (a statement showing the exact amount the buyer will assume),
- affidavits of title, and
- other instruments or documents necessary to clear the title or complete the transaction.

Among a sellers' affidavits is an *affidavit as to debts and liens*, a sworn statement in which the sellers assure the title company (and the buyer) that there are no liens, unpaid bills for repairs or improvements, or undisclosed defects in the title. Required by the title insurance company before it will issue an owner's policy to the buyer, this affidavit establishes the right for the title company to sue the sellers if statements in the affidavit prove incorrect.

Before closing in escrow, *buyers* deposit
- the balance of the cash needed to complete the purchase, usually in the form of a certified check;
- loan documents (if the buyer is securing a new loan);
- a hazard insurance policy, including flood insurance (where required);
- a survey, if requested in the contract or required by the lender; and
- other documents needed to complete the transaction (such as an appraisal).

The escrow agent has the authority to examine the title evidence. When title is shown in the name of the buyers and all other conditions of the escrow agreement have been met, the agent generally is authorized to disburse the purchase price to the seller, minus all the seller's expenses and lien payoffs. The agent then records the deed and deed of trust (if a new loan has been obtained by the purchaser).

There are several advantages of closing a sale in escrow: (1) the buyer's money will not be paid to the seller until the seller's title is acceptable, (2) the seller is assured of getting the purchase price because the buyer's check must clear before title passes, and (3) neither party need be present when title is passed. Under the good funds rule of the Texas Department of Insurance, the title company must require that the buyer provide a cashier's check, certified check, or wired funds at closing if the amount due at closing is $1,500 or more.

> When a seller delivers title into escrow, but dies before closing of escrow, the conveyance still will be accomplished.

Doctrine of Relation Back   If a seller deposits the deed with an escrow agent under the terms of a valid escrow agreement and thereafter the conditions of the escrow are satisfied, the *deed passes title to the purchaser as of the date it was delivered to the escrow agent*. This is called the **doctrine of relation back**—the title relates back to the date on which the deed was deposited in escrow. If the conditions of the escrow agreement have not been met, however, the deed is not considered delivered and title does not pass to the purchaser.

IN PRACTICE   Fees charged by the escrow agent typically are split between buyer and seller according to the agreement of the parties as stated in the sales contract. However, a buyer may not pay charges and fees expressly prohibited by FHA, VA, Texas Veterans Land Board, or other governmental loan program regulations. The promulgated One to Four Family Residential Contract provides that if any expense exceeds the amount stated in the contract to be paid by one party, that party may terminate the contract unless the other party agrees to pay the excess.

Broker's Role at Closing

After the contract is signed and the earnest money is delivered to the title company, the loan company, title company, and attorneys take over. However, a broker's service generally continues all the way through closing. The real estate agents make sure all details are taken care of so the closing can proceed smoothly. This means ensuring that arrangements are made for obtaining title evidence, surveys, appraisals, inspections, repairs, and other items listed in the contract. At the closing itself, the broker's role can vary from simply collecting the commission to conducting the proceedings. In addition, if neither the person who conducts the closing nor the lender provides IRS Form 1099-S to the seller, the broker is required to do so if the transaction is reportable by the closing agent under IRS rules. In most cases, capital gains on a principal residence are not reportable by the title company because they do not exceed the $250,000 (for singles) or $500,000 (for married couples) capital gains exclusion discussed in Chapter 4. Therefore, the IRS permits the title company at closing to obtain certification from the seller that the full gain on the sale is excludable. Closings on other types of property generally would be reportable by the title company.

Lender's Interest in Closing

Whether a buyer obtains new financing or assumes the seller's existing loan, the lender wants to protect its security interest in the property. The lender wants its mortgage lien to have priority over other liens. It wants to ensure that the taxes are paid and that insurance is kept up to date in case the property is damaged or destroyed. For this reason, the lender usually requires a title insurance policy, a fire and hazard insurance policy (along with a receipt for the premium), and a reserve account for tax and insurance payments. In addition, a lender may require other documentation, including a survey, termite or other inspection reports, or a certificate of occupancy and building permit (for a newly constructed building).

IN PRACTICE   Licensees should avoid recommending a specific person or company for any inspection or testing services. If a buyer suffers a financial injury as a result of a provider's negligence, the licensee also may be liable. The better practice is to give clients the sources for names of several professionals who offer high-quality services.

RESPA

As mandated by the Dodd-Frank Act, the CFPB has adopted new rules and disclosure forms, which must be provided to consumers for mortgage applications received on or after August 1, 2015. The Truth in Lending Disclosure Statement and the Good Faith Estimate have been combined into one simpler consumer form called the Loan Estimate, which must be provided to the borrower no more than three days after applying for the loan. The HUD-1 has been replaced with the Closing Disclosure, which must be provided at least three days before closing.

The federal **Real Estate Settlement Procedures Act (RESPA)**, administered by the Consumer Financial Protection Bureau, was enacted in 1974 to protect consumers from abusive lending practices. Specifically, the purposes of RESPA are to

- help consumers become better shoppers for settlement (loan closing) services by requiring disclosures that spell out the costs associated with closing and
- eliminate kickbacks and unearned referral fees that unnecessarily increase the costs of closing a transaction.

RESPA requirements apply when a purchase is financed by a federally related mortgage loan. *Federally related loans* include loans made by banks, savings associations, or other lenders whose deposits are insured by federal agencies. It also includes loans insured by the FHA and guaranteed by the VA; loans administered by HUD; and loans intended to be sold by the lenders to Fannie Mae, Ginnie Mae, or Freddie Mac.

RESPA regulations apply to first-lien mortgage loans made to finance the purchase of one-family to four-family homes, cooperatives, and condominiums for either owner occupancy or investment. RESPA also governs subordinate loans (including loans for home equity and home improvement), refinancings, and reverse mortgages.

RESPA applies to all federally related residential mortgage loans *except*

■ a loan on property of 25 acres or more;

■ a loan for business, commercial, or agricultural purposes;

■ a temporary construction loan;

■ a loan on vacant land;

■ assumption without lender approval;

■ a conversion of a federally related mortgage loan to different terms, if a new note is not required; and

■ transfer of a loan in the secondary market.

Disclosure Requirements Lenders and closing agents have certain disclosure obligations at the time of loan application, before closing occurs, at loan closing, and after closing.

At the time of loan application (or no later than three business days thereafter), mortgage brokers and/or lenders must give the borrowers the following:

■ *Shopping for Your Home Loan: HUD's Settlement Cost Booklet*, which contains general information about closing costs and explains the various RESPA provisions, including a line-by-line discussion of the Settlement Statement, the HUD-1.

■ **Good Faith Estimate (GFE)** of closing costs, which lists the charges the buyer is likely to pay at closing. Quoted costs are subject to "tolerances," which specify the maximum amount by which an actual charge on the HUD-1 closing statement can vary from the estimate on the GFE. There are three tolerance levels. For example, quotes for fees to be charged by the lender (such as discount points, origination fees, underwriting and processing fees) must be exact; there is *zero tolerance* on these items. Estimates for settlement services (including appraisals and recording fees) have a *10% tolerance* if the lender selects the provider or the borrower selects the provider from a list provided by the lender. If the borrower chooses the providers, including escrow and title insurance, there is *unlimited tolerance*. Additionally, reserves for taxes, per diem interest, and the cost of homeowners insurance have *unlimited tolerance*. The terms and prices quoted (except for the interest rate and charges related to the interest rate) must be available for at least 10 business days after the issuance of the GFE. In addition, if the lender requires the use of a particular title company to conduct the closing, the lender must disclose this requirement on the GFE.

■ *Mortgage Servicing Disclosure Statement*, which discloses (a) the possibility of a future transfer of loan servicing to another company and (b) the rights of the borrower if that occurs. Servicing the loan involves duties related to collecting PITI payments, making escrow account disbursements for taxes and insurance, and loan analysis.

Before closing occurs, the borrower must be given the following:

■ **HUD-1 Settlement Statement**, a standard form that shows all charges imposed on borrowers and sellers in connection with the closing. This form is illustrated in Figure 20.4 at the end of the chapter. Items required by the lender that are paid before closing must be marked "paid outside of closing" (POC). Items paid by the buyer or seller outside closing, not required by the lender, are not included on the HUD-1. The HUD-1 statement must be made available for inspection by the borrower one day before closing if requested. No fee can be charged for preparation of the HUD-1 or related statements required by RESPA or the Truth in Lending Act.

In addition to the closing costs, the HUD-1 requires the computation of the tolerances between estimated costs on the GFE and the actual costs on the HUD-1. The data on page 3 of the HUD-1 reflect (1) the various GFE expense categories and their estimated charges, (2) the actual charges for those same expense categories on the HUD-1, and (3) disclosures regarding loan terms, such as "Can your interest rate rise?" RESPA provides a lender with an opportunity to "cure" any violation of the tolerances by reimbursing the borrower any amount by which the tolerances were exceeded, which can be paid either at closing or within 30 days of settlement.

■ *Affiliated Business Arrangement (AfBA) Disclosure* if one closing service provider refers the buyer to another provider with whom the referring party has an ownership or other beneficial interest, such as a lender's referring a buyer to an insurance company that is owned by the lender's spouse. The referring party must give the AfBA disclosure to the consumer at or before the time of the referral. The disclosure must describe the business arrangement that exists between the two providers and give the borrower an estimate of the second provider's charges. With the exception of cases in which a lender refers a borrower to an attorney, a credit reporting agency, or similar provider representing the lender's interest in the transaction, the referring party may not require the consumer to use the particular provider being referred.

At closing, the borrower is given the following:
■ *HUD-1 Settlement Statement,* which shows the actual closing, or settlement, costs for the loan transaction, as discussed previously.
■ *Initial Escrow Statement,* which itemizes the estimated taxes, insurance premiums, and other charges anticipated to be paid from the escrow account during the first 12 months of the loan. It lists the escrow payment amount and any required cushion. Although the statement is usually given at closing, the lender has 45 days from closing to deliver it to the buyer.

After closing, loan servicers must deliver the following to buyers:
■ *Annual Escrow Statement,* which summarizes all escrow account deposits and payments during the servicer's 12-month computation year. It also notifies the borrower of any shortages or surpluses in the escrow account.
■ *Servicing Transfer Statement* if the loan servicer sells or assigns the servicing rights to another loan servicer. The loan servicer must notify the borrower 15 days before the effective date of the loan transfer, including address and telephone contact information for the new servicer. Then the new loan servicer must notify the borrower in writing within 30 days of the transfer. Texas law requires a statutorily prescribed statement that must be included in this notification (S.B. 17, 2011).

New Disclosures and Forms Required by the Dodd-Frank Act Amending RESPA and TILA

As discussed previously, the Dodd-Frank Act and rules adopted by the CFPB require new simplified disclosures when a borrower applies for a mortgage loan and before closing. The new forms and disclosures, some of which are required by

RESPA and some of which are required by TILA must be provided for applications that are received by a mortgage lender on or after August 1, 2015.

No later than three days after the consumer applies for a loan, either a mortgage broker or the lender must provide the consumer with the Loan Estimate form. The Loan Estimate replaces the Good Faith Estimate (GFE) required under RESPA and the "early" TIL disclosure, and incorporates new disclosures required under the Dodd-Frank Act. While a borrower may be provided an early estimate before filing an application for a loan, the estimate must contain a disclaimer noting that the early estimate is not the Loan Estimate required by law. For a sample of the new Loan Estimate form, see Figure 20.1.

Within three days of receiving an application for a loan, the lender must provide the applicant a written list of homeownership counseling organizations using data provided by the CFPB or HUD. The lender may comply with this requirement by using a tool provided on the CFPB's website or using data made available by the CFPB or HUD.

At least three business days before closing, the lender must provide the Closing Disclosure form to the borrower. The Closing Disclosure form replaces the HUD-1 and the TIL disclosure and contains additional new disclosures required by the Dodd-Frank Act. (For a sample of the new Closing Disclosure form, see Figure 20.2.) If the lender increases the annual percentage rate more than ⅛% for most loans, adds a prepayment penalty, or changes the type of loan, the lender must give the borrower a new form and an additional three day period to close. While lenders are ultimately responsible for ensuring that borrowers receive the Closing Disclosure, they may use settlement agents to deliver the disclosure. The tolerances and exceptions described under the discussion of the GFE are the same under the new forms.

RESPA's Consumer Protections
- Settlement Cost Booklet
- Good-Faith Estimate of closing costs
- Uniform Settlement Statement
- Prohibition against kickbacks and unearned fees
- Escrow account limitations
- CLO regulation
- CBA disclosure

Prohibitions and Restrictions RESPA also affords consumer protection through its restrictions placed on brokers, lenders, and title companies.

- *Prohibition against kickbacks*: RESPA explicitly prohibits the payment of kickbacks, or unearned fees, in any real estate settlement service. It prohibits referral fees *when no services are actually rendered*. For example, a mortgage lender would be prohibited from giving money or anything of value to a real estate agent for the agent's referring one of its customers to the lender. A 2010 RESPA rule prohibits a broker or agent from receiving a fee for referring a particular home buyer or seller to a home warranty company; such a payment would be an illegal kickback.
  - This prohibition against kickbacks does *not* include fee splitting among cooperating brokers or members of multiple listing services, brokerage referral arrangements, the division of a commission between a broker and the salespersons, or referrals made by an employee to generate business for the company itself.
- *Selection of the title company*: RESPA makes it illegal for the seller to require that the buyer purchase title insurance from a particular title company as a condition of sale if the property is purchased with the assistance of a federally related mortgage loan.
- *Limitation on escrow (or reserve) account*: RESPA rules allow a lender or a company servicing a mortgage to collect each month, for deposit into an escrow account, a sum equal to one month's annual property taxes, insurance premiums, and other recurring items such as homeowners association

dues and some mortgage insurance premiums. Under the *aggregate analysis accounting method*, the company can also maintain a cushion equal to two months' worth of those payments as long as at least once each year the escrow account does not exceed two times the monthly escrow payment.

■ *Computerized loan origination:* A broker may charge a fee for using a computerized loan origination (CLO) system to help a buyer select and originate a mortgage as long as the fee is disclosed on the good-faith estimate of closing costs and is reasonably related to the value of services provided. Remember that the SAFE Act requires a person who takes a loan application or discusses/negotiates rates or terms to be licensed as a residential mortgage loan originator. (See Chapter 16 for more information on CLOs.)

■ *Controlled business arrangements (CBA):* A service that is increasing in popularity is one-stop shopping for consumers of real estate services. A real estate firm, title insurance company, mortgage broker, home inspection company, or even moving company may agree to offer a package of services to consumers. CBAs are permitted *as long as a consumer is clearly informed of the relationship among the service providers and that other providers are available.* Fees may not be exchanged among the affiliated companies simply for referring business to one another.

No RESPA Violation for Closing Discount   A federal appellate court affirmed an earlier ruling that offering a discount to a buyer if the buyer uses the developer's lender does not violate RESPA (2011).

RESPA Does Not Apply To Fees That Are Not Split   In a unanimous opinion in May 2012, the U.S. Supreme Court ruled that RESPA does not apply to unearned fees that are not split but are charged by a single settlement service provider. In *Freeman v. Quicken Loans*, three couples claimed that loan "discount fees" charged by Quicken did not provide them with lower interest rates and that Quicken had charged them fees for which no services were rendered, violating Section 8(b) by charging a fee that exceeds the reasonable value of goods, facilities or services provided. The Court ruled that a settlement service provider's splitting a fee with one or more other persons would be a violation of RESPA but a single provider's retention of an unearned fee was not a violation.

WEBLINK @ www.hud.gov/offices/hsg/sfh/res/respa_hm.cfm

IN PRACTICE   In addition to RESPA, other laws regulate the closing process, among them are Truth in Lending Regulation Z, particularly as revised by the Mortgage Disclosure Improvement Act discussed in Chapter 16. It requires that

■ the earliest a home purchase transaction can close is seven business days after the homebuyer is issued initial mortgage disclosures from the lender. The waiting period begins when the lender places the early disclosures in the mail;

■ a homebuyer must be provided with a copy of the appraisal a minimum of three business days before closing; and

■ a lender must reissue a Truth in Lending Disclosure (TIL) and wait an additional three days to close if the APR increases beyond a specified percentage from the initial TIL disclosure.

Rebates   In addition to RESPA, TREC and the Texas Department of Insurance have rules prohibiting unearned kickbacks or rebates.

FIGURE 20.1: Loan Estimate

Save this Loan Estimate to compare with your Closing Disclosure.

Loan Estimate

	LOAN TERM
	PURPOSE
DATE ISSUED	**PRODUCT**
APPLICANTS	**LOAN TYPE** ☐ Conventional ☐ FHA ☐ VA ☐ _____
	LOAN ID #
	RATE LOCK ☐ NO ☐ YES, until
PROPERTY	*Before closing, your interest rate, points, and lender credits can*
SALE PRICE	*change unless you lock the interest rate. All other estimated closing costs expire on*

Loan Terms

Can this amount increase after closing?

Loan Amount	
Interest Rate	
Monthly Principal & Interest *See Projected Payments below for your Estimated Total Monthly Payment*	

Does the loan have these features?

Prepayment Penalty	
Balloon Payment	

Projected Payments

Payment Calculation

Principal & Interest	
Mortgage Insurance	
Estimated Escrow *Amount can increase over time*	
Estimated Total Monthly Payment	

Estimated Taxes, Insurance & Assessments *Amount can increase over time*	**This estimate includes** **In escrow?** ☐ Property Taxes ☐ Homeowner's Insurance ☐ Other: *See Section G on page 2 for escrowed property costs. You must pay for other property costs separately.*

Costs at Closing

Estimated Closing Costs	Includes in Loan Costs + in Other Costs – in Lender Credits. *See page 2 for details.*
Estimated Cash to Close	Includes Closing Costs. *See Calculating Cash to Close on page 2 for details.*

Visit **www.consumerfinance.gov/mortgage-estimate** for general information and tools.

FIGURE 20.1: Loan Estimate (continued)

Save this Loan Estimate to compare with your Closing Disclosure.

Loan Estimate

LOAN TERM	
PURPOSE	
PRODUCT	

DATE ISSUED

APPLICANTS

LOAN TYPE   ☐ Conventional ☐ FHA ☐ VA ☐ _____

LOAN ID #

RATE LOCK   ☐ NO ☐ YES, until

PROPERTY

EST. PROP. VALUE

Before closing, your interest rate, points, and lender credits can change unless you lock the interest rate. All other estimated closing costs expire on

Loan Terms

Can this amount increase after closing?

Loan Amount

Interest Rate

Monthly Principal & Interest
See Projected Payments below for your Estimated Total Monthly Payment

Does the loan have these features?

Prepayment Penalty

Balloon Payment

Projected Payments

Payment Calculation

Principal & Interest

Mortgage Insurance

Estimated Escrow
Amount can increase over time

Estimated Total Monthly Payment

Estimated Taxes, Insurance & Assessments
Amount can increase over time

This estimate includes   **In escrow?**

☐ Property Taxes
☐ Homeowner's Insurance
☐ Other:

See Section G on page 2 for escrowed property costs. You must pay for other property costs separately.

Costs at Closing

Estimated Closing Costs

Includes   in Loan Costs +   in Other Costs –
in Lender Credits. *See page 2 for details.*

Estimated Cash to Close

Includes Closing Costs. *See Calculating Cash to Close on page 2 for details.*

Visit **www.consumerfinance.gov/mortgage-estimate** for general information and tools.

FIGURE 20.1: Loan Estimate (continued)

Closing Cost Details

Loan Costs	Other Costs
A. Origination Charges	**E. Taxes and Other Government Fees**
% of Loan Amount (Points)	Recording Fees and Other Taxes
	Transfer Taxes
	F. Prepaids
	Homeowner's Insurance Premium (months)
	Mortgage Insurance Premium (months)
	Prepaid Interest (per day for days @)
	Property Taxes (months)
	G. Initial Escrow Payment at Closing
	Homeowner's Insurance per month for mo.
B. Services You Cannot Shop For	Mortgage Insurance per month for mo.
	Property Taxes per month for mo.
	H. Other
	I. TOTAL OTHER COSTS (E + F + G + H)
C. Services You Can Shop For	**J. TOTAL CLOSING COSTS**
	D + I
	Lender Credits

Calculating Cash to Close

Total Closing Costs (J)	
Closing Costs Financed (Paid from your Loan Amount)	
Down Payment/Funds from Borrower	
Deposit	
Funds for Borrower	
Seller Credits	
Adjustments and Other Credits	
Estimated Cash to Close	

D. TOTAL LOAN COSTS (A + B + C)

FIGURE 20.1: Loan Estimate (continued)

Closing Cost Details

Loan Costs		Other Costs			

A. Origination Charges

% of Loan Amount (Points)

E. Taxes and Other Government Fees

Recording Fees and Other Taxes
Transfer Taxes

F. Prepaids

Homeowner's Insurance Premium (months)
Mortgage Insurance Premium (months)
Prepaid Interest (per day for   days @   )
Property Taxes (months)

G. Initial Escrow Payment at Closing

Homeowner's Insurance	per month for	mo.
Mortgage Insurance	per month for	mo.
Property Taxes	per month for	mo.

B. Services You Cannot Shop For

H. Other

I. TOTAL OTHER COSTS (E + F + G + H)

J. TOTAL CLOSING COSTS

D + I
Lender Credits

C. Services You Can Shop For

Calculating Cash to Close	

Total Closing Costs (J)

Closing Costs Financed (Paid from your Loan Amount)

Down Payment/Funds from Borrower

Deposit

Funds for Borrower

Seller Credits

Adjustments and Other Credits

Estimated Cash to Close

D. TOTAL LOAN COSTS (A + B + C)

Adjustable Payment (AP) Table	
Interest Only Payments?	
Optional Payments?	
Step Payments?	
Seasonal Payments?	
Monthly Principal and Interest Payments	
First Change/Amount	
Subsequent Changes	
Maximum Payment	

Adjustable Interest Rate (AIR) Table
Index + Margin
Initial Interest Rate
Minimum/Maximum Interest Rate
Change Frequency
First Change
Subsequent Changes
Limits on Interest Rate Changes
First Change
Subsequent Changes

FIGURE 20.1: Loan Estimate (continued)

Closing Cost Details

Loan Costs

A. Origination Charges

% of Loan Amount (Points)

B. Services You Cannot Shop For

C. Services You Can Shop For

D. TOTAL LOAN COSTS (A + B + C)

Other Costs

E. Taxes and Other Government Fees

Recording Fees and Other Taxes
Transfer Taxes

F. Prepaids

Homeowner's Insurance Premium (months)
Mortgage Insurance Premium (months)
Prepaid Interest (per day for   days @   )
Property Taxes (months)

G. Initial Escrow Payment at Closing

Homeowner's Insurance   per month for   mo.
Mortgage Insurance   per month for   mo.
Property Taxes   per month for   mo.

H. Other

I. TOTAL OTHER COSTS (E + F + G + H)

J. TOTAL CLOSING COSTS

D + I
Lender Credits

Calculating Cash to Close

Total Closing Costs (J)

Closing Costs Financed (Paid from your Loan Amount)

Down Payment/Funds from Borrower

Deposit

Funds for Borrower

Seller Credits

Adjustments and Other Credits

Estimated Cash to Close

Adjustable Payment (AP) Table	
Interest Only Payments?	
Optional Payments?	
Step Payments?	
Seasonal Payments?	
Monthly Principal and Interest Payments	
First Change/Amount	
Subsequent Changes	
Maximum Payment	

FIGURE 20.1: Loan Estimate (continued)

Closing Cost Details

Loan Costs

A. Origination Charges

    % of Loan Amount (Points)

B. Services You Cannot Shop For

C. Services You Can Shop For

D. TOTAL LOAN COSTS (A + B + C)

Other Costs

E. Taxes and Other Government Fees

Recording Fees and Other Taxes
Transfer Taxes

F. Prepaids

Homeowner's Insurance Premium (months)
Mortgage Insurance Premium (months)
Prepaid Interest (per day for   days @   )
Property Taxes (months)

G. Initial Escrow Payment at Closing

Homeowner's Insurance	per month for	mo.
Mortgage Insurance	per month for	mo.
Property Taxes	per month for	mo.

H. Other

I. TOTAL OTHER COSTS (E + F + G + H)

J. TOTAL CLOSING COSTS

D + I
Lender Credits

Calculating Cash to Close

Total Closing Costs (J)

Closing Costs Financed (Paid from your Loan Amount)

Down Payment/Funds from Borrower

Deposit

Funds for Borrower

Seller Credits

Adjustments and Other Credits

Estimated Cash to Close

Adjustable Interest Rate (AIR) Table

Index + Margin

Initial Interest Rate

Minimum/Maximum Interest Rate

Change Frequency

  First Change

  Subsequent Changes

Limits on Interest Rate Changes

  First Change

  Subsequent Changes

FIGURE 20.1: Loan Estimate (continued)

Additional Information About This Loan

LENDER	**MORTGAGE BROKER**
NMLS/___ LICENSE ID	**NMLS/___ LICENSE ID**
LOAN OFFICER	**LOAN OFFICER**
NMLS/___ LICENSE ID	**NMLS/___ LICENSE ID**
EMAIL	**EMAIL**
PHONE	**PHONE**

Comparisons	**Use these measures to compare this loan with other loans.**
In 5 Years	Total you will have paid in principal, interest, mortgage insurance, and loan costs. Principal you will have paid off.
Annual Percentage Rate (APR)	Your costs over the loan term expressed as a rate. This is not your interest rate.
Total Interest Percentage (TIP)	The total amount of interest that you will pay over the loan term as a percentage of your loan amount.

Other Considerations	
Appraisal	We may order an appraisal to determine the property's value and charge you for this appraisal. We will promptly give you a copy of any appraisal, even if your loan does not close. You can pay for an additional appraisal for your own use at your own cost.
Assumption	If you sell or transfer this property to another person, we ☐ will allow, under certain conditions, this person to assume this loan on the original terms. ☐ will not allow assumption of this loan on the original terms.
Homeowner's Insurance	This loan requires homeowner's insurance on the property, which you may obtain from a company of your choice that we find acceptable.
Late Payment	If your payment is more than ___ days late, we will charge a late fee of _____
Refinance	Refinancing this loan will depend on your future financial situation, the property value, and market conditions. You may not be able to refinance this loan.
Servicing	We intend ☐ to service your loan. If so, you will make your payments to us. ☐ to transfer servicing of your loan.

Confirm Receipt

By signing, you are only confirming that you have received this form. You do not have to accept this loan because you have signed or received this form.

_____   _____   _____   _____
Applicant Signature   Date   Co-Applicant Signature   Date

FIGURE 20.1: Loan Estimate (continued)

Additional Information About This Loan

LENDER	MORTGAGE BROKER
NMLS/___ LICENSE ID	NMLS/___ LICENSE ID
LOAN OFFICER	LOAN OFFICER
NMLS/___ LICENSE ID	NMLS/___ LICENSE ID
EMAIL	EMAIL
PHONE	PHONE

Comparisons — Use these measures to compare this loan with other loans.

In 5 Years	Total you will have paid in principal, interest, mortgage insurance, and loan costs. Principal you will have paid off.
Annual Percentage Rate (APR)	Your costs over the loan term expressed as a rate. This is not your interest rate.
Total Interest Percentage (TIP)	The total amount of interest that you will pay over the loan term as a percentage of your loan amount.

Other Considerations

Appraisal	We may order an appraisal to determine the property's value and charge you for this appraisal. We will promptly give you a copy of any appraisal, even if your loan does not close. You can pay for an additional appraisal for your own use at your own cost.
Assumption	If you sell or transfer this property to another person, we ☐ will allow, under certain conditions, this person to assume this loan on the original terms. ☐ will not allow assumption of this loan on the original terms.
Homeowner's Insurance	This loan requires homeowner's insurance on the property, which you may obtain from a company of your choice that we find acceptable.
Late Payment	If your payment is more than ___ days late, we will charge a late fee of _____
Loan Acceptance	You do not have to accept this loan because you have received this form or signed a loan application.
Refinance	Refinancing this loan will depend on your future financial situation, the property value, and market conditions. You may not be able to refinance this loan.
Servicing	We intend ☐ to service your loan. If so, you will make your payments to us. ☐ to transfer servicing of your loan.

FIGURE 20.1: Loan Estimate (continued)

Additional Information About This Loan

LENDER
NMLS/___ LICENSE ID
LOAN OFFICER
NMLS/___ LICENSE ID
EMAIL
PHONE

MORTGAGE BROKER
NMLS/___ LICENSE ID
LOAN OFFICER
NMLS/___ LICENSE ID
EMAIL
PHONE

Comparisons	Use these measures to compare this loan with other loans.
In 5 Years	Total you will have paid in principal, interest, mortgage insurance, and loan costs. Principal you will have paid off.
Annual Percentage Rate (APR)	Your costs over the loan term expressed as a rate. This is not your interest rate.
Total Interest Percentage (TIP)	The total amount of interest that you will pay over the loan term as a percentage of your loan amount.

Other Considerations

Assumption
If you sell or transfer this property to another person, we
☐ will allow, under certain conditions, this person to assume this loan on the original terms.
☐ will not allow assumption of this loan on the original terms.

Late Payment
If your payment is more than ___ days late, we will charge a late fee of _____

Refinance
Refinancing this loan will depend on your future financial situation, the property value, and market conditions. You may not be able to refinance this loan.

Servicing
We intend
☐ to service your loan. If so, you will make your payments to us.
☐ to transfer servicing of your loan.

Confirm Receipt

By signing, you are only confirming that you have received this form. You do not have to accept this loan because you have signed or received this form.

_____   _____   _____   _____
Applicant Signature   Date   Co-Applicant Signature   Date

FIGURE 20.1: Loan Estimate (continued)

Additional Information About This Loan

LENDER
NMLS/___ LICENSE ID
LOAN OFFICER
NMLS/___ LICENSE ID
EMAIL
PHONE

MORTGAGE BROKER
NMLS/___ LICENSE ID
LOAN OFFICER
NMLS/___ LICENSE ID
EMAIL
PHONE

Comparisons	Use these measures to compare this loan with other loans.
In 5 Years	Total you will have paid in principal, interest, mortgage insurance, and loan costs. Principal you will have paid off.
Annual Percentage Rate (APR)	Your costs over the loan term expressed as a rate. This is not your interest rate.
Total Interest Percentage (TIP)	The total amount of interest that you will pay over the loan term as a percentage of your loan amount.

Other Considerations

Assumption
If you sell or transfer this property to another person, we
☐ will allow, under certain conditions, this person to assume this loan on the original terms.
☐ will not allow assumption of this loan on the original terms.

Late Payment
If your payment is more than ___ days late, we will charge a late fee of _____

Loan Acceptance
You do not have to accept this loan because you have received this form or signed a loan application.

Refinance
Refinancing this loan will depend on your future financial situation, the property value, and market conditions. You may not be able to refinance this loan.

Servicing
We intend
☐ to service your loan. If so, you will make your payments to us.
☐ to transfer servicing of your loan.

FIGURE 20.2: Closing Disclosure

Closing Disclosure

This form is a statement of final loan terms and closing costs. Compare this document with your Loan Estimate.

Closing Information	Transaction Information	Loan Information
Date Issued	**Borrower**	**Loan Term**
Closing Date		**Purpose**
Disbursement Date		**Product**
Settlement Agent	**Seller**	
File #		**Loan Type** ☐ Conventional ☐ FHA
Property		☐ VA ☐ _____
	Lender	**Loan ID #**
Sale Price		**MIC #**

Loan Terms

	Can this amount increase after closing?
Loan Amount	
Interest Rate	
Monthly Principal & Interest *See Projected Payments below for your Estimated Total Monthly Payment*	
	Does the loan have these features?
Prepayment Penalty	
Balloon Payment	

Projected Payments

Payment Calculation	
Principal & Interest	
Mortgage Insurance	
Estimated Escrow *Amount can increase over time*	
Estimated Total Monthly Payment	

Estimated Taxes, Insurance & Assessments *Amount can increase over time* *See page 4 for details*	**This estimate includes** **In escrow?** ☐ Property Taxes ☐ Homeowner's Insurance ☐ Other: *See Escrow Account on page 4 for details. You must pay for other property costs separately.*

Costs at Closing

Closing Costs	Includes in Loan Costs + in Other Costs – in Lender Credits. *See page 2 for details.*
Cash to Close	Includes Closing Costs. *See Calculating Cash to Close on page 3 for details.*

FIGURE 20.2: Closing Disclosure (continued)

Closing Disclosure

This form is a statement of final loan terms and closing costs. Compare this document with your Loan Estimate.

Closing Information	Transaction Information	Loan Information
Date Issued	**Borrower**	**Loan Term**
Closing Date		**Purpose**
Disbursement Date		**Product**
Settlement Agent	**Seller**	
File #		**Loan Type** ☐ Conventional ☐ FHA
Property		☐ VA ☐ _____
	Lender	**Loan ID #**
Appraised Prop. Value		**MIC #**

Loan Terms	**Can this amount increase after closing?**
Loan Amount	
Interest Rate	
Monthly Principal & Interest *See Projected Payments below for your Estimated Total Monthly Payment*	
	Does the loan have these features?
Prepayment Penalty	
Balloon Payment	

Projected Payments	
Payment Calculation	
Principal & Interest	
Mortgage Insurance	
Estimated Escrow *Amount can increase over time*	
Estimated Total Monthly Payment	
Estimated Taxes, Insurance & Assessments *Amount can increase over time* *See page 4 for details*	**This estimate includes** **In escrow?** ☐ Property Taxes ☐ Homeowner's Insurance ☐ Other: *See Escrow Account on page 4 for details. You must pay for other property costs separately.*

Costs at Closing	
Closing Costs	Includes in Loan Costs + in Other Costs – in Lender Credits. *See page 2 for details.*
Cash to Close	Includes Closing Costs. *See Calculating Cash to Close on page 3 for details.*

FIGURE 20.2: Closing Disclosure (continued)

Closing Disclosure

This form is a statement of final loan terms and closing costs. Compare this document with your Loan Estimate.

Closing Information	Transaction Information	Loan Information
Date Issued	**Borrower**	**Loan Term**
Closing Date		**Purpose**
Disbursement Date		**Product**
Settlement Agent	**Seller**	
File #		**Loan Type** ☐ Conventional ☐ FHA
Property		☐ VA ☐ _____
	Lender	**Loan ID #**
Estimated Prop. Value		**MIC #**

Loan Terms

	Can this amount increase after closing?
Loan Amount	
Interest Rate	
Monthly Principal & Interest *See Projected Payments below for your Estimated Total Monthly Payment*	
	Does the loan have these features?
Prepayment Penalty	
Balloon Payment	

Projected Payments

Payment Calculation	
Principal & Interest	
Mortgage Insurance	
Estimated Escrow *Amount can increase over time*	
Estimated Total Monthly Payment	

Estimated Taxes, Insurance & Assessments *Amount can increase over time* *See page 4 for details*	This estimate includes In escrow? ☐ Property Taxes ☐ Homeowner's Insurance ☐ Other: *See Escrow Account on page 4 for details. You must pay for other property costs separately.*

Costs at Closing

Closing Costs	Includes in Loan Costs + in Other Costs – in Lender Credits. *See page 2 for details.*
Cash to Close	Includes Closing Costs. *See Calculating Cash to Close on page 3 for details.*

FIGURE 20.2: Closing Disclosure (continued)

Closing Cost Details

Loan Costs	Borrower-Paid		Seller-Paid		Paid by Others
	At Closing	Before Closing	At Closing	Before Closing	
A. Origination Charges					
01 % of Loan Amount (Points)					
02					
03					
04					
05					
06					
07					
08					
B. Services Borrower Did Not Shop For					
01					
02					
03					
04					
05					
06					
07					
08					
09					
10					
C. Services Borrower Did Shop For					
01					
02					
03					
04					
05					
06					
07					
08					
D. TOTAL LOAN COSTS (Borrower-Paid)					
Loan Costs Subtotals (A + B + C)					

Other Costs					
E. Taxes and Other Government Fees					
01 Recording Fees Deed: Mortgage:					
02					
F. Prepaids					
01 Homeowner's Insurance Premium (mo.)					
02 Mortgage Insurance Premium (mo.)					
03 Prepaid Interest (per day from to)					
04 Property Taxes (mo.)					
05					
G. Initial Escrow Payment at Closing					
01 Homeowner's Insurance per month for mo.					
02 Mortgage Insurance per month for mo.					
03 Property Taxes per month for mo.					
04					
05					
06					
07					
08 Aggregate Adjustment					
H. Other					
01					
02					
03					
04					
05					
06					
07					
08					
I. TOTAL OTHER COSTS (Borrower-Paid)					
Other Costs Subtotals (E + F + G + H)					
J. TOTAL CLOSING COSTS (Borrower-Paid)					
Closing Costs Subtotals (D + I)					
Lender Credits					

FIGURE 20.2: Closing Disclosure (continued)

Calculating Cash to Close	Loan Estimate	Final	Did this change?
Total Closing Costs (J)			
Closing Costs Paid Before Closing			
Closing Costs Financed (Paid from your Loan Amount)			
Down Payment/Funds from Borrower			
Deposit			
Funds for Borrower			
Seller Credits			
Adjustments and Other Credits			
Cash to Close			

Use this table to see what has changed from your Loan Estimate.

Summaries of Transactions
Use this table to see a summary of your transaction.

BORROWER'S TRANSACTION

K. Due from Borrower at Closing
01 Sale Price of Property
02 Sale Price of Any Personal Property Included in Sale
03 Closing Costs Paid at Closing (J)
04
Adjustments
05
06
07
Adjustments for Items Paid by Seller in Advance
08 City/Town Taxes to
09 County Taxes to
10 Assessments to
11
12
13
14
15

L. Paid Already by or on Behalf of Borrower at Closing
01 Deposit
02 Loan Amount
03 Existing Loan(s) Assumed or Taken Subject to
04
05 Seller Credit
Other Credits
06
07
Adjustments
08
09
10
11
Adjustments for Items Unpaid by Seller
12 City/Town Taxes to
13 County Taxes to
14 Assessments to
15
16
17

CALCULATION
Total Due from Borrower at Closing (K)
Total Paid Already by or on Behalf of Borrower at Closing (L)
Cash to Close ☐ From ☐ To Borrower

SELLER'S TRANSACTION

M. Due to Seller at Closing
01 Sale Price of Property
02 Sale Price of Any Personal Property Included in Sale
03
04
05
06
07
08
Adjustments for Items Paid by Seller in Advance
09 City/Town Taxes to
10 County Taxes to
11 Assessments to
12
13
14
15
16

N. Due from Seller at Closing
01 Excess Deposit
02 Closing Costs Paid at Closing (J)
03 Existing Loan(s) Assumed or Taken Subject to
04 Payoff of First Mortgage Loan
05 Payoff of Second Mortgage Loan
06
07
08 Seller Credit
09
10
11
12
13
Adjustments for Items Unpaid by Seller
14 City/Town Taxes to
15 County Taxes to
16 Assessments to
17
18
19

CALCULATION
Total Due to Seller at Closing (M)
Total Due from Seller at Closing (N)
Cash ☐ From ☐ To Seller

FIGURE 20.2: Closing Disclosure (continued)

Additional Information About This Loan

Loan Disclosures

Assumption

If you sell or transfer this property to another person, your lender

☐ will allow, under certain conditions, this person to assume this loan on the original terms.

☐ will not allow assumption of this loan on the original terms.

Demand Feature

Your loan

☐ has a demand feature, which permits your lender to require early repayment of the loan. You should review your note for details.

☐ does not have a demand feature.

Late Payment

If your payment is more than ___ days late, your lender will charge a late fee of _____

Negative Amortization (Increase in Loan Amount)

Under your loan terms, you

☐ are scheduled to make monthly payments that do not pay all of the interest due that month. As a result, your loan amount will increase (negatively amortize), and your loan amount will likely become larger than your original loan amount. Increases in your loan amount lower the equity you have in this property.

☐ may have monthly payments that do not pay all of the interest due that month. If you do, your loan amount will increase (negatively amortize), and, as a result, your loan amount may become larger than your original loan amount. Increases in your loan amount lower the equity you have in this property.

☐ do not have a negative amortization feature.

Partial Payments

Your lender

☐ may accept payments that are less than the full amount due (partial payments) and apply them to your loan.

☐ may hold them in a separate account until you pay the rest of the payment, and then apply the full payment to your loan.

☐ does not accept any partial payments.

If this loan is sold, your new lender may have a different policy.

Security Interest

You are granting a security interest in _____

_____

_____

You may lose this property if you do not make your payments or satisfy other obligations for this loan.

Escrow Account

For now, your loan

☐ will have an escrow account (also called an "impound" or "trust" account) to pay the property costs listed below. Without an escrow account, you would pay them directly, possibly in one or two large payments a year. Your lender may be liable for penalties and interest for failing to make a payment.

Escrow		
Escrowed Property Costs over Year 1		Estimated total amount over year 1 for your escrowed property costs:
Non-Escrowed Property Costs over Year 1		Estimated total amount over year 1 for your non-escrowed property costs: You may have other property costs.
Initial Escrow Payment		A cushion for the escrow account you pay at closing. See Section G on page 2.
Monthly Escrow Payment		The amount included in your total monthly payment.

☐ will not have an escrow account because ☐ you declined it ☐ your lender does not offer one. You must directly pay your property costs, such as taxes and homeowner's insurance. Contact your lender to ask if your loan can have an escrow account.

No Escrow		
Estimated Property Costs over Year 1		Estimated total amount over year 1. You must pay these costs directly, possibly in one or two large payments a year.
Escrow Waiver Fee		

In the future,

Your property costs may change and, as a result, your escrow payment may change. You may be able to cancel your escrow account, but if you do, you must pay your property costs directly. If you fail to pay your property taxes, your state or local government may (1) impose fines and penalties or (2) place a tax lien on this property. If you fail to pay any of your property costs, your lender may (1) add the amounts to your loan balance, (2) add an escrow account to your loan, or (3) require you to pay for property insurance that the lender buys on your behalf, which likely would cost more and provide fewer benefits than what you could buy on your own.

FIGURE 20.2: Closing Disclosure (continued)

Additional Information About This Loan

Loan Disclosures

Assumption
If you sell or transfer this property to another person, your lender
☐ will allow, under certain conditions, this person to assume this loan on the original terms.
☐ will not allow assumption of this loan on the original terms.

Demand Feature
Your loan
☐ has a demand feature, which permits your lender to require early repayment of the loan. You should review your note for details.
☐ does not have a demand feature.

Late Payment
If your payment is more than ___ days late, your lender will charge a late fee of _____

Negative Amortization (Increase in Loan Amount)
Under your loan terms, you
☐ are scheduled to make monthly payments that do not pay all of the interest due that month. As a result, your loan amount will increase (negatively amortize), and your loan amount will likely become larger than your original loan amount. Increases in your loan amount lower the equity you have in this property.
☐ may have monthly payments that do not pay all of the interest due that month. If you do, your loan amount will increase (negatively amortize), and, as a result, your loan amount may become larger than your original loan amount. Increases in your loan amount lower the equity you have in this property.
☐ do not have a negative amortization feature.

Partial Payments
Your lender
☐ may accept payments that are less than the full amount due (partial payments) and apply them to your loan.
☐ may hold them in a separate account until you pay the rest of the payment, and then apply the full payment to your loan.
☐ does not accept any partial payments.
If this loan is sold, your new lender may have a different policy.

Security Interest
You are granting a security interest in _____

_____

_____

You may lose this property if you do not make your payments or satisfy other obligations for this loan.

Escrow Account
For now, your loan
☐ will have an escrow account (also called an "impound" or "trust" account) to pay the property costs listed below. Without an escrow account, you would pay them directly, possibly in one or two large payments a year. Your lender may be liable for penalties and interest for failing to make a payment.

Escrow		
Escrowed Property Costs over Year 1		Estimated total amount over year 1 for your escrowed property costs:
Non-Escrowed Property Costs over Year 1		Estimated total amount over year 1 for your non-escrowed property costs: You may have other property costs.
Initial Escrow Payment		A cushion for the escrow account you pay at closing. See Section G on page 2.
Monthly Escrow Payment		The amount included in your total monthly payment.

☐ will not have an escrow account because ☐ you declined it ☐ your lender does not offer one. You must directly pay your property costs, such as taxes and homeowner's insurance. Contact your lender to ask if your loan can have an escrow account.

No Escrow		
Estimated Property Costs over Year 1		Estimated total amount over year 1. You must pay these costs directly, possibly in one or two large payments a year.
Escrow Waiver Fee		

In the future,
Your property costs may change and, as a result, your escrow payment may change. You may be able to cancel your escrow account, but if you do, you must pay your property costs directly. If you fail to pay your property taxes, your state or local government may (1) impose fines and penalties or (2) place a tax lien on this property. If you fail to pay any of your property costs, your lender may (1) add the amounts to your loan balance, (2) add an escrow account to your loan, or (3) require you to pay for property insurance that the lender buys on your behalf, which likely would cost more and provide fewer benefits than what you could buy on your own.

Adjustable Payment (AP) Table

Interest Only Payments?	
Optional Payments?	
Step Payments?	
Seasonal Payments?	
Monthly Principal and Interest Payments	
First Change/Amount	
Subsequent Changes	
Maximum Payment	

Adjustable Interest Rate (AIR) Table

Index + Margin	
Initial Interest Rate	
Minimum/Maximum Interest Rate	
Change Frequency	
First Change	
Subsequent Changes	
Limits on Interest Rate Changes	
First Change	
Subsequent Changes	

FIGURE 20.2: Closing Disclosure (continued)

Additional Information About This Loan

Loan Disclosures

Assumption
If you sell or transfer this property to another person, your lender
☐ will allow, under certain conditions, this person to assume this loan on the original terms.
☐ will not allow assumption of this loan on the original terms.

Demand Feature
Your loan
☐ has a demand feature, which permits your lender to require early repayment of the loan. You should review your note for details.
☐ does not have a demand feature.

Late Payment
If your payment is more than ___ days late, your lender will charge a late fee of _____

Negative Amortization (Increase in Loan Amount)
Under your loan terms, you
☐ are scheduled to make monthly payments that do not pay all of the interest due that month. As a result, your loan amount will increase (negatively amortize), and your loan amount will likely become larger than your original loan amount. Increases in your loan amount lower the equity you have in this property.
☐ may have monthly payments that do not pay all of the interest due that month. If you do, your loan amount will increase (negatively amortize), and, as a result, your loan amount may become larger than your original loan amount. Increases in your loan amount lower the equity you have in this property.
☐ do not have a negative amortization feature.

Partial Payments
Your lender
☐ may accept payments that are less than the full amount due (partial payments) and apply them to your loan.
☐ may hold them in a separate account until you pay the rest of the payment, and then apply the full payment to your loan.
☐ does not accept any partial payments.
If this loan is sold, your new lender may have a different policy.

Security Interest
You are granting a security interest in _____
_____
_____

You may lose this property if you do not make your payments or satisfy other obligations for this loan.

Adjustable Payment (AP) Table

Interest Only Payments?	
Optional Payments?	
Step Payments?	
Seasonal Payments?	
Monthly Principal and Interest Payments	
First Change/Amount	
Subsequent Changes	
Maximum Payment	

Escrow Account
For now, your loan
☐ will have an escrow account (also called an "impound" or "trust" account) to pay the property costs listed below. Without an escrow account, you would pay them directly, possibly in one or two large payments a year. Your lender may be liable for penalties and interest for failing to make a payment.

Escrow		
Escrowed Property Costs over Year 1		Estimated total amount over year 1 for your escrowed property costs:
Non-Escrowed Property Costs over Year 1		Estimated total amount over year 1 for your non-escrowed property costs: You may have other property costs.
Initial Escrow Payment		A cushion for the escrow account you pay at closing. See Section G on page 2.
Monthly Escrow Payment		The amount included in your total monthly payment.

☐ will not have an escrow account because ☐ you declined it ☐ your lender does not offer one. You must directly pay your property costs, such as taxes and homeowner's insurance. Contact your lender to ask if your loan can have an escrow account.

No Escrow		
Estimated Property Costs over Year 1		Estimated total amount over year 1. You must pay these costs directly, possibly in one or two large payments a year.
Escrow Waiver Fee		

In the future,
Your property costs may change and, as a result, your escrow payment may change. You may be able to cancel your escrow account, but if you do, you must pay your property costs directly. If you fail to pay your property taxes, your state or local government may (1) impose fines and penalties or (2) place a tax lien on this property. If you fail to pay any of your property costs, your lender may (1) add the amounts to your loan balance, (2) add an escrow account to your loan, or (3) require you to pay for property insurance that the lender buys on your behalf, which likely would cost more and provide fewer benefits than what you could buy on your own.

FIGURE 20.2: Closing Disclosure (continued)

Additional Information About This Loan

Loan Disclosures

Assumption
If you sell or transfer this property to another person, your lender
- ☐ will allow, under certain conditions, this person to assume this loan on the original terms.
- ☐ will not allow assumption of this loan on the original terms.

Demand Feature
Your loan
- ☐ has a demand feature, which permits your lender to require early repayment of the loan. You should review your note for details.
- ☐ does not have a demand feature.

Late Payment
If your payment is more than ___ days late, your lender will charge a late fee of _____

Negative Amortization (Increase in Loan Amount)
Under your loan terms, you
- ☐ are scheduled to make monthly payments that do not pay all of the interest due that month. As a result, your loan amount will increase (negatively amortize), and your loan amount will likely become larger than your original loan amount. Increases in your loan amount lower the equity you have in this property.
- ☐ may have monthly payments that do not pay all of the interest due that month. If you do, your loan amount will increase (negatively amortize), and, as a result, your loan amount may become larger than your original loan amount. Increases in your loan amount lower the equity you have in this property.
- ☐ do not have a negative amortization feature.

Partial Payments
Your lender
- ☐ may accept payments that are less than the full amount due (partial payments) and apply them to your loan.
- ☐ may hold them in a separate account until you pay the rest of the payment, and then apply the full payment to your loan.
- ☐ does not accept any partial payments.
If this loan is sold, your new lender may have a different policy.

Security Interest
You are granting a security interest in _____

_____

_____

You may lose this property if you do not make your payments or satisfy other obligations for this loan.

Escrow Account
For now, your loan
- ☐ will have an escrow account (also called an "impound" or "trust" account) to pay the property costs listed below. Without an escrow account, you would pay them directly, possibly in one or two large payments a year. Your lender may be liable for penalties and interest for failing to make a payment.

Escrow		
Escrowed Property Costs over Year 1		Estimated total amount over year 1 for your escrowed property costs:
Non-Escrowed Property Costs over Year 1		Estimated total amount over year 1 for your non-escrowed property costs:
		You may have other property costs.
Initial Escrow Payment		A cushion for the escrow account you pay at closing. See Section G on page 2.
Monthly Escrow Payment		The amount included in your total monthly payment.

- ☐ will not have an escrow account because ☐ you declined it ☐ your lender does not offer one. You must directly pay your property costs, such as taxes and homeowner's insurance. Contact your lender to ask if your loan can have an escrow account.

No Escrow		
Estimated Property Costs over Year 1		Estimated total amount over year 1. You must pay these costs directly, possibly in one or two large payments a year.
Escrow Waiver Fee		

In the future,
Your property costs may change and, as a result, your escrow payment may change. You may be able to cancel your escrow account, but if you do, you must pay your property costs directly. If you fail to pay your property taxes, your state or local government may (1) impose fines and penalties or (2) place a tax lien on this property. If you fail to pay any of your property costs, your lender may (1) add the amounts to your loan balance, (2) add an escrow account to your loan, or (3) require you to pay for property insurance that the lender buys on your behalf, which likely would cost more and provide fewer benefits than what you could buy on your own.

Adjustable Interest Rate (AIR) Table

Index + Margin	
Initial Interest Rate	
Minimum/Maximum Interest Rate	
Change Frequency	
First Change	
Subsequent Changes	
Limits on Interest Rate Changes	
First Change	
Subsequent Changes	

FIGURE 20.2: Closing Disclosure (continued)

Loan Calculations

Total of Payments. Total you will have paid after you make all payments of principal, interest, mortgage insurance, and loan costs, as scheduled.

Finance Charge. The dollar amount the loan will cost you.

Amount Financed. The loan amount available after paying your upfront finance charge.

Annual Percentage Rate (APR). Your costs over the loan term expressed as a rate. This is not your interest rate.

Total Interest Percentage (TIP). The total amount of interest that you will pay over the loan term as a percentage of your loan amount.

Questions? If you have questions about the loan terms or costs on this form, use the contact information below. To get more information or make a complaint, contact the Consumer Financial Protection Bureau at **www.consumerfinance.gov/mortgage-closing**

Other Disclosures

Appraisal
If the property was appraised for your loan, your lender is required to give you a copy at no additional cost at least 3 days before closing. If you have not yet received it, please contact your lender at the information listed below.

Contract Details
See your note and security instrument for information about
- what happens if you fail to make your payments,
- what is a default on the loan,
- situations in which your lender can require early repayment of the loan, and
- the rules for making payments before they are due.

Liability after Foreclosure
If your lender forecloses on this property and the foreclosure does not cover the amount of unpaid balance on this loan,
☐ state law may protect you from liability for the unpaid balance. If you refinance or take on any additional debt on this property, you may lose this protection and have to pay any debt remaining even after foreclosure. You may want to consult a lawyer for more information.
☐ state law does not protect you from liability for the unpaid balance.

Refinance
Refinancing this loan will depend on your future financial situation, the property value, and market conditions. You may not be able to refinance this loan.

Tax Deductions
If you borrow more than this property is worth, the interest on the loan amount above this property's fair market value is not deductible from your federal income taxes. You should consult a tax advisor for more information.

Contact Information

	Lender	Mortgage Broker	Real Estate Broker (B)	Real Estate Broker (S)	Settlement Agent
Name					
Address					
NMLS ID					
___ License ID					
Contact					
Contact NMLS ID					
Contact ___ License ID					
Email					
Phone					

Confirm Receipt

By signing, you are only confirming that you have received this form. You do not have to accept this loan because you have signed or received this form.

_____   _____   _____   _____
Applicant Signature   Date   Co-Applicant Signature   Date

CLOSING DISCLOSURE   PAGE 5 OF 5 • LOAN ID #

FIGURE 20.2: Closing Disclosure (continued)

Loan Calculations

Total of Payments. Total you will have paid after you make all payments of principal, interest, mortgage insurance, and loan costs, as scheduled.	
Finance Charge. The dollar amount the loan will cost you.	
Amount Financed. The loan amount available after paying your upfront finance charge.	
Annual Percentage Rate (APR). Your costs over the loan term expressed as a rate. This is not your interest rate.	
Total Interest Percentage (TIP). The total amount of interest that you will pay over the loan term as a percentage of your loan amount.	

Questions? If you have questions about the loan terms or costs on this form, use the contact information below. To get more information or make a complaint, contact the Consumer Financial Protection Bureau at **www.consumerfinance.gov/mortgage-closing**

Other Disclosures

Appraisal
If the property was appraised for your loan, your lender is required to give you a copy at no additional cost at least 3 days before closing. If you have not yet received it, please contact your lender at the information listed below.

Contract Details
See your note and security instrument for information about
  • what happens if you fail to make your payments,
  • what is a default on the loan,
  • situations in which your lender can require early repayment of the loan, and
  • the rules for making payments before they are due.

Liability after Foreclosure
If your lender forecloses on this property and the foreclosure does not cover the amount of unpaid balance on this loan,
☐ state law may protect you from liability for the unpaid balance. If you refinance or take on any additional debt on this property, you may lose this protection and have to pay any debt remaining even after foreclosure. You may want to consult a lawyer for more information.
☐ state law does not protect you from liability for the unpaid balance.

Loan Acceptance
You do not have to accept this loan because you have received this form or signed a loan application.

Refinance
Refinancing this loan will depend on your future financial situation, the property value, and market conditions. You may not be able to refinance this loan.

Tax Deductions
If you borrow more than this property is worth, the interest on the loan amount above this property's fair market value is not deductible from your federal income taxes. You should consult a tax advisor for more information.

Contact Information

	Lender	Mortgage Broker	Real Estate Broker (B)	Real Estate Broker (S)	Settlement Agent
Name					
Address					
NMLS ID					
___ License ID					
Contact					
Contact NMLS ID					
Contact ___ License ID					
Email					
Phone					

FIGURE 20.2: Closing Disclosure (continued)

Loan Calculations

Total of Payments. Total you will have paid after you make all payments of principal, interest, mortgage insurance, and loan costs, as scheduled.	
Finance Charge. The dollar amount the loan will cost you.	
Amount Financed. The loan amount available after paying your upfront finance charge.	
Annual Percentage Rate (APR). Your costs over the loan term expressed as a rate. This is not your interest rate.	
Total Interest Percentage (TIP). The total amount of interest that you will pay over the loan term as a percentage of your loan amount.	

Questions? If you have questions about the loan terms or costs on this form, use the contact information below. To get more information or make a complaint, contact the Consumer Financial Protection Bureau at **www.consumerfinance.gov/mortgage-closing**

Other Disclosures

Contract Details
See your note and security instrument for information about
- what happens if you fail to make your payments,
- what is a default on the loan,
- situations in which your lender can require early repayment of the loan, and
- the rules for making payments before they are due.

Liability after Foreclosure
If your lender forecloses on this property and the foreclosure does not cover the amount of unpaid balance on this loan,
☐ state law may protect you from liability for the unpaid balance. If you refinance or take on any additional debt on this property, you may lose this protection and have to pay any debt remaining even after foreclosure. You may want to consult a lawyer for more information.
☐ state law does not protect you from liability for the unpaid balance.

Refinance
Refinancing this loan will depend on your future financial situation, the property value, and market conditions. You may not be able to refinance this loan.

Tax Deductions
If you borrow more than this property is worth, the interest on the loan amount above this property's fair market value is not deductible from your federal income taxes. You should consult a tax advisor for more information.

Contact Information

	Lender	Mortgage Broker	Real Estate Broker (B)	Real Estate Broker (S)	Settlement Agent
Name					
Address					
NMLS ID					
___ License ID					
Contact					
Contact NMLS ID					
Contact ___ License ID					
Email					
Phone					

Confirm Receipt

By signing, you are only confirming that you have received this form. You do not have to accept this loan because you have signed or received this form.

_____   _____   _____   _____
Applicant Signature   Date   Co-Applicant Signature   Date

FIGURE 20.2: Closing Disclosure (continued)

Loan Calculations

Total of Payments. Total you will have paid after you make all payments of principal, interest, mortgage insurance, and loan costs, as scheduled.	
Finance Charge. The dollar amount the loan will cost you.	
Amount Financed. The loan amount available after paying your upfront finance charge.	
Annual Percentage Rate (APR). Your costs over the loan term expressed as a rate. This is not your interest rate.	
Total Interest Percentage (TIP). The total amount of interest that you will pay over the loan term as a percentage of your loan amount.	

Questions? If you have questions about the loan terms or costs on this form, use the contact information below. To get more information or make a complaint, contact the Consumer Financial Protection Bureau at **www.consumerfinance.gov/mortgage-closing**

Other Disclosures

Contract Details
See your note and security instrument for information about
  • what happens if you fail to make your payments,
  • what is a default on the loan,
  • situations in which your lender can require early repayment of the loan, and
  • the rules for making payments before they are due.

Liability after Foreclosure
If your lender forecloses on this property and the foreclosure does not cover the amount of unpaid balance on this loan,
☐ state law may protect you from liability for the unpaid balance. If you refinance or take on any additional debt on this property, you may lose this protection and have to pay any debt remaining even after foreclosure. You may want to consult a lawyer for more information.
☐ state law does not protect you from liability for the unpaid balance.

Loan Acceptance
You do not have to accept this loan because you have received this form or signed a loan application.

Refinance
Refinancing this loan will depend on your future financial situation, the property value, and market conditions. You may not be able to refinance this loan.

Tax Deductions
If you borrow more than this property is worth, the interest on the loan amount above this property's fair market value is not deductible from your federal income taxes. You should consult a tax advisor for more information.

Contact Information

	Lender	Mortgage Broker	Real Estate Broker (B)	Real Estate Broker (S)	Settlement Agent
Name					
Address					
NMLS ID					
___ License ID					
Contact					
Contact NMLS ID					
Contact ___ License ID					
Email					
Phone					

TREC   TREC Rule 535.148 prohibits a licensee from entering into a contract with a service provider, such as a home warranty company, if that agreement would prohibit the licensee from offering similar services on behalf of a competing service provider. A licensee is also prohibited from accepting a fee from a service provider to a real estate transaction if the payment is contingent upon a party's purchasing a contract or service from the provider. A Texas licensee who is paid for performing services for a residential service company (home warranty company) must disclose such payments to the party the licensee represents.

The Texas Department of Insurance (TDI)   Procedural Rule P-53 of the TDI prohibits rebates and discounts from title companies to real estate licensees, mortgage lenders, and homebuilders. It is a violation of the law for promotional or educational activities of title company personnel to be conditioned on the referral of title insurance business (H.B. 2408, 2011). For example, the title insurance company cannot directly or indirectly pay for or subsidize, among other things:

- advertising or promotional materials or activities of an individual property, group of properties, or real estate company;
- signs advertising a property or group of properties;
- an event such as an open house, holiday party, seminar, or lecture for an individual real estate company; or
- newsletters, business cards, office supplies or equipment, or secretarial services.

A title company may, however, at market rates, provide continuing education courses (H.B. 2408, 2011) and purchase advertising promoting the title insurance company in any publication, event, or media. In addition, it may participate in or sponsor an event for the local association of REALTORS®, mortgage bankers, or similar group—provided that the level of the company's participation does not exceed normal participation of other volunteer members of the association, is not an activity that would ordinarily be performed by paid staff of the association, and does not defray the expenses that the real estate agent would otherwise incur.

PREPARATION OF CLOSING STATEMENTS

In addition to the purchase price, a typical real estate sales transaction involves numerous expenses for both parties. Some expenses are buyer's charges, others are seller's charges, and still others are split between the parties. On items prepaid by the seller for which reimbursement is due or expenses accrued by the seller and later billed to the buyer, charges must be **prorated** (divided) between the buyer and the seller. After accounting for the purchase price, loan amounts, expenses, and prorated items on the HUD-1 Settlement Statement (see Figure 20.4), the buyer will know how much money to take to the closing and the sellers will know how much money they will get at the closing.

How the Closing Statement Works

The completion of a **closing statement** involves an accounting of the parties' debits and credits. A **debit** is a charge, an amount that the party being debited owes and must pay at the closing. A **credit** is an amount a person gets at closing for (1) a buyer's expense that a seller has already paid and for which the seller must be reimbursed or (2) an accrued seller's expense that a buyer will pay after closing and for which the buyer must be reimbursed. See Figure 20.3 for a listing of some typical credits and debits at closing.

FIGURE 20.3: Credits and Debits at Closing

Item	Credit to Buyer	Debit to Buyer	Credit to Seller	Debit to Seller	Prorated
Principal amount of new mortgage	X				
Payoff of existing mortgage				X	
Unpaid principal balance if assumed mortgage	X			X	
Accrued interest on existing assumed mortgage	X			X	X
Tenant's security deposit	X			X	
Purchase money mortgage	X			X	
Unpaid taxes and utility bills	X			X	X
Buyer's earnest money	X				
Selling price of property		X	X		
Fuel oil on hand (valued at current market price)		X	X		X
Prepaid taxes (possible October to December)		X	X		X

* This chart is based on generally applicable practices. Please note that closing practices may be different in your area.

Normal Closing Charges (Debits)

> A *debit* is an amount to be paid by the buyer or the seller; a *credit* is an amount to be received by the buyer or the seller.

Common expenses incurred in a real estate transaction include the following items. TREC-promulgated contracts specify which party pays which expenses.

Broker's Commission   If the broker is the agent for the seller, the seller is normally responsible for paying the commission. If an agency agreement exists between a broker and a buyer or if two agents are involved (one for the seller; another for the buyer), the commission may be paid by the seller or it may be apportioned between both parties.

Attorney Fees   In most cases, attorney fees are charged to the seller for the preparation of the deed and a release of lien (if the seller's note is being paid off at closing or the buyer is assuming liability for the note). The buyer pays attorney fees for the preparation of the note and deed of trust.

Recording Expenses   The charges for recording all the documents must be paid to the county clerk. If the party to be charged is not specified in the contract, the seller usually pays for recording charges (filing fees) for documents necessary to clear all defects and furnish clear title, such as releases of liens, quitclaim deeds, affidavits, and satisfaction of mechanic's lien claims. The *purchaser* usually pays for recording charges that arise from the actual transfer of the title—the deed and the deed of trust or mortgage. In Texas, each county sets the charges. By statute, the fee for recording the first page is $5, to which a county may add fees for items such as records management and archiving. The usual charge for the first page is $16; for each succeeding page, $4.

Title Expenses   Under the provisions of the TREC sales contract, the seller is required to furnish evidence of good title. If a property is closed on an abstract, the seller usually pays for the expenses of having the abstract prepared or brought up to date; the buyer pays for an attorney to inspect the abstract and issue an opinion of title. If the property closes on a title policy, the seller generally pays for the owner's title policy; if a new loan is involved, the buyer pays for the mortgagee's title policy. However, the promulgated contract form actually allows either party to pay for the owner's title policy. The Texas State Board of Insurance sets the premiums for title policies.

Loan Fees   When the purchaser is securing a new loan to finance the purchase, the lender generally charges a loan origination fee of 1% of the loan amount. The purchaser usually pays the origination fee at the time the transaction is closed. If the buyer assumes the seller's existing loan, an assumption fee will be charged to the buyer.

The lender may also charge discount points, the payment of which is negotiated between the buyer and the seller on the sales contract. In addition, the terms of some mortgage loans require that the seller pay a prepayment charge or penalty for paying off the mortgage loan in advance of its due date.

Tax Reserves and Insurance Reserves (Escrows)   The mortgage lender usually requires that the borrower establish and maintain an *escrow account* so the lender will have sufficient funds to pay ad valorem real estate taxes and to renew insurance policies when these items become due. To set up the reserve, the borrower is required to make a lump-sum payment to the lender when the loan is closed. The amount first paid into this reserve account is limited by RESPA to the amount of year-to-date unpaid real estate taxes (including the month of closing) and two months' reserves for taxes, insurance, and other expenses to be paid by the lender or servicer. Because the lender or servicer must ensure that at least once each year the escrow account does not exceed two times the monthly escrow payment, an aggregate adjustment then must be made to the total to be deposited into the escrow account at the time of closing. The escrow deposit and the interest from the date of closing to the end of the month preceding the buyer's first regular payment are called the *prepaids*.

Appraisal Fees   When the buyer obtains a loan, it is customary for the buyer to pay for a lender-required appraisal. However, in most cases, either the buyer or the seller *may* pay the appraisal fees, as negotiated in the sales contract. An urban residential loan appraisal may cost from $375 to $540; a rural appraisal, $600 to $1,200.

Settlement or Closing Fees   When a transaction is closed through a title company, an escrow fee is charged for the services of the closing agent or escrow agent. A title company will furnish a real estate agent with an estimate of its customary charges for these services. A title insurance company can also pass on to its customers any charges from third-parties for electronic filing fees and ad valorem tax reports.

Survey Fees   A purchaser who obtains new mortgage financing often pays the survey fees because the survey is a lender requirement.

Buyer's Earnest Money   In almost all instances, a buyer pays an earnest money deposit at the time the purchase contract is negotiated. At closing, the buyer receives a credit for the money prepaid.

Prorations

Prorations of expenses between buyer and seller are necessary to ensure that expenses are divided fairly. Expenses that are most frequently prorated include interest on an assumed loan, taxes, rents, and utility bills.

Accrued items are expenses that are owed by the seller but will later be paid by the buyer. Accrued expenses include unpaid ad valorem property taxes, interest on an assumed mortgage, and some utility bills. The seller is debited (charged) for these items at closing and the buyer gets the credit.

Prepaid items are expenses to be prorated, such as fuel oil in a tank, that have been prepaid by the seller but not fully used up. Therefore, the buyer is debited at closing and the seller gets the credit.

FOR EXAMPLE   A sale is to be closed on June 25. Taxes are paid in arrears and will not be billed until late September. Therefore, the seller needs to pay the buyer for taxes from January 1 through June 25 because the buyer will pay the full year's taxes when they come due. If the buyer assumes the seller's existing mortgage, the seller will also owe the buyer the accrued interest for June 1 through June 25. The buyer will make the July payment, which includes interest for the month of June because interest is paid in arrears. Both the taxes and mortgage interest would be debits to the seller and credits to the buyer.

General Rules for Prorating   The provisions of the sales contract establish which items will be prorated and the agreements involved in that process. The Texas promulgated contract forms state in paragraph 13, "Taxes for the current year, interest, maintenance fees, assessments, dues and rents will be prorated through the Closing Date."

The general rules that guide the computation of prorations include the following:
- The seller owns the property on the day of closing, and prorations or apportionments are made *through the day of closing* if the promulgated contract forms are used. This means that the seller pays expenses and receives income for the day of closing.
- Prorations may be based on a statutory year (*360 days in a year and 30 days in a month*) or a calendar year (*365 days in a year and actual days in each month*), depending on local custom and government regulations. Most tax and interest prorations in Texas are based on the calendar year.
- Accrued *general real estate taxes* that are not yet due are prorated at the closing. When the amount of the current real estate tax cannot be determined definitely, the proration usually is based on the last obtainable tax bill. The Texas-promulgated sales contract provides that "if taxes vary from the amount prorated at closing, the parties shall adjust the prorations when tax statements for the current year are available." *Special assessments* for such municipal improvements as streets, alleys, street lighting, and curbs are usually charged in full to the seller and are not prorated at closing.
- *Rents* usually are prorated on the basis of the *actual* number of days in the month of closing. The seller receives the rents for the day of closing and pays all expenses for that day. If the rent has been collected by the seller prior to the closing date, the buyer would receive a credit for rent for the remainder of the month. If any rents for the current month are uncollected when the sale is closed, the buyer may collect the rents and remit a pro rata share to the seller.

- Payments made by tenants in advance to cover the *last month's rent* or the *security deposit* are *not* prorated. Some leases may require the tenant's consent to transfer the deposit.
- Unpaid *wages of building employees* are prorated if the sale is closed between wage payment dates.

The Arithmetic of Prorating   Accurate prorating involves four considerations:
- The nature of the item being prorated
- Whether it is an accrued item that a buyer will pay after closing—a credit to the buyer
- Whether it is an item prepaid by the seller—a credit to the seller
- Whether the proration is for a *360-day statutory year* or a *365-day calendar year*

The following are the steps for calculating the prorated amount.
- *Step 1*: Divide the yearly charge by 12 to determine a monthly charge for the item. For a daily charge, divide the yearly charge by 360 for a *statutory-year* proration or by 365 for a *calendar-year* proration.
- *Step 2*: Determine the number of months and/or days in the proration period; use 30 days per month for a statutory-year proration and actual days per month for a calendar-year proration.
- *Step 3*: Multiply the number of months and/or days in the prorated time period by the monthly and/or daily charges to determine the amount that will be used in the settlement statement.

In some cases when a sale is closed on the 15th of the month, the one-half month's charge is computed by simply dividing the monthly charge by two.

The final proration figure will vary slightly, depending on which computation method is used. The final figure also will vary according to the number of decimal places to which the division is carried. To maintain consistency throughout all real estate computations, the decimal place on a calculator should be set to float or to a minimum of five decimal places. *All computations for prorations round up or down to three decimal places.* The third decimal place is rounded off to the nearest cent only after the final proration figure is determined.

IN PRACTICE   Note that local customs regarding prorations may differ. Prepaid interest calculations for new loans to be sold to Fannie Mae and Freddie Mac must be computed using a 360-day year. Ginnie Mae requires a 365-day year computation. Tax proration factor tables and tax proration calculators are available online. For examples of proration calculations, see the section on prorating in Chapter 19.

RESPA SETTLEMENT STATEMENT

The Settlement Statement, HUD-1, is required by RESPA for almost all transactions involving mortgage loans that are applied for and received by a mortgage lender before August 1, 2015. For mortgage loan applications received on or after August 1, 2015, the Closing Disclosure form must be used. The sample transaction presented on the following pages illustrates the calculations involved in a real estate closing and the resulting HUD-1 form (Figure 20.4). The sales contract for this transaction is shown in Chapter 12, Figure 12.3; the note in Chapter 15, Figure 15.1; and the deed of trust in Chapter 15, Figure 15.4.

FIGURE 20.4: Settlement Statement

OMB Approval No. 2502-0265

A. Settlement Statement (HUD-1)

B. Type of Loan

1. ☐ FHA 2. ☐ RHS 3. ☒ Conv. Unins. 4. ☐ VA 5. ☐ Conv. Ins.	6. File Number: GF #123456	7. Loan Number: 000-0000	8. Mortgage Insurance Case Number:

C. Note: This form is furnished to give you a statement of actual settlement costs. Amounts paid to and by the settlement agent are shown. Items marked "(p.o.c.)" were paid outside the closing; they are shown here for informational purposes and are not included in the totals.

D. Name & Address of Borrower: Blake Redemann and wife, Connie Redemann 7016 Hurst Amarillo, TX 79109	E. Name & Address of Seller: John Iuro and wife, Joanne Iuro 3040 N. Racine Dallas, TX 75340	F. Name & Address of Lender: Thrift Federal Savings 567 Lender's Place Dallas, TX 75240
G. Property Location: 3040 N. Racine Dallas, TX 75340	H. Settlement Agent: ABC Title Co. Place of Settlement: 1234 Settlement Street Dallas, TX 75340	I. Settlement Date: 6/15/xx

J. Summary of Borrower's Transaction		K. Summary of Seller's Transaction	
100. Gross Amount Due from Borrower		**400. Gross Amount Due to Seller**	
101. Contract sales price	$215,000.00	401. Contract sales price	$215,000.00
102. Personal property		402. Personal property	
103. Settlement charges to borrower (line 1400)	12,281.49	403.	
104.		404.	
105.		405.	
Adjustment for items paid by seller in advance		Adjustments for items paid by seller in advance	
106. City/town taxes to		406. City/town taxes to	
107. County taxes to		407. County taxes to	
108. Assessments to		408. Assessments to	
109.		409.	
110.		410.	
111.		411.	
112.		412.	
120. Gross Amount Due from Borrower	**$227,281.49**	**420. Gross Amount Due to Seller**	**$215,000.00**
200. Amounts Paid by or in Behalf of Borrower		**500. Reductions In Amount Due to Seller**	
201. Deposit or earnest money	$15,000.00	501. Excess deposit (see instructions)	
202. Principal amount of new loan(s)	165,000.00	502. Settlement charges to seller (line 1400)	$12,280.00
203. Existing loan(s) taken subject to		503. Existing loan(s) taken subject to	
204.		504. Payoff of first mortgage loan	98,025.67
205. Credits from seller:		505. Payoff of second mortgage loan	
206. Owner's Title Policy	1,462.00	506. Owner's Title Policy	1,462.00
207. Discount Points	2,475.00	507. Discount Points	2,475.00
208.		508.	
209.		509.	
Adjustments for items unpaid by seller		Adjustments for items unpaid by seller	
210. City/town taxes 1/1/xx to 6/15/xx	$305.39	510. City/town taxes 1/1/xx to 6/15/xx	$305.39
211. County taxes 1/1/xx to 6/15/xx	363.65	511. County taxes 1/1/xx to 6/15/xx	363.65
212. Assessments to		512. Assessments to	
213. School Taxes 1/1/xx to 6/15/xx	1,340.08	513. School Taxes 1/1/xx to 6/15/xx	1,340.08
214.		514.	
215.		515.	
216.		516.	
217.		517.	
218.		518.	
219.		519.	
220. Total Paid by/for Borrower	**$185,946.12**	**520. Total Reduction Amount Due Seller**	**$116,251.79**
300. Cash at Settlement from/to Borrower		**600. Cash at Settlement to/from Seller**	
301. Gross amount due from borrower (line 120)	$227,281.49	601. Gross amount due to seller (line 420)	$215,000.00
302. Less amounts paid by/for borrower (line 220)	(185,946.12)	602. Less reductions in amount due seller (line 520)	(116,251.79)
303. Cash ☒ From ☐ To Borrower	$41,335.37	603. Cash ☒ To ☐ From Seller	$98,748.21

The Public Reporting Burden for this collection of information is estimated at 35 minutes per response for collecting, reviewing, and reporting the data. This agency may not collect this information, and you are not required to complete this form, unless it displays a currently valid OMB control number. No confidentiality is assured; this disclosure is mandatory. This is designed to provide the parties to a RESPA covered transaction with information during the settlement process.

FIGURE 20.4: Settlement Statement (continued)

L. Settlement Charges

700. Total Real Estate Broker Fees		Paid From Borrower's Funds at Settlement	Paid From Seller's Funds at Settlement
Division of commission (line 700) as follows:			
701. $ 11,825.00 to Open Door Real Estate			
702. $ to			
703. Commission paid at settlement			$11,825.00
704.			

800. Items Payable in Connection with Loan			
801. Our origination charge *	$1,690.00 (from GFE #1)		
802. Your credit or charge (points) for the specific interest rate chosen $2,475.00 (from GFE #2)			
803. Your adjusted origination charges	(from GFE A)	$4,165.00	
804. Appraisal fee to Swift Appraisal ($500.00 POC) **	(from GFE #3)		
805. Credit report to Acme Credit Bureau ($50.00 POC) **	(from GFE #3)		
806. Tax service to	(from GFE #3)		
807. Flood certification	(from GFE #3)		
808. MLF Law Firm		200.00	

900. Items Required by Lender to Be Paid in Advance			
901. Daily interest charges from 6/15 to 7/1 @ $32.083 /day	(from GFE #10)	513.33	
902. Mortgage insurance premium for months to	(from GFE #3)		
903. Homeowner's insurance $2,026 for 1 years to Basic Insurance	(from GFE #11)	2,026.00	
904.			

1000. Reserves Deposited with Lender			
1001. Initial deposit for your escrow account	(from GFE #9)	2,781.16	
1002. Homeowner's insurance 2 months @ $ 168.833 per month $ 337.67			
1003. Mortgage insurance months @ $ per month $			
1004. Property taxes 9 months @ $ 365.295 per month $ 3,287.66			
1005. months @ $ per month $			
1006. months @ $ per month $			
1007. Aggregate Adjustment –$ 844.17			

1100. Title Charges			
1101. Title services and lender's title insurance	(from GFE #4)	480.00	225.00***
1102. Settlement or closing fee ABC Title	$		200.00
1103. Owner's title insurance ABC Title	(from GFE #5)	1,462.00	
1104. Lender's title insurance ABC Title	$ 205.00		
1105. Lender's title policy limit $165,000.00			
1106. Owner's title policy limit $215,000.00			
1107. Agent's portion of the total title insurance premium	$ 1,416.95, ABC Title		
1108. Underwriter's portion of the total title insurance premium	$ 250.05, Title Underwriters		

1200. Government Recording and Transfer Charges			
1201. Government recording charges	(from GFE #7)	104.00	
1202. Deed $ 26.00 Mortgage $ 78.00 Releases $ 30.00			30.00
1203. Transfer taxes	(from GFE #8)		
1204. City/County tax/stamps Deed $ Mortgage $			
1205. State tax/stamps Deed $ Mortgage $			
1206.			

1300. Additional Settlement Charges			
1301. Required services that you can shop for	(from GFE #6)	550.00	
1302. Survey, Excel Surveying	$ 550.00		
1303.	$		
1304.			
1305.			

1400. Total Settlement Charges (enter on lines 103, Section J and 502, Section K)		$12,281.49	$12,280.00

* Includes Origination Point, 1% or $1,650.00

** POC = Paid Outside of Closing (Borrower)

*** MLF Law Firm (Seller: deed and release)

FIGURE 20.4: Settlement Statement (continued)

Comparison of Good Faith Estimate (GFE) and HUD-1 Charges		Good Faith Estimate	HUD-1
Charges That Cannot Increase	HUD-1 Line Number		
Our origination charge	# 801	$1,690.00	$1,690.00
Your credit or charge (points) for the specific interest rate chosen	# 802	2,475.00	2,475.00
Your adjusted origination charges	# 803	4,165.00	4,165.00
Transfer taxes	#1203		

Charges That in Total Cannot Increase More Than 10%		Good Faith Estimate	HUD-1	
Government recording charges	# 1201	$90.00	$104.00	
Document preparation fees	# 808	150.00	200.00	
Title services	# 1101	460.00	480.00	
Owner's title policy	# 1103	1,462.00	1,462.00	
Appraisal	# 804	500.00	500.00	
Credit Report	# 805	50.00	50.00	
	#			
	#			
Total		$2,712.00	$2,796.00	
Increase between GFE and HUD-1 Charges		$ 84.00	or 3.1	%

Charges That Can Change		Good Faith Estimate	HUD-1
Initial deposit for your escrow account	#1001	$3,230.32	$2,781.16
Daily interest charges	# 901 $ 32.083/day	962.49	513.33
Homeowner's insurance	# 903	2,000.00	2,026.00
Survey	# 1302	500.00	550.00
	#		
	#		

Loan Terms

Your initial loan amount is	$ 165,000.00
Your loan term is	15 years
Your initial interest rate is	7.0 %
Your initial monthly amount owed for principal, interest, and and any mortgage insurance is	$ 1,482.00 includes [X] Principal [X] Interest [ ] Mortgage Insurance
Can your interest rate rise?	[X] No. [ ] Yes, it can rise to a maximum of %. The first change will be on _____ and can change again every _____ after _____ . Every change date, your interest rate can increase or decrease by %. Over the life of the loan, your interest rate is guaranteed to never be **lower** than % or **higher** than %.
Even if you make payments on time, can your loan balance rise?	[X] No. [ ] Yes, it can rise to a maximum of $ _____ .
Even if you make payments on time, can your monthly amount owed for principal, interest, and mortgage insurance rise?	[X] No. [ ] Yes, the first increase can be on _____ and the monthly amount owed can rise to $ _____ . The maximum it can ever rise to is $ _____ .
Does your loan have a prepayment penalty?	[X] No. [ ] Yes, your maximum prepayment penalty is $ _____ .
Does your loan have a balloon payment?	[X] No. [ ] Yes, you have a balloon payment of $ _____ due in _____ years on _____ .
Total monthly amount owed including escrow account payments	[ ] You do not have a monthly escrow payment for items, such as property taxes and homeowner's insurance. You must pay these items directly yourself. [X] You have an additional monthly escrow payment of $ 534.13 that results in a total initial monthly amount owed of $ 2,016.13 . This includes principal, interest, any mortgage insurance and any items checked below: [X] Property taxes [X] Homeowner's insurance [ ] Flood insurance [ ] _____ [ ] _____ [ ] _____

Note: If you have any questions about the Settlement Charges and Loan Terms listed on this form, please contact your lender.

To complete the buyer's side of the closing statement, first the buyer's expenses are listed on page 2 of the HUD-1 form. Then the buyer's expenses are transferred to page 1 and added to the sales price for a "gross amount due from borrower." The borrower's credits are totaled next: earnest money, which has already been paid by the buyer; the balance of a loan to be assumed or the amount of a new loan; and the prorated amounts for items unpaid by the seller (taxes or mortgage interest). The credits are subtracted from the debits, and the difference between the two is the amount of money the buyer needs to take to closing.

A similar procedure is followed to determine how much money the seller will receive at closing. The seller's debits and credits are each totaled. The seller's debits include the balance of any mortgage loan or other lien to be paid off at closing. The credits include the purchase price plus the buyer's share of any prorated items that the seller has prepaid. Finally, the total of the seller's charges is subtracted from the total credits to arrive at the amount the seller will receive at closing. Page 3 of the HUD-1 includes a comparison of anticipated closing expenses shown on the Good Faith Estimate (GFE) and the actual charges on the HUD-1. Terms of the buyer's loan are also disclosed on page 3.

CASE STUDY

John and Joanne Iuro listed their home at 3040 North Racine Avenue with the Open Door Real Estate Company. The listing price was $218,500 and possession could be given within four weeks after all parties had signed the contract. Under the terms of the listing agreement, the sellers agreed to pay the broker a commission of 5½% of the sales price.

On May 16, the Open Door Real Estate Company, under an intermediary agreement, submitted a contract offer to the Iuros from Blake and Connie Redemann, husband and wife. The Redemanns offered $215,000 and agreed to obtain a new mortgage loan. The Iuros signed the contract on May 18. Closing was set for June 15 at the office of ABC Title Company. The title company holds earnest money in the amount of $15,000. (*Use a 360-day year for prorations.*)

Seller's Settlement

The unpaid balance of the Iuros' mortgage after the seller makes the June 1 payment will be $97,700. Principal and interest payments are $807 per month with interest at 8% per annum on the unpaid balance.

The seller submitted evidence of title in the form of title insurance. The cost of the title policy was $1,462. Recording charges of $30 were paid for the recording of the release of seller's lien. In addition, the seller must pay $200 for the escrow closing fee to the title company, $225 attorney fee for document preparation, and 1½ discount points on the buyer's new loan. All these amounts will be paid from the closing proceeds.

Buyer's Settlement

The buyers' new 15-year loan is from Thrift Federal Savings in the amount of $165,000 at 7% interest. In connection with this loan, they will be charged $500 to have the property appraised by Swift Appraisal and $50 for a credit report from the Acme Credit Bureau—both amounts were paid at the time of loan application and will appear as "POC" on the HUD-1. The attorney will charge $200 to prepare the note and deed of trust for the buyer. The buyer is to pay a 1% loan origination fee. The survey fee of $550 is to be paid by the buyer. Finally, the Redemanns will have to pay $104 for recording the deed of trust and the deed, $205 for a mortgagee's title insurance policy to cover the lender's interest in the property, $200 for the escrow closing fee to the title company, $75 for tax certificates, and $40 for courier fees. This year's taxes are estimated at $4,383.55.

In addition, the following prorations and/or deposits will be made into the buyer's escrow account:

- Interest in advance for the last 16 days of June, $513.33, because the first payment will not be due until August 1 and that payment will cover interest for the month of July only: ($165,000 × .07 ÷ 360) = $32.083/day × 16 days = $513.33
- Tax reserves for nine months ($3,287.66), consisting of (1) the seller's payment to the buyer for the seller's taxes from January 1 through June 15 @ $2,009.12; (2) the buyer's expense for the period from June 16 through July 31 @ $547.94 (because the first payment is not until August 1); and (3) the escrow account deposit of $730.60 for two months of the anticipated annual real estate taxes
- Insurance reserves of $337.67 for two months of the annual insurance premium of $2,026.00: $2,026 ÷ 12 = $168.833/mo × 2 = $337.67

Computing the Prorations and Charges

The figures below illustrate some of the various steps in computing the prorations and other amounts to be included in the settlement.

1. *Closing date:* June 15
2. *Commission:* 5½% × $215,000 (sales price) = $11,825
3. Mortgage interest owed by the seller:

   8% × $97,700 (principal due after 6/1 payment) = $7,816 interest per year

   $7,816 ÷ 360 days = $21.711 interest per day
   15 days of accrued interest to be paid by the seller (June 1–15)
   15 × $21.711 = $325.665, or $325.67 *interest owed by the seller*

   $97,700 seller's loan balance + $325.67 interest for June = $98,025.67 loan payoff

4. *Real estate taxes* (estimated based on last year's tax bill of $4,383.55):

   $4,383.55 ÷ 12 months = $365.295 per month
   $365.295 ÷ 30 days = $12.176 per day

   The earned period is from January 1 to and including June 15 and equals 5 months, 15 days:

$365.295 × 5 months =	$1,826.475
$12.176 × 15 days =	$ 182.640
	$2,009.12 *seller owes buyer*

   The buyer's share of prepaid taxes for June 16 through July 31 equals 15 days (including June 16) plus 1 month:

$12.176 × 15 days =	$182.640
$365.295 × 1 month =	$365.295
	$547.94 *buyer's prepaid taxes*

The Settlement Statement is divided into 12 sections. In Section J, the summary of the borrower's transaction, the buyer's/borrower's debits are listed in the 100 series and totaled on line 120 (gross amount due from borrower). The total of the borrower's settlement costs itemized in Section L of the statement is entered on line 103 as one of the buyer's charges. The buyer's credits are listed in the 200 series and totaled on line 220 (total paid by/for borrower). Then the buyer's credits are subtracted from the charges to arrive at the cash due from the borrower to close (line 303).

In Section K, the summary of the seller's transaction, the seller's credits are entered in the 400 series and totaled on line 420 (gross amount due to seller). The seller's debits are entered in the 500 series and totaled on line 520 (total reduction amount due seller). The total of the seller's settlement charges from Section L is on line 520. Then the debits are subtracted from the credits to arrive at the cash due to the seller in order to close (line 603) (unless the total is a negative number, and then it would be cash *from* the seller to close). The seller receives a check from the title company after "closing and funding," that is, after the loan company has sent the money for the buyer's loan to the title company and has given approval for the loan proceeds to be disbursed.

Section L is a summary of all the settlement charges for the transaction; the buyer's expenses are listed in one column and the seller's expenses are listed in the other. On the borrower's side, the first line in a series generally reflects a total of selected items listed "outside the column" as borrower's expenses. For example,

- Line 801 includes origination, document handling, notary, and other lender expenses for advancing the loan; in this case study, it includes a 1% origination fee ($1,650) and courier fee ($40).
- Line 1001 includes the total of all escrow account entries listed "outside the column" ($337.67 = 3,287.66 – 844.17).
- Line 1007 requires an aggregate adjustment that is calculated by the lender to ensure that at least once each year the escrow account does not exceed two times the monthly escrow payment; the amount will always be $0 or a negative number. The aggregate adjustment is deducted from the "Reserves Deposited with Lender" charged to the borrower. For this case study, the aggregate adjustment is computed as follows:
  - Calculate an initial trial balance: Project deposits and disbursements based on starting an escrow account at zero balance. Add $\frac{1}{12}$ of the taxes and insurance into the escrow account each month; deduct taxes in December and an insurance premium in the month of closing.
  - Identify the lowest monthly balance from Year 1 (–$1,712.90), convert it to positive dollars ($1,712.90), and add to the allowable monthly cushion (two months' taxes and two months' insurance) ($1,068.26); the result is the maximum allowable starting balance for the escrow account ($2,781.16).
  - Deduct the total of the "Reserves Deposited with Lender" section shown on the HUD-1 ($3,625.33) from the maximum allowable starting balance in step 2 ($2,781.16). The result is the aggregate adjustment: –$844.17.
- Line 1101 includes the lender's title insurance premium, borrower's escrow fees, tax certificates, and other title service expenses; in this case study, it includes a borrower's escrow fee ($200), lender's title policy ($205), and tax certificates ($75);

- Line 1201 includes the borrower's expense for recording the deed and deed of trust ($26 + 78);
- Line 1301 includes the total of any "additional settlement charges" shown "outside the column."

The comparison of GFE and HUD-1 charges on Page 3 of the HUD-1 indicates that all GFE closing cost estimates were within the tolerances set by RESPA: the *zero tolerance* expenses were exact and the *10% tolerance* expenses were just over 3% of the GFE estimate. On the bottom portion of Page 3, various terms of the buyer's new loan are disclosed.

SUMMARY

Closing a sale involves both title procedures and financial matters. Most closings in Texas take place at a title company. The closing agent assembles all the documents necessary to finalize the purchaser's loan and the seller's transfer of title, prepares the HUD-1 Settlement Statement, arranges the time and place of closing with all parties, conducts the closing, and disburses funds. The real estate agents working with the buyers and the sellers are often present at the closing to see that the sale actually is concluded.

The buyer's attorney may examine the title evidence to ensure that the seller's title is acceptable. The gap in time between the date of the abstract or title commitment and the closing date is covered by the seller's affidavit as to debts and liens.

If a sale is closed in escrow, the buyer can be assured of receiving good title as described in the sales contract and the seller can be assured that all funds due him or her are held in cash by the escrow agent.

The federal Real Estate Settlement Procedures Act (RESPA) requires disclosure of all settlement costs when a real estate purchase is financed by a federally related mortgage loan. RESPA requires lenders to use a HUD-1 Settlement Statement to detail the financial particulars of a transaction. The HUD-1 itemizes the sales price, earnest money deposit, expenses of each party, and prorations between buyer and seller; and it shows the net amount due to the seller and from the buyer at closing. It also reflects the Good Faith Estimate (GFE) estimated costs and the HUD-1 actual costs so the lender can determine that all closing expenses are within their tolerances. If they are not, the lender must pay the buyer for any expenses that exceed the tolerances. The HUD-1 is signed by all parties to evidence their approval.

As described in this chapter, the GFE, the TIL Early Disclosure, the TIL Disclosure and the HUD-1 have been consolidated and replaced; the two new forms—the Loan Estimate and the Closing Disclosure—will be required to be used for mortgage loan applications received on or after August 1, 2015.

CHAPTER 20 QUESTIONS

1. Which statement is *TRUE* of real estate closings in Texas?
   a. The buyer usually receives the rents for the day of closing.
   b. The buyer must reimburse the seller for any title evidence provided by the seller.
   c. The seller usually pays the expenses for the day of closing.
   d. The seller must pay all the closing expenses.

2. Security deposits on rental property being sold should be listed on a closing statement as a credit to the
   a. buyer.
   b. seller.
   c. lender.
   d. broker.

3. The purpose of RESPA (Real Estate Settlement Procedures Act) is to
   a. ensure that buyers do not borrow more than they can pay.
   b. make real estate brokers more responsive to buyers' needs.
   c. disclose kickbacks paid for referrals.
   d. protect consumers from abusive lending practices.

4. Some items included in a closing statement are not prorated but are listed at the full amount. Which of the following is *ALWAYS* prorated?
   a. Special assessments
   b. The unpaid principal balance of the seller's mortgage assumed by the buyer
   c. Accrued interest on the seller's mortgage assumed by the buyer
   d. Rent security deposit

5. Legal title passes from the seller to the buyer
   a. on the date of execution of the deed.
   b. when the closing statement has been signed.
   c. when the deed is delivered and accepted.
   d. when the contract is signed.

6. All encumbrances and liens shown on the title commitment, other than those waived or agreed to by the purchaser and listed in the contract, must be removed so that the title can be delivered free and clear. The removal of such encumbrances is the duty of the
   a. buyer.
   b. seller.
   c. title company.
   d. lender.

7. Which item would *NOT* be prorated between buyer and seller at the closing on an apartment complex?
   a. Recording charges
   b. General taxes
   c. Mortgage interest
   d. Rental income

Questions 8 through 13 pertain to certain items as they normally would appear on a closing statement.

8. The sales price of the property is a
   a. credit only to the seller.
   b. debit only to the buyer.
   c. credit to the seller and a debit to the buyer.
   d. credit to the buyer and a debit to the seller.

9. The earnest money left on deposit with the broker or title company is a
   a. credit to the seller.
   b. credit to the buyer.
   c. debit to the seller.
   d. debit to the buyer.

10. The principal amount of the purchaser's new mortgage loan is a
    a. credit to the seller.
    b. credit to the buyer.
    c. debit to the seller.
    d. debit to the buyer.

11. Unpaid accrued real estate taxes are a
    a. credit only to the buyer.
    b. debit only to the seller.
    c. credit to the buyer and debit to the seller.
    d. credit to the seller and debit to the buyer.

12. The broker's commission is usually shown as a
    a. debit to the buyer.
    b. debit to the seller.
    c. credit to the seller.
    d. credit to the buyer.

13. The interest proration on an existing assumed mortgage is a
    a. credit only to the seller.
    b. debit only to the buyer.
    c. credit to the seller and debit to the buyer.
    d. credit to the buyer and debit to the seller.

14. The doctrine of relation back is MOST closely associated with
    a. escrow.
    b. prorations.
    c. title evidence.
    d. subrogation.

15. The RESPA Settlement Statement must be used to illustrate all settlement charges for
    a. transactions financed by VA and FHA loans only.
    b. residential transactions financed by federally related mortgage loans.
    c. all transactions in which mortgage financing is involved.
    d. all transactions involving commercial property.

16. Which would a lender generally NOT require to be produced at or before the closing?
    a. Title insurance policy
    b. Appraisal
    c. Homestead declaration
    d. Survey

17. When a transaction is to be closed in escrow, before the closing date, the seller generally deposits with the escrow agent all EXCEPT
    a. the deed to the property.
    b. title evidence.
    c. the payoff letter.
    d. a new hazard insurance policy.

18. The annual real estate taxes amount to $1,800, payable in arrears. If closing is set for June 15, which of the following is TRUE, using a statutory year?
    a. Credit buyer $825; debit seller $825
    b. Credit seller $825; debit buyer $825
    c. Credit buyer $975; debit seller $975
    d. Credit seller $975; debit buyer $975

19. The seller collected rent of $400, payable in advance, from a tenant on November 1. At closing on November 15, the
    a. seller owes the buyer $400.
    b. buyer owes the seller $400.
    c. seller owes the buyer $200.
    d. buyer owes the seller $200.

20. A buyer of a $100,000 home has paid $12,000 as earnest money and has a loan commitment for 70% of the purchase price. Disregarding closing costs, how much more cash does the buyer need to bring to the closing?
    a. $18,000
    b. $30,000
    c. $58,000
    d. $61,600

21. Which statement BEST represents the provisions of RESPA?
    a. The required Special Information Booklet lists dollar estimates of closing costs the buyer is likely to pay.
    b. If the seller is paying for the owner's title policy, he may require the buyer to use a specific title company.
    c. The HUD-1 Settlement Statement must be available for the buyer's inspection at least one day before closing.
    d. A mortgage lender may pay a fee to a real estate agent who brings in a loan applicant.

Detailed rationales for the end-of-chapter review questions are available online at www.dearborn.com through the *Instructor Resource Guides* link.

CHAPTER

21

Leases

■ **LEARNING OBJECTIVES** *When you have completed this chapter, you will be able to*

- ■ **discuss** the requirements of laws related to leasing residential real estate;
- ■ **identify** the characteristics of the four types of leasehold estates and the various types of leases;
- ■ **describe** the requirements and general provisions of a valid lease and how a lease may be discharged;
- ■ **explain** the key points of the Texas Landlord and Tenant Act: occupancy limits, rental applications, security deposits, maintenance of premises, smoke alarms, security devices, and breach of lease; and
- ■ **define** the following *key terms*:

actual eviction	habitability statute	periodic estate
constructive eviction	holdover tenancy	reversionary right
estate for years	lease	security deposit
estate from period to period	leasehold estate	sublease
forcible detainer suit	mitigate damages	suit for possession
gross lease	month-to-month tenancy	tenancy at sufferance
ground lease	net lease	tenancy at will
	percentage lease	writ of possession

OVERVIEW

When the owners of real property do not wish to use the property personally or want to derive income from its ownership, they can allow it to be used by another person in exchange for consideration. The person who makes periodic payments for the use of the property *leases* it from the owner. Generally, any type of real property may be leased; the apartment dweller, as well as the commercial or industrial tenant, may find it advantageous to lease real estate for a given period rather than purchase it.

This chapter examines the various leasehold estates a landlord (lessor) and a tenant (lessee) may enter into and the types and specific provisions of lease agreements commonly used in the real estate business. In discussing leases, the terms *owner*, *landlord*, and *lessor* are equivalent. Similarly, *renter*, *tenant*, and *lessee* describe the same person.

Although homeownership is the goal of most Americans, renting may be a better decision than buying for many people. Those who don't want to or have time to maintain a property or who want the flexibility to move quickly when economic opportunities emerge are renters by choice. According to a 2010 Fannie Mae survey, the most common reasons that renters do not buy are (1) not having enough credit to get a loan, (2) not being able to afford the purchase or upkeep of a home, and (3) thinking it is not a good time to buy. To help consumers make the "buy versus rent" decision, the "Homeowners and Renters" pages on the Freddie Mac website include the evaluation page "Is Buying or Renting Right for You?" along with calculators and other tools to compute the financial difference between buying and renting.

LEASING REAL ESTATE

A **lease** is a contract between an owner of real estate (known as the *lessor*) and a tenant (the *lessee*) that transfers the right to exclusive possession and use of the owner's property to the tenant for a specified period of time. This agreement generally sets forth the length of time the contract is to run, the amount to be paid by the lessee for the right to use the property, and other rights and obligations of the parties.

Real estate licensees are prohibited by the License Act from preparing any document that transfers any interest in real estate. This includes leases. Therefore, a real estate licensee must use a lease form promulgated by the Texas Real Estate Commission when one exists. With the exception of leases to be used by a buyer or a seller in connection with a real estate sales transaction, TREC does not have promulgated lease contracts. Therefore, the necessary forms should be prepared by a professional organization (such as the Texas Association of REALTORS® or the Texas Apartment Association), by a Texas attorney, or by the property owner or an attorney and required by the property owner (TRELA §1101.654). A properly drafted lease that is consistently reviewed and revised to incorporate new laws can help to prevent expensive lawsuits. In effect, the lease agreement is a combination of a conveyance (of an interest in the real estate) and a contract (to pay rent and assume other obligations). The landlord (lessor) grants the tenant (lessee) the right to occupy the premises and use them for purposes stated in the lease. In return, the landlord retains the right to receive payment for the use of the premises, as well as a **reversionary right** to retake possession after the lease term has expired. The lessor's interest in leased property is called a *leased fee estate plus reversionary right.*

Several laws that have been previously discussed apply to leases on real property as well as to sales.

Statute of Frauds   The *Texas statute of frauds* requires that a *lease for a term of more than one year be written* to be enforceable. It must be signed by the parties to be charged with its performance—both the lessor and the lessee. A lease for one year or less usually is enforceable if it is entered into orally. However, it is prudent to have *all* leases in writing to avoid relying on the memory of two parties whose recall of the lease essentials may differ.

Agency Disclosure   An Information About Brokerage Services form must be given to prospective tenants at the first substantive dialogue regarding a residential lease for more than one year or when the purchase of the property is contemplated (see Chapter 5).

Sex-Offender Laws   The owners of *single-family rental houses* do not have a duty to disclose to buyers and rental applicants any information about high-risk sex offenders living near the rental dwelling. However, legal counsel for the Texas Apartment Association believes that, under common law, a *multidwelling rental housing* owner must disclose to all rental applicants and existing residents of an apartment community that a convicted sex offender of any level is living in the owner's own apartment community. (For more information about sex offender disclosure, see Chapter 13.)

Lead-Based Paint   A lead-based paint disclosure and the pamphlet *Protecting Your Family* must be given to tenants in properties built before 1978 (with a few specific exceptions). Houses *exclusively* for the elderly or handicapped (unless there are children living there); zero-bedroom units such as lofts, efficiencies, and studios; and properties that have been inspected and found free of lead-based paint are three of the few exemptions from the disclosure requirements. A copy of the disclosure signed by the resident(s), the owner, and any leasing agent must be retained by the owner for at least three years after the lease begins. If renovation or repair work disturbs more than 6 square feet of surface area for interior work or 20 square feet for exterior work, rental residents must be notified and given a copy of the EPA pamphlet *Renovate Right*, and the repairs must be performed by certified renovators. (For more information about lead-based paint disclosures, see Chapter 13.)

Americans with Disabilities Act   The *Americans with Disabilities Act* (ADA) applies to commercial and certain multifamily residential properties in which public goods or services are provided. Multifamily properties of four or more ground-floor units or four or more units with elevators must comply. The ADA requires that such properties either be free of architectural barriers or provide reasonable accommodations for people with disabilities. (For more information about the ADA, see Chapter 6.)

New rules went into effect on January 31, 2013, that may require some pool owners under specific circumstances to install permanent, fixed lifts to improve accessibility under the ADA. While most apartment firms will remain unaffected by the new requirements, some will have to comply if they allow people beyond private residents and guests to use the apartment communities' pools. Pools fall outside the ADA requirements if they are for the exclusive use of residents and their guests.

Fair Housing Laws   The fair housing laws affect landlords and tenants just as they do sellers and buyers. All persons must have access to housing of their choice without differentiation in the terms and conditions because of their race, color, religion, national origin, sex, handicap, or familial status. Withholding an apartment that is available for rent, segregating certain persons in separate sections of an apartment complex or parts of a building, and requiring different amounts of rent or security deposits from persons in the protected classes all constitute violations of the law. Fair housing laws require that the same tenant criteria applied to adults be also applied to families with children, and a landlord cannot charge a higher rent or security deposit because one of the tenants is a child.

For the past several years, discrimination because of disability has been the largest source of housing discrimination complaints. Many housing providers failed to comply with Fair Housing Act requirements of reasonable accommodation and reasonable modifications for a person with a disability (handicap). A person with a disability is an individual with a physical or mental impairment that substantially limits one or more major life activities (such as seeing, hearing, and walking). There must be an identifiable relationship between the person's disability and the requested accommodation or modification.

A disabled rental applicant must be shown the same dwellings as an able-bodied applicant; if an applicant in a wheelchair wants to see an apartment on an upper floor in a building that has no elevator, the applicant has a right to see the unit. If a deaf person uses a relay operator to inquire about available properties, the housing provider must answer the questions and treat the caller the same as a hearing caller. Because the fair housing laws that prohibit discrimination against people with disabilities apply to *all* rental properties, the following is a discussion of a few accessibility specifics:

■ A *modification* is a structural change made to the premises to allow persons with disabilities the full enjoyment of the housing and related facilities. For example, allowing a person with a disability to install a ramp into a rental house might be a reasonable modification. Reasonable modifications are usually made at the tenant's expense, and the owner may condition the permission on the resident's providing a description of the proposed modifications, giving assurances that the work will be done in a workmanlike manner, and obtaining any required building permits. If the modifications would interfere with a future tenant's use, the owner may require that the premises be restored to their original condition at the end of the lease term.

■ An *accommodation* is a change, exception, or adjustment to a rule, policy, practice, or service. For example, a landlord would make a reasonable accommodation for a tenant with mobility impairment by fulfilling a tenant's request for a reserved parking space in front of the entrance to the tenant's unit, even though all parking is unreserved; or a landlord would make a reasonable accommodation for a sight-impaired tenant by permitting a Seeing Eye® dog or other service animal, even though the community has a no-pets rule.

- A request for modification or accommodation may be denied if there is no disability-related need for the accommodation or modification or if providing it is not reasonable. If granting the request would impose an undue financial and administrative burden on the owner or would fundamentally alter the nature of the owner's operations, then it may be unreasonable. A landlord who refuses a requested accommodation because it is not reasonable should discuss the issue with the requester to determine whether an alternative accommodation would effectively address the disability-related needs without imposing an undue burden or fundamentally changing the owner's operations.

- Multifamily dwellings built for first occupancy after March 31, 1991, must meet specific design and construction requirements under the Fair Housing Amendments Act of 1988. The requirements include (1) public use and common areas must be accessible to disabled persons; (2) units designated as *accessible* must have an accessible route to the unit and an accessible entrance; and (3) accessible units must contain adaptive features such as wider doorways and hallways, light switches in accessible locations, reinforced walls for grab bars in bathrooms, and usable kitchens and bathrooms so wheelchairs can maneuver in the spaces.

- The Fair Housing Act does not protect an individual with a disability whose tenancy would constitute a "direct threat" to the health or safety of other individuals or result in substantial physical damage to the property of others, unless the threat can be eliminated or significantly reduced by reasonable accommodation.

Legal counsel for the Texas Apartment Association recommends the following:

> You should assume that every conversation with a prospective applicant and resident is recorded and could be used as evidence in a court of law. You must carefully review every request from a disabled person for a reasonable modification or reasonable accommodation for the person's disability. While you are under no obligation to do more than what the law requires, failure to take pains to ensure that the minimum requirements of the law are met can result in serious legal liability.

In summary, treat all rental applicants and residents with respect and dignity. (For additional information on fair housing, see Chapter 6.)

IN PRACTICE   Most fair housing complaints originate from the rental housing market rather than from the single-family-for-sale sector. Common rental housing discrimination complaints include

- imposing more restrictive rules on minority residents than on others;
- denying families with children or limiting the number of children in units to less than two per bedroom;
- sexual harassment against residents—the U.S. Department of Justice prosecutes landlords who create an untenable living environment by demanding sexual favors from tenants or by creating a sexually hostile environment for them;
- failing to make reasonable accommodations for disabled residents; and
- failing to return telephone messages left by African Americans—an aspect of linguistic profiling that is currently being researched.

In addition to federal fair housing laws, landlords and rental agents must be aware of local laws. Marital status, gender identity, and other factors are protected classes in some cities. Several local governments have approved ordinances that limit smoking in privately owned apartment buildings, and HUD released a notice strongly encouraging public housing authorities to implement non-smoking policies in public housing, emphasizing that there is no "right to smoke." Some local zoning restrictions and local immigration ordinances that require apartment residents to secure government-issued renter licenses and impose criminal penalties upon apartment owners who rent to illegal immigrants are being reviewed by the courts.

LEASEHOLD ESTATES

Estates in land are divided into two major classifications: freehold estates (those involving ownership, as discussed in Chapter 8) and leasehold estates. When a landowner leases real estate to a tenant, the tenant's right to occupy the land for the duration of the lease is called a **leasehold estate**. A leasehold estate is an estate in land that generally is considered personal property. However, when the contract is a lease for life or for 99 years, under which the tenant assumes many of the landowner's obligations, the tenant gets some of the benefits and privileges of a property owner. In addition, the Internal Revenue Service permits certain tax advantages for leases longer than 30 years. A lease may be recorded if signed and acknowledged before a notary public or other officer. Recording will take place in the county in which the property is located. Unless the lease is for three years or longer, it *usually is not recorded*. However, if the lessee intends to mortgage a leasehold interest, recordation is required. If the parties do not want the terms of the lease disclosed to the public, a *memorandum of lease* may be filed with the county clerk. Possession of the property by the lessee provides *constructive notice* to the world of a lessee's rights, and an inspection of the property will result in *actual notice* of the lessee's leasehold interest.

In the discussion of interests and estates in Chapter 8, freehold estates were differentiated from leasehold estates. Just as there are several types of freehold (ownership) estates, there are also various leasehold estates. The four most important are (1) estate for years, (2) periodic estate (or estate from period to period), (3) tenancy at will, and (4) tenancy at sufferance (see Figure 21.1).

FIGURE 21.1: Leasehold Estates

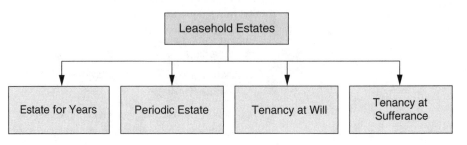

Estate for Years

A leasehold that continues for a *definite period*, whether for years, months, weeks, or even days, is an **estate for years**. An estate for years always has a specific starting and ending time and does not automatically renew at the end of the lease period. When the definite term specified in a written or an oral lease expires, the lessee is required to vacate the premises and surrender possession to the lessor. No notice is required to terminate the lease at the end of the lease period because a specific expiration date already is provided. A lease for years may be terminated before the expiration date by the mutual consent of both parties, but otherwise neither party may terminate without showing that the lease agreement has been breached. Typically, an estate for years gives the lessee the right to occupy and use the leased property—subject, of course, to the terms and covenants contained in the lease agreement itself, which is generally a written document. This right of occupancy is exclusive, which bars even the owner from possession or occupancy.

Periodic Estate

Periodic estates, sometimes called **estates from period to period** or from month to month, are created when the landlord and tenant enter into an agreement that continues for an *indefinite length of time without a specific expiration date*. Rent, however, is payable at definite intervals. These tenancies generally are created by agreement or operation of law to run for a certain amount of time; for instance, year to year, month to month, or week to week. The agreement is automatically renewed for similar succeeding periods until one of the parties gives notice to terminate. In effect, the payment and acceptance of rent extend the lease for another period. A **month-to-month tenancy**, for example, is created when a tenant takes possession with no definite termination date and pays rent on a monthly basis. If the lease agreement on an estate for years provides for the conversion to a periodic tenancy, no negotiations are necessary. The tenant simply exercises the option to begin leasing on a month-to-month basis. If the lease does not provide for a conversion and the tenant remains in possession after the lease term expires, a **holdover tenancy**, or *tenancy at sufferance*, is created. The landlord may either evict the tenant or accept the tenant's rent, which is considered proof of acceptance of the periodic estate. Commercial leases usually provide for a holdover rent rate of 125% to 150% of the lease's stated rental rate.

The courts customarily hold that a tenant who holds over can do so for a term equal to the term of the original lease, provided the period is for one year or less. The courts usually have ruled that a holdover tenancy cannot exist for longer than one year. Thus, if the original lease were for six months and the tenancy were held over, the courts usually would consider the holdover to be for a like period, that is, six months. However, if the original lease were for five years, the holdover tenancy could not exceed one year.

To *terminate* a periodic estate, either the landlord or the tenant must give *proper notice*. Normally, to terminate an estate from week to week, one week's notice is required; to terminate an estate from month to month or longer, one month's notice is required, unless there is an agreement to the contrary.

Tenancy at Will

A **tenancy at will** is a leasehold estate that exists for as long as both lessor and lessee desire it to last. Therefore, it is a tenancy of indefinite duration. It continues until it is terminated by either party's giving proper notice or by the death of either the landlord or the tenant. A tenancy at will may be created by express agreement or by operation of law; during its existence, the tenant has all the rights and obligations of a lessor-lessee relationship, including the duty to pay rent at regular intervals.

FOR EXAMPLE At the end of a lease period, a landlord informs a tenant that in a few months the city is going to demolish the apartment building to make way for an expressway. The landlord gives the tenant the option to move or to continue to occupy the premises until demolition begins. If the tenant agrees to stay, a tenancy at will is created. In a tenancy at will, the tenant remains in possession rightfully; the landlord or tenant "wills" that possession can continue.

Tenancy at Sufferance

A **tenancy at sufferance** arises when a tenant who lawfully possessed real property continues in possession of the premises without the landlord's consent after the rights expire. In this situation, the landlord does not want the tenant in possession but "suffers" or permits the tenant to remain.

Two examples of estates at sufferance are (1) when a tenant in an *estate for years* fails to surrender possession at the expiration of the lease and (2) when a borrower continues in possession after a foreclosure sale (see Chapter 15, deed of trust, ¶22, power-of-sale clause). Eviction procedures will be discussed later in this chapter.

IN PRACTICE The requirement in Section 1101.652(b)(12) of the Texas Real Estate License Act that all contracts must have a definite termination date that is not subject to prior notice does not apply to lease agreements. Landlord and tenant law permits tenancies without definite termination dates for periodic estates, tenancies at will, and tenancies at sufferance.

COMMON LEASE PROVISIONS

In determining the validity of a lease, the courts apply the rules governing contracts. If the intention to convey temporary possession of a certain parcel of real estate from one person to another is expressed, the courts generally hold that a lease has been created. Texas and most other states require no special wording to establish the landlord-tenant relationship. The lease may be written, oral, or implied, depending on the circumstances. The Texas Association of REALTORS® provides a residential real estate lease form for its members' use. Another popular residential lease used in Texas is the TAA lease form used by members of the Texas Apartment Association.

The requirements for a valid lease are essentially the same as those for any other contract, which are as follows:

- *Offer and acceptance*—The parties must reach a mutual agreement on all the terms of the contract.
- *Consideration*—Rent in exchange for possession is the normal consideration granted for the right to occupy the leased premises; however, the payment of rent is not essential as long as consideration was granted in creation of the lease itself. Some courts have construed rent as being any consideration that supports the lease, thus not limiting its definition to the payment of monthly rent (as will be illustrated later in discussions of gross, net, and percentage leases).
- *Capacity to contract*—The parties must have the legal capacity to contract.
- *Legal objectives*—The objectives of the lease must be legal.
- *Legal description*—The leased premises must be clearly described. The legal description of real estate should be used if the lease covers land, such as a ground lease or single-family residence. If the lease is for a multifamily residential property, street address and apartment designation are acceptable.

As discussed earlier in this chapter, the Texas statute of frauds requires that leases for longer than one year be in writing because a lease is considered a conveyance of an interest in real estate. The tenant's signature usually is *not essential if the tenant has taken possession*. Of course, both parties must sign the lease if it is to be enforceable against each party. The courts consider a lease to be a contract and not subject to subsequent changes in the rent or other terms unless these changes are in writing and signed in the same manner as the original lease.

Term of Lease

The term of a lease is the period for which the lease will run. It should be stated precisely, including the beginning and ending dates, together with a statement of the total period of the lease. For instance, a lease might run "for a term of 30 years beginning June 1, 2006, and ending May 31, 2036." A perpetual lease for an inordinate amount of time or an indefinite term might be ruled invalid unless the language of the lease and the surrounding circumstances clearly indicate that the parties intended such a term.

Possession of Leased Premises

Leases carry the *implied covenant of quiet possession* that the landlord will give the tenant exclusive possession of the premises. In Texas, the landlord must give the tenant *actual* occupancy, or possession, of the leased premises. If the premises are occupied by a holdover tenant, or adverse claimant, at the beginning of the new lease period, it is the landlord's duty to bring whatever action is necessary to recover possession and to bear the expense of this action. Additionally, the landlord guarantees that the tenant will not be evicted from the premises by any person who claims to have a title superior to that of the lessor, as might occur in the sale of the property.

Use of Premises

A lessor may restrict a lessee's use of the premises through provisions included in the lease. This is most important in leases for stores or commercial space. For example, a lease may provide that the leased premises are to be used *only* for the purpose of a real estate office *and for no other*. In the absence of such limitations, a lessee may use the premises for any *lawful* purpose.

Improvements

Neither the landlord nor the tenant is required to make improvements to the leased property. In the absence of an agreement to the contrary, the tenant may make improvements with the landlord's permission. Any such alterations generally become the property of the landlord; that is, they become fixtures. However, as discussed in Chapter 2, a tenant may be given the right to install trade fixtures or chattel fixtures under the terms of the lease. The tenant may customarily remove such trade fixtures before the lease expires, provided the tenant restores the premises to the condition that they were in at the time of possession.

Options and Right of First Refusal

Many leases contain an option that grants the lessee the privilege of *renewing* the lease but requires that the lessee give notice on or before a specific date of an intention to exercise the option. Options are generally considered a benefit to the tenant rather than the landlord because the tenant basically has control of the space in the future but does not have to commit for it until the option notification deadline. The *right of first refusal* allows a tenant to match an offer from another party on vacant space in a building. Leases with tenants who foresee a need to expand often contain this clause.

Some leases grant the lessee the option of purchasing the leased premises. Leases with the option to purchase vary widely; competent legal advice should be sought regarding the lease, the note, and the deed of trust.

LANDLORD AND TENANT ACT

Historically, leases were drawn up primarily for the benefit of the landlord. However, consumer awareness has fostered the belief that a lease's validity depends on both parties' fulfillment of certain obligations. To provide laws outlining such obligations, Texas has passed statutes found in Sections 91–94 of the Texas Property Code, known as the *Landlord and Tenant Act*. This law addresses such issues as the landlord's right of entry, maintenance of premises, the tenant's protection against landlord retaliation for complaints, installation of smoke detectors, the landlord's duty to install or rekey a security device, and the disclosure of the property owners' names and addresses to the tenants. The act further sets down specific remedies available to both the landlord and the tenant if a breach of the lease agreement occurs. Some of the major provisions of the Property Code are discussed in the following section.

Occupancy Limits

The "Keating Memo," published by HUD, indicates that a "reasonable" occupancy standard is two persons per bedroom, and, generally, an infant less than six months old may sleep in the same bedroom as the parent or guardian. However, in individual familial status cases, that standard may be adjusted based on "special circumstances," which include size and number of bedrooms, size of the rental unit, ages of any children, and extra rooms such as a den or study. HUD also considers state or local laws concerning occupancy.

The Texas Property Code, 92.010, sets the maximum number of adults (18 years of age or older) that a landlord may allow to occupy a dwelling at three times the number of bedrooms in the dwelling, in most instances. Under the Texas law, *bedroom* means an area of a dwelling intended as sleeping quarters. The term does not include a kitchen, dining room, bathroom, living room, utility room, closet, or storage area of a dwelling. Because local regulations may differ, a landlord or property manager should contact a local code enforcement agency or apartment association to obtain city or county occupancy regulations and ordinances. Housing providers are encouraged to have a written occupancy policy that is consistently followed and justified by the specific characteristics of each property.

Rental Application

By law, at the time an applicant is given a rental application (see Figure 21.2), the landlord must provide the applicant a printed notice of the landlord's tenant selection criteria. If the landlord has an online application process, the website must clearly and conspicuously show the rental qualification criteria. The printed or online notice must include the grounds for which an application may be denied, including the applicant's

- criminal history,
- previous rental history,
- current income,
- credit history, or
- failure to provide accurate or complete information on the application form.

Because the purpose for giving the eligibility criteria is to help people decide whether to submit an application or not, the rental criteria should be available to applicants before they complete the rental application and pay any fees. The applicant must sign an acknowledgment indicating that the notice was made available. Online applications should have an online acknowledgment feature so applicants can acknowledge that the rental criteria were made available before they completed the online application. The acknowledgment must be substantially equivalent to the following statement:

> Signing this acknowledgment indicates that you have had the opportunity to review the landlord's tenant selection criteria. The tenant selection criteria may include factors such as criminal history, credit history, current income, and rental history. If you do not meet the selection criteria, or if you provide inaccurate or incomplete information, your application may be rejected and your application fee will not be refunded.

The acknowledgment may be a part of the rental application if underlined or in bold print. If the landlord does not keep a signed copy of the notice, there is a rebuttable presumption that the notice was not made available to the applicant and an application fee and/or application deposit must be refunded if the applicant is rejected.

FIGURE 21.2: Residential Lease Application

Received on _____ (date) at _____ (time)

TEXAS ASSOCIATION OF REALTORS®
RESIDENTIAL LEASE APPLICATION
USE OF THIS FORM BY PERSONS WHO ARE NOT MEMBERS OF THE TEXAS ASSOCIATION OF REALTORS® IS NOT AUTHORIZED.
©Texas Association of REALTORS®, Inc. 2014

Each occupant and co-applicant 18 years or older must submit a separate application.

Property Address: _____
     Anticipated: Move-in Date: _____ Monthly Rent: $_____ Security Deposit: $_____

Property Condition: **Applicant is strongly encouraged to view the Property prior to submitting any application**. Landlord makes no express or implied warranties as to the Property's condition. Applicant requests Landlord consider the following repairs or treatments should Applicant and Landlord enter into a lease:_____
_____
_____
_____

Applicant was referred to Landlord by:
     ❑ Real estate agent _____(name) _____(phone)
     ❑ Newspaper ❑ Sign ❑ Internet ❑ Other _____

Applicant's name (first, middle, last) _____
     Is there a co-applicant? ❑ yes ❑ no   *If yes, co-applicant must submit a separate application.*
     Applicant's former last name (maiden or married) _____
E-mail _____ Home Phone _____
Work Phone _____ Mobile/Pager _____
Soc. Sec. No. _____ Driver License No. _____ in _____(state)
Date of Birth_____ Height _____ Weight _____ Eye Color _____
Hair Color _____ Marital Status _____ Citizenship _____(country)

Emergency Contact: *(Do not insert the name of an occupant or co-applicant.)*
        Name:_____
        Address:_____
        Phone:_____ E-mail:_____

Name all other persons who will occupy the Property:
Name:_____ Relationship:_____ Age:_____
Name:_____ Relationship:_____ Age:_____
Name:_____ Relationship:_____ Age:_____
Name:_____ Relationship:_____ Age:_____

Applicant's Current Address: _____ Apt. No._____
        _____(city, state, zip)
     Landlord or Property Manager's Name: _____ Email:_____
     Phone:*Day:*_____ *Nt:*_____ *Mb:*_____ *Fax:*_____
     Date Moved-In_____ Move-Out Date _____ Rent $_____
     Reason for move: _____

Applicant's Previous Address: _____ Apt. No._____
        _____(city, state, zip)
     Previous Landlord or Property Manager's Name: _____ Email:_____
     Phone:*Day:*_____ *Nt:*_____ *Mb:*_____ *Fax:*_____

FIGURE 21.2: Residential Lease Application (continued)

Residential Lease Application concerning_____

    Date Moved-In_____ Date Moved-Out _____Rent $_____

    Reason for move: _____

Applicant's Current Employer: _____

    Address: _____(*street, city, state, zip*)

    Supervisor's Name: _____ Phone:_____Fax:_____

    E-mail: _____

    Start Date: _____ Gross Monthly Income: $_____ Position: _____

    Note: If Applicant is self-employed, Landlord may require one or more previous year's tax return attested by a CPA, attorney, or other tax professional.

Applicant's Previous Employer: _____

    Address: _____(*street, city, state, zip*)

    Supervisor's Name: _____ Phone:_____Fax:_____

    E-mail: _____

    Employed from _____to_____ Gross Monthly Income: $_____ Position: _____

Describe other income Applicant wants considered: _____

_____

_____

List all vehicles to be parked on the Property:

Type	Year	Make	Model	License/State	Mo.Pymnt.

Will any pets (dogs, cats, birds, reptiles, fish, and other pets) be kept on the Property? ❑ yes ❑ no
If yes, list all pets to be kept on the Property:

Type & Breed	Name	Color	Weight	Age in Yrs.	Gender	Neutered?	Declawed?	Rabies Shots Current?
						❑ yes ❑ no	❑ yes ❑ no	❑ yes ❑ no
						❑ yes ❑ no	❑ yes ❑ no	❑ yes ❑ no
						❑ yes ❑ no	❑ yes ❑ no	❑ yes ❑ no
						❑ yes ❑ no	❑ yes ❑ no	❑ yes ❑ no

Yes	No	
❑	❑	Will any waterbeds or water-filled furniture be on the Property?
❑	❑	Does anyone who will occupy the Property smoke?
❑	❑	Will Applicant maintain renter's insurance?
❑	❑	Is Applicant or Applicant's spouse, even if separated, in military?
❑	❑	If yes, is the military person serving under orders limiting the military person's stay to one year or less?
		Has Applicant ever:
❑	❑	been evicted?
❑	❑	been asked to move out by a landlord?
❑	❑	breached a lease or rental agreement?
❑	❑	filed for bankruptcy?
❑	❑	lost property in a foreclosure?
❑	❑	had *any* credit problems (including any outstanding debt (e.g., student loans or medical bills)), slow-pays or delinquencies?
❑	❑	been convicted of a crime?
❑	❑	Is any occupant a registered sex offender?
❑	❑	Are there any criminal matters pending against any occupant?
❑	❑	Is there additional information Applicant wants considered?

(TAR-2003) 1-1-14   Page 2 of 4

FIGURE 21.2: Residential Lease Application (continued)

Residential Lease Application concerning_____

Additional comments:_____
_____
_____.

Authorization: Applicant authorizes Landlord and Landlord's agent, at any time before, during, or after any tenancy, to:
   (1) obtain a copy of Applicant's credit report;
   (2) obtain a criminal background check related to Applicant and any occupant; and
   (3) verify any rental or employment history or verify any other information related to this application with persons knowledgeable of such information.

Notice of Landlord's Right to Continue to Show the Property: Unless Landlord and Applicant enter into a separate written agreement otherwise, the Property remains on the market until a lease is signed by all parties and Landlord may continue to show the Property to other prospective tenants and accept another offer.

Privacy Policy: Landlord's agent or property manager maintains a privacy policy that is available upon request.

Fees: Applicant submits a non-refundable fee of $_____ to _____ (entity or individual) for processing and reviewing this application. Applicant ❑ submits ❑ will not submit an application deposit of $_____ to be applied to the security deposit upon execution of a lease or returned to Applicant if a lease is not executed.

<u>**Acknowledgement & Representation**</u>:
   (1) <u>Signing this application indicates that Applicant has had the opportunity to review Landlord's tenant selection criteria, which is available upon request. The tenant selection criteria may include factors such as criminal history, credit history, current income and rental history.</u>
   (2) <u>Applicant understands that providing inaccurate or incomplete information is grounds for rejection of this application and forfeiture of any application fee and may be grounds to declare Applicant in breach of any lease the Applicant may sign.</u>
   (3) <u>Applicant represents that the statements in this application are true and complete.</u>

_____
Applicant's Signature   Date

For Landlord's Use:

On _____, _____ (name/initials) notified

❑ Applicant ❑ _____ by ❑ phone ❑ mail ❑ e-mail ❑ fax ❑ in person

that Applicant was ❑ approved ❑ not approved. *Reason for disapproval:*_____
_____

FIGURE 21.2: Residential Lease Application (continued)

Residential Lease Application concerning _____

TEXAS ASSOCIATION OF REALTORS®
AUTHORIZATION TO RELEASE INFORMATION
RELATED TO A RESIDENTIAL LEASE APPLICANT
USE OF THIS FORM BY PERSONS WHO ARE NOT MEMBERS OF THE TEXAS ASSOCIATION OF REALTORS® IS NOT AUTHORIZED.
©Texas Association of REALTORS®, Inc. 2014

I, _____ (Applicant), have submitted an application

to lease a property located at _____

_____ *(address, city, state, zip).*

The landlord, broker, or landlord's representative is:

_____ *(name)*
_____ *(address)*
_____ *(city, state, zip)*
_____ *(phone)* _____ *(fax)*
_____ *(e-mail)*

I give my permission:

(1) to my current and former employers to release any information about my employment history and income history to the above-named person;

(2) to my current and former landlords to release any information about my rental history to the above-named person;

(3) to my current and former mortgage lenders on property that I own or have owned to release any information about my mortgage payment history to the above-named person;

(4) to my bank, savings and loan, or credit union to provide a verification of funds that I have on deposit to the above-named person; and

(5) to the above-named person to obtain a copy of my consumer report (credit report) from any consumer reporting agency and to obtain background information about me.

_____
Applicant's Signature   Date

Note: Any broker gathering information about an applicant acts under specific instructions to verify some or all of the information described in this authorization. The broker maintains a privacy policy which is available upon request.

(TAR-2003) 1-1-14   Page 4 of 4

Application Deposit   An *application deposit* is a sum of money given to the property owner in connection with a rental application and before a lease is signed. It serves the same function as an earnest money deposit in a sales contract. The applicant puts up enough money that he will not change his mind after the landlord has taken the rental unit off the market to review the application. If the applicant is accepted, the application deposit may be credited toward the security deposit or another fee that is due when the tenant signs a lease. If the applicant is rejected, the deposit must be refunded.

Application Fee   An *application fee* is a sum of money that may be charged by a landlord to offset the actual costs of screening an applicant for acceptance as a tenant. It covers such expenses as the cost of obtaining credit and criminal background checks. The property owner does not have to refund an application fee if the applicant is rejected.

Security Deposits

Most leases require that the tenant provide some form of **security deposit**, to be held by the landlord during the lease term. The security deposit, which primarily safeguards against a tenant's destruction of the premises, is frequently equivalent to one month's rent. As a practical matter, it induces tenants to honor their lease agreement, maintain the premises more carefully during occupancy, and clean the premises thoroughly on leaving.

Under Texas law, within 30 days of the tenant's surrender of the premises, either a security deposit must be refunded to the tenant or the tenant must be provided with an explanation and accounting of damages and other charges being deducted from the deposit and for which the tenant is liable (Texas Property Code, 92.101–.109). However, the landlord is not obligated to return the security deposit until and unless the tenant has furnished the landlord with a written statement of the tenant's forwarding address. If a tenant fails to occupy the premises after signing a lease, a landlord must return a security deposit or rent prepayment after another tenant is secured. A landlord may retain a security deposit for failure to give a move-out notice only if the notice requirement is underlined or printed in conspicuous bold print in the lease. The Texas Association of REALTORS® Residential Lease (TAR-2001) contains such a provision:

> 10(C). Refund: Tenant must give Landlord at least thirty (30) days written notice of surrender before Landlord is obligated to refund or account for the security deposit.

Under a Texas Apartment Association (TAA) lease, however, a security deposit would not be forfeited for failure to give a move-out notice. Instead, the tenant would be charged an agreed *reletting fee* to cover the owner's costs and efforts in attempting to relet. A landlord who in bad faith retains a security deposit or fails to furnish an itemized list of deductions may be held liable for three times the amount of the deposit wrongfully withheld plus $100 and attorney fees.

IN PRACTICE   Although the amount of security deposit is set by the property owner, in reality it is influenced by supply and demand forces. When supply exceeds demand, owners often lower the deposit amount as a marketing tool to increase occupancy. A lease should be clear as to whether a monetary deposit is an application deposit, an application fee, a security deposit, or advance rent. If it is a security deposit, a tenant

A landlord in a commercial lease is obligated to refund or account for a security deposit in a manner similar to that required in a residential lease—but the deadline is within 60 days after the tenant's surrender.

cannot use it to apply to the final month's rent. If it is advance rent, the landlord must treat it as income for tax purposes. In Texas, a landlord does not have to keep tenants' security deposits in a separate account nor is a landlord required to pay interest to a tenant on the security deposit while it is in the landlord's possession.

When a lessor sells a rental property, the seller gives the buyer at closing: the lease; the move-in condition form, if any; and the security deposit (see Figure 12.3, ¶9.B.(5)). A security deposit is not prorated at closing. The buyer must deliver to the tenant a signed statement that he has received the security deposit and is responsible for its return, specifying the exact dollar amount of the deposit. It is the seller's responsibility to see that the new owner gives this written notification to all tenants; otherwise, the seller could still be held liable for the security deposit.

Late Fees

A landlord cannot charge a tenant a late fee for failing to pay rent in a timely fashion unless the notice of the late fee is included in a written lease. The fee must be a reasonable estimate of damages to the landlord as a result of receiving the rent payment after the stated due date. The late fee may include an initial fee and a daily fee for each day the rent continues to remain unpaid. It may be charged after rent has been *unpaid one full day after the initial due date.* Thus, late fees could begin to be charged on the third of the month if rent were due on the first.

Assignment and Subleasing

The lessee may not assign the lease and may not **sublease** without the landlord's consent (Property Code, 91.005). This allows the lessor to retain control over the occupancy of the leased premises. A tenant who transfers all leasehold interests *assigns* the lease. One who transfers less than all leasehold interests by leasing them to a new tenant *subleases* (see Figure 21.3). For example, a transfer of a tenant's interest in a lease wherein the tenant retains a reversionary interest is a sublease, not an assignment. In most cases, the sublease or assignment does not relieve the original lessee of the obligation to make rental payments unless the landlord agrees to waive such liability.

FIGURE 21.3: Assignment versus Subletting

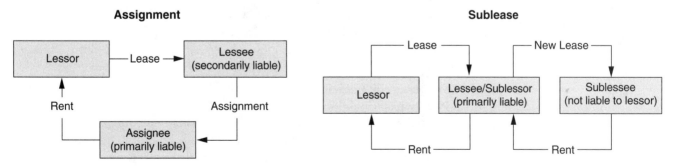

Maintenance of Premises

Historically, under the principle of caveat emptor, a landlord was not obligated to make repairs to leased premises. However, many states—including Texas—now require that a residential lessor maintain dwelling units in a habitable condition and make any necessary repairs to common elements such as hallways, stairs, or elevators. The tenant does not have to make any repairs but, on vacating the premises, must return the premises in the same condition they were received, with allowances for *ordinary wear and tear*.

The **habitability statute** (Texas Property Code, 92.052) states that the landlord "shall make a diligent effort" to repair or remedy any condition that "materially affects the physical health or safety of an ordinary tenant" if the condition arises from normal wear and tear. For this obligation to be enforced, the tenant must give notice to the person to whom rent is paid and must be current in rent payments at the time of notification. All landlords must provide tenants with a telephone number that will be answered 24 hours a day for the purpose of a tenant's reporting emergencies that fall under the habitability statute. An owner who provides a telephone number that is answered by a person or an answering machine or that is forwarded to a pager will be in compliance with this requirement. However, if an answering machine is used, it should be checked reasonably often to ensure that emergency calls from residents are responded to in a timely fashion. If there is an onsite management office, the landlord must post the phone number prominently outside that office; otherwise, the number should be provided on the written rental application or lease. Under the habitability statute, the following apply:

■ The landlord must take reasonable steps to repair the condition in a reasonable period, for which there is a rebuttable presumption of seven days. However, *reasonable time* may vary depending on the availability of labor, materials, and utilities.

■ The condition needing repair must be significant and must affect the *physical* health or safety of the tenant. Claims of mental suffering or anguish are not covered.

■ Conditions that merely cause inconvenience or discomfort, without materially affecting health or safety, are not covered by the statute.

■ The standard is that of an *ordinary* resident rather than a person with extraordinary health problems or needs.

A city with a population of 1.7 million or more (i.e., Houston) can adopt minimum habitability standards, including property inspection, for multifamily rental buildings of three or more units.

Although the statute does not detail all conditions that materially affect the physical health or safety of an ordinary tenant, it does identify the following events:

■ The landlord has failed to remedy the backup or overflow of raw sewage inside the dwelling or the flooding from broken pipes or natural drainage inside the dwelling.

■ The landlord has expressly or implicitly agreed in the lease to furnish water to the dwelling and the water service has totally stopped.

■ The landlord has expressly or implicitly agreed in the lease to furnish heating or cooling equipment; the equipment is producing inadequate heat or cooled air; and the landlord has been notified in writing by the appropriate local housing, building, or health official that the lack of heat or cooling materially affects the health or safety of an ordinary tenant.

■ The landlord has been notified in writing by a local housing, building, or health official that a stated condition materially affects the health or safety of an ordinary tenant.

■ The landlord has failed to provide and maintain a water heater.

If a landlord fails to make repairs within a reasonable time after receiving notice from the tenant, the tenant must send a second notice stating his intention to (1) terminate the lease; (2) repair the property and deduct the cost of such repairs from the rent, for as many months as necessary so long as the total repairs and deductions in any one month do not exceed one month's rent or $500, whichever is greater; or (3) pursue available judicial remedies, including a hearing in a justice of the peace (justice) court to obtain an order for repairs not to exceed $10,000.

If a property condition results from an insured casualty loss, such as fire, smoke, hail, explosion, or a similar cause, the period for repair does not begin until the landlord receives the insurance proceeds.

IN PRACTICE A landlord's insurance policy generally includes coverage for liability claims and damage to the property, but it does not cover a tenant's personal property. It is becoming increasingly common for a landlord to require all tenants to purchase either liability protection or renters insurance. Personal liability insurance refers to a policy that covers a landlord's deductible on her property insurance in the event of resident negligence that results in property damage—such as a resident's causing a fire in a kitchen that spreads to other units. Renters insurance covers not only the resident's liability to the landlord but also the resident's personal property.

Smoke Alarms

The Texas Property Code, Section 92.251, requires that landlords install smoke alarms in all residential rental property regardless of the term of the lease—with the exception of temporary residential tenancies (not to exceed 90 days) created by a contract of sale. Effective January 1, 2013, owners of rental properties first occupied before September 1, 2011, must install at least one smoke alarm in each separate bedroom in a dwelling unit, as well as in a corridor if it serves multiple bedrooms (H.B. 1168, 2011). Smoke alarms must be in good working order at the time the tenant takes possession and are presumed to be in good working order until the tenant requests repair. Replacement of batteries in a smoke alarm is the tenant's responsibility. If a rental property does not have smoke alarms, it is the tenant's responsibility to request compliance from the landlord. If requested by a tenant with a hearing-impairment disability, the smoke alarm provided by the landlord must also be capable of alerting a hearing-impaired person in the bedrooms it serves. If a local ordinance requires a fire extinguisher in each rental unit, it must have the recommended pressure at the beginning of a tenant's possession and is presumed to be in good working order until the tenant requests an inspection in writing (H.B. 1168). If a rental unit has multiple levels, a smoke alarm must be present on each level.

Security Devices

Residential rental dwellings must be equipped at the landlord's expense with specified security devices, including window latches, doorknob locks, sliding door handle latches, sliding door pin locks, keyless deadbolts, and door viewers on each exterior door (Texas Property Code, 92.151–.170). The specific devices required for a particular property are based on the year the property was built. Regardless of the property construction date, all security devices operated by a key, card, or combination must be rekeyed by the landlord at the landlord's expense no later than the seventh day after a new tenant moves in. If a tenant installs a new lock, it must be with the owner tenant moves and with a key given to the owner.

DISCHARGE OF LEASES

Termination of Lease

A written estate-for-years lease expires on the specified ending date; no separate notice is required. Oral and written leases that do not specify a definite expiration date (such as a periodic estate or a tenancy at will) may be terminated by giving proper notice in advance. In Texas, unless otherwise provided by contract, tenancy from month to month may be terminated by one month's notice. Tenancy for a shorter period may be terminated by notice equal to such period. (See the Texas Property Code, Chapter 91.)

Servicemembers may terminate a residential lease upon entering the military or being called to duty. In addition, victims of family violence, sexual assault, or sexual abuse are permitted to terminate a residential lease agreement under certain circumstances. These instances of permissible early lease termination generally require giving a 30-day notice, providing documentation, and vacating the property—unless family violence is committed by a cotenant or occupant of the dwelling, in which case written notice of termination is not required. The tenant has no further liability for future rent or any other future sums due under the lease for early termination of the lease. The tenant would still be liable for any delinquent rent or other sums due before the termination of the lease. However, if the landlord fails to give written notice in the lease of this right to terminate, the tenant is released from liability for delinquent rent. A landlord who violates this law is liable to the tenant for actual damages, a civil penalty equal to one month's rent plus $500, and attorney's fees.

When the conditions of a lease are breached, or broken, by a tenant, a landlord may terminate the lease and evict the tenant. This action must be handled through a Justice of the Peace court. In Texas, a landlord also may terminate a lease if the property is used for prostitution, obscene actions, or sexual performance by a child.

It is possible that the parties to a lease will mutually agree to cancel the lease. For example, the tenant's offer to surrender the lease and the landlord's acceptance will result in termination. A tenant who abandons leased property, however, remains liable for the terms of the lease—including the future rent. By law, however, the landlord has a duty to **mitigate damages** by exercising reasonable care to find another tenant. The vacating tenant remains responsible under the terms of the lease only until another tenant begins rent payments.

What happens to the lease in the event of the death of one party or the sale or foreclosure of the property?

■ When either the owner or the tenant of leased property dies, *the lease does not terminate*, and the heirs are bound by the terms of existing valid leases. The lease "runs with the land," similar to an easement. However, the landlord of a deceased tenant does have a duty to mitigate damages.

■ If a landlord sells or otherwise conveys leased real estate, the new landlord takes the property subject to the rights of the tenants; the lease does not terminate.

■ The Protecting Tenants at Foreclosure Act, as amended in 2010, offers some protection for renters of properties facing foreclosure through December 31, 2014. The law allows a renter who is current on rent to remain in the property until the end of the lease, unless the tenant has no lease contract or the purchaser intends to use the property as a primary residence. Then the lease may be terminated with a 90-day notice to vacate given to the tenant. When the renter protections expire at the end of 2014, Texas law will again be effective; and all leases executed after the date of the mortgage will require a 30-day notice to vacate before a lease can be terminated after foreclosure.

Breach of Lease

When a tenant breaches any lease provision, the landlord may attempt a lockout; may sue the tenant to obtain a judgment to cover past-due rent, damages to the premises, or other defaults; or may file a suit for possession. Likewise, when a landlord breaches any lease provision, the tenant is entitled to remedies against the landlord.

Landlord's Lockout Remedy A landlord may attempt to collect rent on a residence by changing the locks of a tenant who is delinquent in paying all or a part of the rent (Property Code, 92.0081). The landlord must first give the tenant written notice in bold or underlined print, three to five days in advance, that the locks are going to be changed for nonpayment of rent; the time frame is dependent on the method for giving notice. The advance notice must also state the amount of rent that must be paid to prevent the lockout and designate the place where the tenant can pay the rent to avoid the lockout. The lockout remedy can be used only once during a rental payment period, and the landlord cannot change the door locks when the tenant or any other legal occupant is in the dwelling. If the locks are changed, the landlord or the agent must place a written notice on the tenant's front door giving the amount of rent and other charges due and a 24-hour address or phone number for the tenant to obtain a key to get into the property. If there is not an on-site location for the tenant to pick up a key, the owner must deliver the key to the tenant at the dwelling within two hours after the tenant calls the 24-hour phone number, which cannot be answered by an answering machine. The new key must be given to a residential tenant whether or not the delinquent rent is paid; but in many cases, the tenant will pay the delinquent rent as a result of this forced personal contact. However, without a court order, the lockout remedy for nonpayment of rent cannot be used by the owner of a multifamily housing development that receives a low-income-housing tax credit. On a commercial lease, the landlord does not have to give the tenant a key until the rent is paid and then only during the tenant's regular business hours. A landlord should seek legal advice to ensure that all legal requirements for tenant notice are followed.

Utilities Interruption Remedy A landlord may not interrupt electrical service furnished to a tenant as a means for collecting unpaid rent. A landlord may only interrupt utility services furnished to a tenant for purposes of bona fide repairs, construction, or an emergency. If utilities are illegally disconnected, a resident may go to a justice of the peace to seek an order for restoration of service.

A Texas Apartment Association (TAA) lease requires only 24 hours written notice before filing an eviction suit.

Suit for Possession—Actual Eviction When a tenant breaches a lease or improperly retains possession of leased premises, the landlord may regain possession through a **suit for possession**, known as a **forcible detainer suit**, filed in the justice of the peace court in the precinct in which the property is located. This process is known as **actual eviction** and the procedures are outlined in Section 24

As the result of Texas court reform legislation passed in 2011 (H.B. 79), small claims courts have been consolidated with the justice courts.

If a city or a county revokes a certificate of occupancy for a leased property because it is uninhabitable, the landlord must return the security deposit and prorated rent and must reimburse the tenant for expenses incurred (H.B. 1862, 2011).

of the Texas Property Code. The law requires that the landlord serve *notice* on the tenant before commencing the suit. It must include a statement that the suit involves immediate deadlines and that legal assistance is available and must provide the State Bar of Texas toll-free phone number. Justice courts have jurisdiction in matters up to $10,000. In Texas. a notice to vacate may be given to the tenant as early as the date that rent is due if it is not paid; by law, it must give the tenant at least three days' notice that, if rent remains unpaid, the landlord will file a forcible detainer suit. However, if the parties have contracted for a specified notice period in a written lease, the notice period may be shorter or longer than three days. The forcible detainer lawsuit must be heard within 10 days after the filing. When a court issues a judgment for possession to a landlord, the tenant has five days in which to file an appeal, after which the court may issue a **writ of possession** to the lessor. Within 48 hours after receiving the writ of possession, the landlord must deliver written notice that the writ will be enforced on or after a specific date and time, but not sooner than 24 hours after the warning is posted. The tenant must peaceably remove herself and all belongings, or the landlord can have the judgment enforced by a deputy sheriff or constable, who will oversee the forcible removal of the tenant and her possessions. As in other legal processes, additional stipulations in the laws could provide a lengthy tenancy while eviction proceedings are taking place. During or after the eviction suit, the owner can file a separate suit and recover damages, lost rent, attorney's fees, and other sums owed by the resident.

Tenants' Remedies—Constructive Eviction   If a landlord breaches any clause of a lease agreement, the tenant has the right to sue, claiming a judgment for damages against the landlord. If an action or omission on the landlord's part results in the leased premises becoming uninhabitable for the purpose intended in the lease, the tenant has the right to abandon the premises after giving written notice to the landlord. This action, called **constructive eviction**, terminates the lease agreement if the tenant can prove that the premises have become uninhabitable because of the conscious neglect of the landlord (Property Code, 92.056). To claim constructive eviction, the tenant must actually remove himself from the premises while the uninhabitable condition exists. In Texas, the tenant also is entitled to receive a pro rata refund of rent paid or seek a court order requiring repairs to be made and awarding damages to the tenant.

FOR EXAMPLE   If a lease requires the landlord to furnish central heat and the landlord fails to repair a defective heating system rendering the leased premises uninhabitable, the tenant may abandon them.

IN PRACTICE   The Servicemembers Civil Relief Act (2003) affects leases involving military personnel, particularly lease termination rights, evictions, and procedures for collecting delinquent rents. In addition, H.B. 1127 (2011) mandates a statutory notice regarding servicemembers' rights on the first page of an eviction notice. When a lease involves military personnel or their dependents, consult an attorney regarding the laws related to lease termination.

TYPES OF LEASES

The manner in which rent is determined indicates the type of lease in force. The three primary types of leases are (1) the gross lease, (2) the net lease, and (3) the percentage lease (see Figure 21.4).

FIGURE 21.4: Types of Leases

Type of Lease	Lessee	Lessor
Gross lease (residential and commercial office leases)	Pays basic rent	Pays property charges (taxes, repairs, insurance)
Net lease (commercial/industrial building and ground leases)	Pays basic rent plus all or most property charges	May pay some property charges
Percentage lease (large retail store leases)	Pays basic rent plus percentage of gross sales (may pay property costs)	May pay some or all property charges

Gross Lease

In a **gross lease**, the tenant's obligation is to pay a *fixed rental* and the landlord pays all taxes, insurance, mortgage payments, repairs, and other charges regularly incurred through ownership (usually called *property charges*). Tenants generally pay for utilities. Most residential and commercial office leases are gross leases.

Net Lease

The **net lease** provides that in addition to rent, the *tenant pays most or all the property charges*. The monthly rental paid to the landlord is in addition to these charges and, therefore, is net income for the landlord after operating costs have been paid. Leases for entire commercial or industrial buildings and the land on which they are located, ground leases, and long-term leases are usually net leases.

In a *triple net lease*, or *net-net-net lease*, the tenant pays all operating and other expenses, such as taxes, insurance, assessments, maintenance, and other charges.

Percentage Lease

A percentage lease usually requires a tenant to "open its books" so the landlord can verify annual sales figures.

Either a gross lease or a net lease may be a **percentage lease**. This type of lease usually is used in the rental of retail business locations. The percentage lease generally provides for a minimum fixed rental fee plus a percentage of that portion of the tenant's business income that exceeds a stated minimum. The percentage charged in such leases varies widely with the nature of the business and is negotiable between landlord and tenant. A tenant's bargaining power is determined by the volume of business. Of course, percentages vary with the location of the property and general economic conditions.

MATH CONCEPTS

Calculating Percentage Lease Rates

A lease requires a minimum monthly rental of $1,300 per month plus 5% of the business's gross sales exceeding $160,000. On an annual sales volume of $250,000, the annual rent would be calculated as follows:

$1,300 per month × 12 months = $15,600 base rent

$250,000 – $160,000 = $90,000 subject to percentage

$90,000 × 0.05 (5%) = $4,500 percentage rent

$15,600 base rent + $4,500 percentage rent = $20,100 total rent

---

Other Lease Types

Variable Lease   Several types of leases allow for increases in the fixed rental charge during the lease period. Two of the more common ones are the *graduated lease*, which provides for increases in rent at set future dates, and the *index lease*, which allows rent to be increased or decreased periodically based on changes in the government cost-of-living index or some other index.

Ground Lease   When a landowner leases land to a tenant who agrees to *erect a building* on it, the lease usually is referred to as a **ground lease**. It is most often used in commercial property development and is sometimes an attractive alternative to purchasing land because it reduces the amount of cash needed for construction of buildings. A ground lease must be for a long enough term to make the transaction desirable to the tenant making the investment in the building; consequently, such leases often run for terms of 50 years or longer. These leases are generally *net leases* that require the lessee to pay rent as well as real estate taxes, insurance, upkeep, and repairs. Under Texas law a ground leasehold is considered to be an estate in land subject to the rights of a landlord.

> In Texas, hunting leases are not true leases. They are licenses granting access to land in order to hunt.

Oil and Gas Lease   When oil companies lease land to explore for oil and gas, a special lease agreement must be negotiated. Usually the owner of the minerals receives a cash payment, called a *bonus*, for executing the lease. The mineral owner is frequently the landowner. If no well is drilled within a year or other period stated in the lease, the lease expires; however, most oil and gas leases provide that the oil company may continue its rights for another year by paying another flat fee, called a *delay rent*. Such rentals may be paid annually until a well is produced. If oil and/or gas is found, the landowner usually receives one-eighth or more of its value as a royalty. In this case, the lease will continue for as long as oil or gas is obtained in significant quantities. These royalty payments perpetuate the lease so long as production continues.

IN PRACTICE   Because of its long-term nature, as compared with a real estate sales contract, a lease is far more detailed and complicated. The lease document must anticipate and "presolve" many potential problems with the property, as well as possible disagreements between the landlord and the tenant. For the protection of the landlord and tenant, as well as the broker, each should seek competent legal counsel in a lease transaction.

SUMMARY

A lease is an agreement that grants one person the right to use the property of another for a certain period in return for consideration. The lease agreement is a combination of a conveyance creating a leasehold interest in the property and a contract outlining the rights and obligations of the landlord and the tenant. A leasehold estate that runs for a specific length of time creates an estate for years, whereas one that runs for an indefinite period creates a periodic tenancy (year to year, month to month) or a tenancy at will. A leasehold estate generally is classified as personal property.

The requirements of a valid lease include offer and acceptance, consideration, capacity to contract, legal objectives, and a legal description. In addition, the Texas statute of frauds requires that any lease longer than one year be in writing. Leases also generally include clauses relating to such rights and obligations of the landlord and tenant as property improvements and the use of the premises. Landlord/tenant laws cover requirements for maintaining the property, handling security deposits, and installing smoke detectors and security devices.

Leases may be terminated by the expiration of the lease period, the mutual agreement of the parties, or a breach of the lease by either landlord or tenant. However, neither death of the tenant nor landlord's sale of the rental property terminates a lease. The lease "runs with the land," similar to an easement.

Upon a tenant's default on any of the lease provisions, a landlord may, following specific guidelines, utilize the lockout remedy or sue for a money judgment or for actual eviction. If the premises have become uninhabitable due to the landlord's negligence, the tenant may have the right of constructive eviction, that is, the right to abandon the premises and refuse to pay rent until the premises are repaired.

Basic lease types include net leases, gross leases, and percentage leases, which are classified according to the method used in determining the property's rental rate.

CHAPTER 21 QUESTIONS

1. Paul's estate for years lease will expire in two weeks. At that time, he will move to a larger apartment across town. What must Paul do to terminate this lease agreement?
   a. Paul must give the landlord one month's prior notice.
   b. Paul must give the landlord two weeks' prior notice.
   c. Paul needs to do nothing; the agreement will terminate automatically.
   d. The agreement will terminate only after Paul signs a lease for the new apartment.

2. A tenant's right to occupy, or take possession of, leased premises is a(n)
   a. reversionary interest.
   b. equitable title interest.
   c. leasehold interest.
   d. freehold estate.

3. A ground lease is usually
   a. short term.
   b. for 100 years or longer.
   c. long term.
   d. a gross lease.

4. A percentage lease is a lease that provides for
   a. rental of a percentage of a building's value.
   b. definite periodic rent not exceeding a stated percentage.
   c. definite monthly rent plus a percentage of the tenant's gross or net receipts in excess of a certain amount.
   d. a graduated amount due monthly and not exceeding a stated percentage.

5. If a store building collapsed because of conscious landlord neglect and the tenants moved out,
   a. the tenants would be liable for the rent until the expiration date of their leases.
   b. the landlord would not be responsible for any refund of rent.
   c. this would be an actual eviction.
   d. this would be a constructive eviction.

6. Which describes a net lease?
   a. An agreement in which the tenant pays a fixed rent and the landlord pays all taxes, insurance, and related expenses on the property
   b. A lease in which the tenant pays rent plus maintenance and property charges
   c. A lease in which the tenant pays the landlord a percentage of the monthly income derived from the property
   d. An agreement granting an individual a leasehold interest in fishing rights for shoreline properties

7. A lease for more than one year must be in writing to be enforceable because
   a. the landlord or tenant may forget the terms.
   b. the tenant must sign the agreement to pay rent.
   c. the statute of frauds requires it.
   d. it is the customary procedure to protect the tenant.

8. A lease calls for a minimum rent of $1,200 per month plus 4% of the annual gross business over $150,000. If the total rent paid at the end of the year was $19,200, how much business did the tenant do during the year?
   a. $159,800
   b. $250,200
   c. $270,000
   d. $279,200

9. Pablo occupies a building under a written lease for a five-year term with monthly rental payments. The lease expired last month, but Pablo has remained in possession and the landlord has accepted his most recent rent payment without comment. At this point,
   a. Pablo's lease has been renewed for one year.
   b. Pablo's lease has been renewed for another five years.
   c. Pablo's lease has been renewed for one-half the original lease period—2½ years.
   d. there is no extension of the lease.

10. The leasehold interest that automatically renews itself at each expiration is the tenancy
    a. for years.
    b. from period to period.
    c. at will.
    d. at sufferance.

11. Which term refers to a tenant's legal right to occupy leased property against the ownership claims of third parties?
    a. Tenancy at will
    b. Cognovit
    c. Covenant of quiet possession
    d. Constructive eviction

12. A tenant's lease has expired, the tenant has neither vacated nor negotiated a renewal lease, and the landlord has declared that she does not want the tenant to remain in the building. The form of possession is called a(n)
    a. estate for years.
    b. periodic estate.
    c. tenancy at will.
    d. tenancy at sufferance.

13. The requirements of a valid lease include all *EXCEPT* which of the following?
    a. Offer and acceptance
    b. Valuable consideration
    c. Capacity to contract
    d. Recordation in county clerk's office

14. If no special provision is included in the lease regarding permanent improvements made by a tenant, such improvements
    a. are fixtures.
    b. remain the property of the tenant after the lease expires.
    c. are adaptations of space to suit tenants' needs.
    d. are reimbursed to the tenant by the landlord.

15. Adams leased space in her new shopping center to Baker for his dress store. However, Baker's business fails and Baker sublets the space to Davis. If Davis fails to make rental payments when due,
    a. Adams would have recourse against Baker only.
    b. Adams would have recourse against Davis only.
    c. Adams would have recourse against both Baker and Davis.
    d. Davis would have recourse against Baker.

16. In June, Sharisse signed a TAR lease for one year and moved into an apartment. She deposited the required security deposit with the landlord. Six months later, she paid the January rent and mysteriously moved out. Sharisse did not arrange for a sublease or an assignment and made no further rent payments. She left the apartment in good condition. What is Sharisse's liability to the landlord under these circumstances?
    a. Because half the rental amount has been paid and the apartment is in good condition, she has no further liability.
    b. She is liable for one month's additional rent only.
    c. She is liable for the balance of the rent only.
    d. She is liable for the balance of the rent plus forfeiture of the security deposit.

Detailed rationales for the end-of-chapter review questions are available online at www.dearborn.com through the *Instructor Resource Guides* link.

CHAPTER 22

Property Management

■ **LEARNING OBJECTIVES** *When you have completed this chapter, you will be able to*

- **describe** a property manager's functions and the basic elements of a management agreement;
- **explain** the property manager's role in budgeting, renting, and maintaining property;
- **identify** techniques a manager may use to attract, select, and retain quality tenants; the characteristics of an effective rental collection policy; and a property manager's responsibilities regarding compliance with consumer protection and privacy laws;
- **distinguish** the property manager's responsibilities for handling environmental and risk management concerns; and
- **define** the following *key terms:*

business interruption insurance	liability insurance	risk management
casualty insurance	management agreement	surety bond
depreciated cost	multiperil policies	workers' compensation insurance
fire and extended coverage insurance	property manager	
	replacement cost	

OVERVIEW

A real estate owner who rents out the upstairs apartment in the building where she resides generally has no problem with property management—setting and collecting rents, maintenance, and repairs are easy enough with only one tenant. But the owners of large, multiunit developments often lack the time and/or expertise to manage their properties successfully. Enter the *property manager*, a real estate professional hired to maintain the property and ensure profitability of the owner's investment.

This chapter examines the growing property management profession and includes discussions of the types of property insurance available to further protect an owner's real estate investment.

PROPERTY MANAGEMENT

Property management involves leasing, managing, marketing, and overall maintenance of real estate owned by others. The increased size of buildings; the technical complexities of construction, maintenance, and repair; and the trend toward absentee ownership by individual investors and investment groups have led to the expanded use of professional property managers for both residential and commercial properties. In fact, many lenders *require* that investors hire professional property management firms. Property management has become so important that many brokerage firms maintain separate management departments staffed by carefully selected, well-trained people. Some corporate and institutional owners of real estate also have established property management departments. A real estate license is required when a person, for a fee, rents or leases or procures tenants for a property or controls the acceptance or deposit of rent from a resident of a single-family residence (S.B. 747, 2011). An exception to the licensing requirement exists for an onsite apartment manager or an owner or owner's employee (not an agent) who leases the owner's real estate.

IN PRACTICE   The Enforcement Division of TREC has the following statement in a list of FAQs on the TREC website:

> Collecting rent and seeing to the upkeep of the property do not typically require a real estate license. If the duties include showing or leasing the property for the owner for which the manager gets paid, a license would be required. See Rule 535.4. Also, a license is required for any person who controls the acceptance or deposit of rent from a resident of a single-family residential real property unit.

As indicated, S.B. 747 (2011) now requires a license of one who controls the collection or deposit of rent for a single-family residence. Under TREC Rule 535.4(g), a person controls the acceptance or deposit of rent if the person is authorized to use the rent to pay for services related to management of the property, or the person is authorized to deposit the rent into a bank account and either sign checks or withdraw money from the account.

Responsibility of Brokers for Property Management Activities   A broker is responsible for any property management activity and for all advertising conducted by sponsored salespersons (TREC Rule 535.2).

The Property Manager

A **property manager** is someone who *preserves the value of an investment property while generating income for the owners*. More specifically, a property manager is expected to merchandise the property and control operating expenses to maximize income. In addition, a manager should maintain and modernize the property to preserve and enhance the owner's capital investment. The three areas of activities performed by the property manager can be summarized as administration, marketing, and physical management. The manager carries out these duties by

1. securing and retaining suitable tenants,
2. collecting the rents,
3. caring for the premises,
4. budgeting and controlling expenses,
5. hiring and supervising employees, and
6. keeping proper accounts and making periodic reports to the owner.

Securing Management Business

In today's market, property managers may look to corporate owners, apartments and condominiums, investment syndicates, trusts, and absentee owners as possible sources of management business. In securing business from any of these sources, word of mouth is often the best advertising. A manager who consistently demonstrates an ability to increase property income over previous levels should have no difficulty finding new business.

Before contracting to manage any property, the professional property manager should be certain that the building owner has realistic income expectations and is willing to spend money on necessary maintenance. Attempting to meet impossible owner demands by dubious methods can endanger the manager's reputation and prove detrimental to obtaining future business.

The Management Agreement

The first step in taking over the management of any property is to enter into a **management agreement** with the owner. It may take one of two forms: (1) an agency contract in which operational liabilities are shared between the owner and the property manager working as a general agent or (2) an independent contractor agreement in which almost all the operational liabilities are borne by the independent contractor management company. The property manager is charged with the same basic fiduciary duties as the listing broker—care, obedience, accounting, loyalty, and disclosure (see Chapter 5 for a review of agency responsibilities). By law, a license holder who has the authority to bind a party to a lease under a power of attorney or a property management agreement is a party to the lease.

The management agreement should be in writing and cover the following eight points:
■ *Description* of the property.
■ *Time period* the agreement will cover.
■ *Definition of management's responsibilities*—All of the manager's duties should be stated in the contract; exceptions should be noted.
■ *Statement of owner's goals*—This statement should indicate what the owner desires the manager to accomplish with the property. One owner may wish to maximize net income and there instruct the manager to cut expenses and

minimize investment. Another owner may want to increase the capital value of the investment, in which case the manager should initiate a program for improving the property's physical condition.

- *Extent of manager's authority*—This provision should state what authority the manager is to have in such matters as hiring, firing, and supervising employees; fixing rental rates for space; making expenditures; and authorizing repairs within the limits established previously with the owner. Repairs that exceed a certain expense limit may require the owner's written approval.
- *Reporting*—Agreement should be reached on the frequency and detail of the manager's periodic reports on operations and financial position. These reports serve as a means for the owner to monitor the manager's work and as a basis for both the owner and the manager to assess trends that can be used in shaping future management policy.
- *Management fee*—The fee can be based on a percentage of gross or net income, a commission on new rentals, a fixed fee, or a combination of these.
- *Allocation of costs*—The agreement should state which of the property manager's expenses, such as office rent, office help, telephone, advertising, association fees, and Social Security, will be paid by the manager and which will be charged to the property's expenses and paid by the owner.

> Management fees must be negotiated between the owner and the property manager. Standardization of rates would be viewed as price-fixing.

After entering into an agreement with a property owner, a manager must handle the property as if it were his own. In all activities, the manager must be aware that her responsibility is to *realize the highest return on the property that is consistent with the owner's instructions.* Most offsite property managers work as independent contractors.

MANAGEMENT CONSIDERATIONS

A property manager must protect the interest of the property owner by constantly
- improving the reputation as well as the physical condition of the property,
- guarding the owner from insurable losses,
- helping the neighborhood and the community by offering the best possible residential and business environments,
- keeping a check on all expenditures to ensure that costs are kept as low as possible for the results that must be accomplished, and
- adjusting the rental rate as necessary to produce the highest total income.

A property manager must live up to his end of the management agreement in both the letter and the spirit of the contract. The owner must be kept well informed on all matters of policy, as well as on the financial condition of the property and its operation. Finally, a manager must keep in contact with others in the field, improving his knowledge of the subject and staying informed on current policies pertaining to the profession.

Budgeting Expenses

Because the primary focus in property management is the *bottom line*, a property manager should develop an operating budget before attempting to rent any property. The operating budget is based on anticipated revenues and expenses and must reflect the long-term goals of the owner. In preparing a budget, a manager should begin by allocating money for such continuous, fixed expenses as employees' salaries, real estate taxes, property taxes, and insurance premiums.

Next, the manager should establish a cash reserve fund for such variable expenses as repairs, decorating, and supplies. The amount allocated for the reserve funds can be computed from previous yearly costs of the variable expenses.

Capital Expenditures   If an owner and a property manager decide that modernization or renovation of the property will enhance its value, the manager should budget money to cover the costs of remodeling. In the case of large-scale construction, the expenses charged against the property's income should be spread over several years. Although budgets should be as accurate an estimate of cost as possible, adjustments sometimes may be necessary, especially in the case of new properties. Generally, a year-end income statement, such as the one shown in Figure 22.1, would be used as a base for budgeting expenses for the upcoming year.

Renting the Property

Effective rental of the property is essential to the success of a property manager. However, the role of the manager should not be confused with that of a broker or rental agency concerned solely with renting space. The property manager may use the services of a rental agency to solicit prospective tenants or collect rents, but the rental agency does not undertake the full responsibility of maintenance and management of the property.

Setting Rental Rates   In establishing rental rates for a property, a basic concern must be that, in the long term, the income from the rentable space covers the fixed charges and operating expenses and also provides a fair return on the investment. However, consideration also must be given to the prevailing rates in comparable buildings and the current level of vacancy in the property to be rented. In the short term, rental rates are primarily a result of supply and demand. Decisions about rental rates should start with a detailed survey of the competitive space available in the neighborhood. Prices should be noted, and judgment should be applied to adjust for differences between neighboring properties and the property the manager is renting.

Apartment rental rates are stated in monthly amounts on a unit basis. However, office and commercial space rentals are usually stated according to either the annual or the monthly rate per square foot of space.

If a high vacancy level exists, an immediate effort should be made to determine what is wrong with the property or what is out of line in the rental rates. *A high level of vacancy does not necessarily indicate that rents are too high.* The trouble may be inept management or defects in the property. The manager should attempt to identify and correct the problems rather than lower the rent. Conversely, *although a high percentage of occupancy may appear to indicate an effective rental program, it also could mean that rental rates are too low.* Anytime the occupancy level exceeds 95%, serious consideration should be given to raising the rents in an apartment house or office building—but only after conducting a survey of the competitive space available in the neighborhood.

FIGURE 22.1: Income Statement (Accrual) ABC Apartments, Dec. 31

Revenue	Year to Date
Cash Income	
Gross potential rent	458,000
Less: vacancy loss	(22,517)
Laundry income	3,000
Miscellaneous charges income	12,500
Total property revenue	*450,983*
Expenses	
Payroll expense	
Manager	24,000
Maintenance	28,000
Payroll burden	14,581
Total payroll expense	*66,581*
Contract services	
Extermination	1,351
Landscape services	5,881
Contract labor	989
Total contract services	*8,221*
Repairs & maintenance	
Heating, a/c & appliance R&M	6,742
Plumbing	2,414
Electrical R&M	1,971
Building	4,690
Grounds, pools	1,732
Interior renovation	4,832
Total repair-maintenance	*22,381*
Utilities	
Electricity	6,317
Gas	3,900
Water/rubbish/sewer	35,738
Total utilities	*45,955*
Property admin. & advertising	
Advertising, telephone, pagers	2,639
Office supplies, postage, bank chgs, dues, computer	3,318
Property management fees	22,549
Total property administration	*28,506*
Taxes and insurance	
Real estate taxes/franchise taxes	31,583
Property insurance	13,231
Total taxes & insurance	44,814
Total operating expenses	*216,458*
Net operating income	*234,525*
Debt services	
Mortgage interest	135,413
Mortgage principal	20,592
Total debt services	*156,005*
Cash flow	*78,520*

Tenant Selection   Generally, the highest rents can be secured from satisfied tenants. A broker may sell a property and then have no further dealings with the purchaser, but a property manager must continue to deal with each tenant, and the manager's success greatly depends on retaining sound, long-term relationships. In selecting prospective commercial or industrial tenants, a manager should be sure that each person will "fit the space." The manager should be certain that

- the *size of the space* meets the tenant's requirements,
- the tenant will have the *ability to pay* for the contracted space,
- the *tenant's business will be compatible* with the building and the other tenants, and
- *expansion space* will be available if the tenant's business is likely to grow.

As discussed in Chapter 21, the residential landlord must provide the applicant with a printed or online notice of the landlord's tenant selection criteria when the landlord gives the applicant an application form. The printed or online notice must include the grounds for which the application may be denied, including the applicant's criminal history, previous rental history, current income, credit history, or failure to provide accurate or complete information on the application form. Then, the applicant must sign an acknowledgment indicating that the notice was made available; online applications should have an online acknowledgment feature. Some of the most common and legitimate reasons for rejecting prospective tenants include the following:

- Unsatisfactory references from landlords, employers, and/or personal references, including a history of late rental payments
- Evictions
- Frequent moves
- Bad credit report or too many debts
- Length of time at current employment too short
- Smokers
- No verifiable source of income or insufficient income
- Too many vehicles for the available parking space
- Current drug users
- Pets
- Conviction of a crime that was a threat to property in the past five years, including manufacture or distribution of a controlled substance

Several Texas cities—among them Bryan, Dallas, Houston, Irving, and Wichita Falls—have instituted city-wide programs to identify apartment communities with high crime rates and to develop crime-reduction programs in conjunction with the landlords of those properties.

The property manager must comply with all federal, state, and local fair housing laws in the selection of tenants—abiding by the Fair Housing Act, which prohibits discrimination based on race, color, religion, sex, handicap, familial status, and national origin. All applicants must be treated equally. For example, a leasing agent or owner cannot reject someone based on a criminal screening if all applicants are not being screened. Because credit bureaus are tightening access to full credit reports unless a business meets rigid document security requirements, the use of a resident screening provider has become common in the small and independent rental owner marketplace of 1-200 units. Online screening providers search such records as eviction, criminal, credit evaluation, address, sex offender, and social security fraud. Then the findings, if any, in each search category are displayed, along with an overall risk rating. Consistency in the administration of policies and procedures and documentation of conversations and actions will help to protect the leasing agent and the property owner from claims of discrimination while creating and maintaining an open housing market.

Several major state and federal laws affect the landlord in marketing to prospective tenants and in verifying rental history and credit information. Identity theft and privacy issues are of particular importance to property managers, as discussed in the following paragraphs.

Fair Credit Reporting Act　The federal Fair Credit Reporting Act, administered by the Consumer Financial Protection Bureau (CFPB), promotes accuracy, fairness, and privacy of information in the files of consumer reporting agencies.

If a property owner or his representative rejects an application for the rental of a property on the basis of information contained in the applicant's credit report, the applicant must be given the name of the credit reporting agency and must be told that she has a right to get a copy of the credit report. The applicant must also be told that the credit agency did not make the decision to reject the applicant. If the rejection was based on an applicant's specific credit score, that score, along with key factors that adversely affected the credit score, must be included in the rejection notice (Dodd-Frank Act, 2010). If a property owner or his representative rejects an applicant based upon information *other than a credit report or credit score*, the owner or the owner's representative must either disclose the reason or tell the applicant that he has the right to submit a request for disclosure of the reason for rejection.

Fair Credit Reporting Act and the Dodd-Frank Act　The Dodd-Frank Act amended the FCRA to require the disclosure of the credit score when an adverse action (such as a decision not to rent to an applicant) is based in whole or in part on a numerical credit score. This new disclosure requirement applies to "credit scores" and not other types of scores, such as those used by many tenant screening companies. If the rejection was based on an applicant's specific credit score, the "adverse action notice" must include specific "credit score disclosures":

- The credit score used by the person making the credit decision
- The range of possible credit scores under the model used to generate the credit score
- The top four key factors that adversely affected the applicant's credit score
- The date on which the credit score was created
- The name of the consumer reporting agency or other person who provided the credit score
- A statement that a credit score is a number that takes into account information in a consumer report and that a credit score can change over time to reflect changes in the consumer's credit history

Fair and Accurate Credit Transactions Act of 2003 (FACTA)　Enacted as an amendment to the Fair Credit Reporting Act, FACTA established standards to improve the quality of consumer credit information and instituted procedures to help protect consumers against identity theft. Two provisions of FACTA are especially relevant to the business of property management:

1. Because landlords often use credit reports as an evaluation tool during the tenant selection process, prospective tenants can check the accuracy of their credit reports and get errors corrected before filling out rental applications. Consumers may obtain one free credit report per year from all three major credit reporting bureaus: Experian, Equifax, and TransUnion. To obtain the free credit report, consumers can log on to www.annualcreditreport.com or call 877-322-8228.

2. A records disposal rule requires that landlords, lenders, and others who obtain consumer reports take reasonable measures to protect against unauthorized access to, or use of, consumer information during record disposal. According to the FTC, proper disposal includes burning, pulverizing, or shredding paper files; destroying or erasing electronic files or media; or hiring a reputable document disposal company. The business owner must ensure that neither paper nor electronic data can be read or reconstructed after disposal. The disposal rule applies to such documents as credit reports, employment verifications, tenant leases, residential history, and medical history.

On January 1, 2011, the FTC began to enforce its "red flags" FACTA rule. The red-flags alert appears on credit reports to identify potential or detected identity theft. The initial fraud alert remains on credit files for 90 days if there is reason to believe that the consumer is or is about to be a victim of identity theft. If there is a valid identity theft report, the alert remains on the report for up to seven years. Red-flags fraud alert policies developed by a landlord should include *reasonable* measures for identifying and detecting red flags and responding appropriately to mitigate identity theft. Rental owners or property managers have to show that they check IDs of applicants, verify IDs, and follow up when they receive an address discrepancy notice from a consumer reporting agency. Under certain circumstances, any subsequent verification of a correct address must be reported back to the consumer reporting agency. If the property manager cannot work out the discrepancy, the rule states that the rental application is to be denied.

FTC Privacy Rule   Whether a property manager is selecting a tenant or giving a reference for a tenant who is moving, it is important to understand the applicability of the FTC privacy rule to a landlord's actions. Under the privacy rule, companies that are significantly engaged in certain financial activities must make specific disclosures to a consumer before passing the consumer's personal information on to unaffiliated third parties. If a property manager is asked to provide a tenant history and rental reference to another property manager, it would be prudent practice to obtain a written statement from the manager that the information provided will not be used for "credit granting" purposes. Before disclosing any information about a tenant to someone other than another rental housing owner or manager, a law enforcement officer, a consumer reporting agency, or a prospective employer of the tenant, the property manager must have written permission from the tenant.

Texas Privacy Laws   Privacy policy and identity theft laws have also been passed by the Texas Legislature. The highlights of those laws are summarized in the following paragraphs.

Privacy Policy   Anyone who requires an individual to provide a Social Security number (SSN) must adopt a privacy policy. For example, if a landlord requires a potential tenant to provide an SSN on a lease application, the landlord must have a written privacy policy, must make it available to the tenant, and must maintain confidentiality and security for SSNs. The policy must include how the information is collected, how and when it is used, how it is protected, who has access to the information, and how the information is disposed of.

Identity Theft Enforcement and Protection Act   Renters are further protected against identity theft by the Identity Theft Enforcement and Protection Act, which requires a business to implement and maintain procedures to protect and safeguard from unlawful use or disclosure any sensitive personal information in its possession. *Sensitive personal information* is defined as a person's first name or initial and last name in combination with one or more identifiers, including an SSN or other government-issued identification number, driver's license number, mother's maiden name, or any financial data. Information that is publicly available, such as address or phone number, is not considered a confidential identifier. Documents containing sensitive personal information must be safeguarded for confidentiality while they are retained by a business. In addition, a business must destroy these records when it no longer needs to retain them—by shredding, electronically erasing, or other means such that the information is unreadable or indecipherable.

U.S. PATRIOT Act   Knowing who is signing a lease is not only a good business practice but also a requirement under the U.S. PATRIOT Act, which was discussed in Chapter 16 in conjunction with mortgage loan reporting requirements. Apartment owners and managers are required to screen against a list of specially designated nationals and blocked persons—people identified with targeted foreign countries, terrorists, and international narcotics traffickers, and those engaged in activities related to the proliferation of weapons of mass destruction. To verify the identity of persons who do not have an SSN but are in the United States legally, the National Apartment Association lists acceptable forms of ID, including Form I-551, Permanent Resident Card or "Green Card"; Form I-688, Temporary Resident Card; Form I-688A, Employment Authorization Card; and Form I-94, Arrival-Departure Record. The Individual Taxpayer Identification Number (ITIN) and the Matricula Consular cards (Mexican ID cards) are not considered acceptable forms of ID because neither requires verification of the declared identifier information. Matricula Consular cards are accepted by some states to issue a driver's license, but a driver's license alone is also not an acceptable form of ID. Although apartment owners and managers must carefully comply with all fair housing laws, HUD has stated that asking applicants to provide documentation of their citizenship or immigration status during the resident screening process does not violate the Fair Housing Act. The list of specially designated nationals and blocked persons can be obtained at www.treas.gov/offices/enforcement/ofac/sdn.

The FTC has proposed rules and Congress has introduced privacy bills that will limit how online advertisers use behavioral tracking systems.

Telemarketing   If an apartment community decides to launch a telemarketing campaign to solicit new tenants, several laws will apply: federal and state no-call lists, the Junk Fax Prevention Act, and the CAN-SPAM Act, among them. As discussed in Chapter 13, no-call lists permit telephone number registry, prohibiting unsolicited telemarketing *phone calls*. The Junk Fax Prevention Act restricts individuals, businesses, and organizations from sending unsolicited *fax* advertisements. Similarly, the CAN-SPAM Act and the Texas anti-spam statute prohibit unsolicited commercial *email messages*. See Chapter 13 for more details about these laws.

Collecting Rents

A rental property operation will not be profitable unless the property manager can collect all rents when they are due. Any substantial loss resulting from nonpayment of rent will quickly eliminate the margin of profitability.

The best way to minimize problems with rent collection is to make a *careful selection* of tenants in the first place. A property manager's desire to have a high level of occupancy should not override good judgment in accepting only those tenants who can be expected to meet their financial obligations to the property owner. The terms of rental payment should be spelled out in detail in the lease agreement. These details include the time and place of payment, provisions and penalties for late payment, and provisions for cancellation and damages in case of nonpayment. A *firm and consistent collection plan* with a sufficient system of notices and records should be established by the property manager. A property manager who accepts a late payment without charging late fees specified in the contract or reminding the tenant making a late payment that the payment must always be paid on time risks (through "waiver" or "lease modification") losing the legal right to later enforce the charging of late fees or to evict for a late payment.

In cases of delinquency, every attempt must be made to make collections without resorting to legal action. However, for those cases in which it is required, a property manager must be prepared to initiate and follow through with the necessary steps to begin eviction or other appropriate proceedings in conjunction with the property owner's or management firm's legal counsel.

Resident Retention

Studies show that each tenant move-out costs an apartment community between $3,000 and $6,000, a cost that may take 10 or more years to recoup. Additionally, more than 60% of residential tenant turnover is estimated to be controllable. Therefore, it makes more dollars-and-cents sense to keep good residents who are already paying rent than to go after new ones. To retain tenants,

- follow up on move-in experiences because the renewal decision-making process begins at that time;
- communicate, especially regarding service needs and maintenance updates, and follow up on completed work orders;
- deliver a memorable recovery when bad experiences occur;
- provide online communication with the rental staff or property owner; and
- return resident calls and emails immediately.

Increasing resident retention is a key component to controlling revenues and expenses and improving the owner's bottom line.

Maintaining the Property

Maintenance expenses are one of the largest expense categories on a property.

To enable tenants to report property habitability emergencies, all landlords must provide tenants with a telephone number that will be answered 24 hours a day. Residents should be instructed to call 911 for police, fire, and medical emergencies.

However, if maintenance is approached as a process for increasing resident retention, a property manager can maximize income while controlling operating expenses. To maintain the property efficiently, the manager must be able to assess the building's needs and how best to meet them. Because staffing and scheduling requirements vary with the type, size, and geographic location of the property, the owner and manager usually agree in advance on maintenance objectives. In some cases, the best plan may be to operate a low-rental property, with minimal expenditures for services and maintenance. Another property may be more lucrative if kept in top condition and operated with all possible tenant services. A well-maintained, high service property can command premium rental rates.

A primary maintenance objective is to *protect the physical integrity of the property over the long term*. For example, preserving the property by repainting the exterior or replacing the heating system helps decrease long-term maintenance costs. Keeping the property in good condition involves the following four types of maintenance:

- Preventive
- Repair or corrective
- Routine
- Construction

Preventive maintenance includes regularly scheduled activities such as painting and seasonal servicing of appliances and systems. Preventive maintenance preserves the long-range value of the property by warding off future repairs. This is both the most critical and the most neglected maintenance responsibility. Failure to perform preventive maintenance invariably leads to greater expense in other areas of maintenance.

Corrective maintenance involves the actual repair of the building's equipment, utilities, and amenities. Repairing a boiler, fixing a leaky faucet, and mending a broken air-conditioning unit are acts of corrective maintenance.

A property manager also must supervise the *routine maintenance* of the building. Routine maintenance includes such day-to-day duties as cleaning common areas, performing minor carpentry, and providing regularly scheduled upkeep of heating, air-conditioning, and landscaping. Good routine maintenance is similar to good preventive maintenance. Both head off problems before they become expensive.

A commercial or an industrial property manager often is called on to make *tenant improvements*. These are *construction alterations* to the interior of the building to meet a tenant's particular space needs. Such alterations range from simply repainting or recarpeting to completely gutting the interior and redesigning the space by erecting new walls, partitions, and electrical systems. Tenant improvements are especially important when renting new buildings. In new construction, the interiors are usually left incomplete so they can be adapted to the needs of individual tenants. One matter that must be clarified when the lease is negotiated is which improvements will be considered trade fixtures (personal property belonging to the tenant) and which will belong to the owner of the real estate. Trade fixtures were discussed in Chapter 2.

Renovation or modernization of buildings that have become physically or functionally obsolete and thus unsuited to new tenants' needs is also important. (See Chapter 14 for a discussion of obsolescence.) The renovation of a building generally enhances the building's marketability and increases its potential income.

> Onsite employees are not liable for code or ordinance violations on the property as long as they provide the owner's contact information within five business days after a citation is issued.

IN PRACTICE One of the major decisions a property manager faces is whether to contract for maintenance services from an outside firm or hire onsite employees to perform such tasks. The property manager will make the decision on what is most cost-effective for the owner. This decision should be based on a number of factors, including the

- size of the building,
- complexity of the tenants' requirements,
- time and expense involved, and
- availability of suitable labor.

Handling Environmental Concerns

The property manager must be able to respond to a variety of environmental problems. Tenant concerns, as well as federal, state, and local regulations, determine the extent of the manager's environmental responsibilities. The manager may manage structures containing asbestos or radon or be called on to arrange an environmental audit of a property. Managers must see that any hazardous wastes produced by their employees or tenants are disposed of properly. Even the normally nonhazardous waste of an office building must be controlled to avoid violation of laws requiring segregation and recycling of types of waste.

Two environmental issues are of particular concern to the property manager: (1) the Occupational Safety and Health Administration (OSHA) asbestos regulations and (2) mold prevention and remediation. Property owners or managers must determine where asbestos is present (it is presumed to be contained in most structures built before 1981) and either abate the asbestos or develop operation and maintenance procedures for working in areas that might contain asbestos. Educating employees and all residents is the biggest weapon a property manager has in the war against mold. An information sheet on mold prevention and cleaning should be attached to every lease and every lease renewal at the time of signing. Prevention policies should stress the need for residents to keep their rental dwellings clean and to promptly report any signs of leaks or water accumulation. These environmental issues and others are discussed in detail in Chapter 24.

Managing Risks

Because enormous monetary losses can result from certain occurrences, one of the most critical areas of responsibility for a property manager is to protect the property owner against all major insurable risks. Awareness of the purposes of insurance coverage and how to make best use of the many types of insurance available is part of what is called **risk management**.

> The four alternative risk management techniques may be remembered by the acronym **ACTOR**: **A**void, **C**ontrol, **T**ransfer, or **R**etain

Risk management involves answering the question, "What will happen if something goes wrong?" The perils of any risk must be evaluated in terms of options. When considering the possibility of a loss, the property manager and owner must decide whether it is better to

- *avoid it*, by removing the source of risk, such as a swimming pool;
- *control it*, by installing sprinklers, fire doors, and other preventive measures;
- *transfer it*, by taking out an insurance policy—perhaps even *share it*, by insuring with a large deductible; or
- *retain it*, by deciding that the chances of the event's occurring are too small to justify the expense of any other response.

When insurance is considered, a competent, reliable insurance agent who is well-versed in all areas of insurance pertaining to property should be selected to survey the property and make recommendations. If the manager is not completely satisfied with these recommendations, additional insurance surveys should be obtained. The property owner, however, must make the final decision.

IN PRACTICE   There is a growing trend for property owners or managers to require tenants to obtain renters insurance as a means for *transferring* the risk *and sharing it* with the renter. Renters insurance may significantly reduce out-of-pocket expenses to the owner because it may cover the costs for fixing damages caused by a resident's negligence and/or cover the cost of the owner's deductible.

In addition, proactive communication is useful for *controlling* the risk. Residents and employees of all properties should be educated about the proper use of all equipment on the property and should know the procedures for avoiding potential dangers by properly maintaining the property and promptly reporting any issues, such as a water leak.

Commercial real estate leases often include indemnification provisions; the tenant substitutes its liability for the landlord's liability. A landlord's liability for personal injury or property damage is related to the degree of possession and control held by the landlord. In an individual retail space in a shopping center or in a tenant's premises in an office building, a landlord has no possession or control and would not usually have liability for injury or damage. Therefore, it is appropriate for the tenant to indemnify the landlord for injury or damage occurring in or on its premises.

Types of Coverage   To manage the risks, many kinds of insurance coverage are available to owners and managers of income property. Seven of the more common types are listed in the following:

- **Fire and extended coverage insurance**: Fire insurance policies provide coverage against direct loss or damage to property from a fire on the premises. Extended coverage provides insurance to cover hazards such as windstorm, hurricanes, hail, explosion, riot, civil commotion, smoke, aircraft, and land vehicles.
- **Business interruption insurance**: Most hazard policies insure against the actual loss of property but do not cover loss of revenues from income property. Interruption insurance, or rent-loss insurance, covers the loss of income that occurs if the property cannot be used to produce income.
- **Liability insurance**: Public liability insurance covers the risks an owner assumes when the public enters the building. Claims are used to pay medical expenses for a person injured in the building as a result of the landlord's negligence.
- **Workers' compensation insurance**: To provide medical care and a portion of lost wages to employees who have a work-related illness or are injured at work and to protect employers from lawsuits resulting from workplace accidents, most employers carry worker's compensation insurance. Although Texas law does not require an employer to carry workers' compensation insurance, complex legal issues that arise in the event of a workplace injury make it virtually mandatory in practice. *Occupational and disability insurance* is an alternative coverage for employers who choose not to carry workers' compensation insurance.
- **Casualty insurance**: Casualty insurance policies include coverage against theft, burglary, vandalism, and machinery damage. Casualty policies usually are written on specific risks, such as theft, rather than being all inclusive.
- **Surety bonds**: Surety bonds cover an owner against financial losses resulting from employees' criminal acts or negligence while carrying out their duties.
- **Flood and hurricane insurance**: Under certain circumstances, federal law *requires* property owners to obtain flood insurance if a "structure" on the property is located in a floodplain area. Flood insurance policies can be written by any licensed property insurance carrier. Hurricane, or windstorm, insurance can be purchased in Texas coastal counties to cover perils, such as

wind and hail, that are not included in other coastal property policies. For more information about flood and windstorm policies, refer to Chapter 4.

Many insurance companies offer **multiperil policies** for apartment and business buildings. These policies offer the property manager an insurance package that includes such standard types of commercial coverage as fire, hazard, public liability, and casualty. A thorough risk analysis may also indicate the need for specialty insurance coverage such as

- errors and omissions to protect against negligence and innocent mistakes and errors;
- lead liability to protect against accidental contamination;
- employment practices liability for libel, slander, failure to promote, sexual harassment, or wrongful discharge;
- liquor liability for residence-sponsored events or for complexes with onsite bars or restaurants;
- employee benefits liability in the event that an employee's insurance or pension benefits are not kept active;
- onsite pollution liability should chemicals accidentally be disposed of inappropriately;
- tenant discrimination legal expense reimbursement should a resident sue for discrimination; or
- terrorism insurance for catastrophic losses arising from certain terrorism-related events.

Claims When a claim is made under a policy insuring a building or another physical object, there are two possible methods of determining the amount of the claim. One is the **depreciated cost**, or actual cash value of the damaged property, and the other is **replacement cost**. If a 30-year-old building is damaged, the timbers and materials are 30 years old and therefore do not have the same value as new material. Thus, in determining the amount of the loss under what is called *actual cash value*, the cost of new material would be reduced by the estimated depreciation the item had suffered during the time it was in the building.

The alternate method is to cover *replacement cost*. This represents the actual amount a builder would charge to replace the damaged property, including materials, at the time of the loss.

When purchasing insurance, the property owner or the manager must assess whether the property should be insured at full replacement cost or at a depreciated cost. As with the homeowners policies discussed in Chapter 4, commercial policies include *coinsurance clauses* that require the insured to carry fire coverage, usually in an amount equal to 80% of the building's replacement value.

IN PRACTICE Often a property owner pays for small casualty losses out of pocket to avoid rate increases or cancellation of a policy. However, the IRS does not allow the total repair expense to be deducted on an income tax return if the taxpayer voluntarily elected not to claim reimbursement from the insurance company. Because the IRS allows a property owner to deduct losses suffered only up to the deductible portion of the insurance policy, some owners/managers might consider obtaining policies with a higher deductible, which also should result in a lower insurance premium.

Disaster Reporting   The Real Estate Information Sharing and Analysis Center (Real Estate ISAC) was launched after 9/11 as a public-private partnership between the U.S. real estate industry and federal homeland security officials. The partnership facilitates information sharing on terrorist threats, warnings, and incidents; earthquakes; floods; power outages; and other disasters. High-urgency alerts are emailed to building owners and operators as requested by the government. The "Report Incidents" page of the Real Estate ISAC website contains information on the types of incidents that should be reported to local officials, local FBI authorities, and homeland security.

WEBLINK @ www.reisac.org/report.html

THE MANAGEMENT PROFESSION

Most large cities have local associations of building and property owners and managers that are affiliates of regional and national associations. The Institute of Real Estate Management is one of the affiliates of the National Association of REALTORS®. It awards the designations of *Certified Property Manager* (CPM) and *Accredited Residential Manager* (ARM) to persons who have met certain requirements. The Building Owners and Managers Association International (BOMA International) is a federation of local associations of owners and managers, primarily of office buildings. The Building Owners and Managers Institute (BOMI) International, an independent institute affiliated with BOMA, offers training courses leading to several designations: *Real Property Administrator* (RPA), *Systems Maintenance Administrator* (SMA), and *Facilities Management Administrator* (FMA). The International Council of Shopping Centers is the global trade association of the shopping center industry. The National Apartment Association has designations of Certified Apartment Manager (CAM) and Certified Apartment Property Supervisor (CAPS). Also degrees in residential property management are available at a few Texas colleges and universities.

Within Texas, the Texas Apartment Association (TAA) has more than 10,500 members, who manage more than 1.75 million rental housing units statewide. Participation in groups like these allows property managers to use association-prepared lease forms, to gain valuable professional knowledge, and to discuss their problems with other managers facing similar issues. For the latest information on issues affecting property managers in Texas, visit the TAA website.

WEBLINK @ www.taa.org

SUMMARY

Property management is a specialized service to owners of income-producing properties in which the managerial function may be delegated to an individual or a firm with particular expertise in the field. The manager, as agent of the owner, becomes the administrator of the project and assumes the executive functions required for the care and operation of the property. The three areas of activities for the property manager are administration, marketing, and physical management.

A management agreement defines and authorizes the manager's duties and responsibilities. Additionally, it establishes the relationship between owner and manager.

After the management agreement is signed, the first step a property manager should take is to draw up a budget of estimated variable and fixed expenses. The budget also should allow for any proposed expenditure for major renovation or modernization agreed on by the manager and the owner. These projected expenses, combined with the manager's analysis of the condition of the building and the rent patterns in the neighborhood, will form the basis on which rental rates are determined.

After a rent schedule is established, the property manager is responsible for soliciting tenants whose needs are suited to the available space and who are financially capable of meeting the proposed rents. The manager generally is obligated to collect rents, maintain the building, hire necessary employees, pay taxes for the building, and deal with tenant problems.

Once the property is rented, one of the manager's primary responsibilities is supervising its maintenance. Maintenance includes safeguarding the physical integrity of the property and performing routine cleaning and repairs, as well as adapting the interior space and overall design of the property to suit the tenants' needs and meet the demands of the market.

In addition, the manager is expected to protect the owner's interests through effective risk management by securing adequate insurance coverage for the premises. The basic types of coverage applicable to commercial structures include fire and extended coverage insurance on the property and fixtures; business interruption, or rent-loss, insurance to protect the owner against income losses; and casualty insurance to provide coverage against such losses as theft, vandalism, and destruction of equipment. The manager also should secure public liability insurance to insure the owner against claims made by people injured on the premises and workers' compensation policies to cover the claims of employees injured on the job.

The Texas property manager must be a licensed real estate broker, unless exempt by the provisions of the Texas Real Estate License Act; exemptions exist for an onsite apartment manager and for an owner or owner's employee who leases the owner's real estate.

CHAPTER 22 QUESTIONS

1. Which type of insurance coverage insures the property owner against the claims of employees injured while on the job?
   a. Business interruption
   b. Workers' compensation
   c. Casualty
   d. Surety bond

2. Repairing a boiler is classified as which type of maintenance?
   a. Preventive
   b. Corrective
   c. Routine
   d. Construction

3. From a management point of view, apartment building occupancy that reaches as high as 98% might indicate that
   a. the building is poorly managed.
   b. the building may need repairs.
   c. rents should be lowered.
   d. rents should be raised.

4. A deliveryman slips on a defective stair in an apartment building and is hospitalized. A claim against the building owner for medical expenses will be made under which of the following policies held by the owner?
   a. Workers' compensation
   b. Casualty
   c. Liability
   d. Fire and hazard coverage

5. Which should NOT be a consideration in selecting a tenant?
   a. The size of the space versus the tenant's requirements
   b. The tenant's ability to pay
   c. The racial and ethnic background of the tenant
   d. The compatibility of the tenant's business with other tenants' businesses

6. Contaminated groundwater, toxic fumes from paint and carpeting, and lack of proper ventilation are all examples of
   a. issues beyond the scope of a property manager's job description.
   b. problems faced only on newly constructed properties.
   c. issues that arise under the ADA.
   d. environmental concerns that a property manager may have to address.

7. An owner-manager agreement should include all of the following EXCEPT
   a. a statement of the owner's purpose for the building.
   b. a clear definition of the manager's authority
   c. that portion of the property manager's personal operating expenses that will be paid by the owner.
   d. a listing of previous owners of the property.

8. An apartment building burns to the ground. What type of insurance covers the landlord against the resulting loss of rent?
   a. Fire and hazard
   b. Liability
   c. Business interruption
   d. Casualty

9. Apartment rental rates are usually expressed
   a. in monthly amounts.
   b. on a per-room basis.
   c. in square feet per month.
   d. on a prorated yearly basis.

10. Rents should be determined by
    a. supply and demand factors.
    b. the local apartment owners' association.
    c. HUD.
    d. a tenants' union.

11. Property manager Freida hires Albert as the full-time janitor for one of the buildings she manages. While repairing a faucet in one of the apartments, Albert steals a television set. Freida could protect the owner against liability for this type of loss by purchasing
    a. liability insurance.
    b. workers' compensation insurance.
    c. a surety bond.
    d. casualty insurance.

12. A property manager is offered a choice of three insurance policies: one has a $500 deductible, one has a $1,000 deductible, and the third has a $5,000 deductible. If the property manager selects the policy with the highest deductible, which risk management technique is he using?
    a. Avoiding
    b. Sharing
    c. Controlling
    d. Transferring

13. The manager's responsibility for the maintenance of a property includes all of the following EXCEPT
    a. adapting the interior space of the building to meet the requirements of individual tenants.
    b. renovating buildings.
    c. maintaining the present condition of the building and grounds.
    d. meeting the needs of tenants regardless of the expense to the owner.

14. If a property owner rejects an application for the rental of a property,
    a. the applicant must be told that the credit reporting agency did not make the decision to reject the applicant.
    b. the applicant must be told that the credit report is confidential and, therefore, the reasons for rejection cannot be disclosed to the applicant.
    c. the property owner may refuse to give the reason for the rejection if it was based on something *other than* the credit report.
    d. the property owner is not required to provide the name of the credit reporting agency used if the rejection was based on a credit report.

15. A property manager who enters into a management agreement as an agent to an owner is usually a
    a. special agent.
    b. general agent.
    c. universal agent.
    d. designated agent.

16. In preparing a budget, a property manager should set up which of the following for variable expenses?
    a. Control account
    b. Floating allocation
    c. Cash reserve fund
    d. Asset account

Detailed rationales for the end-of-chapter review questions are available online at www.dearborn.com through the *Instructor Resource Guides* link.

CHAPTER 23

Real Estate—A Business of Many Specializations

LEARNING OBJECTIVES   *When you have completed this chapter you will be able to*

- **identify** the various practice areas available in real estate;
- **describe** the ways a salesperson becomes competent to practice in a particular area;
- **explain** a salesperson's scope of practice;
- **list** the various real estate related disciplines; and
- **define** the following *key terms*:

appraisal	financing	residential broker
auctioneer	petroleum landman	real estate counselor
commercial broker	property development	real estate inspector
farm and ranch or land sales broker	property management	residential rental locator

REAL ESTATE—A BUSINESS OF MANY SPECIALIZATIONS

As introduced in Chapter 1, the real estate business is complex and involves a variety of disciplines. In addition to the different specializations or practice areas in real estate brokerage, such as residential, commercial, leasing, and farm and ranch, there are many real estate–related disciplines, including appraising, property management, financing, property inspection, and property development. A real estate licensee will regularly interact with and, therefore, must have knowledge of these interrelated disciplines in order to succeed in the industry. This chapter provides a description of the various real estate–related disciplines and real estate brokerage specializations. In addition, the issue of competency is addressed.

Brokerage

As Chapter 1 explained, the business of bringing together a buyer and a seller who are interested in making a real estate transaction is *brokerage*. Typically, the broker acts as an *agent* of the buyer or the seller (or both) in negotiating the sale, purchase, or rental of property. A salesperson is a licensee who is employed by or associated with a broker and who conducts brokerage activities on behalf of the broker for a fee or commission. Brokerage is discussed in detail in Chapter 5.

Competency

In Texas, prelicense education requirements for a salesperson's license gives the student a well-rounded foundational understanding of real estate with such course requirements as principles, agency, contracts, promulgated contract forms, and finance. While students may take other core or specialization courses before taking the licensing examination, such courses are not required to get a salesperson license. Texas law does not require a specialized designation or coursework to engage in specific practice areas, such as commercial real estate or property management, but the law and rules require that an agent be competent to perform any real estate brokerage activities that require a license. In addition, professional organizations such as the National Association of REALTORS® offer professional designations to brokers and salespersons who complete educational programs in various specialized practice areas. Chapter 1 provides a more detailed explanation of these specialty designation programs.

After obtaining a sales license and a sponsoring broker, new licensees may start to practice in whatever area authorized by their sponsoring brokers; however, brokers must ensure that the agent is sufficiently competent in the practice area. Under Section 535.2 of the TREC Rules, a sponsoring broker is required to advise a salesperson of the scope of that salesperson's authorized activities under the License Act. Although not required to directly supervise a salesperson, the sponsoring broker is responsible for the authorized acts of the sponsored salesperson, unless the broker has limited or revoked such activities in writing. Furthermore, the rule states that if a broker permits a sponsored salesperson to engage in activities beyond the authorized scope, the broker will be responsible for those activities as well.

The sponsoring broker is also required to ensure that the salespersons under their sponsorship meet the statutory minimum continuing education required by the License Act. In addition, a broker is responsible for making sure that sponsored salespersons have sufficient education to competently perform their authorized activities. This means that a broker may require a salesperson to get additional education beyond what is required by law before the salesperson specializes in a practice area.

Residential Brokerage

Residential brokers deal in property used for housing, including small city lots, acreage, and single-family and multifamily units in urban, suburban, and rural areas. The largest majority of persons getting into the industry specialize or at least start their careers in residential sales. According to a survey conducted by the National Association of REALTORS® in 2013, the primary specialty of 79% of REALTORS® in Texas was residential sales. Agents just getting into the business often begin their careers as residential sales trainees, assistants to agents who are well-known in the industry, or members of established teams.

IN PRACTICE Within the residential market, agents may specialize in or deal with on a regular basis foreclosures, short sales, or real estate owned (REO) properties. As detailed in Chapter 15, when a borrower fails to timely pay the mortgage on a property and is considered in default on the loan, the lender may sell the property by foreclosure auction to satisfy the debt. Before the lender forecloses on the property and with the lender's approval, the property may sometimes be sold by the borrower in a short sale for less than the amount owed. If the property fails to sell at a foreclosure auction for at least the amount owed by the borrower, the lender takes possession of the property. Properties owned by lenders and government agencies under this repossession process are called REOs. An REO is typically labeled as a foreclosure in an MLS listing when the lender markets the property to buyers through a real estate agent. Often, REOs and properties subject to foreclosure are purchased by persons looking for investment vehicles. Agents who specialize in these kinds of lender-involved transactions must have a good grasp of financing, investment, tax, and valuation principles. In addition, they must know how to negotiate with lenders.

Leasing/Property Management

A real estate agent who operates a property for its owner is involved in **property management**. According to the National Association of REALTORS® survey in 2013, 9% of Texas REALTORS® indicated that property management was their primary specialty. The property manager may be responsible for soliciting tenants, collecting rents, altering or constructing new space for tenants, monitoring insurance coverage, ordering repairs, and generally maintaining the property. The manager's basic responsibility is to protect the owner's investment and maximize the owner's return on the investment. Property management is discussed in Chapter 22.

Most large cities have local associations of building and property owners and managers that are affiliates of regional and national associations. The Institute of Real Estate Management is one of the affiliates of the National Association of REALTORS®. It awards the designations of *Certified Property Manager* (CPM) and *Accredited Residential Manager* (ARM) to persons who have met certain requirements. The Building Owners and Managers Association International (BOMA International) is a federation of local associations of owners and managers, primarily of office buildings. The Building Owners and Managers Institute (BOMI) International, an independent institute affiliated with BOMA, offers training courses leading to several designations: *Real Property Administrator* (RPA),

Systems Maintenance Administrator (SMA), and *Facilities Management Administrator* (FMA). The International Council of Shopping Centers is the global trade association of the shopping center industry. The National Apartment Association has designations of Certified Apartment Manager (CAM) and Certified Apartment Property Supervisor (CAPS). Also degrees in residential property management are available at a few Texas colleges and universities.

Within Texas, the Texas Apartment Association (TAA) has more than 10,500 members, who manage more than 1.75 million rental housing units statewide. Participation in groups like these allows property managers to use association-prepared lease forms, to gain valuable professional knowledge, and to discuss their problems with other managers facing similar issues. For the latest information on issues affecting property managers in Texas, visit the TAA website.

Apartment Locating

A **residential rental locator** matches landlords and tenants. Working as an independent contractor for several apartment complexes, the locator finds apartment units for prospective tenants, qualifies prospective tenants, and negotiates leases with the apartment complexes. A rental locator is generally paid by the owner of the apartments and must be licensed by the Texas Real Estate Commission (TREC). Apartment locators have specific advertising rules of which they are required to comply.

Commercial Brokerage

Commercial brokers specialize in business property, including offices, shopping centers, stores, theaters, hotels, industrial parks, and parking facilities. According to a survey conducted by the National Association of REALTORS® in 2013, the primary specialization of 3% of Texas REALTORS® was commercial brokerage (see Figure 23.1). Commercial brokers should have knowledge of real estate investment and financing principles because understanding the income-producing potential of commercial properties is key to representing clients in the commercial market. In addition, agents specializing in commercial real estate should have a proper understanding of local zoning laws and commercial property valuation principles.

Within the commercial market, agents in urban areas can further specialize in selling or leasing medical offices, retail, or industrial space to name just a few areas within the commercial market niche.

FIGURE 23.1: Real Estate Specialties

Primary Real Estate Specialty	
Residential brokerage	79%
Commercial brokerage	3
Residential appraisal	3
Relocation	2
Property management	9
Other specialties	4

Source: National Association of REALTORS® Survey of Texas REALTORS®, 2013

Farm and Ranch/Land Sales

Farm and ranch or land sales brokers specialize in farms, timberland, pasture-land, ranches, and orchards. The state of Texas has vast areas of farm and ranch property and other rural land which is regularly bought, sold, and leased both on an individual one-on-one basis and to land developers and businesses in connection with urban, suburban, commercial and industrial growth.

Agents who deal in farm and ranch property should have a good understanding of agricultural production principles, and how crops and timber may affect the sale of such property. In addition, they should have knowledge of such things as hunting and gaming leases, oil and gas and other mineral rights, and water rights on working farms or ranches.

Auctioneers

Both live and online real estate auctions are an integral part of the real estate industry in Texas and across the nation. Live foreclosure auctions are typically conducted on the courthouse steps of the county in which the property is located. Online auction companies such as Auction.com list both residential and commercial real estate for sale by online and live auction. Auction companies may also work with lenders to conduct REO property auctions and bulk property sales, and with sellers on lender-approved short sale auctions.

Under Chapter 1802 of the Texas Occupations Code, a person conducting any type of auction in Texas must have an auctioneer's license. However, under the License Act, a person conducting a real estate auction must be a licensed broker or salesperson. According to the 2013 TREC MCE Legal Update materials,

> [l]ongstanding interpretations harmonizing this provision of TRELA with the licensing requirement in Chapter 1802 recognize that while an auctioneer's license under Chapter 1802 is required for a person to call an auction, a broker or salesperson license is required for a person who handles other facets of the transaction such as negotiating the contract, showing the property, or other activity which typically requires a real estate license.

Under H.B. 3038 (2013), which amended Chapter 1802, an individual auctioneer may now act for a real estate brokerage firm licensed under the License Act. According to the 2013 TREC MCE Legal Update materials, "[t]his change permits the broker and auctioneer to provide the full complement of services related to selling and auctioning real property."

As amended by H.B. 3038, Chapter 1802 now defines *auction* as "the sale of property by competitive bid using any method, format, or venue." The Texas Department of Licensing and Regulation (TDLR) recently amended its rules to clarify that multiple offers to purchase real estate are not considered competitive bids requiring an auctioneer's license if all of the material terms of the transaction other than price are different.

While an auctioneer' license may be necessary to call an auction, a real estate agent specializing in the auctioning of real property and who is regularly involved in auction-related details will need to have knowledge of the auction process, financing and investment principles, and property valuation methods.

Appraisal

The process of developing an opinion of value for a parcel of real estate is **appraisal**. Although brokers must have some understanding of valuation as part of their training, qualified appraisers are employed when property is financed or sold by court order and large sums of money are involved. The appraiser must have sound judgment, experience, and a detailed knowledge of the methods of valuation. Appraiser licensing and the appraisal process are covered in Chapter 14.

Financing

The business of providing the funds necessary to complete real estate transactions is **financing**. Most transactions are financed by means of a mortgage loan, in which the property is pledged as security for the eventual repayment of the loan. Real estate financing and licensing of mortgage professionals are examined in Chapters 15 and 16.

Property Inspection

A **real estate inspector** is generally hired by a prospective purchaser to inspect real property and to give an opinion as to the condition of the structural systems, electrical systems, mechanical systems, plumbing systems, and appliances. Property inspectors must be licensed by the Texas Real Estate Commission.

Property Development

Property development is composed of several different professions. It includes the work of land developers and subdividers who purchase raw land, divide it into lots, build roads, and install utilities. It involves builders and architects who plan and construct the houses and other buildings, and either the developer or the builder who sells the improved real estate, either directly or through brokerage firms.

Counseling

A **real estate counselor** helps clients choose among the various alternatives involved in purchasing, using, or investing in real property. A counselor's role is to furnish clients with the data needed to make informed decisions; a counselor must, therefore, have a broad range of real estate knowledge and experience.

Education

The real estate practitioner and the consumer can learn more about the complexities of the real estate business through education. Colleges, schools, real estate organizations, and continuing education programs conduct courses and seminars in all areas of the business. Experienced real estate professionals often teach these courses.

Title and Abstract

Ensuring good title to the buyer of real estate is the business of title insurance and abstract companies. A broad knowledge of real estate title, conveyancing, and lien law, as well as a good grasp of real estate math are very beneficial. Title insurance escrow officers must be licensed by the Texas Department of Insurance. Title records and closing transactions are discussed in Chapters 18 and 20.

Urban Planning

A rapidly expanding specialization of the real estate profession is urban planning. Urban planners work with local governments to make recommendations for new streets, sewer and water lines, schools, parks, and libraries.

Petroleum Landman

A landman conducts business activities related to oil, gas, and mineral exploration. A landman working for an oil and gas company negotiates and administers purchase or lease contracts with land or mineral interest owners and ensures compliance with governmental regulations. An independent landman, working on a contract basis, researches courthouse records to determine ownership; locates mineral/land owners and negotiates oil and gas purchase contracts, leases, and other agreements with them; and obtains any necessary curative documents. Landmen are not required to have a real estate license.

Other Careers

Many other real estate career options are available. Lawyers specializing in real estate are always in demand. Large corporations with extensive land holdings often have real estate and/or property tax departments. Licensees may be employed as assistants to individual salespersons or brokers to handle the paperwork related to residential or commercial sales. Specialists in real estate finance can work for mortgage banking firms, government agencies, and mortgage brokers, as well as for banks and savings associations. Building managers and superintendents handle real estate belonging to industrial firms, banks, trust companies, insurance firms, and other businesses. Environmental professionals ascertain prior uses of land and assess the potential for environmental hazards for buyers, sellers, and lenders. Government opportunities include, among others, the U.S. Department of Agriculture, the U.S. Department of the Interior, the National Park Service, and the U.S. Department of Veterans Affairs. Local governments have staff personnel in appraisal, land use, inspections, and urban renewal.

SUMMARY

Although residential brokerage is the most often practiced type of brokerage, there are many other real estate practice areas, such as commercial real estate, property management, apartment locating, farm and ranch sales, land sales, apartment locating, and time-share resales, in which real estate agents may specialize.

Specialization in a particular type of brokerage activity requires competency in the practice area. A sponsoring broker must ensure that sponsored salespersons are competent to perform within the scope of activities the broker has authorized the salespersons to engage in. In addition, a broker is responsible for making sure that sponsored salespersons have sufficient education to competently perform their authorized activities. A broker may require that a salesperson obtain additional education beyond what is required by law before the salesperson specializes in a particular practice area.

Real estate brokerage, or the business of representing buyers and sellers in real estate transactions is widely recognized as the core discipline of the real estate industry. Other related disciplines in the real estate industry include appraising, financing, property inspection, property development, counseling, education, title work, and urban planning. A real estate licensee must have a basic understanding of how these highly complex but interrelated disciplines work together in order to understand a real estate transaction from start to finish.

CHAPTER 23 QUESTIONS

1. The business of bringing together a buyer and a seller who are interested in making a real estate transaction is called
   a. leverage.
   b. agency.
   c. brokerage.
   d. arbitrage.

2. Real estate–related disciplines include all of the following EXCEPT
   a. finance.
   b. appraisal.
   c. title work.
   d. tort reform.

3. Which real estate practice area requires a special designation from TREC?
   a. Commercial brokerage
   b. Rental locator service
   c. Property management
   d. None of these

4. A broker is responsible for making sure that sponsored salespersons have sufficient education to perform their authorized activities in what manner?
   a. Facilely
   b. Competently
   c. Fluently
   d. Randomly

5. An REO property is usually owned by all of the following EXCEPT
   a. lender.
   b. government agency.
   c. bank.
   d. title company.

6. A residential rental locator does all of the following EXCEPT
   a. finds apartment units for prospective tenants.
   b. qualifies prospective tenants.
   c. qualifies roommates for existing tenants.
   d. negotiates leases with the apartment complexes.

7. A residential rental locator works in what capacity for apartment complexes?
   a. Independent contractor
   b. Employee
   c. Consultant
   d. Sponsoree

8. Multiple offers to purchase real estate are NOT considered competitive bids requiring an auctioneer's licensure if
   a. all the material terms of the transaction other than price are different.
   b. all the material terms of the transaction other than price are the same.
   c. none of the material terms of the transaction other than price are different.
   d. all the material terms of the transaction regardless of price are the same.

9. A real estate inspector is generally hired by whom to inspect real property?
   a. Lender
   b. Buyer
   c. Seller
   d. Broker

10. A real estate inspector is generally hired to give an opinion as to the condition of all of the following systems EXCEPT
    a. structural.
    b. electrical.
    c. mechanical.
    d. sound.

11. Property inspectors are licensed by which of the following state agencies?
    a. Texas Real Estate Commission
    b. Texas Department of Licensing and Regulation
    c. Texas Property Inspection Licensing Board
    d. None of these

12. A landman conducts business activities related to all of the following EXCEPT
    a. oil.
    b. gas.
    c. mineral exploration.
    d. timber.

13. A landman typically works for which of the following?
    a. Oil and gas companies
    b. Lenders
    c. Real estate brokers
    d. Title companies

14. A landman is licensed by
    a. the Texas Real Estate Commission.
    b. the Texas Department of Licensing and Regulation.
    c. the Petroleum Regulatory Commission.
    d. no one because no license is required.

Detailed rationales for the end-of-chapter review questions are available online at www.dearborn.com through the *Instructor Resource Guides* link.

Control of Land Use and Green Initiatives

■ **LEARNING OBJECTIVES** *When you have completed this chapter, you will be able to*

- **identify** the various types of public and private land-use controls and subdivision regulations;
- **distinguish** the function and characteristics of building codes and zoning ordinances;
- **describe** the environmental issues an agent must understand to protect a client's interests: the basic hazards, the discovery methods, the disclosure responsibilities, and the liability issues;
- **explain** major real estate industry green initiatives and their goals for reducing the overall impact on human health and the environment; and
- **define** the following *key terms*:

buffer zone	green	restrictive covenant
building code	Interstate Land Sales Full	spot zoning
building permit	Disclosure Act	subdivision regulations
comprehensive plan	laches	variance
conditional use permit	nonconforming use	zoning board of
deed restriction	planned unit development	adjustment
developer	property report	zoning ordinance
extraterritorial jurisdiction	public ownership	

OVERVIEW

The various ownership rights a person possesses in a parcel of real estate are subject to certain public land-use controls (such as zoning ordinances, subdivision regulations, and building codes), private controls (such as deed restrictions), and environmental legislation. The purpose of these controls is to ensure that our limited supply of land is being put to its highest and best use for the benefit of the general public as well as private owners.

This chapter discusses the public and private land-use controls and how they help shape and preserve the physical surface of our nation, and it explores environmental issues, including "green" initiatives, that impact the practice of real estate.

LAND-USE CONTROLS

The control and regulation of land use is accomplished in both the public and private sectors through three means: (1) public land-use controls, (2) private land-use controls through deed restrictions, and (3) public ownership of land—including parks, schools, and expressways—by the federal, state, and local governments.

Public Controls

Under the *police powers* granted by the Fourteenth Amendment to the U.S. Constitution, each state, and in turn its counties and municipalities, has the inherent authority to adopt regulations necessary to protect the public health, safety, morals, and general welfare. This includes limitations, or controls, on the use of privately owned real estate. Police power in many areas includes controls over noise, air, and water pollution, as well as population density. Privately owned real estate is regulated through

- zoning;
- subdivision regulations;
- codes that regulate building construction, safety, and public health; and
- environmental protection legislation.

The Comprehensive Plan   In the late 19th and early 20th centuries, some concerned individuals were dissatisfied with the haphazard manner in which metropolitan areas were developing. During this period, unofficial citizens' groups in cities like New York, Boston, and Chicago adopted city plans. One of the first such plans was the McMillan Improvement Plan for Washington, D.C. Adopted in 1901, it set forth the overall strategy for the development of the famous park system of our nation's capital. A few years later, the Burnham Plan for the City of Chicago was published. The Burnham Plan was probably the most influential force in urban planning throughout the country. The subject matter of this plan encompassed rapid transit and suburban growth, a comprehensive park system, forest preserves, transportation and terminals, streets and subdivision control, and problems of the central city.

The City of Dallas developed its first comprehensive plan in 2005.

Today, the country is witnessing a much broader approach to urban planning and development. Local governments recognize development goals primarily through the formulation of a **comprehensive plan** (sometimes called a *master plan*). Cities and counties develop comprehensive plans to ensure that social and economic needs are balanced against environmental and aesthetic concerns. In most cases a city, county, or regional *planning commission* is created for these purposes. A comprehensive plan encompasses all geographic parts of the community and all elements that affect its physical development over a 20- to 30-year period. As a long-range, general framework for making development decisions, the comprehensive plan expresses community goals and objectives; designates areas for residential, commercial, and industrial development; indicates preferred locations for utility systems and for parks, golf courses, cemeteries, schools and libraries, fire stations, and other public facilities; proposes means for transporting people and products (roads, airports, railways); recommends treatment for such special problems as historic preservation, downtown renewal, flood control and drainage, noise mitigation, and other environmental concerns; and lists actions needed to carry out the plan.

Economic and physical surveys are essential in preparing a comprehensive plan. Countywide or regional plans also must include the coordination of numerous civic plans and developments to ensure orderly city growth with stabilized property values.

Tax Increment Reinvestment Zones (TIRZs)   Several cities across the state face difficulties in stimulating economic development in downtown areas due to a large number of structurally obsolete and vacant buildings. Therefore, major planning efforts center around addressing inner-city deterioration, developing raw land in suburban fringe areas, and reversing the decline of major activity centers. One mechanism for accomplishing these goals is the *TIRZ*, also known as a *tax increment financing (TIF)* district, which is created by a city council to attract new business to an area. TIRZs, or TIFs, help finance the cost of redeveloping or encouraging infill development in an area of a city or county that would otherwise not attract sufficient private investment in the reasonably foreseeable future. Homestead preservation districts and reinvestment zones help cities reclaim residential neighborhoods adjacent to central business districts. They provide tools for cities to increase home ownership, provide affordable housing, and prevent the involuntary loss of homesteads in neighborhoods experiencing economic pressures. Taxes attributable to new improvements (the tax increment) are set aside in a fund to finance public improvements in a reinvestment zone—such as parks, street lighting, and building acquisition or rehabilitation costs. For example, if the taxable value for a base year is set at $6 million and improvements to the area increase the taxable value to $7 million, the taxes collected on the additional $1 million, or increment, is earmarked for the TIF fund to pay for project costs. TIFs have no taxing or assessment powers. Major revisions were made to the TIF Act in 2011 to encourage the use of TIFs (H.B. 2853).

S.B. 402 (2011) added another avenue for cities and counties to develop vacant and blighted land for affordable low-to-moderate-income housing: the community land trust (CLT). The CLT, a nonprofit organization, sells a home at a restricted sales price and leases the underlying land to the homeowner through a long-term lease.

Zoning   The **zoning ordinance** is a police power measure in which the private land in a community is divided into districts or zones delimiting the various classes of land use. Zoning is a tool for implementing a local comprehensive plan to *prevent* incompatible adjacent land uses, overcrowding, and traffic congestion; *restrict*

TIRZs in the City of Houston have been created for one of three reasons:

- to address inner city deterioration,
- to develop raw land in suburban fringe areas, or
- to proactively address the decline of major activity centers.

height and size/bulk of buildings; and *promote* aesthetic value. Municipal zoning ordinances may be enacted to specify lot sizes or types of structures permitted, establish setbacks (the minimum distance away from streets and the side and rear property lines that structures may be built), and control density (the ratio of land area to structure area or population).

Zoning powers are conferred by state *enabling acts*. Texas adopted its version of the Standard Zoning Enabling Act in 1927 and delegated zoning powers to municipalities, but not to counties. There are no nationwide zoning regulations; and with the exception of Hawaii, no states have statewide zoning regulations. State and federal governments may, however, regulate land use through special legislation such as scenic easement and coastal management laws.

Typical land-use classifications are agricultural, residential, commercial, and industrial. To ensure adequate control, land-use areas are further divided into subclasses. For example, residential areas may be subdivided to provide for detached single-family dwellings, semidetached structures containing not more than four dwelling units, walkup apartments, highrise apartments, and so forth. A special zoning classification, **planned unit development** (PUD), is used by many communities for *cluster zoning, multiple-use zoning,* or *special-purpose zoning.* It permits a mixed-use zone for properties that would normally not be compatible and creates a unified development in which one or more residence areas is combined with one or more commercial or office areas. Some communities require the use of buffers (such as landscaped parks and playgrounds) or **buffer zones** (zoning districts that gradually change from a higher-intensity use to a lower-intensity use) to separate and screen residential areas from nonresidential areas. For example, a high-density multifamily zone for apartments might be placed between commercial and single-family zones. Some special types of zoning are listed in Figure 24.1.

> The City of Houston is the largest city in the United States without a zoning ordinance, and its residents have voted several times to keep it that way.

FIGURE 24.1: Special Types of Zoning

Type of Zoning	Primary Purpose
Bulk zoning	To control density and prevent overcrowding through restrictions on setback, building height, and percentage of open areas
Aesthetic zoning	To require that new buildings conform to specific types of architecture
Incentive zoning	To require that street floors of office buildings be used for retail establishments
Directive zoning	To use zoning as a planning tool to encourage use of land for its highest and best use

Adoption of Zoning Ordinances The planning and zoning commission (P&Z) recommends zoning ordinances to the city council for final approval. Zoning ordinances must not violate the rights of individuals and property holders (as provided under the due process provisions of the Fourteenth Amendment of the U.S. Constitution) or the various provisions of the state constitution. If the means used to regulate the use of property are destructive, unreasonable, arbitrary, or confiscatory, the ordinances usually are considered void. Tests normally applied in determining the validity of ordinances require that

- power be exercised in a reasonable manner;
- provisions be clear and specific;
- ordinances be free from discrimination;

- ordinances promote public health, safety, and general welfare under the police power concept; and
- ordinances apply to all property in a similar manner.

Requests for an *amendment* to the official *zoning map* may be initiated by a property developer or by the city planning staff in response to the municipality's comprehensive plan. In Texas, each municipal governing body establishes procedures for zoning adoption and enforcement. All property owners within 200 feet of any proposed zoning change must be notified that an amendment to the zoning map has been proposed. Additionally, a 15-day notice published in a local newspaper must be given before a public hearing. The proposed amendment must be heard in a public hearing on the matter and approved by the governing body of the community. If 20% of the owners protest the zoning change, the governing body must approve the change by at least three-fourths vote.

Zoning variations that result in small areas that differ significantly from adjoining parcels in a way that is not in harmony with the general plan for the area might be considered **spot zoning**. An example would be a zoning map amendment that allows a convenience store in the middle of a residential area. If a court determines that changing the zoning was to the excessive benefit of a single property owner, it will not be permitted.

Zoning laws generally are enforced through local requirements that building permits be obtained before property owners can build on their land. A permit will not be issued unless a proposed structure conforms to the permitted zoning, among other regulations. Zoning helps protect private property values because property owners can comfortably invest in a site with reasonable expectation of the type of development that will occur in the adjacent areas.

Conditional Use Permits   In some instances, a property use is only marginally acceptable in a specific zone. For example, a person seeking to build a bed and breakfast inn (B&B) within a single-family residential zoning district would submit a request for approval to the planning and zoning commission. To reduce the impact that the B&B might have on the surrounding areas, the P&Z might approve the property use with certain stipulations by issuing a **conditional use permit** (sometimes called a *special use permit* or *specific use permit*). The stipulated conditions are for the benefit of a neighborhood, not an individual property. In our example, the approval of the B&B would be as a *conditional use*, a use permitted in the appropriate zoning district only when all conditions set forth by the planning and zoning commission are met. The special conditions would be designed to minimize any adverse impact to the surrounding areas by enhancing existing regulations in the zoning ordinance. Because the externalities of the B&B would impose additional burdens that single-family residential properties would not, the P&Z could require a greater setback from the street, additional landscaping, controlled parking, or similar conditions in its approval. A conditional use permit may be issued to either run with the land or run with the ownership.

Conditional use permits allow a property *use* only if stipulated conditions are met. The special conditions are for the benefit of a neighborhood, not an individual property.

Nonconforming Use   After a rezoning process, sometimes the use of an existing building or the building itself no longer conforms to the new zoning classification; such use or property is called a **nonconforming use**. Nonconforming status generally results either from annexation (bringing land into city limits) or amending current regulations. The nonconforming uses or properties, therefore, generally predate the adoption of zoning ordinances for a particular district. Communities

A *nonconforming use* is a use that predates the zoning ordinance or its amendments.

have different ways of dealing with these special cases. The use may be "grandfathered," or allowed to continue, until (1) the current use is discontinued, (2) the improvements are destroyed or torn down, or (3) the ownership of the property is transferred. In other cases, nonconforming uses will be amortized over a specified period, allowing for a return on the owner's investment but setting a definite sunset period for the use to conform with the new zoning ordinances (common with sexually oriented businesses).

Variances   A **variance** is a waiver from compliance with a specific provision of the zoning ordinance; it is for the benefit of one parcel only. A property owner may seek a variance when strict enforcement of a zoning ordinance would cause undue hardship to the property owner because of special circumstances and through no fault of the owner. However, variances are not to be used to help owners cut development costs. Variances may be given for such things as height of a building, setback requirements, minimum square footage of the lot area, percentage of the lot that can be covered by the house or building, or the required number of parking spaces; such variances are called *area variances*. A request for a *use variance*, a change in permitted use, is generally handled through rezoning.

> A *variance* permits an exception to a zoning ordinance; it is for the benefit of one parcel only.

In contrast to most municipality issues, zoning variances are not heard by the city council; they are heard by **zoning boards of adjustment** (ZBAs), which have been established to hear complaints about the effects of zoning ordinances on a specific property. Members of these boards must be free of personal or political influence. If the property owner is not satisfied with the decision of the ZBA, the decision may be appealed to a court of record.

> Zoning variances are heard by zoning boards of adjustment (ZBAs), not by the city council.

FOR EXAMPLE   A builder submits a house plan to the P&Z for approval. However, the fireplace on one side of the house encroaches into the required 15-foot side yard setback. If the builder cannot adjust the floor plan or move the house on the lot, the P&Z may take a request for a variance to the ZBA. Because the fireplace encroaching into the setback occupies only a small portion of the side of the house, the ZBA might approve the variance.

IN PRACTICE   Purchasers of property must be aware of zoning requirements. Licensees should determine whether a buyer's proposed use for the property conforms to existing zoning ordinances. If either the seller or a licensee misrepresents the actual permitted zoning use, the buyer may be able to rescind the transaction on the basis of the misrepresentation.

Extraterritorial Jurisdiction (ETJ)   Texas has enacted legislation providing that the subdivision of land located within one-half to five miles of an incorporated village, town, or city (the distance based on the population size of the municipality) must be approved by the municipality or the county. This is known as **extraterritorial jurisdiction**. In populous counties, regulation of subdivisions in the ETJ is the exclusive responsibility of the county.

A purchaser of property outside the city limits must be notified before executing a sales contract that the property might in the future be annexed by the city. The purchaser is charged with contacting all municipalities in the general proximity of the property to determine whether the property is located within, or is likely to be added to, a city's extraterritorial jurisdiction (see Chapter 13). The disclosures are given to put purchasers on notice that municipalities have no rights to control land use in the extraterritorial jurisdiction; however, if the land is annexed into the city, the city would have that right. Unless an annexation is voluntary or within one of the statute's exceptions, a municipality is required to give a minimum of three years' notice before an annexation, and any land acquired must be contiguous to the city's existing boundaries. It is important to note that a municipality has the power to unilaterally annex adjoining areas; it can bring an adjacent unincorporated area into the city without permission of the persons living in that area.

Subdivision Regulation

Land Development   The process of land development generally involves three distinct stages. These are (1) the initial planning stage, (2) the final planning stage, and (3) disposition, or start-up. During the *initial planning stage*, the **developer** seeks out raw land in a suitable area that can be profitably subdivided. After the land is located, the property is analyzed for highest and best use, and a preliminary subdivision plat is drawn up by a licensed surveyor, as discussed in Chapter 10. The preliminary subdivision plat is then submitted to the city planning staff, who evaluate the preliminary subdivision plat to see that it is consistent with the city's comprehensive plan. Municipal **subdivision regulations** are among the tools used to implement the comprehensive plan. They generally provide for

- location, grading, alignment, surfacing, and widths of streets, highways, and other rights-of-way;
- installation of sewers and water mains;
- dimensions of lots and length of blocks;
- areas to be reserved or dedicated for public use, such as parks or schools; and
- easements for public utilities.

> A *developer* buys undeveloped acreage; subdivides it; puts in utilities, curbs, and gutters; paves the streets; and then either builds and sells homes on the land or sells the lots.

If the project requires an amendment to the zoning map or a zoning variance, negotiations begin along these lines. Surrounding property owners may need to be notified, and public hearings may be required. The developer also locates financial backers and initiates marketing strategies at this point in the process.

> A property developer must receive credit toward capital improvement expenses (streets, curbs, gutters, sewers, etc.) for a portion of the ad valorem tax and utility service revenues that will be generated by the development.

In the *final planning stage*, the final engineering plans and the final subdivision plat are prepared, and approval is sought from the appropriate local officials, usually the planning and zoning commission and/or the city council. Once the plat is approved, it is recorded in the county clerk's office, and the city issues a certificate to the developer. Permanent financing is obtained and the land is purchased. Also, final budgets are prepared and marketing programs are designed.

The *disposition* or *start-up stage* carries the development process to a conclusion. Streets, curbs, gutters, sanitary and storm sewers, and utilities are installed. Open parks and recreational areas are constructed and landscaped if they are part of the subdivision plan. Marketing programs are initiated, and title to the individual parcels of subdivided land is transferred as the lots are sold for home construction.

Building Codes

Most cities and towns have enacted ordinances to *specify construction standards* that must be met when repairing or erecting buildings. These are called **building codes**, and they set the requirements for kinds of materials, sanitary equipment, electrical wiring, fire prevention standards, and the like. Most communities require the issuance of a **building permit** by a city building official before a person can build a structure or alter or repair an existing building on property within the corporate limits of the municipality. Through the permitting process, city officials are made aware of new construction or alterations and can verify compliance with building codes and zoning ordinances by examining the plans and inspecting the work. If the construction of a building or an alteration violates a deed restriction (discussed later in this chapter), the issuance of a building permit will *not* cure this violation. A building permit is merely evidence of the applicant's compliance with municipal regulations. If a structure is built without a permit, city officials may require that it be dismantled. Builders and developers who have filed a development permit with a city need meet only those ordinances applicable at the time the application was filed. Governmental entities may not impose retroactive requirements once the permit application process has begun. After the completed structure has been inspected and found satisfactory, the city inspector issues a *certificate of occupancy*.

If a municipality can provide evidence that new construction in a particular area will result in a shortage of public facilities or prove detrimental to public health, safety, and welfare, a moratorium may be adopted on the issuance of building permits—residential and/or commercial.

The subject of city planning, zoning ordinances, and restrictions on use is extremely technical. Questions concerning any of these subjects in relation to real estate transactions should be referred to competent legal counsel.

Private Land-Use Controls

Deed Restrictions   Not all restrictions on the use of land are imposed by government agencies. Some restrictions to control and maintain the quality and character of a property or subdivision may be created by private entities, including the property owners themselves. A real estate owner can create a **deed restriction**, or **restrictive covenant**, on the *use* of land by including a provision for it in the deed when the property is conveyed or by filing a separate declaration of restrictions with the county clerk. There is a distinction between restrictions on the owner's right to *use* and restrictions on the owner's right to *sell*. In general, a deed conveying a fee simple estate may not restrict the owner's rights to sell, mortgage, or convey it. Such restrictions attempt to limit the basic principle of the *free alienation (transfer) of property*; the courts usually consider them against public policy and therefore unenforceable. For example, private transfer fees included in a deed restriction create a limitation on the free transfer of property. Until June 16, 2011, a developer could place a deed restriction on a property to create a transfer fee, generally 1% of the property's sales price, payable to the developer every time the property was sold. With the exception of transfer fees charged by homeowners and property owners associations and similar entities, new private transfer fees are not allowed (H.B. 8, 2011). Developers who have existing transfer fee restrictions on properties must have filed a notice of the private transfer fee obligation with the county clerk by January 31, 2012. Unless the notice was filed and is updated every three years, existing private transfer fees will be void. A seller of a property subject to a private transfer fee must provide written notice of this obligation to a potential purchaser.

Restrictions are generally placed on a property by the property developer. When a lot in a subdivision is conveyed by an owner's deed, the deed refers to the plat or declaration of restrictions and incorporates these restrictions as limitations on the title conveyed by the deed. In this manner, the restrictive covenants are included

If a substandard single-family or multifamily property is considered a physical or health risk, a city can designate a nonprofit organization to initiate an action for court-ordered receivership to make necessary improvements or order the property demolished.

in the deed by reference and become binding on all grantees. Such covenants or restrictions usually relate to

■ type of building;
■ use to which the land may be put;
■ type of construction, height, setbacks, and square footage; and
■ cost.

For example, the restrictions in one subdevelopment might specify that the home be at least 80% brick with at least 2,000 square feet and that no boat or recreational vehicle may be kept on the street, driveway, or lot.

Restrictive covenants usually run with the land and are binding on subsequent purchasers. Most restrictions have a *time limitation*—for example, "effective for a period of 25 years from this date." After that time, the restrictions become inoperative unless they are extended by majority agreement of the people who then own the property. Frequently, it also is provided that the effective term of the restrictions may be extended with the consent of a majority (or sometimes two-thirds) of the owners in a subdivision. In Texas, a lot owner has the right to opt out of the renewal or extension.

Deed restrictions usually are considered valid if they are reasonable restraints and are for the benefit of all property owners in the subdivision. However, they cannot violate local, state, or federal laws. For example, deed restrictions in violation of fair housing laws, such as restricting the sale of property to a particular color or race, are void. If a restrictive covenant or condition is considered void by a court, the validity of the deed is not affected. The estate simply stands free from the invalid covenant or condition.

IN PRACTICE   In Texas, if a municipality uses zoning as a land-use control tool, the municipality cannot enforce deed restrictions. A deed restriction is a private contract between the developer and the property owner and the city does not get involved in this private contract—unless the city has no zoning ordinances, as is the case with the City of Houston.

> A property owner may apply to a justice of the peace (JP) court for an injunction to enforce a deed restriction.

Enforcement of Deed Restrictions   Developers usually place restrictions on the use of all lots in a subdivision as a *general plan* for the benefit of all lot owners. Such restrictions give each lot owner the right to apply to a justice of the peace (JP) court for an injunction to prevent a neighboring lot owner from violating the recorded restrictions. If granted, the court injunction directs the violator to stop or remove the violation; and the court may punish the violator for failure to obey the court order. If adjoining lot owners stand idly by while a violation is being committed, they can lose the right to obtain a court injunction by their inaction; the court might claim their right was lost through **laches**, the loss of a right through undue delay or failure to assert it. Where extensive and continuing violations of deed restrictions are evident, Texas courts may refuse to enforce them because such violations indicate the lot owners have abandoned the original scheme or plan.

Altering Deed Restrictions   It may be necessary to obtain an alteration of the deed restrictions to use a certain property for a specific purpose. This may or may not be possible, depending on the circumstances. There are two methods of changing deed restrictions: *waiver* and *judicial*. To effect a waiver, a notarized document must be obtained from every property owner, mortgage lender (regardless of lien classification), and the original developer or his estate. Clearly this method is quite impractical for a large subdivision. In such a situation, judicial recourse is more practical. This involves filing a lawsuit to obtain a favorable ruling that declares the offending deed restriction to be void.

Conditions   *Conditions* in a deed are different from restrictions or covenants. A grantor's deed of conveyance can be subject to certain stated conditions whereby the buyer's title may *revert* (go back) to the seller. (This was discussed in Chapter 8 as a defeasible fee estate.)

FOR EXAMPLE   Bill conveys a lot to James by a deed that includes a condition forbidding the sale, manufacture, or giving away of intoxicating liquor on the lot and provides that, in case of violation, Bill can go to court to regain title. If James operates a tavern on the lot, Bill can file suit and obtain title to the property. The *fee simple subject to a condition subsequent* estate is enforced by a *reverter*, or *reversion*, clause.

PUBLIC OWNERSHIP

Over the years, the government's general policy has been to encourage private ownership of land. However, a certain amount of land must be controlled by **public ownership** for such uses as municipal buildings, state legislative houses, schools, and military installations. Other examples of necessary public ownership include publicly owned streets, highways, and parks. Not only do national and state parks and forest preserves create areas for public use and enjoyment, they help conserve our natural resources.

Texas ranks 44th among the 50 states in percentage of land owned by the public (both the state and federal governments). The state owns 825,000 acres—less than 1% of Texas land. Federal land holdings in Texas exceed 6 million acres—about 3.7% of the state, a small percentage considering that the federal government owns approximately one-third of the total area of the United States.

Floodplains

Floodplains and the required insurance for federally related loans were discussed in Chapter 4. In addition, certain statutory water authorities—such as the Brazos River Authority, Trinity River Authority, and Tarrant Water District—control construction within the floodway to permit floodwaters to flow through unimpeded by the structures. In land planning, low-lying areas must be considered because control over these areas is exercised by others.

INTERSTATE LAND SALES FULL DISCLOSURE ACT

To protect consumers from "over-enthusiastic sales promotions" by developers involved in interstate land sales, the U.S. Congress passed the **Interstate Land Sales Full Disclosure Act**. Basically a consumer protection act, the law requires those engaged in the interstate sale or leasing of 25 or more lots to file a *statement of record* and register the subdivision with HUD. The seller is also required to furnish prospective buyers with a property report prior to execution of a contract. A **property report** contains all essential information about the property, such as distance over paved roads to nearby communities, number of homes currently occupied, soil conditions affecting foundations and septic systems, type of title a buyer will receive, and existence of liens.

Any contract to purchase a lot covered by this act may be revoked at the purchaser's option before midnight of the seventh day following the signing of the contract. If the seller misrepresents the property in any sales promotion, a buyer induced by such a promotion is entitled to sue the seller for civil damages under federal law. Failure to comply with the law may also subject a seller to criminal penalties of fines and imprisonment. There is a three-year statute of limitations for fraud that does not begin until discovery of the fraud is made.

ENVIRONMENTAL LEGISLATION AND GREEN INITIATIVES

From the first Earth Day in 1970 when an estimated 20 million Americans attended rallies in support of a *healthy, sustainable environment* to Earth Day 2011 when more than a billion people sent a message for *building a green economy*, citizens of the world have become increasingly aware of the importance of environmental stewardship. Each year another layer of environmental abuse pushes its way into our consciousness; and each year brings new solutions to potential problems as individuals, nonprofit organizations, businesses, and the government attempt to "go **green**." HUD defines *going green* as "a philosophical and social movement centered on a concern for the conservation and improvement of our natural resources." For discussion purposes, this environmental legislation and green initiatives section will be divided into two parts: (1) Texas environmental issues, including discovery, disclosure, and remediation; and (2) green initiatives, including individual, state and federal efforts.

Texas Environmental Issues

Federal and state legislators have passed a number of environmental protection laws in an attempt to respond to the growing public concerns over the improvement and preservation of America's natural resources. Most federal environmental legislation is enforced at the state level by the Texas Commission on Environmental Quality (TCEQ). In addition to the states and the federal government, cities and counties may also pass environmental regulations or ordinances of their own. Understanding environmental issues that affect an agent's market area is essential. Environmental concerns abound—and solutions are forthcoming:

■ As of spring 2011, three Texas regions and 22 counties were still designated by the Environmental Protection Agency (EPA) as "nonattainment for ozone," a failure to meet the standards of the federal Clean Air Act: Beaumont-Port Arthur, Houston-Galveston-Brazoria, Dallas-Fort Worth.

■ In 2010, over 400 water bodies (43% of the water bodies in Texas) were identified as "impaired" (too polluted to support their designated use).

■ The 2002 Water Plan estimated that in 2050 existing supplies of surface and groundwater in Texas will only be able to meet 62.5% of total needs—and 13.5% of the new supplies needed will have to be derived from implementing new conservation measures. To achieve this goal, the Texas Water Conservation Advisory Council has been charged with monitoring and developing water conservation strategies.

■ The 2009 Toxics Release Inventory (TRI), administered by the EPA, documents the toxic chemical releases, transfers, and waste management activities that occur both onsite and offsite for manufacturing plants and other facilities in Texas. McAllen-Edinburg-Mission ranked #1 on Forbes 2011 America's Cleanest Cities list in terms of low toxicity; in contrast, Houston ranked #7 on Forbes 2011 Most Toxic Cities list.

■ As of April 2011, there were 159 Superfund sites in Texas in varying stages of remediation. Superfund projects clean up hazardous waste sites and chemical spills.

■ Texas has 7.6 million acres of wetlands protected by the federal Clean Water Acte—4.4% of the state's area. Wetlands are areas saturated by water, including swamps, marshes, bogs, and similar areas, that often provide a critical habitat for plants, fish, insects, birds, and mammals.

■ Texas has 146 animals and 29 plants on the state endangered and threatened species list—animals ranging from the southwestern willow flycatcher and the Houston toad to the San Marcos salamander and the goose-beaked whale. Endangered plants include the Terlingua Creek cat's eye and Texas snowbells.

Increased public awareness of and concern about environmental problems and their effects on health and economics have had significant consequences on real estate sales and values. From an economic perspective, the actual dollar value of real property can be affected by both real and perceived problems; the marketability of the property may change drastically. Also, the cost of cleaning up and removing environmental hazards may be much greater than the dollar value of the property.

IN PRACTICE The Texas agencies responsible for the administration of most environmental protection laws are the following:

■ Texas Commission on Environmental Quality (TCEQ)—the *primary* environmental agency for the State of Texas; provides technical and compliance assistance for pollution prevention issues; administers clean air, clean water, safe management of waste, resource conservation, Superfund, and toxic release programs; contact TCEQ online or at 512-239-1000.

■ Texas Department of State Health Services (DSHS)—provides direct services to prevent occupational and environmental diseases through identification, evaluation, and control of environmental health hazards including asbestos; lead; indoor air quality (including mold); radiation control; uranium mining, processing, and by-product disposal; contact DSHS online or at 512-458-7587.

■ Texas Parks and Wildlife Department (TPWD)—administers the laws and regulations pertaining to endangered or threatened animal and plant species in Texas; for more information on Texas endangered species, visit the TPWD website or call 512-389-8111.

WEBLINK @
www.tceq.texas.gov
www.dshs.texas.gov
www.tpwd.texas.gov/huntwild/wild/species/endang

Disclosure and Discovery of Environmental Hazards In Texas, a property owner must disclose the presence of specific environmental hazards, as well as "any condition on the Property which materially affects the physical health or safety of an individual." As discussed in Chapter 13, the Seller's Disclosure of Property Condition is the appropriate form for most disclosures. If the property was constructed before 1978, a purchaser must also be given a lead-based paint disclosure form. For unimproved property, the disclosure for conditions under the surface might be required. It is the agent's duty to know which disclosures must be given in each transaction and to ensure that the seller has given them to the purchaser before execution of a contract.

If there is any question about the environmental condition of the property, an environmental assessment addendum promulgated by TREC creates a contract contingency allowing a buyer to get an environmental inspection in a residential transaction. The addendum permits a buyer to terminate a contract if environmental research or reports indicate conditions that adversely affect the use of the property. Real estate licensees are not expected to have the technical expertise necessary to discover the presence of environmental hazards. However, because they are presumed by the public to have special knowledge about real estate, licensees must be aware both of possible hazards and of sources for professional help.

The first step for a licensee is to ask the owner about environmental hazards. The owner may be aware of a potential hazardous condition or have already conducted tests for carbon monoxide, radon, or other hazards. If the owner has already done the detection and abatement work, an environmental hazard can actually be turned into a marketing plus. Potential buyers can be assured that an older home is no longer a lead paint or an asbestos risk. The most appropriate people on whom a licensee can rely for sound environmental information are scientific or technical experts. Developers and purchasers of commercial and industrial properties usually rely on the services of *environmental auditors*. An environmental audit includes the property's history of use and the results of extensive and complex tests of the soil, water, air, and structures. Trained inspectors conduct air-sampling tests to detect radon, asbestos, electromagnetic fields, or soil and water quality. Lead inspectors must be certified, and with a few exceptions, mold assessment consultants and mold remediators must be licensed, as discussed later in this chapter.

While environmental auditors may be called on at any stage in a transaction, they are most frequently brought in as a condition of closing. Not only can such experts detect environmental problems, they can usually offer guidance about how best to resolve the conditions. Some of the pollution and environmental risks in real estate transactions are listed in Figure 24.2.

Mold Remediation   A "black gold rush" was set off when a couple in Dripping Springs, Texas, filed a claim with their insurance company for water damage to a hardwood floor in their 22-room mansion. The claim later grew to include allegations of rampant mold contamination throughout the home and health problems resulting from the mold, which the couple blamed on the insurer's mishandling of the original cleanup project. In 2001, the owners were awarded $32 million in a jury trial; the award was reduced to $4 million by a state appeals court, and the couple settled out of court for an undisclosed amount. As mold-related claims increased exponentially, insurers raised the policy premiums and ultimately stopped covering mold-related claims in homeowner policies unless the damage resulted from a covered water-related event or the homeowner purchased separate mold coverage (Terri Cullen, *The Wall Street Journal*, May 19, 2004).

FIGURE 24.2: Environmental Risks

Environmental Risk	Description/Effect(s)
Asbestos	A mineral that has been used for many years as insulation; it has also been used in floor tile and in roofing material. Although it remains relatively harmless if not disturbed, it can become life-threatening when removed because of the accompanying dust—usually created through remodeling efforts or disintegration of materials. Airborne contaminants may cause respiratory diseases.
Carbon monoxide (CO)	Colorless, odorless gas that occurs as a by-product due to incomplete combustion when burning such fuels as wood, oil, and natural gas. Furnaces, water heaters, space heaters, fireplaces, and wood stoves all produce CO as a natural result of their combustion of fuel. When properly ventilated, the emissions are not a problem. Improper ventilation or equipment malfunction may result in dizziness and nausea, or even death.
Electromagnetic fields (EmFs)	Generated by the movement of electrical current through any electrical appliance. The major concern involves high-tension power lines. EmFs are suspected of causing cancer, hormonal changes, and behavioral abnormalities—although to date there is no proof.
Groundwater contamination	Not only the runoff at ground level but also the underground water systems that are sources for public and private wells. Contamination occurs from a number of sources, including waste disposal sites, underground storage tanks, pesticides, and herbicides.
Lead	A mineral that has been used in paint to protect wood from damage by water; it also has been used in the installation of water pipes. Lead becomes a health hazard when ingested (usually by peeling or flaking paint put into the mouths of small children or contamination through the water supply.) A disclosure notice is required on the lease or sale of properties built before 1978. An elevated level of lead can cause serious damage to the brain, kidneys, nervous system, and red blood cells. Children younger than six are particularly vulnerable.
Mold	Makes up 25% of the earth's biomass; found in all nonsterile environments, both indoors and outdoors. Mold growth is generally associated with flooding, a building defect that has allowed water penetration, excessive humidity, water leaks, or condensation. It is encouraged by warm, humid conditions. To date, no federal or state regulations establish exposure levels for molds as they affect air quality.
Polychlorinated biphenyl (PCB)	Carcinogenic substances used widely before 1977 as coolants and lubricants in transformers, capacitors, and other electrical equipment. Consumer products that may contain PCBs include old lighting fixtures, electrical appliances, and hydraulic oils. Wastes that contained PCBs have been buried in landfills and PCBs have entered the environment from accidental spills and leaks. Because PCBs do not readily break down, they may remain in the environment for a very long time. The effects on human health range from skin conditions, such as acne and rashes, to liver cancer.
Radon gas	An odorless, radioactive gas produced by the decay of other radioactive materials in rocks under the surface of the earth that generally enters a house through cracks in the foundation or through the floor drains. Long-term exposure to radon gas is said to cause lung cancer.
Underground storage tanks (USTs)	Used in both residential and commercial settings. From 3 million to 5 million underground storage tanks in the United States contain hazardous substances such as gasoline or home heating oil. When the containers become old and rust and start to leak, the material can enter the groundwater and contaminate wells and pollute the soil. According to the Environmental Protection Agency (EPA), approximately 40% of the tanks are leaking.
Urea formaldehyde foam insulation (UFFI)	A human-made insulation material that becomes dangerous because of the gases released from the material after it hardens. UFFI is known to cause cancer in animals. In humans, it may cause respiratory problems, as well as eye and skin irritations.
Waste disposal sites	Waste disposal sites for landfill operations or radioactive material disposal that can affect property values in surrounding areas. Landfills constructed on the wrong type of soil will leak waste into nearby wells. Emissions from radioactive waste can sometimes cause cancer or death.

Some research facts may help to relieve some of the anxiety that often results when mold is first discovered. Mold spores are a natural part of the environment and are always present at some level in the air and on surfaces around us. The Centers for Disease Control and Prevention (CDC) indicates that allergic symptoms similar to hay fever are the most common health concern from molds; however, some people are sensitive to molds and can have such symptoms as nasal stuffiness, eye irritation, wheezing, or skin irritation. Severe reactions generally occur only among persons with severely impaired immune systems or chronic lung illnesses and workers exposed to large amount of molds in occupational settings, such as farmers working around moldy hay. Such reactions may include fever and shortness of breath, according to the CDC.

To decrease mold exposure, all property owners, designers, and contractors should develop mold risk mitigation plans and have those plans in place within 24 to 48 hours after a water event. The CDC reports that, in most cases, mold can be removed from hard surfaces by a thorough cleaning with commercial products, soap and water, or a weak bleach solution (1 cup of bleach in 1 gallon of water). Absorbent or porous materials (like ceiling tiles, drywall, and carpet) may have to be replaced. The water problem must be fixed; and after the mold has been cleaned, the areas must be dried thoroughly to prevent mold regrowth. If there is an extensive amount of mold, a licensed mold remediation contractor may need to be hired. When the work is completed, a licensed mold assessment consultant must conduct a post-remediation assessment and issue a *Certificate of Mold Remediation* that
- must be passed along to any buyer of the property within the next five years and
- will prevent an insurance company from using previous mold damage or a claim for mold damage in making an underwriting decision.

For more details about mold assessment and remediation, contact the Texas Department of State Health Services.

WEBLINK @ www.dshs.texas.gov/mold/forms.shtm

Environmental Responsibility and Liability

The Landowner   When the *Comprehensive Environmental Response, Compensation, and Liability Act* (CERCLA) was passed in 1980, it established a $9 billion *Superfund* to clean up uncontrolled hazardous waste sites and to respond to spills. It created a process for identifying potential responsible parties and ordering them to take responsibility for the cleanup action. Under CERCLA and other environmental legislation, a landowner may be liable for cleanup when contamination exists—regardless of whether the contamination is the result of the landowner's actions or those of others. This liability includes the cleanup not only of the landowner's property but also of any neighboring property that has been contaminated. A landowner who is not responsible for the contamination can seek reimbursement for the cleanup cost from previous landowners, any other responsible party, or the Superfund. However, if other parties are not available, even a landowner who did not cause the problem could be solely responsible for the costs.

FOR EXAMPLE   An entrepreneur purchases the site of an abandoned gas station and sets up a small coffee shop. A year later, it is determined that the gasoline storage tanks are still underground—and leaking. The owner of the coffee shop may be faced with the ensuing environmental cleanup costs.

The *Superfund Amendments and Reauthorization Act* created an *innocent landowner immunity*, stipulating that a landowner in the chain of ownership who was completely innocent of all wrongdoing should not be held liable. However, an innocent landowner seeking to be exempted from liability must have no actual or constructive knowledge of the damage. In addition, the landowner must have exercised due care when the property was purchased, making a reasonable search (an environmental Phase I site assessment) to determine that the property was not environmentally damaged.

To provide relief to developers, property owners, project contractors, and lenders who might become involved in remediation projects, new insurance policies have emerged to reduce possible contamination to "just another risk" of doing business:

- *Cleanup cost cap insurance covers* cost overruns that often occur during remediation, when the extent of contamination can be pinpointed.
- *Pollution legal liability* policies protect property owners against losses arising from preexisting and unknown pollution conditions, both on site and off site. Coverage also can be purchased for future pollution conditions that could occur during operation of a facility.
- *Banker's environmental risk insurance* insures lenders when a loan goes into default and there is contamination on the property. It covers either the cost of cleaning up the property or paying off the loan balance.

The Real Estate Professionals   Sellers and purchasers carry the most exposure to environmental liability, but real estate professionals may also be held liable under certain circumstances. Real estate licensees could be held liable for improper disclosure. Therefore, it is essential that licensees be aware of potential environmental risks from neighboring properties, such as gas stations, manufacturing plants, or even funeral homes.

Additional exposure is created for individuals involved in other aspects of real estate transactions. Lenders may end up owning worthless assets if owners default on the loans rather than undertaking expensive cleanup efforts. Real estate appraisers must identify and adjust for environmental problems. Adjustments to market value typically reflect the cleanup cost plus a factor of the degree of panic and suspicion that exists in the current market. The real estate appraiser's greatest responsibility is to the lender, who depends on the appraiser to identify environmental hazards. Although the lender may be protected under certain conditions through the 1986 amendments to the Superfund Act, the lender must be aware of potential problems and may require additional environmental reports. Insurance carriers also might be affected in the transactions. Mortgage insurance companies protect lenders' mortgage investments and might be required to carry part of the ultimate responsibility in cases of loss. More important, hazard insurance carriers might be directly responsible for damages if such coverage was included in the initial policy. An early and careful analysis of the potential environmental risks for each transaction will more likely ensure a positive result for all parties.

Green Initiatives

It seems as though everything is "Going Green." Green Environment. Green Jobs. Green Economy. Green Building. Green Communities. Green Mortgages. GreenScapes. Green Energy. Green Cleanup. Green initiatives range from big projects to small and from individual initiatives to government. Although the discussion of green initiatives here will be limited, some of the key concepts or programs will be mentioned, along with some resources for getting additional information.

Green Building Programs   The U.S. Environmental Protection Agency (EPA) defines *green building* as "the practice of creating structures and using processes that are environmentally responsible and resource-efficient throughout a building's life-cycle from site preparation to design, constructing, operating, maintenance, renovation, and deconstruction." Green buildings are designed to reduce the overall impact of buildings on human health and the natural environment by

■   efficiently using energy, water, and other resources;

■   protecting occupant health and improving employee productivity; and

■   reducing waste, pollution, and environmental degradation.

In a Green Renter Survey conducted in December 2010, 53% of renters said they would pay 10–15% extra for an environmentally friendly apartment. The most important features cited were Energy Star appliances, heaters, and air conditioners and energy-efficient lighting and windows.

For example, green buildings may incorporate reused, recycled or renewable materials in their construction; create healthy indoor environments with minimal pollutants (e.g., not using toxic paints, glues, or dyed materials); and/or feature native landscaping plants that survive without extra watering. In 2008, the City of Dallas adopted a city-wide green building ordinance for new construction; its requirements are designed to reduce greenhouse gas emissions, conserve energy and water, and preserve natural resources. (For more information about green building, check the EPA's site at www.epa.gov/greenbuilding.)

Green Building Certifications   Several programs certify homes as energy efficient. Energy Star is a joint program of the EPA and the U.S. Department of Energy. Components of an Energy Star–qualified home are effective insulation, high-performance windows, tight construction and ducts, efficient heating and cooling equipment, and energy-efficient lighting and appliances. An Energy Star–qualified new home is at least 15% more energy efficient than homes built to the 2004 International Residential Code (IRC). Energy Star offers programs for existing homes also: a do-it-yourself online audit of a home's energy efficiency; professional home energy auditors to make specific recommendations for improving the efficiency of a home (consult a utility provider to see if they offer free or discounted energy audits to customers); and specially-trained contractors who can cost-effectively improve a home's energy efficiency. (See www.energystar.gov for more information.)

Another common green building certification is the Leadership in Energy and Environmental Design (LEED) rating system issued by the U.S. Green Building Council. LEED measures performance in nine key areas that encourage such activities as using a previously developed lot close to community resources and transit; monitoring energy use; reusing and recycling building materials to reduce waste; educating homebuyers; using renewable and clean sources of energy, generated onsite or offsite; and using water-wise landscaping. (Check the U.S. Green Building Council website at www.usgbc.org.)

In response to the growing number of states and localities considering mandatory green building requirements, the National Association of Home Builders, in conjunction with the International Code Council, developed the National Green Building Standard (NGBS), approved in January 2009 as the only consensus-based green building standard for residential properties. Written to be compatible with existing building codes, the NGBS offers uniform guidance on green building practices. (See the National Association of Home Builders website, www.nahbgreen.org, for more information.)

Energy Star seems to have become the most popular new-home energy rating system among homebuilders looking to differentiate themselves from the competition. Energy Star provides a way for consumers to compare one home against another. Posted to the home's electrical box, the Energy Star label is loaded with important information, including annual usage estimates for electricity, natural gas, and CO2 emissions. It also projects the owner's yearly energy savings and includes a HERS (Home Energy Rating System) rating. The standard new home built to 2009 standards would rate a 100. The HERS score drops if builders do anything more than what is required in the way of energy efficiency. Each one-point decrease in the HERS index corresponds to a 1% reduction in energy consumption. Houses with a 72 rating are 28% more efficient than a standard house; a house with a 50 rating would be 50% more efficient, etc. (Lew Sichelman, "Blue Label Signals an Energy-Efficient Home," *Origination News*, September 2012.)

Green Mortgages   An energy-efficient mortgage (EEM) is one that recognizes the added value of energy efficiency; it is typically used to purchase a new home that is already energy efficient such as an Energy Star–qualified home. To get an EEM, a borrower typically has to have a home energy rater verify that the home is energy efficient. An EEM can help a purchaser qualify for a larger loan because a loan company takes into consideration the money saved each month on utility bills. Energy-improvement mortgages (EIMs) allow borrowers to include in the mortgage the cost of energy-efficiency improvements to an existing home without increasing the down payment. EEMs and EIMs are offered on conventional, FHA, or VA loans purchased by Fannie Mae or Freddie Mac. (Additional information on green mortgages is available at www.energystar.gov; then search Energy Efficient Mortgages.)

Tax Incentives   For most Americans, going green can be prohibitively expensive. However, both the state and federal government have incentive programs to encourage homeowners to increase the energy efficiency of their residences and to purchase energy-efficient items. The tax incentives do not cover the total cost of energy improvements; but when coupled with savings on utility bills, they do lessen the financial burden of upgrading a home.

Texas offers an ad valorem property tax exemption for that portion of the appraised property value that arises from the installation or construction of a solar or wind-powered energy device that is primarily for the production and distribution of thermal, mechanical, or electrical energy for onsite use, or devices used to store that energy. Among the eligible renewable technologies are passive solar space heat, solar water heat, wind, and biomass (material derived from plants, animals and their by-products). The tax exemption is available for commercial, industrial, and residential properties. There are dozens of other incentive programs available in Texas for improving energy efficiency; most are offered by cities or utility companies. For example, Austin Energy offers free home-energy improvements to customers with low-to-moderate incomes—including free attic insulation, sealing or replacing ductwork, and installing solar screens. (For more information about incentive programs for Texans, visit www.dsireusa.org/incentives.)

The U.S. government also has many tax incentives—both for businesses and individuals. Periodically, the federal government makes a *Residential Energy Efficiency Tax Credit* available to offset the cost of energy-efficient water heaters, furnaces, boilers, heat pumps, air conditioners, building insulation, windows, doors, roofs, and circulating fans used in qualifying furnaces. It is a personal income tax credit deducted from the tax due to the Internal Revenue Service. Go to www.energystar.gov and click on the *Tax Credits for Energy Efficiency* tab for current program offerings.

The federal *Residential Renewable Energy Tax Credit* is available upon the purchase of renewable energy systems, rather than simply energy-efficient materials and systems. It covers such systems as solar water heaters, wind turbines, fuel cells, and other solar electric technologies. A taxpayer may claim a credit of 30% of qualified expenditures for a system that serves a dwelling unit used as a U.S. residence by the taxpayer. There is no maximum amount that can be deducted for systems placed in service after 2008, and any excess credit may be carried forward to the next tax years. This personal income tax credit is scheduled to expire on December 31, 2016. For more information about other current business and personal tax credits and federal energy loan programs, visit www/dsireusa.org/incentives.

Energystar.gov/rebatefinder is a good source of information on appliances and home improvement products. To encourage customers to buy energy-efficient products, Energy Star partners occasionally sponsor special offers, such as sales tax exemptions or credits or rebates, on qualified products. Partners also occasionally sponsor recycling incentives for the proper disposal of old products.

Remediation Programs   Both Texas and the federal government have laws and programs designed to protect and clean up the environment. Recent developments are listed here.

Texas has legislation
- helping homeowners to make their homes more energy efficient or to install renewable energy devices on their homes by allowing local taxing authorities to offer financing, with payment to be made through an add-on to the owner's property taxes;
- requiring TCEQ to identify cost-effective ways to reduce greenhouse gas emissions;
- authorizing TCEQ to adopt standards for off-shore storage of carbon dioxide emissions;
- creating incentives for the development of clean coal power plants; and
- adding renewable methane to the types of fuels eligible for renewable energy incentives through the Texas Department of Agriculture.

The U.S. government has
- a new Environmental Quality Initiatives Program through which landowners can receive financial assistance from the government when they implement approved environmental measures on their land;
- prohibitions against disposing of specified waste items in a landfill, including fluorescent tubes, batteries, cathode ray tubes, and instruments containing mercury; enter a ZIP Code at www.earth911.com and find the nearest recycling center;
- plans to transform energy use in the nation's commercial buildings by 2050, emphasizing *zero net energy buildings* that produce as much energy as they consume; and
- a program to permit financing energy-efficient home upgrades for up to 10% of the appraised property value; it is available on all Fannie Mae loan products.

Tips for Everyday Green Living   There are dozens of useful tips for green living on a day-to-day basis. Internet sites such as *thedailygreen.com* and *thegreenguide.com* have suggestions for saving energy and money at home, at school, and at the office. Environmentally friendly suggestions include the following:

- When you go out shopping, take your own reusable bags to cut down on the number of paper and plastic bags that are discarded after a single trip.
- Combine your routine shopping trips with other errands to save time and fuel.
- Wash your laundry in cold water instead of hot.
- Unplug unused electronics to counter the "energy vampire" effect.
- Obey the speed limit and avoid rapid, unnecessary acceleration to conserve fuel; every gallon of gasoline burned produces 19 pounds of carbon dioxide.
- Drink water from the tap, instead of buying single-use bottled water, which requires much more energy to produce, store and transport; use filters if you are concerned about the local water supply.
- Use certified recycled paper; replace furnace filters often; switch to greener cleaners; and use reusable fabric towels and napkins rather than paper products.

Where Do We Go From Here?   As a real estate professional, consider obtaining the NAR Green Designation, which provides valuable education on what it means to *go green* in the real estate market and take advantage of the many resources available to become an expert in green housing in your area.

It seems obvious that going green is not optional. Building green communities and implementing environmentally conscious practices is more than just a good idea—it is becoming a necessity for everyone. It is said that if all American households went online to view and pay their bills, it would save over 16 million trees and that moving a thermostat down two degrees in winter and up two degrees in summer would save over 2,000 pounds of carbon dioxide emissions and $100 on a typical home's annual energy bills. And a final point: it has been shown that a green home (any shade of green from small energy improvements to a certified green home) generally sells more quickly and sells for more money per square foot than a standard home—another *green* that most sellers can appreciate.

SUMMARY

The control of land use is exercised in two ways: through public controls and private (or nongovernment) controls. Public controls are ordinances based on the state's police power to protect the public health, safety, morals, and welfare. Through power conferred by state enabling acts, local governments enact comprehensive plans and use tools such as zoning, subdivision regulations, and capital improvement programming to implement the plans.

Zoning ordinances carrying out the provisions of the comprehensive plan segregate residential areas from business and industrial zones and manage not only land use but also height and bulk of buildings and density of populations.

Zoning enforcement involves the city planning staff in issuing conditional use permits and working to resolve nonconforming uses. The zoning board of adjustment hears complaints on zoning administration issues and may issue variances for exceptions to the zoning ordinances. Subdivision regulations are required to maintain control of the development of expanding community areas so that growth will be harmonious with community standards.

Building codes control construction of buildings by specifying standards for construction, materials, and equipment. Building permits are issued to verify compliance with building codes in the construction, alteration, or repair of a building.

Owners, generally developers, exercise private controls through carefully planned deed restrictions that apply to all lot owners. If recorded restrictions are violated, adjoining lot owners may obtain an injunction in JP court to stop the violation. Conditions are imposed by grantors, and violations of conditions stipulated in a deed may allow the grantors or their heirs a reversionary interest in the property.

Public ownership of land provides for such public benefits as parks, highways, schools, and municipal buildings.

In addition to land-use control on the local level, the state and federal governments have intervened when necessary to preserve natural resources through environmental legislation. Concern about environmental risks from asbestos to waste disposal sites is a responsibility of all real estate professionals. Sellers, buyers, real estate agents, appraisers, lenders, and insurance companies all have potential liability related to environmental hazards and to their disclosure.

Concern for the environment has spurred green initiatives at all levels: personal, business, and government. Green building programs, green mortgages, and tax incentives from governments and businesses encourage consumers to invest in both efficient and renewable energy systems. Even small steps on a day-to-day basis can ultimately improve the quality of our environment.

CHAPTER 24 QUESTIONS

1. A covenant in a deed that limits the use of property is known as
   a. a zoning ordinance.
   b. a deed restriction.
   c. laches.
   d. a conditional-use clause.

2. If a landowner wants to use property in a manner that is marginally acceptable under the local zoning ordinance, the planning and zoning commission might approve the request with certain stipulations. This describes
   a. a variance.
   b. downzoning.
   c. a conditional use permit.
   d. an occupancy permit.

3. Public land-use controls include all of the following EXCEPT
   a. subdivision regulations.
   b. deed restrictions.
   c. environmental protection laws.
   d. zoning ordinances.

4. The purpose of a building permit is to
   a. override a deed restriction.
   b. maintain municipal control over the volume of building.
   c. provide evidence of compliance with municipal regulations.
   d. show compliance with restrictive covenants.

5. All of the following would properly be included in a list of deed restrictions EXCEPT
   a. types of buildings that may be constructed.
   b. activities that are not to be conducted at the site.
   c. allowable ethnic origins of purchasers.
   d. minimum size of buildings to be constructed.

6. Zoning powers are conferred on municipal governments
   a. by state enabling acts.
   b. through the comprehensive plan.
   c. by eminent domain.
   d. through escheat.

7. Zoning ordinances control the use of privately owned land by establishing land-use districts. Which is NOT a usual zoning district?
   a. Residential
   b. Commercial
   c. Industrial
   d. Rental

8. Zoning ordinances are generally enforced by
   a. zoning boards of adjustment.
   b. local requirements that building permits will not be issued unless the proposed structure conforms to the zoning ordinance.
   c. deed restrictions.
   d. federal legislation.

9. Zoning boards of adjustment are established to hear complaints about the effects of
   a. restrictive covenants.
   b. a zoning ordinance.
   c. building codes.
   d. laches.

10. Police power allows regulation of all of the following EXCEPT
    a. the number of buildings.
    b. the size of buildings.
    c. building ownership.
    d. building use.

11. A building that is permitted to continue in its former use even though that use does not conform to a newly enacted zoning ordinance is an example of
    a. a nonconforming use.
    b. a variance.
    c. a special use.
    d. inverse condemnation.

12. A restriction in a seller's deed may be enforced by
    a. court injunction.
    b. zoning board of adjustment.
    c. city council.
    d. state legislature.

13. A subdivision declaration reads, "No property within this subdivision may be further subdivided for sale or otherwise, and no property may be used for other than single-family housing." This is an example of
    a. a restrictive covenant.
    b. an illegal reverter clause.
    c. R-1 zoning.
    d. a conditional use clause.

14. Robert owns a large tract of land. After an adequate study of all the relevant facts, he legally divides the land into 30 lots suitable for the construction of residences; puts in utilities, curbs, and gutters; and paves the streets. Robert is a(n)
    a. builder.
    b. developer.
    c. land planner.
    d. urban planner.

15. To protect the public from fraudulent interstate land sales, a developer involved in interstate land sales of 25 or more lots must
    a. provide each prospective purchaser with a printed report disclosing details of the property.
    b. pay the prospective buyer's expenses to see the property involved.
    c. provide preferential financing.
    d. allow a 30-day cancellation period.

16. Asbestos is most dangerous when it
    a. is used as insulation.
    b. crumbles and becomes airborne.
    c. gets wet.
    d. is wrapped around heating and water pipes.

17. Francisco is a real estate salesperson. He shows a pre–World War II house on city water and sewer to Teresa, a prospective buyer. Teresa has two toddlers and is worried about potential health hazards. Which of the following is *TRUE*?
    a. There is very little risk of mold on the premises.
    b. There is probably no asbestos insulation in the home.
    c. Because the house was built before 1978, there is a good likelihood that lead-based paint is present.
    d. Because the house is approximately 60 years old, Teresa should have the water tested for polychlorinated biphenyl.

18. All of the following are true of electromagnetic fields *EXCEPT*
    a. that EmFs are a suspected but unproven cause of cancer, hormonal abnormalities, and behavioral disorders.
    b. that EmFs are generated by all electrical appliances.
    c. that EmFs are present only near high-tension wires or large electrical transformers.
    d. that EmFs are caused by the movement of electricity.

19. Which statement is *NOT* generally connected with green environmental initiatives?
    a. Green buildings are designed to protect occupant health and improve employee productivity.
    b. Green tax incentives are available through the state and federal government to encourage homeowners to increase the energy efficiency of their homes.
    c. Green buildings utilize all new materials rather than old, recycled materials.
    d. Green mortgages permit lenders to adjust qualifying criteria based on lower utility bills.

Detailed rationales for the end-of-chapter review questions are available online at www.dearborn.com through the *Instructor Resource Guides* link.

CHAPTER 25

Real Estate Investment

■ **LEARNING OBJECTIVES**   *When you have completed this chapter, you will be able to*

- ■ **explain** the advantages and disadvantages of investing in real estate;
- ■ **describe** major components of the investment decision: property appreciation, income potential, and the use of leverage and pyramiding;
- ■ **identify** the key tax benefits of investing in real estate;
- ■ **distinguish** the types of real estate investment syndicates and/or trusts; and
- ■ **define** the following *key terms:*

adjusted basis	diversification	real estate investment trust (REIT)
appreciation	exchange	real estate mortgage investment conduit (REMIC)
basis	inflation	
boot	installment sale	
cash flow	intrinsic value	tax credit
capital gain	leverage	tax shelter
depreciation	pyramiding	

OVERVIEW

Real estate is a popular investment. Besides generating income and building up equity, real estate investment can aid in sheltering an owner's income against increasing taxes and the effects of inflation and deflation.

This chapter presents a basic introduction to real estate investment. Major emphasis is placed on investment opportunities open to small or beginning investors, as well as the various tax shelters available to all real estate investors.

Note: The examples and computations given in this chapter are for *illustrative purposes only*, to explain a particular feature or concept of investment, *not to teach the reader how, when, or what amount of money to invest.* Competent legal and tax counsel must be obtained by the investor who desires maximum protection in a very complicated market. Because of this complexity, the practice of brokering investment real estate, although quite alluring, must be restricted to those brokers who are knowledgeable in this specialized field.

INVESTING IN REAL ESTATE

Real estate investments generally fall into one of two types: *real property assets* (such as single-family homes, apartments, shopping centers, and office buildings) and *real estate securities* (such as first-lien mortgage notes, Fannie Mae stocks, Freddie Mac bonds, or Ginnie Mae certificates). Thus, real estate investment means the ownership of one or both types of assets. Based on the experiences of investors during the past few years, investment counselors generally recommend **diversification** within an investment portfolio; among the investment types are savings accounts, individual retirement accounts (IRAs), stocks, bonds, mutual funds, and real estate.

FOR EXAMPLE A family outgrows its first home; rather than sell it, the family decides to keep it and rent it out. This is a form of real estate investment. A couple years later, the family decides to sell the home and, using seller financing, carries back a mortgage on the property. The real estate investment has been converted from dirt to paper, but it is still considered a real estate investment.

Each type of real estate investment meets different objectives for the investor. Real property objectives generally include positive cash flow, equity buildup, tax savings, and property appreciation. Real estate securities generate an income stream without the headaches of property management.

Investment in real estate can also be diversified by varying the forms of ownership: ownership in severalty, in co-ownership, or in trust (which were discussed in Chapter 9), or ownership by syndicates or real estate investment trusts (REITs), which will be discussed later in this chapter.

Often customers ask a real estate broker or salesperson to act as an investment counselor; too often, the licensee is placed in that role by eager, inexperienced investors with high hopes for quick profits. Although it may be the responsibility of real estate licensees to analyze and discuss financial status, future goals, and investment motivations with a potential investor, brokers or salespersons should always *refer a potential real estate investor to a competent tax accountant, attorney, and/or investment specialist* who can give expert, specific advice.

IN PRACTICE   In August 2011, according to NAR, 22% of existing home sales were to investors, and undoubtedly most of those sales were either short sales or foreclosures. Working with real estate investors requires specialized study and training, which can be obtained through professional organizations offering designations recognized in the industry. With research articles, such as "How to Succeed at Short Sales," the NAR website at www.realtor.org provides excellent resources for agents who want to explore the complex, ever-changing world of real estate investing.

Considerations for Prospective Real Estate Investors

In recent years, real estate values have fluctuated widely in various regions of the country. As a result, the ability of investments to produce a return greater than the inflation rate (to serve as an "inflation hedge") has been impaired. This lack of potential profitability has made some real estate investments very unattractive to potential investors.

Still, on a long-term basis, real estate investments have shown an above-average *rate of return*, generally higher than the prevailing interest rate charged by mortgage lenders. Theoretically, this means that an investor can use borrowed money to finance a real estate purchase and feel relatively sure that, if held long enough, the asset will yield more money than it costs to finance the purchase.

In addition, real estate entrepreneurs enjoy many **tax shelters** that are unavailable to investors in other moneymaking activities. These shelters may allow investors to reduce or defer payment of large portions of their federal and state income taxes; however, investments must be analyzed on their *investment merit* rather than as tax shelters for making a good investment out of a poor one. Some of the basic investment tax benefits will be discussed later in this chapter.

Finally, a distinct advantage of real estate investment is that an investor can use borrowed money to finance assets, which significantly increases the investor's buying power. (This concept of *leverage* will be discussed later.) In addition to the advantage of using borrowed money, the portion of an investor's mortgage payments applied to the principal represents *equity buildup* and increases the value of the investor's ownership interest in the asset with each remittance. Careless use of leverage, however, can be disastrous in a declining market.

Unlike stocks and bonds, *real estate is not highly liquid* over a short period. An investor in stocks listed on a stock exchange need only call a stockbroker to liquidate a portion of the assets when funds are needed quickly. In contrast, a real estate investor can raise a limited amount of cash by refinancing the property. If it has to be sold, the property may bring substantially less than market value in a quick sale.

Rarely can a real estate investor sit idly by and watch money grow; *management decisions must be made*. For example: Can the investor effectively manage the property personally, or is it preferable to hire a professional property manager? How much rent should be charged? How should repairs and tenant grievances be handled? Physical and mental energy usually must be invested to make the asset potentially profitable.

Finally, and most important, *a moderately high degree of risk* often is involved in real estate investment. An investor's property may decrease in value or may not generate an income sufficient to make it profitable. The investment may have *negative cash flow* if the income is insufficient to service the debt and pay the operating expenses. Investment decisions must be based on a careful study of all the facts, reinforced by a broad and thorough knowledge of real estate and how it is affected by the marketplace—with legal and tax counsel from the start.

THE INVESTMENT

Traditional income-producing property includes one-to-four-family dwellings, as well as apartment buildings, hotels, motels, commercial properties, shopping centers, office buildings, and industrial properties. These properties may be owned directly by individuals, partnerships, and corporations and managed for appreciation, cash flow (income), and tax shelter purposes.

Appreciation

Property held for **appreciation** generally is expected to increase in value and show a profit when sold at some future date. Income property is just that—property held for current income and an anticipated profit on its sale. Two main factors affect appreciation: inflation and intrinsic value.

Inflation Historically, inflation has been a dominant factor in the growth of our economy. **Inflation** is defined as the *increase in the amount of money in circulation, which results in a decline in its value coupled with a rise in wholesale and retail prices*.

Intrinsic Value *The result of individual choice and preference for a given geographic area, based on features and amenities*, is what defines **intrinsic value**. For example, property located in a well-kept suburb near a shopping center has a greater intrinsic value to most people than similar property located near a sewage treatment plant. As a rule, the greater the intrinsic value, the more money a property can command upon its sale.

Agricultural and Undeveloped Land Quite often, an investor speculates in purchases of either agricultural (farm) land or undeveloped (raw) land located in what she expects will be a major path of growth. In these cases, however, the property's intrinsic value and potential for appreciation are not easy to determine; therefore, this type of investment carries with it many inherent risks. The investor must consider these questions: How fast will the area develop? Will it grow sufficiently to make a good profit? Will the expected growth even occur? More important, will the profits eventually realized from the property be enough to offset the costs of holding the land?

Because technically land cannot wear out, the IRS does not permit an allowance for depreciation of land on an income tax return. Also, land has limited liquidity; few people are willing to purchase raw or agricultural land on short notice. Despite all the risks, land is traditionally a good inflation hedge if held for the long term. It can also generate income to offset some of the holding costs. For example, agricultural land can be leased to tenant farmers for crops, timber production, or grazing. In certain areas of Texas, substantial income can be derived from leasing for recreational uses such as hunting or fishing.

The value of land purchased for appreciation must appreciate at a rate great enough to compensate the owner for the cost of holding it. For example, imagine that an investor purchased raw land for $2,000 per acre with annual real estate taxes of $80 per acre and miscellaneous expenses of approximately 10% per year. For the investor just to break even, the land must appreciate by an average of $280 per acre each year the investor holds the property—an appreciation rate of *14% per year* (10% × $2,000 = $200 + $80 = $280 ÷ $2,000 = 14%).

IN PRACTICE   Most land speculation is based on the principle of present versus future intrinsic value. What was farmland a few years ago could very well be a booming community today. The wise investor knows how to identify, buy, and sell such speculative properties.

Income

Generally speaking, residential rental income property is the wisest initial investment for someone who wishes to buy and personally manage real estate. A single-family dwelling or an owner-occupied duplex-to-fourplex might be a starting point.

Cash Flow   The object of an investor's directing funds into income property is to generate spendable income, usually called *cash flow*. The **cash flow** is the total amount of money remaining after all expenditures have been paid, including taxes, operating costs, and mortgage payments. The cash flow produced by any given parcel of real estate is determined by at least three factors: (1) amount of rent received, (2) operating expenses, and (3) method of debt repayment.

Generally, the amount of *rent* (income) that a property can command depends on a number of factors, including location, physical appearance, and amenities. If the cash flow from rents is not enough to cover all expenses, *a negative cash flow* will result.

To keep cash flow high, an investor should *keep operating expenses reasonably low*. Operating expenses include general maintenance of the building, repairs, utilities, taxes, and tenant services (such as security systems). As with inadequate rental income, poor or overly expensive management can result in negative cash flow.

An investor often stands to make more money by investing borrowed money, usually obtained through a mortgage loan or deed of trust loan. *Low mortgage payments* spread over a long period result in a higher cash flow because they allow the investor to retain more income each month; conversely, higher mortgage payments contribute to a lower cash flow but pay off the loan faster.

Cash-Flow Management   Cash flow may be manipulated as a means of either enhancing the attractiveness of a particular investment to command a higher selling price or producing higher or lower income levels to take advantage of high-income and low-income years for tax purposes. Cash flow may be controlled through the use of various management techniques, such as obtaining high temporary rents through short-term leases or postponing minor repairs to generate a higher cash flow for any given period.

Leverage

Leverage is the use of *borrowed money to finance the bulk of an investment*. As a rule, an investor can receive a maximum return from an initial investment (the down payment) by making a small down payment, paying low interest rates, and spreading mortgage payments over as long a period as possible.

The effect of leveraging is to provide, on sale of the asset, a return that reflects the effect of market forces on the entire amount of the original purchase price but is measured against only the actual cash invested. For example, assume an investor purchases a single-family property with a selling price of $100,000 with $20,000 down, then sells that property five years later for $125,000; the return over five years is $25,000. Disregarding ownership expenses, the return is not 25% ($25,000 compared with $100,000), but 125% of the original amount invested ($25,000 compared with $20,000).

Risks generally are directly proportional to leverage. A high degree of leverage presents the investor and lender with a high degree of risk; lower leverage results in a lower risk. An investor should be prudent in the use of leverage; when property values drop in an area or vacancy rates rise, the highly leveraged investor may be unable to pay even the financing costs of the property.

Equity Buildup   *Equity* is the property's market value minus any debts. *Equity buildup* occurs in two ways potentially: (1) the amount of *principal* payment made each month and (2) any gain in property value due to appreciation. In a sense, equity buildup is like money in the bank to the investor. Although this accumulated equity is not as liquid as money in the bank, it may be sold, exchanged, or even refinanced to be used as leverage for other investments, assuming property values are stable or increasing. Otherwise, equity could decrease.

Pyramiding Through Refinancing   By refinancing existing real estate holdings and using those proceeds to buy additional properties, an investor can increase his assets substantially without investing any additional capital. This practice is known as **pyramiding**. By reinvesting equity borrowed on other properties and doubling holdings periodically, an investor who started out with a small initial cash down payment could own (heavily mortgaged) properties worth hundreds of thousands—even millions—of dollars. Eventually the income derived from such assets could possibly pay off the various mortgage debts and show a handsome profit.

IN PRACTICE   Under some economic conditions, lending institutions will not make loans against the equity in investment properties. In these cases, equity is not available to the investor until the property is sold. Then, the proceeds will be subject to capital gains taxes and the profit tends to be eroded.

TAX BENEFITS

One of the main reasons real estate investments are popular and profitable is that federal law allows investors to use losses generated by such investments to shelter certain portions of their incomes from taxation. Although tax laws change and some tax advantages of owning investment real estate are altered periodically by Congress, with professional tax advice the investor can make a wise real estate purchase.

The discussions and examples used in this section are designed to introduce the reader to general tax concepts. A tax attorney or CPA should be consulted for further details on specific regulations.

Capital Gains

The tax law favors long-term investments by reducing the tax rate on the taxable gain on their sale or **exchange**. A *capital gain* is defined as the difference between the adjusted basis of property and its net selling price.

The steps in calculating the capital gain are as follows:
- **Basis:** The investor's initial cost for the real estate
- **Adjusted basis:** The basis plus the cost of physical improvements and minus depreciation claimed as a tax deduction
- **Capital gain:** Sales price minus selling expenses and adjusted basis

---

MATH CONCEPTS

An investor purchased for $45,000 a single-family dwelling for use as a rental property. The investor is now selling the property for $100,000. Shortly before the sale date, the investor made $3,000 worth of capital improvements to the home. Depreciation of $10,000 on the property improvements has been taken during the term of the investor's ownership. The investor will pay a broker's commission of 7 percent of the sales price and will also pay closing costs of $600. The investor's capital gain is computed as follows:

Selling price:			$100,000
Less:			
7% commission	$ 7,000		
Closing costs	+ 600		
	$ 7,600	– 7,600	
Net sales price		$ 92,400	
Basis:			
Original cost	$ 45,000		
Improvements	+ 3,000		
	$ 48,000		
Less:			
Depreciation	– 10,000		
Adjusted basis:	$38,000	– 38,000	
Total capital gain:		$ 54,400	

Currently, all capital gains on investment real estate are considered taxable.

Capital gains tax rates were modified by the American Taxpayer Relief Act of 2012. The new capital gains tax rates for 2013 and future years are as follows:
- 0% applies to capital gains income if a taxpayer is in the 10% and 15% tax brackets.
- 15% applies to capital gains income if a taxpayer is in the 25%, 28%, 33%, or 35% tax brackets
- 20% applies to capital gains income if a taxpayer is in the new 39.6% tax bracket

Installment Sales

An investor may defer federal income tax on a gain, provided she does not receive all cash for the asset at the time of sale but instead receives payments over two or more years in what is called an **installment sale**. As the name implies, the seller receives payment in installments and pays income tax each year based on the amount received during that year. The installment method often saves an investor money by spreading out the gain over a number of years. The gain may be subject to a lower tax rate than if it were received in one lump-sum payment.

IN PRACTICE   Because part of the tax on the gain can be deferred under an installment sale, the seller can accept a small cash down payment and thus expand the market of potential buyers. This also may put the seller in a position to negotiate for a higher sales price. Note, however, that IRS regulations prohibit a seller from reporting a loss for tax purposes when selling by means of an installment sale.

1031 Exchanges

If an installment sale is not possible in a given transaction, a *1031 exchange* may serve as a means for deferring income tax liability on the sale of investment property. A tax-deferred exchange involves selling investment property and acquiring new investment property without having to pay taxes on the appreciation or having to recapture depreciation at the time of the exchange. Note that the tax is *deferred*, not *eliminated*. An investor can keep exchanging upward in value, adding to assets for as long as he lives without ever personally having to pay any tax on the profits. If the investor's heirs sell the property upon the investor's death, they would pay no capital gains taxes because they would receive the property at current market value. However, if an investor decides to liquidate investments without acquiring replacement property, the investor will be required to pay tax on the total capital gain accumulated since the purchase of the initial property, as well as tax on depreciation recapture.

In a 1031 exchange, the property to be sold is called the "old" or relinquished property. The property to be purchased is the "new" or "replacement" property. The term *sale* refers to the marketing of the relinquished property, and the term *purchase* refers to the acquisition of the replacement property. To qualify as a tax-deferred exchange, the properties involved must be of *like kind*—for example, investment real estate for investment real estate, such as an apartment building for an office building. To defer all the gain in an exchange, (1) the value of the replacement property must be equal to or greater than the value of the old property, (2) all equity from the old property must be used in the purchase of the new property, and (3) the new property must have equal or more debt than the old property. Any additional capital or personal property included with the transaction to even out the exchange is considered **boot**, and the party receiving it is taxed at the time of the exchange. The value of the boot is added to the basis of the property for which it is given. (Refer to the following *math concepts* section.)

Delayed Exchange   A like-kind exchange may be a *simultaneous exchange* or a *delayed exchange*. In a simultaneous exchange, two parties trade properties at the same time, each person relinquishing his own property in exchange for the other person's property. However, if the old and new properties are not both identified at the same time, a simultaneous exchange cannot take place. Therefore, an investor may elect to have a delayed exchange, sometimes called a *Starker Exchange*, in which the taxpayer sells the relinquished property first and then buys the replacement property. For the delayed exchange transaction to qualify for deferral of capital gains, strict rules must be followed. Some of those rules are as follows:

■ *The 45-day rule for identification*—The new (replacement) property must be closed or identified within 45 days after the closing on the old (relinquished) property. One or more potential replacement properties can be identified under the following conditions:

■ *The three-property rule*—Up to three properties can be identified without regard to their combined market values.

■ *The 200% rule*—If more than three properties are on the list, the combined purchase price of all properties on the list cannot exceed twice the selling price of the old property.

■ *The 95% rule*—Any number of replacement properties may be identified if the fair market value of the properties actually acquired is at least 95% of the aggregate fair market value of all the potential replacement properties listed.

■ *The 180-day rule for receipt of replacement property*—The new property or properties (which must be on the list) must be closed within 180 days of the closing on the old property, or up to the date that year's income tax return is due. The 45-day and 180-day periods run concurrently; therefore, normally the investor would have 135 days to close after the 45-day period has expired. For a closing on December 29, however, the investor would only have 109 days to the April 15 tax deadline in which to complete the transactions unless the investor filed an income tax extension with the IRS.

MATH CONCEPTS

Investor Smith owns an apartment building with a market value of $200,000 and an adjusted basis of $90,000. He wants to exchange it for a different apartment building, which has a market value of $250,000 and an adjusted basis of $150,000 and is owned by investor Jones.

	Investor Smith	Investor Jones
Market value	$200,000	$250,000
Debt	0	0
Equity	$200,000	$250,000
To balance equities	$ 50,000	

Investor Smith must pay investor Jones $50,000 (boot) to balance the equities. After the exchange, the basis in investor Smith's new apartment building is $140,000, computed as follows:

Adjusted cost basis of old apartment building	$ 90,000
Boot given in the exchange	+ 50,000
Adjusted cost basis of new apartment building	$140,000

Investor Jones, on the other hand, exchanged a building worth $250,000 with an adjusted cost basis of $150,000 for a building worth only $200,000 plus $50,000 cash. She must pay tax on the $50,000 boot, but her basis in the new building remains the same as for the building she exchanged ($150,000).

Market value of old apartment building	$250,000
Adjusted cost basis of old apartment building	−150,000
Potential gain	$100,000

If investor Jones had received all cash, her gain would have been $100,000. Because she received only $50,000 in cash, she will pay tax only on the $50,000 cash received. The adjusted cost basis of her new apartment building is computed as follows:

Adjusted cost basis of old apartment building	$150,000
Gain recognized	+ 50,000
Cash received	− 50,000
Adjusted cost basis of new apartment building	$150,000

An independent third-party *qualified intermediary*, also known as an *accommodator* or *exchange facilitator*, must handle the exchange. When the sale of the relinquished property is closed, the proceeds from the sale are given to the intermediary—not to the investor. Then, when the replacement property is purchased, the intermediary transfers the proceeds to closing. The investor takes title; and with few exceptions, whoever had title to the old property must take title to the new property: a corporation to a corporation or a husband and wife to a husband and wife.

FOR EXAMPLE   Mary wants to exchange a warehouse that she owns for a small strip mall. However, her warehouse sells before she finds a suitable property for an exchange; therefore, she will have to complete the exchange transaction under the 1031 *delayed exchange* rules. A qualified intermediary will hold the funds from the sale of the warehouse. Mary must identify possible replacement properties within 45 days after closing on the warehouse, and she must close on a replacement within 180 days of the closing on the warehouse. The qualified intermediary will transfer the money from the sale of the warehouse to the closing, and Mary will take title to the new property.

Reverse 1031 Exchange   A *reverse 1031 exchange* is the opposite of a delayed exchange. In a reverse exchange, the investor acquires the new (replacement) property before selling the old (relinquished) property. There are many exchange situations in which the reverse exchange would be applicable, and they are becoming increasingly common in commercial real estate transactions. For example, if an investor wants to find a new property before attempting to market the existing property, a reverse exchange would be conducted through an exchange accommodation titleholder (EAT), who *can be* a qualified intermediary and who will take title to the new property. The investor would then have 45 days from the date of title transfer on the new property to identify the property to be sold and 180 days to close on it, after which the title on the new property will be transferred to the investor. Because the rules for structuring a reverse exchange are more complicated than those for a delayed exchange, it is a more expensive exchange option. Additionally, the investor either must be able to pay for the new property before selling the old property or must get a short-term loan.

Delayed and reverse exchanges require that exact steps be followed. There are generally no exceptions to the rules and no extensions on the timelines. *Careful planning is crucial to the successful execution of a 1031 tax-deferred exchange. It should be entered into only with professional assistance.*

IN PRACTICE   In 2008, the IRS announced that limited personal use will not prevent a rental dwelling unit from qualifying for a tax-deferred like-kind exchange. The relinquished property must be owned by the taxpayer for at least 24 months immediately *before* the exchange. Within each of the two 12-month periods before the exchange, (a) the taxpayer must rent the dwelling to another person at fair market value for 14 days or more, and (b) the taxpayer's personal use must not exceed the greater of 14 days or 10% of the number of rental days in the 12-month period. The replacement property must meet the same requirements: owned 24 months *after* the sale, rented to another person at fair market value for at least 14 days each year, and personal use that cannot exceed 14 days or 10% of the rental days each year. A taxpayer who sells the replacement property within 24 months of acquisition must file an amended tax return.

Depreciation

After a tax-deferred exchange, an investor can depreciate an amount equal to the remaining balance on the relinquished property plus the amount that the new property exceeds the deferred gain. An investor does not get to "start over" with full depreciation on the new property.

Depreciation is an accounting concept that allows an investor to recover the cost of an income-producing asset by way of tax deductions over the period of the asset's useful life as determined by the IRS. Although investors rarely purchase property without the expectation that it will appreciate over time, the view of the IRS is that all physical structures will deteriorate and hence lose value over time. Depreciation may have very little relationship to the actual physical deterioration of the asset. Depreciation deductions may be taken only on personal property and improvements to land and only if they are used in a trade or business or for the production of income. Thus an individual cannot claim a depreciation deduction on a personal residence, with the exception of that portion of a residence used for a business. *Land cannot be depreciated*—technically it never wears out or becomes obsolete.

If depreciation is taken in equal amounts over an asset's useful life, the method used is called *straight-line depreciation*. Since May 13, 1993, the recovery period for residential rental property has been 27½ years; nonresidential property, 39 years.

Normally, in the initial years of a real estate investment, the taxable loss may exceed cash outlays. This happens because depreciation may exceed the gross income generated by the investment. Thus an investor can have a positive cash flow from an investment and still report a loss on a tax return.

Deductions and TRA '86

The Tax Reform Act of 1986 limits the deductibility of losses from rental property. The first $25,000 of loss can be used to offset income from any source, provided the investor *actively participates* in the management and operation of the property and has taxable income of no more than $100,000 before the deduction is made. The deduction is reduced by $0.50 for every dollar of income over $100,000 and is thus eliminated completely when income reaches $150,000. Two examples help illustrate the impact of this law.

■ Harvey has adjusted gross income of $130,000 and losses of $20,000 from three apartment buildings that he owns and personally manages. Harvey is entitled to a deduction of only $10,000 (because the $25,000 maximum is reduced by $0.50 for every dollar of the $30,000 Harvey earned over $100,000), reducing his taxable income to $120,000.

■ Helen has adjusted gross income of $100,000 and losses of $20,000 from rental property that she actively manages. Helen is entitled to a deduction of the full $20,000 (her income does not exceed $100,000), reducing her taxable income to $80,000.

Active participation in management may range from personally managing the day-to-day operation of the rental property with no outside assistance to simply making management decisions (for example, approving new tenants and lease terms) while hiring others to provide services. *Passive* participation includes acting as a limited partner, that is, contributing investment monies but having no voice in management operations.

TRA '86 prevents an investor from using a loss from a passive activity to shelter active income (such as wages) or portfolio income (such as stock dividends, bank interest, capital gains, and royalties). Generally, a passive investor can offset investment losses only against investment income. If the passive investor has no other current investment income, the loss may be carried over to offset investment income in future years. If the investment is sold before the loss is used, it may offset what otherwise would be a taxable gain on the sale.

Special passive loss rules apply to real estate professionals. If a person (1) materially participates in the activities, (2) spends at least 750 hours in real property businesses, and (3) performs more than 50% of personal services for the year in the real property businesses, then the person would be considered a real estate professional and would not be subject to the above passive loss limitations. The requirements must be met on a yearly basis. In one year, a person might be a real estate professional not subject to the passive loss limitations, and in the next year, the person might be an active investor subject to the passive loss rules.

Tax Credits   A tax credit is a direct reduction in tax due, rather than a deduction from income on which tax is computed. A tax credit is therefore of far greater value than a tax deduction.

Investors in older building renovations and low-income housing projects may use designated tax credits to offset tax on a portion of other income. This is a major exception to the rule requiring active participation in the project; even passive investors can take advantage of tax credits. However, there is a maximum income level on which the credits can be taken.

Since 1976, tax credits have been provided for taxpayers who renovate historic property. Historic property is property so designated by the Department of the Interior and listed in the *National Register of Historic Landmarks* or property of historic significance that is located in an area certified by a state as a historic district. The allowable credit is 20% of the money spent on renovation of historic property. The work must be accomplished in accordance with federal historic property guidelines and certified by the U.S. Department of the Interior. After renovation, the property must be used as a place of business or rented—it cannot be used as the personal residence of the person taking the tax credit.

REAL ESTATE INVESTMENT SYNDICATES

A *real estate investment syndicate* is a business venture in which a group of people pools its resources to own and/or develop a particular piece of property. In this manner, people with only modest capital can invest in large-scale, high-profit, high-risk operations such as mixed-use developments and shopping centers. Some profit is realized from rents collected on the investment, but the main return usually comes when the syndicate sells the property after sufficient appreciation.

A syndicate investor enjoys the same federal income tax advantages as a direct ownership real estate investor because no matter how small the interest in the syndicate properties, the investor owns a certain percentage of a particular parcel of real estate. As a real estate owner, the syndicate investor is as much entitled to preferential tax treatment as is a sole owner of a similar property. However, syndicate interests may be more difficult to sell on the open market than real estate. In addition, approval by the syndicate's management may be required before an investor can sell her interest in the project. Some partnership agreements may require that such interest be sold only to another member of the syndicate.

Syndicate participation can take many different legal forms, from tenancy in common to various kinds of partnerships, corporations, and trusts. *Private syndication*, which generally involves a small group of closely associated and/or widely experienced investors, is distinguished from *public syndication*, which generally involves a much larger group of investors who may or may not be knowledgeable about real estate as an investment. The distinction between the two, however, usually is based on the nature of the arrangement between syndicator and investors, not on the type of syndicate.

Federal securities laws include provisions to control and regulate the offering and sale of securities to protect members of the public who are not sophisticated investors. State laws, commonly referred to as *blue-sky laws*, protect investors against securities fraud by requiring sellers of new issues to register their offerings and provide financial details. This allows investors to base their judgments on trustworthy data, avoiding speculative ventures that have "as much value as a patch of blue sky." Real estate securities must be registered with state officials and/or with the federal Securities & Exchange Commission (SEC) when they meet the defined conditions of a public offering. The number of prospects solicited, the total number of investors or participants, the financial background and sophistication of the investors, and the value or price per unit of investment are pertinent facts. Salespersons of real estate securities may be required to obtain special licenses and state registration.

Forms of Syndicates

Real estate investment syndicates usually are organized as general, limited, or limited liability partnerships. These partnership forms were described in Chapter 9 but are recapped here.

A *general partnership* is organized so that all members of the group share equally in the managerial decisions, profits, and losses involved with the investment. A certain member (or members) of the syndicate is designated to act as trustee for the group and holds title to the property and maintains it in the syndicate's name.

Under a *limited partnership* agreement, one party (or parties), usually a property developer or real estate broker, organizes, operates, and is responsible for the entire syndicate. This person is called the *general partner*. The other members of the partnership are passive investors with no voice in the organization and direction of the operation; they are called *limited partners*. The limited partners share in the profits, and out of such profits they compensate the general partner for her efforts. Unlike a general partnership, in which each member is responsible for the total losses (if any) of the syndicate, each limited partner stands to lose only as much as she invests—nothing more. The general partner(s) is (are) totally responsible for any excess losses incurred by the investment. The sale of a limited partnership interest involves the sale of an investment security and, as such, is subject to state and federal securities laws.

The *limited liability partnership* protects individual partners from liability for debts and obligations of the partnership arising from errors, omissions, negligence, and incompetence on the part of one partner—unless there is knowledge of the misconduct at the time of the occurrence.

REAL ESTATE INVESTMENT TRUSTS

A **real estate investment trust (REIT)** is a security that is invested in real estate directly, either through properties or mortgages. By directing funds into REITs, real estate investors can take advantage of the same tax benefits as mutual fund investors. A REIT does not have to pay corporate income tax as long as 90% of its income is distributed to its shareholders and certain other conditions are met. Among the conditions for qualifying as a REIT are the requirements that 100 or more members hold shares in the trust and that 75% of the REIT's assets must be invested in real estate, other REITs, securities, or cash. The three types of investment trusts are equity REITs, mortgage REITs, and hybrid REITs.

Equity REITs Much like mutual fund operations, equity REITs pool an assortment of large-scale income properties and sell shares to investors. This is in contrast to a real estate syndicate, through which several investors pool their funds to purchase one particular property. An equity REIT also differs from a syndicate in that the REIT realizes and directs its main profits through the *income* derived from the various properties it owns rather than from the sale of those properties.

Mortgage REITs   Mortgage REITs operate similarly to equity REITs, except that mortgage REITs buy and sell real estate mortgages (usually short-term junior instruments) rather than real property. A mortgage REIT's major sources of income are mortgage interest and origination fees. Mortgage REITs also may make construction loans and finance land acquisitions.

Hybrid REITs   Hybrid REITs invest shareholders' funds in both real estate assets and mortgage loans. These types of REITs are felt by some to be best able to withstand economic slumps because they can balance their investments and liabilities more efficiently than the other types of REITs.

REAL ESTATE MORTGAGE INVESTMENT CONDUITS

A **real estate mortgage investment conduit (REMIC)** is a tax device that allows cash flows from an underlying block of commercial mortgages to be passed through to security holders without being subject to income taxes at the level of the trustee or agent. Complex rules have been established to create a REMIC, and reports on its activities must be made to the IRS.

SUMMARY

Traditionally, real estate investments command a high rate of return, while at the same time allowing an investor to take advantage of many tax shelters unavailable to other types of investors. In addition, real estate is generally an effective inflation hedge, and an investor can make use of other people's money to make investments through leverage. On the other hand, real estate is *not* a highly liquid investment and often carries with it a high degree of risk. Also, investing in real estate is difficult without expert advice, and a certain amount of mental and physical effort is required to establish and maintain the investment.

Investment property held for appreciation purposes is expected to increase in value to a point where its selling price is enough to cover holding costs and show a profit as well although market conditions do not always permit this. The two main factors affecting appreciation are inflation and the property's present and future intrinsic value. Real estate held for income purposes generally is expected to generate a steady flow of income, called *cash flow*, and to show a profit upon its sale.

For an investor to take advantage of maximum leverage in financing an investment, he should attempt to make a small down payment, pay low interest rates, and spread mortgage payments over as long a period as possible. By holding and refinancing properties, known as *pyramiding*, an investor can substantially increase holdings without investing additional capital.

Under certain conditions, an investor may be able to defer federal income taxes on gain realized from the sale of an investment property through an installment sale. In this situation, the investor pays income tax only on the adjusted portion of the total gain received in any year.

By exchanging one property for another with an equal or greater selling value, an investor can defer paying tax on the gain realized until sometime in the future. A total tax deferment is possible only if the investor receives no cash or other incentive (boot) to even out the exchange. Any cash or property received as boot is taxed. Using a delayed exchange, a person can relinquish property, identify the property to be received in the exchange within 45 days, and take title to the replacement property within 180 days of relinquishing the original property. A reverse exchange allows an investor to purchase the new (replacement) property before selling the old (relinquished) property.

Depreciation allows an investor to recover in tax deductions the basis of an asset over the period of its useful life. Only costs of improvements to land may be recovered, not costs for the land itself.

Individuals also may invest in real estate through an investment syndicate. Syndicates may take many different legal forms, from tenancy in common to various kinds of partnerships, corporations, and trusts. Two additional forms of real estate investment are the real estate mortgage investment conduit (REMIC) and the real estate investment trust (REIT). A REMIC is a vehicle by which commercial mortgages are securitized. REITs can be invested in properties (equity REITs), mortgages (mortgage REITs), or a combination of the two (hybrid REITs).

CHAPTER 25 QUESTIONS

1. When an investor purchases a parcel of real estate through the use of borrowed funds, she is taking advantage of
   a. leverage.
   b. depreciation.
   c. capital gains.
   d. exchanging.

2. An investment syndicate in which all members share equally in the managerial decisions, profits, and losses involved in the venture is an example of a
   a. real estate investment trust.
   b. limited partnership.
   c. real estate mortgage trust.
   d. general partnership.

3. The increase of money in circulation coupled with a rise in prices, resulting in a decline in the value of money, is called
   a. appreciation.
   b. inflation.
   c. deflation.
   d. recapture.

4. For both income and appreciation purposes, Mary is contemplating the purchase of an apartment building as an investment at a price of $150,000. All else being equal, which choice should yield Mary the largest percentage of return on her initial investment after the first year?
   a. Mary pays $150,000 cash for the property.
   b. Mary gives the seller a $75,000 down payment and a 15-year purchase money mortgage for the balance at 11% interest.
   c. Mary gives the seller $15,000 down and obtains a 30-year mortgage for the balance at 12% interest.
   d. Mary gives the seller $20,000 down and agrees to pay the seller 10% of the unpaid balance each year for 10 years, plus 11% interest.

5. For tax purposes, the initial cost of an investment property, plus the cost of any subsequent improvements to the property, less the amount of any depreciation claimed as a tax deduction, represents the investment's
   a. adjusted basis.
   b. gains.
   c. basis.
   d. salvage value.

6. Julia is exchanging her apartment building for an apartment building of greater market value and must include a $10,000 boot to even out the exchange. Which of the following may she use as a boot?
   a. $10,000 cash
   b. Common stock with a current market value of $10,000
   c. An automobile with a current market value of $10,000
   d. Any of the above if acceptable to the exchangers

7. A property's equity represents its current value less
   a. depreciation deductions.
   b. mortgage indebtedness.
   c. physical improvements.
   d. selling costs and depreciation deductions.

8. Barney sold his four-unit apartment building and purchased a six-unit building of the same market value. The gain on the sale of his four-unit apartment building is $28,000. This gain
   a. will not be taxed, because Barney exchanged properties.
   b. will be taxed.
   c. will be amortized over 27½ years.
   d. is called *net debt relief*.

9. In an installment sale, taxable gain is received and must be reported as income by the seller

    a. in the year the sale is initiated.
    b. in the year the final installment payment is made.
    c. in each year that installment payments are received.
    d. at any one time during the period installment payments are received.

10. When investors hold and refinance investment properties, using their equities as leverage, they are taking advantage of which concept?

    a. Pyramiding
    b. Tax sheltered income
    c. Recapture
    d. Useful life

11. A small multifamily property generates $50,000 in rental income with expenses of $45,000 annually, including $35,000 in debt service. The property appreciates about $25,000 a year. On this property the cash flow is

    a. $5,000.
    b. $15,000.
    c. $25,000.
    d. $30,000.

12. Shareholders in a real estate investment trust generally

    a. receive most of the trust's income each year.
    b. take an active part in management.
    c. do not pay IRS taxes on their income from the REIT since the REIT pays taxes as a corporation.
    d. realize their main profit through sales of property.

Detailed rationales for the end-of-chapter review questions are available online at www.dearborn.com through the *Instructor Resource Guides* link.

Glossary

abandonment The voluntary surrender or relinquishment of possession of real property with the intention of terminating one's possession or interest but without the vesting of this interest in any other person, such as when a person moves and abandons leased property before the lease term has expired.

abatement Elimination or reduction of real estate taxes to attract new business to an area.

abstract of title The condensed history of a title to a particular parcel of real estate, consisting of a summary of the original grant and all subsequent conveyances and encumbrances affecting the property and a certification by the abstractor that the history is complete and accurate.

abstract of title with lawyer's opinion An abstract of title that a lawyer has examined and has certified to be, in his opinion, an accurate statement of fact.

acceleration clause The clause in a mortgage or trust deed or note that can be enforced to make the entire amount of principal and interest due immediately if the mortgagor defaults on an installment payment or other covenant.

accession Acquiring title to additions or improvements to real property as a result of the annexation of fixtures or the accretion of alluvial deposits along the banks of streams.

accretion The increase or addition of land by the deposit of sand or soil washed up naturally from a river, lake, or sea.

accrued items On a closing statement, items of expense that are incurred but not yet payable, such as interest on a mortgage loan or taxes on real property.

acknowledgment A formal declaration before a notary public or other authorized public officer that authenticates signatures on a document for the purpose of recording.

acre A measure of land equal to 43,560 square feet, 4,840 square yards, 4,047 square meters, 160 square rods, or 0.4047 hectare.

actual eviction The result of legal action, originated by a lessor, whereby a defaulted tenant is physically ousted from the rented property pursuant to a court order. *See also* eviction.

actual notice Express information or fact; that which is known; direct knowledge.

adjustable-rate mortgage (ARM) A mortgage loan in which the interest rate may increase or decrease at specified intervals over the life of the loan.

adjusted basis *See* basis.

adjusted sales price For income tax purposes, the actual sales price reduced by allowable sales expenses.

administrator/administratrix A man/woman appointed by a court to settle the estate of a deceased person when there is no will; *contrast with* executor/executrix.

ad valorem tax A tax levied according to value; generally used to refer to real estate tax.

adverse possession The actual, visible, hostile, notorious, exclusive, and continuous possession of another's land under a claim of title. Possession for a statutory period may be a means of acquiring title.

agency The relationship between a principal and an agent wherein the agent is authorized to represent the principal in certain transactions.

agency by ratification An agency relationship that is established after the fact.

agent One who acts or has the power to act for another. A fiduciary relationship is created under the *law of agency* when a property owner, as the principal, executes a listing agreement or management contract authorizing a licensed real estate broker to be her agent.

air lot A designated airspace over a piece of land. An air lot, like surface property, may be transferred.

air rights The right to use the open space above a property, generally allowing the surface to be used for another purpose.

alienation The act of transferring property to another. Alienation may be voluntary, such as by gift or sale, or involuntary, as through eminent domain or adverse possession.

alienation clause The clause in a mortgage or deed of trust stating that the balance of the secured debt becomes immediately due and payable at the mortgagee's option if the property is sold by the mortgagor. In effect, this clause prevents the mortgagor from assigning the debt without the mortgagee's approval; also called a *due-on-sale clause*.

allodial system A system of land ownership in which land is held free and clear of any rent or service due to the government; commonly contrasted with the feudal system. In the United States, land is held under the allodial system.

Americans with Disabilities Act A federal law to eliminate discrimination against individuals with disabilities by mandating equal access to jobs, public accommodations, government services, public transportation, and telecommunications.

amortization A loan in which the principal as well as the interest is payable in monthly or other periodic installments over the term of the loan.

amount realized on sale The amount of gain, or profit, subject to the income tax.

antitrust laws Laws designed to preserve the free enterprise of the open marketplace by making illegal certain private conspiracies and combinations formed to minimize competition. Violations of antitrust laws in the real estate business generally involve *price-fixing* (brokers conspiring to set fixed compensation rates), *allocation of customers or markets* (brokers agreeing to limit their areas of trade or dealing to certain areas or properties), or agreement to boycott competitors.

apartment locator A real estate agent who matches landlords and tenants. Usually working as an independent contractor for several apartment complexes, the locator finds apartment units for prospective tenants, qualifies prospective tenants, and negotiates leases with the apartment complexes.

appointed licensee A licensee associated with and appointed by an intermediary broker to communicate with, carry out instructions of, and provide opinions and advice to the parties to whom the licensee is appointed.

appraisal An estimate of the quantity, quality, or value of something. The process through which conclusions of property value are obtained; also refers to the report that sets forth the process of estimation and conclusion of value.

appraisal review board A group of people who hear appeals concerning assessed valuations for tax purposes and recommend or deny changes in values shown of record.

appraised value An estimate of the present worth of a property.

appraiser A person who develops an opinion of value for a parcel of real estate. Licensed by the Texas Appraiser Licensing and Certification Board.

appreciation An increase in the worth or value of a property due to economic or related causes, which may prove to be either temporary or permanent; opposite of depreciation.

apprentice inspector A person who is in training under the direct supervision of a professional inspector or a real estate inspector to become qualified to perform real estate inspections.

appurtenances Those rights, privileges, and improvements that belong to and pass with the transfer of real property but are not necessarily a part of the property, such as rights-of-way, easements, water rights, and property improvements.

area The size in square units (square inches, etc.) of a two-dimensional figure such as a triangle or rectangle.

ARELLO The Association of Real Estate License Law Officials; promotes uniform policies and standards in the field of license law administration and enforcement across the United States.

assemblage The combining of two or more adjoining lots into one larger tract to increase the total value.

assessed value The value set upon property for taxation purposes.

assessment The imposition of a tax, charge, or levy, usually according to established rates.

assessment roll The public record of the assessed values of all lands and buildings within a specific area.

assignment The transfer in writing of interest in a contract, mortgage, lease, or other instrument.

assumption of mortgage Acquiring title to property on which there is an existing mortgage and agreeing to be personally liable for the terms and conditions of the mortgage, including payments; *contrast with* subject to mortgage.

attachment 1. The act of taking a person's property into legal custody by writ or other judicial order to hold it available for application to that person's debt to a creditor. 2. A process of converting personal property to real estate.

attorney One who acts for or represents another; must be licensed as such to give legal advice. No license is required to act under a power of attorney (an attorney-in-fact).

attorney's opinion of title A writing based on a lawyer's reading of an abstract of title that specifies any title defects and names the legal titleholder as the lawyer interprets it; states whether a seller may convey good title.

auctioneer A person who conducts the sale of property by competitive bid using any method, format, or venue; licensed by the Texas Department of Licensing and Regulation.

automated underwriting The process of electronically evaluating a loan application, assessing a borrower's ability to repay, and subsequently providing a recommendation for or against loan approval.

automatic extension　A clause in a listing agreement stating that the agreement will continue automatically for a certain period after its expiration date; illegal in Texas.

avulsion　The sudden tearing away of land, as by earthquake, flood, volcanic action, or a sudden change in the course of a stream.

balloon payment　A final payment of a mortgage loan that is considerably larger than the required periodic payments because the loan amount was not fully amortized.

bargain and sale deed　*See* deed without warranty.

base line　One of a set of imaginary lines running east and west and crossing a principal meridian at a definite point, used by surveyors for reference in locating and describing land under the rectangular survey (or government survey) system of property description.

basis　The dollar amount associated with an asset to determine annual depreciation and gain or loss on the sale of the asset. The owner's basis is the cost of the property; adding the value of any capital expenditures for improvements to the property and subtracting any depreciation claimed as a tax deduction yields the *adjusted basis*.

benchmark　A permanent reference mark or point established for use by surveyors in measuring differences in elevation.

beneficiary　1. The person for whom a trust operates or in whose behalf the income from a trust estate is drawn. 2. A lender who lends money on real estate and takes back a note and trust deed from the borrower.

bequest　The transfer of personal property to a legatee in accordance with a will.

bilateral contract　*See* contract.

bill of sale　A written instrument given to pass title to personal property.

biweekly payment plan　A loan that calls for 26 half-month payments a year, resulting in an earlier loan retirement date and lower total interest costs than with a typical fully amortized loan.

blanket mortgage　A mortgage covering more than one parcel of real estate, providing for each parcel's partial release from the mortgage lien on repayment of a definite portion of the debt.

blockbusting　The illegal practice of inducing homeowners to sell their properties by making representations regarding the entry or prospective entry of minority persons into the neighborhood.

blue-sky laws　Common name for state and federal laws that regulate the registration and sale of investment securities.

boot　Money or property given to make up any difference in value or equity between two properties in an *exchange*.

branch office　A secondary place of business apart from the principal or main office from which real estate business is conducted. A branch office generally must be run by a licensed real estate broker working on behalf of the broker who operates the principal office.

breach of contract　Violation of any terms or conditions in a contract without legal excuse; for example, failure to make a payment when it is due.

broker　One who buys and sells for another for a commission. *See also* real estate broker.

brokerage　For a commission or fee, bringing together parties interested in buying, selling, exchanging, or leasing real property.

broker-salesperson　A person who has passed the broker's licensing examination but works on behalf of another licensed broker.

buffer zone　Zoning districts that gradually change from a higher-intensity use to a lower-intensity use.

building code　An ordinance that specifies minimum standards of construction for buildings to protect public safety and health.

building line　A line fixed at a certain distance from the front and/or sides of a lot beyond which no structure can project. *See also* setback.

building permit　A permission issued by a city for the construction of a building to ensure compliance with building codes.

bundle of legal rights　The concept of land ownership that means *ownership of all legal rights to the land*—for example, possession, control within the law, and enjoyment—rather than ownership of the land itself.

business cycle　Upward and downward fluctuations in business activity through the stages of expansion, recession, depression, and revival.

business interruption insurance　A form of coverage that provides income to a business in the event the premises become untenable.

buydown mortgage　A mortgage on which a cash payment, usually measured in points, has been made to the lender to reduce the interest rate a borrower must pay; usually "bought down" for the first two or three years of the loan.

buyer agency　An agency relationship between the broker and the buyer, with fiduciary duties owed to the buyer.

buyer representation agreement　A contract that establishes a broker-buyer agency relationship.

buyer's broker　A licensee who has declared to represent only the buyer in a transaction, regardless of whether compensation is paid by the buyer or the listing broker through a commission split.

Canons of Professional Ethics and Conduct A code of ethics established by the Texas Real Estate Commission and published in its Rules.

capital gain Income earned from the sale of an asset.

capital investment The initial capital and the long-term expenditures made to establish and maintain a business or investment property.

capitalization A mathematical process for estimating the value of an income-producing property by dividing the annual net operating income by the capitalization rate. The formula is expressed as

$$\frac{\text{Income}}{\text{Rate}} = \text{Value}$$

capitalization rate The rate of return a property will produce on the owner's investment.

cash flow The net spendable income from an investment, determined by deducting all operating and fixed expenses from the gross income. If expenses exceed income, a *negative cash flow* is the result.

casualty insurance A type of policy that protects a property owner or other person from loss or injury sustained as a result of theft, vandalism, or similar occurrences.

caveat emptor A Latin phrase meaning "Let the buyer beware."

chain of title The succession of conveyances from some accepted starting point, whereby the present holder of real property derives title.

channeling The illegal practice of directing people to, or away from, certain areas or neighborhoods because of minority status. *See also* steering.

chattel Personal property; personalty.

Civil Rights Act of 1866 The first and primary law guaranteeing equal rights to all U.S. citizens; prohibits all discrimination based on race or color.

client The person who employs an agent to perform a service for a fee.

closing The consummation of a real estate transaction, when the seller delivers title to the buyer in exchange for payment by the buyer of the purchase price.

closing agent The person responsible for conducting the settlement of a real estate sale.

closing statement A detailed cash accounting of a real estate transaction showing all cash received, all charges and credits made, and all cash paid out in the transaction. *See also* HUD-1.

cloud on the title Any document, claim, unreleased lien, or encumbrance that may impair the title to real property or make the title doubtful; usually revealed by a title search and removed by either a quitclaim deed or suit to quiet title.

Code of Ethics An agreement to which all REAL-TORS® must subscribe and that holds the members to high standards of conduct.

codicil A supplement or an addition to a will, executed with the same formalities as a will, that normally does not revoke the entire will.

coinsurance clause A provision in insurance policies covering real property that requires that the policyholder maintain coverage generally equal to at least 80% of the property's actual replacement cost.

collateral Something of value deposited with a lender as a pledge to secure repayment of a loan.

commercial broker Brokers that specialize in business property, including offices, shopping centers, stores, theaters, hotels, industrial parks, and parking facilities.

commingle The illegal act of a real estate broker who mixes the money of other people with his own money instead of maintaining a separate *trust account* for other parties' funds held temporarily by the broker.

commission Payment to a broker for services rendered, such as in the sale or purchase of real property; usually a percentage of the selling price of the property.

commitment *See* title commitment.

common elements Parts of a property that are necessary or convenient to the existence, maintenance, and safety of a condominium or are normally in common use by all of the condominium residents. Each condominium owner has an undivided ownership interest in the general and limited common elements.

common law The body of law based on custom, usage, and court decisions.

community property A system of property ownership based on the theory that each spouse has an equal interest in the property acquired by the efforts of either spouse during marriage.

community property right of survivorship A declaration made by husband and wife that community property will go to the survivor upon the death of one party; eliminates probate.

Community Reinvestment Act The federal law that requires that federally regulated lenders describe the geographic market area they serve. Deposits from that area are to be reinvested in that area whenever practical.

comparables   Properties listed in an appraisal report that are substantially equivalent to the subject property and are used to compare and establish a value of the subject property.

comparative market analysis (CMA)   A comparison of the prices of recently sold homes that are similar to the subject home in terms of location, style, and amenities. Compiled by a broker or a salesperson to assist a seller in determining a listing price; a competitive market analysis.

competent parties   People who are recognized by law as being able to contract with others; usually those of legal age and sound mind.

comprehensive plan   A master plan to guide the long-term development of a government subdivision, such as a city or county, to ensure that social and economic needs are balanced against environmental and aesthetic concerns.

computerized loan origination (CLO)   A computer network tied into a major lender that allows agents across the country to initiate mortgage loan applications in their own offices.

condemnation   A judicial or an administrative proceeding to exercise the power of eminent domain, through which a government agency takes private property for public use and compensates the owner.

condition   A contingency, qualification, or occurrence on which an estate or property right is gained or lost.

conditional use permit   A grant approved by a planning and zoning commission allowing, with conditions, a special use of property that is in the public interest.

condominium   The absolute ownership of an apartment or a unit (generally in a multiunit building) based on a legal description of the airspace the unit actually occupies, plus an undivided interest in the ownership of the common elements, which are owned jointly with the other condominium unit owners.

consideration   Something of value that induces a person to enter into a contract. Consideration may be "valuable" (money) or "good" (love and affection).

construction loan   *See* interim financing.

constructive eviction   Actions of the landlord that so materially disturb or impair the tenant's enjoyment of the leased premises that the tenant is effectively forced to move out and terminate the lease without liability for any further rent.

constructive notice   Notice given to the world by recorded documents. All people are charged with knowledge of such documents and their contents, whether or not they actually have examined them. Possession of property also is considered constructive notice that the person in possession has an interest in the property.

consumer   An individual, partnership, corporation, or Texas government agency that seeks or acquires, by purchase or lease, any goods or services, as defined by the Texas Deceptive Trade Practices Act.

contents insurance   *See* renters insurance.

contract   An agreement entered into by two or more legally competent parties by the terms of which one or more of the parties, for a consideration, undertake to do or refrain from doing some legal act or acts. A contract may be either *unilateral*, where only one party is bound to act, or *bilateral*, where all parties to the instrument are legally bound to act as prescribed.

contract for deed   A contract for the sale of real estate wherein the purchase price is paid in periodic installments by the purchaser, who is in possession of the property even though title is retained by the seller until final payment. Also called an *installment contract*, *land contract*, or *contract of sale*.

conventional loan   A loan that is not insured by the FHA or guaranteed by the VA.

conveyance   Written instrument, such as a deed or lease, that evidences transfer of some ownership interest in real property from one person to another.

cooperative   A residential multiunit building whose title is held by a corporation that is owned by and operated for the benefit of persons living within the building, who are stockholders of the corporation, each possessing a proprietary lease.

co-ownership   A broad category of ownership by more than one person. Examples are tenants in common and joint tenants.

core real estate course   A real estate course included in the statute or approved by the Texas Real Estate Commission as fulfilling part of the core requirements for licensure. Permitted by statute or Rule: Principles of Real Estate, Real Estate Appraisal, Real Estate Law, Real Estate Finance, Real Estate Marketing, Real Estate Mathematics, Real Estate Brokerage, Property Management, Real Estate Investments, Law of Agency, Law of Contracts, Promulgated Contract Forms, and Residential Inspection for Real Estate Agents.

corporation   An entity or organization, created by operation of law, whose rights of doing business are essentially the same as those of an individual. The entity has continuous existence until it is dissolved according to legal procedures.

corporeal right   A tangible interest in real estate.

corpus   The principal or capital, as distinguished from the interest or income, of a fund or estate.

cost   The capital outlay for land, labor, materials, and profits necessary to bring a property into existence.

cost approach to value An estimate of value based on current construction costs, less depreciation, plus land value. *Contrast with* the income approach to value and the sales comparison approach to value.

cost recovery An Internal Revenue Service term for *depreciation.*

counseling The business of providing people with expert advice on a subject, based on the counselor's extensive, expert knowledge of the subject.

counteroffer A new offer made as a reply to an offer received. It has the effect of rejecting the original offer, which cannot be accepted thereafter unless revived by the offeror's repeating it.

covenant *See* restrictive covenant.

credit On a closing statement, an amount entered in a person's favor—either an amount the party has paid or an amount for which the party must be reimbursed.

curtesy A life estate, usually a fractional interest, given by some states to the surviving husband in real estate owned by his deceased wife. Most states, including Texas, have abolished curtesy.

customer One who purchases or sells property without being represented by an agent.

cycle A recurring sequence of events that regularly follow one another, generally within a fixed interval of time.

datum A horizontal plane from which heights and depths are measured.

debit On a closing statement, an amount charged, that is, an amount that a party must pay.

decedent A person who has died.

Deceptive Trade Practices Act (DTPA) Part of the federal Consumer Protection Act originally passed in 1973 and made specifically applicable to real estate in 1975 prohibiting a number of false, misleading, or deceptive acts or practices.

dedication The voluntary transfer of private property by its owner to the public for some public use, such as for streets or schools.

deductible clause A clause in an insurance policy that limits the exposure to loss for an insured homeowner.

deed A written instrument that, when executed and delivered, conveys title to or an interest in real estate.

deed in lieu of foreclosure A deed given by the mortgagor to the mortgagee when the mortgagor is in default under the terms of the mortgage. This is a way for the mortgagor to avoid foreclosure.

deed in trust A form of deed by which real estate is conveyed to a trustee.

deed of reconveyance The instrument used to reconvey title to a trustor under a trust deed after the debt has been satisfied.

deed of trust An instrument used to create a mortgage lien by which the mortgagor (borrower) conveys title to a trustee, who holds it as security for the benefit of the lender (beneficiary); also called a *trust deed.*

deed restrictions Clauses in a deed limiting the future uses of the property.

deed without warranty A deed that carries with it no warranties against liens or other encumbrances but that does imply that the grantor has the right to convey title; a *bargain and sale deed.*

default The nonperformance of a duty, whether arising under a contract or otherwise; failure to meet an obligation when due.

defeasance clause A provision in leases and mortgages that cancels a specified right on the occurrence of a certain condition, such as cancellation of a mortgage on repayment of the mortgage loan.

defeasible fee estate An estate in which the holder has a fee simple title that may be divested on the occurrence or nonoccurrence of a specified event. The two categories of defeasible fee estates are fee simple determinable and fee simple subject to a condition subsequent.

deficiency judgment A personal judgment levied against the mortgagor when a foreclosure sale does not produce sufficient funds to pay the mortgage debt in full.

delinquent taxes Unpaid taxes that are past due.

delivery and acceptance Title passes when the grantor delivers the deed and the grantee accepts it. The deed may be delivered personally or through a third-party escrow agent; recordation by the county clerk creates an assumption of delivery and acceptance.

demand The amount of goods people are willing and able to buy at a given price; often coupled with *supply.*

demographics The characteristics of human populations, such as size, growth, density, distribution, and vital statistics.

Department of Housing and Urban Development (HUD) Federal agency that administers the Fair Housing Act of 1968.

depreciated cost The value of a property after deducting an allowance for depreciation.

depreciation 1. In appraisal, a loss of value in property due to any cause, including *physical deterioration, functional obsolescence,* and *external obsolescence.* 2. In real estate investment, an expense deduction for tax purposes taken over the period of ownership of income property. *See also* cost recovery.

descent Acquisition of property through inheritance laws when there is no will.

determinable fee estate A fee simple estate in which the property automatically reverts to the grantor upon the occurrence of a specified event or condition.

developer One who converts raw land into a platted subdivision, installs utilities, and paves streets, and who also may construct buildings on lots and sell them.

devise A gift of real property by will. The donor is the devisor and the recipient is the devisee.

discount points An added loan fee charged by a lender to make the yield on a lower-than-market-value loan competitive with higher-interest-rate loans.

discount rate 1. The interest rate charged member banks that borrow from the Federal Reserve System. 2. The rate used to convert future income into present value.

discriminatory housing practice An act that is unlawful under the Fair Housing Act or other fair housing law.

diversification Distribution of investments among several companies or several types of investments (such as savings accounts, individual retirement accounts, stocks, bonds, mutual funds, and real estate) in order to average the risk of loss.

doctrine of relation back Irrevocable deposit of the executed deed, purchase money, and instructions into escrow pending performance of escrow conditions.

dominant tenement A property that includes in its ownership the appurtenant right to use an easement over another person's property for a specific purpose.

dower The legal right or interest, recognized in some states, that a wife acquires in the property her husband held or acquired during their marriage. During the husband's lifetime, the right is only a possibility of an interest; on his death, it can become an interest in land. Dower is not recognized in Texas.

duress Unlawful constraint or action exercised on a person whereby the person is forced to perform an act against her will. A contract entered into under duress is considered voidable.

earnest money deposit An amount of money, deposited by a prospective buyer as evidence of good faith under the terms of a contract, that is to be forfeited if the buyer defaults but applied to the purchase price if the sale is closed.

easement A right to use the land of another for a specific purpose, such as for a right-of-way or utilities.

easement appurtenant An easement that passes with the land on conveyance.

easement by implication An easement that arises when the parties' actions imply that they intend to create an easement.

easement by necessity An easement allowed by law as necessary for the full enjoyment of a parcel of real estate; for example, a right of ingress and egress over a grantor's land.

easement by prescription An easement acquired by continuous, open, uninterrupted, exclusive, and adverse use of the property for 10 years.

easement in gross An easement that is not created for the benefit of any *land* owned by the owner of the easement but that attaches *personally to the easement owner*; for example, a utility easement.

economic life The period of time during which a structure may reasonably be expected to perform the function for which it was designed or intended.

economic obsolescence *See* external obsolescence.

emblements Growing crops, such as grapes and corn, that are produced annually through labor and industry; deemed to be personal property.

eminent domain The right of a government or public entity to acquire property for public use; the entity must make a good faith effort to acquire the real property through direct negotiation and purchase from the owner.

employee One who works under the supervision and control of another. The employer is obligated to withhold income taxes and Social Security taxes from the compensation of an employee. *See also* independent contractor.

employment contract A document evidencing formal employment between employer and employee or between principal and agent. In the real estate business, this generally takes the form of a listing agreement or management agreement.

enabling acts State legislation that confers certain powers, such as zoning, to governmental entities.

encroachment A building or some portion of it—a wall or fence, for instance—that extends beyond the land of the owner and illegally intrudes on some land of an adjoining owner or a street or alley.

encumbrance Any lien (such as a mortgage, tax, or judgment lien) or an easement or a restriction on the use of the land that may diminish the value of a property; a cloud against clear, free title to property.

endorsement 1. An additional document attached to an original insurance policy that amends the original; a rider. 2. Writing one's name, with or without additional words, on a negotiable instrument.

Equal Credit Opportunity Act A federal law to ensure that funds are available to qualified loan applicants without discrimination on the basis of race, color, religion, sex, national origin, age, marital status, or receipt of public assistance.

equal opportunity in housing A federal code ensuring that all U.S. citizens have access to housing without discrimination.

equitable lien A lien arising out of common law. *See* statutory lien.

equitable right of redemption The right to redeem a property *before* a foreclosure sale by paying the full debt plus interest and accrued charges.

equitable title The interest held by a vendee under a contract for deed or an installment contract; the equitable right to obtain absolute ownership to property when legal title is held in another's name.

equity The current market value of a property minus any loans.

equity loan A line of credit made against the equity in the borrower's home.

erosion The gradual wearing away of land by water, wind, and general weather conditions; the diminishing of property caused by the elements.

escheat The reversion of property to the state in the event the property is abandoned or the owner dies without leaving a will and has no heirs to whom the property may pass.

escrow The closing of a transaction through a third party called an *escrow agent*, or *escrowee*, who receives certain funds and documents to be delivered on the performance of certain conditions outlined in the escrow agreement.

escrow agreement A contract, used when a transaction is closed through an escrow, that sets forth the duties of the escrow agent as well as the requirements and obligations of the parties to the transaction.

estate for years A leased interest in property for a certain, exact period of time and for a specified consideration.

estate from period to period *See* periodic estate.

estate in land The degree, quantity, nature, and extent of interest that a person has in real property.

estate taxes Federal taxes on a decedent's real and personal property.

estimate of value An appraisal; the appraised value.

estoppel certificate A document in which a borrower certifies the amount owed on a mortgage loan and the rate of interest.

eviction A legal process to oust a person from possession of real estate. *See* forcible detainer.

evidence of title Proof of ownership of property, commonly a title insurance policy or an abstract of title with an attorney's opinion of title.

exception As used in the conveyance of real estate, the exclusion of some part of the property conveyed, such as a mineral interest held by a previous owner; a deficiency in the grantor's title; *contrast with* reservation.

exchange A transaction in which all or part of the consideration is the transfer of like-kind property (such as investment real estate for investment real estate).

exclusive agency A listing contract under which an owner appoints a real estate broker as his exclusive agent for a designated period to sell a property, on the owner's stated terms, for a commission. The owner reserves the right to sell without paying anyone a commission if the owner sells to a prospect who has not been introduced or claimed by the broker.

exclusive right to sell A listing contract under which an owner appoints a real estate broker as her exclusive agent for a designated period of time to sell a property on the owner's stated terms and agrees to pay the broker a commission when the property is sold, whether by the broker, the owner, or another broker.

executed contract A contract in which all parties have fulfilled their promises; a contract is executed upon closing and funding.

execution The signing and delivery of an instrument. Also, a legal order directing an official to enforce a judgment against the property of a debtor.

executor/executrix The man/woman appointed in a will to carry out the requests of the will; *contrast with* administrator/administratrix.

executory contract A contract under which something remains to be done by one or more of the parties.

express agency An agency created by specific agreement, whether written or oral, of principal and agent.

express contract An oral or a written contract in which the parties state the contract's terms and express their intentions in words.

external obsolescence Reduction in property's value caused by factors outside the subject property, such as social or environmental forces; also called *economic* or *locational obsolescence*.

extraterritorial jurisdiction A half-mile to five-mile area surrounding an incorporated area over which the municipality has the right of subdivision approval and the potential for annexation.

Fair Housing Act of 1968   The federal law that prevents discrimination in housing based on race, color, religion, or national origin; amended in 1974 to include sex and in 1988 to include handicap and familial status in the protected categories.

familial status   One or more persons younger than 18 being domiciled with a parent or other person having legal custody of such individual; the designee of such parent or other person having legal custody through written permission.

Fannie Mae   A privately owned corporation that participates in the secondary market by buying conventional, FHA, and VA loans. Formerly the *Federal National Mortgage Association (FNMA)*.

farm and ranch broker   Brokers that specialize in farms, timberland, pastureland, ranches, and orchards.

Farm Service Agency (FSA)   An agency of the U.S. Department of Agriculture that makes and guarantees loans and provides credit counseling and supervision to farmers and ranchers who are temporarily unable to obtain private, commercial credit.

Farmer Mac   A secondary market for farm real estate loans; the Federal Agricultural Mortgage Corporation.

Federal Agricultural Mortgage Corporation   *See* Farmer Mac.

Federal Emergency Management Agency (FEMA)   A government agency that sets program standards for flood insurance.

Federal Home Loan Mortgage Corporation (FHLMC)   *See* Freddie Mac.

federal judgment lien   Lien obtained by the United States or an agency, department, commission, board, or other U.S. entity that affects all real and personal property of the judgment debtor.

Federal National Mortgage Association (FNMA)   *See* Fannie Mae.

Federal Reserve System   A central banking system designed to manage the nation's economy; "the Fed."

fee simple estate   The maximum possible estate or right of ownership of real property, continuing forever. Sometimes called a *fee* or *fee simple absolute*.

fee simple subject to a condition subsequent   An estate conveyed "provided that" or "if" it is used for a specific purpose. If it is no longer used for that purpose, it reverts to the original grantor or his heirs by their exercise of the right of reentry.

feudal system   A system of ownership usually associated with precolonial England in which the king or other sovereign was the source of all rights. The right to possess real property was granted by the sovereign to an individual as a life estate only. On the death of the individual, title passed back to the sovereign, not to the decedent's heirs.

FHA loan   A loan insured by the Federal Housing Administration and made by an approved lender in accordance with FHA regulations.

fiduciary relationship   A relationship of trust and confidence, as between trustee and beneficiary, attorney and client, or principal and agent.

financing   The business of providing the funds necessary to complete real estate transactions.

financing statement   *See* Uniform Commercial Code.

fire and extended coverage insurance   A type of policy to protect against fire, hail, windstorm, and other damage.

first mortgage   A mortgage that is superior in right to any other mortgage; absent subordination; it must be recorded first.

fiscal policy   The government's policy in regard to taxation and spending programs. The balance between these two areas determines the amount of money the government will withdraw from or feed into the economy, which can counter economic peaks and slumps.

fixture   An item of personal property that has been converted to real property by being permanently affixed to the realty.

flexible-payment loan   A payment plan in which a mortgagor makes lower monthly payments for the first few years of a loan and larger payments for the remainder of the term.

forcible detainer suit   A court suit initiated by a landlord to evict a tenant from leased premises after the tenant has breached one of the terms of the lease or has held possession of the property after the lease's expiration.

foreclosure   A legal procedure whereby property used as security for a debt is sold to satisfy the debt in the event of default in payment of the mortgage note or default of other terms in the mortgage document.

formal will   A written instrument disposing of property on the death of the maker. The testator must be of legal age and sound mind, and not subject to undue influence. The document must be signed and witnessed; also known as a *witnessed will*.

fraud   A misstatement of a material fact made with intent to deceive or made with reckless disregard of the truth, and that actually does deceive.

Freddie Mac A corporation established to purchase primarily conventional mortgage loans in the secondary mortgage market. Chartered as the *Federal Home Loan Mortgage Corporation (FHLMC)*.

freehold estate An estate in land in which ownership is for an indeterminate length of time, in contrast to a lease-hold estate.

fructus industriales Fruits of industry; annual plantings or crops considered personal property.

fructus naturales Fruits of nature; trees and perennial shrubbery and grasses considered real estate.

fully amortized loan A loan in which the principal and interest are payable in monthly or other installments to reduce the loan balance to zero at the end of the loan term.

functional obsolescence A loss of value to improved real property due to inadequate, outmoded, or inappropriate improvements.

future interest A person's present right to an interest in real property that will not result in possession or enjoyment until sometime in the future, such as a reversion or right of reentry.

gap A defect in the chain of title of a particular parcel of real estate; a missing document or conveyance that raises doubt as to the present ownership of the land.

general agent One authorized by the principal to represent the principal in a broad range of matters, for example, a property manager.

general contractor A construction specialist who enters into a formal construction contract with a landowner to construct a real estate building or project. The general contractor often contracts with several subcontractors specializing in various aspects of the building process to perform individual jobs.

general lien The right of a creditor to have all of a debtor's property—both real and personal—sold to satisfy a debt.

general partnership *See* partnership.

general warranty deed A deed in which the grantor fully warrants good clear title to the premises. Used in most real estate deed transfers, a warranty deed offers the greatest protection of any deed; a warranty deed.

Ginnie Mae A corporation within HUD that participates in the secondary market. It sells mortgage-backed securities that are backed by pools of FHA and VA loans. Chartered as the *Government National Mortgage Association (GNMA)*.

good and indefeasible title Title that cannot be defeated by a superior claim, set aside, or made void.

Good Faith Estimate (GFE) A preliminary accounting of expected closing costs given to a buyer from a lender within three business days of loan application; required by RESPA (the Real Estate Settlement Procedures Act).

Government National Mortgage Association (GNMA) *See* Ginnie Mae.

government survey system *See* rectangular survey system.

grantee A person who receives a conveyance of real property from the grantor.

granting clause Words in a deed of conveyance that state the grantor's intention to convey the property at the present time. This clause generally is worded as "convey and warrant," "grant," "grant, bargain, and sell," or "remise, release, and quitclaim."

grantor The person transferring title to or an interest in real property to a grantee.

grantor/grantee indices Public record books that are maintained in the county clerk's office that list all recorded instruments and reference the volume and page where the exact documents can be found.

green Made with little environmental harm; produced in an environmentally and ecologically friendly way by using renewable resources.

gross income multiplier The ratio used to convert annual income into market value in appraising industrial and commercial properties.

gross lease A lease of property under which a landlord pays all property charges regularly incurred through ownership, such as repairs, taxes, insurance, and operating expenses. Most residential leases are gross leases.

gross rent multiplier A figure used as a multiplier of the gross monthly rental income of a property to produce an estimate of the property's value.

ground lease A lease of land only, on which the tenant usually owns a building or is required to build his own building as specified in the lease. Such leases are usually long-term net leases.

groundwater rights Water under the earth's surface below the saturation point and used by a property owner through the rule of capture.

habendum clause That part of a deed beginning with the words "to have and to hold," following the granting clause and defining the extent of ownership the grantor is conveying.

habitability statute A law that imposes a duty on the landlord to make the leased premises habitable and ready for occupancy and to maintain them in a state of repair throughout the term of the lease.

handicap A physical or mental impairment that substantially limits one or more of an individual's major life activities; a record of such an impairment; being regarded as having such an impairment.

heir One who might inherit or succeed to an interest in land under the state law of descent when the owner dies without leaving a valid will.

heterogeneity *See* nonhomogeneity.

highest and best use That possible use of land that would produce the greatest return and thereby develop the highest land value. The optimum use of a site, as used in appraisal.

holdover tenancy A tenancy whereby a lessee retains possession of leased property after the lease has expired and the landlord, by continuing to accept rent, agrees to the tenant's continued occupancy.

holographic will A will that is written, dated, and signed in the testator's handwriting but is not witnessed.

Home Mortgage Disclosure Act A federal law that prevents *redlining* or denial of funds to certain areas; requires that public notices be posted by housing lenders.

homeowners insurance policy A standardized package insurance policy that covers a residential real estate owner against financial loss on a dwelling and its contents and includes liability coverage and loss of use.

homestead Land that is owned and occupied as the family home. In Texas, homestead property is protected or exempt from forced sale by creditors for payments of most debts, with several exceptions.

HUD-1 *See* Uniform Settlement Statement.

hypothecation The pledge of specific real or personal property as security for an obligation without surrendering possession of it.

implied agency An agency created by acts or words of principal and agent; an agency inferred by circumstances.

implied contract A contract under which the agreement of the parties is demonstrated by their acts and conduct.

improvement 1. An improvement *on* land is any structure, usually privately owned, erected on a site to enhance the value of the property; for example, buildings, fences, and driveways. 2. An improvement *to* land is usually a publicly owned structure, such as a curb, sidewalk, street, or sewer.

income approach The process of estimating the value of an income-producing property by capitalization of the annual net income expected to be produced by the property during its remaining useful life.

incorporeal right A nonpossessory right in real estate, for example, an easement or right-of-way.

independent contractor Someone retained to perform a certain act but who is subject to the control and direction of another only as to the end result and not as to the way in which he or she performs the act. Unlike an employee, an independent contractor pays for all her own expenses and both Social Security and income taxes and receives no employee benefits. Most real estate salespersons are independent contractors.

infant A person who has not reached the legal age of majority; a minor.

inflation An increase in the volume of money and credit relative to available goods resulting in a substantial and continuing rise in the general price level.

infrastructure Roads, highways, sewage and drainage systems, and utility facilities necessary to support a concentration of population.

inheritance taxes State-imposed taxes on a decedent's real and personal property.

inspector *See* real estate inspector.

installment contract *See* contract for deed.

installment sale A transaction in which the sales price is paid in two or more installments over two or more years. If the sale meets certain requirements, a taxpayer can postpone reporting such income to future years by paying tax each year only on the proceeds received that year.

insurable title A title that a title company will insure.

interest 1. A charge made by a lender for the use of money. 2. The type and extent of ownership in property.

interest-only loan A loan in which interest is paid periodically but no principal is paid until the due date on the note, when the entire principal amount is due with the final interest payment.

interim financing A short-term loan usually made during the construction phase of a building project (in this case, often referred to as a *construction loan*).

intermediary broker A broker who is employed to negotiate a transaction between both parties and who for that purpose may be an agent of both parties to the transaction, acting fairly so as not to favor one party over the other.

Internal Revenue Service tax lien A general lien imposed by the IRS for the nonpayment of income taxes.

Interstate Land Sales Full Disclosure Act A federal law requiring that a property report be furnished to prospective buyers of certain types of real estate.

intestate The condition of a property owner who dies without leaving a valid will. Title to the property will pass to the heirs as provided in the state law of descent.

intimidation As defined in the fair housing laws, the illegal act of coercing, threatening, or interfering with a person for exercising or enjoying any right granted or protected by federal, state, or local fair housing laws.

intrinsic value An appraisal term meaning the result of a person's individual choices and preferences.

investment Money directed toward the purchase, improvement, and development of an asset in expectation of income or profits.

involuntary alienation See alienation.

involuntary lien A lien that arises by the action of another, such as a judgment lien.

joint tenancy Ownership of real estate between two or more parties who have been named in one conveyance as joint tenants. Upon the death of one joint tenant, the deceased's interest passes to the surviving joint tenant or tenants by the *right of survivorship*. Not automatically created in Texas.

judgment The formal decision of a court on the respective rights and claims of the parties to an action or suit. After a judgment has been entered and recorded with the county clerk, it usually becomes a general lien on the property of the defendant.

junior lien An obligation, such as a second mortgage, that is subordinate in right or lien priority to an existing lien on the same realty.

jurat A person signing a document swears before a notary that the information in the document is true and correct and signs the document in the presence of the notary.

laches An equitable doctrine used by courts to bar a legal claim or prevent the assertion of a right because of undue delay or failure to assert the claim or right.

land The earth's surface, extending downward to the center of the earth and upward infinitely into space.

land contract See contract for deed.

last will and testament See will.

latent defect A hidden structural defect presumably resulting from faulty construction, known to the seller but not to the purchaser and not readily discoverable by inspection.

law of agency See agent.

league In Texas, a tract of land that was granted to a settler by the Mexican government; a league consists of 6.919 square miles.

lease A written or oral contract between a landlord (the lessor) and a tenant (the lessee) that transfers the right to exclusive possession and use of the landlord's real property to the lessee for a specified period of time and for a stated consideration (rent).

leasehold estate A tenant's right to occupy real estate during the term of a lease; generally considered a personal property interest.

legacy A disposition of money or personal property by will.

legal description A description of a specific parcel of real estate complete enough for an independent surveyor to locate and identify it.

legality of object An essential component of a valid contract; a contract must be for a legal purpose and in compliance with public policy.

lessee See lease.

less favorable treatment Any time a person is treated differently on the basis of race, sex, religion, color, national origin, handicap, or familial status, either by act or inaction, in the selling or leasing of real property it is a violation of the fair housing laws. Also known as *unequal treatment* or *different treatment*.

lessor See lease.

leverage The use of borrowed money to finance the bulk of an investment and to magnify the rate of return.

levy 1. To assess; to levy a tax is to assess a property and set the rate of taxation. 2. To seize or collect; to levy an execution is to officially seize an owner's property to satisfy an obligation.

liability coverage Insurance that protects against risks that could render the property owner responsible for certain damages to the property or persons of others.

license 1. A privilege or right granted to a person by a state to operate as a real estate broker or salesperson. 2. The revocable permission for a temporary use of land—a personal right that cannot be sold.

lien A right given by law to certain creditors to have debts paid out of the property of a defaulting debtor, usually by means of a court sale.

lien theory Some states' interpretation of a mortgage as being purely a lien on real property. The mortgagee thus has no right of possession but must foreclose the lien and sell the property if the mortgagor defaults. Texas is a lien theory state.

life estate An interest in real or personal property that is limited in duration to the lifetime of its owner or some other designated person.

life tenant A person in possession of a life estate.

like-kind property See exchange.

limited liability company A business organization in which a member or manager is not generally held liable for debts, obligations, or liabilities of the company.

limited partnership See partnership.

linear measurement A measurement made on a line. The linear measure of a 4-foot square is 16 feet; also called *lineal measure.*

liquidated damages An amount predetermined by the parties to an agreement as the total amount of compensation an injured party should receive if the other party breaches a contract; usually the earnest money in a residential sales transaction.

liquidity The ability to sell an asset and convert it into cash at a price close to its true value in a short period.

lis pendens A recorded legal document giving constructive notice that an action affecting a particular property has been filed in either a state or a federal court.

listing agreement A contract between a landowner (as principal) and a licensed real estate broker (as agent) by which the broker is employed to sell real estate on the owner's terms within a given time, for which service the landowner agrees to pay a commission.

listing broker The broker in a multiple-listing situation from whose office a listing agreement is initiated, as opposed to the *selling broker*, from whose office negotiations leading up to a sale are initiated. *See also* multiple listing.

littoral rights 1. A landowner's claim to use water in large navigable lakes and oceans that are adjacent to the property. 2. The ownership rights to land bordering these bodies of water up to the mean vegetation line.

loan discount *See* discount points.

loan origination fee The amount a lender charges for processing a loan; usually a percentage of the face amount of the loan.

loan to value ratio The ratio of debt to value of a property; the loan amount divided by the lesser of sales price or appraisal.

locational obsolescence *See* external obsolescence.

loss The difference between the purchase price and the selling price of a property if the purchase price exceeds the selling price.

lot-and-block description A description of real property that identifies a parcel of land by reference to lot and block numbers within a subdivision, as specified on a plat of subdivision duly recorded in the county clerk's office.

management agreement A contract between the owner of income property and a management firm or an individual property manager that outlines the scope of the manager's authority to manage the property.

Mandatory Continuing Education (MCE) A requirement for most brokers and all salespersons to complete 15 classroom hours of education once every two years in order to renew a real estate license; becomes effective after the completion of salesperson annual education (SAE) requirements are met.

manufactured home A manufactured home is a single-family house constructed entirely in a controlled factory environment, built to the federal Manufactured Home Construction and Safety Standards (better known as the HUD Code).

market A place where goods can be bought and sold and a price established.

marketable title Good or clear title, reasonably free from the risk of litigation over possible defects.

market data approach to value *See* sales comparison approach.

market price The actual selling price of a property.

market value The highest price a ready, willing, and able buyer would pay and the lowest price a ready, willing, and able seller would accept, neither being under any pressure to act.

mechanic's lien A statutory lien created in favor of contractors, laborers, materialmen, and others (including architects, engineers, or surveyors) who have performed work or furnished materials in the erection or repair of a building.

metes-and-bounds description A legal description of a parcel of land that begins at a well-marked point and follows the boundaries, using direction and distances around the tract back to the place of beginning. *See also* point (place) of beginning.

minority As defined in the Civil Rights Act of 1968 and subsequent amendments as part of the Fair Housing Law, "'minority' means any group, or any member of a group, that can be identified either: (1) by race, color, religion, sex, national origin, handicap, and familial status; or (2) by any other characteristic on the basis of which discrimination is prohibited by a federal, state, or local fair housing law.

misrepresentation An unintentional misstatement of a fact; incorrect or misleading representation.

mitigate damages To take reasonable steps to reduce or eliminate the amount of damages to be incurred by another party. For example, a landlord has a duty to find a replacement tenant for space vacated in breach of a lease.

mixed use Property that accommodates more than one use, such as commercial use and residential use.

monetary policy Governmental regulation of the amount of money in circulation through such institutions as the Federal Reserve Board.

money judgment   A court judgment ordering payment of money rather than specific performance of a certain action. *See also* judgment.

month-to-month tenancy   A periodic tenancy under which the tenant rents for one month at a time. In the absence of a rental agreement (oral or written), a tenancy is generally considered to be month to month.

monument   A fixed natural or artificial object used to establish real estate boundaries for a metes-and-bounds description.

mortgage   A conditional transfer or pledge of real estate as security for the payment of a debt. Also, the document used to create a mortgage lien.

mortgage-backed securities   Securities that are secured by pools of mortgages and are used to channel funds from securities markets to housing markets; Fannie Mae, Freddie Mac, and Ginnie Mae have mortgage-backed securities programs.

mortgage banker   A person or firm that originates, sells, and then services mortgage loans; *contrast with* mortgage broker.

mortgage broker   A person who, for a fee, brings borrowers and lenders together but does not service the loans that have been arranged; *contrast with* mortgage banker.

mortgage (purchase money) lien   A lien or charge on the property of a mortgagor that secures the underlying debt obligations.

mortgagee   A lender in a mortgage loan transaction.

mortgagor   A borrower who conveys property as security for a loan.

multiperil policies   A type of insurance that packages several types of coverage into one policy.

multiple listing   An exclusive listing (generally an exclusive right to sell) with the additional authority and obligation on the part of the listing broker to distribute the listing to other brokers in a *multiple listing service*.

municipal utility district   A defined geographic area created by a developer that levies taxes to pay for providing water and sewer utilities to its inhabitants (usually outside a municipality).

National Association of REALTORS® (NAR)   The largest real estate professional organization in the world, representing all branches of the real estate industry. Active members are allowed to use the trademark REALTOR®.

negative cash flow   *See* cash flow.

negotiable instrument   A written instrument, such as a note, that may be transferred by endorsement or delivery. The holder, or payee, may sign the instrument over to another person or, in certain cases, merely deliver it to the person. The transferee then has the original payee's right to payment.

net lease   A lease requiring that the tenant pay not only rent but also all costs incurred in maintaining the property, including taxes, insurance, utilities, and repairs.

net listing   A listing based on the net price the seller will receive if the property is sold. Under a net listing, the broker is free to offer the property for sale at the highest price obtainable in order to increase the commission. This type of listing is outlawed in many states; it is not recommended in Texas.

nolo contendere   A plea made by a defendant in a criminal action that is equivalent to an admission of guilt and subjects the defendant to punishment; leaves open the possibility for the defendant to deny the alleged facts in other proceedings.

nonconforming use   A use of property that is permitted to continue after a zoning ordinance prohibiting it has been established for the area.

nonhomogeneity   A lack of uniformity; dissimilarity. Because no two parcels of land are exactly alike, real estate is said to be *nonhomogeneous*; also known as *heterogeneity*.

nonrecourse note   A loan for which the sole source of satisfaction for default is the property that was given as collateral; the debtor has no personal liability for any shortfall. Equity loans and reverse-annuity mortgages are nonrecourse.

nonresident broker   A resident broker of another state also licensed in Texas but not a Texas resident.

note   An instrument of credit attesting to a debt and promising to pay.

Notice of Value   States the current market value of a property appraised for a VA loan.

novation   Substituting a new obligation for an old one or substituting new parties to an existing obligation. For example, a lender's modifying note terms for a buyer who fell behind on payments.

objective value   The actual value measured in dollars of an aspect of construction or location.

offer and acceptance   Two essential components of a valid contract; a "meeting of the minds."

open-end mortgage   A mortgage loan that is expandable by increments up to a maximum dollar amount, the full loan being secured by the same original mortgage.

open listing A listing contract under which the broker's commission is contingent on the broker's producing a ready, willing, and able buyer before the property is sold by the seller or another broker.

open market An economic model that allows the price of a commodity to respond freely to the forces of supply and demand.

option The right to purchase property within a definite time at a specified price. There is no obligation to purchase, but the seller is obligated to sell if the option holder exercises the right to purchase.

origination fee *See* loan origination fee.

ostensible agency A form of implied agency relationship created by the actions of the parties involved rather than by written agreement or document.

owelty The difference paid or secured by one cotenant to another for the purpose of equalizing a partition of assets.

package mortgage A method of financing in which the loan that finances the purchase of a home also finances the purchase of certain items of personal property, such as washers, dryers, refrigerators, stoves, and other specified appliances.

panic peddling The illegal practice of inducing panic selling in a neighborhood by making representations of the entry, or prospective entry, of members of a minority group; also called *blockbusting*.

parcel A specific portion of a large tract of real estate; a lot.

partition The division of cotenants' interests in real property when the parties do not agree to terminate the co-ownership voluntarily; takes place through court procedures.

partnership An association of two or more individuals who carry on a continuing business for profit as co-owners. In a *general partnership*, each general partner shares in the administration, profits, and losses of the operation. In a *limited partnership*, the operation is administered by one or more general partners and funded, by and large, by limited or silent partners, who are by law responsible for losses only to the extent of their investments. A *limited liability partnership* limits an individual partner's liability arising from negligence on the part of another partner.

party A prospective buyer, seller, landlord, or tenant, or the person's authorized representative (excluding a real estate licensee).

party wall A wall that is located on or at a boundary line between two adjoining parcels of land and is used or is intended to be used by the owners of both properties.

patent A grant or franchise of land from the U.S. government.

percent By the hundred.

percentage lease A lease, commonly used for retail property, whose rental is based on the tenant's gross sales at the premises; it generally stipulates a base monthly rental plus a percentage of any gross sales above a certain amount.

periodic estate An interest in leased property that continues from period to period—week to week, month to month, or year to year.

personal property Items, called *chattels*, that do not fit into the definition of real property; movable objects; personalty.

personalty Items of personal property, chattel.

petroleum landman A person who conducts business activities related to oil, gas, and mineral exploration.

physical deterioration A reduction in a property's value resulting from a decline in physical condition; can be caused by action of the elements or by ordinary wear and tear.

PITI Principal, interest, taxes, and insurance.

planned unit development A planned combination of diverse land uses, such as housing, recreation, and shopping, in one contained development or subdivision.

plat A map of a town, section, or subdivision indicating the location and boundaries of individual properties.

plottage value The increase in value or utility resulting from the consolidation (*assemblage*) of two or more adjacent lots into one larger lot.

point A unit of measurement used for various loan charges; one point equals 1% of the amount of the loan. *See also* discount points.

point (place) of beginning In a metes-and-bounds legal description, the starting point of the survey, situated in one corner of the parcel; all *metes-and-bounds* descriptions must follow the boundaries of the parcel back to the point of beginning.

police power The government's right to impose laws, statutes, and ordinances, including zoning ordinances and building codes, to protect the public health, safety, morals, and welfare.

power of attorney A written instrument authorizing a person, the *attorney-in-fact*, to act as agent on behalf of another person to the extent indicated in the instrument.

power-of-sale clause A provision in a deed of trust authorizing the trustee to sell a property in the event of the borrower's default.

precedent In law, the requirements established by prior court decisions.

prepaid item Item on a closing statement that has been paid in advance by the seller, such as insurance premiums, which must be reimbursed to the seller by the buyer.

prepayment penalty A charge imposed on a borrower who pays off the loan principal early. This penalty compensates the lender for interest and other charges that otherwise are lost.

price The amount of money paid for an item.

price-fixing *See* antitrust laws.

primary mortgage market *See* secondary mortgage market.

prime rate The interest or discount rate charged by a commercial bank to its largest and strongest customers.

principal 1. A sum lent or employed as a fund or investment, as distinguished from its income or profits. 2. The amount of the note due and payable. 3. A main party to a transaction—the person for whom the agent works.

principal meridian One of 37 north and south survey lines established and defined as part of the rectangular survey (government survey) system.

principle of conformity An appraisal principle holding that the maximum value is realized when a reasonable degree of homogeneity (sameness) exists in a neighborhood.

prior appropriation A concept of water ownership in which the landowner's right to use available water is based on a government-administered permit system.

priority The order in which unpaid debts or obligations will be satisfied if the property goes through a court sale.

private mortgage insurance (PMI) Default insurance on conventional loans, normally insuring the top 20% to 25% of the loan and not the whole loan.

probate A legal process by which a court determines who will inherit a decedent's property and what the estate's assets are; literally means "to prove."

procuring cause The effort that brings about the desired result. Under an open listing, the broker who is the procuring cause of the sale receives the commission.

professional inspector A person who accepts employment for the purpose of performing a real property inspection for a buyer or a seller.

profit The increase in value when the selling price exceeds the purchase price.

promissory note An unconditional written promise of one person to pay a certain sum of money to another at a future specified time.

promulgated contracts Various standard contracts prepared and authorized by the Texas Real Estate Commission that must be used by all licensees when acting as agents in real estate transactions, with limited specific exceptions.

property development A business that includes the work of land developers and subdividers who purchase raw land, divide it into lots, build roads, and install utilities. It also involves builders and architects who plan and construct the houses and other buildings, which are then sold.

property management A real estate agent who operates a property for its owner.

property manager Someone who manages real estate for another person for compensation. Duties include collecting rents, maintaining the property, and accounting for income and expenses.

prorate To divide or distribute expenses, either prepaid or paid in arrears, between buyer and seller at the closing (such as taxes, interest, and rents).

protected class Characteristics of people or factors that cannot be targeted for discrimination and harassment.

public ownership Ownership of land by a government entity.

puffing Exaggerated or superlative comments or opinions not made as representations of fact and thus not grounds for misrepresentation.

pur autre vie For the life of another. A *life estate pur autre vie* is a life estate that is measured by the life of a person other than the grantee.

purchase money mortgage 1. A note secured by a mortgage or trust deed given by a buyer, as mortgagor, to a seller, as mortgagee, as part of the purchase price of the real estate. 2. A mortgage given as part of the buyer's consideration for the purchase of real property.

pyramiding A process of acquiring additional properties through refinancing properties already owned and then reinvesting the loan proceeds in additional property.

quiet title suit *See* suit to quiet title.

quitclaim deed A conveyance by which the grantor transfers whatever interest she has in the real estate, without warranties or obligations.

range A strip of land six miles wide, extending north and south, and numbered east and west according to its distance from the principal meridian in the rectangular (government) survey system of land description.

ready, willing, and able buyer One who is prepared to buy property on the seller's terms and is ready to take positive steps to consummate the transaction.

real estate A portion of the earth's surface extending downward to the center of the earth and upward infinitely into space, including all things permanently attached thereto, whether by nature or by a person.

real estate broker Any person or corporation who sells (or offers to sell), buys (or offers to buy), or negotiates the purchase, sale, or exchange of real estate or who leases (or offers to lease) or rents (or offers to rent) any real estate or the improvements thereon for others and for compensation or valuable consideration. A real estate broker may not conduct business without a real estate broker's license.

Real Estate Center A real estate research center located at Texas A&M University; broker and salesperson licensees pay fees to the center with each renewal. Also known as the *Texas Real Estate Research Center*.

real estate counselor A person who helps clients choose among the various alternatives involved in purchasing, using, or investing in real property.

real estate inspector A person who, under the indirect supervision of a professional inspector, accepts employment for the purpose of performing a real property inspection for a buyer or seller.

real estate investment syndicate *See* syndicate.

real estate investment trust (REIT) Trust ownership of real estate by a group of at least 100 individuals who purchase certificates of ownership in the trust, which in turn invests the money in real property and distributes the profits back to the investors free of corporate income tax.

real estate license law State laws enacted to protect the public from fraud, dishonesty, and incompetence in the purchase and sale of real estate.

real estate mortgage investment conduit (REMIC) A tax device that allows cash flows from an underlying block of commercial mortgages to be passed through to security holders without being subject to income taxes at the level of trustee or agent.

real estate recovery trust account A fund established from real estate license revenues to cover claims of aggrieved parties who have suffered monetary damage through the illegal actions of a real estate or property inspection licensee.

real property The earth's surface extending downward to the center of the earth and upward into space, including all things permanently attached to it by nature or by people, as well as the interests, benefits, and rights inherent in real estate ownership.

Realtist A person who is a member of the National Association of Real Estate Boards.

REALTOR® A registered trademark term reserved for the sole use of active members of local associations affiliated with the National Association of REALTORS®.

realty *See* real estate.

reconciliation The final step in the appraisal process, in which the appraiser weighs the estimates of value received from the sales comparison, cost, and income approaches to arrive at a final estimate of market value for the subject property.

recorded plat A subdivision map filed in the county recorder's office that shows the location and boundaries (lot and block number) of individual parcels of land; *contrast with* rectangular survey system *and with* metes-and-bounds description.

recording The act of entering documents affecting or conveying interests in real estate in the county clerk's records. Until it is recorded, a deed or mortgage generally is not effective against subsequent purchasers or mortgages.

recovery trust account *See* real estate recovery trust account.

rectangular survey system A system established in 1785 by the federal government providing for surveying and describing land by reference to principal meridians and base lines. Also called the *government survey system*. Not used in Texas.

redemption Buying back real estate sold in a tax sale. The defaulted owner is said to have the right of redemption.

redemption period A period established by state law during which a property owner has the right to redeem the real estate from a tax sale by paying the sales price, interest, and costs. Texas law does not permit redemption after a deed of trust foreclosure.

redlining The illegal practice of a lending institution's denying loans or restricting their number for certain areas of a community.

Regulation Z Law requiring credit institutions to inform borrowers of the true cost of obtaining credit; commonly called the *Truth in Lending Act*.

release deed A document that transfers all rights given a trustee under a trust deed loan back to the grantor after the loan has been fully repaid; also known as a *deed of reconveyance*.

release of lien An instrument indicating that a previously existing lien has been released and is no longer enforceable.

remainder interest The future interest in an estate that takes effect after the termination of another estate, such as a life estate; on the death of the life estate owner, ownership will pass to a named third party.

rent A fixed, periodic payment made by a tenant of a property to the owner for possession and use, usually by prior agreement of the parties.

renters insurance The type of insurance that covers the personal property and household goods of renters or condominium owners but does not cover the structure.

replacement cost The construction cost at current prices of a property that is not necessarily an exact duplicate of the subject property but serves the same purpose or function as the original.

reproduction cost The construction cost at current prices of an exact duplicate of the subject property.

reservation Something retained by the seller; for example, minerals, a life estate, or an access easement.

residential broker Brokers who deal in property used for housing, including small city lots, acreage, and single-family and multifamily units in urban, suburban, and rural areas

residential rental locator A person, other than the owner of the property or an onsite manager, who offers, for consideration, to locate a unit in an apartment complex for lease to a prospective tenant.

RESPA The Real Estate Settlement Procedures Act.

restrictive covenant A clause in a deed that limits the way property may be used; generally originated by the owner or developer in a deed. *See also* deed restrictions.

reverse annuity mortgage A form of mortgage that enables homeowners age 62 and older to borrow against the equity in their homes, receiving monthly payments to help meet living costs.

reversion The remnant of an estate that the grantor holds after granting a life estate to another person—the estate will return, or revert, to the grantor; also called a *reverter*.

reversionary interest The future interest in an estate that takes effect after the termination of another estate, such as a life estate; on the death of the life estate owner, ownership reverts to the grantor or the heirs or devisees.

reversionary right An owner's right to regain possession of leased property on termination of the lease agreement.

revocation Termination of licensure privileges for cause.

rider *See* endorsement.

right of survivorship The right for a surviving joint tenant(s) to acquire the interest of a deceased joint tenant; also applies to community property right of survivorship.

right-of-way The right or privilege, acquired through accepted usage or contract, to pass over a designated portion of the property of another.

right-of-way agent A person who sells, buys, leases, or transfers an easement or right-of-way for another for compensation.

riparian rights An owner's rights in land that borders on or includes a stream or river. These rights include access to and use of the water for domestic purposes.

risk management Evaluation and selection of appropriate property and insurance coverage.

rules and regulations As used in this text, those actions taken by the Texas Real Estate Commission that have the net effect of law on licensees. These rules interpret the License Act.

Rural Development An agency within the U.S. Department of Agriculture that makes residential loans in rural communities with populations of 10,000 or less.

sale and leaseback A transaction in which an owner sells improved property and, as part of the same transaction, signs a long-term lease to remain in possession of the premises.

sales comparison approach The process of estimating the value of a property by examining and comparing actual sales of comparable properties.

sales contract A contract containing the complete terms of the agreement between buyer and seller for the sale of a particular parcel or parcels of real estate.

salesperson A person who performs real estate activities while employed by or associated with a licensed real estate broker.

salesperson annual education (SAE) A requirement for education beyond that needed to obtain a real estate salesperson license; continuing education for the first year of licensure.

satisfaction of mortgage A document acknowledging the payment of a debt secured by a two-party mortgage document.

secondary mortgage market A market for the purchase and sale of existing mortgages, designed to provide greater liquidity for mortgages; also called the *secondary money market*. Mortgages are originated in the *primary mortgage market*.

section A square with mile-long sides and an area of one square mile, or 640 acres.

security agreement *See* Uniform Commercial Code.

security deposit A payment by a tenant, held by the landlord during the lease term and kept (wholly or partially) on default or destruction of the premises by the tenant.

seller's broker A real estate broker, also called the *listing broker*, who is employed by and represents only the seller in a real estate transaction. Not to be confused with the *selling broker*.

Seller's Disclosure Notice A notice required of most sellers of real property; must state latent structural defects or any other known structural defects.

selling broker The broker working with or representing a buyer in the purchase of a listed property.

separate property Under community property law, property owned solely by either spouse before the marriage; acquired by gift or inheritance during the marriage, by purchase from separate funds, by sale of separate property, by settlement or judgment for personal injury, or by written contract with a spouse.

servient tenement Land on which an easement exists in favor of an adjacent property (called the *dominant tenement*); also called *servient estate*.

setback The amount of space local zoning regulations require between a lot line and a building line.

severalty Ownership of real property by one person or one legal entity only; also called *sole ownership*.

severance Changing an item of real estate to personal property by detaching it from the land; for example, cutting down a tree.

shared-appreciation mortgage A mortgage loan in which the lender, in exchange for a loan with a favorable interest rate, participates in the profits (if any) the mortgagor receives when the property is eventually sold.

short sale A sale of a house in which the proceeds fall short of what the owner still owes on the mortgage; the lender agrees to accept the proceeds of the sale and forgive the balance on the loan.

situs The personal preference of people for one area over another area, not necessarily based on objective facts and knowledge.

sole ownership *See* severalty.

sole proprietorship A method of owning a business in which one person owns the whole business and reports all profits and losses on his personal income tax return.

special agent One authorized by a principal to perform a single act or transaction; a special agent for a seller is authorized to find a ready, willing, and able buyer for a particular property; a special agent for a buyer is authorized to assist a buyer in locating and negotiating the purchase of a property.

special assessment A tax or levy customarily imposed against only those specific parcels of real estate that will benefit from a proposed public improvement like a street or paved alley.

special warranty deed A deed in which the grantor warrants, or guarantees, the title only against defects arising during her tenure and ownership of the property and not against defects existing before that time, generally using the language, "by, through or under the grantor but not otherwise."

specific lien A lien affecting or attaching only to a certain, specific parcel of land or piece of property.

specific performance A legal action brought to compel a party to carry out the terms of a contract.

spot zoning A change in a local zoning ordinance to permit a particular use that is inconsistent with the area's zoning classification. Spot zoning is not favored in the law.

statute of frauds That part of state law that requires certain instruments, such as deeds, real estate sales contracts, and certain leases, to be in writing to be legally enforceable.

statute of limitations That law pertaining to the period of time within which certain actions must be brought to court.

statutory lien A lien imposed on property by statute—a tax lien, for example—in contrast to an equitable lien, which arises out of common law.

statutory right of redemption The right of a defaulted property owner to recover the property after its sale by paying the appropriate fees and charges; available in Texas for tax foreclosures and homeowners' associations assessment liens; not available for a deed of trust foreclosure.

statutory year A year composed of 12 months, each with 30 days, for a total of 360 days in a statutory year. Also known as a *banker's year; contrast with* a calendar year, which has 365 days, or 366 in a leap year.

steering The illegal practice of channeling homeseekers to particular areas, either to maintain the homogeneity of an area or to change the character of an area to create a speculative situation. *See also* channeling.

straight-line method A method of calculating depreciation for tax purposes; computed by dividing the adjusted basis of a property by the estimated number of years of remaining useful life.

subagent A licensee who represents a principal through cooperation with and consent of a broker representing the principal and who is not sponsored by or associated with the principal's broker.

subcontractor *See* general contractor.

subdivision A tract of land divided by the owner, known as the *developer*, into blocks, building lots, and streets according to a recorded subdivision plat, which must comply with local ordinances and regulations.

subjective value The perceived value of an item based on the relative benefits expected to be derived from its use.

"subject to" clause A provision in a deed specifying exceptions and reservations affecting the title.

subject to mortgage The buyer of an already mortgaged property makes the payments but does not take personal responsibility for the loan. Should the mortgage be foreclosed and the property sold for a lesser amount than is owed, the grantee-buyer is not personally liable for the deficiency, but the grantor-seller is; *contrast with* assumption of mortgage.

sublease The leasing of premises by a lessee to a third party for part of the lessee's remaining term. *Contrast with* assignment.

subordination Relegation to a lesser position, usually in respect to a right or security.

subordination agreement A written agreement between holders of liens on a property that changes the priority of mortgage, judgment, and other liens under certain circumstances.

subpoena A legal process ordering a witness to appear and give testimony or to present documents under penalty of law. TREC has subpoena powers.

subrogation The substitution of one creditor for another, with the substituted person succeeding to the legal rights and claims of the original claimant. Subrogation is used by title insurers to acquire the purchaser's rights to sue to recover any claims they have paid.

substitution An appraisal principle stating that the maximum value of a property tends to be set by the cost of purchasing an equally desirable and valuable substitute property, assuming that no costly delay is encountered in making the substitution.

subsurface rights Ownership rights in a parcel of real estate to the water, minerals, gas, oil, and so forth that lie beneath the surface of the property.

suit for possession *See* forcible detainer.

suit to quiet title A court action intended to establish or settle the title to a particular property, especially when a cloud on the title exists.

supply The amount of goods available in the market to be sold at a given price. The term often is coupled with *demand*.

surety bail bond A pledge of real estate instead of cash as security for bail.

surety bond An agreement by an insurance or bonding company to be responsible for certain possible defaults, debts, or obligations contracted for by an insured party; used to ensure that a particular project will be completed at a certain date or that a contract will be performed as stated.

surface rights Ownership rights in a parcel of real estate that are limited to the surface of the property and do not include the air above it (*air rights*) or the minerals below the surface (*subsurface rights*).

survey The process by which boundaries are measured and land areas are determined; the onsite measurement of lot lines, dimensions, and position of a house on a lot, including the determination of any existing encroachments or easements.

syndicate A combination of people or firms formed to accomplish a business venture of mutual interest by pooling resources. In a *real estate investment syndicate*, the parties own and/or develop property with the main profit generally arising from the sale of the property.

tacking Adding or combining successive periods of continuous occupation of real property by adverse possessors. This strategy enables someone who has not been in possession for the entire statutory period to establish a claim of adverse possession.

taxation The process by which a government or municipal quasipublic body raises monies to fund its operation.

tax basis The amount on which future gain is measured. Also the amount of remaining depreciation.

tax credit An amount by which tax owed is reduced directly.

tax levy *See* levy.

tax lien A charge against property created by operation of law. Tax liens and assessments take priority over all other liens.

tax rate The rate at which real property is taxed in a tax district or county. For example, in a certain county, real property may be taxed at a rate of 0.056 cents per $1 of assessed valuation.

tax sale A court-ordered sale of real property to raise money to cover delinquent taxes.

tax shelter A legal means by which an investor may reduce or defer payment of part of her federal income tax.

tenancy at sufferance The tenancy of a lessee who lawfully comes into possession of a landlord's real estate but who continues to occupy the premises improperly after lease rights have expired.

tenancy at will An estate that gives the lessee the right to possession until the estate is terminated by either party; the term of this estate is indefinite.

tenancy in common A form of co-ownership by which each owner holds an undivided interest in real property as if the sole owner. Ownership shares must be equal; and upon the death of an owner, the interest passes to heirs.

tenant One who holds or possesses lands or tenements by any kind of right or title.

term loan *See* interest-only loan.

testate Having made and left a valid will.

testator A person who makes a last will and testament.

Texas Deceptive Trade Practices–Consumer Protection Act (DTPA) Makes it illegal to use false, misleading, or deceptive acts or practices in the advertising, offering for sale, selling, or leasing of any real or personal property.

Texas Department of Housing and Community Affairs A Texas governmental agency that has financing programs to help low-income and moderate-income families acquire housing.

Texas Fair Housing Act A "substantially equivalent" fair housing law that allows complaints to be heard by the Texas Workforce Commission Civil Rights Division (TWCCRD) or in state courts.

Texas Real Estate Broker-Lawyer Committee A committee that drafts and revises standard contract forms to be used by real estate licensees.

Texas Real Estate Commission (TREC) A group of people appointed by the governor to set policy in implementing the License Act.

Texas Real Estate Commission Canons of Professional Ethics and Conduct A code of ethics, adopted by The Texas Real Estate Commission, that establishes a basis for professional conduct of licensed real estate brokers and salespersons and that has the force and effect of the law.

Texas Real Estate License Act The statute that controls the licensing of persons permitted to practice real estate brokerage in Texas.

Texas Veterans Home Improvement Program This program assists Texas veterans in the repair and improvement of their principal residence by providing low-interest home improvement loans.

Texas Veterans Housing Assistance Program (VHAP) Established by a constitutional amendment in 1984, the VHAP assists Texas veterans in the purchase of a principal residence.

Texas Veterans Land Board (VLB) Created in 1946 to administer a program to provide low-interest, long-term loans to Texas veterans for the purchase of land (the Land Program). Also administers the Housing Assistance Program and the Home Improvement Program.

Texas Veterans Land Program Established to assist Texas veterans to buy land with a small down payment, long-term mortgages, and low interest rates.

Texas Workforce Commission Civil Rights Division (TWCCRD) The organization authorized to receive, investigate, and seek to conciliate complaints of violations of the Texas Fair Housing Act.

time is of the essence A phrase in a contract that requires the strict performance of a certain act within a stated time frame; most Texas contracts require *reasonable time*.

timesharing A form of ownership where permission is given to use certain property for certain intervals of time; may be fee simple title or merely a right to use (license).

title 1. The right to or ownership of land. 2. The evidence of ownership of land.

title commitment A statement of the terms and conditions on which a title insurance underwriter is willing to issue a title insurance policy.

title insurance A policy insuring the owner or mortgagee against loss by reason of defects in the title to a parcel of real estate, other than encumbrances, defects, and matters specifically excluded by the policy.

title search An examination of the public records to determine what, if any, defects are in the chain of title; usually performed by a title company or abstracter.

title theory Some states' interpretation of a mortgage to mean that the lender is the owner of mortgaged land. On full payment of the mortgage debt, the borrower becomes the landowner; not recognized in Texas.

township line Lines running at six-mile intervals parallel to the base lines in the rectangular survey (government survey) system; not used in Texas.

township square The principal unit of the rectangular survey (government survey) system. A township is a square with six-mile sides and an area of 36 square miles; not used in Texas.

township tier A strip of land running east and west in the government (rectangular) survey system; not used in Texas.

trade fixture Article installed by a tenant under the terms of a lease and removable by the tenant before the lease expires. These remain personal property and are not true fixtures.

TREC *See* Texas Real Estate Commission.

trigger terms Specific credit terms, such as down payment, monthly payment, the amount of finance charges, or the term of the loan, which, if included in an advertisement, trigger full disclosure of all financing terms under Regulation Z.

trust A fiduciary arrangement whereby property is conveyed by a *trustor* to a person or institution, called a *trustee*, to be held and administered on behalf of another person, called a *beneficiary*.

trust account *See* commingle.

trust deed A deed of trust.

trustee *See* trust.

trustee's deed   A deed executed by a trustee conveying land held in a trust.

trustor   *See* trust.

undivided interest   A unity of possession among co-owners or cotenants.

unenforceable contract   A contract that has all the elements of a valid contract, yet neither party can sue the other to force performance of it. For example, an oral listing agreement is generally unenforceable.

Uniform Commercial Code   A codification of commercial law that attempts to make uniform throughout the United States all laws relating to commercial transactions. Security interests in personal property are created by an instrument known as a *security agreement*. To give notice of the security interest, a *financing statement* must be recorded.

Uniform Settlement Statement   A closing cost statement required by RESPA for the closing of certain real estate transactions; the HUD-1 form.

unilateral contract   A one-sided contract wherein one party makes a promise in order to induce a second party to do something. The second party is not legally bound to perform; however, if the second party does comply, the first party is obligated to keep the promise.

unity of ownership   The four unities traditionally needed to create a joint tenancy—unity of title, time, interest, and possession.

useful life   A period of time over which an asset, such as a building, is expected to remain economically feasible to the owner.

usury   Charging interest at a rate higher than the maximum rate established by state law.

valid contract   A contract that complies with all the essentials of a contract and is binding and enforceable to all parties to it.

VA loan   A mortgage loan on approved property made to a qualified veteran by an authorized lender and guaranteed by the U.S. Department of Veterans Affairs to limit the lender's possible loss.

value   The amount of goods or services considered to be a fair and suitable equivalent for something else.

vara   In Texas, a measurement of length; one vara equals 33⅓ inches.

variable-rate mortgage   A mortgage loan in which the interest rate may increase or decrease at specified intervals within certain limits, based on an economic indicator.

variance   A waiver from compliance with a specific provision of the zoning ordinance; for the benefit of one parcel only.

vendee   A buyer.

vendee's lien   A buyer's claim against a seller's property when the seller has not delivered title to the buyer, as in an installment contract or contract for deed.

vendor   A seller.

vendor's lien   The equitable lien of the grantor upon the land conveyed, in the amount of the unpaid purchase price.

voidable contract   A contract that seems to be valid on the surface but may be rejected or disaffirmed by one or both parties.

void contract   A "contract" that has no legal force or effect because it does not meet the essential elements of a contract and therefore is not a contract.

volume   The size in cubic units (cubic inches, etc.) of a three-dimensional figure such as a cube.

voluntary alienation   *See* alienation.

voluntary lien   A lien that arises because of actions permitted by a person, such as when signing a deed of trust or mortgage.

wage lien   A lien ordered by the Texas Workforce Commission against all real and personal property of an employer who owes back wages to an employee.

warehousing agency   An agency that purchases a number of mortgage loans and assembles them into one or more packages of loans for resale to investors; Fannie Mae, Freddie Mac, and Ginnie Mae are warehousing agencies.

warranty clause   The part of a deed in which the seller warrants the title conveyed to the buyer.

warranty deed   *See* general warranty deed.

waste   An improper use or an abuse of a property by a possessor who holds less than fee ownership, such as a tenant, life tenant, mortgagor, or vendee. Such waste generally impairs the value of the land or the interest of the person holding the title or the reversionary rights.

will   A document providing for the transfer of title to property owned by the deceased, called the *testator*. *See* formal will and holographic will.

workers' compensation insurance   Insurance carried by an employer to provide medical care and a portion of lost wages to an employee who has a work-related illness or is injured at work.

wraparound mortgage   A method of refinancing in which the new mortgage is placed in a secondary, or subordinate, position; the new mortgage includes both the unpaid principal balance of the first mortgage and whatever additional sums are advanced by the lender.

writ of execution   A court order that authorizes and directs the sheriff to sell property of a defendant to satisfy a judgment.

writ of possession A court order authorizing a sheriff to return leased premises to the owner following an eviction suit, pursuant to a *judgment for possession.*

zero lot line A term generally used to describe the positioning of a structure on a lot so that one side rests directly on the lot's boundary line (no setback). Where allowed by zoning, a zero lot line is used for "garden homes."

zoning board of adjustment Group established to hear complaints about the effects of zoning ordinances on specific parcels of property.

zoning ordinance An exercise of police power by a municipality to regulate and control the character and use of property.

Answer Key

Detailed rationales for the end-of-chapter questions are available online at www.dearborn.com under the Instructor Resources material for this title.

CHAPTER 1
Introduction to Modern Real Estate Practice

1. d (8)
2. d (4–5)
3. c (5)
4. c (6)
5. a (5)
6. c (6)
7. c (6)
8. c (9)
9. c (3)
10. d (3)
11. a (3)
12. a (2)

CHAPTER 2
Real Property

1. d (16)
2. b (18)
3. c (16)
4. b (17–18)
5. b (20)
6. d (14)
7. b (15)
8. b (19)
9. c (14)
10. c (17)
11. b (17)
12. b (17)
13. c (15)
14. a (17)
15. b (19)
16. b (15)
17. a (15)

CHAPTER 3
The Real Estate Market

1. c (28)
2. a (30–31)
3. c (31)
4. a (29)

5. c (27)
6. c (28)
7. d (28)
8. c (32)
9. a (28)
10. c (26)
11. d (26)
12. d (27)
13. c (27)
14. b (26)

CHAPTER 4
Concepts of Home Ownership

1. d (39)
2. d (42)
3. b (40)
4. d (38)
5. d (45)
6. a (37)
7. b (46)
8. a (47)
9. c (44)
10. d (36)
11. a (39)
12. c (42)
13. b (42)
14. d (42)
15. a (42)
16. b (37)

CHAPTER 5
Real Estate Brokerage and the Law of Agency

1. a (54–55)
2. b (56)
3. b (71)
4. c (70)
5. b (71)
6. c (58)
7. b (70)
8. b (59)
9. b (59)
10. a (71)

11. c (62)
12. c (73)
13. a (55)
14. b (57)

CHAPTER 6
Fair Housing Laws and Ethical Practices

1. b (86)
2. a (99)
3. d (86)
4. c (86–87)
5. c (91)
6. b (92)
7. a (83)
8. d (87)
9. c (91)
10. b (92)
11. d (88)
12. d (102)
13. c (101)
14. c (102)
15. a (85)
16. b (91)
17. c (83)
18. c (85)
19. c (95)
20. d (106)
21. d (108)

CHAPTER 7
Texas Real Estate License Act Analysis Form

1. 1949 (120)
2. 2011 (120)

3.

Broker	Salesperson
a. 18 years	18 years
b. day of filing	day of filing
c. four years as licensed salesperson	
d. 900 classroom hours	180 classroom hours
e. Yes	yes
f. $10	$10 (139–159, 179)

4. Auction (if performing an act of a broker or salesperson in addition to conducting the auction sale); sell; exchange; purchase; rent; assist in procuring prospects; assist in finding listings; collect rent (if for a single-family residential unit); serve as a hostess at an open house (if engaging in any activity for which a license is required); trade; lease; buy; locate renters. All assume "performing for someone else for a fee." (120–126)

5. A real estate broker includes any person or business entity that for another person and in expectation of receiving compensation performs any action listed in section 1101.002(1). (120–121)

6. Any person employed by or engaged by a licensed real estate broker to do any of the actions that a broker is licensed to perform (122)

7. a. A property owner buying and selling for himself
   b. An owner and his or her regular employees who do not conduct or appear to conduct a real estate brokerage business
   c. An attorney-in-fact under a power of attorney

d. An attorney at law licensed in Texas
e. An escrow holder; receiver; trustee in bankruptcy; administrator; executor; person acting under order of court; trustee under trust agreement, deed of trust, or will, or the regular salaried employee thereof; or public officer or employee while performing duties as such
f. On-site manager of an apartment complex
g. Sale of cemetery lots
h. Transactions involving mining and mineral interests
i. A person who conducts a real estate auction
j. Transactions involving leasing or managing a hotel or motel
k. A builder's employees selling structures erected by the owner (124–125)

8. List any nine reasons cited in Sections 1101.651 and 1101.652 (note also Rule 541.1, which lists offenses that demonstrate lack of ability to perform with honesty, trustworthiness, and integrity); among those:
a. Accepting an undisclosed rebate or profit on an expenditure for a principal
b. Acting in the dual capacity of broker and an undisclosed principal in any transaction
c. Pursuing a continued and flagrant course of misrepresentation
d. Making false promises
e. Failing to make clear to all parties for whom the licensee is acting

f. Failing to remit or account for funds belonging to others
g. Using misleading advertising or an ad without the broker's name
h. Failing to use a contract form required by the commission
i. Procuring a license by fraud
j. Willfully disregarding or violating any provisions of the act
k. Paying a commission to any unlicensed person in violation of the act
l. Inducing a party to break a sales contract or lease to substitute a new one
m. Being convicted of a felony
n. Displaying a For Sale sign without the seller's proper written authority
o. Knowingly preparing an inaccurate statement or invoice
p. Dishonest dealings, bad faith, untrustworthiness, or incompetency in conduct
q. Employing unlicensed salespersons
r. Discriminating on the basis of race, color, religion, sex, disability, familial status, or national origin
s. Soliciting, selling, or offering for sale by means of a deceptive practice
t. Commingling funds of others with his or her own
u. Failing to deposit the money of others in an escrow or trustee account within a reasonable time
v. Failing to advise a purchaser in writing to have the abstract examined or

to obtain a title insurance policy

w. Accepting compensation from someone other than the agent's broker

x. Violating the intermediary statute (163–167)

9. Class A misdemeanor: Punishable by a fine up to $4,000 or imprisonment for up to one year or both (176)

10. Nine members appointed by the governor with the advice and consent of the senate; staggered terms of six years (126–127)

11. Section 1101.552 of the act requires that every licensed real estate broker maintain a definite place of business in this state. In addition, Section 1101.553 requires that a residential rental locator display the locator's license. (155)

12. Section 1101.367 and Rule 535.121 provide that the broker shall immediately return the salesperson's license to the commission. Notice of termination of sponsorship must be in writing—from the broker or from the salesperson. It may be reactivated by filing a request for new broker sponsorship with TREC along with a transfer fee. (145)

13. Section 1101.654 defines the unauthorized practice of law: For consideration, reward, or monetary benefit, a licensee drew a deed, note, deed of trust, or other written instrument that may transfer or affect title to real estate; does not include completion of promulgated contract forms. (167)

14. The Recovery Trust Account (Sections 1101.601–.615) is established by a $10 deposit from each broker and salesperson licensee to reimburse aggrieved persons who suffer actual damages by reason of acts committed by a licensed broker or salesperson, provided recovery is ordered by a court of competent jurisdiction. Limits are $50,000 for claims arising out of the same transaction and $100,000 for claims against any one licensee.

When recovery is ordered by a court against a licensed broker or salesperson and the licensee cannot pay the full amount of the judgment ordered by the court, the aggrieved person may apply to the court in which the judgment was entered for an order directing payment out of the real estate recovery trust account of the amount unpaid on the judgment. (159–163)

15. The Broker-Lawyer Committee has 13 members: 6 appointed by the Texas Real Estate Commission, 6 appointed by the president of the State Bar of Texas, and one public member appointed by the governor. The primary function of the committee is to prepare contract forms, including special addenda, which are presented to the Commission for possible approval or promulgation. (Sections 1101.252–.254.) (137)

16. As a condition for the first renewal of a salesperson license (SAE requirement), the applicant shall furnish proof of completing at least 6 additional semester hours (60 classroom hours) of real estate core during the two-year initial license period, effective on or after September 1, 2012. Real estate core requirements for SAE are 18 total hours, including the prelicense core requirements. (Prior to September 1, 2012, the SAE requirement is 4 semester hours in the first year of licensure—a total of 18 hours, 14 of which must be core courses.)

Persons who have completed SAE requirements must furnish proof of completing at least 15 classroom hours of Mandatory Continuing Education (MCE) during the two-year period preceding license renewal. MCE hours must include TREC-approved non-elective 3-hour legal update and 3-hour legal ethics courses. In some instances, exemptions from MCE requirements apply to persons holding a broker's license for at least ten years as of September 1, 1991. For licenses issued or renewed on or after September 1, 2012, a broker who sponsors a salesperson or a broker or salesperson who supervises another licensee must take at least 6 hours of broker responsibility education each two years, which may be used to meet MCE requirements. (150–151)

CHAPTER 7
Texas Real Estate License Act

1. c (119)
2. b (119)
3. a (163)
4. d (124)
5. b (124–125)
6. d (126)
7. b (132)
8. a (141)
9. b (130)
10. c (162–163)
11. a (131)
12. b (166)
13. a (167)
14. c (167–168)
15. d (178)
16. b (153)

CHAPTER 8
Interests in Real Estate

1. b (187)
2. b (186)
3. b (197)
4. a (191)
5. a (188–189)
6. c (198)
7. d (191–192)
8. b (189)
9. c (195–196)
10. d (194)
11. b (191)
12. a (190)
13. c (192)
14. a (193)
15. a (189)
16. a (197–198)
17. b (192)
18. d (192)

CHAPTER 9
How Home Ownership Is Held

1. a (221)
2. b (207)
3. d (208)
4. d (209)
5. a (218)
6. b (206)
7. c (208)

8. c (215)
9. a (213)
10. a (212)
11. b (207–208)
12. c (210)
13. b (218–219)
14. a (212)
15. a (210)
16. a (218–219)
17. b (208–209)
18. c (210)
19. c (211)
20. c (216)
21. b (210)
22. d (214)
23. c (215)

CHAPTER 10
Legal Descriptions

1. b (233)
2. d (233)
3. b (228)
4. b (229)
5. c (236)
6. c (230)
7. c (234)
8. b (235)
9. d (238)
10. d (233,238)
11. c (230)
12. b (232)
13. d (232–233)
14. a (236)
15. a (233)
16. a (238)
17. c (236)
18. c (232)
19. c (234–235)
20. c (234–235)
21. c (234–235)
22. b (233)
23. b (238)

CHAPTER 11
Real Estate Taxes and Other Liens

1. c (246)
2. c (260)
3. c (258)
4. c (263)

5. b (247)
6. b (258)
7. b (249)
8. c (255)
9. c (249)
10. c (260)
11. b (246, 259)
12. d (259, 261)
13. b (247)
14. b (247)
15. d (257)
16. c (247)
17. b (247)
18. b (262)
19. b (264)
20. a (247)
21. d (249)

CHAPTER 12
Real Estate Contracts

1. c (271)
2. c (272)
3. a (278)
4. d (271)
5. d (277)
6. b (276)
7. c (273)
8. b (271)
9. b (272–273)
10. a (275)
11. b (278)
12. d (296)
13. b (297–298)
14. d (275)
15. b (276–277)
16. c (276)
17. a (278)
18. b (278)
19. a (295–296)
20. d (296)
21. b (279)
22. d (296)
23. b (277)
24. a (272)

CHAPTER 13
Listing Agreements

1. a (304)
2. c (305)
3. a (305, 317)
4. c (317)
5. c (320)
6. b (305)
7. b (320)
8. a (319)
9. c (319–320)
10. a (305)
11. b (317)
12. b (320)
13. b (304)
14. c (305, 317)
15. b (317)

CHAPTER 14
Real Estate Appraisal

1. b (356)
2. b (345)
3. b (347)
4. a (346)
5. d (357)
6. a (347)
7. b (355)
8. b (351)
9. a (352–353)
10. c (352–353)
11. b (350)
12. c (352)
13. a (345)
14. b (353)
15. a (350)
16. a (348)
17. d (348)
18. b (352)
19. c (351)
20. c (354)
21. b (351)

CHAPTER 15
Real Estate Financing Principles

1. a (369)
2. d (364)
3. b (364)
4. c (371)
5. b (369)
6. b (376)
7. b (371–372)
8. b (370)
9. a (382)
10. d (376)
11. d (378)
12. b (381)
13. a (365)
14. b (381–382)
15. c (381)
16. a (371)
17. d (379)

CHAPTER 16
Real Estate Financing Practice

1. b (418)
2. a (401)
3. b (422)
4. c (417)
5. d (419)
6. d (416)
7. a (420)
8. b (405)
9. b (421)
10. d (415)
11. c (406)
12. d (430)
13. b (405)
14. b (425)
15. c (422–423)
16. b (418)
17. b (403)
18. b (403)
19. b (403)
20. b (403)
21. c (405)
22. a (430)
23. d (428)
24. a (408)
25. d (425)

CHAPTER 17
Transfer of Title

1. c (447)
2. a (439)
3. d (439)
4. a (443)
5. c (450)
6. b (442)
7. a (447)
8. b (443)
9. b (442)
10. a (451)
11. a (444)
12. b (439–440)
13. c (451)
14. b (443–444)
15. d (447)
16. d (447)
17. b (451)
18. b (438)
19. a (442)

CHAPTER 18
Title Records

1. b (467)
2. c (466)
3. a (462)
4. d (465)
5. b (466)
6. b (465)
7. c (462)
8. d (465)
9. a (464)
10. b (462)
11. a (460)
12. d (465)
13. a (465)
14. a (462)
15. c (463)
16. a (462)
17. a (462)

CHAPTER 19
Real Estate Mathematics

1. c **$4,350 due at closing**

100% total value − 90% loan = 10% down payment

down payment (part) = ?	
$88,500 (total)	10% = 0.1 (rate)

$88,500 (total) × 0.1 (rate) = $8,850 down payment

$8,850 down payment − $4,500 earnest money = $4,350 due at closing (475–476)

2. b **$88,100 original cost**

100% total original cost + 12% profit = 112% sales price

$98,672 sales price (part)	
original cost (Total) = ?	112% = 1.12 (rate)

$98,672 (part) ÷ 1.12 (rate) = $88,100 (original cost) (479)

3. c **27%**

$80,000 + $87,500 + $87,500 = $255,000 invested by three people

$350,000 − $255,000 = $95,000 fourth investor's share

$95,000 (part)	
$350,000 (total)	rate = ?

$95,000 (part) ÷ $350,000 (total) = 0.2714 = 27% fourth investor's share (475–476)

4. b **$40,843.83 principal balance**

$391.42 monthly interest × 12 = $4,697.04 annual interest

$4,697.04 annual interest (part)		
Principal (Total) = ?	11½% = 0.115 (Rate)	1 Year (Time)

$4,697.04 (part) ÷ [0.115 (rate) × 1 (time)] = $40,843.83 principal balance (481)

5. d **$135.38 monthly taxes**

annual taxes (part) = ?	
$95,000 (total)	$1.71 ÷ 100 = 0.0171 (rate)

$95,000 (total) × $0.0171 (rate) = $1,624.50 annual taxes

$1,624.50 ÷ 12 = $135.38 monthly taxes (482)

6. **c**   **$1,194.00 total cost**

   Concrete:

   4" ÷ 12 = 0.333'

   15' × 40' × 0.333' = 199.8 cubic feet ÷ 27 = 7.4 cubic yards

   7.4 cubic yards × $60/cubic yard = $444 concrete cost

   Labor:

   15' × 40' = 600 square feet × $1.25/square foot = $750 labor cost

   $444 concrete cost + $750 labor cost = $1,194.00 total cost (484)

7. **d**   **$51,000 sales price**

   $47,300 net to seller + $1,150 closing costs = $48,450 net after commission

   100% (total rate) – 5% (commission rate) = 95% net after commission

$48,450 net after commission (part)	
sales price (total) = ?	95% = 0.95 (Rate)

   $48,450 (part) ÷ 0.95 (rate) = $51,000 sales price (479)

8. **d**   **$652.08 average monthly rent**

   $75,000 gross annual sales – $50,000 = $25,000 annual sales subject to 2.5%

annual percentage rent (part) = ?	
$25,000 (total)	2.5% = 0.025 (rate)

   $25,000 (total) × 0.025 (rate) = $625 annual percentage rent

   $625 ÷ 12 = $52.08 monthly percentage rent

   $600 monthly minimum rent + $52.08 monthly percentage rent = $652.08 average monthly rent (475–476)

9. **a**   **$657 commission to Elisha**

total commission (part) = ?	
$73,000 sales price (total)	6% = 0.06 (rate)

   $73,000 (total) × 0.06 (rate) = $4,380 total commission (part)

   $4,380 ÷ 2 = $2,190 broker's share of the commission

commission to Elisha (part) = ?	
$2,190 broker's commission (total)	30% = 0.3 (rate)

   $2,190 (total) × 0.3 (rate) = $657 commission to Elisha (477–478)

10. **d 27,225 square feet per lot**

    1/8 = 0.125 for streets

    100 acres × 0.125 = 12.5 acres for streets

    100 total acres – 12.5 acres for streets = 87.5 acres for lots

    87.5 acres for lots × 43,560 = 3,811,500 square feet

    3,811,500 square feet ÷ 140 lots = 27,225 square feet per lot (483–484)

11. **a $127.11 interest proration (credit buyer; debit seller)**

Step 1: Calculate the daily rate.

$43,580 (total) × 10½% (rate) × 1/12 (time) = $381.325 month's interest

$381.325 ÷ 30 = $12.711 day's interest

Step 2: Calculate time.

August 1 through August 10 = 10 days

Step 3: Multiply the daily amount by the number of days.

$12.711 × 10 = $127.11 interest proration (486–487)

12. **c $5,512.50 for points**

2.5 points loan discount + 1 point origination fee = 3.5 points

loan amount (part) = ?	
$175,000 sales price (total)	90% = 0.9 (rate)

$175,000 (total) × 0.9 (rate) = $157,500 loan amount (part)

points (part) = ?	
$157,500 loan amount (total)	3.5% = 0.035 (rate)

$157,500 (total) × 0.035 (rate) = $5,512.50 for points (481)

13. **b $316.67 interest**

interest (part) = ?		
$5,000 loan (total)	9½% = 0.095 (rate)	$^8/_{12}$ (time)*

$5,000 (total) × 0.095 (rate) × 8 months ÷ 12 = $316.67 interest (480)

*   When the "time fraction" would convert to a "repeating decimal" (for example, 8 ÷ 12 = 0.6666666), don't convert the fraction to a decimal. Multiply the total by the rate and then by the fraction's numerator; then, divide by the denominator.

14. **b $502.22 tax proration**

Step 1: Calculate monthly and daily rates.

$1,282 annual tax ÷ 365 = $3.512 daily tax

Step 2: Calculate time.

Seller owes the buyer for January 1 through May 23 =

(J = 31) + (F = 28) + (M = 31) + (A = 30) + (M = 23) = 143 days

Step 3: Multiply daily rates by the number of days.

$3.512 × 143 days = $502.22 tax proration (487–488)

15. **b $1,197.92 monthly net operating income**

annual net operating income (part) = ?	
$115,000 investment (total)	12½% = 0.125 (rate)

$115,000 (total) × 0.125 (rate) = $14,375 annual net operating income

$14,375 ÷ 12 = $1,197.92 monthly net operating income (476)

16. b 9% annual interest rate

$450 semiannual interest (part)		
$10,000 loan (total)	Rate = ?	$\frac{6}{12}$ = 0.5 (time)

$450 (part) ÷ [$10,000 (total) × 0.5 (time)] = 0.09 = 9% annual interest rate (480)

17. b $571,500 price

$68,580 annual net operating income (part)	
price (total)	12% = 0.12 (rate)

$68,580 (part) ÷ 0.12 (rate) = $571,500 price (476)

18. b $80,000 sales price

$5,200 commission (part)	
sales price (total)	6.5% = 0.065 (rate)

$5,200 (part) ÷ 0.065 = $80,000 sales price (477–478)

19. a $2,072 monthly PITI payment

$60,000 annual salary ÷ 12 = $5,000 Duc Van's monthly salary + $2,400 Lan's monthly salary = $7,400 total monthly salary

monthly PITI payment (part)	
$7,400 monthly salary (total)	28% = 0.28 (rate)

$7,400 (total) × 0.28 (rate) = $2,072 monthly PITI payment (476)

20. c 30% rate of profit

$10,500 + $93,000 = $103,500 cost of the home

$134,550 sales price – $103,500 cost of the home = $31,050 Profit

$31,050 profit (part)	
$103,500 cost (total)*	rate = ?

$31,050 (part) ÷ $103,500 (total) = 0.3 = 30% rate of profit (479)

* Profit and loss are based on cost or a prior year's figure. For example, to calculate the profit from year 2009 to 2010, *total* will be the year 2009 figure.

21. d 950 running feet

125' + 350' + 125' + 350' = 950 running feet (482)

CHAPTER 20
Closing the Real Estate Transaction

1. c (528)
2. a (526)
3. d (497)
4. c (526)
5. c (496)
6. b (492)
7. a (526)
8. c (526)
9. b (526)
10. b (526)
11. c (526, 528)
12. b (526)
13. d (526, 528)
14. a (496)
15. b (497)
16. c (495)
17. d (495)
18. a (529, 534)
19. c (529, 534)
20. a (525)
21. c (498)

CHAPTER 21
Leases

1. c (545)
2. c (544)
3. c (562)
4. c (561)
5. d (560)
6. b (561)
7. c (541)
8. c (562)
9. a (545)
10. b (545)
11. c (547)
12. d (545)
13. d (547)
14. a (548)
15. a (555)
16. d (558)

CHAPTER 22
Property Management

1. b (580)
2. b (578)
3. d (571)
4. c (580)
5. c (573)
6. d (579)
7. d (569)
8. c (580)
9. a (571)
10. a (571)
11. c (580)
12. b (579)
13. d (577)
14. a (574)
15. b (569)
16. c (571)

CHAPTER 23
Real Estate—A Business of Many Specializations

1. c (588)
2. d (592)
3. d (588)
4. b (588)
5. d (589)
6. c (590)
7. a (590)
8. a (591)
9. b (592)
10. d (592)
11. a (592)
12. d (593)
13. a (593)
14. d (593)

CHAPTER 24
Control of Land Use and Green Initiatives

1. b (604)
2. c (601)
3. b (598, 604)
4. c (604)
5. c (604)
6. a (600)
7. d (600)
8. b (601)
9. b (602)
10. c (598)
11. a (601)
12. a (605)
13. a (604)
14. b (603)
15. a (606)
16. b (610)
17. c (610)
18. c (610)
19. c (613)

CHAPTER 25
Real Estate Investment

1. a (626)
2. d (634)
3. b (624)
4. c (626)
5. a (627)
6. d (629)
7. b (626)
8. b (628)
9. c (628)
10. a (626)
11. a (625)
12. a (634)

Index